CHILD
SEXUAL ABUSE

CHILD
SEXUAL ABUSE
New Theory and Research

David Finkelhor

THE FREE PRESS
A Division of Macmillan, Inc.
NEW YORK

Collier Macmillan Publishers
LONDON

FOR
My sister, Sarah
and
My brother, Ben

The Free Press
A Division of Macmillan, Inc.
866 Third Avenue, New York, N.Y. 10022

Collier Macmillan Canada, Inc.
Printed in the United States of America

printing number

4   5   6   7   8   9   10

Library of Congress Cataloging in Publication Data

Finkelhor, David.
  Child sexual abuse.

  Bibliography: p.
  Includes index.
  1. Child molesting.   2. Sexually abused children.
I. Title.   [DNLM: 1. Child abuse.   2. Sex offenses.
WA 320 F499c]
RC560.C46F55   1984   616.85'83   84–47889
ISBN 0–02–910020–8

Contents

Preface

THE SUBJECT OF SEXUAL ABUSE has inspired a great number of books
since the late 1970s. This book, however, is quite different from the
others. It is not a personal account of sexual abuse or a description of
the experience of its survivors and victims. Also, it is not a guidebook on
how to treat or intervene in cases of sexual abuse. The need for books of
these two sorts is slowly, but surely, being filled by talented people in the
field who have personal and clinical experience with this problem.

This book is intended to fill two other needs: a need for theory and a
need for research. In the area of theory, there are a host of important questions about sexual abuse that have not received much concerted attention.
Why is there so much sexual abuse, in spite of what were once thought of
as strong taboos against such activity? Why do some children suffer victimization while others do not? What is it about our ethical concepts that makes
sexual contact between adults and children abhorrent? Why is it that some
adults can sexually molest a child when most find such an idea repellent?
While this book hardly provides full answers to any of these questions, it is
the intention of the following chapters to raise these issues and speculate upon
them.

In the area of research, the needs of this field are, perhaps, even more
pressing. Partly because the topic is so new and partly because of the urgency
it inspires, most efforts in this field have been directed toward treatment.
Little effort has been reserved for the painstaking tasks of data collection,

systematic observation, and statistical analysis. Thus some of the most fundamental questions in the field—What are the long-term effects of abuse? What groups of children are at high risk?—have been studied hardly at all.

To stimulate research on sexual abuse, I believe a number of things must occur. For one, the field needs more researchers and more research projects. People are likely to think that "money" is the simple answer to those problems, and it is undeniable that an infusion of research funds would make a dramatic difference. But even if massive new funding is not forthcoming (as it may not be given the current political attitude toward social welfare and social science), the growth of research can be fostered in other ways. New researchers are attracted to fields where interesting theoretical questions have been identified, where a tradition of good research has already started to grow, and where some fundamental methodological problems have been conquered. This book is dedicated to the goal of identifying these issues, inaugurating this tradition, and showing a path through some of these methodological problems.

The book is roughly divided into a theoretical section and an empirical section. The first five chapters are devoted to the development of new ideas on subjects that in the past have been either neglected or treated in confused fashion. Chapter 1 looks at sexual abuse from a sociological, rather than the conventional psychological, point of view: as a social problem that has come to attention in a particular place at a particular time. Chapter 2 urges a more careful consideration of the taken-for-granted question of why we consider sexual activity between adults and children to be wrong and thus a social problem worthy of attention. Chapter 3, based on some previously unpublished empirical findings, speculates about why some children are more at-risk to sexual victimization than others. Chapter 4 organizes and develops theory about sexual abuse perpetrators based on the long-standing but largely neglected and confused literature on sex offenders that already exists. Chapter 5 integrates everything up to this point, giving special attention to the theories of Chapter 3 and 4. Chapter 5 also presents a four-preconditions model of sexual abuse as a valuable tool for understanding this complex problem.

The second section of the book is devoted to new research based on several studies in which I have been engaged. Chapters 6, 7, 8, and 9 are all reports from a survey of Boston parents which I completed in 1981. These chapters present valuable new information on a variety of subjects, many of which have never before been researched. Chapters 10 and 11 deal with two types of sexual abuse that have been the subject of much speculation, but not much research: the abuse of boys and abuse by women. The chapters advance discussion of these two types of abuse by reviewing the literature, showing that more is known about these subjects than is usually alleged.

Chapters 12, reporting some additional findings from the student survey which was the subject of *Sexually Victimized Children* (1979), brings forth some clear survey evidence that sexual abuse does have long-term effects. Chapter 13 discusses professionals and documents, through a previously unreported survey conducted in Boston, many of the serious problems that plague service delivery in this field. Finally, Chapter 14 looks back over some of the important themes and findings from the book and draws out some implications for the field.

Since the book attempts to advance both theory and research, chapters vary a great deal in tone and level of generality. Not all chapters will serve the needs of all readers. Some chapters, dealing with theory, especially in the first part of the book, may seem speculative and general to research-oriented readers. Others, dealing with research, may seem narrow, even technical. Chapters 8, 12, and 13 may seem overly academic to people with little interest in research, and may be skipped. For those interested primarily in new concepts, I would recommend focusing on Chapters 1, 2, 4, and 5.

Acknowledgments

REFLECTED IN THIS BOOK is work I did over a five-year period from 1978 to 1983, while I was a research scientist and, for four years, Assistant Director of the Family Violence Research Program at the University of New Hampshire. Some material has appeared in article form in *Child Abuse and Neglect* and in the *American Journal of Orthopsychiatry*.

During those five years, my work was supported by the National Center for Prevention and Control of Rape (NCPCR) at the National Institute of Mental Health (under grant MH34109), and during the last two years, by the National Center for Child Abuse and Neglect (NCCAN) (under grant 90CA840/01). Mary Lystad, the chief, and Marvin Feuerberg, project officer at the NCPCR, helped me a great deal with their interest and faith in my research. Joseph Wechsler and Aeolian Jackson at NCCAN have also been very helpful.

Over the years I have developed a number of colleagues in this field, from whose ideas I have benefited and whose acquaintance is an important answer to the perennial question, "How can you spend your time studying a subject so depressing?" Kee MacFarlane is perhaps the most knowledgeable person I know in this field; her quick insights and friendship have been an indispensable resource. Diana Russell is another person whose friendship and critical thinking have inspired my work. I feel privileged to have had her collaboration on one of the chapters included in this book. Lucy Berliner is another one of the really innovative and committed clinicians working in this field who has encouraged me in the belief that my work was of more than academic concern.

The problem of sexual abuse has attracted many people, most of whom have struck me as remarkable in the quality of their caring and commitment. A number of these people—Judith Herman, Jon Conte, Nick Groth, Ann Burgess, Roland Summit, Lynn Sanford—have been extraordinarily generous with their encouragement of my work. Beverly Gomes-Schwartz and Jonathan Horowitz were generous in soliciting my collaboration on their grant from the Office of Juvenile Justice, which resulted in jointly authored Chapter 13.

A number of people at the Family Violence Research Program have made essential contributions to my work. Murray Straus, the director, has been a wonderful colleague and mentor, and he has provided hours of useful comment on my research and writing. Dennis Redfield, who was my data analyst for three-and-a-half years, taught me a great deal about data and statistics while untangling many a knotty problem. Chapter 8 of this volume, which he co-authored, owes a great deal to his methodological sophistication. Ruth Miller has been an extraordinarily conscientious and devoted secretary whose efforts lie behind every comma in this book. Sigi Fizz has navigated my projects out of many tight squeezes with many bureaucracies. Gerry Hotaling's humor has put it all in perspective on many occasions. Other members of the program, past and present, who deserve thanks are Rich Sebastian, Dan Saunders, Alan Lincoln, Kersti Yllo, Jean Giles-Sims, Barbara Carson, Susan Herrick, Campbell Harvey, Larry Baron, Sharon Araji, Angela Browne, Elaine Hashem, Gretchen Stevens, and Kathy Hersh.

Other researchers contributed in very fundamental ways to the research reported in this book. The Boston survey on sexual abuse was conducted by the Center for Survey Research at the University of Massachusetts. Jack Fowler helped immensely with the design and execution of the study. Barbara Thomas did a top-notch job as project director. The rest of the staff and the interviewers worked above and beyond the call of duty to make it a success. Data reported in Chapter 10 come from the American Humane Association; Pat Schene and John Fluke helped make them available to me. Peter Rossi assisted with methodological questions in Chapter 8. Miriam Ornstein, Rebecca Newberry, and Tony Rao helped in the data analysis for Chapter 13.

CHAPTER 1

Sexual Abuse as a Social Problem

S EXUAL ABUSE IS emerging as one of the major forms of child abuse. As recently as ten years ago, sexual abuse was regarded as a rather uncommon problem. But in the late 1970s, official reports of sexual abuse began to mushroom at a much more rapid rate than reports of other forms of abuse. The number of cases being reported to the nationwide data collection system of the American Humane Association increased from 1,975 in 1976, and 4,327 in 1977, to 22,918 in 1982 (the last data available at the time of writing; Schene, 1983).[1] A more systematic effort to estimate the number of new cases of sexual abuse known to professionals concluded with a figure of 44,700 for the year starting in April 1979. Yet almost universally the problem is conceded to be far greater than statistics on reported cases would indicate.

Studies of the prevalence of child sexual abuse in the general population suggest that sexual abuse is still extremely undercounted by official reports. At least three random sample surveys had been done on adults by 1981 which asked about histories of child sexual abuse. A 1980 mail survey of 1054 Texas driver's license holders reported rates of 3% for males and 12% for females (Kercher, 1980).[2] A 1981 survey of 521 Boston parents (see Chapter 5) found that 6% of the males and 15% of the females had had an experience of sexual abuse before age 16 by a person at least five years older.

Finally, a meticulous 1978 survey that used 14 separate questions to probe for a variety of forms of child sexual abuse found that, before age 14, 28% of 930 San Francisco women had been victimized, meaning that they had experienced unwanted sexual touching (Russell, 1983). Twelve percent of these

930 women had been victimized by a relative. When the researcher added attempted and completed forcible rapes plus all forms of unwanted contact by relatives between the ages of 14 and 17, the figure for total sexual abuse before age 18 rose to 38%.

In addition to these random-sample surveys, other surveys of nonclinical populations have found similarly high rates of sexual victimization. For example, one found 19% for females and 9% for males in a college student sample of 796 (Finkelhor, 1979); another found 8% of females and 5% of males in a student sample of 952 (Fritz, Stoll & Wagner, 1981); still another found 22% of females in a student sample of 482 (Fromuth, 1983). Even in the Kinsey study of a generation ago, 9% of the 4441 females mentioned a sexual contact with an adult before the age of 14 (Kinsey et al., 1953). While the exact figures in all these studies vary because of the populations surveyed, the definitions used, and the sensitivity of the questions asked, they clearly establish that sexual victimization occurs in the lives of an important minority of all children.

Unfortunately, because all these prevalence studies have been done on populations now fully grown, they are not directly applicable to the experience of today's children. However, there is no strong reason to believe that rates of true prevalence have declined in the last 10 years, especially since the numbers of reported cases have increased dramatically. Even if no more than 10% of all girls and 2% of all boys were destined to be sexually abused, it would lead to the prediction (based on 60 million children currently under 18) that roughly 210,000 new cases of sexual abuse were occurring every year. This statistic gives a sense of how small a fraction of cases are currently reported, even given the recent surge.

Accompanying the rise in reported cases, the problem of sexual abuse has received increasing coverage by the press and media. Between 1978 and 1982 at least a dozen highly publicized books appeared on the subject of sexual abuse—about half of which were first person accounts by individuals who were victims. (For example, see: Allen, 1980; Armstrong, 1978; Brady, 1980; Butler, 1978; Forward, 1978; Geiser, 1978; Herman, 1981; Justice & Justice, 1979; Meiselman, 1978; Rush, 1980; Sanford, 1980; Walters, 1975). In addition to books, there were many films, major network television documentaries, and newspaper articles on the subject. A survey reported in Chapter 6 suggests that most American respondents remembered seeing a media discussion of the problem in 1980.

New, popular attention to this problem can be ascribed not only to the discovery of its true dimensions, but also to the idea that sexual abuse is a different sort of a problem than was once thought (Finkelhor, 1979). We now know that a great deal of sexual abuse occurs at the hands of close family members, particularly fathers and stepfathers. Not uncommonly, abuse goes on for an extended period of time. Most victims never tell anybody about it, and abuse can leave substantial psychological scars on its victims in the form of disturbed self esteem and an inability to develop trust in intimate relationships (Herman, 1981; Meiselman, 1978; Tsai, Feldman-Summers & Edgar, 1979).

EARLY ATTENTION TO THE PROBLEM

Whenever a social problem appears suddenly and of great magnitude we are apt to wonder why. More than any other social problem in recent memory, sexual abuse has risen precipitously in public awareness from virtual obscurity to extremely high visibility. Why has this emergence been so dramatic?

It is somewhat misleading to say that sexual abuse was entirely ignored in the past. Actually, from time to time it was promoted as a problem, but by a segment of the population that had little credibility in the eyes of many professionals and policymakers. At certain times in the past, moralists did express concern that children were being sexually abused as a result, in their view, of the liberalization of sexual values (Hoover, 1947; "Horror Week," 1949). Since they used the issue of child molesting as a way of campaigning against other kinds of progressive reforms that most social welfare professionals supported (e.g., sex education, humane treatment of sex offenders, end to censorship), the professionals tended to discount these alarms. Moreover, in many respects the moralists were mistaken about the problem, since they portrayed the greatest danger to children as coming from strangers and depraved individuals outside the family, not from within the family where, as recently documented (DeFrancis, 1969; Finkelhor, 1979), the more serious threat is.

THE CHILD ABUSE MOVEMENT AND THE WOMEN'S MOVEMENT

Sexual abuse has recently entered the public spotlight not because the true prevalence has increased, nor because reporting suddenly mushroomed (this was an effect rather than a cause), but, primarily, because the problem has been ·championed by a coalition of groups who are well experienced in promoting social problems—specifically the women's movement and the children's protection movement. Each of these groups has had success promoting a number of other social policy concerns. Since they already had the attention of both the public and the policymakers, when these groups joined forces, they had little difficulty drawing public attention to the issue of sexual abuse.

Interestingly, however, the child abuse movement and the women's movement have tended to focus on different aspects of the sexual abuse problem.
They have put the problem into somewhat different theoretical perspectives
and have suggested different remedies for it.

The child protectors have tended to view sexual abuse in the context of
other forms of child abuse and neglect (Avery-Clark, O'Neil & Laws, 1981).
"The sexual and physical abuse of children" is a common way the problems are
mentioned in the literature (Walters, 1975). Focusing on the family, child protectors tend to concentrate their attention on sexual abuse committed by
parents and other caretakers. Their analyses of incest take the view that incest is
a "product of family pathology and, except on the rarest occasions, all family
members contribute in some way to the pathology that breeds incest" (de
Young, 1982).

Feminists, by contrast, tend to identify sexual abuse with the phenomenon
of rape rather than with child abuse (Brownmiller, 1975). They emphasize that
the scope of the problem is larger than incest and includes much abuse from
non-family members and even strangers. Stressing the fact that most abuse is
committed by men against girls (De Francis, 1961; Finkelhor, 1979), the
feminists have chosen to explain sexual abuse as a function of the inferior status
of women and children and of predatory attitudes directed toward them by the
media and pornography (Herman & Hirschman, 1977; Rush, 1980). Rather
than blaming dysfunctional families, feminists tend to blame patriarchal social
structure and male socialization (Nelson, 1982), taking particular umbrage at
theories that focus on the mother's role or the victim's complicity (McIntyre,
1981).

The two groups have also proposed somewhat different ways of dealing
with the problem. The child abuse movement argues for whole-family treatment programs (Giaretto, 1982), with an emphasis on reconciling and
reconstituting the family. Although most of the child protectors recognize the
importance of criminal justice participation, they generally argue against incarceration of offenders on the grounds that it increases family denial and
retaliation against the victim while decreasing willingness to report.

Feminist-oriented intervention adopts a more "victim advocacy" approach,
based on the model of rape crisis counseling and victim witness programs. The
key goal in this approach is to protect victims against further victimization by
the offender, family, or community agencies. Victim advocates sometimes express strong reservations about the idea of family reconciliation on the grounds
that it subjects victims to the risk of further psychological and sexual abuse. Victim advocates have been more enthusiastic about vigorous criminal justice sanctions applied to offenders as a way of deterring future abuse and reinforcing
public standard about sexual conduct (Nelson, 1982).

International Scope of the Program

Unlike physical child abuse, which became a matter of international concern almost simultaneously to its "discovery" in the United States, interest in child sexual abuse has remained primarily American. Facts about the international dimension have been difficult to obtain. Prior to 1980 studies of sexual abuse had been conducted in a number of other countries. For example, see Riemer (1940) on Sweden, Szabo (1958) on France, Pilinow (1970) on Poland, Maisch (1972) on Germany, Devroye (1973) on Belgium. Yet, in no other country was the concern as great as it was in the United States, and until recently, in no other country had attempts been made to gather national statistics.

The argument could be made that the United States is exceptional in its large child sexual abuse problem compared to other countries. For example, the argument could be based on international statistics, which show extraordinary American rates of reported rape (Geis, 1977; Schiff, 1973). These reported rape rates do include a substantial number of assaults against children. However, reported rape rates are a very doubtful proxy for reported or particularly unreported child sexual abuse. There are even reasons to believe that the available international figures are not very accurate (Geis, 1977).

Moreover, the opposite argument, that the United States is *not* an exception, has a number of plausible points in its favor:

1. *Prior to the late 1970s it would have been hard to distinguish levels of the problem of sexual abuse in the United States from any other Western society.* In all places it was considered rare, yet we now know from adult prevalence studies that the problem was widespread in the United States even then. Other societies may well have rates as high as the United States without its being evident at the public level.

2. *Social conditions which we might imagine to promote sexual abuse—like social isolation, arbitrary parental authority over children, patriarchal values—seem to prevail in many other societies.*

3. *Finally, we are beginning to hear reports of widespread prevalence of sexual abuse revealed in other countries.* For example, an effort to mobilize professional attention to this problem is gaining momentum in Great Britain (Mrazek, Lynch & Bentovim, 1981, 1983). A recent survey of over 3000 readers of a British teenage women's magazine found that over one-third had experienced sexual victimization as a child (Baker, 1983). A survey of British professionals identified 1072 cases in a one-year period (Mzarek, Lynch & Bentovim, 1983). In Sweden, too, figures are emerging about widespread prevalence. Radda Barnen, a Swedish children's rights organization, commissioned a probability sample of close to 1000 adult Swedes, and found that 9% of the women and

3% of the men said they had been sexually abused before the age of 18 (Ronstrom, 1983). The nature of the experiences reported in the survey closely paralleled the findings from equivalent American studies. Thus, the existence of widespread child sexual abuse in other countries seems established, but we will probably have to wait another five years, or perhaps more, before we can really evaluate the situation in the United States based on good international comparisons.

SEXUAL ABUSE IN HISTORICAL PERSPECTIVE

The current flood of reports in the United States has prompted many people to wonder whether sexual abuse is on the rise. It is certainly possible that it is, but it is also possible that the recent flood can be entirely accounted for by people's new willingness to report what was previously an unmentionable experience. Arguments can be made on both sides.

Looked at in long-term historical perspective, for example, there are plausible arguments that sexual abuse is actually declining, not increasing. Making their arguments in reference to the problem of child maltreatment in general, some historians have drawn attention to how dreadful life circumstances were for most children prior to modern times (De Mause, 1974). In the past children were forced to do arduous and dangerous work. They were badly neglected by their families; they were sold or indentured or married off at an early age for economic gain. It is plausible that given such an unprotected status, children were vulnerable to much more abuse of all sorts, including sexual abuse.

Some evidence of sexual abuse is available in historical accounts of children being used as prostitutes and favored sexual companions in Greek, Roman, and medieval times, as well as later periods (Rush, 1980; Schultz, 1982). The fact that until fairly recently, children could be placed in various forms of servitude suggests that sexual abuse in this form may have been very widespread.

On the matter of incest, Linda Gordon (1982) has pointed to features of family life that existed up until the 20th century in America which she believes were probably conducive to greater levels of incestuous sexual abuse in the past. The absence of compulsory education meant that it was typical for adolescent girls to remain closely tied to the home. It would have been normal in pre-20th-century American families for girls to carry much of the domestic responsibility and to assume unquestioning obedience to a father's commands. Kept in the home outside social scrutiny and subject to strict paternal authority, the girl's vulnerability to sexual abuse was probably great.

It seems plausible that many of the historical changes that have benefited children—laws against child labor and harsh physical punishment, age-of-consent laws, educational reforms, child welfare agencies, as well as greater scientific knowledge about child development—have resulted in a decline of both physical and sexual child abuse. But it is hard to be certain.

The debate about the history of childhood will undoubtedly continue and grow, although whether it will cast any new light on the question of historical trends in the prevalence of sexual abuse is questionable. It is a long step from saying that the general status of children has improved to proving that, therefore, the amount of child sexual victimization has declined. Unfortunately, given the particularly secret nature of this social problem, it is unlikely that we are going to uncover social records prior to the 20th century that will ever decide this issue convincingly, thus leaving most of our discussion to the realm of speculation.

DIVORCE AND REMARRIAGE

Arguments about more recent historical trends in the prevalence of sexual abuse usually draw implications from changes in contemporary family life and sexual mores. Probably the most dramatic recent development in family structure (in the West and elsewhere) has been the increasing ease with which conjugal pairings can be formed and dissolved (Goode, 1963). There has been a widespread increase in divorce all over the world, accompanied by high rates of remarriage and informal coupling. Probably, this increase has had an impact on the problem of sexual abuse, but its impact has not been solely positive or negative.

On the one hand, a consistent finding in sexual abuse research has been that children are at higher risk of abuse when they live with a stepfather or mother's boyfriend than with a natural father (see Chapter 3) (Finkelhor, 1979; Miller, 1976; Russell, 1984). Since today children are exposed to more stepfathers, mothers' lovers, and boyfriends as a result of an increasing number of divorces and recouplings, their vulnerability to sexual abuse may have increased.

On the other hand, the increasing accessibility of divorce works in the opposite manner, too. For example, many children are no longer subjected to arbitrary authority and abuse merely because their mother has no alternative and is unable to leave the abusive family situation. The availability of divorce has certainly rescued many children from what might have once been chronic and inescapable torment and abuse. So the high rate of divorce and recoupling has probably increased vulnerability for some children, while decreasing it for others.

CHANGING SEXUAL NORMS

Along with changes in family structure in recent years, there have also been dramatic changes in sexual attitudes and behaviors, which have possibly contributed to the problem of sexual abuse. Although these changes, it can be argued, have aggravated the problem somewhat, I do not think they created it.

The so-called "sexual revolution" has accomplished a number of things: a dramatic increase in public talk about sex and an undercutting of certain kinds of traditional sexual prohibitions in particular groups—prohibitions on premarital sex, extramarital sex, and other kinds of sexual activity (Hunt, 1974). The sexual revolution has also gone hand in hand with the new assertiveness of women and their demand for a more active role in determining the nature and course of sexual encounters.

Certainly one major effect of the sexual revolution has been the erosion of traditional, externalized controls over sexual behavior. Forces such as the religion, parental authority, and tradition no longer have as much legitimacy in controlling behavior and enforcing sexual norms as in the past. One result has been that many people are confused about the state of sexual norms. What are permissible and what are taboo types of sexual behavior? Standards are unclear and in flux.

One group for whom this state of confusion is particularly serious are those whose sexual behavior in the past was regulated primarily by strong external controls. The loss of these controls may have propelled them in an antisocial direction. This group might conclude, logically, that there are no longer rules. If, for example, prohibitions no longer govern premarital sex or extramarital sex, are the prohibitions against sex with children still in force?

The erosion of these taboos may have been aided and abetted by the availability of popular pornography. The world of pornography always needs new frontiers to conquer to promote new sales. This medium has been quick to exploit the theme of sex with children. In the late 1970s in the United States, we saw a rapid escalation in the quantity of pornography portraying children as sex objects (Baker, 1978; Burgess, 1982, 1984; Dillingham & Melmed, 1982; Guio, Burgess & Kelly, 1980; McCaghy, 1979; Tyler, 1982). In some pornography stores in some areas, as many as a quarter or a third of the book titles refer to incestuous sex or sex with underage children (Stone, 1983). So even the man who was slow to draw his own conclusion that the sexual revolution now permits sex with children might certainly get that message quickly from pornography (Densen-Gerber & Hutchinson, 1978).

CHANGE IN EXPECTATIONS

Two other contributions of the sexual revolution to this problem should not be overlooked. Although from its portrayal in the media one might conclude that today sex is more readily available, the sexual revolution has heralded a more dramatic rise in expectations than in actual sexual activity. Although everybody is exposed to the sexualization of life as portrayed in the media, not everyone can actualize these new expectations. For many, the opportunities for sexual variety or sexual fulfillment have not increased. Men, feeling a sense of sexual deprivation in the face of these expectations, but locked in situations where they felt few other options were available, might turn to children for the sexual gratification promised by the sexual revolution.

Added is the fact that women are no longer acting out innocent, childlike sexual roles. Women have become more critical of male sexual performance and have pressed for equality and mutuality in sexual encounters. This assertiveness may threaten many men who have been raised to prefer passivity and uncritical compliance from sexual partners. For these men, children may represent a very attractive sexual alternative. Children are not critical of a man's sexual performance. They expect no mutuality. They are taught to obey adults and can easily be cajoled into sexual activity. So through its impact on sexual norms, pornography and women's roles, the sexual revolution may have exacerbated the problem of sexual abuse.

Nonetheless there are countervailing tendencies. The sexual revolution needs to be credited with creating an environment where this problem could come to public attention in a previously unheard of way. In the current public environment, matters such as sexual abuse can be talked about in the media, people can bring sexual problems to the attention of professionals. It is possible to argue that as a result of this climate children are getting better protection from the possibility of sexual abuse than ever before (Sanford, 1980). Certainly the statistics indicate that victims of all sorts are being able to reach out for help as they never have in the past. So at the same time that it may have increased the potential for sexual abuse, the sexual revolution also enabled the problem to come out into the open.

Although the current discussion is almost entirely in the realm of conjecture, it is hoped that, as time goes by, some of the questions about recent historical trends in sexual abuse can be answered more definitively. One way of doing this is to look at the experience of different generations who are still alive today. Using this approach, Russell (1983) has indeed found evidence for the idea that sexual abuse may have been increasing during the course of the 20th century. Younger women in her survey reported more *intrafamilial* sexual abuse than did older women. For example, only 7.9% of women in their sixties and 11.7% of women in their fifties at the time of her survey reported such abuse compared to 23.8% of those in their thirties and 22.3% of those in their twenties. This apparent increase over time might be explained by the younger women's better recall and greater willingness to report. However, Russell also found no comparable increase over time in reports of *extrafamilial* abuse, suggesting that better recall and willingness to report might not account for the growth in rates of intrafamily abuse. Obviously more research needs to be done on this crucially important sociological question.

SEXUAL ABUSE IS DIFFERENT FROM PHYSICAL ABUSE

As a problem that has come to light through the child welfare system, sexual abuse is frequently thought of in the same context as physical abuse. However, sexual abuse has many complexities that it does not share with physical abuse. One of them concerns the role of the medical community. Physicians have been extremely important allies in the issue of physical abuse. They have been crucial in the identification of victims and also in the recognition of the problem as a social issue. As a matter of fact, in the United States, at least, it was primarily the adoption by pediatricians of physical abuse as a medical problem which allowed it to become a major public issue.

Interestingly, sexual abuse does not mobilize the activism of physicians to nearly the same extent as physical abuse. In part this is because sexual abuse remains an emotional subject that sets off conflicts for almost everyone, professionals included. Yet, physical abuse is an emotional subject too. If physicians have been slow to mobilize against sexual abuse (Goodwin & Geil, 1982), an important reason is that so few victims of sexual abuse show any medically significant physical trauma (Rogers, 1982). Physicians are trained to minister to physical ailments, and conditions that do not pose major medical challenges—like sexual abuse—fall outside their interest.

Second, the group of physicians who might be most appropriately concerned about sexual abuse—psychiatrists—have been slow to react to the problem. Although pediatricians and gynecologists also could have been more active in researching the problem, sexual abuse—as a primarily interpersonal rather than physical problem—falls most directly into the expertise of the psychiatric branch of medicine. That psychiatry has not adopted sexual abuse as a priority problem has to do, in part, with its ideological foundations, which have been skeptical traditionally with regard to sexual abuse (Masson, 1983).

The conventional Freudian viewpoint on sexual abuse, going back to his own writings, was that these experiences were, most often, fantasies that expressed a child's Oedipal conflicts and not real events (Rush, 1977, 1980). The focus on the sexual interests of the child tended to put blame for the situation on the child's seductiveness and not on the adult's irresponsibility. This particular ideology has much less hold than it used to; in fact much of the American psychiatric community has abandoned it. But it still works to reinforce any natural ambivalence about the problem by psychiatry as a profession.

In short, given the not-exclusively-physical nature of the abuse and the ambivalence of psychiatry, physicians have not been and will not be the professionals to galvanize interest in the problem of sexual abuse. In the United States we have seen that the problem has been promoted more often by psychologists and social workers than physicians. Since physicians can be a very prestigious group in the lobby against any social problem, their absence leaves an important gap. Their absence is already noticeable in terms of public policy response. While the "discovery" of physical child abuse was heralded with new government legislation, new appropriations, new agencies, and new attention to the problem in major medical and research centers around the country, no equivalent mobilization of established institutions has occurred around sexual abuse. The lesser involvement of the medical community is part of the reason.

Men, Women, and Sexual Abuse

Another very important difference between sexual abuse and physical abuse also explains the more cautious institutional response to the problem: sexual abuse is committed primarily by men. Virtually all data collected show this male preponderance (see Chapter 11). Moreover, the male preponderance is not simply a matter of abuse by women going undetected, since even in nonclinical surveys of adults reporting retrospectively on childhood sexual experiences, the male perpetrators vastly outnumbered the women (Finkelhor, 1979). Also it is not a question of sexual contact between children and women being defined differently. Studies that have simply asked about sexual contacts with older partners, and have not used terms like "abuse" or "molestation," also show that the vast majority of sexual contacts between adults and children are between men and children (Bell & Weinberg, 1978). After reviewing all the studies, Diana Russell and I conclude in Chapter 11 that men constitute about

95% of the perpetrators in cases of abuse of girls and 80% in cases of abuse of boys.

These facts, which are well appreciated on a psychological level, make sexual abuse a subject to which men and women have different reactions. Sexual abuse is a problem which incriminates a particular sex—men—a rather uncomfortable fact for many men to deal with. It makes it harder for them to work enthusiastically on this problem and to avoid defensive responses which can transfer blame from the male offenders to the (often female) victims. Since men occupy powerful policy-making positions, the gender politics of sexual abuse can often hamper effective policies and public action.

To state this another way, while physical abuse may be seen, correctly, as a problem of parenting, sexual abuse should, perhaps to a larger extent, be described as a problem of *masculine socialization*. When we understand why women do not sexually abuse children to the same extent as men do, we may reach some important conclusions about how to help prevent men from committing this kind of abuse.

SEXUAL ABUSE AND MASCULINITY

I would like to outline several differences between men and women which I think help explain why women are much less likely to abuse children sexually. (Several others are mentioned in Chapter 11.)

1. *Women learn earlier and much more completely to distinguish between sexual and nonsexual forms of affection.* In part because of their preparation for motherhood, women are sensitized to appreciate the distinction involved in affection without a sexual component (Person, 1980). Men are not given as many legitimate opportunities to practice nurturing and to express dependency needs except through sex (Zilbergeld, 1978). So when men need affection and are feeling dependent, they are much more likely to look for fulfillment in a sexual form, even with an inappropriate partner. Women can get such needs met also with children, but without sexualizing the relationship.

2. *Men grow up seeing heterosexual success as much more important to their gender identities than women do* (Person, 1980). When their egos or their competencies suffer any insult, men are much more likely than women to feel a need for sex as a way of reconfirming their adequacy, even if the only easily available sexual partner is a child. Sex with children may be a weak confirmation, but it is some confirmation.

3. *Men are socialized to be able to focus their sexual interest around sexual acts isolated from the context of a relationship.* Women, by contrast, are taught to focus on whole romantic contexts and whole relationships. This ability of men

to relate concretely to sexual acts is illustrated in their greater interest in pornography, as well as their ability to be aroused by children. For women, the fact that a partner was a child would make it more difficult to experience sexual interest in that partner. Men, however, could experience arousal because the partner, even though a child, had the right kind of genitals or could engage in the desired sex act.

4. *Finally, men are socialized to see as their appropriate sexual partners persons who are younger and smaller than themselves, while women are socialized to see as their appropriate sexual partners persons older and larger.* It is less of a contortion for a man to find a child sexually attractive because children are merely an extension of the gradient along which his appetites are already focused.

If one thinks about these as some of the reasons why men abuse children while women do not, there are clear implications about social changes that could help to eliminate sexual abuse. First, men might benefit from the opportunity to practice affection and dependency in relationships that did not involve sex, such as male-to-male friendships and nurturant interaction with children. Second, the accomplishment of heterosexual sex might be de-emphasized as the ultimate criterion of male adequacy. Third, men might learn to enjoy sexual relationships based on equality. Men who are comfortable relating to women at the same level of maturity and competence will be less likely to exploit children sexually. As men's relations with women change, so will their relations with children.

A corollary of these ideas is very important. Based on the sex distribution of offenders, it would be easy to imagine someone's suggesting that to protect children from sexual abuse, we should keep them as far away from men as possible. Although in its extreme form this is ridiculous, such attitudes reach expression in prejudices against male babysitters and single-parent fathers. In fact, the exact opposite might be what is needed. As they take more and more equal responsibility for the care of children, men may well come to identify more closely with children's well-being and learn how to enjoy deeply affectionate relationships that have no sexual component. This step may be one of the most important we need to take toward transforming men from offenders against children to defenders of their well-being.

CHAPTER 2

Sexual Abuse as
a Moral Problem

I N ADDITION TO the combined support of feminists and child protectors, the problem of sexual abuse has another feature which contributed to its dramatic appearance as a social problem. The moral issue was already well established. In public discussion at least, people readily agreed that sex between adults and children was wrong. Still, advocates for the problem have had to prove that it is widespread. But unlike advocates for some other social problems, such as marital rape, they have not had to expend so much effort arguing publicly that sexual abuse is wrong.

Unfortunately, that advocates for the problem of sexual abuse have been able to assume this moral consensus has led to fuzzy thinking. They have not had to examine the assumptions of their position. They have not had to think through the moral issues clearly in their own minds because the weight of traditional morality supported their point of view.

This chapter intends to criticize some of the more complacent arguments made about what is wrong with sex between adults and children, and then to suggest a sounder line of reasoning in favor of such a position.

Before starting, it should be made clear what we are discussing. For purposes of this discussion, "sex" refers to activities, involving the genitals, which are engaged in for the gratification of at least one person. Thus "sex" is not limited to intercourse. Second, "adult" refers to persons 18 or over, either related or not, to the child. "Child," at least in the first part of this discussion, means a prepubertal child.

Simple Arguments Are Not Sufficient

There are at least two "intuitive" arguments that are often made against the idea of sex between adults and children, both of which fall short of being convincing. One argument states simply that such sex is intrinsically wrong. It is unnatural from a biological and psychological point of view. As evidence, such an argument would cite such facts as the following: (1) A little girl's vagina is too small to accept a mature male's penis. (2) The thought of such relations inspires an innate disgust in many people. (3) Almost all societies either taboo or tightly regulate sexual contact between the mature and immature. However, this argument against sex between adults and children is too categorical. It does not make reference to any more general ethical notions that would give this prohibition meaning. Many assertions of "intrinsic wrong" made about other sexual behavior, such as homosexuality or masturbation, have been called into question in recent years.

A second argument rejects adult-child sexuality because it entails a premature sexualization of the child. From this point of view, childhood should be a time of relative immunity from sex, where a child enjoys freedom from an often problematic aspect of life. When adults approach children sexually, they draw them into a world for which children are not yet ready. Unfortunately for this argument, however, children are sexual. Most children are curious about sex. Many explore sexuality with one another. There is increasing professional and scientific agreement that sexual interest and activity among children is healthy and perhaps even salutary to later sexual functioning (Yates, 1978). This argument seems inadequate also.

A third argument about what's wrong with sex between adults and children remains, simply, that it is harmful. This one is probably the most common argument one hears currently, and it is an argument containing a good deal of validity. Certainly clinicians are encountering an increasing number of both children and adults who appear to have been badly traumatized by childhood sexual contacts with adults. Clinicians are convinced that sexual abuse can result in long-term effects on a child's self-esteem and on a child's ability to develop healthy sexual and intimate relationships (Herman, 1981).

Research studies do support the idea that sexual abuse can have serious negative consequences (DeFrancis, 1969; Kaufman, Peck & Taqiuri, 1954; Tsai, Feldman-Summers & Edgar, 1979). Studies among populations of prostitutes, drug abusers, and adolescent runaways suggest that a high proportion of such people have a history of sexual abuse. In Chapter 12 we review evidence on long-term effects, showing that the group of ordinary college students who were sexually victimized as children are significantly impaired in terms of their feelings about their own sexual behavior compared to a nonvictimized group.

However, the research is somewhat more equivocal on the issue of whether the effects of sexual contact between adults and children are inevitably negative. In our own research we found that the vast majority of adults who reported that they had such sexual contacts as children said the effects were negative (Finkelhor, 1979). It is also true that some children who have sexual contacts with adults report these as positive. In our student study (Finkelhor, 1979) 7% of the women, for example, rated the experience as a positive one. (Only about half of these positive experiences were with actual adults, the rest being with other children at least five years older.) Some researchers have recently captured media attention reporting what they call "positive incest" (Farrell, 1982; Nelson, 1981; Nobile, 1977). It turns out that most of what these researchers are terming positive incest are experiences between two children or two mature partners, not cross-generational incest. But it is probably true that a small number of children do have sexual experiences with adults that they feel are positive (Sandfort, 1982).

Given that positive experiences between adults and children may be possible, can one still argue that sexual contact between adults and children is wrong because it is harmful? Yes, I think one can. The evidence suggests that such sexual contact can be harmful, often extremely so. The evidence also suggests that such sexual contact is frequently felt to be negative and unpleasant even if it does not always leave permanent scars. On the other side, the evidence of positive or therapeutic effects is small—and controversial. In short, most people would agree that even if not inevitably harmful, sexual contact between adults and children carries high risks. These high risks justify the prohibitions society places on this activity.

Even though one can argue against sexual contact between adults and children on the basis of the risk involved, it remains, however, that such an argument underemphasizes the real extent of the wrong and the basic ethical issue at stake. Whether such activity should be sanctioned or not is not just an empirical issue like whether we should allow children to ingest caffeine, something to be decided by a balancing of negative and positive consequences. Thinking about the question in these terms misses the whole moral dimension, which also ought to be addressed.

For example, we would bridle at the notion that the question of slavery should be decided on the empirical question of whether black people or any other slave group experience more well-being under slavery than in freedom. Something about slavery is so offensive to our fundamental notion about human relationships, to our system of ethics, that we do not decide the issue on purely empirical grounds. Testimony from even large numbers of slaves that they preferred the condition of slavery would not convince us that "consensual" slavery should be allowed. Similarly, there is an ethical dimension beyond the empirical dimension that needs to be included in our understanding of what is wrong with sex between adults and children.

The Issue of Consent

The ethical dimension of the problem can be approached through the issue of consent. Consent is one of the key notions around which we organize the ethics of our social interactions. As a society, we are moving toward a sexual ethic that holds that sex of all sorts between consenting persons should be permitted, but sex in situations where a person does not consent should be considered illegal and taboo. Rape is clearly a crime whose wrong lies in the fact that it is a sex act done to a person without his or her consent. Sex between adults and children can be condemned for the same reason.

But don't many children "consent" to sex acts with adults? It is true that sex between adults and children commonly is much less coercive than rape because, in many cases, children appear to consent passively or even cooperate. If we say that sex is "Okay" if consent is present, doesn't this legitimize much adult-child sex?

The key argument we make is that children are incapable of truly consenting to sex with adults because they are children. For this reason, sex between an adult and a child cannot be sanctioned under our moral standard, which requires that consent be given. However, to make this statement, a more detailed discussion of consent is necessary.

For consent truly to occur, two conditions must prevail. A person must know what it is that he or she is consenting to and must have true freedom to say yes or no.

Can children fulfill these conditions in relation to sex with adults? It is fairly evident they cannot. For one thing, children lack the information necessary to make an "informed" decision about the matter. They are ignorant about sex and sexual relationships. It is not only that they may be unfamiliar with the mechanics of sex and reproduction. More important, they are generally unaware of the social meanings of sexuality. For example, they are unlikely to be aware of the rules and regulations surrounding sexual intimacy—what it is supposed to signify. They are uninformed and inexperienced about what criteria to use in judging the acceptability of a sexual partner. They do not know much about the "natural history" of a sexual relationship—what course it will take. And finally, children have little way of knowing how other people are likely to react to the experience they are about to undertake—what likely consequences it will have for them in the future.

Children may know that they like the adult, that the physical sensations feel good, and on this basis may make a choice. But they lack the knowledge the adult has about sex and about what they are undertaking. This "ignorance" stems from the very fact of being a child and inexperienced. In this sense, a child cannot give informed consent to sex with an adult.

For another thing, a child does not have the freedom to say yes or no. This is true in a legal sense and also in a psychological sense. In a legal sense, a child is under the authority of an adult and has no free will. In a more important psychological sense, children have a hard time saying "no" to adults, who control all kinds of resources that are essential to them. Food, money, freedom all lie in adult hands. In this sense, the child is like the prisoner who volunteers to be a research subject. The child has no freedom in which to consider the choice.

This lack of freedom is especially true when the adult propositioning the child is a parent or a relative or another important figure in the child's life, as is so often the case. Most of what we see as "consensual" behavior among children is a response to the powerful incentives and authority that such adults hold. As one of my interviewees said, "He was my uncle. He told me what to do and I obeyed. I was taught to obey adults." Thus a child cannot consent, in a moral sense, to sex with an adult because a child is not truly free to say no.

The basic proposition here is that adult–child sex is wrong because the fundamental conditions of consent cannot prevail in the relationship between an adult and a child. The proposition seems to be an important supplement to other arguments, particularly the argument that such acts are wrong solely because they harm the child. It adds a moral dimension to the empirical one. Thus even if someone could demonstrate many cases where children were not harmed by such experiences, one could still argue that the experiences were wrong because the children could not consent. The wrongness is not contingent upon proof of a harmful outcome.

A somewhat analogous situation, I think, is that of sex between therapists and patients. Many patients may benefit from sex with their therapist, but the argument that such sex is wrong does not hinge on the positive or negative outcome that results. Rather it lies in the fundamental assymmetry of the relationship. A patient, I would argue, cannot freely consent to sex with a therapist. The main consideration here is that, in the context of a therapeutic relationship, a patient is not really free to say yes or no. Even if the patient liked it, a moral wrong would have been committed.

The child-adult sex situation is similar, with the addition that not only the child could not freely consent, but also the child could not give *informed* consent. An adult patient is somewhat more aware of the social significance of sexuality, probably foreseeing some of the consequences of sex with a therapist. A child, however, is less aware of both these things and is thus even further handicapped from being able to give informed consent.

OBJECTIONS

Various arguments have been raised in objection to children being incapable of fulfilling conditions of true consent to sex with adults. I would like to mention them briefly.

First, objectors have pointed out that the conditions of consent, as I have outlined them here, not only do not prevail in adult-child contacts, but they do not prevail in many adult-adult contacts (NAMBLA, 1981). Do all adults really have full knowledge of consequences when entering into a sexual relationship? Obviously not. Is a secretary being propositioned by her boss truly free to refuse? In many cases, no. Full consent probably is not present in all adult-adult encounters. Some adults probably deserve protection along with children. However, the greater potential access that adults have to both knowledge and freedom puts them in a different category. Children constitute a clearly identifiable *class* where these conditions do not prevail; they deserve special protection.

Second, some people argue that the notion of "inability to consent" involves an oppressive type of paternalism. Most of the new champions of eliminating so-called "age-of-consent laws" have made their arguments on behalf of the "rights of children," such as the right of children to express themselves sexually and choose whomever they wish for sexual partners (O'Carroll, 1980; Presland, 1981). It may be true that children are oppressed by arbitrary adult-imposed controls. But it seems extremely doubtful that any large group of children are complaining that they are not "allowed" to engage in sex with adults. If polled, we suspect children would vote for better protection against adult sexual overtures, not more "freedom."

These self-proclaimed children's liberationists tend to minimize two parts of the problem. They do not truly believe that adults are vastly more powerful than children. They think, for example, that the fact that the adult badly wants the child to like him, or the fact that the child's disclosure could put the adult in jail, really equalizes the power imbalance that exists between an adult and a child. They also do not acknowledge the enormous manipulativeness and callous lack of regard for children's well-being that characterize the behavior of many persons who try to seduce children. Most children are not capable of protecting their own interests in the face of this power and this guile (Gay Left Collective, 1981). There is nothing wrong with paternalism where it provides children with protection they need and cannot give themselves.

Still another line of objection to the "inability to consent" argument accepts the fact that adults do have a tremendous power advantage over children, but argues that only in the area of sex are such adult prerogatives viewed in a negative light. For example, one pedophile writes:

> One might have expected that there would be an equal concern in government, at least as great as that in relation to sex, that children should not be subjected to "manipulation" by ruthless adult salesmen of every kind of creed. . . . Adults are free to fill a child's mind with any prejudice or bigotry they like, without any danger of facing a sentence for corrupting a minor. . . . If it is true that children are incapable of making judgements about sexual relationships, how much more adept are they likely to be at judging the rival claims of Protestant and Catholic, or Jehovah's Witnesses and the Exclusive Brethren? (O'Carroll, 1980, pp. 155-156).

It is true that adults are allowed awesome power to influence children in ways that may be detrimental to their development. Government is concerned about some other abuses of such power besides sexual abuses—the reason, for example, why we have laws that require parents to send children to school and laws that forbid child labor. Nonetheless, sex is a special domain requiring some special restraints on the free exercise of adult power, and there are good reasons why this should be so.

First of all, in part because of the emotions they mobilize, we know that sexual relationships often come into conflict with other kinds of roles and other kinds of social responsibilities. (This conflict becomes apparent, for example, in incestuous fathers who try to keep their daughters from having normal teenage social lives with their peers.) To make sure that adults fulfill important responsibilities toward children, society needs to restrict the kinds of sexual involvement permitted between them. According to some theorists (Parsons, 1949), it is the need for this separation of roles which has resulted in widespread evolution of incest taboos.

Second, the sexual arena is a special domain for restriction of power because of the risks involved. We may believe that bringing a child up in a bizarre religious sect or with unusual political beliefs is detrimental to a child's well-being. However, although strong scientific evidence is still lacking on the subject, the particular concern the public feels about the greater potential for psychological harm that can result from early sexual involvement with an adult is probably well-founded. Special limits on adult prerogatives in regard to sex are justified on this account.

Finally, the sexual realm is a special realm for restricting adult power because of the stigmatization that occurs. People in our society react with both alarm and prejudice toward a child who has been sexually involved with an adult (even after the child grows up). Critics may argue that if society accepted child-adult sexuality, such a stigma would not exist. But it does exist, and it is unfair of adults who wish it didn't to inflict such stigma on children, who cannot be fully cognizant of its existence. To rear a child in a stigmatized status cannot be considered a crime in and of itself, or else we would have to support laws that would make it a crime to bring a child up to believe in communism. But in the absence of any clearly countervailing benefit and in the presence of apparent risk, the fact of potential stigma is an additional argument for limitation on adult prerogative in the area of sexuality.

A final argument some have used to object to children's inability to consent is that it is too categorical: Can *all* children be said to lack power and knowledge in relation to *all* adults? Aren't there exceptions where conditions of consent might prevail, and why should these exceptions be penalized?

This problem holds for all legal and social rules. Some underage persons undoubtedly have the capacity and judgment to drive cars, vote, drink responsibly, and protect themselves in sexual encounters with adults. In all these cases a few persons are unfairly restricted because the majority are judged to lack certain capacities. However, as opposed to the questions of driving, voting, and drinking, we do not see the idea of prohibiting adults from having sex with children as being very restrictive to children (primarily these laws are restrictive to adults).

The question arises, then, at what age a person might be judged capable of consent. We have limited our discussion up to now to the situation of prepubertal children with adults. However, it is also our sense that many postpubertal children also do not have the power and knowledge necessary to give true consent, especially in situations where the adults are persons in authority.

We are not exactly sure how age of consent should be determined. We feel certain that consent cannot occur between any child up to age of majority and a person in authority over that child, such as any guardian, teacher, or administrative official. Perhaps an adolescent of 15 or 16 is capable of consent in relation to an adult who is not in authority. Research can and should be done to evaluate whether the younger partners in such relationships end up being harmed.

In regulating sex among children, we also favor the notion of "age differentials," such as the law in the state of Washington which makes intercourse with a victim under 11 criminal only if the perpetrator is over 13; with a victim 11, 12, or 13 only if the perpetrator is over 16; and so on (Kocen & Bulkley, 1981).

Under any scheme some capable children will be unfairly restricted. However, we believe the argument for a relatively conservative approach is strong. The restrictions imposed on children by such laws are not onerous, whereas the risks they seek to protect against appear relatively great.

CONCLUSION

In this chapter we have tried to provide some clarity for the moral arguments about what is wrong about sex between adults and children. There are two important reasons for ethical clarity on this issue. One is to be able to explain convincingly to victims and perpetrators of sexual abuse why drastic interference is being made in their affairs. Adults who take sexual advantage of children are notorious for the justifications they give and for their stubborn refusal to admit to any wrongdoing. "No harm was caused," they often say. Although argument is unlikely to convince them, both they and their victims may benefit in the long run from being exposed clearly to the moral issue involved.

Second, ethical clarity is important on this issue for the benefit of society as a whole. In America today, sexual ethics are increasingly confused. Taboos have fallen by the wayside and new standards have not been articulated to replace the old ones. A polarization has taken place, and many people have the impression that one is either broadly in favor of sexuality or broadly opposed. Moral confusion about sex may be in part responsible for the occurrence of sexual abuse, since some people interpret the current sexual revolution as an exhortation that "all is permitted."

But concern about sexual abuse of children is not part of a Victorian resurgence. It is compatible with the most progressive attitude toward sexuality currently being voiced, a position which urges that consent be the only standard by which the legitimacy of sexual acts is evaluated. Ethical clarity in this issue can help society move toward some more coherent outlook on sexual matters and by doing so combat at least one source of the problem of abuse.

CHAPTER 3

Victims

A STREAM OF STUDIES describing the age and sex of children who are sexually abused is steadily accumulating. As we now know from many reports, victims include both girls and boys, although girls predominate (for more on the exact ratio see Chapter 10). The most common ages are between 8 and 12, although younger and older children are also well represented.

Unfortunately, these facts about age and sex are not enough to illuminate why it is that some children get abused while others do not. To develop theories about victims, we need to know many other things. Do victims tend to come predominantly from certain social-class or ethnic backgrounds? Do they live in particular kinds of household arrangements? Is their family life characteristic in any way? Have they experienced any other life events in common? Information about these kinds of questions has been very hard to come by.

One of the few attempts to gather detailed information about the backgrounds of victims and how they might be different was one I made in an earlier study. In 1979, I published a book, *Sexually Victimized Children*, which was, in part, a report on a study of 796 college students and the sexual abuse that some of them had experienced. For those familiar with the study, it will be recalled that 19% of the women and 9% of the men in that sample had had some kind of sexual victimization during childhood. These victimization experiences were defined as sexual encounters of children under age 13 with persons at least 5 years older than themselves and encounters of children 13-16 with persons at least 10 years older. Sexual encounters could be intercourse, oral-genital contact, fondling, or an encounter with an exhibitionist.

Quite a large pool of information about the family backgrounds of the student participants was gathered in that study. Initially I had time to include only a portion of this information in the original report. Much of the rest of the information was analyzed subsequently and has provided some revealing directions, suggesting why some children are victimized. I want to present those findings here and comment on some of their theoretical implications.[1]

Table 3–1 gives a list of most of the background factors that were investigated in the student study. For each characteristic, the table indicates whether it distinguished between girls who were victims and those who were not. (All the following data will be limited to girls. There were too few boy victims for the analysis to be productive.) If the characteristic did distinguish significantly between victims and nonvictims, the victimization rate is given for the subgroup that contained the characteristics.[2] Thus for girls from families with incomes of less than $10,000, 33% were sexually victimized, compared to a rate of 19% for the sample as a whole. In other words, lower-income girls were two-thirds more likely to be victimized than the average girl.

No one should be surprised at this finding. Reported cases of sexual abuse come predominantly from lower-socioeconomic-strata families. The median income for families of sexual abuse cases officially reported in 1979 was approximately $9,285 compared to $19,661 for all U.S. families in the same year (Brown, 1978). Moreover, this association with lower social class status has been confirmed in studies of family violence and child abuse in nonclinical populations (Straus, Gelles & Steinmetz, 1980). The actual added risk to lower-class children indicated in the college student study is certainly underestimated because college students from lower-income backgrounds are obviously a special, possibly healthier, group than lower-income persons who do not go to college.

However, by no means should this finding lead people to the conclusion that sexual victimization is rare among the affluent. On the contrary, the high prevalence in this college student group implies the opposite. For example, among girls from families with incomes of over $20,000, nearly 20% encountered sexual victimization.

Social isolation, too, was a risk factor in sexual victimization. A large percentage of children who grew up on farms were victimized. Similarly, when a girl reported that she had only a small number of friends, she was more vulnerable. Presumably, the physical presence of friends and neighbors acts as a deterrent to potential abusers. But even more than that, lonely children may be more susceptible to offers of attention and affection in exchange for sexual activities. The connection between social isolation and both physical and sexual abuse is one that has been frequently noted in the child abuse literature (Justice & Justice, 1979).

FATHERS AND STEPFATHERS

The background factors most strongly associated with sexual victimization involved characteristics of the child's parents. For example, having a stepfather, one of the strongest risk factors, more than doubled a girl's vulnerability. Virtually *half* the girls with stepfathers were victimized by someone (not necessarily their stepfather). Moreover, this risk factor remained the strongest correlate of victimization, even when all other variables were statistically controlled.

Apparently there is substance to the notion that stepfathers are more sexually predatory toward their daughters than are fathers (de Young, 1982; Gruber & Jones, 1983). In our study, a stepfather was five times more likely to sexually victimize a daughter than was a natural father. This corresponds with findings of other studies (de Young, 1982; Gruber and Jones, 1983), particularly Russell's (1984). Russell found that one out of six women who had a stepfather as a principal figure in her childhood was sexually abused by him, compared to a rate of one out of forty for abuse by biological fathers.

Stepdaughters are even more vulnerable than these comparisons might suggest. Only a quarter of their added vulnerability in the present study was due to the intrusions of their stepfathers. Girls with stepfathers are also more likely than other girls to be victimized by other men. In particular, they are five times more likely to be victimized by a friend of their parents.

Why do girls with stepfathers suffer at the hands of parents' friends? Two things appear to be going on. Being a stepdaughter puts a girl into contact with other sexually predatory men besides her stepfather. Some of these men are friends of her stepfather, men who may not feel the same kind of restraint they might if this were the *real* (rather than the step) daughter of a friend.

But paradoxically some of these stepdaughters were victimized prior even to meeting their stepfather. The parents' friends who took advantage of them were probably friends of their mothers. Thus a mother who is courting may bring sexually opportunistic men into the home who may have little compunction about sexually exploiting the daughter if the chance arises. So the high vulnerability of girls who have stepfathers is a function of both the presence of a stepfather and the earlier exposure to a mother who was dating actively and may have put her daughter in jeopardy through the men she brought into the home. (For other studies suggesting risks to stepdaughters, see Langner, 1962, and Pope & Mueller, 1976).

The study also suggests that the quality of a daughter's relationship to a father, whether natural or stepfather, makes a difference in her vulnerability to abuse. When a father has particularly conservative family values, for example, believing strongly in children's obedience and in the subordination of women, a daughter is more at risk. Moreover, when he gives her little physical affection, the same is true. Such daughters have a harder time refusing the intrusions of an older man, even when they suspect them to be wrong, because they have been taught to obey. Moreover, a child who is starved for physical affection from a father may be less able to discriminate between a genuine affectional interest on the part of an adult and a thinly disguised sexual one.

IMPORTANCE OF THE MOTHER

The study also confirmed the idea that mothers are very important in the protection of daughters. Girls who ever lived without their natural mother were three times more vulnerable to sexual abuse than the average girl. Similarly, if a girl reported that her mother was emotionally distant, often ill, or unaffectionate, the girl was also at much higher risk. Part of the problem here may be a lack of adequate supervision. However, daughters of mothers who worked were *not* at higher risk, so it is not simply a matter of a mother's not being around the house.

Another part of the problem of absent and unavailable mothers may be a lack of communication. When daughters report to interested mothers about their activities, such mothers may alert them to potential dangers in their environment. Girls without mothers or with distant, ill, or unaffectionate mothers may not get such assistance. However, it wasn't simply a matter of sex education, because victimized daughters got just as much (or, more accurately, just as little) sex information from their mothers as any daughters.

It may have been that girls with absent or unavailable mothers have many unmet emotional needs that make them vulnerable. This is not to say that they seek out victimization. But they may be more susceptible to the ploys of a sexual offender. Their neediness may make them conspicuous as potential victims of such men.

The study also suggests a connection between the oppression of wives and the victimization of daughters. Girls whose mothers are powerless may more easily fall into the victim role themselves. Although no direct measure of marital power was available, we could look at relative distribution between husbands and wives of one important power resource: education. A wife who has substantially less education than her husband is much more likely to be subordinate to and dependent on him. The lesson a daughter learns from observing her parents may be that she, too, is powerless and must obey.

Educational inferiority in a wife did indeed prove to be an important correlate of a daughter's sexual victimization. The most dangerous parental combination for a daughter is not when her mother and father are both poorly educated, but when her father is well educated and her mother is not (see Table 3-2). If a poorly educated mother is married to a well-educated father (a situation indicating that she is on the short end of a power relationship), her daughter is significantly more vulnerable than if both parents have little education (44% vs. 30% victimized). Here is concrete testimony of how inequality between the sexes may be dangerous to the health and well-being of children.

A mother's importance may also lie in the specifically sexual messages that she transmits to her daughter. Victimized girls were much more likely to have mothers who were punitive about sexual matters. These mothers warned, scolded, and punished their daughters for asking sex questions, for masturbating, and for looking at sexual pictures much more often than usual. A girl with a sexually punitive mother was 75% more vulnerable to sexual victimization than the "typical" girl in the sample. It was the second most powerful predictor of victimization, after having a stepfather, and was still highly significant when all other variables were controlled.

This indication makes clear that sexually repressive practices backfire, although we can only speculate about why. It is possible that girls most bombarded with sexual prohibitions and punishments have the hardest time developing realistic standards about what constitutes danger. Blanket taboos often incite rebelliousness, and such girls may discard all the warnings they receive from their mothers about sex, including ones about sexual victimization. Moreover, if mothers have repressed all the healthier ways of satisfying sexual curiosity, these daughters may be more vulnerable to an adult or authority figure who appears to give them permission and opportunity to explore sex, albeit in the process of being exploited.

Whatever the precise mechanism, it is clear from this finding that it is not sexually lax, but sexually severe, families that foster a high risk for sexual exploitation, and some priority should be given to investigating this connection further.

OTHER FACTORS

Besides some of the factors that seemed to be associated with abuse, it is important to mention a few that appeared not to be associated. Perhaps most important, there was not much evidence of physical abuse being connected with sexual abuse. Girls who were victimized did not report any higher levels of violence in their family (either directed against themselves or between their parents) than did nonvictims. There was somewhat more spanking in the background of victimized girls, but the difference was slight and it washed out when other factors such as social class and parental education were controlled. Many people have wondered whether physical abuse and sexual abuse are closely related, and on the basis of these data and other research (Finkelhor & Hotaling, 1983), the conclusion we would make is that they are not.

We also note that religion, ethnicity, family size, and crowdedness were not related to victimization. These are all factors which have, at times, been speculated about in the literature, but which had no relationship to sexual abuse in the sample we surveyed. It should be said, however, on matters of religion and ethnicity in particular, that the sample was students from New England and therefore not especially varied, containing a small representation of blacks and very few Hispanics.

RISK FACTORS CHECKLIST

Putting some of the above findings together, we were able to construct a tool that is surprisingly effective in helping to identify children at risk for sexual victimization: The Sexual Abuse Risk Factor Checklist. The checklist includes eight of the strongest independent predictors of sexual victimization. Figure 3–1 shows that among children with none of the factors present in their backgrounds, victimization was virtually absent. Among those with five factors, two-thirds had been victimized. The presence of each additional factor increased a child's vulnerability between 10% and 20%. The relationship is fairly linear and quite dramatic.

The factors included in the checklist were arrived at by using a stepwise multiple regression analysis. These were the factors which made the strongest independent contribution to the explanation of sexual victimization. A checklist containing only four or five factors would have had about equivalent predictive value, but a longer list was viewed as preferable because in using such a checklist in field situations, information on some of the variables may be missing. Usually a more precise prediction can be achieved by weighting the "predictor" variables according to their regression coefficients, rather than the uniformly weighted checklist illustrated here. However, in this case both the weighted scale and the checklist had a multiple R of .32. Moreover, the checklist is much easier to visualize and use, therefore it was chosen over the coefficient approach.

The checklist is still in the process of formulation and refinement. It needs to be validated on a sample different from the one from which it was derived. It should not be seen as an instrument for predicting precisely in advance who will

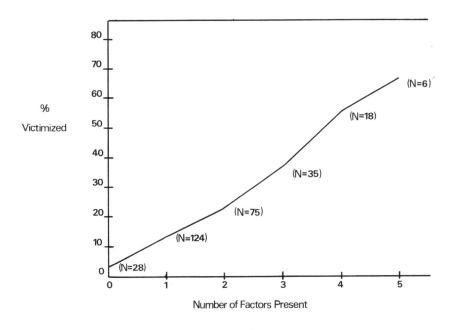

Factors :   Stepfather
            Ever live without mother
          ˜ Not close to mother
            Mother never finished high school
          ˜ Sex–punitive mother
          ˜ No physical affection from father
            Income under $10,000
          ˜.2 friends or less in childhood

Figure 3-1 Likelihood of Girls' Sexual Victimization by Presence of Eight Vulnerability Factors in Childhood

be sexually victimized. We are skeptical of the possibility or advisability of ever devising such a screening test for the problem of physical or sexual abuse (Light, 1974). However, it can be a device for sensitizing professionals about the kinds of backgrounds which put a child at-risk for sexual victimization. Also, it can be a tool for further research and theorizing about the causes of abuse.

BLAMING THE VICTIM

An important caveat needs to be raised about the approach taken in this chapter. The research reported here is on victimization as seen through the eyes of the victim. Large quantities of information were gathered on the victims and their families. Little information was gathered directly, nor could be, given the research design, about the offenders, their backgrounds, or their family situations. Hence the findings tend to overemphasize the victims' role in the experience. The role of the perpetrators is obscured. This type of emphasis can create the impression of blaming the victims for their own victimization.

It is important to keep in mind that moral and factual responsibility for the victimization experiences studied here lies with the offenders. They initiated the activities in 97% of the cases, according to our respondents. The most immediate and relevant "cause" of the victimization was a decision made by an offender.

Some might argue on the basis of this logic that, not to implicate victims unfairly, we should only study offenders. However, that is not a satisfactory solution. Offenders are harder to study, especially offenders who have not been caught. To limit our studies to offenders would severely curtail the amount of information we could obtain about sexual abuse. Victims can give us a lot of knowledge about the problem, knowledge we would be foolish to ignore, but even more important, we have to learn to identify children who may be at high risk. It is only through identifying characteristics of children at high risk that we can develop prevention programs targeted at the populations which are the most vulnerable. We have to do this by studying victims.

Clearly we cannot confine ourselves to studies of victims. One of the evident shortcomings of a great deal of research on child sexual abuse is that knowledge about offenders and victims is rarely brought together. Studies are done on victims, and the conclusions make it appear that the victims were the cause of the abuse. Or studies are done on offenders, and we get no useful information on what might have put some potential victims at greater risk than others. Obviously a melding of these two approaches is needed, something the next two chapters will try to accomplish.

The next chapter, Chapter 4, to supplement this one, presents a review of knowledge about offenders. Chapter 5 presents a model: the Four-Preconditions Model of Sexual Abuse, which brings together knowledge about offenders and victims. As we point out in a section called "Putting 'Responsibility' in Perspective," it is only when these two perspectives are juxtaposed that it becomes clear that victims who are at special risk are not to blame. So the findings of the present chapter should be taken into account with those of the two that follow.

TABLE 3–1
Family Characteristics and Sexual Victimization of Girls

Family Characteristic	Association		% Victimized[a]	N
	Yes (+)	No (0)		
Whole Family Characteristics				
Income under $10,000	+		33	(72)
Lived on farm	+		44	(16)
Religious background		0		
Ethnic background		0		
Family size		0		
Crowded home		0		
Parents had unhappy marriage	+		25	(155)
Parents showed little mutual affection	+		27	(162)
Father's Characteristics				
Child ever lived without father	+		29	(86)
Child had a stepfather	+		47	(30)
Child not close to father		0		
Blue collar	+		26	(179)
Never finished high school		0		
Often ill		0		
Often drank		0		
General inadequacy		0		
Little affection toward child	+		31	(42)
Conservative family values	+		38	(37)
Conservative sexual values		0		
Sexually modest or immodest		0		
Gave no sex education		0		
Punitive sexually		0		
Violent toward child or mother		0		
Spanked child at age 12		0		
Mother's Characteristics				
Child ever lived without mother	+		58	(19)
Child had a stepmother	+		35	(17)
Child not close to mother	+		34	(105)
Employed		0		
Never finished high school	+		38	(77)
Often ill	+		35	(134)
Often drank		0		
General inadequacy		0		
Little affection toward child	+		32	(108)
Conservative family values		0		
Conservative sexual values		0		

(Continued)

TABLE 3–1 Continued

FAMILY CHARACTERISTIC	ASSOCIATION		% VICTIMIZED[a]	N
	Yes (+)	No (0)		
Mother's Characteristics				
Sexually modest or immodest		0		
Gave no sex education		0		
Punitive sexually	+		35	(97)
Violent toward child or father		0		
Spanked child at age 12	+		24	(241)
N =			530	

[a] The total rate of victimization for all girls was 19%. A positive association was considered to exist only if subgroup in table had significantly higher percentage of victimized children than the rest of the sample, as tested by chi-square at p < .05.

TABLE 3–2

Mother's and Father's Education and Sexual Victimization of Girls

PARENT'S EDUCATION	% VICTIMIZED	(N)
Father finished high school Mother *did not* finish high school	44	(34)
Father *did not* finish high school Mother *did not* finish high school	30	(47)
Father *did not* finish high school Mother finished high school	28	(43)
Father finished high school Mother finished high school	16	(394)

Analysis of Variance

Source of variance	F	df	p
Father's education	0.35	1	N.S.
Mother's education	10.20	1	.001
Father's × mother's	5.80	1	.020

CHAPTER 4

Perpetrators

THERE IS NOTHING in the field of child sexual abuse more perplexing than the question, "Why would someone molest a child?". Although people are no longer apt to see offenders as crazed sex fiends, they still lack some alternative framework that makes sense of offender behavior. This chapter tries to present an organized framework for looking at and understanding the behavior of sex abusers.

Unlike the previous chapter, this chapter contains no new empirical findings. There is a large body of research theories about sexual abuse perpetrators which this chapter will try to summarize, synthesize, and integrate. (See also Finkelhor & Araji, 1983; Araji & Finkelhor, 1983.)

IS SEXUAL ABUSE SEXUALLY MOTIVATED?

One of the first controversies encountered in the literature on sexual abusers is the question of whether sexual abuse is sexually motivated. In recent years, writers have chosen to emphasize the nonsexual motives involved in child sexual abuse. For example, Groth (1979, p. 146) writes that "distorted expression of identification and affiliation needs, power and control issues, and hostile and aggressive impulses, *rather than sexuality* [italics added], were the underlying issue in pedophilia." Sgroi (1982, pp. 1–2) states, "Individuals who are sexual offenders against children do not seem to be motivated primarily by sexual desires . . . it is far more appropriate to regard child sexual abuse as a power problem."

This emphasis on sexual abuse as, in Groth's terminology, "pseudo-sexual" behavior has been an important antidote to the exclusive focus on sexual abuse as a "sexual deviation." We cannot recognize the social or psychological significance of adults relating sexually with children unless we analyze the broad emotional and developmental meaning that such behavior has for its perpetrators.

However, to go to the other extreme and deny the sexual component to sexual abuse, as some interpreters of Groth have done, is also a mistake (Frude, 1982). This approach overlooks important realities about sexual behavior in general and child sexual abuse in particular.

First, all sexual behavior, not just child sexual abuse, is laden with nonsexual motivation. Even the most innocuous and socially conventional coupling between a husband and wife is heavily motivated by nonsexual needs—need for affection, need for confirmation of masculinity or femininity, need for assertion of allegiance, and so on. Sex is always in the service of other needs. Just because it is infused with nonsexual motives does not make child sexual abuse different from other kinds of behavior we readily call "sexual."

Of course, different sexual acts contain different "alloys" of sexual and nonsexual components. Many rapes, including those against children, should be characterized as acts where the sexual element is low and the nonsexual element—the desire to punish, humiliate, and retaliate—is high. But there is a sexual element, nonetheless, even if small: the rapist decides to rape, not just to abuse. In much pedophilic-type behavior, in contrast to rape, the evidence suggests that there is often a quite strong erotic component (Groth, 1979), with offenders caressing, touching, and being strongly aroused by the object of their fantasies. Many offenders have clearly documented deviant patterns of sexual arousal and fantasy (Freund 1967a, 1967b, 1972).

Moreover, even in cases of sexual abuse where the erotic component seems to be less prominent, a full account of the behavior must explain why the interaction took a sexual rather than nonsexual course. If the abuse were merely an expression of a need for dominance or affiliation, the adult should be content to bully or befriend the child. But the fact that the needs took a sexual form of expression reveals an erotic component. The sexual act and the sexualization of the child were important to the expression of the need. This sexualization is something that needs to be explained too.

In my view the debate about the sexual motivation of sexual abuse is something of an unfortunate red herring. Sexual abuse does have a sexual component; sometimes it is strong, sometimes weak, sometimes primary, sometimes secondary. Along with nonsexual motivations, it does need to be taken into account. The goal should be to explain how the sexual component fits in.

SEXUAL ABUSE AND PSYCHOPATHOLOGY

Another feature of past theories about sexual abusers becomes clear as one reads through the literature. These theories tend to emphasize psychopathology. The dominant model is that sexual interest in children is a specific deviant psychological state that afflicts a small group of men who have had traumatizing developmental experiences (Gebhard et al., 1965). A current incarnation of this model is the popular view that the behavior of most sex abusers can be explained by the fact that they themselves were victims of sexual abuse as children.

There is much insight in these types of accounts. However, no doubt they overemphasize psychopathology because they are based on studies of a very unrepresentative population: caught and convicted sex offenders. Caught and convicted sex offenders are those who are the most compulsive, repetitive, blatant, and extreme in their offending, and thus also those whose behavior stems from the most deviant developmental experiences.

We now know much better than before how widespread sexual abuse is and how small a fraction of offenders are ever apprehended, let alone convicted. Although they have not been studied, it seems very probable that undetected offenders are persons with much less conspicuous psychological abnormality. The widespread existence of abuse forces one away from an exclusive focus on theories of psychopathology and toward the possibility that normative factors are at work. Widespread and conventional patterns of socialization and cultural transmission also play a part in creating sexual abusers.

A similar expansion of a theoretical perspective from a psychopathological model to include social and cultural factors has taken place in recent years on the subject of physical child abuse. Child abusers were at one point considered primarily very emotionally disturbed individuals who themselves had suffered from serious early childhood trauma (Gelles, 1973). Current theorizing about child abuse gives much more weight to the influence of normal social processes which induce child abuse. For example, they stress the positive valuation our culture puts on obedience and the use of physical punishment to elicit it, and the nature of family organization which tends to isolate parents with their heavy child-care burdens (Gil, 1973).

It is clear that cultural forces can modify the propensity of large numbers of adults to be sexually interested in children. According to Ford and Beach

(1951), among the Lepcha people of India, many adults and adolescents have sexual intercourse with young girls by cultural prescription. It is believed among this group that only through early sexualization do young girls come to physiological puberty.

Similar cultural forces are at work in American society. Writers have pointed out, for example, the tendency in our society to sexualize children in the media and elsewhere (Goldsen, 1978; Klemusrud, 1981; Rush, 1980; Vermeulen, 1981; Winn, 1981). It is possible, although we have no empirical evidence yet, that such media portrayals and the culture they represent may stimulate adult sexual interest in children.

Child pornography is another cultural feature that may stimulate sexual interest in children (Baker, 1978; Densen-Gerber & Hutchinson, 1978; McCaghy, 1979). It is true that no strong empirical evidence yet exists linking child pornography to the development of a sexual interest in children, but the connection is plausible enough to warrant serious and concerted scientific investigation.

The point remains that sexual abuse needs to be seen within a social and cultural framework, as pointed out in Chapter 1. Most of the literature about abusers has neglected this perspective.

NEED FOR A MULTIFACTOR ANALYSIS

Another problem in the literature on sexual abusers is that few theories have tried to address the full complexity of the behavior. Most approaches have tended to emphasize a few factors such as deviant patterns of sexual arousal or psychosexual immaturity. However, there is a large range of behaviors that needs to be explained. It includes the man who spends his whole life fixated on ten-year-old boys, or the man who after many years of heterosexual fidelity to his wife is possessed by a strong impulse to caress his granddaughter's genitals, or the man who persuades his girlfriend to help bring a child into their bed in order to "experience something new," or the adolescent, preoccupied with his lack of sexual experience, who forces his younger sister to have sex with him, or the father who promiscuously fondles all his daughters and all the friends they bring home. To explain all this diversity, a multifactor model that matches a variety of explanations to a variety of different kinds of abusers is needed.

The multiple explanations are available. The problem is putting them into some organizing framework. Our reading of the literature on sexual abusers suggests that this oganizing framework consists of four separate underlying factors that theories are attempting to explain. These appear to be four components that contribute, in different degrees and forms, to the making of a child molester. Formulated as questions, these factors are:

1. Why does a person find relating sexually to a child emotionally gratifying and congruent.
2. Why is a person capable of being sexually aroused by a child?
3. Why is a person blocked in efforts to obtain sexual and emotional gratification from more normatively approved sources?
4. Why is a person not deterred by conventional social inhibitions from having sexual relationships with a child?

We call these factors "emotional congruence," "sexual arousal," "blockage," and "disinhibition," respectively. The first three factors explain how a person develops a sexual interest in a child or children in general. The last factor explains how this interest is translated into actual behavior.

In the past these factors have tended to be seen as competing theories which theorists of different persuasions debated. However, they can also be seen as complementary components, several of which may come into play in the making of a particular abuser. Viewing them as complementary processes, which may work antagonistically or synergistically, can be useful in explaining the diversity of the behavior. Not all may necessarily play a role in the case of every abuser, but they are good places to start an inquiry into the source of child molesting.

A variety of mechanisms have been proposed in the literature that operate at each one of these levels. Most of the mechanisms relate to the individual psychology of the offender. However, the social and cultural processes that have been hypothesized to be connected to sexual abuse also fit into the typology. In the following sections of this chapter, the various psychological as well as sociocultural theories will be organized according to the four general factors.

This is by no means an exhaustive inventory. New explanations are likely to be proposed. Moreover, hypothesized explanations are included even when empirical evidence for them is not strong. There has been painfully little research on any explanation of sexual abuse, and the lack of empirical support may simply reflect this vacuum. When explanations do have some empirical evidence that clearly confirms or disconfirms them, it will be indicated. (For more detail, see Araji & Finkelhor, 1983).

Finally, it needs to be pointed out that the literature reviewed here refers exclusively to male offenders. There have been virtually no studies of female offenders. The presumption of maleness in discussions of sexual abusers does make sense because of the clear preponderance of males among offenders (for more discussion of this issue, see Chapter 11). But theories applicable to female offenders are badly needed.

FACTOR 1: EMOTIONAL CONGRUENCE

A large number of familiar theories about sexual abusers are essentially attempts to explain why an adult would find it emotionally satisfying to relate sexually to a child. We have called this "emotional congruence" because it conveys the idea of a "fit" between the adult's emotional needs and the child's characteristics, a fit for which the theories are trying to account. These are not explanations of a sexual proclivity. They are more accounts of the nonsexual motivations surrounding pedophilic sexual behavior.

Theorists like Hammer and Glueck (1957) and Groth, Hobson, and Gary (1982), for example, talk about child molesters as having arrested psychological development. They experience themselves as children, they have childish emotional needs, and thus they wish to relate to other children.

Another version of this theory points out not just the immaturity but the general sense of low self-esteem and low sense of efficacy that molesters feel in their social relationships. Relating to a child is congruent because it gives them the feeling of power, omnipotence, and control (Loss & Glancy, 1983; Hammer & Glueck, 1957). Several studies have demonstrated the sense of inadequacy and immaturity experienced by child molesters (Hammer & Glueck, 1957; Stricker, 1967; Peters, 1976; Panton, 1978). Even more to the point, Howells (1979) has shown that what is most salient for child molesters when they describe victims is the child's "lack of dominance."

In another variation on this theme, Howells (1981) has adapted to pedophilia Stoller's (1975) general theory of sexual deviance. According to this theory, the child-molesting fantasy comes to serve as a "scene of symbolic mastery over childhood-induced psychological traumas." In other words, a molester needs the relationship to children to overcome a sense of shame, humiliation, or powerlessness that he had experienced as a small child at the hands of an adult. This process is called by other theorists "identification with the aggressor."

> One way in which the male child may try to combat the feelings of powerlessness inherent in being a victim is to ultimately identify with the aggressor and reverse roles; that is, to become the powerful victimizer rather than the helpless victim. The child molester then re-enacts in his offense the characteristics of his own victimization in an attempt to restore to himself a feeling of being in control. (Groth, Hobson & Gary, 1982, p. 138)

Another type of theory that is essentially about emotional congruence is that which uses the notion of narcissism or identification with the self. In this type of theory, as a result of either emotional deprivation or even overprotection, an adult remains emotionally involved with himself or his likenesses.

> He narcissistically remains in love with the child he then was. This is impossible so he must project his love on to other children of a similar age to his lost childhood who thus become love objects for him. (M. Fraser, as quoted in Howells, 1981, p.61)

Some feminist explanations of sex abuse have a surprisingly similar underlying theme to these individual psychological theories, although they are focused on the sociocultural level. These theories point to themes in male socialization and male culture, such as those mentioned in Chapter 1 that make children "appropriate" or, in our terms, emotionally congruent objects for sexual interest. Primary among these themes, for example, is the value that male socialization puts on being dominant, being powerful, and being the initiator in sexual relationships (Gross, 1978; Hite, 1981; Russell 1982b). Thus, men prefer to relate to partners who are younger, smaller, and weaker than themselves. Children fit in or are an inevitable extension of these role requirements. In fact, they may "fit" the demands of male cultural expectations better than many adult women would. Some men are more affected by these socialization experiences than others or may belong to subcultures which give more or less emphasis to these normative themes (Gebhard et al., 1965; Summit & Kryso, 1978).

FACTOR 2: SEXUAL AROUSAL TO CHILDREN

A second component to the development of child-molesting behavior is reflected in theories of why a person finds children sexually arousing. "Sexually arousing" would mean a physiological response (such things as penile tumescence) to the presence of children or to fantasies of children in sexual activities. There are good experimental data, using physiological measurements, that child molesters, including incest offenders, do show unusual levels of sexual arousal to children (Abel et al., 1981; Atwood & Howell, 1971; Freund, 1967a, 1967b; Freund & Langevin, 1976; Freund et al., 1973; Quinsey et al., 1975).

This issue of sexual arousal in explanations of child molesting is, however, as indicated earlier, a controversial one. Many of the theories cited for emotional congruence seem to presume that what they are explaining is sexual arousal. If a person wants his emotional needs met by relating to someone much younger than himself, this, to these theorists, seems a sufficient explanation of why a person would seek to have sexual relations with a child. However, it does not seem fully convincing. For one thing, the evidence suggests that there do exist such things as sexual preferences or sexual proclivities which have an existence autonomous from people's emotional needs. Certainly, this is the premise of a group of sex therapists who have been relatively successful at changing people's sexual proclivities when these proclivities are experienced by clients as being at odds with their basic emotional needs (Langevin, 1983; Masters & Johnson, 1979).

For another thing, as we mentioned earlier, people who have emotional needs to relate to children, to be with children, to love children, to control children, to have children dependent on them do not necessarily find children sexually arousing even when these emotional needs are extraordinarily strong. Most such people get their emotional needs met by being mothers, fathers, grade-school teachers, pediatricians, and such—in other words, in nonsexual ways. The fact of finding children sexually stimulating would seem to be a component that needs to be explained independent of, or in addition to, having a strong emotional need that can be met only by children.

In addition, some theories do not treat arousal to children as needing an explanation because they presume such arousal is intrinsic. Freud's (1953) concept of polymorphous attraction posited that in the course of development all people find children sexually attractive, and need to be weaned away from such "perverse" attractions by social conditioning and repression. But social conditioning can fail or these perverse elements can get called forth owing to "regression." They do not need to be explained; they are just there.

One major argument against this point of view is that a great many people deny having sexual interest in children (Freund et al., 1972; Glueck, 1965; Henson & Rubin, 1971; Laws & Rubin, 1969). They simply do not find themselves sexually aroused when they see naked children.

Moreover, even if most adults could be shown to have some degree of arousal to children under some circumstances, this still would not eliminate the need for explanation. What needs to be explained is why such arousal is stronger in some adults than in others, or why it occurs for them in a wider variety of circumstances with a wider variety of children.

A set of theories have tried to account for why some people are aroused by or have stronger arousal to children. These theories have relied primarily on tenets of social learning theory, and have treated sexual arousal as a kind of response that can be evoked or conditioned under the right set of circumstances (Howells, 1981).

One general theory is that some people have early sexual experiences which cause them, through conditioning or imprinting, to find children arousing later when they become adults (Money, 1981a; Wenet, Clark & Hunner, 1981). However, well over half of all children have childhood sexual experiences with other children (Finkelhor, 1979), and since not all these people become sex abusers, it would suggest that there are some special circumstances under which such experiences condition a later sexual interest in children.

Several suggestions exist as to what special circumstances might work to give such early childhood sexual experiences the special compelling quality they seem to have for many child molesters. One possibility is that the critical experiences are those where some special kind of fulfillment or frustration is involved. Humbert Humbert in Nabokov's *Lolita*, for example, traced his sexual interest to the particularly intense, but frustrated romance he had with Annabel Leigh when he was a child himself.

Another possibility is that the critical experiences might be ones associated with traumatic victimization. Several researchers have found more childhood sexual victimization in the backgrounds of sex abusers than in a variety of comparison groups (Bard et al., 1983; de Young, 1982; Gebhard et al., 1965; Groth, Hobson & Gary, 1982; Langevin et al., 1983; Prentky, 1983). It may be that the traumatic experience facilitates an imprinting or conditioning process.

McGuire, Carlisle, and Young (1965), in their general model of sexual deviation, suggest that what is important in the development of a fixation is that the early experience of arousal be incorporated into a fantasy that is repeated and becomes increasingly arousing in subsequent masturbatory repetitions (see also Wenet, Clark & Hunner, 1981). It may be that any feature of the experience that makes it prominent in the person's awareness—such as being associated with great pleasure, or great embarrassment or shame—will make it likely to come to attention in the course of masturbation. Since masturbation is highly reinforcing, the components of the memory, in this case children, come to be associated with sexual arousal through a process like "operant conditioning" even in cases where the original experience itself might not have been pleasurable.

Another social learning process—modeling—has been proposed to account for some aspects of sexual arousal to children (Wenet, Clark & Hunner, 1981). According to a suggestion by Howells (1981), what may be important about the experience of being victimized oneself is not the conditioning, but having a model who finds children sexually stimulating. A similar process may be at work for children who grow up in families where other children besides themselves, such as their sisters or cousins, are the objects of sexual exploitation at the hands of adults.

Howells (1981) has also speculated about how a process of "attributional error" may play a role in creating sexual arousal to children.

Children appear to elicit strong emotional reactions in many people, reactions usually labelled as "parental" or "protective" or "affectionate," but potentially definable as sexual love. The fact that the initial stages of the adult sexual response cycle are not distinct physiologically from patterns of arousal produced by other emotions allows for such misattribution in some individuals and in some (as yet unknown) situations. (pp. 68-69)

Thus, perhaps certain socialization experiences or subjectively felt sexual deprivation may prompt individuals to label any emotional arousal as a sexual response. Once having labeled a response as sexual, they may find ways to reinforce it through repetition and fantasy, and thus come to have a much more general sexual arousal to a child in particular or children in general.

There has also been recent clinical work suggesting that biological factors, such as hormone levels or chromosomal make-up, contribute to child molesting (Berlin, 1982; Goy & McEwen, 1977; Money, 1961). Such theorizing stems from findings of physiological abnormalities among molesters (Berlin, 1982; McAuliffe, 1983) and from evidence of some success in treating them with antiandrogenic drugs (Berlin & Meinecke, 1981; Money, 1981b). However, these theories are not yet developed enough to specify how biological factors affect the choice of a child as an object of sexual arousal. At the current level of conceptualization, biological factors are seen as a source of instability which may predispose a person to develop deviant patterns of arousal (Money, 1981a). Or they are seen as having a generalized effect on levels of sexual interest and sexual arousability. At this level of generality, however, such theories, useful as they may be for treatment, are not really specific explanations of how a person comes to find children arousing.

The process of how persons come to find children arousing has a social as well as an individual component. Mentioned earlier was the possible role that child pornography and advertising play in pedophilia (Densen-Gerber, 1983; Dworkin, 1983; McCaghy, 1979; Rush, 1980). We were talking in part about a form of social learning. It is possible, as Russell (1982b) notes, that exposure to pornography involving children creates new converts or teaches such arousal to people who would not otherwise have become so. In some pornography, themes of sex with children are mixed in with themes of sex with adults. In masturbating to this material, the consumers may come to find children arousing.

More often, however, pornography involving children is bought by those who have some established interest in this form of arousal already. For these consumers, pornography depicting sex with children might increase the strength of their arousability and the variety of child objects to which they become aroused. However, the predominant effect of such media is probably to increase the legitimacy and remove the inhibitions about having and acting on such fantasies (Densen-Gerber, 1983; Russell, 1982b). If this is the primary process at work—and we must caution that there is little if any research concerned with the effects of child pornography—then this process is better classified under disinhibition (factor 4, see below).

FACTOR 3: BLOCKAGE

A third component to an understanding of sex abusers is reflected in theories that are essentially explanations of why some individuals are blocked in their ability to get their sexual and emotional needs met in adult relationships. Individual psychological theories that rely on Oedipal dynamics fall into this category of explanation. Child molesters are described in such theories as having intense conflicts about their mothers or "castration anxiety" that makes it difficult or impossible to relate to adult women (Fenichel, 1945; Gillespie, 1964; Hammer & Glueck, 1957).

Sometimes the source of blockage is not seen so much in Oedipal dynamics as in early traumatic forays into sexual behavior. The man who finds himself to be impotent in his first sexual attempts, or abandoned by his first lover, may come to associate adult sexuality with pain and frustration. This avenue having been filled with trauma, he chooses children as a substitute gratification. According to Kinsey et al. (1948), for example, "the usual professional interpretation describes these offenders as sexually thwarted, incapable of winning attention from older females and reduced to vain attempts with children who are unable to defend themselves" (p. 238).

Indeed, child molesters are often described as timid, unassertive, inadequate, awkward, even moralistic types with poor social skills who have an impossible time developing adult social and sexual relationships (Frisbie, 1969; Gebhard et al., 1965; Glueck, 1965; Guttmacher & Weihofen, 1951; Hammer & Glueck, 1957; Langevin, 1983).

Theories that try to account for incest offenders rely heavily on this blockage model. In the family dynamics model of incest, for example, the marital relationship has broken down; the wife has become alienated for some reason; the father is too inhibited or moralistic to find sexual satisfaction outside the family. Thus blocked in other avenues of sexual or emotional gratification, he turns to his daughter as a substitute (de Young, 1982; Gebhard et al., 1965; Meiselman, 1978).

Repressive sexual norms may act as a form of blockage. They may operate to make adults feel guilt and/or some conflict about engaging in adult sexual relationships, and this may push some into choosing child partners. For example, some have argued that, in the incestuous family, norms tabooing extramarital affairs may block the father from seeking out other *adult women*, rather than his child, to substitute for the deteriorating relationship with his wife (Weinberg, 1955). There is also a norm that makes masturbation seem inappropriate for adults, and this norm may block what would otherwise be another alternative and benign sexual outlet. Goldstein, Kant, and Hartman (1973) do report a finding that child molesters were among the most repressed of all sex offenders and were "the least permissive...regarding premarital and extramarital intercourse" (p. 144).

In general, this review of blockage theories suggests a further subdivision of the category into two types: developmental blockages and situational blockages. Developmental blockages refer to theories like those involving Oedipal conflicts, where the person is seen as prevented from moving into the adult sexual stage of development. Situational blockages refer more to theories, such as those related to incest, where a person with apparent adult sexual interests is blocked from normal sexual outlets because of the loss of a relationship or some other transitory crisis.

FACTOR 4: DISINHIBITION

A final factor that needs to be explained about child molesters is why conventional inhibitions against having sex with children are overcome or are not present. Among sex abusers, apparently, ordinary controls are circumvented or there is a higher level of acceptability for such behavior.

On the individual psychological level, theories have talked about child molesters as people who had generally poor impulse control (Gebhard et al., 1965; Glueck, 1965; Groth, Hobson & Gary, 1982; Hammer & Glueck, 1957; Knopp, 1982). In addition, a number of personality factors have been cited: senility (Cushing, 1950; Karpman, 1954), alcoholism and alcohol abuse (Anderson & Shafer, 1979; Frisbie, 1969; McCaghy, 1968; Rada, 1976; Virkkunen, 1974) and psychosis (Gebhard et al., 1965; Hammer & Glueck, 1957; Marshall & Norgard, 1983; Mohr, Turner & Jerry, 1964).

The evidence for these various characteristics is mixed. It is generally negative on the matter of senility and mental retardation (Gebhard et al., 1965; Mohr, Turner & Jerry, 1964). It is explanatory only for some small number of offenders in the case of lack of impulse control and psychosis (Gebhard et al., 1965; Hammer & Glueck, 1957). However, it is supported in a large percentage of cases for the contribution of alcohol and alcoholism (Aarens, 1978; Morgan, 1982). The presumed mechanism at work in all these conditions is the lowering or disappearance of inhibitions against acting on pedophilic impulses.

Sometimes situational factors, as well as personality factors, are used in disinhibition-type explanations to account for child molesting. For example, when a person with no prior history of such behavior commits sexual abuse under conditions of great personal stress, the stressors—unemployment, loss of love, death of a relative—are viewed as factors which lowered inhibitions to deviate types of behavior (Gebhard et al., 1965; Mohr, Turner & Jerry, 1964; Swanson, 1968).

Theories of incest also often rely on mechanisms that fall into this category. Men are seen as engaging in sexual acts with girls in their family because these girls are stepdaughters or because the men were away from the family during the child's early life (Gebhard et al., 1965; Lustig et al., 1966). Being a stepdaughter or being separated presumably works to reduce the ordinary inhibition that would exist against sex between a natural father and a daughter who had lived with each other continuously since the child's birth. These inhibitory mechanisms are sometimes viewed as quasibiological in nature, coming into play merely as the result of proximity during early stages of development (Shepher, 1971; Van den Berghe, 1983). Others view them as developing out of the empathy and concern anticipatory to and resulting from a caretaking role (Herman, 1981). Incest occurs when these inhibitory mechanisms are disrupted.

There are also feminist theories of sex abuse that are essentially disinhibition arguments too. These theories highlight certain social and cultural elements which encourage or condone sexual behavior directed toward children and thus weaken inhibitions (Densen-Gerber, 1983).

For example, Rush (1980) has written extensively about the way in which sexual interaction with children has been sanctioned by religion and law throughout history. Armstrong (1983) argues that the reluctance of the contemporary legal system to prosecute and punish offenders gives a green light to potential molesters. These and other feminists (McIntyre, 1981; Nelson, 1982) have also criticized the tendency among both the public and professionals to blame victims rather than offenders, pointing out that this feeds into the justifications that offenders provide for their own violations (Rush, 1980; Russell, 1982b). Anything that reinforces excuses for sexal abuse, according to these theories, acts to reduce inhibitions.

In accounting for incest, a common feminist theme has been to show how inhibitions are lowered by social approval for the excesses of patriarchal and parental authority (Rush, 1980). According to feminists, many men see families as private institutions where the fathers have socially sanctioned authority over women and children to treat as they wish.

[The] seduction of daughters is inherent in a father-dominated family system, where the man expects to have his will obeyed as head of household and ex-

pects his family to provide him with domestic and sexual services. When patriarchal beliefs about rights of fathers provide further excuse for initiating sexually gratifying relationships within the family, it is not hard to see how many
"Mr. Averages" can manage to *overcome all the social and emotional barriers* to
committing incest with their daughters. (Nelson, 1982, pp. 69-70; italics
added)

In our terms, such social norms and values disinhibit offenders.

VALUE OF THE FOUR FACTORS

The four-factor model just outlined is useful for giving some order to the variety of theories that have been proposed to account for child molesters. It shows
the commonalities among the various ideas that have been proposed and also
reduces the complexity of the theories to four basic factors. However, it would
seem that the model can be used as more than merely a classification scheme. It
can be used also to generate theory about sexual abuse.

First, the model shows how many theories of child molesters imply other
processes which are not fully specified. As we pointed out earlier, for example,
theories of emotional congruence seem to imply that sexual arousal naturally
follows. But the model suggests that arousal needs to be explained, not just
taken for granted. Blockage theories show why a person shuns more normative
sources of sexual and emotional gratification, but not why children are chosen
as the substitute. Similarly, theories of disinhibition seem to imply prior levels
of sexual interest in children that would otherwise be inhibited. But the theories
do not themselves specify where these sexual interests come from. This prior interest needs to be explained too.

Second, the model suggests that a complete theory needs to address issues
on a number of different levels. Child molesting is not adequately explained
simply by the fact that an adult is sexually aroused by children. There may be
adults who are so aroused but who have alternative sources of sexual gratification or who are inhibited by ordinary social controls from acting on their
arousal. A full explanation has to show why the adult was capable of being
aroused, why he directed his impulse toward a child, and why no inhibitions
halted the enacting of the impulse.

Similarly, many adults are blocked in their ability to gain sexual and emotional gratification from adults. However, most of those adults may have little
emotional congruence for children or little sexual arousal to children, and may
be inhibited from acting on such feelings even if they had them. An adequate
theory needs to explain child molesting using several, if not all, these levels
simultaneously.

Third, this multiple-level model of child molesters suggests, as in some of the above examples, that many people may have important prerequisite components to engaging in child molesting, but never do. Theories from only one level of the model will never accurately discriminate between those who engage and do not engage in such behavior. Sex abusers will always show up as having some of these characteristics, such as arousal to children, shyness, impulsivity, or need for dominance, but there will also be large numbers of nonabusers in the population at large who have these characteristics too. The abusers should differ by fulfilling requirements at all levels of the model, not just one or two.

Do Abuse Victims Become Abuse Perpetrators?

A good illustration of the need for a complex theory can be seen by looking at the currently popular idea that child molesters are persons who themselves were the victims of sexual abuse. This theory has a long history (Gebhard et al., 1965; Seghorn & Boucher, 1980), but has been given new credence by recent studies which find a large number of child molesters reporting abuse experiences from their own childhood. For example, Groth and Burgess (1979) found that 32% of a group of 106 child molesters reported some form of sexual trauma in their early development compared to 3% of a comparison group of 64 police officers. Researchers at the Bridgewater Massachusetts Treatment Center (Bard et al., 1983; Prentky, 1983) compared a group of rapists and child molesters and found that significantly more child molesters (57%) than rapists (23%) had been sexual assault victims. Pelto (1981) found 10 times as many and Langevin et al. (1983) over 5 times as many childhood sexual abuse experiences in the backgrounds of incest offenders as compared to nonoffender controls.

Large as these numbers seem, there are of course problems with them. We cannot really be certain that these child molesters suffered so much more abuse than other children in their neighborhoods or in their families who did not become molesters. We need better control groups in these studies of the abuse experiences of offenders.

Nonetheless, it appears plausible that a history of molesting may play a role in the creation of some child molesters. However, such a theory quickly becomes an all-encompassing explanation. Why is someone a child molester? Well, because he himself was abused. But fortunately for society and unfortunately for such a simple theory, most children who are molested do not go on to become molesters themselves. This is particularly true among women, who whether victimized or not rarely become offenders. Obviously, if victimization is a causal factor it interacts with some other factors. Looking toward the typology, it may be that a history of victimization needs to be combined with a blockage of alternative sources of gratification and a low level of inhibition before it produces a child molester. A full explanation of child molesting needs to take into account a variety of factors.

EXPLAINING DIFFERENT TYPES OF CHILD MOLESTERS

The best reviews of theories of child molesting (Howells, 1981; Langevin et al., 1983; Mohr, Turner & Jerry, 1964; Quinsey, 1977) have generally emphasized the importance of developing different theories to explain different types of molesting behavior. Howells (1981), for example, believes distinctions need to be made between molesters who prefer boys and those who prefer girls, molesters who are aggressive and those who are not, and molesters who have a strong "sexual preference" for children and those whose interest is more transitory. The four-factor model we have suggested here can be utilized readily in developing explanations for these differences, as will be shown below.

SEXUAL PREFERENCE

Let us look at how a preference for a boy or girl child could be determined at each of the various levels of the model.

1. *Emotional Congruence.* Different types of developmental experiences may make it more emotionally congruent for a molester to relate to a boy or a girl child. For example, if the underlying mechanism is a kind of "narcissistic" identification, a person would be most likely to be attracted to a child of the same sex as himself (Fraser, 1976; Kraemer, 1976; Storr, 1965). If the issue is one of needing to feel powerful and omnipotent, on the other hand, the adult may be more inclined to choose a girl, less imposing or threatening than a boy. Similarly, if the molestation grows out of an extension of male sexual socialization, here too, the man may choose a girl, in keeping with a masculine script (Rush, 1980).

2. *Sexual Arousal.* Preference for a boy or girl child may be affected by conditioning processes surrounding early sexual experiences. Thus, an early pleasurable experience with a girl may lead to sexual preference for girls, an early experience with a boy may lead to preference for boys.

3. *Blockage.* Developmental and situational blockages may lead toward different sex object choices. For example, if the person is experiencing an Oedipal conflict which makes his mother threatening, this anxiety may generalize to all contacts with women, even girls, and lead to a preference for boys. If, however,

a man is blocked situationally, his normal heterosexual partner unavailable because of marital disruption—as in theories of incest—he may prefer a girl, an object that is most similar to his preferred partner.

4. *Disinhibition.* For given individuals, inhibitions may be stronger for one sex than for another. It may be easier for many men to have sexual contact with girls because they have been brought up with strong homophobic taboos (Knopp, 1982). On the other hand, some offenders may prefer to have sex with boys because they presume boys can "take care of themselves better," and they are disturbed and inhibited by the rape and seduction taboos that surround the idea of sex with "helpless" girls.

It would seem from this inventory that no one mechanism necessarily explains all preferences for boys or girls. There are a variety of possible mechanisms. Moreover, we can use them to show why one molester may be exclusive in his sex preference, while another may not have a preference at all.

Exclusivity and Strength

According to Howells (1981), the classificatory distinction that is the most "pervasive" in the research literature on pedophilia is that between "offenders whose deviant behavior is a product of a deviant sexual preference for children and those whose deviant behavior is situationally induced and occurs in the context of a normal sexual preference structure" (p. 76). Howells (1981) calls the former "sexual preference mediated" and the latter "situational" pedophilic incidents. Others have called the former "pedophilic" and the latter "nonpedophilic" types. Groth, Hobson, and Gary (1982), in the terminology that has probably gained the widest usage, call the former "fixated" and the latter "regressed" offenders.

Different theories have been used to explain each type. Groth, Hobson, and Gary (1982) account for fixated offenders with an emotional congruence theory which stresses "that they identify with the child and appear to want to remain children themselves." They account for regressed offenders with a blockage theory which stresses that the "molesters turn to a child sexually as a substitute for their adult relationship which has become conflictual and emotionally unfulfilling."

A somewhat different approach can be applied to this distinction. The two distinct categories (fixated and regressed) into which all child molesters fall can be replaced by two continuous dimensions. The first dimension is the strength of a person's sexual interest in children, that is, how strongly motivated they are to have sex with children, as evidenced, for example, by the number of contacts they have and the persistence of this interest over time. The second dimension is the exclusivity of a person's interest, that is, what percentage of their total sexual experiences and fantasies is involved with children as opposed to other partners. Fixated offenders in Groth, Hobson, and Gary's (1982) terms would obviously be at the high end of both dimensions, having a strong and relatively exclusive sexual interest in children. Regressed offenders would be at the other end, having rather weak and rather nonexclusive interest.

The idea of a continuum on each of two dimensions has a number of advantages.

1. *The issues of exclusivity and strength of sexual interest in children are separable and need to be looked at separately.* Although it seems plausible that strong and exclusive interests tend to co-occur, consideration needs to be given to the question of whether this is always the case. For example, take the case of a rather asexual man who under a great deal of stress fondles a young boy, but does not repeat the behavior. His interest in children may be exclusive but rather weak. Take, for another example, a hypersexual individual who has many sexual contacts with children as well as sexual contacts with adults. His sexual interest in children may be strong but relatively nonexclusive. We believe many individuals fit into these types, showing that strength and exclusivity are different dimensions.

2. *A continuum, as opposed to a dichotomy, allows a focus on the degree of sexual interest in children in terms of its strength and exclusivity.* Besides people who have a very strong sexual interest and those who have a very weak interest, there are undoubtedly many in the middle. A continuum reflects reality better in that it allows relative rather than only absolute distinctions.

3. *The two-dimensional scheme gets away from a reliance on one particular theoretical approach to explaining types of pedophilia.* (One theory is not enough.) What is at work is that a variety of processes at the various levels of the model combine to produce molesting behavior that is more or less strong and more or less exclusive. The variety needs to be explored.

For example, a man who was sexually victimized when he was a child may have the potential for having a strong pedophilic interest. But suppose that, as an adolescent, he has good heterosocial skills, has no pattern of masturbation to fantasies of children, and follows peer pressure into heterosexual behavior. His emotional congruence for children (factor 1) may be offset by countervailing influences of having no strong sexual arousal to children (factor 2) and no blockage in his adult relationships (factor 3). His pedophilic interest may be very weak. Another man with the same kind of childhood victimization, who had a sense of inadequacy and poor social skills (factor 3) and lived in a subculture where impulsivity was tolerated (factor 4), might end up with a very much stronger pedophilic interest.

As illustrated in this example, one source of child-molesting behavior will not always lead to the same kind of outcome. Depending on the other countervailing or reinforcing factors, similar initial processes may lead to very different outcomes.

INCEST OFFENDERS AND PEDOPHILES

The approach illustrated here also has implications for the analysis of incest offenders and their relationship to other kinds of perpetrators. Other theorists have taken two basic approaches to incest offenders. In a great deal of the literature, incest offenders have been analyzed as an entirely distinct group from other kinds of sex offenders against children (de Young, 1982; Gebhard et al., 1965; Langevin, 1983) and separate theories have been used to explain them. In another segment of the literature and in the approach advocated here, general theories about child molesters are developed and incest offenders are integrated into those theories (Groth, 1979; Howells, 1981). These two might be called the separate theory versus the unified theory approach.

There is no disagreement between the two schools that incest offenders, at least incarcerated incest offenders, as a group appear to be somewhat different from other incarcerated child molesters. The disagreement would appear to revolve around the question of how much similarity there is. There is no denying that there is some (Langevin et al., 1983). Almost all those who have studied incest offenders have noted a group who molested their children as part of a general attraction to underage children. Some have maintained this group was very small (Gebhard et al., 1965), however, while others have implied that it characterized a significant fraction of the reported incest offenders (Weinberg, 1955). In a recent phallometric study, Abel et al. (1981) found that incest offenders were aroused to young children—other than their daughters or stepdaughters—in a pattern similar to that of heterosexual pedophiles. Although an earlier study by Quinsey et al. (1975) found differently, the current empirical evidence does not rule out a unified theory approach.

Another consideration that has not often been raised, however, is whether there are many extrafamilial child molesters who have patterns similar to incest offenders'. Many teachers, babysitters, and neighbors who molest are not persons with primary sexual interest in children, but are acting in response to such things as stress and opportunity. If they do not offend repetitively and compulsively, they are not likely to end up in prison. Because they do not include many of this type, groups of incarcerated extrafamilial child molesters look more different from incest offenders than they really are. If there are many extrafamilial child molesters who are similar to incest offenders, this would also argue for the unified theory approach.

The typology that has been suggested in this chapter is obviously of the unified theory approach. According to it, there are many different types of child molesters: those attracted to boys, those attracted to girls; those who molest aggressively, those who molest nonaggressively; those with relatively exclusive sexual interest in children, those with sexual interest in other types of partners; those who molest their own children, those who molest other people's children. There is no advantage to or clear empirical imperative for taking one of these dichotomies—incest versus nonincest—and creating a wholly separate framework for each side.

Within the single framework proposed here, however, obviously many incest offenders will cluster in certain areas. They will be situated at the "less exclusive" end of the exclusivity continuum and toward the "weaker" end of the strength of sexual interest continuum. Situational blockages and disinhibitions may be more important than sexual arousal factors in accounting for their behavior. But the multifaceted nature of the model will encourage a complex view of incest offenders that will do more justice to the variety of etiologic factors involved in their behavior.

CONCLUSION

This chapter has introduced a typology for thinking about the sources of child molesting with two particular goals in mind. One is to create some order to the diverse array of ideas that have been forwarded about molesters. Another is to illustrate how more complex models need to be used to account for molesting behavior.

Unfortunately, no new information about child molesters is uncovered here. These are just old ideas packaged in a different way. We desperately need new information about child molesters. Many of the ideas catalogued here may be wrong and may need to be discarded. Many other ideas accounting for molesting behavior may have yet to be unearthed. We are particularly uncomfortable with the fact that so much of what we know about sexual abusers comes from men in prison and in treatment. When information is gathered about undetected molesters, the picture may change drastically.

It is also important to keep in mind that understanding what makes a molester is not the same as understanding why a child is sexually abused. The molester is only part of the process. Factors related to the child and to the environment also need to be understood. It is toward adding these dimensions that we turn next.

CHAPTER 5

Four Preconditions: A Model

THERE IS A PRESSING need for new theory in the field of sexual abuse. What theory we have currently is not sufficient to account for what we know. Nor is it far-reaching enough to guide the development of new empirical research.

Two types of theory currently prevail in the field. On the one hand, there are a collection of partially developed ideas, catalogued in the previous chapter, about what creates a child molester. On the other hand, there is a highly specific family-systems model of father-daughter incest.

Taken as a whole, the current level of theoretical development displays a number of important shortcomings. For one, the theories we have are not very useful for collating what is known about offenders with what is known about victims and their families. Research and theory about offenders have been developed by psychologists working with offenders in prison settings in isolation from other workers who were protecting and treating children.

For another, currently available theories are not comprehensive. The theories about offenders have been developed from work mostly with men who molested multiple children outside their own families. In contrast, the family-systems theories have been developed almost exclusively from work with father-daughter incest families. Unfortunately, there is much sexual abuse, such as that committed by older brothers, uncles, and neighbors, which falls outside either domain. Theory to account for such abuse is missing.

Finally, currently available theories tend to neglect sociological factors. They have mostly developed from clinical work and are aimed at helping to direct therapeutic interventions. However, sexual abuse as a widespread social problem has sociological dimensions that need to be included in theory.

In this chapter we build on the foundation of the last chapter and propose a model of sexual abuse that tries to address these shortcomings. It brings together knowledge about offenders, victims, and families. It is at a level of generality capable of accommodating many different types of sexual abuse from father-daughter incest to compulsive and fixated molesting. Finally, it incorporates explanations at both the psychological and sociological level. The model is called the Four-Preconditions Model of Sexual Abuse.

The model was developed by reviewing all the factors that have been proposed as contributing to sexual abuse (Lukianowicz, 1972; Lystad, 1982; Tierney & Corwin, 1983), including factors related to victims and families as detailed in Chapter 3 and factors related to offenders as detailed in Chapter 4. This review suggested that all factors relating to sexual abuse could be grouped as contributing to one of four preconditions that needed to be met before sexual abuse could occur:

1. A potential offender needed to have some motivation to abuse a child sexually.
2. The potential offender had to overcome internal inhibitions against acting on that motivation.
3. The potential offender had to overcome external impediments to committing sexual abuse.
4. The potential offender or some other factor had to undermine or overcome a child's possible resistance to the sexual abuse.

These factors suggested a model of sexual abuse portrayed in Figure 5–1. What follows is a more detailed description of the components of the model and how it operates to account for a wide variety of sexual abuse.

PRECONDITION I: MOTIVATION TO SEXUALLY ABUSE

A model of sexual abuse needs to account for how a person (an adult or adolescent) becomes motivated for or interested in having sexual contact with a child. This question is essentially the one we took up in the previous chapter. Following along the lines of the previous chapter, we suggest that there are three components to the source of this motivation: (1) emotional congruence—relating sexually to the child satisfies some important emotional need; (2) sexual arousal—the child comes to be the potential source of sexual gratification for that person; and (3) blockage—alternative sources of sexual gratification are not available or are less satisfying. (The fourth factor from the previous chapter—disinhibition—is isolated as a separate precondition for reasons detailed below.)

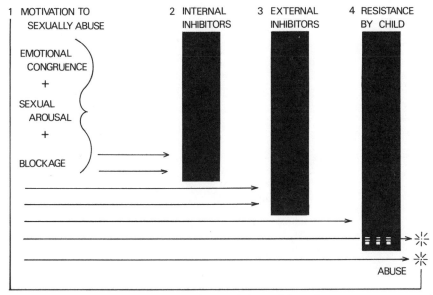

Figure 5–1   Four Preconditions of Sex Abuse

These three components are not themselves preconditions. That is, some contribution from each is not required in order for the sexual abuse to occur. For example, an offender may sexually abuse a child without necessarily being sexually aroused by the child; he may do so simply because such abuse satisfies an emotional need to degrade. Or an offender may sexually abuse a child for the sake of variety without necessarily being blocked from alternative sources of gratification.

However, in many cases elements are present from each of the three components in accounting for the motivation. As we illustrated in the previous chapter, the mixture of elements may help explain a variety of aspects of the motivation: whether it is strong and persistent or weak and episodic, whether it focuses primarily on boys or girls or both.

The first section of Table 5–1 lists some factors that may help account for the presence of Precondition I. These are some of the more common theories catalogued here, apportioned according to whether they occur at the invididual or social-cultural level.

Precondition II: Overcoming Internal Inhibitors

In order for sexual abuse to occur, a potential offender not only needs to be motivated to commit abuse, but the offender must overcome internal inhibitions against acting on those motives. We presume that most members of soci-

TABLE 5–1
Preconditions for Sexual Abuse

	LEVEL OF EXPLANATION	
	Individual	*Social/Cultural*
Precondition I: Factors Related to Motivation to Sexually Abuse		
Emotional congruence	Arrested emotional development Need to feel powerful and controlling Re-enactment of childhood trauma to undo the hurt Narcissistic identification with self as a young child	Masculine requirement to be dominant and powerful in sexual relationships
Sexual arousal	Childhood sexual experience that was traumatic or strongly conditioning Modeling of sexual interest in children by someone else Misattribution of arousal cues Biologic abnormality	Child pornography Erotic portrayal of children in advertising Male tendency to sexualize all emotional needs
Blockage	Oedipal conflict Castration anxiety Fear of adult females Traumatic sexual experience with adult Inadequate social skills Marital problems	Repressive norms about masturbation and extramarital sex
Precondition II: Factors Predisposing to Overcoming Internal Inhibitors	Alcohol Psychosis Impulse disorder Senility Failure of incest inhibition mechanism in family dynamics	Social toleration of sexual interest in children Weak criminal sanctions against offenders Ideology of patriarchal prerogatives for fathers Social toleration for deviance committed while intoxicated

TABLE 5–1 *Continued*

	LEVEL OF EXPLANATION	
	Individual	*Social/Cultural*
		Child pornography Male inability to identify with needs of children
Precondition III: Factors Predisposing to Overcoming External Inhibitors	Mother who is absent or ill Mother who is not close to or protective of child Mother who is dominated or abused by father Social isolation of family Unusual opportunities to be alone with child Lack of supervision of child Unusual sleeping or rooming conditions	Lack of social supports for mother Barriers to women's equality Erosion of social networks Ideology of family sanctity
Precondition IV: Factors Predisposing to Overcoming Child's Resistance	Child who is emotionally insecure or deprived Child who lacks knowledge about sexual abuse Situation of unusual trust between child and offender Coercion	Unavailability of sex education for children Social powerlessness of children

ety have such inhibitions. If there are those who do not, then the absence of inhibitions needs to be explained.

This precondition is essentially the same as the disinhibition factor identified in Chapter 4. It is established as a precondition separate from the other three factors relating to offenders for two reasons. First, emotional congruence, sexual arousal, and blockage are sources of the motivation to sexually abuse. Disinhibition is not in itself a source of motivation, but the reason the motivation is unleashed. It is not sufficient in itself to create abuse. A person who has no inhibitions against sexual abuse, but also no inclination to do so, will not abuse.

Second, unlike the other three, disinhibition itself *is* a requirement for sexual abuse. No matter what the motivation to abuse sexually, if a potential offender is inhibited by social taboos from acting, then abuse will not occur. Many people probably have a strong sexual interest in children but do not commit abuse precisely because they are inhibited. To account for the abuse, we need to account for why the inhibitions were overcome. The disinhibition may have been temporary, and the person may ordinarily have very strong controls, but an explanation for the disinhibition is an important element in a full explanation of sexual abuse.

Table 5–1 also lists the major reasons for disinhibition of sexually abusive behavior as found in the literature reviewed in Chapter 4.

PRECONDITION III: OVERCOMING EXTERNAL INHIBITORS

The first two preconditions try to account for the behavior of perpetrators. But it is quite clear that such accounts do not fully explain to whom or why abuse occurs. A man fully motivated to abuse sexually who is also disinhibited may not do so, and he certainly may not do so with a particular child. There are factors outside himself that control whether he abuses and whom he abuses. Preconditions III and IV are about these.

Precondition III concerns external inhibitors in the environment outside the offender and outside the child. The most important of these external forces is the supervision a child receives from other persons. Family members, neighbors, and children's own peers all exert a restraining influence on the actions of a potential abuser.

It might appear that, given an offender motivated to commit abuse, the supervision of other persons is a rather fragile form of deterrent. A child cannot always be in the presence of others. Yet, it is interesting how frequently in both the clinical and empirical literature the influence of third parties appears as an important factor in creating a vulnerability to abuse. Some of the most important external inhibitors of sexual abuse noted in the literature are included in the table of preconditions.

Mothers appear to be especially crucial in protecting children from abuse. Of course, there has been criticism that mothers have been blamed too frequently for abuse. This criticism has some validity, which was discussed in Chapter 3 and will be discussed further later in context of the full four-preconditions model. But findings related to the importance of mothers in protecting children appear too regularly to be dismissed simply as sexism. There is growing evidence that when mothers are incapacitated in some way, children are more vulnerable to abuse.

That incapacitation may take various forms. When a mother is absent from a family because of divorce, death, or sickness, as seen in Chapter 3, children appear to suffer more abuse. (See also Kaufman, Peck & Tagiuri, 1954; Machotka, Pittman & Flomenhaft, 1966; Maisch, 1972; Raphling, Carpenter & Davis, 1967). Mothers may also be psychologically absent because they are alienated from children or husband or suffering from other emotional disturbances, with similar consequences.

One form of maternal incapacitation, it is also interesting to note, may come from the relationship between mother and father. Mothers may be unable to protect children because they themselves are abused and intimidated by tyrannical and domineering men. Even large power imbalances that may stem from differences in education may undercut a woman's ability to be an ally for her children.

Just what are all the forms of protection that a mother provides is not entirely clear. Supervision does not mean simply being present with the child at all times. It also includes knowing what is going on for a child, knowing when a child is troubled, and being someone to whom the child can readily turn for help. It can be seen how a potential offender might well be inhibited from abusing a child if he realized that the mother would quickly suspect or know what was going on. Judith Herman (1981) has found that the main difference between families where father and daughter have a "seductive" relationship and families where that relationship becomes actual incest is that in the incestuous families, the mother is incapacitated in some way. In the seductive relationship situation, mothers seem to exert some inhibiting force.

Other people besides mothers act as deterrents to sexual abuse. To the degree that neighbors, siblings, friends, and teachers interact closely with a child and are familiar with his or her activities, they also inhibit abuse. This idea would appear to be supported by findings that children who live in isolated settings or who have few friends and few social contacts are at greater risk to abuse (Chapter 3; Henderson, 1972). The absence of general public scrutiny of family and children may be one of the factors that accounts for the reportedly high level of abuse in the stereotypical "backwoods" family environments (Summit & Kryso, 1978).

One other form that external inhibition may take is simply the absence of physical opportunity for abuser and child to be alone together. In situations where such opportunities are more available, abuse is more likely to occur. The literature on sexual abuse has, for example, mentioned household conditions as factors which may facilitate abuse. When family members are required to sleep together in the same bed or in the same room, abuse may be facilitated. Similarly, one of the reasons why a father's unemployment may precipitate abuse is that, in addition to lowering his internal inhibitions because of emotional stress, it leaves him at home alone with a child for extended periods. When a potential abuser and a child are left alone in the absence of supervising persons, it may help to overcome the *external inhibitions* that often exist against sexual abuse.

PRECONDITION IV: OVERCOMING THE RESISTANCE OF THE CHILD

Children themselves play an important role in whether or not they are abused, and any full explanation of why abuse occurs needs to take into account factors related to the child. Children have a capacity to avoid or resist abuse. Unfortunately, since professionals are mostly in contact with children who were abused, the importance of this capacity is not often realized. If professionals dealt with more children who had had close calls but escaped, this capacity might be more apparent. Some of the factors noted in the literature as compromising children's capacity to resist are listed in Table 5–1.

The notion of a capacity to resist or avoid must not be seen in a narrow way. It means much more than a child who says no to a potential abuser when asked to play a sexual game, or who runs away or fights back when accosted. It involves many subtle aspects related to children's behavior and personality.

Much abuse is undoubtedly short-circuited without the child's knowing anything about it because a potential abuser chooses not to approach that particular child, but goes on to another. This even occurs within a family, where some children will be molested by a father while others are left alone. Abusers undoubtedly sense that some children do not make good targets. They sense that a child will not play along, will not keep a secret, will say no, cannot be intimidated. One might call this a "front of invulnerability." Some molesters who pick victims out in public situations, such as in school yards, have been quoted as saying they know almost instinctively who is a promising target and who is not. Many children may resist abuse without even being aware they are resisting.

A great many things may overcome the ability of children to avoid or resist becoming victims of abuse, and usually one or more of these things are present in every abuse situation. One large class of risk factors is anything that makes a child feel emotionally insecure, needy, or unsupported (Burton, 1968; DeFrancis, 1969; Weiss et al., 1955). A child who feels needy will be more vulnerable to the ploys of a potential abuser: the offers of attention, affection, or bribes. A child who feels unsupported will not have someone to turn to about the abuse or will be more afraid to tell. Children who are emotionally abused, who are disabled or disadvantaged, or who have poor relationships to their parents are all at-risk for these reasons. Several of the factors we found associated with abuse in Chapter 3—having few friends, not receiving physical affection from a father, not being close to a mother, or having her be punitive—fall into this category. They all erode a child's ability to resist.

Children's ability to resist or avoid abuse may be undercut because they are young, are naive, or lack information. It may also be undercut because they have a special relationship to the potential offender. A child who might object to a sexual game when proposed by a stranger may comply because the proposal comes from a family member, a person the child trusts. Because the adult knows the child, the adult may frame the proposal in such a way that the child will agree. That same familiarity may allow the adult to formulate a threat which will thwart any resistance by the child.

Of course, it is important to recognize that however the child behaved or whatever the child did may not make a difference in some situations. All that may have been simply irrelevant because the adult used force and coercion to involve the child in sexual activity. In such cases, the factor overcoming a child's resistance had nothing to do with the child or the child's relationship with the adult. The key factor was force.

Whether or not force was present, it is important in understanding why abuse occurs to account for factors related to the victims. Such factors will continue to appear among those which are found empirically to predict a child's risk of becoming a victim of sexual abuse. These factors seem to be best conceptualized as explaining something about the ability of children to resist or avoid abuse. The absence of such resistance or its being overcome in some fashion are a fourth precondition to the occurrence of sexual abuse.

Operation of the Model

The operation of the four-preconditions model is illustrated in Figure 5-1. It suggests that the various preconditions come into play in a logical sequence.

Only some individuals have strong motivation to become sexually involved with children. Of those that do, only some overcome their internal inhibitions to act on these motives. Of those who overcome their internal inhibitions, only some overcome external inhibitions—the surveillance of other family members or the lack of opportunity—and act on the motives.

At this point, three things can happen. (1) Any particular child may resist either directly or indirectly, for example by running away or by having a confident, assertive, or invulnerable demeanor, and in such a way avoid abuse. This is shown by the arrow that stops before Precondition IV. (2) Any particular child may fail to resist and be abused. This is shown by the lowest line in the figure. (3) Any particular child may resist but may have his or her resistance overcome through coercion. This is shown by the line drawn through Precondition IV.

All four preconditions have to be fulfilled for the abuse to occur. The presence of only one condition, such as lack of protection by a mother or social isolation or emotional deprivation, *is not enough in itself to explain abuse. To explain abuse requires the presence of all four prior conditions.*

This model of sexual abuse, with its four preconditions, is useful for categorizing and integrating many of the suggestions in the literature about individual, family, and cultural factors which predispose to sexual abuse. But the model also has other uses.

No Distinction Between Intra- and Extrafamilial Abuse

As we indicated earlier, much prior theorizing about sexual abuse has revolved around either (1) the psychodynamics of sex abusers or (2) the family-systems model of father-daughter incest. However, a great deal of sexual abuse falls in neither category. Many children are abused by members of their extended family who are not pedophiles and not fathers: for example, brother, uncles, and grandfathers. No current theory even attempts to explain why this abuse occurs. Many other children are abused by babysitters and neighbors who are also not pedophiles. Moreover, the family-systems theory, which is entirely about father-daughter incest, is virtually useless in trying to account for the sexual abuse of boys in their own family (Conte, 1982).

By contrast, the four-precondition model is at a sufficiently general level that all kinds of abuse can be integrated within it. It suggests that abuse by fathers and abuse by pedophiles both require an explanation of how the sexual interest in the child arose, why there were no effective inhibitors, and why a child's resistance was either absent or insufficient. It is an approach which applies to both "fixated" and "regressed" offenders (Groth, 1979), both intrafamilial and extrafamilial sexual abuse.

Family-Systems Model

The four-preconditions model should not be seen necessarily as an alternative to the family-systems model. Rather the family-systems model is just one particular instance of the four-preconditions model, an instance that applies to the dynamics of father-daughter incest. All the dynamics of the family-systems model are encompassed within the four-preconditions model. The four-preconditions model is simply at a higher level of generality.

If the family-systems model is reformulated in terms of the four-preconditions model, it sounds something like the following:

PRECONDITION I Father is motivated to take a sexual interest in his daughter because his relationship with his wife has deteriorated (blockage). Perhaps he sees in his daughter someone who has qualities similar to what he liked in his wife, but someone who can give him uncritical admiration and whom he can manipulate easily to fulfill his sexual and emotional needs (emotional congruence). Father may have himself been sexually abused, but certainly has fantasized about daughter and perhaps masturbated to these fantasies (sexual arousal).

PRECONDITION II Father's internal inhibitions against committing abuse are overcome either by alcohol or by a setback in his job or career aspirations. He rationalizes to himself that he really loves his daughter, or that no great harm will be caused, or that committing incest is preferable to having an affair.

PRECONDITION III External inhibitions against committing abuse are low because mother is not readily protective of daughter. Father may have cultivated a rivalry between mother and daughter. Or mother may be alienated from daughter for her own reasons. Daughter does not feel close to or readily confide in mother.

PRECONDITION IV Daughter's resistance to father's advances is undermined because she trusts him, because she enjoys the attention, affection, and favored status. She may even feel she is holding the whole family together.

This is just one example of how family dynamics can be encompassed within the four-preconditions model. In other families, somewhat different dynamics prevail. But the basic mechanisms are the same.

PUTTING RESPONSIBILITY IN PERSPECTIVE

One of the most persistent criticisms of explanations of sexual abuse is that they tend to take responsibility for the abuse off the offenders and displace it onto either victims, third parties, or society as a whole (Armstrong, 1978, 1983; Conte, 1982). For example, the family-systems model, which finds that mothers are unsupportive and unprotective of daughters in many incestuous families, is frequently criticized for blaming the mother (McIntyre, 1981;

Nelson, 1982). Similarly, research that has found that emotionally deprived children are more vulnerable to abuse has been criticized for putting unnecessary blame on the victims.

The four-preconditions model of sexual abuse puts the issue of responsibility into a somewhat better perspective. In this model the problem of a mother's failing to protect her child or a child's failing to resist victimization are taken seriously as contributing elements. However, it is clear that these factors are not germane to the situation until after the potential offender has already taken some giant strides on the road toward committing the offense. The matter of victim's and mother's behavior are relevant only because the offender is already embarked on an antisocial train of events, better showing where responsibility lies.

Combining Psychological and Sociological Explanations

Another advantage to the four-preconditions model is that it is able to accommodate explanatory factors at both a psychological and a sociological level. This seems to be an important prerequisite for a model that can adapt to new developments in our knowledge about sexual abuse. A great deal of the theorizing about sexual abuse occurred at a time when it was believed to be a rather unusual problem. These theories reflected the ideas of abnormal psychology mentioned earlier. However, since that time we have come to realize how many adults molest children and how many children suffer abuse. A problem that is so widespread certainly needs to be accounted for in sociological as well as psychological terms.

Social factors can be incorporated into the four-preconditions model just as easily as psychological ones. Some of these factors have already been illustrated in the discussion of offenders.

Precondition I Identifiable characteristics of our society tend to motivate adult men to interact sexually with children. These include the erotic premium that males place on youth, smallness, and submissiveness in sexual partners and the tendency of males to eroticize all their affectionate relationships. Such social factors make sexual relations with children more emotionally congruent for potential offenders.

In Chapter 3, we also mentioned social factors related to other components of the motivation to abuse. For example, pornography plays a possible role in the conditioning of sexual arousal to children. Repressive social norms about masturbation and alternative sexual outlets may also contribute to the blockage that directs offenders toward children.

PRECONDITION II Social factors may influence large groups of men to ignore or discount conventional social inhibitions against becoming sexually involved with children. These include child pornography, again, which promotes the idea that sex with adults is enjoyable and educational for children. The social norm that a father has the prerogative to demand what he wants from his children may act as a disinhibitor of sexual abuse within the family. Another such social factor may be the widespread belief that people are not socially accountable for behavior they engage in while drunk (McCaghy, 1968). Such a belief may facilitate the disinhibition of sexually abusive behavior among adults while they are drinking.

PRECONDITION III Several social factors in particular may help account for the failure of external inhibitors to protect large numbers of children. First, to the extent that mothers are dependent on husbands and deprived of social resources by virtue of their sex, they are less effective protectors of children. Second, as traditional, stable communities and neighborhoods have disappeared, many children have fewer adults who supervise and monitor their activities and thus serve as protectors. Finally, a traditional ideology of family sanctity deters outsiders from interfering in family affairs on behalf of children whom they might suspect of being abused.

PRECONDITION IV Social factors play a role in undermining the ability of many children to resist or avoid the enticements of sexual abusers. For example, a pervasive society-wide anxiety about sex makes it common for children not to receive important information about human sexual behavior that would alert them to abuse situations before they occurred.

By drawing attention to sociological factors that contribute to sexual abuse, the model also highlights proposals for changing social systems in ways that would reduce the prevalence of abuse.

USE OF THE MODEL IN TREATMENT

The four-preconditions model also has implications for working with abusive families and abusive individuals. It suggests that evaluation and intervention can operate at four separate sites to prevent sexual abuse from re-occurring. Therapists can evaluate the strengths of each of the four mechanisms in the individual or family situation and develop strategies that can be useful in reinforcing areas that are weak.

For example, in the case of a father who has been abusing his daughter, a clinician might use the model as follows:

PRECONDITION I   What motivates the offender to take a sexual interest in his daughter? In many cases of incest, therapists conclude that the emotional congruence and sexual arousal elements of the situation are not strong and that the blockage of relationship to the wife is the key to understanding why the husband turns to the daughter. However, the model urges clinicians to look carefully at these other sources of sexual interest. The relationship with the daughter may be fulfilling very strong emotional needs for the father (emotional congruence) that arise from much earlier life experiences. They may be the reason why the relationship with the wife is poor. Without the daughter, the father may simply turn to other inappropriate partners, including other children. The clinician needs to look also at the component of sexual arousal, since some research indicates that incestuous fathers have or develop deviant sexual arousal patterns that make them similar to nonincest pedophiles (Abel et al., 1981). To avoid repetition of the abuse, it may be appropriate for the therapist to consider specific behavioral manipulation of the father's sexual proclivities.

PRECONDITION II   An evaluation of the strength and quality of the offender's internal inhibitions may be the key to assessing how likely he is to re-abuse. He may be a generally well-controlled individual who acted under intense stress and who feels great guilt about his actions. On the other hand, he may be full of denial or be someone whose inhibitions are readily overwhelmed by frustrations or alcohol. Of course, the strength of the inhibitions must be examined in the context of the strength of the motives. Even some strongly inhibited offenders are overwhelmed by powerful compulsions. The strength of the internal inhibitors will probably be a good index of how motivated an offender is to participate in treatment voluntarily.

PRECONDITION III   Many of the immediate issues for child welfare workers concern evaluation of factors related to external inhibitors. Workers want to know whether, now that the abuse has been uncovered, other adults are capable of protecting the child from re-abuse. The child's welfare seems better assured when the mother reacts by believing the child, kicking the father out of the household, and allowing the father access to the daughter only under supervised conditions. If the mother sides with the father, refuses to acknowledge the abuse, or appears ineffectual and emotionally devastated, then workers will worry that external inhibitors to re-abuse are weak. They will look for other adults, such as grandparents, who can help to protect the child. Or they can remove the child from the family. Removal from access to the perpetrator is the ultimate external inhibitor. But in general, external inhibitors are the ones easiest to manipulate and thus most readily assessed in crisis intervention.

PRECONDITION IV Clinicians sometimes neglect to analyze the degree to which children are capable of protecting themselves. Sometimes the revelation of the abuse gives the child knowledge and support that reinforce the ability to resist the offender. Knowing she or he can tell the caseworker that it has happened again may be just enough to help the child stand up to the father. Some treatment programs find it very valuable to train victims in abuse prevention skills. If the child now knows that adults clearly should not do such things and has practiced saying no in various situations, the child may be much less vulnerable to re-abuse. If, on the other hand, the child is filled with guilt and remorse for creating problems for the family, this may be a sign that ability to resist is not yet great.

By using the four-preconditions model as a framework for assessment, clinicians may be able to plan the most effective strategy in working with a family. The model directs attention to a variety of vulnerable points. A comprehensive strategy will try to address them all. Some preconditions are easier to manipulate than others. A worker may be able to create external inhibitors to re-abuse much more quickly than reduce an offender's motivation to abuse. On the other hand, some interventions promise more comprehensive results. To simply introduce more external inhibitors may protect some children, but the offender, still motivated to abuse and still disinhibited, may simply turn to other children.

Decisions about the advisability of criminal prosecution can also be made in the context of the model. The threat of criminal action may be exactly the kind of external constraint that will deter an offender from abusing again. On the other hand, if other constraints are as effective and prosecution risks traumatizing the child, then it may not be called for.

The model has a great many other uses as a guide for assessment and intervention, and we have given only some brief illustrations here as an encouragement to others to adopt it and utilize it.

CONCLUSION

This chapter has integrated much of what we currently know about child sexual abuse into a four-preconditions model. Models of this sort have a variety of uses beyond simply being a way of organizing knowledge to make it useful and accessible, uses which we have tried to illustrate here.

One thing this model should do is remind us that sexual abuse is a complex phenomenon. Factors at a number of levels, regarding a number of individuals, come into play in determining its occurrence. Keeping such a model in mind should keep us from being seduced by simple explanations.

At the same time, this model should help us to keep from getting discouraged by that complexity. Sexual abuse is a problem with causes and explanations. Many of these we do not yet fully understand. The four-preconditions model is open-ended; new findings and new ideas can be added to it. By having given some structure to what is already known, this model enables us to use that knowledge.

CHAPTER 6

Child Sexual Abuse in a Sample of Boston Families

I N THE SPRING of 1981, under a grant from the National Center for the Prevention and Control of Rape, a survey of parents was conducted in the
Boston metropolitan area. The study was undertaken to fulfill a number of
important objectives.

First, there had not been enough studies of sexual abuse based on population surveys. Most knowledge of sexual abuse had come from clinical cases and
reported cases. Since everyone believed these cases represented only a fraction
of the true number of cases, it was important to gather information on sexual
abuse from a systematic survey of the population at large, as this survey intended to do.

Second, we wanted to survey parents. Parents play an important part in the
sexual abuse problem in a number of ways. Parents abuse their own children.
Parents are often the ones to hear reports from their children about sexual
abuse. Parents are the most important sources of information from which
children can learn to protect themselves from sexual abuse. In particular, we
wanted to know what might be keeping parents from reporting cases of sexual
abuse they knew about, and how good a job parents were doing in giving information to their children about the problem. Therefore, the study focused on
parents.

The study broached a number of questions concerning sexual abuse that
had never really been asked before. For example, it tried to find out what kinds
of things the public-at-large (represented by the parents surveyed) regards as
sexual abuse. It also tried to find out what kinds of myths and misconceptions

about sexual abuse are still in widespread circulation. The survey also tried to
tap how much sexual abuse parents had heard about that had occurred to their
own children or even to other children that they knew. At the same time, we
were gathering information, similar to that which had been gathered in other
surveys (Finkelhor, 1979; Russell, 1983), about how many adults had themselves been abused when they were young.

The survey was limited to the Boston area for reasons of cost, convenience,
precision, and concern for our respondents. A national survey has an attractive
feature, in that it allows one to make generalizations that apply to the whole
country. However, national surveys are more expensive. Moreover, they are
harder to monitor and supervise, and we believed that the training and supervision of interviewers would be important in a survey on such a sensitive issue
as sexual abuse. Finally, we wanted to make information on services available
to survey respondents in case they needed them, and this was feasible only if we
were limiting our survey to one locale.

STUDY DESIGN

The "sample frame" of the study consisted of all adults in the Boston
metropolitan area who were the parents of children age 6 to 14 and were living
with them currently. The Center for Survey Research of the University of
Massachusetts, which conducted the survey in the spring of 1981, drew an area
probability sample of 4344 households, all of which were screened for the
presence of a child between the ages of 6 and 14. Of the 700 households that fit
the study requirements, interviewers were able to conduct interviews with 521
parents: a response rate of 74%. Trained interviewers conducted the interviews, which lasted approximately an hour.

The survey was designed to include both fathers and mothers. However,
because 20% of the families were single-parent households headed by women,
the sex ratio of the study was somewhat skewed and included just 187 men
compared to 334 women.

On other characteristics, the sample was quite typical of the Boston population as a whole. Eighty-nine percent of the parents were white, 6% black, and
3% Hispanic. (Boston has a small minority population for a large city.) The majority (56%) of the respondents were Catholic, 26% were Protestant, 9% were
Jewish, and 7% were other or no religion. In terms of total family income, 16%
of the sample fell below $10,000, while 25% made $35,000 or more.

Because of the requirement that the adult be a parent and have a child at
least 6 years old, the sample was somewhat older than the adult population of
Boston in general. The median age was 38, with only 8% of the sample under

age 30. At the same time, since a parent still had to be living with his or her child to be included in the study, not many older adults were included. Only 7% of the sample was 50 or over.

Seventy-two percent of the respondents were employed, only 3% considered themselves unemployed, and the rest were primarily homemakers. In terms of education, only 12% of the respondents had not completed high school, 33% had a high school diploma but no more, 33% had some college or a college degree, and 15% had been to graduate school.

Sexual Abuse Questions

A series of questions were asked designed to gain data on the respondents' exposure to incidents of child sexual victimization. First they were asked if they knew of any children of their neighbors or friends who had been sexually abused. Then they were asked if they knew of any relatives or friends who had been abused. Finally, they were asked, "To your knowledge, has anyone ever sexually abused any of your own children?"

On pretesting our study, we had found that many parents revealed victimization experiences that had occurred to their children, but were reluctant to term them sexual abuse. In many cases they would say that these had been "attempts." From the child's account the parents inferred that the child had escaped before something "more serious" had happened, so they chose to see what happened as attempted abuse rather than abuse. Thus, in the final survey we also asked parents, "To your knowledge, has anyone ever *attempted* to sexually abuse any of your own children?" If the parent reported abuse or attempted abuse, another series of questions were posed about what had happened and how the parent had handled it.

(Subsequent analysis confirmed the wisdom of asking about attempts. We contrasted the experiences that parents had labeled "attempts" with those they had labeled actual abuse. Although "attempts" included a somewhat larger number of experiences where no physical contact took place between the abuse and the victim, the difference was not statistically significant. No other characteristic of the experience—age of victim, sex of victim, age of offender, sex of offender—differentiated between experiences labeled attempts and those labeled abuse. So for purposes of our analysis we amalgamated the two.)

The parents in the survey were also asked about their own sexual abuse experiences. In a self-administered section of the questionnaire, respondents were asked, "During the time before you were 16, were any sexual things done to you or with you by a person at least 5 years older than you?" A similar question was asked pertaining to "attempts to do sexual things." If respondents reported any such sexual things or attempts to do sexual things, they filled out a more detailed questionnaire on up to three such experiences. As part of this question-naire, respondents were asked, "Do you consider these experiences to have been *sexual abuse.*" Only those experiences considered by respondents to have been sexual abuse are reported here as sexual abuse.

FINDINGS

Table 6–1 shows the exposure that the Boston parents had had to child sexual abuse. Twelve percent (15% of the women and 6% of the men), said they themselves had been sexually abused. Nine percent said their child had been the victim of abuse or attempted abuse: 4.5% said abused; 4.5% said attempted. Substantial percentages also knew about sexual abuse of a relative, friend, or child of a friend or neighbor. Altogether 47% had some personal knowledge of sexual abuse themselves or through some person in their social network.

It needs to be pointed out that direct comparisons among the percentages in Table 6–1 should be made cautiously. The questions ascertaining the extent of abuse among the different groups were different. Moreover, for several categories we do not know what the base population was. We do not know, for example, how many relatives or friends each respondent had.

Fortunately we do know the base population for children of the respondents. The 521 parents interviewed had a total of 1428 children (living both in and outside the house), so that the actual prevalence of sexual abuse or attempted abuse *known to parents* in this Boston sample was 4% of all their children. (Four parents had had two children abused.) However, many of the children of these parents were still quite young, and will undoubtedly suffer from sexual victimization at a later point in childhood. So the full rate of child victimization that these parents will know about by the time they have raised all their children is certainly greater than 4%.

There are at least two facts that should be kept in mind in looking at data reported by parents about the sexual victimization of their own children.

1. We know that children are frequently sexually abused by their own parents. We doubted that many parents would tell us that they themselves had abused their child, and indeed we got no such report. By the same token, parents may well have withheld information about abuse that they knew had occurred to their children at the hands of their partners or other family members. Data presented later suggest that this may well have happened.

2. A great deal of victimization that occurs to children is never revealed to parents. To get a sense of how many children are sexually victimized but

do not tell their parents, we can examine the experience of the parents themselves. Only 39% of the parents who said they themselves had been victimized told anyone about it within a year of its occurrence. If children of the new generation are like their parents, then the number of children who are actually victimized might easily be double the number that parents know about.

Still, parents are the adults to whom children frequently do report cases of sexual abuse when they do report. (In Table 6–2 we see that most parents find out about the abuse directly from their children.) Parents are the people who are most often in the position to decide what action to take about sexual victimization. So in spite of the previously mentioned limitations on the data, it is instructive to see what parents do hear from their children and how they react. The children's reports will also be compared with what the parents reported about their own victimization experiences.

Nature of the Abuse Being Reported

First, it is interesting to note that boys were well represented in experiences reported by both the children and the parents. Boys accounted for 39% of the children who had told parents about victimization incidents. Males accounted for 16% of the adults who reported they had been victimized as children—but since the sample did not have an equal number of men and women, the adjusted percentage would be 26%. Police and social agencies rarely relate that this many of their reports come from boys, clearly suggesting how much abuse of boys is not reported. (See Chapter 10 for more about abused boys.)

While the sex of the victims was relatively mixed, the sex of the perpetrators was virtually entirely male (94%). In only three of the accounts from the children was a female implicated in the victimization. This corresponds with findings from the self-reported experiences of parents (97% male perpetrators) and from almost all other sources, and adds additional evidence against the idea that there is a large volume of abuse by females that simply never comes to public attention (for more on female perpetrators, see Chapter 11).

Table 6–3 shows that children reporting victimization to their parents can be fairly young. Of cases parents knew about, in 37% the child was under age 7. The mean age of the child victims known to parents was 8.6 years (7.9 for boys, 8.9 for girls). Note that this age distribution is younger than the age distribution estimate for sexually abused children if we were using the parents' reports of their own childhood victimization (mean 9.9; 11.4 for males and 9.7 for females). This difference has to do with the fact that many of the children in the survey families had not yet reached the age where they might be victimized, so that the average age was reduced compared to a group which had completely finished with childhood.

The abuse experiences and attempts that the parents knew about included an extremely large number of experiences that did not involve physical contact (Table 6-4). Fifty-four percent constituted encounters with exhibitionists or adults who propositioned the children without actually succeeding in touching them. These data suggest that what most parents consider "sexual abuse" in reference to their own children includes many things that professionals in the field would not consider such. They are close calls. Certainly the fact that we asked about attempts as well as actual abuse increased somewhat the number of these noncontact experiences we heard about. (However, a large number of the experiences reported as abuse—not just attempted abuse—were also of this sort.) We need to consider another possibility as well: children may be more likely to tell parents about thwarted attempts than about attempts that succeed.

The cases of sexual abuse which occurred to the parents themselves give a picture more in keeping with other studies of sexual abuse. Here about 20% of the experiences parents called "sexual abuse" did not involve any contact. The majority, 53%, involved sexual fondling of some sort. Nineteen percent involved intercourse or attempted intercourse and another 8% oral-genital contact.

Identity of Perpetrators

Concerning the identity of offenders, the information from the child reports shows an interesting contrast to the information from parents' reports. The children told their parents about an especially high number of experiences with strangers (Table 6-5).

Table 6-5 confirms our concern, expressed earlier, that parents may have balked at telling our interviewers about abuse that occurred at the hands of relatives, especially when we see from the self-report sample how frequently we might have expected abuse at the hands of relatives to occur. Only 10% of the child reports were about relatives, while 32% of the parents had been victimized by a relative. It may be in part that children do not disclose to their parents abuse at the hands of relatives. Children may anticipate that telling about relatives will provoke a crisis of loyalty for parents and that parents may end up taking the adult's side.

Another feature of the abuse experiences that get revealed to parents is that they often involve other youngsters as the perpetrators. In Table 6-6, we see that half the perpetrators in the child report group were under the age of 20, while young perpetrators constituted a much smaller proportion of the self-report sample. Here again, children are probably more comfortable telling about an experience at the hands of another child. In the case of abuse by an adult, the child has greater cause to fear retaliation and may doubt that he or she will be believed in the face of a perpetrator's denial.

Parents' Reactions

One of the main objectives of this portion of the study was to find out how parents reacted to and dealt with experiences of sexual abuse and attempted sexual abuse that occurred to their own children. We wanted to know how they felt about the abuse and whether or not they reported the experience to any professionals. At the same time it seemed to be worthwhile to gather similar, but hypothetical information from the other parents, those whose children had not (or had not yet) been sexually victimized. So we asked these parents to "suppose your child were to tell you that he/she had been sexually fondled on several occasions, say by a relative." Then we asked them to imagine how they would react.

The purpose of this hypothetical example was to see if parents who were anticipating dealing with a problem of sexual victimization—as they might in a parents' education class—would be accurate in predicting how they would react compared to parents who had actually faced the experience. So Tables 6–7, 6–8, and 6–9 indicate both how the parents of the abused children reacted and also how the parents in the hypothetical case thought they might react.

The predominant immediate reactions of parents to sexual abuse (and attempted sexual abuse) of their children were anger at the perpetrator, emotional upset, fright, and guilt (Table 6–7). Only infrequently did they admit to being annoyed with the child or embarrassed about the event. Even less frequently did they initially reject the child's story and deny that the abuse had occurred, but such denials are probably underrepresented because they would not admit any abuse to the interviewers either.

The group of parents trying to predict their own responses to sexual abuse said they would react in much the same way. The predominant reactions were anger, upset, fright, and guilt. The only major difference between the two groups was that in imagining an abuse situation, "hypothetical" parents expected to feel more embarrassment than did the parents who actually had a victimized child.

Reporting Patterns

A key question was whether parents would report to any community agency abuse that had occurred to their children. A little over half the parents who had encountered abuse said they had reported it (Table 6–8). Primarily they had reported these experiences to the police. A quarter also said they had reported the abuse to the school. Rather few had reported to agencies which specialize in work with child abuse: the child protection agency or the child abuse hotline.

The reasons for not reporting the victimization were varied (Table 6-9). The most commonly cited factors were a desire to "handle the situation by myself" and a belief that it was "no one else's business." Another frequently cited reason for not reporting was that the parents felt the incident was "not serious," which may have meant that because the parents felt the child had escaped real abuse, they thought an agency might not take a report seriously. Another reason for not reporting that received frequent mention was "feeling sorry for the abuser," a surprising sentiment in light of the fact that anger toward the abuser was one of the most frequently mentioned immediate reactions among parents.

It is interesting to note that some of the reasons that received the least frequent mention are often cited by professionals as the reasons for low levels of reporting. Nonreporters did not agree with the cynical view that "agencies never do anything." Nor did they feel strongly that "police or social workers will frighten the child."

One of the main reasons for not reporting to police could be inferred from looking at which kinds of experiences did get reported. The variable that most differentiated reported experiences from nonreported experiences was the relationship between the victim and the abuser. When the abuser was a relative, none were reported to police. When the abuser was an acquaintance, 23% were reported. By contrast, when the abuser was a stranger, 73% of the incidents were reported (F = 6.88, p < .001). This demonstrates clearly how loyalty to an intimate makes it difficult for a parent to report even if the intimate is a child molester.

We also wondered whether reporters and nonreporters could be differentiated by their demographic characteristics. We looked at education, income, occupation, race, marital status, place of birth, size of town. Reporting rates were not significantly higher or lower for any particular group. This seems to show that the dilemmas posed by reporting are similar for families from all backgrounds.

In comparison to parents dealing with actual abuse, the parents reporting on hypothetical child abuse were much more "report minded." Over three-quarters of these parents said they would report the case, and they cited different agencies among their choices (Table 6-8). The police were still the most frequently chosen agency (somewhat less than for actual reporting parents). But many more parents in the hypothetical situation thought they would report to a child protective agency or child abuse hotline.

The survey does raise the possibility that people's intentions about reporting need to be taken with a grain of salt. Many people who say they will report probably do not. And in crises, people turn more often to the police than to social welfare agencies. However, it is also true that the people answering about a hypothetical case were responding to a more serious form of abuse than many of the actual cases that parents encountered. This may explain some of their greater willingness to report.

Concerns About Effects on Children

We also asked parents to tell us about their concerns regarding the effects of sexual victimization on their children. We read them a list of effects that we thought would worry parents (drawn from our pretest) and asked them if they agreed that these were concerns. Parents did not admit to a great number of concerns about the effects of child sexual victimization (Table 6–10). In general they did not think their children were going to suffer ill effects.

The effects that worried parents the most, if any, were emotional problems and being afraid of sex. Other concerns such as fear of adults, homosexuality, school problems, sexual difficulties were cited by a few parents. But no one particular concern stood out above all the rest.

The parents who were asked about a hypothetical abuse situation were also presented the same list of concerns, and in contrast to the parents whose children had really been victimized, they showed a great deal of concern. The vast majority said they would be concerned that their children might develop emotional problems, might be afraid of sex, might be afraid of adults, and might develop school problems. Even the outcome of least concern—that their child would become a homosexual—was expressed by a third of the hypothetical parents.

The more serious concerns of the parents in the hypothetical case probably reflect two differences. For one thing, the hypothetical case involved a relative, but most of the actual cases involved strangers and acquaintances. Parents may have perceived abuse by a relative to be more potentially traumatizing and thus showed more concern in the hypothetical case.

But even more important, the parents whose children had actually been victimized were in a quite different situation. Their child had actually experienced abuse. On the one hand, these parents may have minimized the possible effects of the experience because to contemplate these effects was frightening. On the other hand, they may have had a more realistic assessment of the situation based on being able to actually see how their child coped with and reacted to the events which had occurred. Their children may have seemed so little ef-

fected by the experiences that the probability of serious long-term consequences from the victimization might have struck the parents as extremely
remote.

Children Vulnerable to Abuse

We were interested in knowing whether the children who had experienced victimization came predominantly from any particular background. We looked at
the social class, ethnic, and racial background of the families they came from.
We also looked at family composition, where the family was from, and where
they lived in the Boston metropolitan area.

The children who, according to parents, had been victimized did not come
disproportionately from any identifiable social, class, ethnic, religious, or racial
background. Almost no variable we collected differentiated between families
with a victimized child and those without. It seemed as though sexual victimization was widely and broadly distributed.

In looking at the parents who had been victimized, the situation was similar
with one exception. Education, ethnicity, religion, and race did not make a difference in rates of victimization. Income, however, did. Women from families
with incomes under $10,000 had somewhat higher rates of victimization and
women from families with incomes above $35,000 had clearly lower rates
(Table 6–11). However, we are not certain that this is evidence that sexual
abuse is related to social class. The income levels measured here are levels of
their current families, not the families in which they grew up. The finding may
mean that sexual abuse increases one's likelihood of ending up poor, not the
other way around. However, considering the finding from the student study
(Chapter 3) that family income and sexual abuse are related, we think low income probably does increase risk.

One other family variable showed a relationship to sexual abuse: children in
stepparent families (essentially step*father* families) showed a higher rate of sexual victimization. In these families a child was about twice as likely to have been
sexually victimized (17% vs. 8% for families without a stepparent) according to
parents. Stepparent families have been shown to be associated with high
vulnerability to sexual abuse in other studies (see Chapter 3). The reason is *not*
just that the stepparents themselves abuse the child. In the present sample, for
example, only one of the victimized children had been victimized by any kind
of parent. Unfortunately, the real reason for this greater vulnerability is not
clear. In Chapter 3 we suggested two possible factors. Having a stepfather
means in most cases that the child's mother has gone through a courting process. As part of her dating, she may bring into the home sexually opportunistic
men who molest her children. A second possibility is that a stepfather brings

into contact with his new family a network of friends and acquaintances who may not feel the same kind of restraint they might if these were the natural children of a friend. However, both these are matters of speculation. More research needs to be done on why there seems to be a higher vulnerability to sexual abuse in stepparent families.

SOME IMPLICATIONS FROM THE SURVEY

The survey demonstrated that a small but significant number of parents in the community discover that someone has abused or attempted to abuse their children. The kind of abuse and abuse attempts they are most likely to hear about are those that occur at the hands of strangers, acquaintances, and other children and those where no touching occurs. Comparison to parents' own experiences of childhood sexual victimization makes it clear that their children's experiences involving relatives, intercourse, and older offenders are the ones that parents are least likely to discover.

It is easy to speculate on why parents find out only about selective types of abuse. Clearly, children have a greater fear of retaliation when the offender is a relative and an adult. They also have a greater and realistic fear of not being believed or not being supported. The relatives and adult offenders themselves are probably more adept than would be a stranger or acquaintance or younger child at keeping the sexual abuse a secret and manipulating the child into staying silent too.

All this evidence points to the need for more parent education on the problem of sexual abuse. Unless parents make it clear to children that they are receptive to hearing about sexual abuse and will support them even if the abuser is a trusted person, children are going to be reluctant to tell.

The study findings also point to a need for educating parents about the handling of sexual abuse incidents. Only a little more than half the families reported the abuse to any agency. Among the nonreporters there was a strong sentiment that the incident was not anyone else's business and that they could handle it themselves.

Although parents do not express strong anxieties about what would happen if they did report, they were probably not aware of some of the possible benefits of seeking professional help. If reporting served any purpose at all for them, it seemed to be part of their desire to punish the offender and perhaps protect other children from a similar fate. This idea is supported by the fact that reporters overwhelmingly turned to the police rather than any social agency in the aftermath of an abuse incident. Very few parents consulted doctors or mental health or child protection agencies. They did not seem to have much interest in consulting someone who might help assure the child's well-being. In fact, they did not express many concerns at all about the child's well-being. Either they were denying their concerns, or their children's resiliency persuaded them that there was little to worry about.

One part of the problem, possibly, is that parents do not know that other professionals besides the police might be interested in helping in situations of child sexual abuse. From other sections of the survey, we know that parents do not spontaneously mention child protection services, mental health agencies, or physicians as possible sources of assistance. When such agencies are brought to their attention, however, parents do acknowledge them as valuable help sources, but rarely do they spontaneously associate them with the problem. In communities like Boston, where other agencies do provide help to families where children have been sexually victimized, these agencies will apparently need to do a better job of educating parents and advertising their availability. This education may be one important step to insure that children suffer less in the long run from some of the potential effects of childhood sexual victimization.

In another important result of the survey, the finding that 15% of the mothers and 5% of the fathers had themselves been victims of sexual abuse adds to a growing number of studies that show that an important fraction of the population is affected by this social problem. The Boston finding is important in that it is an estimate that grows out of a random-sample survey. At the same time, however, the estimate is lower than in some other studies: lower than in a number of student surveys (Finkelhor, 1979; Fromuth, 1983) and lower than in another random-sample survey (Russell, 1983).

The Russell study is particularly noteworthy because of its much higher figures. Russell found that 38% of a sample of 930 San Francisco women reported at least one experience of intrafamilial or extrafamilial sexual abuse before reaching 18 years of age; 28% reported one such experience before reaching 14 years of age. Twelve percent of the San Francisco women had been abused by a relative before the age of 14 and 4.5% had been abused by a father or stepfather. These figures are twice as high as the Boston figures for overall abuse and more than twice as high for intrafamilial abuse and for abuse by fathers and stepfathers.

There are some differences between the studies in the definition of abuse, but not enough to account for much of the disparity. Russell's definition, for example, included unwanted sexual touching by peers before the age of 14 and any unwanted experiences with same-aged relatives, while the Boston study included only experiences with partners (relatives or others) who were five or more years older. This means that the San Francisco study included some experiences with peers that can legitimately be called abuse, but that were not counted in the Boston study. The Boston study also required that in order to be included, the respondent had to label the experience as "abuse", something that was not required in the San Francisco study.

On the other hand, the 38% figure from the San Francisco study is based only on experiences which involved physical contact, whereas in the Boston study, a fifth of the experiences that were counted as abuse did not. When Russell added noncontact abuse experiences to make her definition more comparable to the Boston study, her figures jumped to 48% of the women before age 14 and 54% before age 18, over three times the Boston figures. So in some important ways, the definition used in San Francisco was more conservative and cannot explain the higher figures.

Some of the disparity in the two studies probably has to do with the study populations. The San Francisco study is more truly representative of the whole female population. In the Boston study, because only mothers of children were interviewed, the age range was more restricted, and also some women whose lives were perhaps more traumatized and disorganized by their history of abuse may have been excluded. It is also possible that the number of victimized women living in San Francisco is higher than the number living in Boston.

One other important source of the disparity between the studies, however, concerned the interview. The San Francisco study was entirely devoted to respondents' various kinds of sexual assault and abuse experiences. Fourteen separate questions asked about situations where child sexual abuse might have occurred. For example, respondents were asked specifically if anyone had ever tried to have sexual intercourse with them against their wishes before age 14, specifically if anyone had tried to touch their breasts or genitals, and also more general questions about whether they had had any other upsetting sexual experiences before 14. It seems likely that all this probing turned up experiences that are either not remembered or not seen as relevant when more general screening questions are asked. The findings from the San Francisco study do suggest that the prevalence figures from the Boston survey are underestimates and that multiple-question approaches need to be used in the future.

TABLE 6–1

People Respondent Knew Who Had Been Sexually Abused

IDENTITY OF VICTIMS	% RESPONDENTS WHO KNEW SUCH A VICTIM (N = 521)
Self	12
Own child	9
Relative	9
Friend	21
Child of friend or neighbor	20

TABLE 6–2

Manner in Which Parent Learned of Child's Abuse/Attempted Abuse

MANNER	% (N = 48)
Child told parent	63
Someone outside household learned and told parent	13
Child told some other household member	8
Another household member discovered abuse	8
Parent discovered abuse	4
Something in child's behavior suggested abuse	4

TABLE 6–3

Age of Child and Age of Parent (Self-Report) at Time of Abuse/Attempted Abuse

AGE IN YEARS	% CHILDREN (N = 52)	% PARENT SELF-REPORTS (N = 78)
0–6	37	15
7–12	44	65
13–16	19	19

$\chi^2 = 8.30, p < .05$

TABLE 6–4
Sexual Activities in Child Reports and Parent Self-Reports

ACTIVITIES	% CHILD REPORTS (N = 52)	% PARENT SELF-REPORTS (N = 78)
Intercourse	2	9
Attempted intercourse	8	10
Oral–genital	6	8
Touching sex organs	10	26
Fondle through clothes	20	27
Exhibit sex organs	26	11
Sexual request	28	9

$\chi^2 = 16.79$, $p < .05$

TABLE 6–5
Identity of Perpetrators in Child Reports and Parent Self-Reports

IDENTITY	% CHILD REPORTS (N = 49)	% PARENT SELF-REPORTS (N = 78)
Parent	2	8
Relative	8	24
Acquaintance	45	35
Stranger	45	33

$\chi^2 = 7.99$, $< .05$

TABLE 6–6
Age of Perpetrator in Child Reports and Parent Self-Reports

AGE IN YEARS	% CHILD REPORTS (N = 52)	% PARENT SELF-REPORTS (N = 78)
Under 13	23	3
14–20	27	18
21 +	50	79

$\chi^2 = 17.37$, $p < .001$

TABLE 6–7
Parents' Reactions to Discovery of Sexual Abuse

| | % OF PARENTS | |
REACTION	Real Case (N = 48)	Hypothetical Case (N = 469)
Angry at perpetrator	90	99
Emotionally upset	88	98
Frightened	81	89
Guilt (felt bad for not protecting child)	77	91
Embarrassed that others might know	10	38*
Annoyed with child	10	12
Thought child might be inventing story	4	13

*p = .06

TABLE 6–8
Parents' Reporting to Agencies About Sexual Abuse of Own Child

| | % OF PARENTS | |
	Real Case (N = 48)	Hypothetical Case (N = 435)
Reported it outside family	56	78***
Of those reporting:	(N = 27)	(N = 334)
Agency		
Police	74	47**
School	27	3***
Clergy	15	6
Doctor	12	11
Mental health agency	12	17
Child protection agency	8	30*
Child abuse hotline	4	22*

*p < .05
**p < .01
***p < .001

TABLE 6–9

Parents' Reasons for Not Reporting

REASON	% PARENTS (N = 20)
Incident was not serious	45
No one else's business	75
Didn't want neighbors and friends to find out	45
Police or social workers might frighten child	15
Retaliation by abuser	15
Child may have been at fault	15
Wished to forget incident	50
Wanted to handle situation by self	90
Felt sorry for abuser	50
Did not wish to get abuser into trouble	50
Agencies rarely do anything	11

TABLE 6–10

Parents' Concerns About Effects of Sexual Abuse

EFFECTS	% PARENTS	
	Real Case (N = 48)	Hypothetical Case (N = 469)
Develop emotional problems	29	94*
Be afraid of sex	23	91*
Be afraid of adults	17	81*
Become homosexual	15	34*
Develop school problems	13	84*
Develop frigidity/impotence in later life	13	56*
Be teased by friends	10	78*
Engage in more sex activity	8	50*

*$p < .01$

TABLE 6–11

Current Family Income and Women's Self-Reports of Sexual Abuse

INCOME	% SEXUALLY ABUSED	(N)
Under $10,000	22	(68)
10,000–24,999	15	(119)
25,000–34,999	16	(56)
35,000+	6	(67)

F = 2.37
p = .07

CHAPTER 7

What the Public Knows About Sexual Abuse

B OOKS AND ARTICLES on the subject of child sexual abuse regularly start by debunking the popular "myths" about the problem. Among the most commonly targeted myths are: that children are molested primarily by strangers; that girls are the exclusive targets of sexual abuse; and that sexual abusers are violent, aggressive, senile, or mentally ill (Adams & Fay, 1981; Groth, 1979; Justice & Justice, 1979; Sanford, 1980; Walters, 1975).

In the typical article on sexual abuse, writers cite these and various other myths that are thought to be widespread and go on to show how mistaken they are. As many writers point out, the myths about sexual abuse can be an important contributing factor to the problem itself. For example, parents who are not aware of the true nature of the problem cannot give their children useful information to help avoid abuse. If they warn children about strangers, and a more serious danger comes from adults the child knows, then the child is poorly advised.

Moreover, adults who misunderstand the problem are more likely to overlook abuse that is occurring or to contradict a child who tries to seek help. For example, if a parent does not believe that boys are victims of sexual abuse, he or she may just ignore a child who is giving obvious signals of alarm and distress. If these misconceptions about sexual abuse are as widespread as most authors imply, it would indicate that sexual abuse is indeed one of the most misunderstood social problems in contemporary America. However, no one has ever established empirically that these myths are prevalent or just how prevalent they are. Rather, authors on the subject of sexual abuse have tended to infer these myths anecdotally, from conversations or from the questions which they face regularly in the course of public speaking and clinical consultation.

Some of the myths can also be traced to the writings of journalists and public officials in the past. For example, the following advice appeared in *PTA Magazine* in 1971:

> Parents should ask children to observe three simple rules to avoid molesters:
>
> 1. Never get into an automobile with a stranger.
> 2. Never accept candy or anything else from a stranger.
> 3. Never go with a stranger anywhere—no matter what the stranger promises in return or what reason he gives for the pickup. (Randall, 1971)

The image of the child molester as a stranger near the schoolyard could hardly be stated more explicitly.

However, the various "myths" of sexual abuse are also a handy pedagogical device. They help authors expound on the nature of sexual abuse, and if the myths did not actually exist, they might have to be invented. It may be that the myths of sexual abuse are not as widespread as the constant reference to them might suggest. These myths may live on in the professional literature about sexual abuse, at least in part, because they are "straw men," easy to debunk.

To find out how informed or uninformed the public is about child sexual abuse, we included in the 1981 Boston survey many questions related to this subject. We wanted to know how much exposure the Boston parents had had, what they thought sexual abuse was, why they thought it happened, and what they thought needed to be done about it. The answers surprised us in some cases. (For a parallel study concerning physical abuse, see Gil & Noble [1969].)

EXPOSURE TO SEXUAL ABUSE

Virtually all (93%) the parents had been exposed to a discussion of sexual abuse in the previous year (1980). It was by no means a new subject for them. Ninety percent said they had seen something about the problem on TV during the last year (see Table 7–1). Eighty-five percent said they had also read something about the problem in the newspaper. Others had heard about it from other media sources or friends.

In about 1978 the media started to present an increasing amount of information about sexual abuse. Incest victims and offenders appeared on the Phil Donahue Show. Family magazines carried articles on how to protect children from abuse. Episodes involving sexual abuse were aired on TV series. Information on sexual abuse touched a wide audience, and the survey of parents in the Boston area corroborated it.

Some parents in the Boston area had an even more intimate exposure to the problem of sexual abuse, however. As we saw in the last chapter, either they themselves or someone they knew had been abused. Altogether, close to half the parents knew about sexual abuse in this way. Twelve percent said they themselves had been victimized (see Table 6–1). Nine percent said it had been their child. Nine percent knew of a relative who had been abused, 21% knew of a friend, and 20%, the child of a friend or neighbor. So sexual abuse was not an alien subject for Boston parents. Most had read or heard something about it, and a large number had experienced it firsthand or in their immediate social network.

SERIOUSNESS OF THE PROBLEM

There was also no question that the parents saw sexual abuse as a serious problem, both in terms of its scale and in its effects on children. For example, we asked parents to rate a series of different kinds of traumatic events that could befall children. Parents consistently ranked sexual abuse as the most harmful experience on the list, significantly more harmful than having a friend die or more harmful than having his or her parents get a divorce. The high ranking of sexual abuse in terms of seriousness held for boy victims as well as girl victims. If Boston parents erred on the question of sexual abuse, it was, if anything, on the side of being too alarmist.

Similarly, the parents did not minimize (by too much) the scope of the problem. Even though until recently, official estimates seriously underestimated the real frequency of sexual abuse (the *Comprehensive Textbook of Psychiatry* [Freedman, Kaplan & Sadock, 1975] estimated one case per million), parents did not see sexual abuse as a rare occurrence by any means. Almost half estimated that it occurred to at least one girl in every ten (see Table 7–2). Forty percent said it occurred to one boy in ten or more. Only a minority guessed that sexual abuse was a rare event: 21% thought it relatively rare among girls (1 in 500 or less) and only 30% thought it similarly rare among boys.

How often sexual abuse actually does occur is not yet a matter of established scientific fact. No national survey has yet been done. Nonetheless, virtually all surveys have shown sexual abuse to occur to well over one in ten of girls (Chapters 1 and 5; Finkelhor, 1979; Russell, 1981). So while Boston parents may be somewhat low in their estimates, they do not tend to see it as rare or unusual.

VIEWS OF THE OFFENDER

Parents may have been relatively well-informed (or good guessers) on the matter of prevalence, but when it came to the identities of the offenders, they were not so accurate. The most prevalent misconception about sexual abuse was still widespread despite all the media exposure they claimed to have had. When asked to think of a sexual abuser, a majority of parents still thought in terms of an offender who was a stranger. We asked respondents this question in two different ways. In the first instance, we mentioned the term "sexual abuse" and then asked what type of offender came to mind. Fifty percent said a stranger, while only 22% mentioned a relative and only 28% someone the child knew, but not a relative. In a second instance, later in the survey, we also asked parents to rate different types of offenders as to how often they thought these types sexually abused children. Here again, strangers were rated as the most frequent perpetrators of sexual abuse (Table 7–3).

Virtually all studies of sexual abuse have shown that strangers make up only a minority of persons who offend against children. Studies of cases reported to the police as well as surveys of the general population come to the same conclusion (DeFrances, 1969; Finkelhor, 1979). In the last chapter, we saw that even in these respondents' own reported victimization experiences only a third occurred at the hands of strangers. The fact that Boston residents are misinformed on this issue is all the more glaring because it contradicts their own experience.

The survey does show, however, that the public has heard some of the news about the identity of offenders. The kind of offenders most likely to be cited after strangers are stepparents and parents (Table 7–3). This is an indication of more up-to-date knowledge about sexual abuse. It has been only very recently that incest has been acknowledged to be a major component of the problem of sexual abuse. For a long time, abuse by parents or stepparents was thought to be extremely uncommon (Weinberg, 1955). That parents in the study mention parents and stepparents as frequent abusers suggests that accurate information has reached some segment of the community.

The reality that sexual abuse is often committed by parents has been recognized by some groups more than others. Higher socioeconomic respondents for example, more often acknowledged that relatives and parents are often abusers. Older persons and more religious persons, however, did not. The myth that strangers are the most common abusers is strongest among the working class, people with lower incomes and less education—people who might have less access to the findings of recent research.

Although parents still had many misconceptions about offenders being strangers, they were not misinformed about their sex or their age. Professionals have often implied that many people saw child molesters as "dirty old men" (Groth, 1979; Sanford, 1980), in spite of the fact that offenders are most likely to be young and middle-age adults. Yet, our survey would indicate that the "dirty old man" image is not prevalent, not at least at present. Seventy-eight percent of the respondents said that only in rare cases or almost never would an elderly person sexually abuse a child. They saw children as more likely to be victimized by adults between 30 and 40 than by older persons. The "dirty old man" stereotype apparently was not given much credence.

That most sex abusers are men, however, the survey respondents had little doubt. When asked to estimate the number of abusers who might be women, the median estimate was 20%. If anything, this estimate is high. Surveys of victimization in the general population have regularly shown that over 90% of abusers are men (see Chapter 11). When women appear as abusers, it is most often as accomplices to men, not as abusers themselves. It is rather infrequent for women on their own to turn to children for direct sexual gratification.

SEXUAL ABUSE VICTIMS AND THE NATURE OF ABUSE

Our respondents' perceptions of the sexual abuse victims were rather accurate too. Professionals have taken some pains in recent years to warn parents, for example, of the early age at which sexual abuse can occur. One presumed popular misconception was that parents saw children as relatively immune from sexual victimization until they started to develop secondary sexual characteristics (Sanford, 1980). But contrary to this stereotype, most sexual abuse occurs before adolescence. In the literature peak ages tend to fall between 8 and 12 (Finkelhor, 1979).

Parents are apparently cognizant of the young age of many sexual abuse victims. We asked the respondents to indicate what they saw as the range of peak vulnerability of children to sexual abuse. Respondents saw more than 50% of abuse occurring before age 11. They saw more than a quarter of abuse occurring before age 8. There was no evidence that a large number of parents held the misleading idea that vulnerability to abuse was a problem brought on only by the arrival of physical maturation.

Although they know that young children are frequently abused, there was evidence that parents still do not acknowledge just how extremely young victims can be. To illustrate this we superimposed two graphs in Figure 7–1. One line shows the ages of children whose actual abuse experiences came to light in the Boston study (this included experiences of respondents, their children, their friends, relatives, and the children of friends and neighbors). The second line shows the percentage of respondents who saw children as vulnerable at that age. As the figure reveals, parents are fairly accurate in estimating the risk of

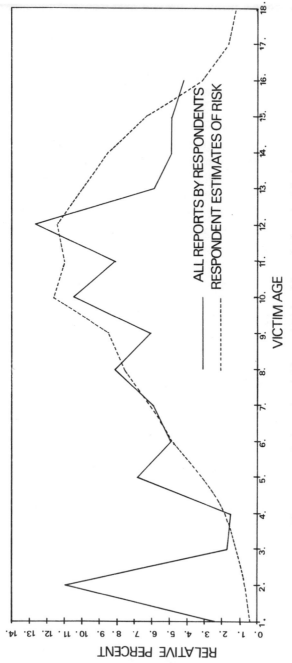

Figure 7-1 Estimated and Observed Risk of Sexual Abuse by Victim Age

abuse except for some of the very youngest children. Children under the age of 5 have a fairly serious risk of victimization, yet the public is not really aware of it.

We also asked parents some questions to test whether they could distinguish readily between sexual abuse and rape. Unlike rape, sexual abuse does not nearly so often involve physical force or attempts to achieve sexual intercourse. Many sexual abusers entice children into sexual activity through the authority they hold over the child, through rewards or enticements they offer the child, or through misrepresenting the nature of moral standards. The sexual acts they initiate often involve only touching and manipulating the genitals, not actual penetration (Finkelhor, 1979).

These realities of the nature of sexual abuse were relatively well understood by Boston parents. Only 41% thought that force was involved in most cases. Although many mentioned intercourse as coming to mind when they thought of sexual abuse, 63% mentioned some *other* sexual activity beside (or in addition to) intercourse. This would seem to indicate that a large proportion of parents had heard accurate accounts of specific cases of sexual abuse and could clearly envision it as something different from rape.

One of the most serious aspects of sexual abuse is that so few victims feel able to tell anyone about it. Research indicates that a majority of children keep the knowledge of their abuse experiences to themselves and do not tell parents or other adults (see Chapter 6; Finkelhor, 1979). This secrecy about the event can be part of what creates developmental difficulties for a child, since it contributes to a sense of isolation and stigma (Burgess et al., 1978).

We were interested in knowing if parents recognized this aspect of the problem. Many parents might assume that children would tell them if they were sexually victimized, and this might give them a false complacency about the problem. However, our respondents did not seem to take this view. They guessed that children were not very forthcoming in talking about sexual abuse experiences. Forced to pick a number, our respondents on the average estimated that only 33% of victimized boys and 39% of victimized girls would tell their parents about their experience soon afterwards. This number is close to figures found in actual studies. (In Chapter 6, we saw that only 39% of the victimized parents themselves told.) Also, it shows a fairly high degree of awareness on the part of parents about how children react to sexual victimization.

Source of the Problem

That adults will sexually exploit a child is a disturbing fact for many people, and they often admit to having difficulty understanding why someone would do such a thing. When pressed, however, there are various kinds of popular "explanations" that people use to help account for this phenomenon to themselves. They range from seeing sexual abuse as a result of unbearable sexual frustration to blaming it on senility, alcohol, or homosexuality. We gave our respondents a list of common popular "explanations" (developed from a pretest) and asked them which ones explained for them most cases of sexual abuse.

There was an overwhelming and broadly agreed upon inclination among the Boston parents to see sexual abuse as a mental health problem. Sixty-two percent said that in most cases sexual abusers are mentally ill. This was two and a half times more people than cited any other explanation (Table 7–4). Moreover, the idea that mental illness explains sexual abuse cut across all educational, social class, and other backgrounds.

Other stereotypical explanations of sexual abuse did not garner much support. Only 22% saw sexual abusers as alcoholics in most cases. Only 2% cited senility as a factor in most cases. The connection between homosexuality and child molesting (which has been exploited by antihomosexual campaigns such as the recent California referendum attempting to bar homosexuals from teaching jobs) did not claim many adherents. Boston parents were also very reluctant to blame any part of the sexual abuse on the children themselves. Only a small percentage (5%) saw it as resulting from children who "act in a sexy way." Instead, most respondents attributed sexual abuse to mental illness in the abuser.

REPORTING SEXUAL ABUSE

Although our respondents seemed genuinely concerned in the abstract about the problem of sexual abuse, we needed to know whether they were prepared to do something about it. There is evidence that a great deal of sexual abuse is covered up and not reported by people who have a knowledge that it is occurring (James, Womack, & Strauss, 1978; National Center for Child Abuse and Neglect [NCCAN] 1981). There are strong norms against "informing" on others, especially when family matters are concerned, so we wondered whether the general public is inclined to report sexual abuse.

We gave respondents a hypothetical situation. "A man from the neighborhood where you live was found to be fondling the sex organs of his 12-year-old daughter over a period of three years. I know it is hard to say what you would do about such a situation without knowing more about it, but just say what you would do *in most cases*. If you were the only person who knew about this happening, would you try to report it to anyone?" Ninety-three percent said they would.

This is quite an impressive response. The vast majority of the sample said they would try to report a neighbor who they knew to be committing abuse. Unfortunately, it is hard to know how much credibility to give a person's expression of good intentions in a hypothetical situation. No doubt more people say they would report than would actually do so. When faced with a real situation, and the doubts about whether abuse is really occurring, the hope that somebody else knows and will make the report, and the fear of being seen as an "informer," many well-intentioned neighbors would probably falter in their resolve to report. However, it is interesting that so many people would have at least the intention and inclination to report. It suggests that they believe it to be the right thing to do.

To get a sense of what might keep people from reporting, we asked the "nonreporters" why they would hesitate. The answers they gave (Table 7–5) probably reflect the concerns of many of those who in the hypothetical instance said they would report. There was no single reason that stood out for not reporting. Not wanting to interfere in other people's business was a frequently cited reason. Ignorance about where to report also stopped people from reporting. Almost half felt they would like to handle the situation on their own without outside interference. (Just *what* these people planned to do is not clear.) Finally, about a third cited fear of retaliation.

It is interesting that very few people in this survey mentioned another reason for not reporting that is frequently mentioned by actual nonreporters. Real nonreporters when questioned about their behavior often say, "I wasn't sure enough that abuse was really occurring" or some variant on this refrain. This uncertainty is a reality in most child abuse situations, since outside observers are not always sure of what is happening exactly and mostly have suspicions to go on. The fact that few of our respondents cited this reason as a cause for nonreporting is probably related to the artificial situation we created. By telling them in advance that the abuse was occurring, we eliminated any ambiguity. They knew it was occurring. The excuse of uncertainty was not open to them as a reason for not reporting.

WHICH AGENCY?

We were also interested in finding out where people would report a case of sexual abuse. In many ways this was a more productive question than the question about whether they would report or not. People might well renege on an intention to report, but they obviously could not report a case of sexual abuse to an agency they had never heard of. So by asking them where they would report, we hoped to learn more about what community resources for dealing with the problem of sexual abuse people saw at their disposal.

We gathered two kinds of information about where Bostonians would report sexual abuse. In one question we simply asked them to give us the name of the person, place, or agency to whom they would first report the abuse. This was called the "spontaneous mention." After they mentioned one such person, place, or agency, we read them a list of several other agencies and asked if they would report it to any of these other places in addition. The responses are indicated in Table 7–6.

Table 7–6 shows that when asked where they would first report, the agency that comes to mind most immediately is the police. A fairly large group of people also think of the state child protective agency (what people called the "welfare department" or "human services"). The police and the child protective agency are the two main agencies people think of spontaneously.

What Table 7–6 also shows, however, is that when people are told or are reminded about the range of possible agencies which might be consulted, their priorities change. Thus, when forced to find an agency on their own, the police are the first community resource to be consulted when a person knows of a case of sexual abuse. But when people are reminded that there is a child abuse hotline (as there is in Massachusetts) and that there is a state child protective agency, more people see those as appropriate agencies for reporting than the police. Thus, adding both columns in Table 7–6 together, we see that all together, 88% mentioned using the child abuse hotline, 86% mentioned contacting the child protective agency, while only 67% mentioned the police. This suggests that although many people contact the police when they hear about abuse, more would contact child abuse agencies and hotlines if they were more aware of their existence.

MENTAL HEALTH AND CRIMINAL JUSTICE

An on-going debate in the field of sexual abuse concerns whether child sex abuse offenders ought to be treated or punished (Bulkley, 1981a; Conte, 1982; MacFarlane & Bulkley, 1982). Few professionals actually see the question in such stark either/or terms, and the most successful programs to deal with offenders are, in fact, ones which contain both treatment and punishment components (such as the Child Sexual Abuse Treatment Program of Santa Clara County, California; Giaretto, 1982). Still many people argue hotly whether the main emphasis should be on criminal justice or on mental health.

To get a reading of popular opinion on this debate, we forced parents to choose between a mental health or a criminal justice option. We posed the question this way:

> Some people say that a man [who had fondled the sex organs of his 12-year-old daughter over a period of 3 years] needs to be brought to trial because he has done something very wrong. Other people think someone like that needs to get psychological help for his problem. If you had to choose one or the other, which do you think is most important—being brought to trial or getting psychological help?

Overwhelmingly people chose "getting psychological help." Only a scant 12% opted for prosecution. This is important because many professionals have worried that the public harbors a powerful retributive rage against any man who would molest a child. Apparently not: Bostonians, at least, say they prefer treatment over punishment.

The absence of a vindictive impulse toward sexual abusers was also indicated by the kind of punishment people said they would mete out. Such punishments were not very severe. We asked respondents (even those who preferred psychological treatment to criminal punishment) to suppose that the offender was brought to trial. "Which one of these choices would be an appropriate punishment for such an offense" (the father-daughter sexual abuse mentioned earlier). The choices are shown in Table 7–7.

Over 50% of the parents did not see jail as an appropriate punishment for sexual abuse. Of these, 20% said punishment was not appropriate at all (these were the core of those who preferred psychological treatment) and another 32% opted for probation alone. Forty-eight percent did recommend a jail sentence but only a third of these called for a severe jail sentence (more than five years). Just two respondents wanted the death penalty. As might be expected, higher-status respondents opted for leniency and treatment. Catholics, Protestants, and lower-status respondents tended to be more punitive.

However, in spite of more punitive sentiments among some groups, parents, on the whole, were rather lenient toward the child sexual abuser. In the last few years, movements have arisen in both California and New York, one called Society's League Against Molesters (SLAM), another called Reform All Sexual Child Abuse Laws (RASCAL) (Curry, 1982), lobbying legislators to stiffen substantially penalties against child molesters. These movements would probably not have strong public support in Boston.

SEXUAL ABUSE AND PUBLIC POLICY

The controversy over whether to treat or punish child sex offenders is but one policy issue that currently confronts professionals dealing with sexual abuse.

Another concerns the emergency handling of cases of sexual abuse that come to public attention. In the past the tendency has been for child protective workers to intervene quickly by removing children from families where they were the victims of sexual abuse. State workers have tended to rely on such protective custody because alternative ways of intervening have not been readily available. However, protective custody has come under severe criticism from some quarters on the grounds that such action punishes the child rather than the abuser (Finkelhor, 1983).

How to handle cases of child sexual abuse when they are first discovered is a complicated policy matter. Many factors, such as the nature of the abuse, the resources of the family, and the alternatives available, need to be taken into consideration before a rational decision can be made. However, we wished to see whether the public had any strong overall bias toward one position in this policy controversy. So we asked the following question:

> Some people say that in a situation [where the father has abused 12-year-old daughter over a period of 3 years], the child should be removed from the home at least for a while to make absolutely sure that she is not molested again. Other people say that the father should be removed from the home at least for a while because he is the one who did the wrong. Still other people think that the first priority needs to be to try to keep the family together. What action do you think is most important—to remove the child, remove the father, or try to keep the family together?

Only a small number of respondents (15%) recommended removing the child. The majority (51%) thought the best option was removing the father, thus keeping him from the child and making him suffer the burden of being homeless. What was interesting was that a relatively large number (35%) thought the best course was trying to keep the family together. This group (which included a disproportionate number of Jews and professionals) seemed to believe that family togetherness was a more important value than assuring that the child would not be molested again.

OVERVIEW OF KNOWLEDGE AND MYTH

Taken together, the findings reported from this survey suggest that the public is relatively knowledgeable and concerned about the problem of sexual abuse. Parents ranked it as a serious problem affecting children. They also believed it to be alarmingly common.

They seem to be aware of some of the most important realities about sexual abuse: the fact that it affects both boys and girls, the fact that it occurs at the hands of trusted family members, the fact that it can happen to young children, the fact that it involves fondling and touching as well as intercourse, the fact that many children do not tell, the fact that it can take place without brute force being used. Some of the classic myths about sexual abuse cited by professionals do not seem highly prevalent.

It is perhaps possible that people never had these misconceptions, that parents have always been more enlightened about the nature of sexual abuse. Our preferred explanation, however, is that people have learned a great deal about the problem in just the last few years. Whatever myths were prevalent in the population a few years ago have probably been greatly reduced by a wave of media attention to the problem.

Unfortunately, we do not have comparative data. We do not know for sure that accurate knowledge about sexual abuse is relatively recent. But we can make a strong inference that this is the case from two other facts. First of all, even the professional literature itself was, until a few years ago, riddled with misconceptions about child sexual abuse. Professionals themselves wrote about child molesting as though it primarily occurred in schoolyards and playgrounds. The information contained in the popular media was also rife with myths.

Second, our respondents reported being exposed to a great deal of recent discussion of child sexual abuse in the media and among friends. It makes sense that their enlightened information comes from this recent exposure. Professionals and researchers newly concerned with the problem of sexual abuse have been relatively successful in getting the word out to the public. The level of public awareness seems to reflect up-to-date knowledge and information.

On one important matter, however, misconception appeared to prevail. There was still a large group of people who tended to associate the notion of sexual abuse primarily with strangers rather than people known to the child. The problem here, we guess, is not entirely one of misinformation. If the public has gotten other accurate information about sexual abuse, it has certainly heard the truth that abusers are more likely to be intimates than strangers. The problem is, rather, that this truth is a very difficult one to accept. It is unpleasant for people to harbor suspicions about friends, neighbors, relatives, members of their own family. So people continue to hold the image of the sexual abuser as a stranger, because the other image is so disconcerting.

Our survey also suggests that people still do not know enough about what to do when they have suspicions about a child being abused. There appears to be an unfamiliarity with the social agencies which are available to deal with abuse. These agencies do not readily come to mind to the majority of people thinking about reporting a case of child abuse. So they tend to think of the police as the first line of defense. Further analysis showed this tendency to be particularly strong among males, the less educated, low-income workers, and Catholics. Our questions suggest that if these and other people knew more about agencies specifically geared to deal with child abuse, they would utilize these agencies more often and more readily.

Sex Abuse and Mental Illness

Another dominant image of sexual abuse revealed by the survey is that it is committed by people who are mentally ill. The respondents in our survey had a great preference for ascribing sexual abuse to mental illness over any other explanation. Writers have often cited this belief as one most important misconception about sexual abuse (Groth, 1979; Walters, 1975). But whether it is a real misconception or not is open to discussion.

When writers say that sexual abuse offenders are not mentally ill, they usually cite the fact that very few of them show evidence of clinical disorders such as schizophrenia. In fact, as an increasingly large number of cases of sexual abuse have come to light, clinicians have found many examples of what they term "normal" men among the ranks of those who sexually molest children. If saying that a child molester is mentally ill means picturing him as a crazed, bizarre, sadistic person, then it is certainly a myth.

But this picture may not be at all what people mean when they say that sexual abusers are mentally ill. Saying that someone is mentally ill has two other popular meanings, neither of which means "insane."

On one hand, "mentally ill" has increasingly come to be used by people to explain deviant behavior which they fail to understand in any other way (Howells, 1980). It is a kind of residual category. If a person cannot explain another person's behavior with the usual "vocabulary" of motives, they apply the term "mentally ill." Someone who robs a house would not be likely to be termed mentally ill, because a plausible motivation—money—is immediately identifiable to most people. When someone molests a child, the motive is more difficult for many people to apprehend, so they use the term "mentally ill." The popularity of this response may just be another way of people saying that they are confused and unsure about just why a person sexually abuses.

The second meaning of "mentally ill" is "being in need of psychological treatment." In this sense, people apply the term "mental illness" not just to psychotics and other clinically disordered people, but to anyone whom they think ought to be in treatment. Mental health professionals have in recent years claimed expertise over a growing number of personal and social problems and argued that they have technology to change all kinds of behavior from overeating to homosexuality. The public apparently believes some of these claims and is willing to turn over to psychiatrists and psychologists many people who behave in deviant and antisocial ways. This tendency is reflected, for example, in the strong preference our respondents showed for treatment rather than punishment of sexual abusers. When people say that such abusers are mentally ill, they do not mean psychotic. They mean that abusers need treatment. Since most mental health professionals agree with this assessment, it may be a mistake to say that this public opinion about sexual abusers is a "misconception."

The preference that people show for treatment rather than punishment of sexual abusers is more than just strong (and perhaps naive) faith in the curative powers of contemporary psychology and psychiatry. People turn toward the treatment option in part to escape from a conflict they feel. People seem to be reluctant to criminalize acts that occur between family members (Armstrong, 1983). Thus, the act of rape has not in the past been legally considered a crime when perpetrated by a husband against his wife. Assaults between family members are treated as much less serious and criminal than assaults between non-family members (Rossi et al., 1974). The idea of polarizing the family in the criminal justice arena challenges a strongly held belief that family problems should be resolved by some less impersonal mechanism than the law. Thus the strong preference we noted among Bostonians for treatment over punishment in part reflects the case that people were considering—a father who was abusing his daughter. If the example had been that of a stranger molesting a little girl, we think that the sentiment for punishment rather than treatment might have increased.

PUNISHMENT FOR SEXUAL ABUSE

The fact that the offender was the father may also help explain the relative leniency of the punishment our respondents were willing to inflict on the abuser. The most frequent choice of our interviewees was for nothing more serious than probation, and less than half opted for any jail sentence at all. This judgment would seem to be substantially less punitive than most penalties specified by the criminal laws which govern sexual abuse.

Sexual abuse is outlawed by a complex tangle of statutes that vary from state to state and even within the same state, so it is not easy to generalize about penalties. But penalties can, at least in theory, be very severe. For sexual inter-course with a child, for example, "most states provide for a maximum of be-tween 10 and 12 years imprisonment" according to a recent comprehensive review on the subject (Kocen & Bulkley, 1981). A number of states *including Massachusetts* allow life imprisonment and at least three states still provide the death penalty.

In the example we provided for the Boston residents, however, intercourse did not occur. State laws are on the whole a good deal less severe in punishing sexual abuse which does not involve intercourse, a crime that goes under the various names of "indecent assault," "sexual contact," "indecent liberties" or "lewd and lascivious acts." In such cases "maximum penalties average 5 to 15 years" (Kocen & Bulkley, 1981). The penalty in Massachusetts, for indecent assault for example, is two-and-one-half to ten years imprisonment. In New Hampshire, sexual contact with a child under 13 has a maximum penalty of only one year in jail and $1000 fine.

However, it also must be borne in mind, these penalties are entirely theoretical. We do not know of any studies that have shown what kinds of sentences child sex offenders actually do receive (as opposed to what they could receive). There have been suggestions that judges in practice are a good deal more lenient with child sex abusers, and rarely impose maximum sentences (Conte & Berliner, 1981; Dowben, 1979). So it is not entirely fair to compare sentences recommended by Massachusetts citizens with the maximum penalties mandated under the criminal law. We would guess that the actual penalties meted out to child sex abusers are probably much more in line with the attitudes of our sample of Bostonians than a comparison with theoretical sentences would indicate. In any case, any future study of this issue needs to compare the punishments that the public would mete out to sexual abusers who are not related to their victims, as well as those who are.

Conclusion

The survey indicates that it is probably time for writers on the subject of sexual abuse to take a new approach. The old myths about sexual abuse are not as widespread as these writers have implied. A modern view of the subject has been disseminated to a large segment of the public. Even if myth was still widespread, the literary device of debunking the myths has worn thin and could use some rest.

Still much educating remains to be done on the subject of sexual abuse. One matter that ought to receive some priority according to this study is helping parents know what agencies are available to receive reports of child abuse. Another priority need (as shown by an aspect of this study which will be reported elsewhere) is helping parents talk to their children about sexual abuse. Indeed, parents say they would like help. In our survey 89% supported the idea of providing education about child sexual abuse in the schools. They believe it is a serious problem and they are open to ideas and suggestions. In general, the climate would seem to be good now for talking with parents about this important subject and recruiting them to be more effective allies in the battle against sexual abuse, which up until recently has been a much neglected problem.

TABLE 7–1

Sources of Information About Sexual Abuse

SOURCE	% PARENTS (N = 478)
TV	90
Newspaper	85
Radio	48
Magazine	43
At work[a]	39
In a book	17
Conversation with friend, relative	14

[a] % of those who worked (N = 350)

TABLE 7–2

Parents' Estimate of Number of Sexually Abused Children

ESTIMATE	% PARENTS	
	Girl Victims (N = 507)	Boy Victims (N = 507)
1 in 4 or more	19	17
1 in 10	30	23
1 in 100	30	30
1 in 500 or less	21	30

TABLE 7–3

Parents' Rating of Most Probable Offenders

OFFENDER	% PARENTS[a] (N = 521)
Stranger	35
Stepparent	28
Parent	22
Friend or acquaintance of child	13
Other relative	5
Older brothers or sisters	3

[a] Does not sum to 100. Respondents could choose more than one category.

TABLE 7-4
Reasons Why People Sexually Abuse Children

REASON	% PARENTS ENDORSING[a] (N = 518)
Mental illness	62
Offenders do not believe it wrong	25
Too highly sexed	25
Loneliness and isolation	22
Get ideas from books and magazines	14
Alcoholism	12
Homosexuality	11
Not enough sex from their partners	10
Children act in sexy way	5
Senility	2

[a] Respondents could choose more than one category.

TABLE 7-5
Main Reasons for Not Reporting Hypothetical Case of
Sexual Abuse

REASON	% (N = 43)
Rather handle it by self	47
Wouldn't know where to report	44
Do not wish to interfere in people's affairs	44
Afraid of retaliation	30
Not serious enough to report	9

TABLE 7–6

Agencies to Which Parents Would Report a Hypothetical Case of Sexual Abuse

	% MENTIONED SPONTANEOUSLY[a] (N = 510)	% FROM LIST[a] (N = 510)
All who would report 93%		
Agency		
Police	37	30
Child protective agency	24	52
Child abuse hotline	8	80
Mental health agency	5	39
Doctor[b]	3	—
Clergy[b]	6	—
School[b]	2	—

[a] Could choose more than one.
[b] Doctor, clergy, school were not choices available on the list read to respondents.

TABLE 7–7

Appropriate Punishment for Father–Daughter Sexual Abuse

PUNISHMENT	% PARENTS ENDORSING (N = 500)
Capital punishment	0.4
Jail for more than 5 years	18
Jail for 6 months–5 years	18
Jail for 6 months or less	12
Probation	32
Punishment not appropriate	20

CHAPTER 8

How the Public Defines Sexual Abuse

COAUTHORED WITH
Dennis Redfield

NOT EVERYONE AGREES about what is and what is not sexual abuse. Is it sexual abuse when a 14-year-old girl fondles her 11-year-old brother's penis? Is it sexual abuse when a 37-year-old stranger exposes himself to a 15-year-old girl in the subway? Is it sexual abuse when a 15-year-old boy asks to fellate a 21-year-old neighbor and the neighbor accepts?

People also disagree about how serious different forms of abuse are (Giovannoni & Beccera, 1979). Is sexual abuse of a 4-year-old child more or less serious than sexual abuse of a 12-year-old? Is sexual abuse by an uncle more serious than sexual abuse by a neighbor? Is sexual abuse less serious if intercourse is only attempted, but doesn't actually occur?

These questions are not academic ones. What people think sexual abuse is and how seriously they take it affects how they behave. For example, it may affect what kinds of sexual behaviors get reported to authorities. Researchers have noted that sexual activities involving adults and boys get reported less often than sexual behavior involving adults and girls. They have speculated that this is because people see sexual activities with girls as more serious and more abusive than the same activity with boys (Groth, 1979).

What people think is abusive may also affect how they react toward the participants. If people think having an encounter with an exhibitionist is extremely abusive they will react with more alarm when a child reports such an encounter, even if the child is not upset. If they think that a sexual encounter between a 12-year-old boy and a 27-year-old woman is not very abusive, they may laugh about it even though the child feels very exploited.

To illustrate with a real life example, in January 1982 a judge in Lancaster, Wisconsin, sentenced a man to 90 days in a work-release program on a charge of sexually assaulting the five-year-old daughter of the woman with whom he lived. In explaining this lenient sentence, the judge said: "I am satisfied we have an unusually sexually promiscuous young lady. And he [the defendant] did not know enough to refuse. No way do I believe he initiated sexual contact" (Nyhan, 1982).

Shortly afterward a citizens group in Wisconsin announced they were trying to gather signatures for a petition to recall the judge. They and many news commentators expressed outrage that a judge could hold a five-year-old girl responsible for such a sexual relationship, even in part (Nyhan, 1982). The controversy revealed the question of whether, according to public norms, anything a five-year-old child might do would mitigate the abusiveness of an adult having sexual relations with her. Obviously the judge—one representative of public norms—thought it did.

In addition to explaining how people may react to victims, some writers have felt that public norms about sexual abuse might also explain a great deal about who gets sexually abused and who doesn't, or who does the sexual abusing and who doesn't. Herman and Hirschman (1977), for example, have argued that public norms determine why it is that fathers commit so much more sexual abuse than mothers. They write:

> A patriarchal society, then, most abhors the idea of incest between mother and son, because this is an affront to the father's prerogatives. Though incest between father and daughter is also forbidden, the prohibition carries considerably less weight and is, therefore, more frequently violated. We believe this understanding of the assymetrical nature of the incest taboo under patriarchy offers an explanation for the observed difference in the occurrence of mother-son and father-daughter incest. (p. 741)

In other words, public norms are more tolerant of father abuse, and that is why there is more of it.

Herman and Hirschman and some other feminists (Rush, 1980) have also made a somewhat different but related argument on the question of why men abuse more than women. It may be that men and women learn different kinds of norms about sexual abuse. Rush points to the pornography men consume that sanctions sex with children. She also describes a male culture, dating back to Greek and biblical times, which has either tolerated or encouraged sex between men and children. It may be these different norms men learn that help account for the male monopoly on sexual abuse.

Nine Variables of Sexual Abuse

When we looked at the kinds of debates that had gone on about the public norms surrounding sexual abuse, we were able to identify nine important variables that had been the subject of some controversy:

1. *Age of victim.* It would seem to be unclear in the public mind how old a child can be and still be a victim of sexual abuse merely by virtue of age. Laws defining statutory rape, for example, have varied from 12 to 18, and this subject has always provoked great legislative controversy.
2. *Age of perpetrator.* Some definitions of sexual abuse limit themselves to acts where perpetrators are adults. Others include acts perpetrated by teenagers and older children as well as adults.
3. *Relationship between victim and perpetrator.* Violations of the incest taboo are often cited as inspiring particular horror and disgust. Child welfare professionals, too, generally regard abuse within the family as more serious than abuse outside the family. However, in characterizing the degree of abusiveness, it is unclear how negatively a sexual contact is viewed simply because it occurs between family members.
4. *Sex of victim.* As we mentioned earlier, some people think the small number of cases of victimized boys coming to professional attention stems from the fact that people do not take such abuse very seriously.
5. *Sex of perpetrator.* As we also mentioned earlier, some theorists propose that the lesser taboo on sexual acts by men and fathers accounts for their greater likelihood to commit offenses. However, it is also true that in recent years, the popular media have given very romanticized portrayals of sexual relationships between boys and older women (films: *Private Lessons, Summer of '42, Harold and Maude, Murmur of the Heart*). It is not clear whether it is male or female older partners who are most tabooed.
6. *Sexual act.* There has been some controversy over what kinds of sexual activities should be considered abuse both for legal and for social welfare purposes. For example, an encounter with an exhibitionist is sometimes defined as sexual abuse, sometimes not. Some have argued that exposing a child to a sexually unconventional lifestyle, such as prostitution, is sexual abuse. Some have argued that when adults have sex in a child's presence, it is abuse.
7. *Consent.* Under the theory of statutory rape, children under a certain age cannot consent to sexual activity with an older person. In theory, whether the child propositioned the adult or whether the child resisted strenuously are considered irrelevant to determining if abuse occurred.

In reality, however, observers, such as the judge in Wisconsin, do take the child's behavior into account in assigning degrees of abusiveness. Is this a stance with support in public norms?

8. *Consequence.* Sometimes when people are not sure whether a situation is abuse or not, they judge it in terms of its outcome. We wondered how much weight people give, in assessing abusiveness, to the question of whether the experience has had a negative consequence for the child.

9. *Sex of respondent.* As indicated earlier, some suggestion has been made that men and women are socialized into different normative cultures around the question of sexual activities with children. We wondered whether men would see sexual incidents as less serious than women would.

A VIGNETTE STUDY

We decided to find out about public definitions of sexual abuse through a "vignette experiment." (A more detailed and technical description of our procedure for the vignette experiment is provided in an appendix to this chapter.) In the vignette experiment, we gave people hypothetical situations of sexual contact involving children and asked them to decide whether or not they considered these examples to be abuse. The usefulness of the vignette experiment was that we could mix up characteristics of the vignettes arbitrarily to see how a change in one characteristic, all by itself, would affect people's reactions to it.

We created categories for each of the variables we were interested in, and these categories (or values) are listed in Table 8–1. Then we programmed the computer arbitrarily to make up vignettes based from these categories. We put 20 of these made-up vignettes together in one questionnaire (plus four others at the beginning to give people practice) and gave each of the parents in our Boston survey a questionnaire consisting of a different set of 20 vignettes. The task for each respondent was to indicate on a scale from 1 to 10 whether they saw the vignette as definitely sexual abuse, definitely *not* sexual abuse, or something in between. A portion of one of the questionnaires is shown in Table 8–2.

One thing people will notice immediately is that the kinds of situations portrayed in the questionnaires bore very little relationship to the common kinds of sexual abuse that a child protective worker, for example, would be likely to see. In fact, many of the vignettes seemed extremely unusual and unlikely. Ironically, this was exactly the purpose of the experiment: to explore the *boundaries* of people's definitions of sexual abuse. By giving people situations that were unlike the usual real life situations that they have to classify, we found out just what the rules were that they used to make the classifications.

THE MAIN FINDINGS

The respondents in the Boston survey took fairly well to the task we gave them. All together they rated 9839 different vignettes, or about 94% of the ones we gave them. One thing that was interesting was that they tended to see most of the vignettes we gave them as very sexually abusive. Sixty percent of all ratings were either an 8, 9, or 10. The mean score for all vignettes was 7.5. Also interestingly, men and women did not rate vignettes the same way. Women consistently gave higher ratings to vignettes than men did. The mean for women was 7.66 while for men it was 7.29.

In Table 8–3, we have chosen some of the most common kinds of sexual situations involving children, and shown how the sample of parents rated these. These scores are a kind of "composite score" and represent what the consensus of the sample was about these situations. (They are not the score that any particular person gave to that particular vignette.) We can see how women tended to score vignettes higher than did men, and we can also see what kinds of situations people tended to regard as more serious.

Relative Importance of Each Variable

The first thing we wanted to know was which of the various variables was most important to people in determining the seriousness of sexual abuse. We entered all the variables into a regression equation, and the results of that equation are shown in Table 8–4. By looking at the values under the heading "R^2 change" we can see the relative importance of each one. (R^2 change is the amount of additional variance explained when that variable was entered into the regression equation *last*.)

Clearly the two most important variables in determining a respondents' judgment of abusiveness were the age of the perpetrator and the type of act committed. While other variables contributed to people's definitions of sexual abuse, their influence was considerably smaller. Age of perpetrator and type of sex act were the main determinants. This means that once people knew that the perpetrator was an adult, they were pretty certain to rate it as "definitely sexual abuse," no matter what the other variables were. It also means that once they knew the act involved was intercourse or attempted intercourse the same held true. On the other hand, if the perpetrator was another child, or if the act was "calling the child a whore" they were almost just as certain to rate a vignette less abusive. Such matters as whether the consequence was harmful or not did not make much of a difference.

Let us look specifically at all the categories in each variable.

Age of Perpetrator

Figure 8–1 shows a model of how people rated vignettes according to the age of the perpetrator. Essentially, among adult perpetrators (those over 20) people made no distinction according to age. There was little difference in abusiveness between a 25-year-old and a 75-year-old perpetrator. Among child perpetrators (those under 20), however, the age of the perpetrators was crucial. Sexual acts initiated by teenagers were considered more abusive than those initiated by younger children regardless of the younger partner's age.

Sexual Acts

Table 8–5 shows the scores for the nine types of sexual acts which were included in the experiment. (The table can be read, for example, to say that when an act of intercourse is involved, respondents, independent of any other knowledge, rated a vignette .74 points higher than they would an average vignette in this sample. It must be emphasized that a negative score in Tables 8–5 through 8–9 does not mean that the condition was viewed as nonabusive. Because scores are expressed as deviations from the grand mean, a negative score only indicates that a given condition was viewed as *less abusive* than the average vignette by that many units.)

The table shows a large spread of scores. The presence of intercourse, not surprisingly, adds substantially to the definition of a vignette as abuse. But it is interesting to see that attempted intercourse and fondling the child's sex organs are also rated as highly abusive, nearly as abusive as intercourse. This seems to mean that respondents think that the abusiveness of sexual touching is similar to the abusiveness of intercourse, at least when a child is involved.

At the other extreme, verbal abuse with a sexual theme is clearly not considered sexual abuse. Calling a child a "faggot" or "whore" resulted in an automatic two-point lower rating of a vignette, the largest effect created by any variable value in the whole experiment. Similarly, respondents on the whole did not think that the exposure of a child to an adult engaged in prostitution or pimping constituted sexual abuse.

The ratings of some of the other acts are also revealing. Being exposed to an exhibitionist was considered a relatively more abusive act among the choices we gave. However, being the object of sexual picture-taking was scored fairly

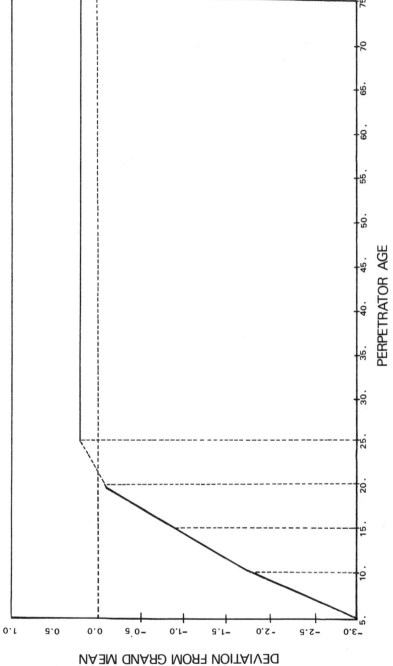

Figure 8–1 Estimated Independent Effect of Perpetrator Age

low. This surprised us since the use of children in the making of pornography has recently received attention as one of the more serious and ever increasing kinds of child sexual abuse. It is possible that respondents were not thinking of child pornography when they read the phrase "took sexual pictures of . . ." and were thinking instead of sexually suggestive pictures more along the lines of designer jean advertisements.

For sexual acts, there were differences between the ratings given by men and women on only two of the items. Women saw having sex in the presence of a child as more serious than did men, probably a reflection of the greater acceptance men show toward the viewing and depiction of sex of any kind. On the other hand, men saw being called a "whore" or "faggot" as more abusive than did women (although neither saw it as very abusive).

Conditions of Consent

Table 8–6 presents the estimated scores for the conditions of consent. It is quite evident that people take a child's behavior into account in assessing the degree of abuse. When a child objects strenuously, respondents rated the vignette significantly higher than even a situation where a child acts in passive compliance. When a child collaborates to any extent, respondents rate a situation as less abusive. Respondents did not accept the notion that all sexual exploitation of a child is equally abusive regardless of the child's role.

We wanted to see whether these judgments about consent conditions applied to children at different ages, so we constructed Figure 8–2, which shows consent conditions for three groups of children (age 0–6, age 7–13, and age 14–16). We can see that consent conditions are taken into account by respondents for even the youngest, the most naive, and presumably least able to consent group. That is, for even the children 0–6, a situation where a child reacts passively is rated as less abusive than a situation where a child "objects strenuously." (We did not allow conditions where a child under six asked or agreed to sexual acts with an older partner.) However Figure 8–2 does show some difference between the group of children 7–13 and the group 14–16. Consent conditions make more of a difference in judging the abusiveness for the older group than for the younger group, resulting in a line whose slope is steeper for the former. This result suggests that people do feel that younger children are somewhat less capable of true consent than older ones.

Age of Victim

Figure 8–3 shows an interesting public perception about sexual abuse at different ages. People considered vignettes less abusive when they involved either very young victims or adolescent victims. In the case of very young victims,

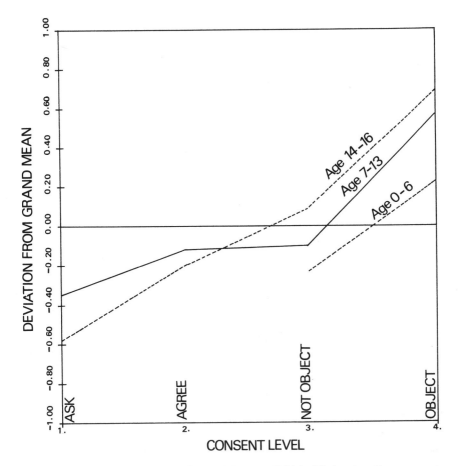

Figure 8-2   Estimated Effects of Consent Within Victim Age Groups

people probably saw them as naive about sex and therefore less tainted and abused by being involved in sexual activity with an older person. In the case of adolescents, they were probably viewed as quasi-adults and therefore less abused by sexual activity with adults.

People were most willing to apply the term abuse to children in preadolescence and early adolescence, because this is an age where children are old enough to be aware of sexual meanings but too young, in respondents' judgment, to be sexually involved. As children get to be 15 and 16, people see them capable of engaging in sexual activity with older partners under conditions of consent without its automatically being a form of abuse. Unfortunately, because people's view of adolescents changes gradually, not abruptly, as the adolescents get older, the results do not give a clear cut answer to the question of what an exact age limit for statutory rape should be.

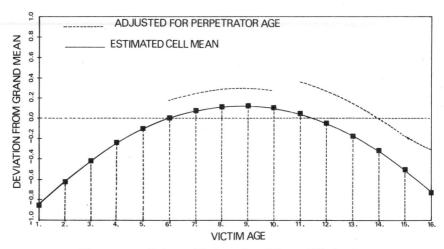

Figure 8–3   Estimated Independent Effect of Victim Age

Relationship

Tables 8–7 and 8–8 show how men and women rated the seriousness of abuse in various types of relationships. What is interesting is that they did not make major differentiations among them. Most of the values shown in Tables 8–7 and 8–8 are *not* significantly different (statistically) from the grand mean (represented in these tables by 0.0). Thus only the relationships marked with asterisks are significantly different from the grand mean.

We need to caution against misinterpreting Tables 8–7 and 8–8. For example, although father–daughter is ranked above male relative–girl in Table 8–7, we cannot truly say that this ranking is due to something beside chance. We can say only that father–daughter incest is significantly more abusive than relationships with scores below .19. Comparisons among relationships that have small differences in score (like father–daughter vs. male relative–girl) are not really warranted by these tables.

It is interesting to note nonetheless that father–daughter and male relative-girl were scored very high by both men and women. These are the kinds of sexual contacts that are most often coming to public and professional attention.

By contrast, the relationships considered as the least abusive were those involving women as perpetrators. The sex of victim–sex of perpetrator combinations for the full sample are shown in Table 8–9, and we see there that male perpetrator–female victim combinations are considered the most abusive, and female perpetrator–female victim combinations the least abusive.

One surprising finding was that people made only a weak and inconsistent distinction between intrafamilial and extrafamilial relationships. Some incestuous contacts, like those involving fathers and daughters, were considered significantly more abusive than nonfamily contacts. But other family relationships, especially where the older partners were female, or the partners were siblings, were not treated as specially serious. The overall score for family relationships was +.05 compared to −.07 for nonfamily relationships, a small and nonsignificant difference.

Men and women did rate the relationships differently. To capsulize the differences between male and female respondents on the question of relationship, the relationships showing the largest difference are listed in Table 8–10. Men tend to see situations involving older women as *less* serious. In particular, they view mother–son incest as substantially less serious than do women.

What men tend to see as more serious than women are those abuse situations that occur *outside the family*. Thus men scored higher than women those relationships involving strangers and some involving neighbors. Women scored higher relationships involving female family members. This may reflect the fact that for women more of the abusiveness inheres in the betrayal of the family bond rather than in the sexual violation. The men may be more focused on the violation caused by a sexual intruder, as in the situation of rape.

Consequences

We included three conditions where negative consequences were attendant to the abuse and one condition (comprising 50% of vignettes) where no consequence was mentioned. This variable turned out to be the least important and exerted a very minimal influence over respondents in their rating of the vignettes. The inclusion of a negative consequence resulted in an increase of .15. The exclusion of a negative consequence resulted in a net decrease of .15.

SOME INTERPRETATIONS

Our findings appear to demonstrate that the way in which people judge the seriousness of sexual contacts with children is complex. People take into account a wide variety of factors in assessing how abusive any given situation is.

Certain of the findings are quite anticipated. Incidents involving adult perpetrators are taken much more seriously than those involving child perpetrators. Acts such as intercourse and attempted intercourse are viewed as more abusive than acts which involve no contact. It would be fair to say that age of perpetrator and type of act are the factors which most readily define sexual abuse.

Other findings are quite plausible, even if they could not necessarily be predicted. It is interesting that when the victims are either very young children or older adolescents, people tend to discount the abusiveness somewhat. When the sexual activities are purely verbal or are matters of lifestyle, people do not consider them sexual abuse.

Some of the findings seem quite surprising, though, and deserve more attention. Perhaps the most surprising findings revolve around the issue of the type of relationships.

Relationships

Our analyses showed that the exact relationship between the child and the perpetrator was not a consistently important factor in affecting people's assessment of abuse. That a perpetrator was a family member, for example, rather than a neighbor did not in and of itself drastically or systematically increase people's sense of seriousness. That a perpetrator was an adult rather than a child made much more difference than the nature of the relationship that adult had to the younger partner.

This finding is important. It suggests that in practice the notion of "incest" is not one of the stronger norms governing people's judgment of sexual abuse of children. That is, people do not automatically place any sexual relationship involving a relative in a category of special seriousness. They may do so for some particular family relationships, such as father–daughter incest, but not for family relationships as a whole. Other factors about the sexual contact, the ages and sexes of participants, for example, outweigh and complicate the simple issue of whether or not it was incest.

This reality about attitudes toward incest has some practical implications. Some of those most actively involved in alerting the public to the problem of child sexual abuse have relied heavily on the term "incest." The word has a shock value which has often appealed to journalists, who would rather write a story about the alarming rise in "incest" than about the alarming rise in "child sexual abuse."

However, the current study suggests that incest is not simply a subcategory of sexual abuse in the public mind and that it may not be the best term to define the phenomenon about which the public is concerned. First of all, there are categories of incestuous sexual contact which people rank as fairly low on the scale of abusiveness, particularly contacts among similarly aged children. Second, there are categories of nonincestuous sexual contact, such as contacts between adult neighbors and young children, which people rank as very seriously abusive, much more seriously so than many types of incest. In defining what people see as abuse, the age dimension is much more important than the family dimension. Exclusive emphasis on incest may muddle this concern.

Consent

Another surprising finding from the study concerns the matter of consent. In spite of laws that presume the contrary, the public apparently does feel that children bear substantial responsibility in matters of sexual contact with older persons. The respondents in this survey tended to downrate the abusiveness of any situation where the child did anything less than object strenuously. This finding held true even in the case of very young children. The judge from Wisconsin who put some of the blame on the 5-year-old girl for her own victimization was reflecting an attitude that has some general support.

The weight that public norms give to the matter of consent probably stems from several sources, some of which are valid and some of which are based on prejudice and ignorance. First, our variable measuring consent was also a measure of coercion and force. "[P] did it even though [V] objected strenuously" implies the presence of coercion. There is something that is intrinsically frightening about coercion, and it is not surprising or inappropriate that public opinion regards such situations as particularly alarming. There is some evidence that sexual abuse situations which involve force are also seen as more traumatic by the victims of the abuse themselves (Finkelhor, 1979). Certainly in situations (such as in some of our vignettes) where no great age disparity existed between the partners, it was quite reasonable that respondents should judge abusiveness on the basis of the degree of coercion or consent.

However, it is also true that the weight people gave to the matter of consent betrays some popular ignorance and some popular prejudices about child sexual abuse. A popular prejudice on the subject of sexual assault has been that victims wish, on some level, to be raped or that victims, because of some imputed moral flaw, deserve to be raped, and that the failure to resist to the utmost reveals the existence of this complicity (Burt, 1980). Undoubtedly some of this prejudice transfers to people's thinking when the victims are children as well as when the victims are adults.

But people not readily acquainted with the subject of child sexual abuse are also probably ignorant of just why it is that a child might not "object strenuously." In a great deal of child sexual abuse, children do not resist, but it is not because these children seduce adults. Children passively comply or accept sexual advances from an adult because they are intimidated or cowed by the adult's authority, especially when the adult is a family member. Young children, particularly, are gullible and easily manipulated, and adults give them rewards or misrepresent moral standards to get them to comply with sexual requests (Burgess et al., 1978). These are the kinds of realities about sexual abuse which workers in the field may need to convey more explicitly to the public, so that children are not unfairly blamed for situations of sexual exploitation.

Do Norms Account for Rates of Abuse?

Finally, what can the findings tell us about the causes of abuse itself. Does it appear to be true, as some theories say, that when a form of abuse is treated as less serious, it will make that type of abuse easier to engage in.

One specific prediction of this type of theory appears to be false. There is no evidence that fathers exploit daughters, for example, because this is a more normatively tolerated type of contact. In fact we found the opposite. Father–daughter abuse was rated the most serious form of sexual abuse. In general, abuse at the hands of men was rated as more serious than abuse at the hands of women. So it would not appear that normative toleration explains why we see so much more abuse by men.

However, there is some support in these findings for the idea that there are dual cultures, one male and one female, which may contribute to the higher rates of abuse by males. It does appear to be true that men as a group do not see the kinds of activities described in our vignettes as sexually abusive to the same degree as do women. Men's overall ratings were significantly lower than the ratings women gave. This may well be the influence of a long history of subtle toleration of this kind of behavior in the male subculture. It may be the result of pornographic media which have tended to legitimize such behavior. It may also be that males, who are less frequently sexually victimized than women, are thus less alarmed and take the problem less seriously. It is also consistent with our theory that male sexual socialization plays a part in the male monopoly of sexual abuse (see Chapter 1).

It does not appear to be true, however, that this male toleration of abuse applies selectively—to only some preferred kinds of relationships. That is, male culture is not more "permissive" only toward abuse where males are the offenders. Nor are they more alarmed toward abuse where males are the victims. In terms of rank orders, males tended to observe a relatively similar hierarchy of abusiveness as did females, and where there were exceptions they were not in the expected direction. Overall, the main difference between men and women was that men saw all acts of abuse—regardless of sex, act, relationship, and age—as less serious.

APPENDIX

The objective of a vignette experiment is to determine how one variable influences respondent judgment independent of the influence of any other variable. Thus designs for vignette studies try to dissociate each variable from each other variable and create a condition of complete orthogonality among variables.

Two main designs have been employed toward this end. In the most common design, variable conditions are systematically *assigned* in such a way as to be independent of each other. One conventional way of doing this is to combine each level of each variable with each level of each other variable, thus creating a design that is fully crossed and balanced (equal number of appearances for each level of each variable).

However, in a fully crossed design, the number of vignettes is equal to the product of the number of values each variable can take, so the total number of required vignettes grows very quickly with the addition of new variables and new variable values. To include all the variables and variable levels we wanted in the current study would have required 345,600 vignettes in a fully crossed design. To keep the number of vignettes to a more manageable size, most experimenters are forced to restrict drastically the number of variables and variable values used.

An alternative vignette experiment technique, the "factorial survey," has been developed by Rossi (Rossi & Nock, 1982; see also Garrett & Rossi, 1978; Jasso & Rossi, 1977), which allows for the possibility of many more variables and more variable values. Under the factorial survey technique, the investigator creates a hypothetical universe of all possible combinations of all variables. Then the investigator draws a random sample of this universe, still a large number, but not nearly the full universe. The random sample should presumably maintain the overall characteristics of this universe—independence among the component variables and equal combinations of the variable values. The drawback to the factorial survey is that not all possible combinations are represented in the random sample. Thus higher order interactions, such as those involving five, six, or seven variables, cannot be measured. But the approach is excellent when higher order interactions are not an important issue in the research.

In the present study, we used a combination of the assigned condition and factorial survey designs. We chose four variables whose interactions we anticipated would be quite important—victim sex, perpetrator sex, relatedness, and force—and we ensured that all possible combinations of these four variables would appear in equal frequencies. We also ensured that each respondent would see all possible combinations of three of these variables (victim sex, perpetrator sex, and relatedness). All combinations of each of the three variables were presented to every four respondents.

The other variables (sexual act, perpetrator age, victim age, consent, and consequence) were assigned on a random basis across the three variables which were fully crossed, as in the Rossi technique.

In theory, this created a set of vignettes where all variables were orthogonal to each other and where each value of each variable appeared a nearly equal number of times. Unfortunately, we needed to depart somewhat from this theoretical design because some combinations of some variables were just not realistically possible or created confusion for respondents. For example, in the real world, a parent perpetrator with a 5-year-old child could not himself be 15. Thus after pretesting we were obliged to exclude certain combinations. The major exclusions were as follows:

1. Sexual intercourse was not applied in a vignette involving two males or two females.
2. A parent had to be between the ages of 20 and 50 (and at least 15 years older than the child).
3. Cousins and siblings needed to be under the age of 30.
4. Grandparents needed to be over the age of 55.
5. Children could not agree to or ask: a) an adult to engage in pimping or prostitution; b) an adult to have sex in their presence; or c) an adult to call them a whore/faggot.
6. The perpetrator had to be the same age or older than the child.
7. Intercourse or attempted intercourse could take place only with a child who was above 11 and a perpetrator who was above 10.
8. A child under age 6 could not ask or agree to engage in sexual acts. He or she could only object or not object.

The task set for the respondent was to rate each vignette on a scale provided below each vignette. The dimension we chose for the respondent to consider was the extent to which he or she saw the incident as "definitely sexual abuse" or "definitely *not* sexual abuse." We decided to use a 10-point scale as something that had intuitive meaning for respondents.

The packet of 20 experimental vignettes was preceded by four fixed vignettes which were the same for all respondents. These fixed vignettes had several purposes. First, these fixed vignettes gave the respondents practice for the task we were asking them to do. Second, they gave everyone the same four vignettes on which to define the range. We were concerned that if, by random selection, a set of very unusual vignettes happened to fall first it might skew the sense of scale that respondents would use. Finally, the first four vignettes were all very plausible situations, which would avoid a problem we discovered in pretesting, that of demoralization or distrust created when the respondent's first few vignettes were bizarre cases. However, the four fixed vignettes were not included in the data analysis.

The vignette study was part of the larger study of parents' attitudes and reactions to the problem of sexual abuse described in Chapter 5. About halfway through that interview, the interviewers gave the parents a packet containing the 20 experimental and four fixed vignettes. The respondents rated the vignettes on their own and returned the sheet to the interviewer.

A total of 10,420 experimental vignettes were distributed to respondents. However, we excluded from the analysis any completed set which did not include at least 15 out of 20 codable vignettes. Taking into account the excluded sets and uncompleted vignettes, we were left with a total of 9839 codable vignettes, the sample on which the subsequent analysis is based.

Although respondents could rate vignettes anywhere on a 10-point scale, the distribution of ratings that they actually made was highly skewed. The mean score was 7.5 (S.D. = 2.7) and the modal score was 10. Sixty percent of all ratings were an 8, 9, or 10. This meant that respondents were confident that a large number of the vignettes did constitute sexual abuse. Unfortunately, this skewedness added some imprecision to the data analysis. It created a ceiling effect, a lessening of the spread of ratings among those vignettes that the respondents saw as most abusive. This, in turn, made it more difficult to measure the effect of the independent variables.

To ameliorate this problem to some extent, we transformed all vignette scores into deviation scores for *each respondent*:

$$\text{Respondent Deviation Score} = DY_{ij} = Y_{ij} - \frac{\Sigma Y_{ij}}{n}$$

where Y = scores
j = respondents
i = vignettes within respondents
n = number of valid scores within respondents

This produced a more normal distribution of scores and a grand mean of 0.

Table 8–11 shows the intercorrelations among the independent variables. Since we were dealing with some dichotomous, some nominal, and some interval variables, the values in Table 8–11 are not all simple correlation coefficients. In the case of two nominal variables, for example, what is shown in Table 8–11 is the largest r value between any two of the values of the two nominal variables (for example, the correlation between "had intercourse" under the act variable and "agreed to it" under the consent variable). Thus Table 8–11 shows the *maximum amount of relationship* that exists among variables.

Many of the relationships among the variables in Table 8–11 show the desired independence from one another, but others do not. This reflects the conditions we had to place on possible combinations of variables. (For example, the association between acts and victim age represents the limitation we placed on intercourse, that it could occur only to children at least 11 or older.) This lack of true orthogonality among variables means greater imprecision in the measurement of the effects of some of the independent variables.

Conditions placed on variable combinations also resulted in some unequal cell frequency. In particular, two acts, sexual intercourse and attempted sexual intercourse, were somewhat underrepresented. We corrected for this in the regression analysis by weighting.

The analysis of effects was carried out using regression technique. Values for the nominal variables were coded as orthogonal contrasts, which allowed two benefits: (1) the multiple regression would approximate the results of a multiple analysis of variance, and (2) the regression coefficients could be used to make estimates of the cell means for the various variable values (Kerlinger & Pedhazur, 1973).

Initial analyses revealed that important interaction effects existed among the variables victim sex, perpetrator sex, and relatedness. It was thus decided not to enter these variables into the regression separately, but rather to create a new variable, "relationship," which had 20 separate values (each possible combination of the other three variables).

Initial analyses also revealed significant difference between the ratings made by males and females. Females consistently rated vignettes as more serious than males. The mean for females was 7.66 compared to 7.29 for males. This suggested analyzing male and female subjects separately. However, after running separate regression equations by sex, we found that the results were extremely similar with the exception of one variable: relationship. This suggested that while men saw the vignettes overall as less abusive than did women, within the experiment they tended to apply the same norms for deciding the relative ranking of abusiveness. Thus, most of the results, except for the one "relationship," are reported for the full sample. Because the sample contained fewer men than women, we weighted the sexes in the full sample regression to simulate a sample of 50% males and 50% females.

TABLE 8–1
Variables and Variable Levels Used in Vignette Construction

Victim Sex

1. Boy
2. Girl

Perpetrator Sex

1. Male
2. Female

Victim Age

Ages 1 through 16
Increments of 1 year

Perpetrator Age

Ages 5 to 75
Increments of 5 years

Relatedness

1. Parent
2. Sibling
3. Other relative (male cousin, female cousin, aunt, uncle, grandmother, grandfather, were varied randomly)
4. Neighbor
5. Stranger

Sex Act: (P) Perpetrator   (V) Victim

1. (P) had intercourse with (V)
2. (P) attempted to have intercourse with (V)
3. (P) fondled the sex organs of (V)
4. (V) fondled the sex organs of (P)
5. (P) deliberately showed his/her sex organs to (V)
6. (P) took sexual pictures of (V)
7. (P) had sexual intercourse in the presence of (V)
8. (P) was engaged in pimping/prostitution with the knowledge of (V)
9. (P) repeatedly called (V) a whore/faggot

Consent

1. (P) did it even though (V) objected strenuously
2. (V) was uncomfortable but did not object
3. (V) agreed to it
4. (V) asked (P) to do it

Consequence

1. Nothing (50% of vignettes)
2. One of the following: (50% of vignettes)
   a. Later (V) had nightmares about it
   b. Later (V) was upset that it had happened
   c. (V) was ashamed about it for many years afterward

TABLE 8-2

Example of a Portion of a Vignette Questionnaire
(First four vignettes are fixed for all questionnaires.)

Give each incident a score on the following scale by placing an "X" above the appropriate category.

<---- — — — — — — — — — ---->
$\quad$ 1 $\quad$ 2 $\quad$ 3 $\quad$ 4 $\quad$ 5 $\quad$ 6 $\quad$ 7 $\quad$ 8 $\quad$ 9 $\quad$ 10

Definitely NOT sexual abuse $\qquad\qquad$ Definitely sexual abuse

A $\qquad\qquad$ A

A 35 year old male fondled the sex organs of his 8 year old daughter. He did it even though the girl objected strenuously.

<---- — — — — — — — — — ---->
$\quad$ 1 $\quad$ 2 $\quad$ 3 $\quad$ 4 $\quad$ 5 $\quad$ 6 $\quad$ 7 $\quad$ 8 $\quad$ 9 $\quad$ 10

B $\qquad\qquad$ A

A 40 year old female had intercourse with her 15 year old son. The boy asked her to do it.

<---- — — — — — — — — — ---->
$\quad$ 1 $\quad$ 2 $\quad$ 3 $\quad$ 4 $\quad$ 5 $\quad$ 6 $\quad$ 7 $\quad$ 8 $\quad$ 9 $\quad$ 10

C $\qquad\qquad$ A

A 12 year old boy deliberately showed his sex organs to his 8 year old sister. The girl was uncomfortable but did not object. Later the girl was upset that it had happened.

<---- — — — — — — — — — ---->
$\quad$ 1 $\quad$ 2 $\quad$ 3 $\quad$ 4 $\quad$ 5 $\quad$ 6 $\quad$ 7 $\quad$ 8 $\quad$ 9 $\quad$ 10

D $\qquad\qquad$ A

A 50 year old male stranger deliberately showed his sex organs to a 13 year old girl. The girl was uncomfortable but did not object.

<---- — — — — — — — — — ---->
$\quad$ 1 $\quad$ 2 $\quad$ 3 $\quad$ 4 $\quad$ 5 $\quad$ 6 $\quad$ 7 $\quad$ 8 $\quad$ 9 $\quad$ 10

1 $\qquad\qquad$ A

A 45-year-old male deliberately showed his sex organs to his 15-year-old nephew. The boy agreed to it.

<---- — — — — — — — — — ---->
$\quad$ 1 $\quad$ 2 $\quad$ 3 $\quad$ 4 $\quad$ 5 $\quad$ 6 $\quad$ 7 $\quad$ 8 $\quad$ 9 $\quad$ 10

2 $\qquad\qquad$ A

A 15-year-old girl took sexual pictures of her 4-year-old sister. She did it even though the younger girl objected strenuously.

<---- — — — — — — — — — ---->
$\quad$ 1 $\quad$ 2 $\quad$ 3 $\quad$ 4 $\quad$ 5 $\quad$ 6 $\quad$ 7 $\quad$ 8 $\quad$ 9 $\quad$ 10

3 $\qquad\qquad$ A

A 10-year-old-boy stranger deliberately showed his sex organs to a 2-year-old boy. The younger boy was uncomfortable but did not object. Later on the younger boy had nightmares about it.

<---- — — — — — — — — — ---->
$\quad$ 1 $\quad$ 2 $\quad$ 3 $\quad$ 4 $\quad$ 5 $\quad$ 6 $\quad$ 7 $\quad$ 8 $\quad$ 9 $\quad$ 10

TABLE 8–2 *Continued*

4   **A**

A 50-year-old female deliberately showed her sex organs to her 15-year-old son. The boy agreed to it. Later on the boy had nightmares about it.

<———— —— —— —— —— —— —— —— —— ——>
      1   2   3   4   5   6   7   8   9   10

5   **A**

A 30-year-old male deliberately showed his sex organs to his 2-year-old son. He did it even though the boy objected strenuously.

<———— —— —— —— —— —— —— —— —— ——>
      1   2   3   4   5   6   7   8   9   10

6   **A**

A 35-year-old male attempted to have intercourse with his 16-year-old niece. The girl was uncomfortable but did not object.

<———— —— —— —— —— —— —— —— —— ——>
      1   2   3   4   5   6   7   8   9   10

7   **A**

A 70-year-old-female stranger deliberately showed her sex organs to an 11-year-old boy. The boy asked her to do it.

<———— —— —— —— —— —— —— —— —— ——>
      1   2   3   4   5   6   7   8   9   10

8   **A**

A 15-year-old boy had intercourse in the presence of a 4-year-old-neighbor girl. The girl was uncomfortable but did not object. Later on the girl was upset that it had happened.

<———— —— —— —— —— —— —— —— —— ——>
      1   2   3   4   5   6   7   8   9   10

9   **A**

A 35-year-old male had his sex organs fondled by his 7-year-old daughter. The girl asked to do it. Later on the girl had nightmares about it.

<———— —— —— —— —— —— —— —— —— ——>
      1   2   3   4   5   6   7   8   9   10

10   **A**

A 5-year-old-boy stranger deliberately showed his sex organs to a 1-year-old girl. He did it even though the girl objected strenuously. The girl was ashamed about it for many years afterward.

<———— —— —— —— —— —— —— —— —— ——>
      1   2   3   4   5   6   7   8   9   10

TABLE 8–3
Male and Female Ratings of Common Vignettes

VIGNETTE	ESTIMATED MEAN RATING[a]	
	Male	Female
40-yr.-old male had intercourse with his 12-yr.-old daughter	9.19	9.46
30-yr.-old male fondled the sex organs of his 4-yr.-old daughter	8.79	8.97
50-yr.-old male had his sex organs fondled by his 10-yr.-old niece	8.68	9.14
30-yr.-old female fondled the sex organs of her 5-yr.-old son	8.38	8.94
40-yr.-old male stranger deliberately showed his sex organs to a 12-yr.-old girl	8.38	8.58
25-yr.-old male stranger attempted to have intercourse with a 15-yr.-old girl	8.34	8.58
35-yr.-old male had his sex organs fondled by his 8-yr.-old son	8.21	8.60
15-yr.-old boy fondled the sex organs of his 8-yr.-old sister	7.61	7.75
15-yr.-old boy had intercourse with his 12-yr.-old sister	7.42	7.76
15-yr.-old girl had intercourse with her 12-yr.-old brother	7.24	7.90
30-yr.-old female had sexual intercourse in the presence of her 5-yr.-old daughter	7.13	8.12
30-yr.-old female engaged in prostitution with the knowledge of her 12-yr.-old daughter	6.75	7.37

[a] Scale of 1 to 10, where 1 = Definitely not sexual abuse, and 10 = Definitely sexual abuse.

TABLE 8–4

Regression Analysis on Abusiveness

Variable	R² Change (additional variance)
Perpetrator age	.09**
Act	.08**
Consent	.02**
Victim age	.01**
Relation[a]	.008**
Consequence	.005**

** p < .01

Multiple R = .52

Multiple R^2 = .28

Adjusted multiple R^2 = .28

Standard error = 1.90

[a] "Relation" is composite of "sex of perpetrator," "sex of victim," and "relationship."

TABLE 8–5

Rating Scores for Sexual Activities

Activities	Score[a]
Intercourse	.74**
Attempted intercourse	.61**
Perpetrator fondled sex organs of victim	.60**
Victim fondled sex organs of perpetrator	.31**
Perpetrator deliberately displayed sex organs	.22**
Perpetrator had sexual intercourse in presence of victim	−.24**
Perpetrator took sexual pictures	−.57[b]
Perpetrator engaged in pimping/prostitution	−.93**
Perpetrator called victim faggot/whore	−2.00**

** p < 0.1

[a] Score reflects deviation from grand mean associated with independent effect of this condition.

[b] Reference category used in effect coding. No significance test possible.

TABLE 8–6

Rating Scores for Consent Conditions

CONDITION	SCORE[a]
Victim objected strenuously	.57[b]
Victim was uncomfortable but did not object	.01
Victim agreed to do it	−.15**
Victim asked perpetrator to do it	−.43**

**p < 0.1

[a] Score reflects deviation from grand mean associated with independent effect of this condition.

[b] Reference category used in effect coding. No significance test possible.

TABLE 8–7

Rating Scores for Relationship (Female Respondents Only)

TYPE OF RELATIONSHIP	SEX OF VICTIM	SCORE	SCHEFFÉ'S TEST
Father	Girl	.42**	(−.14)[a]
Male relative	Girl	.41**	(−. 5)[a]
Mother	Boy	.25**	
Older brother	Girl	.14	
Older sister	Boy	.04	
Male stranger	Girl	.02	
Female relative	Girl	.01	
Mother	Girl	.00	
Female neighbor	Girl	.00	
Older brother	Boy	.00	
Male neighbor	Girl	−.01	
Male relative	Boy	−.08	
Female relative	Boy	−.08	
Male stranger	Boy	−.08	
Father	Boy	−.11	
Female stranger	Boy	−.15	(.41)[b]
Female stranger	Girl	−.16	(.40)[b]
Male neighbor	Boy	−.16	(.40)[b]
Female neighbor	Boy	−.16	(.40)[b]
Older sister	Girl	−.25*	(.31)[b]

*p < .05

**p < .01

[a] Row factor level is significantly different from all factor level means less than the value indicated.

[b] Row factor level is significantly different from all factor level means greater than the value indicated.

TABLE 8–8
Rating Scores for Relationship (Male Respondents Only)

TYPE OF RELATIONSHIP	SEX OF VICTIM	SCORES	SCHEFFÉ'S TEST
Father	Girl	.55**	(.19)[a]
Male relative	Girl	.33*	(− .41)[a]
Male stranger	Girl	.32*	(− .42)[a]
Older brother	Boy	.29*	(− .45)[a]
Male stranger	Boy	.18	
Female stranger	Girl	.16	
Male neighbor	Boy	.14	
Male relative	Boy	.10	
Older brother	Girl	.07	
Female neighbor	Girl	.05	
Male neighbor	Girl	− .05	
Mother	Boy	− .08	
Female relative	Girl	− .08	
Female relative	Boy	− .09	
Father	Boy	− .13	
Mother	Girl	− .21	(.50)[b]
Older sister	Boy	− .23	(.51)[b]
Female stranger	Boy	− .28*	(.47)[b]
Older sister	Girl	− .47**	(.27)[b]
Female neighbor	Boy	− .55**	(.19)[b]

*p < .05
**p < .01

[a] Row factor is significantly different from all factor level means less than the indicated value.
[b] Row factor level is significantly different from all factor level means greater than the indicated value.

TABLE 8-9

Rating Scores for Sex of Perpetrator
and Sex of Victim Combinations

COMBINATION	SCORE[a]
Male perpetrator Female victim	.20**
Male perpetrator Male victim	.03
Female perpetrator Male victim	−.10[b]
Female perpetrator Female victim	−.13**

**p < .01

[a] Score reflects deviation from grand mean associated with independent effect of this condition.

[b] Reference category used in effect coding. No significance test possible.

TABLE 8-10

Difference in Seriousness Rating by Relationship by Sex
of the Respondent

TYPE OF RELATIONSHIP	VICTIM	AMOUNT OF DIFFERENCE[a]
Men See as Less Serious than Women		
Female neighbor	Boy	.39
Mother	Son	.37
Older sister	Girl	.22
Older sister	Boy	.19
Men See as More Serious than Women		
Female stranger	Girl	.32
Male stranger	Girl	.30
Male neighbor	Boy	.30
Male stranger	Boy	.26
Mother	Girl	.22
Male relative	Boy	.18
Older brother	Boy	.15

[a] Absolute value of estimated rating score for males minus estimated rating score for females. Only difference scores greater than .10 are included.

TABLE 8–11

Intercorrelation Matrix of Variables

	(P) SEX 2	CONSEQ. 3	(V) AGE 4	(P) AGE 5	REL. 6	CONSENT 7	ACT 8
1. Victim sex	.00	.01	.00	.01	.00	.00	.02
2. Perpetrator sex		.01	.02	.01	.00	.01	.02
3. Consequence			.02	.02	.01	.01	.00
4. Victim age				.33***	.00	.24***	.27***
5. Perpetrator age					.20***	.05***	.03**
6. Relatedness						.00	.03**
7. Consent							.03**

**p < .01

***p < .001

Region I: Normal r

Region II: Value given is largest r between row variable and any level of column variable.

Region III: Value given is largest r between any pair of row variable and column variable levels.

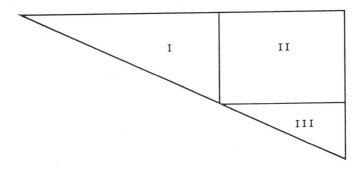

CHAPTER 9

What Parents Tell
Their Children
About Sexual Abuse

S EVERAL FEATURES OF the sexual abuse problem make it a particularly
important one to approach through a strategy of prevention.

1. The high prevalence figures cited earlier (see Chapter 6) make it clear
   that sexual abuse is a major public problem that needs to be combatted
   through an approach that will reach a wide segment of the population.
2. Since most incidents of child sexual abuse are not reported to any adult
   when they occur (see Chapter 6), most victimized children are unlikely
   to be helped after their victimization. This underlines the importance of
   reaching children before victimization occurs.
3. Even when they are identified, there is no assurance that most victims
   are helped in the aftermath. Not many child care or mental health
   workers yet have the training and expertise to treat child sexual abuse.
   Treatment programs do not exist in many communities.
4. Work with children who have been abused suggests that abuse could be
   prevented in many instances if children had had prior instruction. Lack
   of knowledge or uncertainty about norms of behavior often play a role
   in a child's victimization. For example:

   - children often say they were confused and misled by the offender's in-
     sistence that the sexual activity was proper and normal;
   - children often say they did not know they had a right to refuse;

- children often say they did not believe they would be defended by other adults (including parents) if they refused or complained.
- children often say they were thrown off their guard when the adult behaved in a way that they had never been led to expect.

Accounts of these sorts suggest that children properly educated about the problem of sexual abuse might be substantially less vulnerable to victimization.

But are children being properly educated? Those concerned with prevention of child sexual abuse have been worried about the kind of education most children receive. They have pointed out that children rarely get sufficient information to arm them against sexual victimization and that what information they do receive is usually misleading and poorly timed.

ROLE OF PARENTS

The concern about the education of children has focused particularly on the role parents play. Professionals sense the enormous opportunity and advantage that parents have to influence the situation, compared to the limited opportunities enjoyed by the professionals themselves. Parents are clearly in a pivotal position to make a large contribution to efforts of prevention for a number of reasons.

First, sexual abuse can occur to a child very early in life. Parents may be the only adults who are in a position to help a child of such a young age avoid abuse.

Second, an ideology that has a strong hold on American families is that information on sexual subjects should be imparted to children only by their parents. Professionals, cowed by this ideology, often feel a great deal of reticence about discussing such subjects with children. Thus, if parents do not mention certain matters to children, there is no assurance that other adults will.

Third, much abuse is committed by family members, and parents may be the only authorities who can engage in prevention activities that are effective against this kind of family abuse. How credible, for example, is a teacher who warns a child about the behavior of certain close relatives? A child is much more apt to believe such cautions when warned by a parent.

Fourth, parents have a great advantage in being able to integrate discussions of sexual abuse with what the child already knows. Parents are aware of children's level of knowledge with regard to sex and adults. Children will be better able to understand information that is presented in the context of knowledge they already have.

Finally, part of any prevention of child sexual abuse is to enable a child to feel that he or she can appeal for help from a parent. When parents tell children about child sexual abuse, it opens this line of communication. The mere fact that children feel confident that they can go to their parent for help or information about the problem may make them less vulnerable to abuse.

All the above are important reasons why information about child sexual abuse is more meaningful and effective when it comes from a parent. Yet the assumption is widespread that parents neglect this responsibility and opportunity. The parent study was a golden opportunity to assess just what kinds of prevention information gets exchanged in most households, and what seem to be the obstacles to a more effective exchange.

TALKING ABOUT SEX ABUSE

Our most important objective was to find out whether parents had ever talked with their children about child sexual abuse. We approached the subject by first asking parents whether they had talked with their children about a whole range of emotionally laden subjects, ranging from suicide to abortion. The question read, "Can you remember a situation where you talked to your child about ——?" The list of topics, accompanied by the precentage of parents who had discussed them, is shown in Table 9–1.

Some emotional topics—death, kidnapping, pregnancy and birth, and even drugs—seemed to be relatively easy to discuss and had been brought up by the vast majority of parents. Sexual abuse, however, was not one of the easy topics. It was the next-to-least-often-discussed subject on the list, being a little easier to talk about than birth control and a little more difficult than abortion. Only 29% of the parents said they had talked with their children about sexual abuse.

Although few parents had talked to their children explicitly about sexual abuse, this was not the full story. We had found in our pretesting that many parents insisted on qualifying their answer to our question. "No," they would say, "I haven't talked about sexual abuse, at least not *in so many words*." Or they might say, "Well, I sort of talked about it."

Besides the 29% who had discussed sexual abuse directly, an additional 31% of the parents we interviewed said they had had some conversation with their child where they believed they were talking about sexual abuse, but perhaps not in a direct way.

We asked people for more specifics about these conversations, and they gave us examples of what they meant. "I told him not to get into strangers' cars," said one parent. "I cautioned him about talking to strange people and getting into cars or taking candy." "Some people are mentally ill and do bad things to children," said another.

A very common pattern was for parents to talk about kidnapping and think they were warning a child about sexual abuse at the same time. They would caution children about getting into cars or going with strangers into the woods. The image of sexual abuse would be part of what was on their mind, but they would not mention it specifically. The emphasis they gave the child was not to accept favors or rides from strangers.

A number of other parents (11%) hastened to tell us that although they themselves had not talked with the children about sexual abuse, some other person had. In most cases this other person was the respondent's spouse.

It is hard to know exactly how accurate that figure (11%) is. Some spouses may not have really known whether their partner had really talked about it. Other spouses may have assumed that the partner had, when in fact the partner's discussion was very vague or indirect.

Our impression was that it was socially desirable for a parent to say that they or someone else had indeed told the child. Our figures suggest that only a minority of children got told and that even these estimates were inflated by people's good intentions.

MOTHERS VERSUS FATHERS

As might be expected, mothers did a much better job of talking with their children about sexual abuse than did fathers. Thirty-six percent of the mothers said they had discussed the subject compared to only 15% of the fathers ($F = 26.44$, $p < .001$). This is very consistent with everything we know about child-rearing and sexual socialization. Warning children about the dangers in the world and giving them information about sex both seem to be more the province of mothers than fathers (Roberts, Kline & Gagnon, 1978). This does not occur necessarily because mothers are more concerned about the potential danger than are fathers. Both men and women expressed equal levels of concern and awareness about the problem of abuse. Rather, according to the division of responsibilities in American families, it seems to fall to mothers to translate these concerns to their children.

Compared to the difference between mothers and fathers, the difference between sons and daughters was negligible. In spite of the fact that sexual victimization is generally seen as a problem that affects girls more than boys, both sons and daughters were talked to (or perhaps we should say, ignored) in roughly equal proportions. If there was a difference it concerned primarily the fathers. Fathers had a slightly more difficult time mentioning anything about sexual abuse to their daughters than their sons. Only 11% spoke to their daughters compared to 19% who spoke to sons (a difference that was not significant at the .05 level). For mothers there was no difference.

The age of the child was a factor, but not a very strong factor, in whether a parent had talked with their child about sexual abuse. Naturally older children were somewhat more likely to have been enlightened than younger ones. Prior to age nine, the number of parents who had said something to their children hovers between 14% and 20%. From 10 up, the number of parents who have talked with their children shoots to between 32% and 40%.

Age nine seems to be something of a watershed. When we asked parents, in another question, what age they thought was the most appropriate for talking about sexual abuse, the mean answer they gave was 9.1. The age of a child does bear some relationship to whether parents have talked with him or her about sexual abuse, but it is only one factor. Some parents talk to their very young children about it. And many parents do not do so even with their very mature children.

Here again, mothers differed from fathers in what they saw as the appropriate age for telling children. Mothers tended to advise talking to children more than a year earlier than fathers, choosing a mean age of 8.6, compared to the father's 9.8 (F = 22.34, p < .001). There were no significant differences in estimates for boy as opposed to girl children.

We were interested in whether the parents remembered any specific event or concern that precipitated their decision to talk to their child about sexual abuse. We knew from other questions in the survey for example, that many parents had seen stories about sexual abuse on TV or in the newspaper during the previous year. We also knew that many of them had heard about some other person in their social network who had been the victim of sexual abuse. We wanted to know if these kinds of concerns were influential in prompting a parent to discuss sexual abuse with their child.

We asked parents four specific questions about why they chose that moment to discuss sexual abuse with their children. Most (70%) just said that they decided the time had come to have such a discussion—an ambiguous answer that gives us little additional understanding. Stories in the media or something that happened to another child did appear to be catalysts in 51% and 48% of the families, respectively. However, the simple fact that the child was spending more time by him or herself was not an important consideration (only 19% of families).

On the whole, we would say that parents were not extremely reflective about what prompted their discussions. But it would appear that things they hear about sexual abuse through the media or from neighbors, relatives, and the school may provide part of the stimulus to do something they wouldn't otherwise be inclined to do: bring up the difficult subject of sexual abuse.

WHAT PARENTS SAID

It was not possible, unfortunately, to take much encouragement from the fact that at least 29% of the parents had talked to their children about sexual abuse. When we asked parents what they actually had said to their children, their answers made us very skeptical of how well children had, in fact, been instructed, and whether the information they got would be of any real use.

Those parents who had talked about sexual abuse had not been shy about the subject. Most said they had had several discussions with the child about it. The median number of discussions was actually 5.3 and one-fourth of the parents said they had had 10 discussions or more. If discussions had really been that frequent, there should have been much opportunity for the child to pose questions and become familiar with the subject.

Unfortunately, in spite of the quantity of the discussions, the quality of discussions seems to have left much to be desired. Many of these discussions appeared to be little more than an extension of the discussions of kidnapping. The reticence about the actual nature of sexual abuse crept into the conversations of even those who said they had talked about the subject directly. The result was that many children did not hear an entirely accurate or useful account of the subject.

For example, we gave parents a list of possible matters they might have mentioned to their children when they had their discussion about sexual abuse (Table 9–2). The matter that received the most attention according to parents was the warning not to be lured into someone's car. In truth, only a small amount of child sexual abuse occurs in offenders' cars. This subject was obviously more appropriate to a discussion of kidnapping than a discussion of sexual abuse.

By contrast, the sexual parts of the discussion of sexual abuse, in other words, the information that identified the real nature of the problem, was the information that was most often left out. One-third of the parents in their discussion of sexual abuse did not mention the possibility of someone trying to remove the child's clothes. One-quarter did not mention a situation where an adult might try to exhibit their sex organs inappropriately to the child. This suggests that important pieces of information were in many cases missing from the parent-child discussions.

The most serious omission in the discussions of sexual abuse concerned the nature of the persons who might try to molest the child. It is abundantly evident that most parents only talked to their children about the possibility of abuse by strangers. The possibility of abuse by friends and particularly the possibility of abuse by family members, went largely unmentioned.

We asked people in two ways about what kinds of offenders they had warned their children about. First we just asked parents, "What people or kind of people did you tell him/her to watch out for?" and then wrote down their spontaneous answers. Then we read them a list of possible people they could have mentioned as offenders and asked them if they had specifically mentioned any of these. Column 1 of Table 9–3 shows their spontaneous answers, and column 2 shows their choices after we gave them a list.

Overwhelmingly people remembered their discussions of sexual abuse as revolving around strangers. One in five said they warned the children about possible acquaintances. Very few mentioned anything about family members. When we "reminded" them about the subject of offenders who the child might already know, a little over half "remembered" that they had said something about such people. However, even with prompting, only 22% of the respondents said that they had warned their children about the possibility of sexual abuse at the hands of a family member.

Even these numbers may be misleading. The large difference between the figures for "spontaneous mention" and "cite on prompt" in Table 9–3 suggests that even if parents did mention acquaintances or family members, we doubt they were strongly emphasized. The parents obviously had not remembered them spontaneously as an important part of the conversation. What they had primarily remembered was that they had warned the child about strangers. Strangers were probably who got emphasized to the child.

We also asked parents what they had told their child to do in case someone tried to molest them (Table 9–4). The answers showed that parents had emphasized two things: (1) get away from the offender, and (2) tell someone about the experience. In general, these are good things for a child to do. But the first suggestion, at least, is useful primarily in dealing with molestation by strangers. We suspect parents did not give enough attention to such things as saying no in an assertive way, something that is much more relevant in the case of a friend or relative who is attempting to abuse.

WHICH PARENTS TALK

We anticipated that some kinds of parents would be more apt to talk to their children about child sexual abuse than others. Perhaps having more education, or being a professional, or being a member of a younger generation might make a parent better able to discuss the problem. Or perhaps being working-class and in touch with the realities of surviving might make a parent more likely to talk. So we analyzed the likelihood of a parent talking to his or her child by all the background and demographic variables collected in the survey.

Surprisingly, few of the background variables made any difference. Parents' education, income, age, occupation, race, place of residence, religion, or degree of religiousity were inconsequential in predicting their likelihood of talking to their child about sexual abuse. Middle-class parents did no better job than lower-class parents, and professionals did no better than blue-collar workers. All this attests to the real difficulty of talking to children about the problem. It was a difficulty that cut across educational backgrounds and class lines.

However, one group of parents did do a significantly better job of talking to their children about sexual abuse. These were the parents who had themselves been victimized. Forty-six percent of the parents who were abused themselves had talked to their children, compared to only 26% of the other parents ($F = 10.20$, $p < .05$). This difference can be seen as both an encouraging and a discouraging finding. It is encouraging that former victims try to stop the cycle of abuse by alerting their own children to the problem. It is discouraging because it suggests that in our current culture only a major traumatic personal history can jolt parents into overcoming their reticence. And even then, less than half the parents who themselves had been directly affected by abuse broke the dominant pattern of avoidance.

WHAT KEEPS PARENTS FROM TALKING

The evidence that parents avoid talking to their children about sexual abuse is quite dramatic as is the evidence that this avoidance cuts across most social groupings. The important question for people interested in the field of sexual abuse prevention then becomes "why?" We know from other parts of our survey that people think that sexual abuse is a serious problem (see Chapter 6). They rated it much more serious than other potentially traumatic events of childhood such as having a friend die or having parents get a divorce. They acknowledged that it occurs to a great number of children. They know many people in their social network who have been victimized (including themselves) or who have children who have been victimized. Yet they do not put this knowledge or concern into action. Faced with their own children, they avoid the subject.

The most direct way to find out why people do not talk to their children about sexual abuse is to ask them. So we asked them. When we did this in our pretesting, we found that certain answers came up again and again. So in the larger survey these were the main answers we gave the parents in the full survey to choose from. Those answers along with the number of parents in our survey who chose them (divided between those who talked to their children, "tellers," and those who did not, "nontellers") are shown in Table 9–5.

It is apparent from Table 9–5 that parents have many reasons for not talking about sexual abuse. They say it is a difficult subject to discuss. They said they did not wish to frighten their child. Some saw their child as being in little danger of being abused. Some said the child was still too young to talk about the subject. Several of these explanations deserve some more detailed discussion.

Child Is in Little Danger

It is logical for parents to see no need to discuss a danger with a child if they honestly believe the child is very unlikely to encounter such a danger. And 55% of the parents who did not talk to their child said just that: they felt there was little danger that their child would be abused. When we ran a discriminant analysis on the parents who did and did not talk, this was the question above all others that was most effective in distinguishing between the two groups. Apparently a great many parents do not see their children as being in any danger, and as a result decline to talk to them about the problem.

Certainly this would suggest the need to raise the level of public knowledge about the prevalence of the problem. But what is surprising about this idea is that from other data in the survey we would have said that public alarm is already quite high. For example, when we asked parents to estimate how often they thought sexual abuse occurred, about half the parents said it occurred to one girl in 10 or more often. When we asked them whether they knew someone who had ever been abused, 47% said yes. Sexual abuse was prevalent in their environment. The parents knew that.

However, it is one thing to acknowledge that children in general are at-risk to sexual abuse and another to acknowledge that the danger extends to your own child. People often maintain a false sense of security about unpleasant events by believing that they only happen to other people. For example, 61% of our parents believed they lived in a neighborhood that was safer than average in terms of their child's risk of being sexually abused. Only 4% said they thought that their neighborhood was more dangerous than average. Obviously parents minimize the danger of sexual abuse to their own children even in the face of knowledge that sexual abuse is prevalent.

Fear of Frightening Child

Many of the parents, and many professionals, point out that sexual abuse is a hard topic to raise because it can easily and unnecessarily frighten a child. What adult is eager to give the child the disturbing news that there are people in the world who wish to do him or her harm. But the comparison with kidnapping is instructive. Almost all the parents had talked to their children about kidnapping. It is hard to imagine that a child's conception of kidnapping could be any less frightening than their conception of sexual abuse. To give children the idea that someone may try to take them away from their family and not let them see their family again seems a far scarier thing than to let children know that there are people in the world who may try to touch their sex organs. To a young child with a rather vague conception of sex, but a distinct and alarming conception of separation, kidnapping would seem like a far more potent fear to plant in a child's mind. The irony is that kidnapping is a relatively rare event (if we exclude parental kidnapping—this is not what children are being warned about anyway), yet parents warn their children about it in great numbers.

In contrast to kidnapping, sexual abuse is estimated to happen to hundreds of thousands of children every year (see Chapters 1, 10, and 14). Sexual abuse occurs much more frequently than kidnapping and we suspect parents know this.

So it is not just the fact that sexual abuse is thought to be an unlikely and frightening possibility that explains why parents do not talk. It would seem more likely that parents persuade themselves that their child is not in much danger and that the child will be unduly frightened because, in part, the parents find the prospect of warning about the danger so anxiety-producing.

Child Is Too Young

Thirty-six percent of the parents said that they thought their child was too young to be told about sexual abuse. Indeed parents did show a general tendency to give more information about sexual abuse to older children. When asked what was the best age to tell a child about sexual abuse, most parents said nine.

The unfortunate problem here is that many young children do become the victims of sexual abuse. This fact is clearly revealed from the parents' own experiences. We asked the parents in another part of the survey whether they themselves had ever been victimized and 12% said they had. About a third of these parents had been victimized before the age of nine. Moreover, when we asked parents to estimate the age of greatest vulnerability to sexual abuse, 55% indicated great vulnerability under the age of nine. Parents know that young children are at-risk.

If parents wait until nine or later to talk about sexual abuse, it is not that they doubt the risk to young children. Rather, we think they postpone discussions because they think that it will become easier to tell an older child. They think that the disturbing sexual content in the discussion will be better handled by a nine-year-old than a six-year-old.

Unfortunately, once they start postponing it until the right time, many parents just keep on postponing. In many families the older the child gets, the older the parent thinks he or she has to be before it is appropriate to talk. So parents in our sample who had eight-year-old children thought the best age for discussing was age nine. But parents who had nine-year-old children thought the best age for telling was age 10. This inflationary spiral often ends with the parent never talking with the child about sexual abuse. For the most part, we think parents say children are too young, not out of a realistic assessment of the child's needs or ability to understand, but rather as a rationalization for the sense of discomfort parents feel about the subject.

Difficulty in Talking About Sex

Obviously much of the discomfort that parents feel in talking about sexual abuse concerns sex. Parents have a notoriously difficult time talking to their children about sexual topics of all sorts. Other research indicates that parents neglect to discuss with their children a wide variety of sex-related subjects such as contraception, intercourse, venereal disease, masturbation, and so forth (Roberts, Kline & Gagnon, 1978). One obvious reason why sexual abuse may be more difficult to talk about than kidnapping is the fact that kidnapping does not involve sex.

However, we were surprised to find in our survey of parents that sexual abuse was not just harder to talk about than kidnapping, it was apparently harder to talk about than a wide assortment of other sexual subjects. Parents in our survey talked about homosexuality, intercourse, and even abortion more frequently than they did about sexual abuse. Only contraception was a subject more difficult to discuss. So sexual abuse may be even more difficult to talk about than other sexual subjects.

However, before we theorize about why sexual abuse might be more difficult to talk about than homosexuality, we should hasten to say that our findings on this matter do not agree with the Roberts, Kline, and Gagnon study, the one other research that surveyed parents discussions with children on a variety of sexual issues. In that Cleveland study, parents apparently found it *easier* to talk with their children about "molestation" than about such subjects as abortion, homosexuality, masturbation, and intercourse. Nevertheless, all sexual topics are hard for parents to discuss, and sexual abuse may be one of the harder ones.

Parents have a hard time talking about sex for a number of reasons. For one thing, parents often feel they lack the knowledge, vocabulary, and practice to speak about sexual matters comfortably. They fear embarrassing themselves in front of children by appearing to be ignorant, tongue-tied or confused.

Secondly, sexual topics usually trigger many strong emotional feelings for parents. They may remind parents of sexual embarrassments from their own life. They may provoke feelings about sexual dissatisfactions or disappointments that still concern them today. Parents may be aware of the fact that they are confused about certain issues of sexual values—like the advisability of premarital sex. Parents are aware that discussions of sex may call upon them to talk about their own experience or give opinions about these troublesome issues. Since discussions of sex seem like such an emotional minefield, many parents choose to skirt this territory entirely.

Moreover, children often collaborate in the avoidance of sexual discussions. It is not just that children sense parents reticence and embarrassment. Children, too, learn early the culture's paradoxical message about sex: it is bad to appear to be interested in sex, but it is also bad to appear to be ignorant of it. To talk with parents about sex often implies both that one is interested in sex, and also that one lacks knowledge. So they not only avoid bringing up sex with parents, they sometimes resist even when the parent takes the initiative.

Discussions of sexual abuse do not really need to be concerned with a great deal of sexual information, something most parents don't realize. A parent can tell children that they should not let an older person put his or her hands in their pants or play with their private parts without a lengthy discussion about sex (Sanford, 1980). Parents can also tell children that their body is their own and they have a right not to be touched in ways that make them feel uncomfortable or bad (Sanford, 1980). This too does not require a lengthy discussion of other sexual matters.

However, it is undoubtedly true that the more sexual information a child has, the better protected they are against sexual abuse. Just a few warnings about "hands in the pants" without a more general context in which to make sense of this may be of limited help. But since there are probably some parents who will never be able to have very complete discussions about sex with children, it is better that they be able to give them some warnings about sexual abuse rather than none at all.

What many parents may apparently need to give information about such sensitive subjects as sexual abuse are some easy formulas, possibly like this "hands in the pants" warning. This may have been part of what parents had in mind when they responded so readily to the answer that it "just had not occurred to them to talk about the subject" (see Table 9–5). We suspect that one reason why kidnapping receives such universal comment from parents, for example, is that such formulas do exist on this subject, for example: "don't get into a car with a stranger," or "don't take candy from a stranger." The formulas of this sort give parents a specific and limited message to pass on to their children. Although parents may have imagined that such formulas were protecting their child against sexual abuse, we now know that this was largely not the case. Obviously some new formulas need to be popularized to help parents broach the subject. One particularly good effort in this direction is Linda Sanford's book for parents *The Silent Children* (New York: Doubleday, 1980). Another useful, if less detailed book, which condenses some of Sanford's earlier ideas is Caren Adams and Jennifer Fay, *No More Secrets* (San Luis Obispo: Impact, 1981).

CONCLUSION

In spite of some surprising knowledgeability about the problem of sexual abuse, it would appear from our Boston survey that parents are doing a very poor job of communicating with their children about it. This failure is serious. We know that child sexual abuse is a large scale problem that will touch the lives of many children. If we have any ambition to reduce the toll of the problem, we must begin to insure that children get better instruction about what sexual abuse is and how to avoid it.

From talking to our Boston parents, it would appear that a number of steps may be useful in helping parents to do this. First of all, parents need to be impressed with the seriousness and the immediacy of the problem. Although they are knowledgeable about it, it may still be too easy for them to relegate it to a dusty corner of their awareness. In particular, they need to be persuaded that their own child could be victimized. In spite of their knowledge, parents seemed to be relatively complacent, doubting that abuse would occur to their child in their own neighborhood. However, they said that one of the things that most motivated them to talk with their children was hearing about abuse that had occurred to someone else in their neighborhood or extended social network. Moreover, the parents with the best records of talking with their children were those who had been victimized themselves. These are the parents who really are familiar with the risk, so they do not leave the matter to chance.

Another strategy that needs to be pursued is helping parents break through their persistent reticence about bringing up sexual matters with their children.

Although it may be only a second best approach, parents can be taught to give warnings about sexual victimization that do not require engaging their children in elaborate discussions of sex. As some parents are persuaded that education about sexual abuse can be done prior to and separate from general sex education, they may do more of it. One thing that will assist parents a great deal in this task is if educators provide them with simply remembered formula phrases and contexts through which they can provide warnings about sexual abuse. These formulas may be a good vehicle for getting help to children even from the most inhibited parents.

Ultimately, the responsibility for educating children about the problem of sexual abuse will have to be shared by other people outside the family as well. In this regard, it is encouraging to note from the survey that parents seem to be very willing to accept help. There was a very widespread support among the Boston parents for the schools providing information on sexual abuse to children. This support has been also recognized by educators, such as those from the Illusion Theater program (Kent, 1979) in Minneapolis or the Child Assault Prevention Program in Columbus (Cooper, Lutter & Phelps, 1983), who have gone into schools with specially formulated programs dealing with the problem. In spite of these successes, relatively few school systems have made a conscious effort to insert education about sexual abuse into their curriculum. Those concerned about the problem should intensify their efforts to get schools to help. It will probably take a concerted effort on the part of child welfare professionals, parents, schools, and even the media to bring about the changes necessary, and in this way insure that children get sufficient and accurate information about the problem of sexual abuse and how to avoid it.

TABLE 9–1

Difficult Subjects Parents Discussed
with Their Child

SUBJECT	% PARENTS (N = 517)
Death	92
Kidnapping	87
Pregnancy and birth	84
Drugs	81
Mental illness	66
Homosexuality	44
Sexual intercourse	43
Suicide	36
Abortion	33
Sexual abuse	*29*
Birth control	26

TABLE 9–2

Subjects Mentioned in Discussion of Sexual Abuse

SUBJECT	% PARENTS (N = 147)
Someone tempting child with rewards	86
Someone luring child into car	96
Someone taking child away	84
Someone trying to remove child's clothes	65
Someone touching child's sex organs	80
Someone exhibiting their sex organs to child	74

TABLE 9–3

Perpetrators Mentioned in Discussion of Sexual Abuse

PERSON	% PARENTS	
	Spontaneously (N = 148)	*With Prompting (N = 148)*
Strangers	77	97
Adults child knows	21	53
Other children	14	44
Family members	7	22

TABLE 9–4
Instructions to Child in Case of Sexual Abuse

	% PARENTS	
ACTION	Spontaneously (N = 148)	With Prompting (N = 148)
Run away	69	91
Tell parent	49	98
Tell someone else	29	77
Fight back	16	45
Come home	4	
Scream	7	

TABLE 9–5
Attitudes About Talking About Sexual Abuse Among Tellers and Nontellers

	% AGREEING		
ATTITUDE	Tellers (N = 146)	Nontellers (N = 359)	Significance
Your child is too young to really understand about sexual abuse	16	44	**
There is little actual danger that your child will be sexually abused	21	55	**
You are concerned that discussions of sexual abuse can frighten your child unnecessarily	31	56	**
Sexual abuse is a difficult subject to talk about with a child	61	74	**
It has just not occurred to you to talk to your child about sexual abuse	4	65	**
Your child does not want to talk about the subject of sexual abuse	35	37	N.S.

**χ^2: $p < .01$

CHAPTER 10

Boys as Victims
Review of the Evidence

PAST INTEREST IN the sexual abuse of boys has been limited for a variety of reasons. Perhaps most important, until recently, clinicians saw fairly few such cases, and those they did see appeared to be anomalies in the general tide of cases involving girls. Few people knew much about the sexual abuse of boys, and there was little pressure from clinicians for information or understanding about such cases.

But the sexual abuse of boys has been overlooked for two other reasons, as well. First, much of the attention paid to the problem of sexual abuse has resulted from the sponsorship it has received from the women's movement. It was only after the women's movement had raised the general public's consciousness about the problem of rape that public and professionals began to take increasing interest in the problem of sexually abused children. But the rape paradigm primarily sensitized people to inquire about the victimization of girls at the hands of men. The paradigm did not encourage consideration of abused boys, especially since they were not coming to public attention.

Second, the clinical information about the problem of sexual abuse quickly coalesced around one particular model which appeared to typify and explain it: the incestuous family. In the dynamics of this model, fathers become sexually involved with their daughters when their marital relationship has broken down and an eldest daughter replaces the mother in certain maternal and domestic responsibilities. A large number of cases appeared to fit this model. It quickly became the "classic" model and much sexual abuse was thought about in relation to it. However, it is clearly a model that applies predominantly, if not exclusively, to girls. In the absence of any obvious model to accommodate it, the sexual abuse of boys appeared as something of an anomaly.

New Interest in Abused Boys

Now, however, increasing numbers of questions are being asked about the sexual abuse of boys, resulting primarily from the fact that the number of such cases have mounted rapidly in some clinical settings. Whereas five years ago, many treatment programs saw only a few cases of abused boys, today some programs report that as many as a quarter or a third of their cases are of that sort (Gentry, 1978; Rogers, 1979; Swift, 1979).

This increasing number of cases has prompted interest in understanding more about the sexual abuse of boys. Up until the present, the literature which has appeared on the subject has consisted almost entirely of a few case histories (Awad, 1976; Dixon, Arnold & Calestro, 1978; Kaufman et al., 1980; Langsley, Schwartz & Fairbairn, 1968). Clinicians, administrators, and policy planners have begun to seek more information about the nature and scope of the problem.

Quite naturally, many of the questions being asked concern how the sexual abuse of boys compares to the sexual abuse of girls. Is it as widespread? Does it occur at the same age? Does it involve the same types of offenders? Or different ones? Are the effects of the experience similar?

Fortunately, recordkeeping about cases of sexual abuse has progressed to the point where we now have information about great numbers of sexual abuse cases, including cases of abused boys. Moreover, research on sexual abuse has progressed to the stage where we have information from normal populations as well as clinical ones.

The purpose of this chapter is to try to draw together available data on the sexual abuse of boys from these sources. It will try to answer some questions about how widespread the problem is and how the sexual abuse may compare in character with the sexual abuse of girls.

Defining Sexual Abuse of Boys

Some uneasiness appears in simply defining the sexual abuse of boys in the same way as the sexual abuse of girls. This uneasiness, when articulated, usually stems from two presumptions. One is that sexual activities between boys and older persons is more often initiated by the boys themselves. The second is that boys are less negatively affected by what sexual contacts they may have with older persons.

Not a great deal of evidence exists concerning either of these presumptions. Some of my own prior research suggests that neither of these presumptions should be taken for granted. In the 1978 survey, college students were asked about childhood sexual experiences with a much older person—defined as five or more years older for a child under 13 and 10 or more years older for a child under 17. The prevalence figures for such experiences are discussed below. In terms of frequency of initiation, the boys reported that the older person had initiated the contact in 91% of the encounters, only slightly (and nonsignificantly) less than in the case of girls, where 98% of the experiences had been initiated by the older person. When boys were involved with older persons, these were not self-initiated encounters.

In terms of the negative effect, the findings from the college survey were less straightforward. The boys did indeed rate their experiences as being less negative than did the girls: 38% of the boys as opposed to 66% of the girls said they were negative experiences. Moreover, boys were more likely than girls to cite interest and pleasure as reactions they had to experiences at the time. However, when we looked at long-term effects of the experience as measured by impact on sexual self-esteem, the boys seem to have been effected as much, if not more, than the girls (see Chapter 12).

Thus we need to be careful about these two presumptions concerning sexual abuse of boys. These presumptions have their roots in several sources which may not be entirely trustworthy. For one thing, the male ethic itself has tended to portray youthful male sexuality in very positive, adventuresome terms. As we point out below, it may be this very ethic that is partly responsible for the serious underreporting of sexual victimization experiences involving boys. This ethic may have depicted boys' experiences with older persons and adults as much less victimizing than they actually are.

Second, a body of opinion and research has emerged in recent years which is trying hard to vindicate homosexual pedophilia (O'Carroll, 1980; Sandfort, 1982). These reports have given accounts of seductions initiated by boys as seen through the eyes of pedophiles or as told by boys recruited through pedophile networks. Undoubtedly such boy-initiated sex does occur, but there is no evidence that the major proportion of boy–adult sexual encounters are of this sort. Available evidence suggests the opposite: most are not.

Still, the possibility that some such encounters may be child-initiated and may be positive raises the question of how sexual abuse should be defined. As suggested in Chapter 2, a good case can be made for calling encounters between children and much older persons abuse, no matter who initiates them and no matter what effect they have. These encounters involve older persons who have great power and knowledge about sex compared to the children. All indications are that although some such encounters may not be harmful, they are nonetheless high-risk. Probably the best argument for calling them abuse is that under current law and social mores they are considered illegal and taboo. Most older persons engaged in sexual activities with children know this.

Thus I favor an approach to defining child sexual abuse that simply uses an age difference or presence of coercion. What that age difference should be is a matter of some dispute; however, encounters between prepubertal boys and adults are clearly sexual abuse.

PREVALENCE OF SEXUAL ABUSE AMONG BOYS

Estimating the true prevalence of any kind of sexual abuse is difficult at best, but estimating the prevalence for boys is riskier still. Few prevalence studies exist, and those that do generally suffer from methodological limitations including the problem of defining what is and what is not sexual abuse. But sexual abuse of boys suffers under an additional burden: some of the better studies of the prevalence of sexual abuse have limited themselves to females (Kinsey et al., 1953; Russell, 1983) or have had quite small samples of men (Bell & Weinberg, 1978; Finkelhor, 1979). So resources are more limited when one attempts to estimate the true prevalence of sexual abuse of boys.

Bell and Weinberg Survey

One methodologically plausible estimate comes from a study that was not about sexual abuse at all—Bell and Weinberg's widely cited study of homosexuality in San Francisco (Bell & Weinberg, 1978, 1981). These researchers needed a control group of heterosexuals to compare with their large homosexual sample, so they commissioned an area probability survey of heterosexual men in San Francisco. This was a "random" sample obtained by field interviewers knocking on doors. Its main limitations were that it specifically excluded homosexuals and that it was relatively small for a study of this sort. Nonetheless, of this group of 284 men who were interviewed face-to-face about a wide variety of sexual matters, 2.5% said they had had a "prepubertal sexual experience with a male adult involving physical contact" (see Table 10–1).[1]

Bell and Weinberg give a somewhat higher figure for sexual abuse of boys in their homosexual sample. The homosexual sample, however, was not a random one, but was collected from volunteers recruited by paid recruiters. The fact that the figure for abuse is almost twice as high for the homosexual than the heterosexual men (4.9% vs. 2.5%) may be because the homosexual sample was composed of volunteers more willing to confide whereas the heterosexual was composed of respondents selected randomly. But it also may reflect the fact that more homosexual men have had such experiences. For more discussion of the possible connection, see Chapter 12.

Finkelhor Boston Survey

As indicated in Chapter 6, I also have data on sexual abuse of boys from a random community sample. The figures cited there, based on the 185 fathers of children 6 to 14 in the Boston area, show that 6% said they had had an experience involving physical contact with a person five or more years older prior to age 17 that they would have termed "abuse." However, in Table 10-1 I have used a definition of abuse more consistent with that of Bell and Weinberg, for purposes of comparison: Abuse is defined as an experience before the age of 13 with a partner at least five years older involving physical contact and labeled by the respondent as "abuse." In my survey, 3.2% of the men reported such an experience, quite in line with Bell and Weinberg's findings.

Finkelhor Student Survey

My survey on sexual abuse among college students (Finkelhor, 1979) also reported figures for the prevalence of sexual abuse among boys. In that survey, I gave self-administered questionnaires to whole classes of students at seven New England colleges and universities.

The main figure reported in the student survey was that 8.7% of the boys had had either an experience under 13 with a partner five or more years older or an experience between 13 and 16 with a partner at least 10 years older. Once again, for comparison with Bell and Weinberg, I have included in Table 10-1 only the experiences of boys under 13 with partners who were actual adults. The result was 4.1% of the boys.

Fritz, Stoll, and Wagner Student Study

Another group, this one at the University of Washington, also conducted a survey of sexual abuse among a student population. Fritz, Stoll, and Wagner (1981) gave questionnaires to subjects enrolled in psychology courses and collected results from a total of 410 males. Of these, 4.8% described at least one sexual encounter involving physical contact with a postadolescent individual before the subject had reached puberty.

Texas Survey

Finally, in 1978 a mail survey about sexual abuse was sent to a random sample of Texas residents who held valid driver's licenses, as part of a legislatively mandated study of sexual abuse in that state (Kercher, 1980; Kercher & McShane, 1983). Unfortunately, sexual abuse was left rather broadly defined for the respondents as

> contacts or interactions between a child and an adult when the child is being used for the sexual stimulation of the perpetrator or another person. Sexual abuse may be committed by a person under the age of 18 when that person is significantly older than the victim or when the perpetrator is in the position of power or control over another "child."

No other specific age parameters were given. Of the 461 male respondents in this survey, 3% indicated that they had been sexually abused.

Estimating Prevalence

Even though none of the surveys in Table 10–1 are national samples and two are not even random samples, the consistency of their figures is intriguing. It does suggest that the true prevalence figure for abuse experiences to boys *under 13 or before puberty* might be between 2.5% and 5%. Just as an exercise in relative magnitudes, see what those figures might show when extrapolated to a national level. Suppose, for example 2.5% to 5% boys are being victimized by the time they reach 13. (This assumes that the rate for boys who are now children will be the same as the rate found among boys who are now adults, an assumption we have no way of knowing is accurate.) That should mean a total of 550,000 to 1,100,000 of the currently 22 million boys under 13 (census estimate 1980) would eventually be victimized. Now, suppose also that the rate of victimization remains relatively constant from year to year. To produce that many victims, approximately 46,000 to 92,000 new victimizations would have to occur each year. That gives us an idea of what the annual incidence might be in the population of boys under 13.

No figure near this number of boy victims is currently being reported. The National Incidence Study of Child Abuse and Neglect (NCCAN, 1981) estimated approximately 7600 cases of sexually abused boys known to professionals in the country for 1979. That study used an unfortunately restricted definition of sexual abuse,[2] but even doubling or tripling it does not come close to the predicted incidence based on a conservative estimate like 2.5% of all boys. Rough and unscientific as this kind of estimation is, it illustrates the fact that the vast majority of abused boys are not coming to public attention.

COMPARING ABUSE OF BOYS AND GIRLS

Another way of approaching the problem of the scope of abuse among boys is to compare the amount of sexual victimization of boys and girls that has been reported in different studies. All of the studies shown in Table 10–2 recruited their male and female groups, whether clinical or nonclinical, from the same sources.

The studies are quite diverse. They include statistics drawn primarily from child protective sources, studies done at three hospitals, two studies based on police reports, and four studies based on some nonclinical population. Altogether, the findings in Table 10–2 do show some interesting regularities.

First, sexually victimized boys are reported by *all* sources. In some cases they make up a fairly small proportion of the cases seen, but they are present nonetheless.

Second, some studies show quite a few more boys than girls compared to other studies. Larger numbers of boys tend to show up in general surveys and in the *police*-based studies.

The fact that general surveys tend to show higher rates of male-to-female sexual abuse than the clinical studies suggests strongly that the sexual abuse of boys is not coming to public attention to the same extent as the sexual abuse of girls. Agencies may not be seeing the boys who are being abused.

UNDERREPORTING OF ABUSE OF BOYS

There are several factors which singly and in combination would help explain why fewer abused boys than girls ever reach public attention.[3]

1. *Boys grow up with the male ethic of self-reliance.* When they are hurt, when they are offended, it is generally harder for them to seek help. The general masculine ethic says, "Don't have others fight your battles," "Don't complain," "Keep your injuries to yourself." It is not a surprise then that fewer boys than girls told anyone about their victimization experiences in our student survey (25% vs. 33%). When experiences are never talked about, they cannot get reported.

2. *Boys have to grapple with the stigma of homosexuality surrounding so much sexual abuse.* The preponderance of abuse boys suffer is at the hands of men (see below) and for many boys this may create serious qualms about their

masculinity. Homosexuality is one of the more fearsome stigmas among many male peer groups, and boys may be very concerned about being labeled "queer" as a result of people finding out about a sexual abuse experience. Parents, too, when they find out about abuse of their sons, may be concerned about the stigma of homosexuality, and this may deter them from taking the report any further. One result of the whole society-wide anxiety about homosexuality may be that a large number of victimized boys fail to ever talk about their experiences and therefore they never get the information and reassurances that might save them years of silent suffering.

3. *Boys may have more to lose from reporting their victimization experiences.* Boys in general are allowed more independence and unsupervised activity than are girls of a similar age. Boys may be justifiably afraid that, if parents were to find out about instances of sexual molestation, it would mean some curtailment of their freedom and independence. Rather than risk that curtailment, they let the incident pass unmentioned.

All these factors may help explain findings shown in Table 10–2, which confirm the generally held clinical opinion, that sexually abused boys are much less likely to come to agency attention than the frequency of such abuse would lead one to expect (Kempe, 1978; Nasjleti, 1980).

Is Ratio Affected by Service Provided?

Another interesting finding in Table 10–2 is that hospital and child protective agencies see proportionately fewer boys compared to girls than do the police. In fact, the police show a ratio that just about duplicates the ratio found in the general surveys.

The different ratios of boys to girls indicated in Table 10–2 are probably best explained by variations in the type of populations each agency sees. The child protective agencies for example are primarily receiving reports about *intrafamilial* sexual abuse. It is likely (in fact, there is other evidence we will report later to indicate it) that intrafamilial sexual abuse occurs less frequently to boys. Since the child protective agencies deal more exclusively with the intrafamilial cases, they tend to see more girls.

The disproportion of girls in studies limited to intrafamilial cases also shows up in the National Incidence Study. The National Incidence Study cannot really be categorized with any of the other studies. Its cases of sexual abuse were based on reports to many kinds of agencies: child protective, hospital, police, schools, courts. It is interesting that the boy–girl ratios of the National Incidence study are closer to the child protective agencies' and hospitals' than to the police's. This probably stems from the fact that the National Incidence study defined abuse as limited to acts committed by caretakers and parents (Finkelhor & Hotaling, 1983). When studies focus on intrafamilial abuse alone, we believe they are likely to show a lower proportion of boys than when they focus on abuse both within and outside the family.

In contrast to child protective agencies, hospitals for their part are not limited to seeing only intrafamily sexual abuse. Hospitals also see many stranger rape cases where the victim is a child and other types of nonfamily child molesting. Nonetheless, there is probably some bias in hospital based programs toward seeing children who require a medical exam or some medical intervention. When they have been forced to have intercourse, girls may be very likely to end up at a medical facility, either to take evidence or to test for pregnancy or to repair damage caused by penetration. Boys, who do not suffer the risk of pregnancy, may be less likely to be seen by hospitals.

Police probably receive the most reports about what would be characterized as the stereotypical extrafamilial "child molester" experience. These involve the stranger in the school yard, the exposer in the park, or the neighbor who lures the children into his house with offers of money or favors. Such events are not seen as cause for social work intervention but rather as the province of the police. Boys may well be exposed to more of these kinds of abuse situations proportionately and therefore show up in larger proportions in police statistics.

THE NATIONAL REPORTING STUDY

To answer some of the most important questions about the sexual abuse of boys, we need to analyze a fairly good size sample of such cases. Unfortunately few such samples exist. Although the earlier cited surveys have been useful for calculating prevalence figures, they have uncovered too few cases to submit to detailed analysis. However, one large repository of cases of sexual abuse of boys does exist, the National Reporting Study of Child Abuse and Neglect. It is appropriate to describe here the nature of these data.

Every state in the United States has a law which mandates professionals to report cases of known or suspected child abuse to some child protective agency in that state. Since 1973, the American Humane Association has collected data from each of these state agencies and compiled them into a national summary. By 1978 all states participated in this data gathering.

The American Humane Association (AHA) was generous in providing me with the data for the 6096 substantiated cases of sexual abuse (including 803 cases involving boys) that were included in the aggregated statistics for 1978. Not all states provide individual case data on sexual abuse, so the 6096 cases represent the contributions of only 31 states and territories. Some important states with a large number of reported cases, such as California and Washington, are missing from the data base.

There are certain severe limitations to these data from the AHA study on sexually abused boys. First of all, these are "officially reported cases," so it is doubtful that they are representative of all sexual abuse cases. As we saw earlier, only a small fraction of all sexual abuse cases come to professional attention, and only a fraction of these are "officially reported." The fraction that gets reported is probably very different from the large pool that does not. It is probably more severe. It is probably more long-term. It is probably more like the stereotype of what professionals and child welfare workers think the sexual abuse of boys should look like. So conclusions drawn from these cases cannot be readily extrapolated to the problem as a whole.

Second, one of the biases that we know for certain is built into these data is a bias toward sexual abuse committed by parents and family members. The child abuse that is mandated for reporting in most states is only child abuse committed by parents and other caretakers. This means that much abuse committed by strangers, neighbors, or other children, for example, is not included in this sample. This limitation is particularly problematic in dealing with sexual abuse of boys, which, as we pointed out earlier, tends to be more nonfamily than the sexual abuse of girls.

Finally, there are questions about the reliability of the data. The information on the cases in the study are provided by the caseworkers who are assigned to the cases in a large number of far-flung offices and agencies. It is not known how consistent or accurate these official reports are.

Still the AHA study is an extremely large collection of sexual abuse cases, and it is readily available for analysis. The 803 cases of abused boys are numerous enough to provide the opportunity for elaborate statistical analysis. Moreover, they are probably representative of the kinds of cases that many workers commonly see, especially those who work with "reported cases." But keep in mind that the remainder of this section deals with *reported cases.*

SEX OF THE ABUSER

Some of the most interesting evidence of the AHA study concerns the perpetrators of sexual abuse against boys. However, some prior discussion of the use of the term "perpetrator" in the AHA study is required.

When child protective workers, the "respondents" in the AHA study, fill out the reporting forms used to collect data, they are asked on the form to report all caretakers involved in child abuse *and neglect.* In situations where a child has been sexually abused, the workers frequently feel that acts of neglect by a parent, particularly the mother, contributed to the situation where the sexual abuse occurred. For example, the mother might have known about the abuse but failed to take steps to stop it. Or the mother may have left the child alone for long periods with a recent boyfriend. In these kinds of cases, mothers are often listed on the forms as co-perpetrators. But it is not because they molested the child themselves; rather it is because they were involved in the circumstances that permitted the abuse.

This reporting practice shows up in the AHA data as a high percentage of cases where a woman (usually a mother) is cited as a perpetrator in sexual abuse. In Table 10-3, we see that a female was listed as involved in 41% of cases where males were victimized and even 31% of cases where females were victimized.

However, in most of these cases where a female is listed as involved, a male was also involved, and he was the one doing the actual molesting (NCCAN, 1981). A more accurate picture of the number of children who were actually molested by women comes from looking at the number of cases where a woman was the perpetrator *alone*, without a male also being listed. These constitute a much smaller proportion of the cases, 14% of boys and 6% of girls (Table 10-3). These percentages jibe better with the findings of other studies (see Chapter 11) and confirm that, in spite of some misconceptions, boys, like girls, are abused primarily by men.

BOYS AND NONFAMILY ABUSE

The AHA data also shows that the sexual abuse of boys appears more likely than in the case of girls to come from outside the family. Boys were victimized by a male non-family member 23% of the time while girls were 14%. Since this sample still deals primarily with *caretakers*, these non-family members were not strangers. Most of these offenders were individuals like teachers, institutional staff, coaches, mother's boyfriends, babysitters, and others who had some caretaking responsibility for the children.

These findings are confirmed by the earlier findings in the Finkelhor student survey. There, because the offenders were not limited to caretakers, the difference was even greater. About 83% of the persons who victimized boys in that sample were non-family members. In the case of girls, only 56% were non-family. The comparable figures in the Boston parents survey was 77% non-family for boys, 66% non-family for girls, not so great a difference but one in the same direction.

In their current work Burgess and some of her colleagues are uncovering a large amount of victimization that occurs to children in the form of "sex rings" (Burgess, 1984; Burgess, Groth & McCausland, 1981). These are groups of children who become involved with the same adult usually through some recreational or neighborhood activity, and the adult trades favors with many of the children for sexual activities. It may be that boys are more likely to be abused in this way, and this may be one of the common sites where boys are victimized outside the family by people who know them.

BOY VICTIMS ARE MUCH YOUNGER THAN GIRLS

One of the most striking characteristics of the boy victims in the AHA study sample is how young they are. Thirty-two percent of the incidents occurred to boys who were under age six. This contrasts sharply with girls in this sample, only 18% of whom were under six and most of whom were adolescents at the time of reporting. Forty-seven percent of the girls in this sample were 13 or over, but only 26% of the boys were of this age. The median ages were 8.46 for boys and 12.40 for girls. One gets the impression that sexual abuse occurs to boys at a much earlier age than to girls.

Unfortunately, the findings from the AHA study on this subject are not consistent with conclusions from other sources. For example, in the New England college student survey (Finkelhor, 1979), the median age for the victimized boys was *older* than for the girls (11.2 vs. 10.2). The same was true among parents' self-reports from the Boston survey (11.4 for boys vs. 9.7 for girls.) In three studies of incarcerated sex offenders (Frisbie, 1969; Gebhard et al., 1965; Mohr, Turner & Jerry, 1964) the median age of the boy victims of these offenders was also older than the median age for girls, sometimes by more than three years. In the Queen's Bench study (1975) of sexual abuse incidents reported to the police, the median age was virtually identical for boys and girls (8.7 and 8.5). Could the AHA study figures be misleading?

One of the main problems with the AHA study data is that they are made up of cases that have come to the attention of public welfare agencies. The age of the children recorded in the case reports was the age of the children *at the time the case was investigated and substantiated*. So the age information tells us more about the age of the children at the time the abuse was discovered than about the age of the children at the time it first occurred or went on.

This would help to explain the extremely high median age for victimized girls in this AHA study sample, about a year higher than any other study. About three-quarters of the instances of sexual abuse of girls in this sample are instances of abuse by fathers. From clinical accounts, we know that many cases of father–daughter abuse go on for a substantial period of time before they end or are discovered; Meiselman (1978) calculated the average duration to be about three-and-one-half years. So most of the cases of girls in the AHA study sample undoubtedly began when the girls were several years younger than the age reported in the study data.

By contrast, there are other characteristics of this reported data which might tend to skew the median age for boys downward. First of all, a substantially smaller proportion of the boys are victimized by parents within their nuclear family. Although the clinical accounts of boy abuse are much less readily available than the accounts of girls, it is plausible that abuse outside the nuclear family does not go on so long and comes to light more quickly, if at all. A boy's own parents are not so often participating in covering up and maintaining the secret. So abuse outside the family probably goes on for shorter periods than abuse inside. And since more of the abuse of boys is outside the family, when it does come to light, it will be after a shorter time and the boys will be younger.

The statistics can be read to confirm this idea. In the AHA study figures, boys who are abused inside their family are older than boys abused outside. Fifty-four percent of the boys abused inside the family are over 10 compared to only 36% of boys abused outside the family. This may be because the abuse inside the family goes on for a longer period of time and takes longer to discover. So boys' ages in the reporting study may be lower than girls' because more of their abuse occurs outside the family.

A second reason why reported statistics might show an artificially low median age for boy victims is that older boys may be even less likely than younger boys to reveal sexual abuse situations. If the masculine ideology of self-sufficiency and reluctance to get help applies at all, it is certain to apply more strongly to the preadolescent and adolescent boys. So older boys who have been abused may be much less likely to tell anyone about it or report the abuse than an older girl, who is looking for some support in ending the abuse. This would also have the effect of reducing the average age of boys compared to girls among a collection of reported cases. Confirming this, it is interesting to note that in the Boston survey, among the reports that children had made to their parents, boys were younger than girls (mean age 7.9 vs. 8.9).

In short, although from reported cases boys appear to be victimized at an earlier age than girls, much of this difference could be explained by differences in the way the abuse of boys and the abuse of girls is discovered. Information from general surveys shows, if anything, a higher age for victimized boys among unreported cases. It may be that more older boys are abused but these are the cases least likely to become official reports. Obviously we need more good data about how the age of children affects their likelihood of abuse and chances of coming to public attention.

Family Backgrounds of Abused Boys

Reported child abuse is a heavily lower-class phenomenon. This does not mean that abuse does not occur in other social classes. It does. But the cases coming to the attention of authorities originate overwhelmingly among very disadvantaged groups. In 1979, for example, the median income for general child abuse cases reported to the National Incidence Study was $8,435. In the same year the median income for U.S. families was $19,661 (Brown & Holder, 1980).

Of the various forms of child abuse, however, sexual abuse is among the most middle-class. For example, the sexual abuse cases reported to the National Incidence Study came from families with median incomes of $9,285, 10% higher than other child-abusing families as a whole. Moreover, families where a father sexually abuses a daughter are even more middle-class than the rest (Brown & Holder, 1980).

In contrast to girls, however, sexually abused boys come from backgrounds *much more typical* of other child abuse cases. Families of boy victims are poorer. They are more likely to be broken. Consistent with this general picture, these families are more likely to evidence physical abuse in addition to the sexual abuse.

First, boys who are abused come from poorer backgrounds than girls. Sixty-two percent of the boys' families were receiving public assistance, compared to only 40% of the girls' families. Income comparisons show a similar differential.

Second, boys who are abused also come more often from single-parent households (48% for boys vs. 31% for girls). Most of these families, like most single-parent households, are headed by women who are divorced, separated, or never married. The female-headed condition helps account for the generally lower income of these boys' families and their presence on the welfare rolls. Since girls are, to a larger extent than boys, abused by fathers, a much larger proportion of abused girls have either natural, common law, or stepfathers living in their households.

Since sexually abused boys have more characteristics of physically abused children in general and they come, to a larger extent, from lower-income and broken families, it is not surprising that sexually abused boys do suffer from more physical abuse than girls. There was evidence of physical abuse in only a small number of families of sexually abused girls (5%). The level of physical abuse was higher (20%) in the families of sexually abused boys. In fact, this suggests that for some boys, their sexual abuse may come to light in the course of an investigation that begins by being alerted to signs of physical—not sexual—abuse. For girls, this appears to be a much less common route to discovery.

Boys Victimized in Conjunction with Girls

One of the other remarkable differences between sexually abused boys and girls according to the AHA data is that boys are relatively *less likely to be abused alone.* The difference is most striking in regard to abuse by a parent (see Table 10–4). If a girl is abused by a parent, in 65% of the reports she will be the *only reported victim.* If a boy is abused, 60% of the time there will be another victim. These other victims are usually sisters.

It is hard to know whether what we are seeing here is a true difference between the victimization pattern of girls and boys, or whether it is an artifact of reporting. Other evidence has suggested that boys are less likely to come forward or be identified as having been a victim (Finkelhor, 1979). It may be that one of the main ways in which boys are identified as having been abused is if a sister comes forward or the abuse of a sister is discovered. Then, in the course of an investigation, it is also discovered that a boy in the family has suffered abuse. In the situation where a boy is being abused and where there are no sisters or no sister is also being abused, it may be that the sexual victimization is less likely to be discovered.

On the other hand, this difference may be a true characteristic of the victimization of boys. When boys are sexually victimized within their family, it may be much more often in tandem with sisters.

Abuse of Solo Boys Is Quite Different

The finding that so many of the abused boys were abused along with girls has some implications for our analysis of differences between the abuse of boys and girls. In many of the statistics where we have compared boys with girls, almost a third of the boys used in the comparison came from the same families as the girls we were comparing them to. This would tend to dilute any difference. If we compared the income of families where boys were abused with the income of families where girls were abused, differences would be obscured by the fact that some of the same families were counted in both sides.

What is interesting is that if we look at the cases of boys who were victimized alone, these are very different cases on the whole from girls who were victimized alone or from boys who were victimized along with some girls. When we look at the group of boys who were victimized apart from any girls, the differences between abuse of boys and abuse of girls becomes even more striking.

For example, in Table 10–5, we see that boys victimized alone were 2.5 times more likely than girls to be victimized by a non-family member. Boys victimized alone were also over 4 times more likely to be victimized by a non-family member than boys victimized in tandem with girls. Lone boy victims were also much more likely than girl or mixed boy–girl victims to be victimized by someone under the age of 25. These are cases of being victimized by an older brother, a babysitter, or a young adult in the neighborhood. Lone boys are also much more likely to be victimized at a very early age. Almost two-fifths were under six years old at the time the victimization was *reported*. This suggests that clinically, too, important distinction should be made between boys victimized alone and those victimized in conjunction with siblings and others.

ABUSE BY MOTHERS AND FATHERS

Abuse of boys appears to differ by whether or not they are abused in conjunction with sisters. In addition, abuse of boys appears to differ by whether they are abused by a male or a female parent.

Although most boys abused by a parent are abused by a father, enough mothers also abuse to make possible some interesting comparisons. In Table 10–6, we have arrayed the four possible combinations of parent–child sexual abuse: father–daughter, father–son, mother–daughter, and mother–son. Each form shows some distinctive characteristic.

Table 10–6 shows again that girls tend to be older than boys at the time that the abuse goes on record. But it also shows that children of both sexes victimized by mothers are younger than children victimized by fathers. Sons abused by fathers are about four years younger, when discovered, than girls victimized by fathers. Boys victimized by mothers are the youngest of all the four groups.

Sons who are victimized by fathers are distinctive in that so often they are being abused in conjunction with the abuse of an older sister. This helps explain why, in Table 10–6, a smaller number of the father–son cases involve an only child or an oldest child. Because these boys are younger brothers of older victimized sisters, it also helps explain why the median age of victims in father–son cases is lower than in father–daughter cases.

Mothers, although they appear to take advantage of very young children, appear to have a tendency, like fathers, to pick the oldest child.

The mother abuse cases are also remarkable for their distinctive family background characteristics (Table 10–7). Mothers who abuse—both sons and daughters—are dramatically poorer than fathers who abuse. Also they are heavily black. This characteristic is interesting because, on the whole, sexual abuse, especially father–daughter abuse, is one of the most white-dominated forms of child abuse. But when mothers sexually abuse, a large number of them are black.

Consistent with this picture of families who are more like typical child-abuse families, mother abusers are also more likely than father abusers to combine physical and sexual abuse. Over half the cases of mother sexual abuse was combined with physical abuse, something less characteristic of father abuse cases.

So these figures paint an interesting portrait of children abused by a mother. The victims tend to be young children, and the mothers tend to be poor, single, black, and prone to physical abuse. These features seem to set off abuse by mothers as quite distinct from sexual abuse by fathers.

SUMMARY

This chapter has reviewed available data for information about sexually victimized boys. The most important findings about sexually abused boys that can be gleaned are:

1. Estimates drawn from surveys of men in the general population would indicate that perhaps 2.5%–8.7% of men are sexually victimized as children. Comparison with similar studies of girls would suggest 2–3 girls are victimized for every boy.
2. Boys, like girls, are most commonly victimized by men.
3. Boys are more likely than girls to be victimized by someone outside the family.
4. Boys are more likely than girls to be victimized in conjunction with other children.
5. Victimized boys are more likely than girls to come from impoverished and single-parent families and are also more likely to be victims of physical abuse as well.
6. The abuse of boys is more likely to be reported to the police than to a hospital or child protective agency.

TABLE 10-1
Prevalence Surveys of Sexual Abuse Among Boys

SURVEY/DEFINITION OF ABUSE	RATE PER 100	N	TYPE OF SAMPLE
Bell & Weinberg (1981)			
Prepubertal sexual experience with male adult involving physical contact			
a. Heterosexual sample	2.5	284	Probability
b. Homosexual sample	4.9	275	Convenience
Finkelhor (1979)			
Child under 13 with adult	4.1	266	College students (whole classes)
Finkelhor (1981)			
Prepubertal experiences with person 5 years older involving physical contact	3.2	185	Probability
Fritz, Stoll & Wagner (1981)			
Prepubertal sexual contact with postadolescent involving physical contact	4.8	410	College psychology students
Kercher & McShane (1983)			
Sexual abuse (see text)	3.0	461	Probability (Texas driver's license holders)

TABLE 10–2
Ratio of Boy to Girl Victims Across Various Studies

STUDY	NUMBER OF BOYS PER 100 GIRLS	N
Child Protective Agencies		
DeFrancis (1969)	11	250
American Humane Assn. (1978)	15	6096
Hospitals		
Jaffe, Dynneson & Ten Bensel (1975)	13	291
Rogers (1979)	33	114
Ellerstein & Canavan (1980)	12	145
Police		
Queen's Bench (1976)	47	131
Swift (1979)	~ 50	?[a]
Mixed Agency		
National Incidence (NCCAN) (1981)	20	3124
General Surveys		
Bell & Weinberg		
Heterosexual (1978)	32	385[b]
Homosexual (1978)	47	804[b]
Finkelhor (1979)	48	796[b]
Kercher & McShane (1979)	27	1056[b]
Finkelhor (1981)	40	521[b]

[a] Estimate cited without giving N.

[b] N for entire survey, not N of victims.

TABLE 10-3

Women as Perpetrators of Sexual Abuse

	% MALE VICTIMS (N = 757)	% FEMALE VICTIMS (N = 5052)
Female involved	41	31
Female alone	14	6
Mother involved	36	27
Mother alone	12	5

SOURCE: Data from American Humane Association (AHA), National Reporting Study of Child Abuse and Neglect, 1978.

TABLE 10-4

Abuse by Parents: Single- and Multiple-Victim Situations

VICTIM SITUATION	% BOYS (N = 516)	% GIRLS (N = 3770)
Sole victim	40	65
Multiple victim, same sex	17	28
Multiple victim, opposite sex	43	7

SOURCE: Data from American Humane Association (AHA), National Reporting Study of Child Abuse and Neglect, 1978.

TABLE 10-5

Comparison of Boys Abused Alone to Boys Abused in Conjunction with Girls, and Girls Abused Alone (Various Conditions)

CONDITION	% BOYS ALONE (N = 424)	% MIXED GROUP (N = 581)	% GIRLS ALONE (N = 3095)
Victim under 6 years	38	18	19
Perpetrator non-family member	35	8	13
Perpetrator under 25	34	11	16
Initial report to doctor or hospital	22	13	18

SOURCE: Data from American Humane Association (AHA), National Reporting Study of Child Abuse and Neglect, 1978.

TABLE 10–6
Comparison of Characteristics in Abuse by Parents

CHARACTERISTIC	FATHER–DAUGHTER (N = 1818)	FATHER–SON (N = 199)	MOTHER–DAUGHTER (N = 193)	MOTHER–SON (N = 66)
Median age of victims	13.48	9.36	9.04	7.81
Oldest child	66%	49%	66%	63%
Only child	23%	14%	23%	24%

SOURCE: Data from American Humane Association (AHA), National Reporting Study of Child Abuse and Neglect, 1978.

TABLE 10–7
Comparison of Family Situations in Abuse by Parents

CHARACTERISTIC	% FATHER–DAUGHTER (N = 1818)	% FATHER–SON (N = 199)	% MOTHER–DAUGHTER (N = 193)	% MOTHER–SON (N = 66)
Income under $5,000	15	18	45	36
Income over $13,000	33	25	5	4
Black	8	8	31	33
Physical abuse present	27	32	53	50

SOURCE: Data from American Humane Association (AHA), National Reporting Study of Child Abuse and Neglect, 1978.

CHAPTER 11

Women as Perpetrators:
Review of the Evidence

COAUTHORED WITH

Diana Russell

J UST AS IT HAS been assumed, until recently, that boys were rarely victims of sexual abuse, so was it assumed that very few women were perpetrators. Past studies that collected data on the gender of perpetrators confirmed this assumption. However, some researchers and scholars have begun to question that this is the case.

For example, Nicholas Groth, a prison psychologist, reporting that he had encountered in his professional work to date only three women out of 253 adult offenders against children (i.e., 1%), nevertheless concluded his discussion of the female offender by arguing that sexual victimization of children by women "may not be as infrequent an event as might be supposed from the small number of identified cases" (1979, p. 192). He offered the following reasons for his view: (1) women may "mask sexually inappropriate contact with a child through the guise of bathing or dressing the victim"; (2) the sexual offenses of females are "more incestuous in nature, and the children are more reluctant to report such contact when the offender is a parent (i.e., their mother) and someone they are dependent upon"; (3) it may be that boys are more frequently the targets of female offenders than girls and that "boys are less likely to report or disclose sexual victimization than girls."

Sociologist of sexual behavior, Kenneth Plummer (1981), refers to the notion that pedophiles are men (rather than women and men) as a "stereotype." He believes that there is a "considerable degree of adult female–child sexuality." Like Groth, Plummer argues that such activity (he appears to deliberately avoid using the word "abuse") is hidden "because of the expectations of the female role which simultaneously expect a degree of bodily contact between woman and child and deny the existence of sexuality in women" (p. 228). He maintains that "what may be socially prescribed for the woman may lead the man to a term of imprisonment" (p. 228).

In explanation of the very few cases of mother–son incest reported in the literature, psychologists Blair and Rita Justice (1979) suggest that this form of incest may be less likely to come to light. They write,

> In our experience, mothers engage more frequently in sexual activity that does not get reported: fondling, sleeping with a son, caressing in a sexual way, exposing her body to him, and keeping him tied to her emotionally with implied promises of a sexual payoff. (p. 179)

In addition to statements like those just cited which have appeared in print, the view that the amount of abuse by females has been seriously underestimated is commonly expressed at conferences and elsewhere by experts in the field. In light of such opinions, it would appear appropriate to review the data available on this subject, as well as the arguments about the meaning of those data.

STUDIES BASED ON REPORTED CASES

Most of the early studies of sexual abuse were consistent in the very small number of cases of abuse by females which they reported (see Table 11–1). For example, DeFrancis's (1969) early study based on cases coming to the attention of the Brooklyn Humane Society found only 3% of perpetrators to be women. Another early study, based on reports to the San Francisco Police Department, found similarly few women perpetrators (Queen's Bench, 1976). However, these and other early studies also found very low rates of abuse against boys. Many observers wondered whether, as abuse of boys became more evident, many more cases of abuse committed by women would also surface.

More abuse of boys, but not much more abuse by women, did surface in later, more comprehensive studies. The two most systematic efforts to collect data about reported cases of sexual abuse have been the American Humane Association study and the National Incidence Study of Child Abuse and Neglect. Let us consider their findings in regard to women perpetrators.

The National Incidence Study was a multimillion dollar effort sponsored by special congressional mandate to try to estimate the extent and nature of child abuse. The study chose 26 counties to be representative of the entire United States and developed procedures for collecting data from professionals in these counties on both reported and unreported cases of child abuse (NCCAN,

1981). The study concluded that 44,700 cases of sexual abuse were known to professionals in 1979, 17% of which occurred to boys.

Unfortunately, the initial report on the study gave misleading information about the sex of perpetrators for reasons similar to those mentioned in regard to the American Humane Association study cited in Chapter 10. From figures provided in the main report of the study findings (Table 55), a reader might conclude that 46% of the sexual experiences encountered by children included a female perpetrator. A subsequent reanalysis of the data from the report is summarized below and provides a more accurate breakdown (Finkelhor & Hotaling, 1983).

One major problem in interpreting National Incidence Study figures on perpetrators is that according to study definitions a caretaker could be a perpetrator not only if he or she had sexual contact with a child, but also if he or she "permitted acts of sexual abuse to occur." Since it is true that, in many cases of intrafamily sexual abuse, mothers (or other female caretakers) know that abuse is occurring and fail to stop it, these women are listed in the study as perpetrators. When these "perpetrators" are subtracted, as can be done by reanalyzing the data, leaving only those who actually committed abuse, the percentage of female abusers drops dramatically to *13% in the case of female victims and 24% in the case of males.*

However, even these percentages of female abusers are inflated for two reasons. First, the study did not clearly link perpetrators with the type of maltreatment they were guilty of. Thus, if in one family a mother neglected a child while a father sexually abused the child, both mother and father were listed as perpetrators. Since sexual abuse is listed as one of the abuses that occurred, it is impossible to determine just who did what. Possibly, some of the women who are included as perpetrators of sexual abuse were really only perpetrators of some other kind of maltreatment.

Second, the study considered an adult caretaker to be an active perpetrator of sexual abuse if the adult provided "inadequate or inappropriate supervision . . . of child's voluntary sexual activities" in a situation where a child was involved with a person at least two years older and where negative consequences ensued for the child. So here also, some mothers listed as active perpetrators may very well not be persons who engaged in sexual contact with the child.

There was a final problem: many of the women who are listed as perpetrators in the figures quoted above (and in Table 11–1) were perpetrators in situations where a male was also listed as a perpetrator. Twelve of the 22 cases involving male children and 60 of the 87 cases involving female children involved both male and female perpetrators. Even if these are not situations, as mentioned above, where the female was committing some other kind of abuse besides sexual abuse, most clinical accounts of situations which include both male and female perpetrators usually show the interest and initiative for the sexual abuse to come from the male. Frequently the female partner is participating under duress. It is certainly not justified to consider these situations as straightforward instances of sexual abuse of children by females. For all these reasons we suspect that the figures for female abusers from the National Incidence Study—24% in the case of boys and 13% in the case of girls—are too high.

The American Humane Association (AHA) study mentioned in the last chapter was another large-scale collection of sexual abuse cases that included some female perpetrators. As we mentioned in the last chapter, determining the exact number of female perpetrators in the AHA study was also complicated by the fact that many women were listed as perpetrators for "allowing" sexual abuse, not for having sexual contact themselves. Unlike the National Incidence Study, in the AHA study it was not possible to distinguish clearly between perpetrators who committed abuse and those who simply allowed it. The best we could do was isolate situations where only one perpetrator was listed and that perpetrator was a female. This approach left figures of 14% of the perpetrators against boys and 6% of the perpetrators against girls as being females acting alone. Interestingly, these figures are similar to the equivalent figures that could have been derived from the National Incidence Study if only cases of sole female perpetrator had been counted.

Both these studies indicate that female perpetrators more frequently sexually abuse girls than boys. While the percentage of female offenders against boys is higher (14% vs. 6% in the AHA study), there are also a great many more girl victims than boy victims. Thus 6% of 5052 girls is substantially higher than 14% of 803 boys. Thus even the stereotype that women are most likely to abuse boys is not supported by the data from these studies.

STUDIES BASED ON SELF-REPORTS

Of course, the data based on reported cases have a great number of well-recognized shortcomings. People who believe that there is much unreported abuse by females usually argue that such abuse rarely comes to public attention, and thus has yet to show up in statistics on reported cases such as those cited above.

Fortunately, there are, by now, a number of studies that have collected data on sexual abuse and adult sexual contacts with children from the self-reports of the children themselves. All these studies, most of which were described in Chapter 10 (see Table 11-2), are based on interviews with adults, recalling childhood experiences. From the studies that have inquired about it (Russell,

1983), it is clear that only a small minority of cases located in this manner were ever reported as cases of sexual abuse or child molestation to public agencies.

Three studies listed in Table 11–2 were not described in the last chapter: Gebhard et al. (1965), Fromuth (1983), and Russell (1983). Gebhard and colleagues (1965) recruited 477 men using a Kinsey-style methodology and asked these volunteers about prepubertal sexual contacts with adult males and females. The men were used as a nonoffender control group in a study of incarcerated sex offenders. Fromuth (1983) studied psychology students at Auburn University using the exact definition used in the Finkelhor student survey.

Russell's study involved a random-sample survey in which face-to-face interviews were conducted with 930 adult women residents in San Francisco. Those surveyed were asked about experiences of intrafamilial and extrafamilial child sexual abuse. Intrafamilial child sexual abuse was defined to include any kind of exploitive sexual contact that occurred between relatives, no matter how distant the relationship, before the victim turned 18 years old. Experiences with a relative that were wanted *and* were with a peer (less than five years older) were regarded as nonexploitive. Extrafamilial child sexual abuse was defined as *unwanted* sexual experiences with persons unrelated by blood or marriage, ranging from petting (touching of breasts or genitals or attempts at such touching) to rape, before the victim turned 14 years, and completed or attempted forcible rape experiences from the ages of 14 to 17 years (inclusive).

Kinsey and his colleagues, interestingly, also collected data on this subject, but were missing some important information, so did not report on experiences by sex of offender. Nonetheless, they wrote of the male sample, "The record includes some cases of preadolescent boys involved in sexual contact with adult females, and still more cases of preadolescent boys involved with adult males" (Kinsey et al., 1948).

Almost all the studies clearly agree with Kinsey. The bulk of evidence from the self-report studies is that sexual contact between children and older women is a distinct minority of child–adult contacts. For boys, with but one exception, the figures show approximately a quarter or less of all contacts. For girls, with again but one exception, the figures show one tenth or less.

Of the two exceptions, one is the study by Fritz, Stoll, and Wagner (1981), which surveyed the undergraduate psychology students at the University of Washington. In that sample 4.8% of the boys reported they had had a "sexual interaction with a postpubescent person at least five years older than (themselves) before they reached puberty," and 60% of these experiences were with females, largely older female adolescents.

It is interesting that this finding is so dramatically at variance with the findings of the Finkelhor (1979) student sample, which used a similar type of population, a similar definition of molestation, and a similar questionnaire methodology. Unfortunately, the principal investigator (Nathaniel Wagner) of the Fritz, Stoll, and Wagner study has since died, many of the questionnaires have been lost, and it is no longer possible to reanalyze the findings to try to find the source of the discrepancy (Stoll, 1981). In the face of the consensus of the other studies shown in Table 11–2, it seems likely that the Fritz, Stoll, and Wagner findings resulted from an unusual sample or an error in tabulation.

The other somewhat discrepant figure in Table 11–2 is for female children from the Bell and Weinberg (1981) homosexual sample. Of the 62 female homosexuals who reported a childhood experience with a person over 16, 22% of them reported these to be with older women. An obvious possible explanation of the discrepancy is that female homosexuals have different patterns of childhood sexual contacts. It is not known whether the sexual contact with the older women influenced them to become lesbians, or whether their early sexual orientation made them more vulnerable to have experiences with adult women rather than adult men, or a combination of both. But this finding cannot be taken to confirm high rates of abuse by females in the general population.

There are some other reports of higher rates of victimization of children by older females from less representative populations, for example, from studies of the childhood experiences of sex offenders who have been apprehended and/or incarcerated. Groth (1983), for example, found that 51% of a sample of sex offenders had been victimized when they were young and of these 25% had been victimized by a female. MacFarlane (1982) also found that 51% of a sample of attendees at a Parents United National Conference (an organization for incest offenders and their families) had been victimized and of these 33% had been victimized by females. However, both these are unusual groups for whom victimization (and perhaps victimization by females) may have played a role in their becoming offenders. They are not samples that can be used to estimate how widespread victimization and victimization by females is in the general population.

Because figures from sources similar to Groth's and MacFarlane's are often quoted, it is important to emphasize just how unrepresentative such samples of sex offenders in jail or in treatment are. First of all, they are not representative of sex offenders in general, since most sex offenders are never reported, let alone caught or persuaded to get help. In Russell's study, for example, according to victim recollections, only 2% of the perpetrators of intrafamily sexual abuse and 6% of the perpetrators of extrafamily sexual abuse were ever reported to the police. The number who actually were prosecuted and convicted was even smaller, 1%. Those who do get caught or who end up in treatment are almost certainly very unusual. One might speculate that they were either so repetitive or conspicuous in their behavior that they were caught, or so guilty or remorseful that they reported themselves or sought treatment, or so flagrantly bizarre in their behavior that their denial of sexual abuse had no credibility. In addition, because of racial and class prejudices, they are more likely to be lower class or members of minority groups, a conclusion supported by Russell's (1983) data on convictions.

Not only are apprehended offenders unrepresentative of perpetrators in general, but incarcerated or in-treatment sex offenders who were themselves sexually abused in their childhood are hardly likely to be representative of sexual abuse victims either. It has frequently been suggested that having a history of victimization puts someone at-risk of becoming a perpetrator. But not all victims become perpetrators, so those who do probably had victimization experiences that were different in some way, more severe, more unusual, more disturbing. So it seems very unlikely that the victimization experiences of a group of incarcerated offenders would be typical of the victimization experiences of other people.

SOME POSSIBLE OBJECTIONS

The data collated from a variety of studies seem to support clearly the presumption that most sexual offenses against children are perpetrated by males. However, it also appears to be true that some of the earliest studies presented unrealistically low estimates of the numbers of female offenders and that even today many studies based on reported cases may still be underestimating such offenses. The best estimates, based on a variety of surveys of the general population, put the percent of sexual contacts by older females to be about 20% (range 14% to 27%) for male children and about 5% (range 0 to 10%) for female children. Especially since contacts with female children occur with at least twice or three times the frequency as contacts with male children (Chapter 10), the presumption that sexual abusers are primarily men seems clearly supported.

However, various objections have been raised against using any of the available data to resolve the issue of male preponderance, and these objections need to be addressed.

1. *Is sexual abuse by adult female perpetrators less often perceived as abusive?* An important question raised by some observers is whether there is a great amount of contact between children and older or adult women that goes unnoticed in surveys because the younger partners do not consider it abuse or victimization or even upsetting, in fact, may consider it positive and pleasurable. However, several of the studies in Table 11–2 do give evidence against even such a possibility as this, because they did not use terms such as sexual abuse or sexual

victimization. Bell and Weinberg (1978), for example, asked only about sexual contacts that respondents had had before puberty, and then asked for the age of the other partner. The Bell and Weinberg figures listed in Table 11-2 are based on contacts with partners older than age 16, whether these contacts were positive and pleasurable or negative.

Similarly, in the Finkelhor (1979) student sample, students were asked simply to note experiences that they had had before the age of 12 with a person over 16. Experiences were included in the tally of sexual abuse if they met certain age difference criteria, not according to whether they were considered to be positive or negative, upsetting or pleasurable. Thus the figures in both Bell and Weinberg and Finkelhor samples were not limited to those perceived as abusive by the respondents. If there were positive experiences with older females, they were included in these figures.

The question of what difference it makes whether the experiences examined are considered abusive by the respondent can be looked at with some of the data from the Finkelhor Boston survey too. In that survey, adult respondents were asked to list any experiences they may have had before the age of 16 with a person five years older than themselves (irrespective of whether it was considered abusive). The males listed 24 such experiences, five of which (or 21%) were with older females. Later the respondents were asked whether they considered the experience to be abusive. Thirteen of the experiences were considered abuse including two (or 15%) of the experiences with females. So asking only about abusive experiences made some difference (not significant statistically), but one could not say that a much larger percentage of experiences with older women becomes apparent when respondents are asked about both positive and negative experiences.

2. *Can women mask sexually inappropriate behavior more easily than men?* A possibility raised by both Groth (1979) and Plummer (1981) is that since women have more socially prescribed and accepted physical intimacy with children, they might carry on sexual contacts with children that would go unnoticed. For example, a woman could presumably have an inappropriately old child suck on her breast as a way of gaining sexual gratification, but the behavior might not be noticed as abuse.

It is true that there are a few caretaking activities which women engage in that could mask some abuse, breast-feeding and washing being two of these. However, it seems very unlikely that women could mask very well the kinds of activities which compose the vast majority of kinds of abuse engaged in by men: having the child fondle the adult's genitals, putting the penis on or in the vagina, engaging in oral sex. A woman engaging in such activities would have a hard time disguising these as normal mothering.

Part of the issue is: from whom would the woman be masking the abuse?

Perhaps it is true that other persons would be unlikely to notice that an unhealthy kind of physical contact was occurring between mother and child. But it seems extremely implausible to think that the women could be masking the sexual activity from the children themselves.

Professionals who work with children believe for the most part that children are very good at distinguishing touch that is affectionate from touch that is sexual and intended for the adult's genital gratification. Especially in the case of preadolescent boys, who tend to be particularly inclined by their peer culture to see sexual content in behavior, it is hard to imagine an older woman being sexual with them without their noticing.

Not just women, but men, too, try to disguise the sexual nature of their activities with children when they engage in them, telling the children that it is just a game or a way of expressing affection. Children even believe these deceptions for a short time, but then later come to realize what they were. While women might, perhaps, deceive children more easily than men at the time of the activities, we think much of such activity would show up in reports of older children who, looking back on their younger years, now realize that women were being sexual with them. Few such reports occur.

In fact, what this discussion really reveals is that, despite the ample opportunities for sexual abuse mothers have, remarkably few seem to take advantage of them. An activity such as breast-sucking is one that is commonly part of sexual lovemaking and also one of the most basic nurturant activities between mother and child. It seems fraught with possibilities for abuse. Yet reports from clinical populations or general surveys reveal extremely few cases of inappropriate breast-sucking between mothers and older children. By contrast, suppose that it was somehow a basic part of the early nurturing process for children to fondle their father's penis. Given the nature of male sexuality common in this culture, we might expect that many fathers would be reluctant to give up this activity and would try to get a child to repeat this act after the child had outgrown it. The contrast shows well the apparent restraint that is the norm in relations between women and children. Although some measure of sexual activity may be masked, it would seem small.

3. *Do women commit special kinds of abuse that go unnoticed and unmeasured?* In discussions of abuse by women, certain activities are mentioned that are not otherwise often considered in discussions of abuse. Justice and Justice (1979), for example, talk about "sleeping with a son, caressing in a sexual way, exposing her body to him, and keeping him tied to her emotionally with implied promises of sexual payoff" as forms of sexual abuse by women that go unrecorded. The giving of frequent enemas is also sometimes mentioned.

It is true that studies of sexual contacts between adults and children have not usually asked about such behaviors. If they have not been asked about, however, part of the reason is that such behaviors are generally judged to be in a different category. In their extreme forms, these activities are types of psychological abuse rather than situations where children are used for the direct physical gratification of an adult's sexual needs. They are different from having intercourse with a child or having the child engage in oral sex.

But more important, it is not at all clear that women engage in more of this psychological abuse than men do. Herman (1981) points out that a large number of fathers have "seductive" relationships with daughters that border on abuse but never actually cross the line. Also men have their own forms of psychological abusiveness: making sexual references to a daughter's breasts or body, or inappropriately exposing children to pornography. Women seem to engage in such behavior far less frequently.

The point about male preponderance is not that women never do harmful things to children's sexuality. It is only that women do not seem to use children for their direct physical sexual gratification as often as men do. If the question of abuse is to be broadened to a wider range of psychological sexual abuses, then the behavior of both men and women, not just women, needs to be submitted to this kind of broader scrutiny.

4. *Are sexual offenses by females less likely to be reported because they are primarily intrafamilial?* Some have speculated that the quantity of abuse by females could be obscured because it is more likely to occur within the family, and intrafamilial sexual abuse itself is less subject to public reporting. However, there is no good evidence to substantiate the idea that abuse by females is preponderantly intrafamilial. In self-report studies by both Finkelhor (1979) and Russell (1983) the ratio of female perpetrators involved in intrafamily abuse was not significantly different from that of extrafamily abuse. Moreover, this speculation would not explain why sexual abuse by females is so rarely evident in the self-report studies.

5. *Is sexual abuse by females obscured because they more often abuse boys who, compared to girls, are more reluctant to report?* Some have speculated that sexual abuse by females does not appear very frequently because it occurs predominantly to boys, and boys are less likely to report. While it does appear to be true from prior research that boys are less likely to report abuse either to parents or to public agencies (Finkelhor, 1979), it is not necessarily true that most abuse by females occurs to boys. In studies done on both reported cases and self-reports, a greater *absolute* number of cases involved females abusing girls, not boys.

Moreover, this explanation would apply only to underreporting of abuse in public records. We do not see a very convincing argument that boys would fail to report sexual experiences with older females in self-report studies. In fact, if anything, since sexual contacts between young boys and older women would seem to be among the least stigmatized of the cross-generational contacts (see Chapter 8), we might expect candor about such experiences in self-report studies to be even higher.

THEORIES FOR LOW RATES OF ABUSE BY WOMEN

The previous review leads fairly persuasively to the conclusion that the traditional view about child molestation as a primarily male deviation is essentially correct. Women do not use children for their own direct sexual gratification very frequently.

In spite of the fact that the traditional view on child molestation has always accepted it as a male deviation, this fact has hardly ever been the subject of theoretical interest. Until feminist theorists entered the field, it was not treated as something that needed to be explained. This perhaps most well-established truth about child molestation was not used for insights it might offer about the source of the problem.

However, the explanation of male preponderance is important to virtually every theory of child molesting. Gender, as a variable, interacts with every other variable proposed by every other theory. Every theory of child molesting needs to explain not just why adults become sexually interested in children, but why that explanation applies primarily to males and not females.

For example, one popular theory invoked to explain child molesting is that a victimized child becomes a victimizer in an attempt to master the trauma and take on the power of the adult perpetrator. One problem with this theory as stated here (for others see Chapter 4) is that many more girls than boys are the victims of sexual abuse. If being the victim of sexual abuse increases the risk of becoming a perpetrator, then there should be more women perpetrators than there are. Obviously it is mainly boy victims of sexual abuse who grow up to be child molesters. But the theory says nothing about this phenomenon. There is no reason implicit in the theory to explain why girls should not master their trauma through an identification with the perpetrator, just as boys do. If this identification occurs, at least it happens in a different way. Perhaps girls do not so readily identify with perpetrators who are usually male. However, the sex of the perpetrator has not been cited as an important contingency when the theory is applied to boys. Sexual victimization by both women and men is mentioned as likely to contribute to a boy's becoming a perpetrator (de Young, 1982).

Some people have pointed out, in reaction to this dilemma, that while girl victims may not often grow up to be perpetrators, they do often seem to grow up to be the mothers of victims. The rates of victimization in the mothers of victims do seem to be very high (Goodwin, McCarthy & DiVasto, 1981). However, while this may be a parallel phenomenon, a different kind of theory needs to explain it. Every theory of child molesting, just like this one, must have a way of accounting for the different operation of its dynamics in males as opposed to females.

Thus the question of why men abuse so much more than women needs to be the subject of theoretical inquiry. We would like to discuss 10 theories: one theory that is probably not useful, and nine others that have some possible truth.

Perhaps the theory that people mention most colloquially to account for low rates of female offenders is one that might be termed the "problem of the limp penis." Many people assume that an erection cannot be forced on a victim and therefore that potential women offenders cannot gain satisfaction from sexual aggression in the way men can. This is thought to discourage abuse by women.

This theory has many problems. Erections can be forced, as accounts of sexually abused boys and homosexual rape clearly show (Groth, 1979). Moreover, much abuse by women occurs, as we have indicated, against female children. But most important, the problem of the limp penis simply does not take into account very significant facts about sexual abuse. First, many sexual abusers trick or bribe children into collaborating with them to some extent, and can thus produce sexual arousal in children. Women can do this as well as, if not better than, men. Second, most sexual abusers get their satisfaction not from intercourse but from either manipulating the child's genitals or having the child manipulate their own. Women could do this too, getting satisfaction from touching the child or having the child manually stimulate them. The child does not need to be aroused. Thus, the "limp penis" is not a valid theory of why women are less likely to abuse sexually.

Several other theories do deserve consideration, however:

1. Women are socialized to prefer partners who are older, larger, and more powerful than themselves. Being in a position of dominance or authority is antagonistic to the role relationship which most women find sexually arousing. Men, on the contrary, are socialized to prefer partners who are younger, smaller, innocent, vulnerable, and powerless. Clearly, children would be more sexually attractive to men than to women.

2. Women do not generally act as initiators in sexual relationships. Since they would rarely be invited by children to engage in sex, such contacts must be thus less likely to arise. Males, on the other hand, are expected not only to take the initiative, but also to overcome resistance and sometimes even to consider resistance as a cover for sexual desire.

3. Men appear to be more promiscuous than women, a fact that has been ascribed by some to biological factors (Symons, 1979). Whatever its source, if women are less inclined to have multiple sexual partners, they may be less likely to sexualize relationships with children.

4. Men seem to be able to be aroused more easily by sexual stimuli divorced from any relationship context—by pornography, for example. Women, on the other hand, may rely more on a totality of cues including the nature of the relationship with the sexual partner. The fact of a partner being a child may interfere more with women's ability to experience sexual arousal.

5. Men appear to sexualize the expression of emotions more than women. Thus women seem better able to distinguish situations of affection and intimacy that do not involve sex (such as family relationships) from those that do. Men are more likely to define all affectional contacts as sexual and thus become aroused by them.

6. Men and women appear to react in different ways to the unavailability of sexual opportunities. Having sexual opportunities seems to be more important to the maintenance of self-esteem in men than in women (Person, 1980). Thus, when other alternatives are blocked, men may more readily turn to children (or other sexual outlets) to maintain their sense of self-esteem.

7. Because of preparation for a role presumed to include maternal responsibilities, women may be more sensitive to the well-being of children, and may be more inhibited from sexual contact by the possibility that such contact would be harmful to the child (Herman, 1981). Another closely related explanation is that because women tend to interact much more with children, including their own children, a kind of bonding occurs between women and children that involves a sense of protectiveness and responsibility toward them that fewer men have the opportunity to develop.

8. Since women are more often victims of sexual exploitation of various kinds, they may be better able to empathize with the potential for harm that may result from such contact and more likely to control their sexual impulses toward children.

9. As we saw in Chapter 8, sexual contact with children may be more condoned by male subculture than female subculture. Rush (1980) has documented how sexual involvement between men and children has been accepted or encouraged throughout Western history. Without equivalent encouragement, women may be less likely to develop sexual interest in children.

CONCLUSION

Our review of both the evidence and the arguments suggests that there appear to be no sound reasons to believe that we have been wrong in presuming the amount of sexual abuse by adult female perpetrators to be small. There is every reason to believe that child sexual abuse is primarily perpetrated by males and that male perpetrators may be responsible for more serious and traumatic levels of sexual abuse than female perpetrators (Russell, 1983). The question then is, Why are so many experts in the field arguing that the number of female perpetrators has been seriously underestimated?

At least two factors account for this wave of speculation about hidden abuse by females. On the one hand, clinicians are seeing (and also noticing) more cases of abuse by females than ever before. The number of such cases may even have jumped dramatically. But, in fact, the number of cases *of all types* of sexual abuse coming to light has increased dramatically. The types of cases coming to attention are therefore more varied. Because very few or no cases of female perpetrators were coming to light in the past, now as they appear in proportion to their actual prevalence, it may seem at first like a dramatic new development. Certainly because they were absent in the past, these cases may be receiving particular notice when seen. This increase or, in some settings, sudden appearance has led to the speculation that we need re-evaluate the traditional wisdom about female perpetrators.

Certainly in the past some people have assumed that sexual abuse at the hands of females *never* occurred. If this is how people have interpreted past research, then it is wrong and does require correction in the direction that some of the current commentators indicate. Sexual abuse by women does occur in some fraction of cases, probably 5% in the case of girls and 20% in the case of boys. But by the same token, to take the appearance of some cases of sexual abuse by women to mean that sexual abuse is not primarily committed by men is also wrong and has no support in any of the data.

In addition to this, however, we see another important reason for the current questioning of the long-held presumption of a male preponderance. We believe that some workers and researchers are ideologically uncomfortable with the idea of a male preponderance and thus have been quick to rush to the possibility that it might not be true. The fact that primarily men commit sexual abuse does have discomforting ideological implications. In a cultural climate where feminists have called upon men to relinquish certain traditional modes of behavior, such facts bolster feminists arguments and thus may create defensiveness in those who oppose feminist claims. For some people the problem of sexual abuse might be an easier cause to promote if it was not entangled in "gender politics." Political support for matters of general "human" concern is easier to mobilize than for matters that appear to benefit some social group more than others, particularly when that group is a lower-status, stigmatized one. But reality cannot be twisted to suit any particular ideological or political need. The solution to the widespread and destructive problem of child sexual abuse can be found only if we face the truth about it—a truth we believe to be well-documented by the evidence and well-fitted to our current understanding of sex roles and male and female sexuality.

TABLE 11-1

Percentage of Women Perpetrators: Case Report Studies

STUDY	% WOMEN OFFENDERS	TOTAL OFFENDERS N
Male Children		
National Incidence Study	24[a]	91
American Humane Assn.	14	757
Griffith et al.	6	245
DeJong et al.	4	103
Ellerstein and Canavan	0	16
Female Children		
National Incidence Study	13[b]	664
American Humane Assn.	6	5052
Male and Female Children		
Queen's Bench	4	123
DeFrancis	3	250
Jaffe, Dynneson & Ten Bensel	0	291

SOURCES:

National Incidence Study (1981)
Cases known to professionals in 26 counties (chosen to represent U.S.) and reported anonymously to study in year starting April 1979.

American Humane Association (1979)
Cases reported to mandated reporting agency in 31 states for 1978.

Griffith et al. (1981)
Cases coming to attention of hospital-based sexual assault unit.

Ellerstein and Canavan (1980)
Cases coming to attention of hospital-based sexual assault unit.

DeJong, Hervada, and Emmett (1983)
Cases coming to attention of hospital-based sexual assault unit.

Queen's Bench (1976)
Cases coming to attention of San Francisco Police Department July 1, 1975 to June 30, 1976.

DeFrancis (1969)
Cases coming to attention of Society for Protection Against Cruelty to Children.

Jaffe, Dynneson & Ten Bensel (1975)
Cases coming to attention of hospital-based sexual assault unit.

[a] Including 10 female-only and 12 female and male perpetrator cases.
[b] Including 27 female-only and 60 female and male perpetrator cases.

TABLE 11-2
Percentage of Women Perpetrators: Self-Report Studies

Study	% Women Offenders	Total Offenders N
Male Children		
Bell & Weinberg		
Heterosexual sample	27	20
Homosexual sample	14	11
Finkelhor		
Student sample	16	84
Boston sample	15	23
Fritz, Stoll & Wagner	60	20
Gebhard, Gagnon, Pomeroy		
& Christenson	27	22
Female Children		
Bell & Weinberg		
Heterosexual sample	7	15
Homosexual sample	22	62
Finkelhor		
Student sample	6	119
Boston sample	0	65
Fritz, Stoll & Wagner	10	42
Fromuth	5	139
Russell	4	651

SOURCES:

Bell & Weinberg (1981), Heterosexual
Random sample of 336 male and 150 female San Francisco residents.

Bell & Weinberg (1981), Homosexual
Volunteer sample of 684 male and 292 female San Francisco homosexuals.

Finkelhor (1979), Student
796 students in social science courses in 7 New England colleges.

Finkelhor (1981), Boston
Random sample of 187 male and 334 female residents of Boston.

Fritz, Stoll & Wagner (1981)
412 male and 540 female psychology students.

Fromuth (1983)
482 female psychology students.

Gebhard, Gagnon, Pomeroy & Christenson (1965)
Volunteer sample of 477 men (data on experiences with female perpetrators available in only 269 cases)

Russell (1983)
Random sample of 930 San Francisco females.

CHAPTER 12

Long-Term Effects of Childhood Sexual Abuse

Some New Data

THE DEBATE OVER the effects of childhood sexual victimization spans almost a century. It was a question of some lengthy consideration for Freud and has been taken up again in several of the landmark studies of sexuality since then (Hamilton, 1929; Kinsey et al., 1953; Terman, 1938).

If the debate has heated up in recent years, it is because the issue neatly embodies much of the contemporary public policy dilemma concerning sexuality and childhood. On one hand, there is a body of opinion that sees childhood as a relatively treacherous time in the development of sexuality. During this period, children need protection from the common sexual traumas that our civilization inflicts on them, one of the most common of these being sexual victimization by adults.

This viewpoint has been reinforced in recent years by the women's movement, which has sought to highlight the high frequency of sexual victimization. Feminists have been instrumental in drawing attention to the unrecognized suffering of victims of both rape and child sexual abuse, traumas that have often been exacerbated by the social stigmas attached to such victims and the social taboos around discussing such experiences. Their conclusion is clearly that the extent of victimization and the trauma produced by such victimization have been insufficiently recognized in the past (Armstrong, 1978; Butler, 1978; Herman & Hirschman, 1977).

On the other hand, another point of view has urged the public and professionals to give up alarmist concerns about child sexual development (Farson, 1974; Menninger, 1942; Pomeroy, 1968, 1974). Quoting Storr (1965, p. 91), "there is no doubt that, in the past, far too much emphasis has been placed upon childhood seduction as the cause of subsequent neurosis." Although they do not discount the idea that children can be harmed by early exploitation, they are critical of what they see as an exclusive preoccupation with harm in discussions of child sexuality. They appear to fear that if child sexuality is viewed as so fragile and subject to ruin, the positive element of child sexuality will become neglected (Currier, 1977). In particular, these writers have argued, probably more restrainedly than they would if they did not feel in the minority, that children's sexuality needs to be encouraged and developed (Constantine & Martinson, 1982; Yates, 1978). Some of these writers have tended to minimize the dangers of sexual victimization (Pomeroy, 1978).

Those who wish to stress the seriousness of child sexual abuse have plenty of clinical evidence to which to turn. There have been many reports—for example, those reviewed and supplemented by De Young (1982), Herman (1981), and Meiselman (1978)—of adults with substantial psychological problems, which seem very plausibly connected to a history of child sexual abuse (Courtois & Watts, 1982). Studies of various troubled populations such as drug abusers (Benward & Densen-Gerber, 1975), juvenile offenders (Jones, Gruber & Timbers, 1981; Youth Policy and Law Center, 1982), adolescent runaways (Nakashima, 1982; Weber, 1977), prostitutes (James & Meyerding, 1977; Janus, Seanlon & Price, 1984; Silbert & Pines, 1981), and adults with sexual dysfunctions (McGuire & Wagner, 1978) show that high proportions of these troubled individuals were sexually victimized as children. The case seems easily made that some fraction of those who are sexually victimized in childhood are affected quite badly by these experiences.

On the other hand, there has been plenty of room for critics to argue that conclusions from clinical samples such as these could be misleading. In spite of the number of victims judged by clinicians to have been badly affected by childhood victimization, it is possible these may be skewed samples and not representative of the vast majority of children who have sexual contact with adults. It is also possible that the long-term effects seen in these cases are a function not of the sexual abuse but of other pathological elements, such as psychological abuse, parental neglect, or family disorganization. Critics are correct to point out that studies of nonclinical cases are needed, hopefully studies that allow a comparison between victimized and nonvictimized children controlling for various background factors to be able to assess whether and where there exist any long-term effects of sexual abuse.

Some retrospective evaluations of the long-term effects of sexual abuse have been attempted with fairly large nonclinical populations, but the implication of these studies is widely contested. Gagnon (1965), for example, looked at the Kinsey data on 333 women who had been childhood victims of sex offenses, most of which had never been reported. He found that about 75% of women had "no apparent adult maladjustment." Nine to 12% had minor complaints "which incapacitated them from playing an adequate social and occupational role in the community." Another 4% to 7% showed "major psychological or other disturbance."

Although Gagnon concluded that this was a "small amount of negative outcome," many would challenge his conclusion based on these data. First, Gagnon appears to have begun his investigation with the expectation that there would be nearly universal effects, so that a finding of only 25% with impairment, which might otherwise seem to be significant fraction, could be dismissed as a "small amount." It is not clear that 25% is either small or large. Second, Gagnon appeared to be evaluating only the grossest and most readily apparent forms of adult "maladjustment" (his criteria are described only vaguely). Effects that might cause suffering and unhappiness but which did not "interfere with social role performance or cause major psychological disturbance" were not counted as impairment. This seems an important insensitivity in his outcome measure. Most important, Gagnon's study lacked a control group, so one does not really know how the victimized women fared with respect to their nonvictimized peers.

In Landis's (1956) retrospective study of college students, there was the possibility of comparisons with a control group of nonvictimized students, but he did not use it to much advantage. His estimate of the long-term effects of sexual victimization were based largely on uncontrolled victim self-evaluations. Of the men, "19% thought temporary damage had resulted and 81% said no damage had resulted. Of the women, 3% felt permanent damage had resulted, 30% temporary and 66% no damage." Little effort was made to compare victim or nonvictim groups on any outcome measure. In one departure from this pattern, Landis did find that more of the victimized than nonvictimized women had had orgasms, and from this he concluded that "the present data suggest that in most cases sex deviate experiences do not do permanent damage to sex responses." However, this finding is irremediably confounded by the fact that many more of the nonvictims were still virgins, and the orgasm the victims were referring to may well have occurred in the sexual abuse they had experienced. Moreover, since sexual promiscuity has been hypothesized as one possible response to early childhood victimization, it would hardly seem that the experience or capacity for orgasm can be treated as a complete measure of whether sexual abuse has long-term effects on sexuality. (In this regard, one could also fault Terman's 1951 study.)

Tsai, Feldman-Summers, and Edgar (1979) conducted what has been the most sophisticated study to date of the long-term effects of child sexual victimization, using both a control group of nonvictims and more sensitive measures of psychosexual functioning, including the MMPI. In that study, the victim group as a whole did not differ from the nonvictim group on any of the outcome measures, orgasmic capability, number of sexual partners, sexual responsiveness, satisfaction with sexual relations, MMPI scores, or overall self-rated adjustment. However, the half of the victim group that was interested in therapy did differ quite significantly from the controls (and from the non-therapy seekers) on these same measures.

Tsai, Feldman-Summers, and Edgar's research suffers unfortunately from certain design problems. The victim subjects were recruited by regional "television, radio, and newspaper announcements" while the control sample was recruited in a very different way by the circulation (presumably among friends and colleagues) of a "wanted list" of women with designated characteristics matching the victims'. The ads for victims "emphasized that the project was not restricted to women who wanted therapy but was open to women who considered themselves well-adjusted and not in need of therapy."

What cannot be determined about this study is, How representative *was* the sample of childhood sexual abuse victims? It seems possible that the ad, which emphasized both an offer of therapy for some and a call to others who considered themselves well-adjusted, would recruit from two extreme ends of the spectrum. Setting a quota of 30 for the non-therapy seekers as well as the therapy seekers may have further distorted the representativeness of this group. We really have little way of knowing how the group of respondents would compare to a less self-selected group of sexual abuse victims in the population as a whole.

PRESENT RESEARCH

Using some of my own data from the college student study of child sexual victimization (Finkelhor, 1979), it is possible to take still another look at the question of long-term effects. In one particularly important way my data constitute an improvement over other studies such as Gagnon's and Tsai, Feldman-Summers, and Edgar's. This study could compare 121 victims to 685 nonvictims within the same population. Moreover, while the college students questioned were not necessarily representative of the population at large, nonetheless, whole classes filled out the questionnaire and the participation rate was 92%; it was not a highly self-selected population of either victims or controls.

Also there were opportunities to exert other controls not present in previous attempts to estimate the effect of sexual abuse. Enough background information on the students in the sample was gathered to statistically control for

a wealth of background variables, making sure that any difference between victims and nonvictims was not spurious.

EFFECTS OF SEXUAL SELF-ESTEEM

It has been noted in clinical studies of sexual abuse victims that the experience
often seems to have a particular effect in sexual feelings and sexual behavior
(Herman, 1981; Herman & Hirschman, 1977; Meiselman, 1978). Victims
report feeling sexually stigmatized. They report being confused about sexual
and nonsexual encounters. Some report experiences of compulsive sexual activity or else wanting to avoid all sexual activity.

To tap the possible effects of sexual abuse on sexual feelings and behavior, a
measure called "sexual self-esteem" was developed. This scale is composed of
six items intended to capture attitudes toward current sexual feelings and activity among a group of young people. The items included:

a. I find I spend too much time thinking about sex.
b. I often find myself in awkward sexual situations.
c. I really like my body.
d. If I'm sexually interested in someone, I usually take the initiative to do
   something about it.
e. After sexual experiences, I often feel dissatisfied.
f. Someone my age should be having more sex than I am.

Agreement or disagreement was indicated on a 4-point Likert scale. The directions of items *c* and *d* were reversed for scoring.[1]

This sexual self-esteem scale is the most comprehensive outcome measure in
the study, since it captures a broad evaluation of a person's current level of sexual satisfaction and sexual adjustment. Therefore, it was of no little importance
to find that: students who had been sexually victimized as children, both
women *and* men, had lower levels of sexual self-esteem than other people in the
sample. Results can be seen in Table 12–1.

Victimized women were six points lower and men 11 points lower than
nonvictims, both results being statistically significant. The victimized women
were especially likely to report that they often got into awkward sexual situations. The victimized men revealed especially high feelings of dissatisfaction
after current sexual experiences.

However, the relationship could have been a spurious one. Suppose all
lower-class respondents had lower self-esteem, and lower-class respondents
were also more likely to have been sexually victimized, as *has been* indicated in
previous research (Finkelhor, 1979). In that case there might be a statistical rela-

tionship between being victimized and a low score on sexual self-esteem, but no causal one.

To test such possibilities, we ran a regression analysis including all the background factors measured in the study that might possibly be related to both sexual self-esteem and sexual victimization. These included class, ethnic background, family size, family values, parents' attitudes, education, and so on.

Sexual victimization made a contribution to explaining sexual self-esteem, independent of family income, emotional deprivation, or family sexual practices and all other variables controlled for. This result held in the case of both boys and girls.

The results of this regression certainly reinforce the likelihood that the reduction in self-esteem shown among victims of childhood sexual abuse is a result of the experience itself and its aftermath.

Forced Sex

There is repeated suggestion in the literature that women who are victims of childhood sexual abuse become victims later in life as well. Several investigators have found unusually large incidences of childhood sexual victimization in the histories of rape victims (Miller et al., 1978), including marital rape victims (Finkelhor and Yllo, forthcoming; Frieze, 1980; Russell, 1982a) and also in the histories of women who become victims of wife abuse (Doron, 1981; Russell, 1982a; Thyfault, 1980).

The current study has only weak evidence in support of this assertion. Women who were sexually victimized before the age of 13 were more likely to be the victims of another forced sex experience[2] after the age of 13 (32% of the child victims compared to 22% of the rest of the sample). The difference is statistically weak (p = .07), however, as indicated by the results of the t-test comparing the two proportions, and should be taken with some caution.

Moreover, unlike the case with self-esteem, the results did not stand up when other variables were entered as controls. For example, any relationship between childhood victimization and later victimization disappears when controlled for sexually punitive mothers. Having a mother who frequently punished sexual curiosity or masturbation, for instance, makes a woman vulnerable to both early and later sexual victimization. It cannot be said, on the basis of this study at least, that the early victimization experience plays a part in causing the later one.

Even though the finding here is a negative one, the increasing number of reports that point to some connection between childhood and adulthood victimization should not be dismissed. The women in the student study were very young. The association might have appeared more strongly with an older group.

Even if researchers ultimately establish such associations, they need to be careful. They need to be very alert to the possibility that women who report one form of victimization, particularly sexual victimization, may also report another: The statistical associations between child sexual abuse and later sexual victimization may result from candid respondents willing to talk about both. Thus it is a finding which needs careful scrutiny before being fully accepted.

If, after such careful scrutiny, the connection between childhood and later victimization is firmly established, a number of factors could be at work.

1. There is evidence that childhood sexual victimization may force children out of their families at an earlier age, as they seek to escape the abuse or the blame associated with it. Some marry early, probably men who have little else to recommend them than the fact that they are willing. Being young and unable to return to their families, these women are in extremely dependent positions and vulnerable to physical and sexual abuse. Those that do not marry immediately but run away from home, may also find themselves living a dire existence that makes them more vulnerable to rape.

2. Childhood sexual abuse may have a corrosive effect on self-esteem. Women who feel bad about themselves may be conspicuous "targets" for sexually exploitative men. They may also lack assertiveness to short-circuit at an early stage encounters where they sense some risk.

So the sexual abuse–adult rape connection has some plausibility. A careful untangling of this relationship should be an important research priority.

HOMOSEXUAL ACTIVITY

Part of the traditional mythology about child molestation is that when it happens to boys, it leads to homosexuality. Parents, whose sons have been victimized, often ask professionals about this notion before anything else. There are clinical reports that also note connections between child molestation and later homosexuality (Brunold, 1964; Finch, 1967).

Some clinical research has concluded that childhood sexual victimization can result in homosexuality among women, too (Finch, 1967; Gundlach, 1977). The explanation suggested is that a woman who has a traumatic childhood sexual encounter with a man will conclude that men are undesirable sexual partners and opt to conduct her relationships with other women.

When we looked at this question in our student study, we indeed found evidence that there may be a connection between childhood victimization and adult homosexual activity for boys at least. We could find no such relationship for girls. Boys victimized by older men were over *four times* more likely to be currently engaged in homosexual activity than were nonvictims (Table 12–2). Close to half the male respondents who had had a childhood sexual experience with an older man were currently involved in homosexual activity.[3]

It is important to note that this relationship did not hold for respondents who had had peer homosexual experiences as children. Those who had peer homosexual experiences were somewhat more likely to be currently engaged in homosexual sex, but the difference was not statistically significant. It was only for those with sexual experiences with much older partners that there appeared to be some carry-over effect into adulthood.

The results of a regression analysis run on the relationship reinforce this conclusion. Once again, no other variable in the study could "explain" or eliminate the relationship between sexual victimization and current homosexual activity for boys. In fact, controlling for other variables, sexual victimization appeared to be the most powerful predictive variable in the regression equation. Peer homosexual experience had no significant contribution.

Why might a childhood sexual experience with an older man be associated with later homosexual activity? Current literature on adult homosexual behavior suggests that in many cases it has roots in early childhood or maybe even in a genetic inheritance (Bell and Weinberg, 1981). Many men who currently identify themselves as homosexuals report being aware of that sexual interest from an early age. Related to these findings, it may be that men whose homosexual interest reached far back into childhood may have made themselves vulnerable or accessible to older men. They may have developed an infatuation for an older man which he capitalized on. They may have had an intense sexual curiosity directed toward men which made them vulnerable or open to sexual suggestions by older men.

The problem with this reasoning is that it does not explain well why peer homosexual experiences also are not predictive of later homosexual behavior. Shouldn't a childhood interest in homosexuality lead to experiences with peers as well as with older partners?

Another explanation involves stigma. Childhood victimization experiences may be stigmatizing for the children to whom they occur. It may be common for a boy who has been involved in an experience with an older man to label himself a homosexual (1) because he has had a homosexual experience and (2) because he was found to be sexually attractive by a man. Once he labels himself homosexual, the boy may begin to behave consistently with the role and gravitate toward homosexual activity.

Several factors could explain why the labeling impact of an experience with an adult would be greater than with a peer. (1) The adult is sexually mature and represents some social authority in the eyes of the child. Thus a homosexual experience with an adult may confer a more irrefutable "homosexual" label on the child (than a peer experience). The child may receive a stronger confirmation of his homosexual attractiveness. (2) The experience with the adult is likely to be more emotionally upsetting and may therefore become the basis of an unresolved preoccupation.

Although these explanations have some plausibility, great caution should be used in adopting either of them. For one thing, the number of victimized men in this sample was small, and although the results are quite significant statistically, changes in the reports of only a few respondents could alter findings. For another thing, it must be emphasized that these data show a "correlation" between sexual victimization and later homosexuality, but this is by no means saying that the former *causes* the latter.

Third and most broadly, much theorizing has taken place about the "causes" of homosexuality that has harmed homosexuals and their public image. A great many assumptions have been made about something called homosexuality or some people called homosexuals, when in fact we are only beginning to understand enough about homosexual activity to make such definitions. Also, it has been assumed that social science could explain "homosexual" behavior, when no theory yet exists explaining heterosexual behavior. In such a vacuum, explanations of "homosexuality" only stigmatize it as a deviant developmental pattern which it may not be.

Another thing that should be clarified is even if childhood victimization sometimes leads to later homosexual behavior, this victimization cannot be seen as a simple matter of homosexual men "recruiting" young boys. Although the data are sparse, the evidence suggests that a great number of the men who victimize young boys are not self-identified homosexuals (Newton, 1978). On the one hand, many abusers of boys appear to be married and have lengthy heterosexual histories (Gebhard et al., 1965). Others are exclusive pedophiles, who have no interest in adult males at all and do not consider themselves to be gay (and in fact often bridle at such a label) (Groth & Birnbaum, 1978). In short, these kinds of findings cannot and should not be used to increase our culture's already intense fear of homosexuals.

SOME IMPLICATIONS

That some children have long-term reactions to childhood sexual victimization has never really been in dispute. Clinical experience is rich in this regard. The contribution of the current research is to show, however, that as a group those who have been victimized have demonstrable long-term deficits compared to those who have never been victimized. Unfortunately, it is not possible to say on the basis of this study just what these deficits are. The main variable of interest, "sexual self-esteem," is a limited, somewhat vague construct and does not touch on many areas of possible adult adjustment. But the impression of impairment is inescapable, and this research is one of the first to marshall statistical evidence that the culprit is something to do with experience itself, not a common background factor.

Some observers have concluded that the true trauma of sexual victimization results not so much from the experience itself as from the alarmed reaction that such victimization elicits from a child's family, friends, and the community. The study was also not well-equipped to answer this question by distinguishing among the various possible long-term traumatizing aspects of the experience. Supporting this claim, there is some weak evidence from the study that those who told their parents about the experience may have fared worse than those who did not. But, true or not, the more general issue is that it should not be assumed that a victimized child is destined for difficulty. It may be that by providing a calm and supportive reaction to victimization, the risks of long-term effects on the child can be completely dissipated.

The finding of the contribution of childhood sexual victimization to later homosexual activity in boys is reported here with some trepidation. It is possible that such evidence may contribute to the very intense reactions by parents and community that are conducive to exacerbating trauma. It is also possible that such results could fuel the phobia about homosexuality which plagues many parents and professionals.

It needs to be made clear that even if sex abuse does contribute to later homosexuality, this process would explain only a small fraction of adult homosexuality. In the recent Bell and Weinberg (1981) study, only 5% of the homosexual men reported childhood sexual experiences with adults. Such a small figure means that childhood sexual victimization can have little to do with the source of most homosexual behavior.

Moreover, even in cases where victimization might be causally related to homosexuality, it could not necessarily be argued that the homosexuality was a *traumatic* outcome of the victimization. In some cases the victimization may affect sexual orientation and also be traumatizing, in other cases it may not. Independent measures of other kinds of functioning need to be made to judge harm. All the effects of an unpleasant experience (for example, death of a parent) cannot be presumed to be negative.

In practical terms, what would be suggested by this connection, if borne out elsewhere, is not that parents or professionals try to thwart a boy who shows an interest in homosexual sex. Rather, they should make sure that the boy is not under any misconceptions that he "must be a homosexual" as a result of his experience.

ADULT ETHNOCENTRISM

To some extent, however, the whole debate over the effects of child sexual victimization is misplaced. In the study of this childhood experience, as in the study of many others, researchers and theoreticians persistently focus on the question of long-term effects. Did the experience result in psychopathology, in marital instability, in sexual dysfunction, or in homosexuality. On this score, the issue of sexual victimization has been treated no differently from such issues as the effects on children of divorce, school failure, or racial integration. The bottom line is always how does this event affect adult adjustment, adult feelings, adult capacities, and adult attitudes.

This preoccupation is a kind of ethnocentrism on the part of adults. The impact of an event on childhood itself is treated as less important. It is only "childhood," a stage which, after all, everyone outgrows.

Note, however, that this attitude is not taken toward traumatic events in adulthood. Does the seriousness of rape depend on whether it has a disruptive effect on old age? No. In fact, rape is treated as a serious life event whether or not it causes long-term effects. Research demonstrating that the negative effects of rape attenuate after a year or two (Burgess & Holstrom, 1979; Feldman-Summers, Gordon & Meagher, 1979; Kilpatrick, Veronen & Resnick, 1979) is greeted with relief by everybody, rape activists included. Few people would try to conclude from such research that rape is really a less traumatic experience than was previously thought.

Comparable research on the subject of child sexual abuse, however, would stir a storm of controversy. It would immediately be cited as evidence that the anxiety over childhood sexual victims had been exaggerated. In short, different standards are used to evaluate the seriousness of life events occurring to children.

Rape is traumatic because adults consider it so. Adults can speak eloquently about their experience and communicate its pain. Child sexual abuse should be similarly viewed (Ruch and Chandler, 1982), especially because children cannot speak for themselves. It is a noxious event of childhood, serious for its immediate unpleasantness, if nothing else, not necessarily for its long-term effects.

TABLE 12–1

Sexual Self-Esteem of Abuse Victims and Nonvictims

Sex	Sexual Self-Esteem Score for Victims	(N)	Sexual Self-Esteem Score for Nonvictims	(N)
Boys	40.9**	(17)	52.4	(243)
Girls	45.7*	(104)	51.6	(432)

*p< .01
**p< .05

TABLE 12–2

Homosexual Activity for Boys Who Engaged in Different Kinds
of Childhood Homosexual Experiences

Kind of Childhood Homosexual Experience	% Engaging in Homosexual Activity in Last Year	(N)
None	11	(174)
With peer	20	(30)
With much older partner	45*	(11)

*p < .01

CHAPTER 13

Professionals' Responses

COAUTHORED WITH
Beverly Gomes-Schwartz
Jonathan Horowitz

T HE MANAGEMENT AND treatment of cases of child sexual abuse have posed a serious challenge to communities across the country. A number of factors have coalesced to make sexual abuse more complicated and vexing than many other family and human service problems with which professionals have had to cope.

1. The problem has emerged in the human service realm rather suddenly. Prior to 1975 such cases were relatively rare in the files of community professionals. Then, suddenly, between 1976 and 1979 official reports of sexual abuse more than tripled (American Humane Association, 1981). In some communities the rise was even more precipitate. Communities have had a hard time developing expertise, experience, and procedures for handling a so quickly emerging problem.

2. The scope of the problem has grown rapidly, and the demand for services has tended to outstrip quickly the available community resources and agency capacities. Communities have found, for example, that as they develop people and agencies with specialized capabilities in the area of sexual abuse, these resources are quickly swamped.

3. Sexual abuse provokes strong emotional reactions in the public and professionals, so it tends to be either denied or treated as an emergency (Summit, 1981a). When workers want to take quick action, they often do not want to wait for consultations and evaluations and the normal pace of bureaucratic operation. They often act before they fully know what needs to be done. Such rush actions or the denials that are the

other side of the problem often have complicated cases for other agencies and other workers.

4. Sexual abuse falls into competing professional and institutional domains. On one hand, it is a serious child welfare problem—one of the types of child abuse which is mandated for reporting to state child protective agencies. On the other hand, it is a serious crime—eliciting community outrage and action by police and district attorneys. It is also a mental health and, in some cases, even a medical problem. Professionals in all these domains feel they have some responsibility to handle sexual abuse. Yet in most communities, no formalized division of roles exists. In fact, many of these agencies and professionals have little experience cooperating with each other and often a great deal of distrust.

Complicating matters, these competing professions do not necessarily view the problem of sexual abuse in the same light. A variety of philosophies about the nature and handling the problem of sexual abuse have developed (MacFarlane & Bulkley, 1982). For example, those who see sexual abuse primarily as a crime see punishment as the main objective. Those who see it as mental illness usually regard psychotherapy for the offender as the proper approach. Those who see it as a form of family dysfunction look to family-systems interventions as the approach of choice. Very often professionals from different domains (and sometimes even the same domain) have different prescriptions for action.

The result of these strains is that sexual abuse cases are not always well handled. Anecdotal reports from around the country suggest that many professionals are frustrated and concerned (Blose, 1979). They cite a lack of uniformity in handling cases, conflict among agencies, and cases being handled ineptly by people without experience (Berliner & Stevens, 1982; MacFarlane & Bulkley, 1982).

However, little systematic evidence has been collected on how professionals and agencies are responding to the problem. How knowledgeable are they about it? Are they using the resources that are available? How deep are the differences in philosophy among various agencies? Are some agencies and professionals more conspicuously successful than others? We decided to take advantage of an opportunity to contact a large number of professionals in the Boston area as a vehicle for gathering systematic information on some of these questions.

A SURVEY OF PROFESSIONALS

Questionnaires were distributed to 790 professionals who worked in the Boston metropolitan area. These were professionals who were attending meetings and teaching conferences designed to provide information to the community about child sexual abuse and about the community resources available to deal with it. They completed the questionnaires prior to the meetings, which were held in a variety of settings from September 1980 to May 1981.

Such a procedure for recruiting respondents had a number of drawbacks. It did not produce a sample of professionals that was systematically representative of professionals in the Boston area. Moreover, we had no way of knowing in what ways it might have been unrepresentative. Since it consisted of people who were motivated to attend meetings about the subject of sexual abuse, it probably overrepresented those who were more knowledgeable about, more sensitized to, and had more experience with the problem.

On the other hand, these recruitment procedures had some advantages. We were able to collect a fairly large and diverse sample of professionals quickly and inexpensively. With a virtually captive audience at meetings, the survey drew a high participation rate from the people who were approached. Finally, since we were interested in the handling of cases, the fact that this group of professionals may have had prior experience with sexual abuse was, in one way, an advantage rather than a drawback.

Turning to the composition of the sample, the group was predominantly female (80%) and white (93%). The median age of the sample was 31.8 years and the median professional experience was 5.5 years. Respondents came from a variety of professions including social work, psychology, medicine, law, education, nursing, and law enforcement. However, for purposes of this study we categorized respondents according to the type of agency in which they worked rather than their professional affiliation. Analyses by both agency and profession showed agency to be a more powerful predictor of behavior and attitudes.

Respondents were distributed within six basic types of agencies. The *mental health* clinics from which 14% of respondents came were located throughout several urban and suburban communities. Staff were predominantly social workers or psychologists and psychiatrists. Nine percent of respondents were from *medical* agencies including freestanding community health centers and hospital units (e.g., pediatrics, emergency room). Respondents from medical agencies were primarily nurses with a smaller group of physicians and a sizable group of mental health professionals (social workers, psychologists, and psychiatrists).

Staff from the Department of Social Services (*DSS*) composed 25% of the sample and overwhelmingly identified themselves as social workers. The 9% of respondents from *criminal justice* agencies included police, district attorneys' staff, and court-related personnel such as probation officers and victim-witness assistants. Professionally, these respondents were about equally divided among police (most serving special assignments related to sex crimes), lawyers, and mental health professionals. It is noteworthy that the criminal justice sample included more younger people (67% under 30), more women (62%), and more individuals who could be expected to be knowledgeable about mental health than a typical group of criminal justice professionals. Nonetheless, fewer of the criminal justice respondents (48%) regularly worked with children under 14 than did the professionals from other agencies (85%).

Thirty percent of the sample were *school* professionals including teachers, school nurses (21%), and counseling staff (32%) from elementary and high schools throughout the area. The school respondents tended to be older (33% over 40) than the other groups. Ten percent of the respondents we called *"Other Social Service"* because they came from private agencies and state agencies other than DSS involved in child protection and/or public welfare. This group included a large number of social workers, some psychiatrists and psychologists, and other mental health workers, such as rehabilitation therapists and child advocates.

Exposure to Problem

Sexual abuse was not a problem foreign to the professionals who completed our questionnaire. Most had seen cases of sexual abuse in their career. In fact, most had seen a case in the previous year.

Workers from different agencies, however, had had differing amounts of experience, as is illustrated in Table 13-1. DSS workers tended to have had the greatest amount of experience with both victims and offenders. School personnel tended to have had the least. The pattern held whether we were asking about their whole career or just cases in the last year. Criminal justice workers had seen a greater proportion of offenders to victims than did other workers, but almost everyone saw more victims than offenders. Sexual abuse has obviously been appearing at the doorstep of a wide variety of agencies, and no particular agency or professional group has been left out.

Agencies also showed characteristic patterns in the kinds of sexual abuse cases they were most likely to see. For example, note in Table 13-2 that the criminal justice personnel are distinguished by the large percentage of their cases (55%) in which the abuse was committed by a non-family member. In contrast, cases seen by DSS, mental health, and other social service workers tended to be predominantly parent–child incest.

This pattern has been noted elsewhere (Finkelhor, 1983). When abuse occurs at the hands of someone outside the family, such as a stranger or a neighbor, families and agencies give priority to catching the offenders, punishing them, and referring cases to criminal justice agencies. When abuse occurs at the hands of a parent, however, those involved often wish to avoid the prosecution of the offender. In these cases, there is much more concern about the well-being of the child, so that child protective, mental health, and social service agencies are called into play.

Agencies also tended to differ in terms of whether the cases they saw were of recently occurring abuse (see Table 13–3). Although in most cases workers had seen, the abuse had occurred fairly recently, in 29% of the cases, workers were hearing about abuse that had happened over a year before (sometimes over 5 years before) the referral took place. These delayed cases most often were seen by mental health workers. Undoubtedly a large proportion of these cases were adolescent and adult psychotherapy clients who confided in therapists that they had been sexual abuse victims when younger. By contrast, the cases coming to the attention of criminal justice workers were most likely to be active emergencies. In 93% of the criminal justice cases the abuse had occurred within the last year, and in 55% of the cases, it had occurred within the last month. These criminal justice cases probably included encounters with exhibitionists and rapists, the kinds of cases which tend to get relayed to police fairly quickly.

Our main interest was how agencies managed cases of sexual abuse and how they collaborated or tried to collaborate with one another. We gathered data in two ways. First, we asked workers specific questions about the most recent case of sexual abuse they had handled. How had it been referred to them and who had they drawn upon for help? Second, we gave workers a hypothetical case of sexual abuse, and we asked them what kinds of interventions they would recommend in managing such a case. The first question tapped actual practices, the second, workers' beliefs and intentions.

MANDATED REPORTING

A first question for the study concerned the degree to which agencies appeared to be complying with child abuse reporting statutes. All states, including Massachusetts, have such laws, which require professionals to report known and even suspected cases of child abuse to mandated authorities. Ever since these laws have been passed they have been controversial. Many professionals feel they compromise their confidential relationships with clients. Many others are distrustful of what the mandated reporting authorities do once they receive a report. As a result, many professionals do not comply with the law. In a recent study sponsored by the National Center for Child Abuse and Neglect, it was found that in 1979 only about one third of the cases of child abuse and neglect known to community professionals were officially reported to child protective service (NCCAN, 1981). For sexual abuse cases alone, the estimate of the reporting rate was 56% of those known to professionals. A study of family physicians in Washington State had similarly discouraging findings: 44% of the discovered cases were not reported to the official reporting agency (James, Womack & Strauss, 1978). Clearly many professionals do not comply with the reporting laws.

Table 13–4 gives findings on how agencies in the Boston area handle their official reporting obligations. Each worker in our sample indicated whether he or she had reported his or her last case to DSS (the mandated authority in Massachusetts). Only a minority of workers had (86 of 327 cases). However, there were at least two very legitimate reasons why a worker might not have reported his or her last case: someone else already reported the case, or the victim in the case was no longer a child. After subtracting all of those cases from consideration, in column 6 in Table 13–4 we show what percentage of the cases that *should have been* reported actually were reported.

Boston professionals we surveyed had a reasonable record of reporting child abuse, at least if some of the previously mentioned studies are used in comparison. They actually did report over 64% of the cases they should have reported.[1] However, a report was not made when it should have been in 36% of the cases. This finding shows that compliance with the mandatory reporting statutes is far from complete.

What is interesting to note is which agencies had the best and the worst records of compliance (Table 13–4). Two groups that stood out for their low levels of compliance were criminal justice agency personnel and mental health professionals. We can only speculate on why these two groups stood out. In the case of mental health workers, we suspect that the high nonreporting rate reflects the contradiction they feel that reporting poses to the promise of confidentiality which they offer to clients. In the case of criminal justice, it reflects a belief that they have all the legal and bureaucratic tools necessary to protect the child and punish the offender. Both types of workers may be distrustful of the child abuse investigation, doubtful of its effectiveness, and wary of the interference that it may provoke in their own plans. In any case, the statistics show that there are still major problems in gaining compliance with child abuse reporting laws at least in the area of sexual abuse.

PATTERNS OF COLLABORATION

A second issue in the analysis of actual practices was how agencies collaborated with one another around cases of sexual abuse. We found a marked tendency for agencies to operate on cases in an isolated way within their own restricted professional network.

For example, we asked respondents to indicate from what source their most

recent cases had been referred. While all agencies received a substantial proportion of referrals from victims and offenders themselves or their families, when a
case came from some other agency, there was a distinct insularity in the pattern
of referral. That is, agencies received a large number of their referrals from
other agencies of the same type. The insularity was most pronounced in the
case of criminal justice agencies, which received 49% of their cases from other
criminal justice sources compared to only 6% from non-criminal justice
sources. The insularity is apparent among the schools and medical agencies too,
who also receive a disproportionately large number of cases from agencies and
personnel within their own professional spheres. Only mental health, DSS, and
other social service agencies showed a more heterogeneous pattern in the
sources of their cases.

The relative insularity of agency operation around sexual abuse was confirmed when we asked workers what resources they had consulted in the handling of their most recent cases (Table 13-5). Criminal justice personnel stood
out from other agencies for their high use of other criminal justice resources.
DSS staff were most likely to call upon "mental health" resources, while other
social service staff were the most frequent users of "psychiatrists."

One of the most important findings from Table 13-5 is the low level of interagency cooperation. In many cases respondents consulted no one else about
the case, including DSS, the mandated reporting agency. Close to half the
school and other social service staff and 40% of the mental health staff sought
no outside assistance.

Although differences in the cooperation patterns of different types of agencies are striking, the data on the handling of actual cases have an important
limitation. Agencies were not dealing with precisely the same kinds of cases.
We know, for example, that mental health agencies dealt with an unusually
large number of adults reporting childhood abuse experiences from the distant
past. We also know that police dealt with a large number of cases of abuse at the
hands of strangers and non-family members. The type of case often dictates a
referral pattern. A case in which childhood abuse occurred in the distant past
would not warrant a criminal justice investigation. A case of a child who encountered a stranger exhibitionist might be less likely than a case of father–child
incest to need a mental health consultation.

PROPOSED INTERVENTION IN A HYPOTHETICAL CASE

To compensate for this limitation in the data on actual case handling, we attempted to access the manner in which workers respond to sexual abuse in a
second way—with a hypothetical case. We gave each worker a short vignette.

A mother from a middle-class family comes to the office where you work and says that she believes her daughter is being sexually molested by her stepfather. The woman is convinced that this is happening, and does not know what to do.

Then we asked a series of questions to assess what attitudes and what interventions a worker might bring to the case.

One advantage to the use of a hypothetical vignette is quite clear. Differences among workers could not be attributed to the fact that they were dealing with different kinds of cases. They had all received a uniform stimulus; they had the same facts. Differences should reflect real differences in workers' training, attitudes, knowledge, and predispositions concerning sexual abuse.

On the other hand, such a hypothetical vignette carries with it an obvious disadvantage. What a worker *thinks* he or she would do when faced with a sexual abuse case is not the same as what he or she actually *would* do. Many good intentions and good ideas are short-circuited in practice. Good intentions may be thwarted by lack of time, lack of interest, lack of support from agency or superiors, or simply by ingrained habit patterns. Thus what workers said they would do is not necessarily indicative of actual practices. Rather, what we think it tends to tap is workers' attitudes and ideologies about what should be done about the problem of sexual abuse.

To assess how workers would intervene in such a hypothetical case, we gave them a list of possible interventions and asked them to circle the ones they would be most likely to take. The answers, broken down by agency, appear in Table 13–6.

Certain interventions appeared to have greater popularity among workers. For example, most workers thought a high priority should be given to interviewing the child. Many also thought the mother ought to be interviewed again. A majority also recommended a physical exam.

Interestingly enough, while the majority also said they would report the case to DSS, at least one third failed to indicate reporting to DSS as an intervention they would choose. This seems to be a more alarming commentary on the issue of mandated reporting than the evidence we presented earlier. The vignette was clearly a situation covered by the child abuse reporting act. The fact that a third of workers did not mention this intervention suggests the degree to which there is resistance to and ignorance of the law, and confirms our earlier finding on the problem that exists in the reporting of actual cases.

Although certain interventions seemed to be more popular than others, Table 13–6 is also impressive for the diversity it displays. Workers were not by any means in agreement about what ought to be done in the hypothetical case of sexual abuse. Moreover, workers from different agencies did show distinctly different patterns and different preferences in the interventions they chose.

DSS workers, for example, tended to be characterized by the sheer quantity of interventions they recommended. They gave priority to doing many things which did not appeal to other workers. For example, DSS workers were much more likely to make a home visit. They were more likely to recommend a psychiatric evaluation of the child and the family. They were more likely to recommend a physical exam. And they were the only group to give a high priority to interviewing the offender. DSS workers' enthusiasm for interventions is undoubtedly related to their special position within the child welfare system. DSS is the agency with ultimate responsibility for the disposition of sexual abuse cases. DSS workers also have experience and established contacts with the network of possible service providers. This gives them both the motivation for making a thorough investigation and the resources for carrying it out.

In contrast to DSS, school personnel were conspicuous for their low number of recommended interventions. School personnel had the lowest percentage of workers who wished to interview the mother again, interview the child, interview the offender, or arrange for a physical exam. They were wary of other interventions too. What school personnel seemed to want to do was report the cases to DSS (they were tied for highest on this intervention), but do little else.

School personnel seemed to be very reluctant to engage in any social work or mental health interventions. This may be in part because they felt it was not their function; their primary objective was education. But it may also reflect a conflict they felt. School personnel often believe that they have to maintain a good relationship with children's families. They are very concerned about interventions they might take that would alienate parents. So in many difficult child welfare situations, school personnel would rather delegate interventions to other agencies that are better insulated from parental anger and criticism.

Confirming our earlier analysis, the figures in Table 13–6 also reveal a remarkable isolation and distinctiveness of criminal justice agencies compared to all others. For example, all other agencies were extremely wary of reporting this case of sexual abuse—one involving a stepfather—to the police. Only among the criminal justice workers themselves was there a substantial inclination to involve the police.

For their part, criminal justice workers showed a parallel reticence to propose interventions that went outside their own realm. They were somewhat more reluctant than other agencies to report to DSS (although this difference was not statistically significant). And curiously, they were reluctant to make a home visit or interview the stepfather. (These are two interventions that one might think criminal justice personnel would find more comfortable than would many social work or mental health workers.) In short, criminal justice workers were isolated, both because they had different approaches to handling sexual abuse cases and because other agencies tended to steer clear of them.

Attitudes About Goals of Intervention

The isolation of criminal justice workers was further illustrated by questions we asked to probe the kinds of goals professionals brought to their interventions in child sexual abuse.

Several major debates about the goals in handling child sexual abuse have preoccupied the professional community. One concerns whether it is important to bring criminal charges to bear against the abuser. Another concerns what priority should be given to removing either the child or the offender to prevent a recurrence of the sexual abuse.

On the matter of criminal charges, some groups have argued that such practices are highly countertherapeutic (DeFrancis, 1969; MacFarlane & Bulkley, 1982). They have pointed out that prosecution usually only subjects victims to more trauma while further polarizing the family and hardening the offender in his resistance and denial. Others, however, have insisted that prosecution is important: first, to create in the offender the motivation to stop and to change; second, to establish clear community norms that such behavior is wrong; and third, to give the victim the clear message that the community acknowledges that she or he has been victimized (MacFarlane & Bulkley, 1982). Different communities have built treatment approaches to sexual abuse based on differing philosophies concerning the wisdom of prosecution of family sexual abuse offenders (Brant & Tisza, 1977; Giaretto, 1982; Sgroi, 1982).

A similar debate rages concerning the priority that should be given to preserving the family unit in the aftermath of sexual abuse. Some professionals insist that unless the offender and victim are separated after discovery, the victim is often subjected to continuing abuse and also to retaliation for having revealed the secret (Herman, 1981). Moreover, they argue, preserving family unity obviates any pressure on the offender to seek help or change his ways, and may allow destructive family patterns to continue unabated. On the other hand, other professionals give high priority to keeping families together in the wake of sexual abuse (Giaretto, 1982). Victims, they say, do not want to lose their fathers; they just want the sexual abuse to stop. Moreover, they say, separation instills guilt feelings in the victim over breaking up the family and often subjects the family to the kinds of social and economic hardships that follow separation and divorce.

We asked workers in our survey several questions pertaining to the goals of intervention in the hypothetical case involving incest by a stepfather. For example, we asked them whether, among their recommended interventions, they would "Encourage the parent to press criminal charges" or "Try to get the child removed from the family" or "Try to get the stepfather removed from the family." We also asked them whether they agreed with two statements concerning the case: "Every effort should be made to keep the family together" and "It would be important to bring criminal charges against the alleged offender." (The way in which workers from various agencies responded to these questions is shown in Tables 13–7 and 13–8.)

According to the responses, there appeared to be consensus on only one thing: nobody thought that removing a child from his or her family was an intervention that ought to be encouraged. Aside from that there was a great deal of disagreement. Criminal justice workers in particular appeared to hold a minority position. They were noticeably out of step with all other workers in that they favored pressing criminal charges and trying to remove the stepfather, and placed relatively low priority on trying to keep the family together. DSS workers were at the other end of the spectrum, having a positive attitude toward trying to keep the family together and a negative attitude toward pressing criminal charges.

The biases of criminal justice workers on these questions are easily understood. It made sense that they should urge pressing charges, since that is the institutional framework in which they work. Moreover, the criminal justice approach is very oriented toward isolating and punishing offenders, so their willingness to see offenders removed from their households also makes sense.

Why DSS workers should vote so readily for preserving family unity is somewhat more perplexing. DSS workers are the ones held responsible when children are hurt or reabused, and they also are very familiar with the many situations in which keeping a family together is just not possible. On the other hand, DSS workers also have firsthand experience of the havoc sometimes created by breaking up a family. They may feel, on the basis of experience, that it should be a last resort intervention.

Moreover, they may have another reason for so strongly emphasizing the need to keep the family together. DSS workers are often criticized and stigmatized for being "child stealers." Much of the public mistakenly thinks that the main thing that child protective workers do is remove children from their homes. It may be in part in reaction to this stigma that DSS workers, when given the opportunity, wish to show their commitment to the goal of keeping families together.

IMPLICATIONS FOR PRACTICE

The data presented here seem to reinforce two important concerns about the management of child sexual abuse, at least as it occurs in Boston agencies.

1. There is a high degree of institutional insularity. Agencies do not readily cooperate with one another. They tend to rely heavily on other professionals within their own immediate institution. There appear to be some strong barriers to interaction, particularly between criminal justice and child protective professionals, but also to some extent between other agencies as well.
2. There exists a high degree of disagreement among agency personnel about the proper approach to handling sexual abuse. Different agencies give priorities to different kinds of interventions and are at odds with one another about basic objectives in the management of cases.

We suspect that this disagreement has three unfortunate implications for community-wide handling of child sex abuse. First of all, it means that how a case of sexual abuse is handled is heavily affected by the often arbitrary factor of which agency finds out about it first. The particular needs and circumstances of a case may be less important in determining what is done than the nature of the agency which first discovers the case. Second, it means that certain kinds of interagency collaboration that might be beneficial in the handling of some cases are probably the exception rather than the rule, because of institutional barriers to cooperation. Third, the lack of consensus on goals means that it may be rather difficult for the Boston community to develop a community-wide plan and some uniform procedures for dealing with sexual abuse.

A good example of the problems that arise when agencies do not cooperate was furnished by workers at the Sexual Trauma Treatment Program (STTP) in Hartford, Connecticut. We will quote at length here from their case example, comments, and conclusions (Bander, Fein & Bishop, 1982).

CHRONOLOGY *(Workers' comments in parentheses)*

AUG. 9.   Ann, a 14-year-old, told her mother, age 36, that her 41-year-old father had been fondling her breasts and touching her. The mother, Mrs. P., called the Child Abuse Hotline, which contacted the child protection agency five days later. (Delayed interagency response.)

Previously, the child had told her priest, family doctor, and school counselor of these occurrences. (Nonreporting of cases to child protection agency.)

SEPT. 20.   The case was referred to STTP six weeks after the original call. (Further delay in referral.)

SEPT. 28. STTP had its first contact with the family, one week later. (Third delay in response.)

OCT. 4. STTP contacted other professionals who were aware of the abuse. (Attempts to obtain corroborative information and coordinate with others.)

OCT. 5. STTP met with Ann, who was frightened about the molestation and angry at the time lapse since she had reported the incest. STTP suggested to Mrs. P. and Ann that they contact the police. This action was supported by a youth officer who knew the family. The STTP worker, Mrs. P., Ann, and the youth worker went to the police to make a statement. The detective refused to allow the STTP worker to remain with the child. (Support for child not available during questioning.)

STTP expected an arrest and an order restraining Mr. P. from returning to the home. Although there was enough information for a warrant, the detective suggested counseling for the father, with arrest at a later date only if Mr. P. did not comply with the treatment. Mrs. P. agreed, but Ann was upset and afraid. (Police and STTP had different expectations about police action and gave different messages to family.)

Mrs. P. and Ann went home. They were given the telephone number of a battered women's shelter.

OCT. 14. Mr. P. signed a confession for the police and agreed to treatment and conditional probation if they did not arrest him. Mr. P. called Ann's school and told her to come home so that he could apologize. Ann was so upset that the school counselor called the priest who in turn called STTP. STTP recommended separation of the family either by placing the child in a foster home, removing the mother and children to a safe place, or having the father leave the home. The counselor and the priest were resistant to separation. (Conflicting treatment goals.)

The priest then accompanied Ann home to talk with her father. That night Ann phoned STTP frantically stating that Mr. P. had put Mrs. P. and the children out of the house. All emergency shelters were filled. They stayed with a friend of Mrs. P.'s.

OCT. 21. The family was reunited against STTP's advice. (Child protection subordinate to goal of keeping family together.)

NOV. 5. Mr. P. offered Ann money in an attempt to have her withdraw the allegation.

NOV. 22. Mr. P. began his treatment at the community hospital, where the psychiatrist was hostile to STTP's involvement. At the hospital Mr. and Mrs. P. began marital counseling. Ann began attending the STTP adolescent group, and she and her mother were seen together in treatment. (Coordination of treatment providers lacking.)

DEC. 10. Ann withdrew from treatment under pressure from her father.

JUNE 5. Ann was molested again with violence. Mrs. P. reported the incident to the police. Mr. P. was to be arrested but instead was returned to the home to await arraignment. The police told the family to call if Mr. P. attempted to harm them. Ann's fear of physical harm resulted in emergency foster home placement for her. (Conflicting goals and expectations.)

JULY 13. Mrs. P. filed for divorce and the family became reinvolved in therapy with STTP.

SEPT. 5. Both Mrs. P. and Ann were hospitalized to prevent their threatened suicides. The hospital psychiatrist was unwilling to share information with STTP. STTP tried to coordinate continued treatment, but the goals were different. Hospital personnel suggested family treatment and marital therapy despite the father's pressure on the child, his violent outbursts and lack of remorse for his actions, and Mrs. P.'s readiness for divorce. (Different goals for treatment.)

The divorce action was withdrawn. The family withdrew from STTP. Later it was learned that Ann had fled the hospital and could no longer be located by STTP.

WORKERS' CONCLUSION

In this case, there were 11 months of periodic, interrupted treatment. There were many delays in obtaining treatment, and every agency involved had a different treatment philosophy. The youth services officer, the priest, the psychiatrist, and STTP were not in harmony over treatment goals; the protection of the child became secondary to efforts to reunite the family. This family lost all chances for maintaining its integrity through the conflicting concerns of the professionals. The more critical issues appeared to lie with the difficulty of making many systems work together. Other agencies, such as the police, the family doctor, the school counselor, the shelter for battered women, did not participate in the service network in a way that might have assisted the family.[*]

What can be done to improve the degree of cooperation among community agencies? Part of the difficulty agencies have in planning cooperative efforts may be that they imagine that the differing goals of other agencies necessarily conflict with their own. Criminal justice personnel may think that because mental health workers are interested in therapy, they will necessarily sabotage efforts aimed at prosecution. Mental health workers, by contrast, think that because prosecutors are worried only about convictions they are not concerned about the treatment of either offenders or victims.

*Reprinted with permission from *Child Abuse and Neglect*, Vol. 6, K. Bander, E. Fein, and G. Bishop, "Child Sexual Abuse Treatment: Some Barriers to Program Operation," Copyright © 1982, Pergamon Press, Ltd.

However, the experience from some communities around the country is that collaboration can actually help agencies achieve their goals simultaneously. For example, police and prosecutors in most localities currently find sexual abuse cases difficult to prosecute. For one thing, child victims often make poor witnesses. In addition, in many cases the children come under great pressure from family members to recant their story, and cases often evaporate before they get to trial. By contrast, in communities where prosecutors have developed collaborative arrangements with mental health and child protective workers, prosecutors often find their conviction rate going up (Bulkley & Davidson, 1981). If children are in treatment, they get help and support from their counselors and, in the end, they make better witnesses. If offenders are also in treatment, or anticipate treatment as a substitute for incarceration, they are often more willing to plead guilty, avoiding the need for a costly trial. In short, criminal justice agencies find that collaboration with mental health agencies can promote their own objectives.

Conversely, lack of cooperation can impede the efforts of all agencies. Many social service professionals believe that collaborating with prosecutors only makes cases more complicated and increases the jeopardy to child and family. But in actual practice, these professionals find they have a terribly difficult time holding the offenders in treatment. Men quit treatment programs, leaving the social service agency unsure about whether the abuse will continue (MacFarlane & Bulkley, 1982).

In locales where social service professionals have worked out collaborative arrangements with courts and prosecutors, they often find markedly increased effectiveness in working with offenders. Using the threat of prosecution or parole revocation, the social service and mental health workers report that men stay in treatment longer and the workers are able to achieve more lasting and extensive changes in families (Giaretto, 1982). The collaboration can work to improve treatment outcome as well as conviction rates.

The experience of some communities is that a combination of different goals can be achieved through greater collaboration. However, such collaborations are not always easy to initiate. They often require the surmounting of institutional mistrust that has grown up over many years. Kee MacFarlane (1982), who formerly was a specialist in charge of sexual abuse programs with the National Center for Child Abuse and Neglect and who had a broad overview of communities around the county, has noted that these collaborations can develop in a great variety of ways. The initiative can come from many agencies—prosecutor's offices, mental health agencies, sometimes the state child protective service.

What most of the successful collaborations had in common, according to MacFarlane, is that they were the work of a small number of workers, who pioneered the arrangements through personal contacts among themselves. They tended not to result, at least initially, from decisive agency policy changes or high-level community planning efforts.

This observation is encouraging. It suggests that the opportunity exists for creative restructuring of service systems by individual workers who are willing to take the initiative. As workers continue to be frustrated over the handling of child sexual abuse, and as models for other modes of cooperation become better known, it is possible that more and more of these efforts will take hold and succeed in communities across the country.

TABLE 13-1
Experience with Sexual Abuse Victims or Offenders During Professional Career

AGENCY	% SEEING ONE OR MORE VICTIMS	% SEEING ONE OR MORE OFFENDERS	(N)
Mental health	81	57	(96)
Medical	76	39	(63)
DSS	87	75	(172)
Criminal justice	70	62	(60)
School	60	27	(194)
Other social service	83	54	(67)
	$\chi^2 = 73.02$, $p < .0001$	$\chi^2 = 106.90$, $p < .0001$	

TABLE 13-2
Identity of Offender in Most Recent Case of Sexual Abuse

AGENCY	% OF OFFENDERS WHO WERE			(N)
	Parents	Other relatives	Nonfamily	
Mental health	69	15	16	(75)
Medical	45	31	24	(42)
DSS	75	10	15	(148)
Criminal justice	36	9	55	(42)
School	58	17	25	(115)
Other social service	68	10	23	(53)

$\chi^2 = 48.57$, $p < .001$

TABLE 13-3
Interval Between Occurrence of Sexual Abuse and Contact with Agency for Most Recent Case

AGENCY	% CASES WHERE ABUSE OCCURRED OVER 1 YEAR BEFORE REFERRAL	(N)
Mental health	40	(73)
Medical	26	(42)
DSS	30	(146)
Criminal justice	7	(42)
School	29	(105)
Other social service	33	(54)

$\chi^2 = 15.58$, $p < .01$

TABLE 13–4

Agencies' Compliance with Reporting of Sexual Abuse

Agency	# Cases Seen	# Cases Reported	# Cases Not Reported Because		# Cases Should Have Been Reported[a]	% Reported of Those Which Should Have Been[b]
			Already Reported	Victim No Longer Child		
Mental health	76	13	38	15	27	48
Medical	42	16	17	3	23	70
Criminal justice	42	9	18	3	21	43
School	116	35	67	7	46	76
Other social service	51	13	27	8	18	72
Total	327	86	167	36	135	64%

$\chi^2 = 10.73$

[a] "# cases should have been reported" deletes all those in which the case was already reported or the victim was no longer a child. Respondents could note multiple reasons for not reporting, so N's do not reflect simple subtraction of appropriately nonreported cases.

[b] Column 2 ("# cases reported") as a percentage of column 5 ("# cases should have been reported").

TABLE 13-5
Resources Consulted to Aid in Handling Most Recent Case: % Using Other Agency or Professional

RESPONDENT'S AGENCY	NO OTHER AGENCY	POLICE	MENTAL HEALTH	PHYSICIAN	PSYCHIATRIST	DSS	COURT
Mental health	40	5	26	5	8	17	13
Medical	38	7	23	23	19	38	12
DSS	20	10	43	19	19	na	24
Criminal justice	19	31	26	12	14	21	50
School	47	8	28	8	7	30	8
Other social service	45	11	24	24	20	25	19
χ^2	31.04**	22.94***	13.50*	18.59**	13.86**	N.S.*	41.05*****

*p < .05
**p < .01
***p < .001
****p < .0001

TABLE 13-6
Percentage Advocating Actions in Handling Reports of Abuse I

AGENCY	INTERVIEW MOTHER	INTERVIEW CHILD	INTERVIEW STEPFATHER	INTERVIEW FAMILY	REPORT TO POLICE	REPORT TO DSS	HOME VISIT	PHYSICAL EXAM	CHILD PSYCH. EVAL.	FAMILY PSYCH. EVAL.
Mental health	62	77	55	55	9	68	27	59	26	32
Medical	61	86	52	43	12	72	38	75	45	45
DSS	68	82	70	50	5	63	75	66	50	55
Criminal justice	60	81	31	20	52	59	17	58	37	20
School	44	60	29	22	11	72	33	50	34	39
Other social service	67	65	46	40	6	56	28	55	32	32
All agencies	58	73	48	38	12	66	42	59	38	40
χ^2	29.48***	39.21***	80.16****	58.54****	109.50****	N.S.	124.61***	20.00*	21.29*	33.74***

N = 725

*p < .01
**p < .001
***p < .0001

TABLE 13–7

Percentage Advocating Actions in Handling Reports of Abuse II

Agency	Encourage Criminal Charges	Remove Child	Remove Stepfather
Mental health	6	7	10
Medical	9	5	6
DSS	5	8	9
Criminal justice	35	6	35
School	7	7	11
Other social service	11	3	11
All agencies	10	7	12
χ^2	37.69*	N.S.	37.83*

N = 725

*p < .0001

TABLE 13–8

Percentage Advocating Objectives in Handling of Sexual Abuse Cases

Agency	Keep Family Together[a]	Bring Criminal Charges[b]	(N)
Mental health	73	26	(78)
Medical	68	44	(50)
DSS	85	31	(164)
Criminal justice	34	74	(53)
School	52	48	(175)
Other social service	60	50	(65)
	$\chi^2 = 67.34,$ $p < .0001$	$\chi^2 = 45.00,$ $p < .0001$	

[a] Item: Every effort should be made to keep the family together.

[b] Item: It would be important to bring criminal charges against the alleged offender.

CHAPTER 14

Implications for Theory, Research, and Practice

I NTEREST IN THE problem of child sexual abuse is not merely a fad. As this book has shown, the problem is substantial, not just in terms of its scope and its impact on victims and their families, but also in terms of the issues it raises for scholars, practitioners, and policy makers. Interest in the problem is destined to grow because it poses many challenges to people engaged in a variety of endeavors, challenges that they will want to confront rather than avoid. Although these challenges will not appeal to everyone, they will draw in committed and idealistic people looking for new solutions to old dilemmas.

As new people are drawn, we will undoubtedly see the field develop rapidly in new directions. Older ideas and approaches may become obsolete. While it is impossible to predict all the new directions the field may take, I think certain directions will prove more fruitful than others. I would like to conclude this book by outlining some of the developments that I think will be most important to the field. They fall into three areas: theory, research, and practice. I will address each one in turn.

THEORY DEVELOPMENT

Theories about child sexual abuse have been slow to emerge, and this slowness has in turn hampered research as well as practice. New theories have a way of generating a sense of intellectual excitement as well as practical activity—two developments the field could desperately use.

One way to foster new theory is to attract people with a theoretical bent into the field. Such people are often from academic backgrounds, and have been in short supply in the field partly because sexual abuse treatment and research have grown up outside academic institutions. Instead, interest in sexual abuse has developed in social service agencies, prosecutors' offices, and rape crisis centers. The major medical and mental health centers which sponsor a great deal of new thinking and research (and which have been active in the field of physical child abuse) have been slow to become involved.

However, more theoretically oriented people will increasingly get involved, either on their own or with some major institutions. As such people become more interested in sexual abuse, they will apply new theoretical approaches to the problem. We can speculate on what some of those new theoretical approaches might be.

Borrowing Theory from Other Fields

A variety of theoretical perspectives in the field of social psychology might be applied usefully to the problem of sexual abuse, as they have been applied to some other social and psychological problems. One example is attribution theory. Attribution theory concerns itself with the interpretations and assumptions that people as "naive psychologists" make about their own and other people's behavior (Bem, 1972). Attribution theorists have taken an interest in such questions as what prompts people to hold rape victims responsible for their own rapes (Cann, Calhoun & Selby, 1979) or what prompts battered women to see themselves at fault for being beaten (Frieze, 1978). There are many parallel questions in the field of child sexual abuse: What factors contribute to abused children's seeing themselves as to blame for their victimization? What factors contribute to professionals' or the public's feeling unsympathetic toward child sexual abuse victims (as in the case of the Wisconsin judge cited in Chapter 8). Another question is, What contributes to sexual abusers' and others' seeing many children's normal affectionate behavior as sexually provocative and sexually motivated? These questions are ripe for theoretical work.

Another theoretical framework that might be well borrowed is from the field of moral development. The literature on moral development, which was originally conceived to explain how children acquire the capacity to solve ethical dilemmas, has recently been applied to adults, who may also display different levels of complexity in their moral thinking. Newberger (1980; Newberger & Cook, 1983) has recently developed theory suggesting that physical abusers are characterized by a more primitive level of moral development than nonabusers. Sexual abusers appear unable to identify with the potential harm their actions may cause their child victims (Summit & Kryso, 1978).

This suggests that deficits in moral development may exist in sexual abusers as well. Writers on moral development also have theorized about the different patterns of moral development that are displayed by men versus women (Gilligan, 1982). These different patterns may be part of what explains the low incidence of women engaging in sexual abuse (see Chapter 11). If we can identify the sources of some of the deficits or differences in moral development, we may be able to better identify the individuals at high risk to become abusers.

These are but two examples of theory-borrowing that might prove fruitful. Unfortunately, theory-borrowing is sometimes more difficult than it might seem at first glance. Some of the difficulties can be seen by looking at two other fields from which theory-borrowing would seem to have been natural, but which have been quite problematic.

It would seem natural to look for new insights about sexual abuse by borrowing theories concerning sexual behavior in general. Yet of all the branches of behavioral sciences, this is one of the least developed (Gagnon, 1977). Imagine how useful it would be to have a general understanding of how sexual proclivities develop and thus why some individuals come to be sexually interested in children. Instead we have only some very sketchy, ad hoc clinical theories of why some men become pedophiles and practically no understanding of how people in general come to choose certain sexual objects.

For another example, imagine how useful it would be to have an understanding of how sexual dynamics are managed in healthy, nonabusive families so we could see clearly what is different about incestuously abusive ones. Imagine how useful it would be to know how ordinary, nonabused children develop conceptions of their own sexuality, so we could restore a normal process to those who had been abused. Instead we know practically nothing about either of these matters.

The field of sexual abuse will be greatly enriched by theoretical developments in the general field of human sexual behavior. We need to keep this in mind and try to encourage the development of knowledge and theory in that field.

Another field from which theory-borrowing has been problematic is anthropology. At one time, writers in the field of sexual abuse regularly tried to draw from anthropology (Bagley, 1969). Articles from anthropology journals regularly cascaded out in literature searches giving "incest" as a key word. But in retrospect this literature has turned out to be of fairly limited usefulness.

The main problem concerns the fact that although anthropologists share the term "incest" with sexual abuse researchers, in reality, the two groups are concerned with very different and rather unrelated problems. Anthropologists are primarily interested in explaining the development and existence of a social institution—the incest taboo—whereas sexual abuse researchers are interested in explaining a certain form of deviant behavior among specific individuals and families.

Moreover, the term "incest" itself means something very different for each group. For anthropologists, in addition to sexual behavior, it also covers violation of rules of marriage, and it applies to relationships between blood relatives, whatever their age and relationship. Sexual abuse researchers, however, are not very interested in 26-year-old cousins who marry each other. Incest for them means sexual contacts between adults and dependent children, and matters of consensual sex among adults, marriage, blood relations, or even whether actual intercourse occurred are of little importance.

In the end, I think the sharing of the term "incest" between these two fields has been more confusing than helpful. Sex abuse researchers are continually thrown off base when they find people using the anthropological definition of "incest" to make some point that seems offensive to their perspective (Cohen, 1978); for example, "such and such a culture practices incest [e.g., cousin marriages] with no bad effects."

In the past, I have tried to encourage people in the field of sexual abuse to relinquish the word "incest" and talk about "family or intrafamilial sexual abuse" (which is what they mean). But this advice has made little headway, especially given the evocative character of the word "incest," which makes it attractive to everyone from journalists to graduate students.

While I believe that researchers in the field of sexual abuse need to recognize the irrelevance of much of the anthropological literature of the past, they may still look to anthropology to offer some extremely valuable insights in the future. But these insights will require new anthropological research.

What is curious about the field of anthropology is that it has dwelt so extensively on the question of incest (meaning marriage and sexual intercourse among blood kin) and so briefly on the question of sexual contacts between adults and children. How society regulates sexual behavior between the mature and the immature is of substantial theoretical interest, as much as how it regulates sexual behavior among blood kin. Anthropologists have debated whether all societies have some form of incest taboo. Do they also all have some form of taboo or regulation on sex between adults and children? My guess is that this latter is as widespread as the former. Anthropology could obviously be of great assistance to the field of sexual abuse if it were to investigate and theorize about this question.

There are many other potential questions to answer as well. For example, if in some societies, sexual contact does occur, as it seems to, between the mature and the immature, how is it controlled, what effects does it have, and how is it regarded? Does some violation of the norms against adults having sex with children occur in all societies? What factors may account for such violations being more or less widespread? For example, anthropologist Peggy Sanday (1981) analyzed 95 societies according to their prevalence of rape and found that rape was part of a cultural configuration of societies that had high levels of interpersonal violence, male dominance, and sexual separation. Is there a cultural configuration that produces high levels of child sexual abuse in addition to rape? It will be an exciting development when anthropologists turn attention to questions such as these.

Some of the most active transfer of theory into the field of sexual abuse has come from feminism. In fact, it was in part the feminist postulate that sexual assault was endemic to American society that prompted attention to sexual abuse in the first place. Indeed, feminism has proposed a variety of theoretical speculations about sexual abuse, many of which are waiting to be refined and investigated.

For example, feminists have argued that the large disparities of power between men and women in American society contribute to the occurrence of sexual abuse (Herman, 1981; Rush, 1980). There is some evidence, including evidence reported earlier here (Chapter 3), that this is true. Part of what is still needed, though, is detailed articulation of the various ways in which these power inequities create offenders, make children vulnerable, increase the trauma, and inhibit reporting.

Feminists have also suggested the notion that the different ways in which men and women are socialized contribute to the problem (Herman, 1981). Differences in male and female socialization are still being actively explored in theory and in research (Gilligan, 1982). As new insights develop concerning sexual socialization, they should be tested as quickly as possible for their applicability to the problem of sexual abuse.

Feminists have recently turned a substantial amount of attention to pornography and have suggested that it may play a role in the promotion of sexual exploitation of children (Rush, 1980). Most detailed analysis of pornography, however, has concentrated on its contribution to rape. The connection between pornography and child victimization deserves a similar kind of serious scholarly investigation. It seems likely that such attention is simply a matter of time, and that many of the new directions in feminism, such as its interest in pornography, will provide intriguing potential for theory in the field of sexual abuse.

Theory Building Within the Field

Borrowing theory from outside the field is not the only route to developing new theory. Theories can be developed from within the field by combining, expanding, and adding on to what already exists. There are some obvious ways for this to proceed.

Currently, there are two virtually separate and unconnected bodies of theory: theories developed from work with offenders and theories developed from work with victims and their families. These two fields need to be reconciled. The reconciliation has been hampered for several reasons. First, the theorists work with very different populations. Most of the offender theory has been developed through work with incarcerated pedophiles, men who have sexually abused outside the family. Most of the victim-related work has been done with incestuous families or with families where offenders were no longer present. Second, the theorists have little professional contact with one another. They attend different professional meetings and write for different journals.

Two things need to happen. These groups have to begin collaborating on clinical work and on research. Offender researchers need to look at offenders together with their victims and the victims' families. They need to study incest offenders as well as pedophiles. Victim researchers need to pay much closer attention to understanding the offenders, and begin to delve into the offenders' backgrounds. Moreover, a dialogue needs to be encouraged professionally among these researchers. Conferences need to be organized to bring the two groups together.

One factor in particular that has hampered the pooling of offender and victim research is family-systems theory. Family-systems theory has been one of the most eagerly welcomed theoretical developments in the field of mental health in generations. It has proven useful for clinicians working with families where sexual abuse has occurred, and has been widely adopted throughout the field.

But the family-systems perspective has also introduced two unhealthy biases into the field. First, it has created strong theoretical interest in one form of sexual abuse, father–daughter incest, to the exclusion of all other forms. Second, it has discouraged interest in studies of offenders.

Family-systems theory concentrates on one form of sexual abuse, because that is the form of sexual abuse that its theory best explains. In father–daughter incest, according to the theory, the marital relationship has broken down, the mother is alienated from the roles of wife and mother, and the father makes an alliance with the oldest daughter that substitutes for the marital relationship and becomes sexual. This theory encompasses some of the most cherished principles of the family-systems perspective, including the danger of cross-generational alliances and the collusion of all family members in family pathology.

Many criticisms have been made of the theory, including raising the question of whether it unfairly makes the mother and the daughter responsible for the incest. But one additional criticism is that the theory tends to focus all attention on one form of sexual abuse. Father–daughter incest is a common form of sexual abuse, but it probably accounts for less than a third of all abuse. Other forms of sexual abuse, by older brothers, uncles, grandparents—not to mention abuse by non-family members such as neighbors, teachers, and friends, all of which is also common—are not so easily explained. Theoretical attention needs to be devoted to these types of abuse too.

One reason why some of these other forms of abuse have not received attention is that family-systems theory also makes an implicit theoretical distinction between family sexual abuse and nonfamily abuse. Family abuse can utilize family dynamics and family-systems theory to explain it; nonfamily abuse has to look elsewhere. Because family-systems is the dominant paradigm, theorists have not tackled nonfamily abuse.

But is this theoretical division warranted? No, not at least in light of theoretical and empirical work done to date. Abuse by a grandfather who lives across town may not be so different from abuse by a neighbor who lives next door or down the street. More attention needs to be paid to developing theory that can apply to broader categories of abuse than simply father–daughter or intrafamily contacts.

The popularity of family-systems theory has also led to a relative neglect of theorizing about offenders. For the most part, family-systems theory has treated sexual abuse as a problem of family dynamics. Questions about the history, attitudes, and motivations of offenders have been considered matters for traditional individual psychology, which family-systems theory avoids. This has been another reason for the lack of communication between offender researchers, who are individual-oriented forensic psychologists, and victim researchers, who are more often of the family-systems persuasion.

However, focus on family dynamics alone is not adequate. Clinicians are finding that offenders need individual work as well as family treatment to stop their abusing. Some research has found that incest offenders are less different from other pedophiles than was once thought (Abel et al., 1981). Family-systems theory has many insights about how family dynamics may contribute to the abuse situation, but this theory needs to be melded with other theoretical insights about offenders.

New Directions in Research

Research on child sexual abuse is so badly needed that it is hard to think of any kind of study that would not be welcome. Yet some particular undertakings should be given priority. Certainly some of the findings highlighted in this book have obvious implications for research still to come.

Prevalence and Incidence Studies

As more people have become aware of the problem of sexual abuse, the demand for accurate statistics about its scope has intensified. A few studies, including the one reported here in Chapter 6, do make a start at meeting this demand. But there are still important shortcomings to all of these studies, and any future efforts should be directed toward trying to remedy these shortcomings.

The study reported in Chapter 6, as well as Russell's San Francisco study (1983), establish that adults in the community can be surveyed about their own childhood sexual abuse experiences. In both these surveys, the majority of cases uncovered had never been reported to any professional. This type of study clearly gives a more accurate picture of sexual abuse than studies based entirely on reported cases.

However, this adult survey design has the disadvantage of not being current. We have no way of knowing whether the present cohort of children is experiencing the same level of sexual abuse as a cohort who are now adults. One improvement on the adult survey design which would make it more current would be to concentrate on the youngest cohort of adults available. Thus, for example, a survey of 18-year-olds would give a more accurate picture of the sexual abuse experience of children for the last decade. It is even conceivable that children, particularly older children, could be surveyed. If the interviewees were children, certain ethical problems would have to be confronted, such as protecting them from possible retaliation by abusers and providing them with services when cases were uncovered.

Another design alternative is to interview parents about the victimization of their own children, as we did in the Boston survey. The results of this survey suggest, however, that parents either do not know about or are reluctant to volunteer information about the abuse of their children by intimates. But by refining and experimenting with interview techniques (such as allowing parents to fill out self-administered forms or giving them a great deal of specific encouragement to be candid), it may be possible to improve reporting of intrafamilial abuse. Certainly the success of the National Survey of Family Violence (Straus, Gelles & Steinmetz, 1980) in getting parents to reveal that they had used serious force against their children (3% said they had threatened to use a knife or gun on their child sometime in the child's life) suggests that it is possible to get parents to confide embarrassing, serious normative violations. We should not yet discount the possibility that we might be able to coax parents to reveal sexual abuse incidents that they, their partners, or other close relatives have committed.

Even if we find we cannot get sufficient candor from perpetrators, we can certainly gather much more information about sexual abuse from other individuals in the community besides the perpetrator or victim. In our Boston survey, 20% of the adult respondents knew of a child of a friend or a neighbor who had been sexually abused. We did not gather enough information to allow us to judge the quality or the source of these respondents' knowledge, but clearly much information about cases unknown to professionals can be obtained from the general public. Some statistical problems naturally exist in going from such third-party reports to a true incidence rate (Light, 1974), but the large number of cases uncovered from these sources would, undoubtedly, provide a completely different perspective on the sexual abuse problem, as well as on the possibilities for increasing levels of official reporting.

Ultimately, of course, some restraint needs to be put on the demand for more and better incidence and prevalence figures. Although they do alert people to the size of the problem, such figures are of limited usefulness to social scientists, clinicians, and policy makers. They do not necessarily add to our understanding of how to identify or prevent abuse. Since precise figures on prevalence may be difficult and expensive to obtain, they should not be emphasized in research to the exclusion of other important issues. Once we have figures making an unambiguous and persuasive case that the problem is widespread, then they will be accurate enough.

Risk Factors

The line of research that would be most productive for both theory and practice would focus on identifying what characteristics put children at high risk for abuse. The identification of such characteristics would give practitioners some markers that could direct their efforts toward prevention and detection and would push researchers to develop theories to account for why these characteristics are associated with abuse. Think, for example, of how important to the field of child abuse it has been to discover that teenage mothers and mothers whose bonding with their children is interrupted are at particularly high risk to abuse. Whole programs of research and intervention have developed as a result of such a finding. No similar risk factors are, as yet, so clearly identified in the case of sexual abuse.

A broad range of risk factors need to be explored, including class and ethnic variables, demographic variables, family constellation variables. We also need to look at characteristics of adults that make them high-risk to offend and characteristics of children that make them highly vulnerable targets. At present, we have only rough hypotheses about a small number of risk factors and very little evidence.

Explorations of risk factors can occur in many ways. The design illustrated in Chapter 3 is an example of one kind of study that can be done fairly readily. Nonclinical populations—students, organization members, professionals, whole communities—can be sampled and the victims of sexual abuse compared with nonvictims on a wide range of suspected or possible risk factors. Random sampling of populations, as in Russell's (1983) study, makes for much better designs, but it is not necessary for the kinds of exploratory studies that are needed at this stage.

Risk factor studies can be done also with clinical samples if a plausible comparison or control group can be found within the same setting. This type of design has the obvious problem that all the sexual abuse cases are reported cases, but such studies still are eminently worth doing given the current level of knowledge.

Given what hunches we already have about sexual abuse through clinical work and preliminary studies such as that reported in Chapter 3, certain types of risk factors should be looked at particularly carefully.

1. Any type of physical or emotional challenge to a child—illness, handicap, learning disability, stigma, psychological disturbance—that may compromise a child's ability to avoid molestation
2. Any type of impairment in parenting capacities, particularly ways in which mothers may be incapacitated, that may reduce the supervision and support that would protect against sexual abuse
3. Characteristics of potential offenders that may allow them to be identified from the general population: a history of other forms of sexual deviance, alcohol problems, social isolation, having been the victim of sexual abuse, hypersexuality

The identification of risk factors within these broad categories will be a major advance on the road to identifying where sexual abuse occurs.

Topics in Need of Research

Several additional questions, some of which have been highlighted in earlier sections of the book, are in crying need of research. One is the sexual abuse of boys. Probably the most serious question in regard to boys is how their response to victimization differs from that of girls and how clinicians can take this difference into account. Even purely descriptive accounts of work with sexually abused boys would be an important resource given the current state of ignorance on the subject.

Questions surrounding the long-term effects of abuse also need much greater elaboration. What is desperately needed is a study which follows a cohort of victimized children throughout their development and charts the ongoing effects at different stages of development. One of the most important points made by recent research on the long-term effects of divorce on children (Wallerstein, 1983) is that traumatic childhood experiences have different effects at different stages of the life cycle. While these effects are somewhat predictable from what we know of the demands of different developmental stages, how a particular child will respond to those demands cannot be specified. A child who seems relatively free from effects at one stage may develop symptoms in response to the demands of another, depending on the nature of the abuse, personality, and other stresses posed by the developmental process. Researchers need to follow children throughout their development and document the impact of abuse at each point.

The nature and diversity of research on offenders also needs to be expanded. Almost all research to date on offenders has been on incarcerated populations, who are clearly not representative of all offenders. To study a more diverse group of offenders, researchers need to broaden the subject pool to include those who are just entering the criminal justice system, those who plea bargain out of jail sentences, offenders in diversion programs, offenders in voluntary treatment, and those who have been detected by child protection workers but are not the subject of criminal justice action. It is also possible to try to study undetected offenders. Studies have been conducted on undetected rapists (Kanin, 1957), and at least one qualitative study interviewed a large number of undetected pederasts (Rossman, 1976). Work needs to be done on the possibility of studying adults who have had sexual contact with children, but who are not the subject of child welfare or criminal investigation.

Finally, there is a pressing need to evaluate the effects of various intervention strategies. Communities around the country are currently struggling to set up programs to respond to the challenge of sexual abuse. A variety of longstanding programs offer themselves as models, but policy makers have little objective evidence to guide them in decisions about what are the relative advantages and disadvantages of different models. Such outcome research will greatly advance the welfare of sexual abuse victims.

NEW DIRECTIONS IN PRACTICE

Up to this point, little of this book has been devoted to issues of practice (with the exception of Chapter 13). The book is not without implications for the practitioner, so in this last section of the last chapter, I would like to draw out in greater detail a few implications of the current work for the practitioner.

Unreported Cases

Any research such as that reported here, which attempts to assess how widespread abuse really is, cannot help underline the fact that a great deal more sexual abuse occurs than ever gets reported. A little arithmetic demonstrates this fact clearly. Suppose 10% of all girls were victims of sexual abuse and one boy was victimized for every five girls. (These are conservative figures since the figures from our Boston survey were actually 15% for girls and one boy for every three girls. Russell's (1983) figures for girls are even higher—38%.) Such a prevalence rate in a population of about 60 million children under 18 should result in over 210,000 new cases of sexual abuse every year. The National Incidence Study (NCCAN) (1981) estimated that approximately 44,700 cases of sexual abuse are uncovered by professionals in a year. This would mean that only *only one out of every five* cases are coming to the attention of professionals.

However, such mathematics are not needed to convince us of the extent of the problem: nearly everyone is in agreement that sexual abuse is terribly underreported. Moreover, nearly everyone is engaged in some form of activity designed directly or indirectly to increase the level of reporting. The problem is that we know relatively little about which of these efforts pay off and which do not.

There are three distinct levels at which efforts can be directed: (1) Children themselves need to be encouraged to reveal sexual abuse. (2) Other adults, such as parents and relatives, who know of sexual abuse, need to be encouraged to take their suspicions to professionals. (3) Finally, professionals who know of or suspect cases must be encouraged to pass such information on to official reporting agencies.

There is reason to think that the biggest bottleneck is at the first level: children who do not reveal abuse. Retrospective surveys of adults have never shown that any more than half of them told about the abuse that was occurring. Our survey of parents' knowledge about their own children also provided evidence that parents do not seem to be hearing from their children about abuse of the same type and in the same quantity that they themselves experienced in their own childhoods. This evidence points toward giving a high priority to reaching children themselves and urging them to tell someone.

Such a message has been one of the main objectives of a variety of sexual abuse prevention programs that have tried to educate school children. These programs have had a great deal of success in Minneapolis, Washington State, the Bay Area in California, and Columbus, Ohio, but they need to receive wider distribution. In another innovative development, sex abuse educators in Seattle, Washington, have recently made a television spot featuring basketball star Bill Russell, who tells children to report anyone who tries to molest them. Efforts are under way to gain national exposure for these messages, and this is a very encouraging development. Efforts that try to reach children through school, television, and other media appear to have the greatest potential to whittle away at the most serious obstacle to greater reporting.

Underreported Groups

Efforts to increase reporting must pay attention to certain groups in which nonreporting is particularly severe. For example, a variety of evidence, some of it presented in Chapter 10 on sexually abused boys, suggests strongly that the abuse of boys is less likely to come to public attention. This stems from a greater reluctance on the part of boys and their guardians to reveal abuse and a greater reluctance on the part of professionals to suspect it. To increase the reporting of such abuse, special efforts will undoubtedly have to be made. Such efforts should broadcast explicitly the fact that abuse of boys is common. Boys and their families need public reassurance that boys are not at fault for such abuse and that such abuse does not mean that the boys will become homosexuals. However, the underreporting of abuse of boys has deep roots in sex-role stereotypes and homophobia that will not be easily changed short of a direct assault on these attitudes. Boys will be less likely to report abuse as long as it is considered unmanly to ask for help or suffer a hurt and as long as being the victim of a sexual assault is a threat to masculinity. So those who would work to increase reporting must help change these attitudes as well.

Young children are another group whose victimization is less likely to be reported. This tendency shows up in the generally younger age of victimization revealed in nonclinical than clinical samples. It also is manifested by the trend for average age of victims to drop as treatment programs become more widespread and better trusted. As trust and awareness build, less easily reported cases of young children being abused slowly get revealed.

Cases involving young children do not get reported for a variety of familiar reasons. Younger children are more intimidated and don't tell. Parents are fearful of the effects of disclosure on the child. Finally, parents and professionals do not entertain suspicions of abuse with such young children.

The methods for combatting these tendencies are also familiar. The fact that younger children are victims needs to be widely publicized, as do some of the symptoms that can be used to diagnose sexual abuse. Parents and children need to hear reassurances about reporting. Perhaps most important, programs need to develop their expertise in dealing with cases involving young children so that parents and professionals in the community have a sense of trust that such cases will be skillfully handled. Such trust will foster greater reporting.

Focus on Prevention

The realization that most sexual abuse goes unreported leads to other implications besides the idea that reporting effort needs to be increased. As was indicated in Chapter 9, one of these implications is that we need to put more effort into prevention to forestall abuse before it occurs.

The argument for prevention is bolstered by other facts we have uncovered about sexual abuse. Enough children in all segments of society are at-risk that general prevention certainly is worth the effort. Moreover, our Boston survey reinforces the general impression that educators have: most children are currently receiving little accurate or useful information. Parents, according to our results, are eager for their children to receive more education about sexual abuse.

It is an encouraging sign that the challenge of sexual abuse prevention is being taken up. Since 1980, a raft of curricula, children's books, school programs, films, puppet shows, and theater performances have appeared. These efforts demonstrate a great deal of creativity and diversity, which has resulted in their adoption and dissemination.

As of the end of 1983, however, there were some obvious gaps in prevention. First, prevention efforts were still highly localized, with areas like Minnesota, California, and Washington State out in front, while in many other areas little or nothing was being done. Second, prevention efforts have yet to receive much in the way of national endorsement or promotion. Virtually no federal funding had been directed to sexual abuse prevention and no national organization is actively coordinating or promoting the field.

A key question of prevention waiting to be addressed is whether such efforts can be targeted at particularly high-risk groups. In the case of physical abuse, for example, prevention strategies have focused on educating and monitoring teenage, unmarried, and economically stressed parents. What would be parallel strategies for the field of sexual abuse?

One possible parallel direction might come from the fact that children who live with stepparents are at apparently higher risk of abuse (see Chapter 3). If information could be targeted at families where parents were remarrying, to alert them to some of the foreseeable strains that contribute to vulnerability, some sexual abuse in these families might be avoided. Another group of possibly high-risk children, the developmentally disabled, have been the focus of a well-designed prevention program put together by officials in Minnesota (O'Day, 1983). Still other high-risk groups who might be specially targeted include foster children, adopted children, and those who live in rural or isolated circumstances.

Offender Treatment

Some of the most glaring deficits in the field of sexual abuse currently concern work with offenders. While programs that treat victims and families have proliferated rapidly (Giaretto, 1981), there have been many fewer advances in work with offenders.

The reasons for the difficulty are readily recognized. Offenders generally deny their offense; they are hard to bring to justice or to treatment; and therapists and criminal justice officials do not relish working with them. Unfortunately, techniques for working with offenders have not received widespread dissemination, and many communities lack any concerted approach. However, expertise in working with offenders is improving, and the conclusions from experience around the country need to be made available. Some of the most important conclusions from such work include the following.

1. *Success for both prosecutors and therapists seems to be enhanced by mutual cooperation.* This notion has received increasing endorsement in jurisdictions throughout the country, and new models are being developed and implemented, although entrenched institutional patterns have slowed their adoption.

2. *It is not true that effective treatment can occur only with offenders who are "motivated" to get help, even though this attitude is widespread.* Programs have been successful in treating offenders who were pressured into treatment through threats of prison or parole revocation.

3. *Many incestuous abusers require more than family therapy to insure against re-occurrence of abuse.* Some of the important issues that lead to incestuous abuse, such as a history of childhood trauma, may not be adequately dealt with in family therapy and require individual treatment of offenders as well.

4. *There now exists a wide variety of treatment technologies for dealing with child sex offenders, many of which have proven successful* (Kelley, 1982). These include such techniques as masturbatory reconditioning (Laws & O'Neil, 1979), desensitization (Abel, 1978), heterosocial skills training (Marshall & McKnight, 1975; Whitman & Quinsey, 1981), insight therapy (Kelley, 1982), and antiandrogen drug therapy (Berlin & Meinecke, 1981). While there are controversies about the effectiveness of various approaches, the issue for many experts is not whether any effective approach exists, but rather how to mix and match approaches to types of offenders.

5. *The treatment of child sex offenders is a highly specialized field, and most clinicians, including many who treat other types of offenders, are not skilled enough to treat them.* In spite of this, many child sex offenders are routinely remanded by courts and attorneys to therapists with only limited experience in this kind of treatment. This misplacement needs to be monitored and changed.

In summary, in all regions, there is a desperate need for development of specialized child sex offender treatment programs and training of clinicians with expertise in this area. Along with that, research needs to focus on evaluating the effectiveness of various programs and treatment strategies.

Obviously a great deal needs to be done, and not everything can be done at once. Sexual abuse is a field which in terms of social problems is just being discovered. But its newness can be an asset. In a new field, thinking and practices are not yet set in concrete. We owe it to the children who suffer from this abuse, and who will suffer in the future, to apply our best thinking and our best effort, making sure that what we do has the greatest potential for relieving the present and future toll of sexual abuse.

Notes

CHAPTER 1

1. Unfortunately the changes shown in the American Humane Association data cannot be taken as anything but a very rough indicator of the magnitude of the real increase in reported cases. Among other problems, the increase in the AHA figures has been dramatically affected by changes in the number of states contributing data to the reporting system and changes in the completeness of that data. Given these considerations, for someone to draw the inference from the AHA figures that the actual number of sexual abuse reports has increased by a factor of 10 between 1976 and 1982 would be quite unwarranted.

2. The question in the Texas study was "Were you ever sexually abused as a child?", sexual abuse being defined as "contacts or interactions between a child and an adult when the child is being used for the sexual stimulation of the perpetrator or another person. Sexual abuse may be committed by a person under the age of 18 when that person is significantly older than the victim or when the perpetrator is in the position of power or control over another child." There was no specified age range for "child" and no specified age difference for "significantly older."

CHAPTER 3

1. Some of these findings appear in the article "Risk Factors in the Sexual Victimization of Children," *Child Abuse and Neglect,* 1980, 4:265-273.

2. One serious limitation of data is that we cannot be certain of temporal sequence. It is conceivable, for example, that the low family income or the girl's having a step-

237

father resulted from the child's having been sexually abused rather than the other way around. However, we believe that most of the factors listed in Table 3–1 are more plausibly seen as conditions antecedent to the child's sexual victimization.

CHAPTER 10

1. The magnitude of the potential underestimate in Bell and Weinberg's survey is conveyed by comparing it with another survey of the San Francisco area. Russell (1983) conducted a survey in 1978 of 930 San Francisco *women* only, where the focus of the interview was on sexual assault experiences. Russell found 28% of the women had had some sexual abuse experience with a family member or non-family member before the age of 14. Bell and Weinberg's smaller sample of women for the same geographical area (N = 101) found only 7.9% who had had a prepubertal sexual experience with a male adult involving physical contact.

   Of course, the definitions used in the two studies were not quite the same. Russell's figures count some experiences with offenders who were not adults and also some experiences where the offenders were women. But aside from this their definitions are roughly equivalent. The additional nonadult and women offenders in Russell's tabulation are not enough to account for the large 20% difference between her findings and those of Bell and Weinberg. The difference more likely stems from the fact that Russell gave her interviewers meticulous training in how to talk specifically about sexual abuse with respondents. She also embedded the question in a questionnaire whose whole intent was to bring up recollections of victimization experiences.

   If Bell and Weinberg's figures do underestimate the number of abused girls, as comparison to Russell would suggest, then their figures on the number of abused boys may be underestimates too. It is hard to say by how much.

2. This comparison is made simply to obtain some gross proportions. Serious caution needs to be observed.

   The National Incidence Study did not define sexual abuse in the same way as the prevalence studies shown in Table 10–1. The National Incidence Study excluded most cases where sexual abuse was not committed by a parent or caretaker, obviously a large number of cases, especially in dealing with sexually abused boys. At the same time, if the National Incidence Study were replicated year after year, many of the 7600 cases coming to the attention of professionals would undoubtedly be cases that had come to attention in earlier years. Thus the two figures that were compared to form a ratio of the known cases to the actual existing cases are not necessarily measures of the same thing and should be regarded with caution.

3. I am indebted to Nicholas Groth for elaborating on much of the following section.

CHAPTER 12

1. The index was intended to be applicable equally to the self-esteem of men and women. But it had to be standardized to the norms of each sex. For example, although the confidence to act assertively about sexual interest is a sign of self-esteem, women score lower on this question, not because they have lower self-esteem, but because norms on this behavior differ for men and women. Thus, to create the scale, each question was normalized by sex, then summed, then the whole scale was normalized by sex and transformed to a percentage scale (Straus, 1979). Thus the mean for men and women was 50 and the standard deviation for each was 20. The scale reliability, tested by Cronbach's alpha, was .48 for men and .54 for women, not a high reliability but high enough for use in an exploratory study (Nunnally, 1967).

2. Forced sex is something more general than rape. The question asked was whether women had had a sexual experience in adulthood that took place as a result of force or threat.

3. We would like to emphasize that the measure used here is whether the respondent engaged in any homosexual *activity* in the previous year. Such respondents would not necessarily be considered by themselves or others as homosexuals.

CHAPTER 13

1. There is one additional valid reason why some cases might not have been reported. Approximately 12% of the sexual abuse cases cited by respondents as their most recent were cases in which abuse occurred at the hands of a non-family member. There is some ambiguity about whether workers are required by Massachusetts law to report nonfamily sexual abuse. On one hand, the law (119 S 51A) does not limit reporting to cases which involve family members. On the other hand, some state child abuse officials believe that is how the law is to be interpreted. Curiously, the professionals in our sample did not show a different reporting rate for nonfamily sexual abuse compared to family sexual abuse. Moreover, when asked in an open-ended section of the questionnaire to explain why they did not report a case of sexual abuse, none of them mentioned the fact that the abuser was not a family member as a reason for not reporting. Therefore, it is our belief the distinction between family and nonfamily abuse is not a distinction that Boston professionals make when considering whether they have an obligation to report.

References

AARENS, M., CAMERON, T., ROIZEN, J., ROOM, R., SCHNERBERK, D. & WINGARD, D. *Alcohol, casualties and crime.* Berkeley: Social Research Group, 1978.

ABEL, G. Treatment of sexual aggressives. *Criminal Justice and Behavior,* 1978, *5:* 291–293.

ABEL, G., BECKER, J., MURPHY, W. D. & FLANAGAN, B. Identifying dangerous child molesters. In R. B. Stuart (Ed.), *Violent behavior.* New York: Brunner/Mazel, 1981.

ADAMS, C. & FAY, J. *No more secrets: Protecting your child from sexual assault.* San Luis Obispo, CA: Impact, 1981.

ALLEN, C. V. *Daddy's girl.* New York: Wyndham, 1980.

AMERICAN HUMANE ASSOCIATION. *National Study on Child Neglect and Abuse Reporting.* Denver: American Humane Association, 1981.

AMIR, M. *Patterns in forcible rape.* Chicago: University of Chicago Press, 1977.

ANDERSON, L. & SHAFER, G. The character disordered family: A community treatment model for family sexual abuse. *American Journal of Orthopsychiatry,* 1979, *49:* 436–445.

ARAJI, S. & FINKELHOR, D. Explanations of pedophilia: Review of empirical research. Durham, NH: University of New Hampshire, 1983.

ARMSTRONG, I. *Kiss daddy goodnight.* New York: Hawthorn, 1978.

———. *The home front.* New York: McGraw Hill, 1983.

ATWOOD, R. & HOWELL, R. Pupillometric and personality test scores of female aggressing pedophiliacs and normals. *Psychonomic Science,* 1971, *22:* 115–116.

AVERY-CLARK, C., O'NEIL, J. A. & LAWS, D. R. A comparison of intrafamilial sexual and physical child abuse. In M. Cook & K. Howells (Eds.), *Adult sexual interest in children*. London: Academic Press, 1981.

AWAD, G. Father–son incest: A case report. *Journal of Mental and Nervous Diseases*, 1976, *162*: 135–139.

BAGLEY, C. Incest behavior and incest taboo. *Social Problems*, 1969, *16*: 1186–1210.

BAKER, C. D. Preying on playgrounds: The sexploitation of children in pornography and prostitution. *Pepperdine Law Review*, 1978, *5*: 816.

BAKER, T. Report on reader survey: Child sex abuse—"19" confidential survey. London: St. George's Hospital (Mimeo), 1983.

BANDER, K., FEIN, E. & BISHOP, G. Child sexual abuse treatment: Some barriers to program operation. *Child Abuse and Neglect*, 1982, *6*: 185–191.

BARD, L., CARTER, D., CERCE, D., KNIGHT, R., ROSENBERG, R. & SCHNEIDER, B. A descriptive study of rapists and child molesters: Developmental, clinical and criminal characteristics. Bridgewater, MA: (Mimeo), 1983.

BELL, A. & WEINBERG, M. *Homosexualities*. New York: Simon and Schuster, 1978.

———. *Sexual preference: Its development among men and women*. Bloomington, IN: Indiana University Press, 1981.

———. *Preliminary data: Childhood and adolescent sexuality San Francisco study*. Bloomington, IN: Institute for Sex Research (Mimeo), (n.d.)

BEM, D. Self-perception. In Leonard Berkowitz (Ed.), *Experimental advances in social psychology*, Vol. 7. New York: Academic Press, 1972.

BENDER, L. & GRUGETT, A. A follow-up report on children who had atypical sexual experiences. *American Journal of Orthopsychiatry*, 1951, *22*: 825–837.

BENWARD, J. & DENSEN-GERBER, J. Incest as a causative factor in anti-social behavior: An exploratory study. Paper presented at the American Academy of Forensic Sciences, 1975.

BERLIN, F. S. Sex offenders: A biomedical perspective. In J. Greer & I. Stuart (Eds.), *Sexual aggression: Current perspectives on treatment (Vol. 1): Victim treatment (Vol. 2)*. New York: Van Nostrand Reinhold, 1982.

BERLIN, F. & MEINECKE, C. F. Treatment of sex offenders with antiadrogenic medication: Conceptualization, review of treatment modalities and preliminary findings. *American Journal of Psychiatry*, 1981, *138*: 601–607.

BERLINER, L. & STEVENS, D. Clinical issues in child sexual abuse. In J. R. Conte & D. Shore (Eds.), *Social work and child sexual abuse*. New York: Haworth, 1982.

BLOSE, J. *The sexual abuse of children in Massachusetts*. Boston, MA: Massachusetts Committee on Criminal Justice, 1979.

BRADY, K. *Father's day*. New York: Dell, 1980.

BRANDT, R. & TISZA, V. The sexually misused child. *American Journal of Orthopsychiatry*, 1977, *44*: 80–87.

BROWN, L. Analysis of official reports of sexual abuse in 1976, presented to CAUSES Conference on Incest, Chicago, October, 1978.

BROWN, L. & HOLDER, W. The nature and extent of sexual abuse in contemporary American society. In W. Holder (Ed.), *Sexual abuse of children*. Englewood, CO: American Humane Association, 1980.

BROWNMILLER, S. *Against our will: Men, women and rape*. New York: Simon and Schuster, 1975.

BRUNOLD, H. Observations after sexual traumata suffered in childhood. *Excerpta Criminologica*, 1964, *4*: 5–8.

BULKLEY, J. *Child sexual abuse and the law*. Washington, D.C.: American Bar Association, 1981a.

BULKLEY, J. (Ed.). *Innovations in the prosecution of child sexual abuse cases*. Washington: American Bar Association, 1981b.

BULKLEY, J. & DAVIDSON, H. *Child sexual abuse—legal issues and approaches*. Washington, D.C.: National Resource Center for Child Advocacy and Protection, American Bar Association, 1981.

BURGESS, A. Research on the use of children in pornography. Executive summary report to National Center on Child Abuse and Neglect. Washington, 1982.

BURGESS, A. (Ed.) *Child pornography and sex rings*. Lexington, MA: Lexington Books, 1984.

BURGESS, A., GROTH, N., HOLMSTROM, L. & SGROI, S. *Sexual assault of children and adolescents*. Lexington, MA: Lexington Books, 1978.

BURGESS, A., GROTH, N. & McCAUSLAND, M. Child sex initiation rings. *American Journal of Orthopsychiatry*, 1981, *51*: 110–118.

BURGESS, A. W. & HOLMSTROM, L. Sexual disruption and recovery. *American Journal of Orthopsychiatry*, 1979, *49*: 648–657.

BURT, M. Cultural myths and support for rape. *Journal of Personality & Social Psychology*, 1980, *38*: 217–230.

BURTON, L. *Vulnerable children*. London: Routledge and Kegan Paul, 1968.

BUTLER, S. *Conspiracy of silence*. San Francisco: New Glide, 1978.

CANN, A., CALHOUN, L. & SELBY, J. Attributing responsibility to the victim of rape: Influence of information regarding past sexual experiences. *Human Relations*, 1979, *32*: 57–67.

COHEN, Y. The disappearance of the incest taboo. *Human Nature*, July 1978, 72–78.

COOPER, S., LUTTER, Y. & PHELPS, C. *Strategies for free children*. Columbus, OH: Child Assault Prevention Project, 1983.

CONSTANTINE, L. & CONSTANTINE, J. M. *Group marriage*. New York: Macmillan, 1973.

CONSTANTINE, L. & MARTINSON, F. *Children and sex: New findings and new perspectives*. Boston: Little, Brown, 1982.

CONTE, J. R. Sexual abuse of children: Enduring issues for social work. In J. R. Conte & D. Shore (Eds.), *Social work and child sexual abuse*. New York: Haworth, 1982.

CONTE, J. R. & BERLINER, L. Sexual abuse of children: Implications for practice. *Social Casework*, 1981, *63*: 601–616.

——. Prosecution of the offender in cases of sexual assault against children. *Victimology*, 1981, *6*: 102–109.

COURTOIS, C. & WATTS, D. Counseling adult women who experienced incest in childhood or adolescence. *Personnel and Guidance Journal*, 1982, pp. 275–279.

CRIME IN CALIFORNIA. *Time*, March 2, 1953.

CURRIER, R. L. Debunking the doublethink on juvenile sexuality. *Human Behavior*, September, 1977, p. 16.

CURRY, W. Grass roots waging war on molesters. *Los Angeles Times*, April 21, 1982.

CUSHING, J. G. N. Psychopathology of sexual delinquency. *Journal of Criminal Psychopathology*, 1950, *49*: 26–34.

DE FRANCIS, V. *Protecting the child victim of sex crimes committed by adults.* Denver: American Humane Association, 1969.

DEJONG, A., HERVADA, A. & EMMETT, G. Epidemiological variations in childhood sexual abuse. *Child Abuse and Neglect*, 1983, *7*: 155–162.

DE MAUSE, L. (Ed.). *The history of childhood.* New York: Psychohistory Press, 1974.

DE YOUNG, M. *The sexual victimization of children.* Jefferson, NC: McFarland, 1982.

DENSEN-GERBER, J. Why is there so much hard-core pornography nowadays? Is it a threat to society or just a nuisance. *Medical Aspects of Human Sexuality.* New York: Hospital Publications, Inc., 1983.

DENSEN-GERBER, J. & HUTCHINSON, S. F. Medical–legal and societal problems involving children—child prostitution, child pornography and drug–related abuse; recommended legislation. In S. M. Smith (Ed.), *The maltreatment of children.* Baltimore: University Park Press, 1978.

DEVROYE, A. L'inceste: Revue de Donnees Bibliographiques. *Acta Psychiatrica Belgica*, 1973, *73*: 6, 661–712.

DILLINGHAM, J. & MELMED, E. *Child pornography: A study of the social sexual abuse of children.* Executive summary report to National Center on Child Abuse and Neglect. Washington, 1982.

DIXON, K. N., ARNOLD, L. E. & CALESTRO, K. Father–son incest: Unreported psychiatric problem? *American Journal of Psychiatry*, 1978, *135*: 835–838.

DORON, J. Multiple victimization: Those who suffer more than once. Paper presented at the National Research Conference on Family Violence, Durham, NH, 1981.

DOWBEN, C. Legal tolerance of incest. Paper presented to the CAUSES Conference on Child Sexual Abuse, Chicago, 1979.

DWORKIN, A. Pornography and male supremacy. Address presented at the University of New Hampshire, Durham, NH, March, 1983.

ELLERSTEIN, N. & CANAVAN, W. Sexual abuse of boys. *American Journal of Diseases of Children*, 1980, *134*, 255–257.

FARRELL, W. Myths of incest. Paper presented to Conference on Family and Sexuality, Minneapolis, MN, 1982.

FARSON, R. *Birthrights: A bill of rights for children.* New York: Macmillan, 1974.

FELDMAN-SUMMERS, S., GORDON, P. & MEAGHER, J. Impact of rape on sexual satisfaction. *Journal of Abnormal Psychology,* 1979, *88:* 101–105.

FENICHEL, D. *The psychoanalytic theory of neurosis.* New York: Norton, 1945.

FINCH, S. Sexual activities of children with other children and adults. *Clinical Pediatrics,* 1967, *3:* 102.

FINKELHOR, D. *Sexually Victimized Children.* New York: Free Press, 1979.

———. Removing the child—prosecuting the offender in cases of child sexual abuse. *Child Abuse and Neglect,* 1983, 7: 195–205.

FINKELHOR, D. & ARAJI, S. Explanations of pedophilia: A four factor model. Durham, NH: University of New Hampshire, 1983.

FINKELHOR, D. & HOTALING, G. Sexual abuse in the National Incidence Study of Child Abuse and Neglect. Report to the National Center for Child Abuse and Neglect, 1983.

FINKELHOR, D. & YLLO, K. *License to rape: Sexual violence against wives.* New York: Holt, Rinehart, forthcoming.

FORD, C. S. & BEACH, F. *Patterns of sexual behavior.* New York: Harper & Row, 1951.

FORWARD, S. *The trauma of incest.* New York: Tarcher, 1978.

FRASER, M. *The death of narcissus.* New York: Paul Hoeber, 1976.

FREEDMAN, A. M., KAPLAN, H. I. & SADOCK, B. (Eds.), *Comprehensive textbook of psychiatry,* 2nd ed. Baltimore: Williams and Wilkins, 1975.

FREUD, S. Three essays on the theory of sexuality. *Standard edition of the complete psychological works of Sigmund Freud, Vol. 7.* London: Hogarth Press, 1953.

FREUND, K. Diagnosing homo- or heterosexuality and erotic age-preference by means of a psychophysiological test. *Behavioral Research and Therapy,* 1967a, *5:* 209–228.

———. Erotic preference in pedophilia. *Behavioral Research and Therapy,* 1967b, *5:* 339–348.

FREUND, K. & LANGEVIN, R. Bisexuality in homosexual pedophilia. *Archives of Sexual Behavior,* 1976, *5:* 415–423.

FREUND, K., LANGEVIN, R., CIBIRI, S. & ZAJAC, Y. Heterosexual aversion in homosexual males. *British Journal of Psychiatry,* 1973, *122:* 163–169.

FREUND, K., McKNIGHT, C. K., LANGEVIN, R. & CIBIRI, S. The female child as surrogate object. *Archives of Sexual Behavior,* 1972, *2:* 119–133.

FRIEZE, I. Self-perceptions of the battered woman. Paper presented at the Annual Meeting of the Association for Women in Psychology, Pittsburgh, PA, 1978.

———. Causes and consequences of marital rape. Paper presented at the American Psychological Association, Montreal, 1980.

FRISBIE, L. *Another look at sex offenders in California*. California Department of Mental Hygiene, Research Monograph No. 12, Sacramento, CA, 1969.

FRITZ, G., STOLL, K. & WAGNER, N. A comparison of males and females who were sexually molested as children. *Journal of Sex and Marital Therapy*, 1981, 7: 54–59.

FROMUTH, M. F. The long term psychological impact of childhood sexual abuse. Ph.D. Dissertation, Auburn University, 1983.

FRUDE, N. The sexual nature of sexual abuse. *Child Abuse and Neglect*, 1982, 6: 211–223.

GAGNON, J. Female child victims of sex offenses. *Social Problems*, 1965, 13: 176–192.

GAGNON, J. *Human Sexualities*. Glenview, IL: Scott, Foresman, 1977.

GARRETT, K. A. & ROSSI, P. Judging the seriousness of child abuse. *Medical Anthropology*, 1978, 1: 1–48.

GAY LEFT COLLECTIVE. Happy families? Pedophilia examined. In D. Tsang (Ed.), *The age taboo*. Boston: Alyson Publications, 1981.

GEBHARD, P., GAGNON, J., POMEROY, W. & CHRISTENSON, C. *Sex offenders: An analysis of types*. New York: Harper & Row, 1965.

GEIS, G. Forcible rape: An introduction. In D. Chappell, G. Geis & R. Geis, *Forcible rape: The crime, the victim and the offender*. New York: Columbia, 1977.

GEISER, R. *Hidden victims*. Boston: Beacon, 1978.

GELLES, R. Child abuse as psychopathology. *American Journal of Orthopsychiatry*, 1973, 43: 611–621.

GENTRY, C. Personal communication concerning the Project Against Sex Abuse of Appalachian Children, Knoxville, TN, 1978.

GIARETTO, H. A comprehensive child sexual abuse treatment program. *Child Abuse and Neglect*, 1981, 6: 263–278.

———. *Integrated treatment of child sexual abuse*. Palo Alto: Science and Behavior Books, 1982.

GIL, D. *Violence against children*. Cambridge: Harvard, 1973.

GIL, D. & NOBLE, J. H. Public knowledge, attitudes and opinions about physical child abuse in the U.S. *Child Welfare*, 1969, 48: 395–426.

GILLESPIE, W. H. The psycho-analytic theory of sexual deviation with special reference to fetishism. In I. Rosen (Ed.), *The psychology and treatment of sexual deviation*. New York: Oxford University Press, 1964.

GILLIGAN, C. *In a different voice*. Cambridge: Harvard, 1982.

GIOVANNONI, J. & BECCERA, R. *Defining child abuse*. New York: Free Press, 1979.

GLUECK, R. C. Pedophilia. In R. Slovenko (Ed.), *Sexual behavior and the law*. New York: Harper & Row, 1965.

GOLDSEN, R. Letter to the editors of *Human Behavior*, February 1978, pp. 7–8.

GOLDSTEIN, M. J., KANT, H. S. & HARTMAN, J. J. *Pornography and sexual deviance*. Los Angeles: University of California Press, 1973.

GOODE, W. *World revolution and family patterns.* New York: Free Press, 1963.

GOODWIN, J. & GEIL, C. Why physicians should report child abuse: The example of sexual abuse. In J. Goodwin, (Ed.), *Sexual abuse: Incest victims and their families.* Boston: John Wright–PSG, 1982.

GOODWIN, J., McCARTHY, T. & DiVASTO, P. Prior incest in mothers of abused children. *Child Abuse and Neglect,* 1981, *5:* 87–95.

GORDON, L. Incest, social work and daughters resistance, 1880-1930. Boston: University of Massachusetts (Mimeo), 1982.

GOY, R. & McEWEN, B. S. *Sexual differentiation of the brain.* Cambridge, MA: MIT Press, 1977.

GREENE, N. B. A view of family pathology involving child molest—from juvenile probation perspective. *Juvenile Justice,* 1977, *13:* 29–34.

GRIFFITH, S., ANDERSON, S., BACH, C. & PAPERNY, D. Intrafamilial sexual abuse of male children: An underreported problem. Paper presented at the Third International Congress of Child Abuse and Neglect. Amsterdam, 1981.

GROSS, A. The male role and heterosexual behavior. *Journal of Social Issues,* 1978, *34:* 87–107.

GROTH, N. *Men who rape.* New York: Plenum, 1979.

———. Personal communication, 1983.

GROTH, N. & BIRNBAUM, J. Adult sexual orientation and the attraction to underage persons. *Archives of Sexual Behavior,* 1978, *7:* 175–181.

GROTH, N. & BURGESS, A. Motivational intent in the sexual assault of children. *Criminal Justice and Behavior,* 1977, *4:* 253–264.

GROTH, N. A. & BURGESS, A. W. Sexual trauma in the life histories of rapists and child molesters. *Victimology,* 1979, *4:* 10–16.

GROTH, N. A., HOBSON, W. & GARY, T. The child molester: Clinical observations. In J. Conte & D. Shore (Eds.), *Social work and child sexual abuse.* New York: Haworth, 1982.

GRUBER, K. & JONES, R. Identifying determinants of risk of sexual victimization of youth. *Child Abuse and Neglect,* 1983, *7:* 17–24.

GUIO, M., BURGESS, A. & KELLY, R. Child victimization: Pornography and prostitution. *Journal of Crime and Justice,* 1980, *3:* 65–81.

GUNDLACH, R. Sexual molestation and rape reported by homosexual and heterosexual women. *Journal of Homosexuality,* 1977, *2:* 367–384.

GUTTMACHER, M. & WEIHOFEN, H. *Sex offenses: The problem, causes and prevention.* New York: Norton, 1951.

HAMILTON, G. V. *A research in marriage.* New York: Lear, 1929.

HAMMER, E. F. & GLUECK, B. C., JR. Psychodynamic patterns in sex offense: A four-factor theory. *Psychiatric Quarterly,* 1957, *3:* 325–345.

HENDERSON, J. Incest: A synthesis of data. *Canadian Psychiatric Association Journal,* 1972, *17:* 299–313.

HENSON, D. E. & RUBIN, H. B. Voluntary control of eroticism. *Journal of Applied Behavior Analysis*, 1971, *4*: 37–44.

HERMAN, J. *Father–daughter incest.* Cambridge: Harvard, 1981.

HERMAN, J. & HIRSCHMAN, L. Father–daughter incest. *Signs*, 1977, *2*: 1–22.

HITE, S. *The Hite report on male sexuality.* New York: Knopf, 1981.

HOOVER, J. E. How safe is your daughter? *American Magazine*, July 1947, 32.

Horror Week. *Newsweek*, November 28, 1949.

HOWELLS, K. Some meanings of children for pedophiles. In M. Cook & G. Wilson (Eds.), *Love and attraction.* Oxford: Pergamon, 1979.

———. Social reactions to sexual deviance. In D. J. West (Ed.), *Sex offenders in the criminal justice system.* Cambridge, U.K.: Cropwood, 1980.

———. Adult sexual interest in children: Considerations relevant to theories of etiology. In M. Cook & K. Howells (Eds.), *Adult sexual interest in children.* New York: Academic Press, 1981.

HUNT, M. *Sex in the 1970's.* Chicago: Playboy Press, 1974.

JAFFE, A. C., DYNNESON, L. & TEN BENSEL, R. Sexual abuse: An epidemiological study. *American Journal of Diseases of Children*, 1975, *129*: 689–692.

JAMES, J. & MEYERDING, J. Early sexual experiences as a factor in prostitution. *Archives of Sexual Behavior*, 1977, 7: 31–42.

JAMES, J., WOMACK, W. & STRAUSS, F. Physician reporting of sexual abuse and children. *Journal of the American Medical Association*, 1978, *240*: 1145–1146.

JANUS, M.-D., SCANLON, B. & PRICE, V. Youth prostitution. In A. Burgess (Ed.), *Child pornography and sex rings.* Lexington, MA: Lexington Books, 1984.

JASSO, G. & ROSSI, P. H. Distributive justice and earned income. *American Sociological Review*, 1977, *42*: 639–652.

JONES, R., GRUBER, K. & TIMBERS, G. Incidence and situational factors surrounding sexual assault against delinquent youths. *Child Abuse and Neglect*, 1981, *5*: 431–440.

JUSTICE, B. & JUSTICE, R. *The broken taboo.* New York: Human Sciences, 1979.

KANIN, E. Male aggression in dating–courtship relations. *American Journal of Sociology*, 1957, *63*: 197–204.

KARPMAN, B. *The sexual offender and his offenses.* New York: Julian Press, 1954.

KAUFMAN, A., DiVASTO, P., JACKSON, R., VOORHEES, D. & CHRISTY, J. Male rape victims: Noninstitutionalized assault. *American Journal of Psychiatry*, 1980, *137*: 221–223.

KAUFMAN, I., PECK, A. & TAGIURI, C. K. The family constellation and overt incestuous relations between father and daughter. *American Journal of Orthopsychiatry*, 1954, *24*: 266–279.

KELLEY, R. J. Behavioral re-orientation of pedophiliacs: Can it be done? *Clinical Psychology Review*, 1982, *2*: 387–408.

KEMPE, H. C. Sexual abuse, another hidden pediatric problem. *Pediatrics,* 1978, *62:* 382–389.

KENT, C. *Child sexual abuse project: An educational program for children.* Minneapolis, MN: Hennepin County Attorney's Office Sexual Assault Services, 1979.

KERCHER, G. *Responding to child sexual abuse.* Huntsville, TX: Sam Houston State University, Criminal Justice Center, 1980.

KERCHER, G. & McSHANE, M. The prevalence of child sexual abuse victimization in an adult sample of Texas residents. Huntsville, TX: Sam Houston State University (Mimeo), 1983.

KERLINGER, F. & PEDHAZUR, E. *Multiple regression in behavior research.* New York: Holt, 1973.

KINSEY, A., POMEROY, W. & MARTIN, C. *Sexual behavior in the human male.* Philadelphia: Saunders, 1948.

KINSEY, A., POMEROY, W., MARTIN, C. & GEBHARD, P. *Sexual behavior in the human female.* Philadelphia: Saunders, 1953.

KILPATRICK, D., VERONEN, L. & RESNICK, P. The aftermath of rape: Recent empirical findings. *American Journal of Orthopsychiatry,* 1979, *49:* 658–669.

KLEMESRUD, J. 'Lolita syndrome' is denounced. *New York Times,* March 3, 1981, p. B14.

KNOPP, F. H. *Remedial intervention in adolescent sex offenses: Nine program descriptions.* New York: Safer Society Press, 1982.

KOCEN, L. & BULKLEY, J. Analysis of criminal child sex offense statutes. In J. Bulkley (Ed.), *Child sexual abuse and the law.* Washington: American Bar Association, 1981.

KRAEMER, W. A paradise lost. In W. Kraemer (Ed.), *The forbidden love: The normal and abnormal love of children.* London: Sheldon Press, 1976.

LANDIS, J. Experiences of 500 children with adult sexual deviants. *Psychiatric Quarterly Supplement,* 1956, *30:* 91–109.

LANGEVIN, R. *Sexual strands: Understanding and treating sexual anomalies in men.* Hillsdale, NJ: Erlbaum Associates, 1983.

LANGEVIN, R., HANDY, L., HOOK, H., DAY, D. & RUSSON, A. Are incestuous fathers pedophilic and aggressive? In R. Langevin (Ed.), *Erotic preference, gender identity and aggression.* New York: Erlbaum Associates, 1983.

LANGNER, T. *Life stress and mental health.* New York: McGraw-Hill, 1962.

LANGSLEY, D. G., SCHWARTZ, M. N. & FAIRBAIRN, R. H. Father–son incest. *Comprehensive Psychiatry,* 1968, *9:* 218–226.

LAWS, D. R. & O'NEIL, J. A. Variations on masturbatory conditioning. Paper presented at the 2nd National Conference on Evaluation and Treatment of Sexual Aggressives. New York, 1979.

LAWS, D. R. & RUBIN, H. B. Instructional control of an automatic sexual response. *Journal of Applied Behavior Analysis,* 1969, *2:* 93–99.

LEVINE, R. A. Gusii sex offense: A study in social control. In D. Chappell, R. Geis &

G. Geis (Eds.), *Forcible rape: The crime, the victim and the offender.* New York: Columbia University Press, 1977.

LIGHT, R. Abused and neglected children in America: A study of alternative policies. *Harvard Educational Review,* 1974, *43:* 556–598.

LOSS, P. & GLANCY, E. Men who sexually abuse their children. *Medical Aspects of Human Sexuality,* 1983, *17:* 328–329.

LUKIANOWICZ, N. Incest. *British Journal of Psychiatry,* 1972, *120:* 301–313.

LUSTIG, N., DRESSER, J. W., SPELLMAN, S. W. & MURRAY, T. B. Incest. *Archives of General Psychology,* 1966, *14:* 31–40.

LYSTAD, M. H. Sexual abuse in the home: A review of the literature. *International Journal of Family Psychiatry,* 1982.

MACFARLANE, K. Personal communication, 1982.

MACFARLANE, K. & BULKLEY, J. Treating child sexual abuse: An overview of current program models. In J. Conte & D. Shore (Eds.), *Social Work and Child Sexual Abuse.* New York: Haworth, 1982.

MACFARLANE, K., JONES, B. & JENSTROM, L. *Sexual abuse of children: Selected readings.* Washington: DHHS, 1980.

MACHOTKA, P., PITTMAN, F. S. & FLOMENHAFT, K. Incest as a family affair. *Family Process,* 1966, *6:* 98–116.

MADEN, M. & WRENCH, D. Significant findings in child abuse research. *Victimology,* 1977, *2:* 196–224.

MAISCH, H. *Incest.* New York: Stein and Day, 1972.

MARSHALL, P. D. & NORGARD, K. E. *Child abuse and neglect: Sharing responsibility.* New York: Wiley, 1983.

MARSHALL, W. I. & McKNIGHT, R. D. An integrated program for sexual offenders. *Canadian Psychiatric Association Journal,* 1975, *20:* 133–138.

MARTINSON, F. M. *Infant and child sexuality.* St. Peter, MN: The Book Mark, 1973.

MASSON, J. M. *The assault on truth: Freud's suppression of the seduction theory.* New York: Farrar, Straus & Giroux, 1984.

MASTERS, W. H. & JOHNSON, V. E. *Homosexuality in perspective.* Boston: Little, Brown, 1979.

McAULIFFE, S. Is sexual deviance a biological problem? *Psychology Today,* 1983 (March), p. 84.

McCAGHY, C. H. Drinking and deviance disavowal: The case of child molesters. *Social Problems,* 1968, *16:* 43–49.

——. The moral crusade against child pornography: Some reflections. Paper presented to the American Society of Criminology, Philadelphia, November 1979.

McGUIRE, I. S. & WAGNER, N. N. Sexual dysfunction in women who were molested as children: On response patterns and suggestions for treatment. *Journal of Sex and Marital Therapy,* 1978, *4:* 11–15.

McGuire, R. J., Carlisle, J. M. & Young, B. G. Sexual deviations and conditioned behavior: A hypothesis. *Behavior Research Therapy*, 1965, *2*: 185–190.

McIntyre, K. Role of mothers in father–daughter incest: A feminist analysis. *Social Work*, 1981, *26*: 462–466.

Meiselman, K. *Incest: A psychological study of causes and effects with treatment recommendations.* San Francisco: Jossey-Bass, 1978.

Menninger, K. *Love against hate.* New York: Harcourt, Brace & World, 1942.

Miller, J., Moeller, D., Kaufman, A., DiVasto, P., Pathak, D. & Christy, J. Recidivism among sex assault victims. *American Journal of Psychiatry*, 1978, *135*: 1103–1104.

Miller, P. Blaming the victim of child molestation: An empirical analysis. Doctoral dissertation, Northwestern University, 1976. Dissertation Abstracts International, 1976. University Microfilms No. 77-10069.

Mohr, J. W., Turner, R. E. & Jerry, M. B. *Pedophilia and exhibitionism.* Toronto: University of Toronto, 1964.

Money, J. Sex hormones and other variables in human eroticism. In W. C. Young (Ed.), *Sex and internal secretions, VIII.* Baltimore: Williams and Wilkins, 1961.

———. Paraphilias: Phyletic origins of erotosexual dysfunction. *International Journal of Mental Health*, 1981a, *10*: 75–109.

———. Paraphilia and abuse martyrdom: Exhibitionism as a paradigm for reciprocal couple counseling combined with antiandrogen. *Journal of Sex and Marital Therapy*, 1981b, *7*: 115–123.

Morgan, P. Alcohol and family violence: A review of the literature. National Institute of Alcoholism and Alcohol Abuse, Alcohol consumption and related problems. *Alcohol and Health Monograph 1.* Washington, D.C.: DHHS, 1982.

Mrazek, P. & Kempe, H. *Sexually abused children and their families.* New York: Pergamon, 1981.

Mrazek, P., Lynch, M. & Bentovim, A. Recognition of child sexual abuse in the United Kingdom. In P. Mrazek & H. Kempe (Eds.), *Sexually abused children and their families.* New York: Pergamon, 1981.

———. Sexual abuse of children in the United Kingdom. *Child Abuse and Neglect*, 1983, *7*: 147–153.

Nabokov, V. *Lolita.* New York: Putnam, 1955.

Nakashima, I. Runaway girls. *Medical Aspects of Human Sexuality*, August 1982, *16*(8): 49–50.

Nasjleti, M. Suffering in silence: The male incest victim. *Child Welfare*, 1980, *59*: 269–275.

National Center for Child Abuse and Neglect (NCCAN). *Study findings: National study of incidence and severity of child abuse and neglect.* Washington, D.C.: DHEW, 1981.

NELSON, J. The impact of incest. In L. L. Constantine & F. Martinson (Eds.), *Children and sex*. Boston: Little, Brown, 1981.

NELSON, S. *Incest: Fact and myth*. Edinburgh: Stramullion, 1982.

NEWBERGER, C. Cognitive structure of parenthood. In R. Selman & R. Yando (Eds.), *New directions in child development, Vol. 7*, 1980.

NEWBERGER, C. & COOK, S. J. Parental awareness and child abuse and neglect: A cognitive developmental analysis of urban and rural parents. *American Journal of Orthopsychiatry*, 1983, *53*: 512–524.

NEWTON, D. Homosexual behavior and child molestation: A review of the evidence. *Adolescence*, 1978, *13*: 29–43.

NOBILE, P. Incest: The last taboo. *Penthouse*, January, 1977, p. 117.

NORTH AMERICAN MAN/BOY LOVE ASSOCIATION (NAMBLA). The case for abolishing the age of consent laws. In D. Tsang (Ed.), *The age taboo*. Boston: Alyson Publications, 1981.

NUNNALLY, J. D. *Psychometric theory*. New York: McGraw-Hill, 1967.

NYHAN, D. For three girls, justice takes a holiday. *Boston Globe*, February 11, 1982.

O'CARROLL, T. *Paedophilia: The radical case*. Boston: Alyson Publications, 1980.

O'DAY, B. *Preventing sexual abuse of persons with disabilities*. St. Paul, MN: Minnesota Department of Corrections, 1983.

PANTON, J. MMPI profile configurations associated with incestuous and non-incestuous child molesting. *Psychological Reports*, 1979, *45*: 335–338.

PANTON, J. H. Personality differences appearing between rapists of adults, rapists of children, and non-violent sexual molesters of children. *Research Communications in Psychology, Psychiatry and Behavior*. 1978, *3*(4): 385–393.

PARSONS, T. Social structure of the family. In R. N. Anshen (Ed.), *The family: Its function and destiny*. New York: Harper, 1949.

PELTO, V. Male incest offenders and non-offenders: A comparison of early sexual history. Dissertation, United States International University. Ann Arbor, MI: University Microfilms, 1981.

PERSON, E. S. Sexuality as the mainstay of identity. *Signs*, 1980, *5*: 605–630.

PETERS, J. J. Children who are victims of sexual assault and the psychology of offenders. *American Journal of Psychotherapy*, 1976, *30*: 398–412.

PILINOW, A. Cynniki rozktadu I technika rozbijania podstowowych wiezi spoteczych. In A. Podgorecki (Ed.), *Socjotechnika*, Ksiazka i Wiedza, 1970.

PFOHL, S. J. The discovery of child abuse. *Social Problems*, 1977, *24*: 310–323.

PLUMMER, K. Pedophilia: Constructing a sociological baseline. In M. Cook & K. Howells (Eds.), *Adult sexual interest in children*. London: Academic Press, 1981.

POMEROY, W. *Boys and sex*. New York: Delacorte, 1968.

——. *Your child and sex*. New York: Delacorte, 1974.

——— A new look at incest. *The Best of Forum*, 1978, pp. 92–97.

POPE, H. & MUELLER, C. W. Intergenerational transmission of marital instability: Comparisons by race and sex. *Journal of Social Issues*, 1976, *32*: 49–66.

PRENTKY, R. A. Personal communication. 1983.

PRESCOTT, J. W. Body pleasure and the origins of violence. *The Futurist*, 1975, pp. 64–74.

PRESLAND, E. Whose power? Whose consent? In D. Tsang (Ed.), *The age taboo*. Boston: Alyson Publications, 1981.

QUEEN'S BENCH FOUNDATION. *Sexual abuse of children*. San Francisco, CA: Queen's Bench Foundation, 1976.

QUINSEY, V. L. The assessment and treatment of child molesters: A review. *Canadian Psychological Review*, 1977, *18*: 204–220.

QUINSEY, V. L., STEINMAN, C. M., BERGENSEN, S. G. & HOLMES, T. F. Penile circumference, skin conduction, and ranking responses of child molesters and "normals" to sexual and nonsexual visual stimuli. *Behavior Therapy*, 1975, *6*: 213–219.

RADA, R. T. Alcoholism and the child molester. *Annals of New York Academy of Science*, 1976, *273*: 492–496.

RANDALL, G. Safe in the streets. *PTA Magazine*, 1971, *65*: 5–7.

RAPHLING, D., CARPENTER, B. & DAVIS, A. Incest: A geneological study. *Archives of General Psychiatry*, 1967, *16*: 505–511.

RIEMER, S. A research note on incest. *Comprehensive Psychiatry*, 1940, *2*: 338–349.

ROBERTS, E., KLINE, D. & GAGNON, J. *Family life and sexual learning*. Cambridge, MA: Project on Human Sexual Development, 1978.

ROGERS, C. Findings from a hospital-based sexual abuse treatment program. Paper presented at Children's Hospital Medical Center Conference on Sexual Victimization of Children, Washington, D.C., December 1979.

———. Child sexual abuse and the courts: Preliminary findings. In J. R. Conte & D. Shore (Eds.), *Social work and child sexual abuse*. New York: Haworth, 1982.

RONSTROM, A. Sexuella overgrepp po barn I sverige. Paper delivered to Radda Barnens Nordiska Seminarium om Barnmisshandel, Tallberg, Sweden, 1983.

ROSENFELD, A. Incest: The victim-perpetrator model. Unpublished paper, Stanford University, 1978.

ROSSI, P., WAITE, E., BOSE, C. & BERK, R. The seriousness of crimes: Normative structures and individual differences. *American Sociological Review*, 1974, *39*: 224–237.

ROSSI, P. H. & NOCK, S. L. *Measuring social judgements: The factorial survey approach*. Beverly Hills: Sage, 1982.

ROSSMAN, P. *Sexual experience between men and boys*. New York: Association Press, 1976.

RUCH, L. O. & CHANDLER, S. M. The crisis impact of sexual assault on three victim groups: Adult rape victims, child rape victims and incest victims. *Journal of Social Service Research*, 1982, 5: 83–100.

RUSH, F. The Freudian cover-up. *Chrysalis*, 1977, 1: 31–45.

———. *The best kept secret.* New York: Prentice-Hall, 1980.

RUSSELL, D. The prevalence and impact of marital rape in San Francisco. Paper presented to the American Sociological Association, New York, 1980.

———. Preliminary report on some findings relating to the trauma and long-term effects of intrafamily childhood sexual abuse. Paper presented to the Conference on Child Prostitution and Pornography, Boston, 1981.

———. *Rape in Marriage.* New York: Macmillan, 1982a.

———. Rape, child sexual abuse, sexual harassment in the workplace: An analysis of the prevalence, causes and recommended solutions. Final report for the California Commission on Crime Control and Violence Prevention, March 1982.

———. Incidence and prevalence of intrafamilial and extrafamilial sexual abuse of female children. *Child Abuse and Neglect*, 1983, 7: 133–146.

———. *Sexual exploitation: Rape, child sexual abuse, and sexual harassment.* Beverly Hills: Sage, 1984.

SANDAY, P. The socio-cultural context of rape: A cross cultural study. *Journal of Social Issues*, 1981, 37: 5–27.

SANDFORT, T. *The sexual aspect of paedophile relations.* Amsterdam: Pan/Spartacus, 1982.

SANFORD, L. *The silent children.* New York: Doubleday, 1980.

SCHENE, P., Associate Director, Children's Division, American Humane Association. Personal communication. March 3, 1983.

SCHIFF, A. Rape in foreign countries. *Medical Trial Technique Quarterly*, 1973, 20: 66–74.

SCHULTZ, L. Child sexual abuse in historical perspective. In J. R. Conte & D. Shore (Eds.), *Social work and child sexual abuse.* New York: Haworth, 1982.

SEGHORN, T. & BOUCHER, R. Sexual abuse in childhood as a factor in adult sexually dangerous criminal offenses. In J. M. Samson (Ed.), *Childhood and sexuality.* Montreal: Editions Vivantes, 1980.

SGROI, S. An approach to case management. In *Handbook of clinical intervention in child sexual abuse.* Lexington, MA: Lexington Books, 1982.

SHEPHER, J. Mate selection among second generation kibbutz adolescents and adults. *Archives of Sexual Behavior*, 1971, 1: 293–307.

SHEPPARD, D., GIACINTI, T. & TJADEN, C. Rape re-education: A citywide program. In M. Walker & S. Brodsky (Eds.), *Sexual assault.* Lexington, MA: Lexington Books, 1976.

SILBERT, M. & PINES, A. Sexual child abuse as an antecedent to prostitution. *Child Abuse and Neglect*, 1981, 5: 407–411.

STOLL, K. Personal communication, 1981.

STOLLER, R. *Perversion: The erotic form of hatred.* New York: Pantheon, 1975.

STONE, L. Child pornography: A content analysis. Dissertation proposal, International College, 1983.

STORR, A. *Sexual deviation.* London: Heineman, 1965.

STRAUS, M. Indexing and scaling for the social sciences with SPSS. Unpublished manuscript, University of New Hampshire, 1979.

STRAUS, M. A., GELLES, R. & STEINMETZ, S. *Behind closed doors: Violence in the American family.* New York: Doubleday, 1980.

STRICKER, G. Stimulus properties of the Blacky to a sample of pedophiles. *The Journal of General Psychology,* 1967, 77: 35–39.

SUMMIT, R. Beyond belief: The reluctant discovery of incest. In M. Kirkpatrick (Ed.), *Women in context.* New York: Plenum, 1981a.

———. Recognition and treatment of child sexual abuse. In C. Hollingsworth (Ed.), *Providing for the emotional health of the pediatric patient.* New York: Spectrum, 1981b.

SUMMIT, R. & KRYSO, J. Sexual abuse of children: A clinical spectrum. *American Journal of Orthopsychiatry,* 1978, 48: 237–251.

SWANSON, D. W. Adult sexual abuse of children: The man and circumstances. *Diseases of the Nervous System,* 1968, 29: 677–683.

SWIFT, C. Prevention of sexual child abuse: Focus on the perpetrator. *Journal of Clinical Child Psychology,* 1979, 8(2): 133–136.

SYMONS, D. *The evolution of human sexuality.* New York: Oxford University Press, 1979.

SZABO, D. L'inceste en milieu urbain. *L'année Sociologique* (3eme serie), 1958.

TERMAN, L. *Psychological factors in marital happiness.* New York: McGraw-Hill, 1938.

———. Correlates of orgasm adequacy in a group of 556 wives. *Journal of Psychology,* 1951, 32: 115–172.

THYFAULT, R. Sexual abuse in the battering relationship. Paper presented to the Rocky Mountain Psychological Association, Tucson, 1980.

TIERNEY, K. & CORWIN, D. Exploring intra-familial child sexual abuse: A systems approach. In D. Finkelhor, R. Gelles, G. Hotaling & M. Straus (Eds.), *The dark side of families: Current family violence research.* Beverly Hills: Sage, 1983.

TSAI, M., FELDMAN-SUMMERS, S. & EDGAR, M. Childhood molestation: Variables related to differential impacts on psychosexual functioning in adult women. *Journal of Abnormal Psychology,* 1979, 88: 407–417.

TSANG, D. *The age taboo.* Boston: Alyson Publications, 1981.

TYLER, T. Child pornography. Paper presented at the Fourth International Congress on Child Abuse and Neglect, Paris, 1982.

VAN DEN BERGHE, P. L. Human inbreeding avoidance: Culture in nature. *Behavioral and Brain Sciences,* 1983, 6: 91–123.

VERMEULEN, M. Turning kids into sex symbols. *Parade*, March 8, 1981, pp. 4–6.

VIRKKUNEN, M. Incest offenses and alcoholism. *Medicine, Science and Law*, 1974, *14:* 124–128.

WALLERSTEIN, J. Children of divorce: Preliminary report of a 10-year follow-up. Paper presented at the American Academy of Law and Psychiatry, Portland, OR, 1983.

WALTERS, D. *Physical and sexual abuse of children.* Bloomington, IN: Indiana University Press, 1975.

WEBER, E. Sexual abuse begins at home. *Ms.*, April 1977, pp. 64–67.

WEINBERG, K. *Incest behavior.* New York: Citadel, 1955.

WEISS, J., ROGERS, E., DARWIN, M. & DUTTON, C. A study of girl sex victims. *Psychiatric Quarterly*, 1955: *29:* 1–2.

WENET, G. A., CLARK, T. R. & HUNNER, R. J. Perspectives on the juvenile sex offender. In R. J. Hunner & Y. E. Walker, (Eds.), *Exploring the relationship between child abuse and delinquency.* Montclair: Allanheld, Osmun, 1981.

WHITMAN, W. & QUINSEY, V. Heterosocial skill training for institutionalized rapists and child molesters. *Canadian Journal of Behavioral Science*, 1981, *13:* 105–114.

WINN, M. What became of childhood innocence? *New York Times Magazine*, January 25, 1981, pp. 15–17, 44–68.

YATES, A. *Sex without shame: Encouraging the child's healthy sexual development.* New York: Morrow, 1978.

YOUTH, POLICE AND LAW CENTER, Wisconsin Female Juvenile Offender Study Project. Summary report. Madison: PPLC, 1982.

ZILBERGELD, B. *Male sexuality.* New York: Bantam, 1978.

Index

257

Doubleday

New York London Toronto Sydney Auckland

Joy
Fielding

Missing
Pieces

PUBLISHED BY DOUBLEDAY
a division of Bantam Doubleday Dell Publishing Group, Inc.
1540 Broadway, New York, New York 10036

DOUBLEDAY and the portrayal of an anchor with a dolphin
are trademarks of Doubleday, a division of
Bantam Doubleday Dell Publishing Group, Inc.

Book design by Maria Carella
Title page illustration copyright © 1997 by Marcie Wolf-Hubbard

Library of Congress Cataloging-in-Publication Data
Fielding, Joy.
    Missing pieces: a novel / by Joy Fielding. — 1st ed.
       p.   cm.
       I. Title.
PR9199.3.F518M57   1997
813'.54—dc21   96–40901
                              CIP

ISBN 0-385-48521-2

Printed in the United States of America

First Edition

August 1997

10   9   8   7   6   5   4   3   2   1

For Carole

Acknowledgments

I wish to thank officials at the Union Correctional Institution and the Florida State Prison who provided me with much needed information. I would especially like to thank the staff of the medical examiner's office of Palm Beach County who were so generous with both their time and expertise. A special thank-you to Lawrence L. Lewis, a volunteer at the Palm Beach County Courthouse, who gave me directions, pamphlets, and a much-appreciated cup of coffee at the end of a very long day.

My heartfelt gratitude to Larry Merkin and Beverley Slopen, both of whom read earlier drafts of the manuscript and offered invaluable advice and encouragement.

Thank you to Janet Tanzer and Sally Muir, two of the world's great family therapists, whose wit and wisdom changed my life. And to my daughters, Shannon and Annie—I couldn't have written this book without them.

Lastly, my thanks to my husband, Warren, for everything.

Missing Pieces

Chapter

1

Another woman is missing.

Her name is Millie Potton and she was last seen two days ago. According to today's paper, Millie is tall and thin and walks with a slight limp. She is fifty-four years old, which isn't surprising. Only women over fifty have names like Millie anymore.

The small article on page three of the local news section of the *Palm Beach Post* states that she was last seen wandering down the street in her bathrobe by a neighbor, a woman who obviously saw nothing particularly peculiar in the incident. Millie Potton, the article continues, has a long history of mental problems, the implication being that it is these mental problems that are responsible for her disappearance and are not therefore anything the rest of us have to be concerned about.

Over two dozen women have disappeared from the Palm Beach area in the last five years. I know because I've been keeping track, not con-

sciously, at least not at first, but after a while their numbers just started adding up, and a vague figure affixed itself to my conscious mind. The women range in age from sixteen to sixty. The police have dismissed some as runaways, especially the younger ones, girls like Amy Lokash, age seventeen, who left a friend's house at ten o'clock one evening and was never seen or heard from again. Others, and Millie Potton will undoubtedly be among them, have been dismissed for any number of indisputably logical reasons, even though the police were wrong about Amy Lokash.

Still, until a body turns up somewhere, stuffed into a garbage bin behind Burger King like Marilyn Greenwood, age twenty-four, or floating facedown in a Port Everglades swamp like Christine McDermott, age thirty-three, there really isn't anything the police can do. Or so they say. Women, it seems, go missing all the time.

It's quiet in the house this morning, what with everybody gone. I have lots of time to tape my report. I call it a report, but really it isn't anything so clearly defined. It's more a series of reminiscences, although the police have asked me to be as specific and as orderly as I can, to be careful not to leave anything out, no matter how insignificant—or how personal—something may seem. They will decide what is important, they tell me.

I'm not sure I understand the point. What's done is done. It's not as if I can go back and change any of the things that have happened, much as I'd like to, much as I tried to before they occurred. But I was just hitting my head against a brick wall. I knew it at the time. I know it now. There are certain things over which we have no control—the actions of others being the prime example. Much as we may not like it, we have to stand back and let people go their own way, make their own mistakes, no matter how clearly we see disaster looming. Isn't that what I'm always telling my clients?

Of course, it's much easier to give advice than it is to follow it. Maybe that's one of the reasons I became a family therapist, although that certainly wasn't the reason I gave on my college entry application. There, if memory serves me correctly, and it does so with alarmingly less frequency all the time, I listed my intense desire to help others, my

reputation among friends as someone to whom they could always turn in times of trouble, my experience with my own dysfunctional family, although the term "dysfunctional" had yet to be coined at the time I entered university way back in 1966. It's so common now, so much a part of the everyday vernacular, that it's hard to imagine how we managed for so long without it, despite the fact that it's essentially meaningless. What constitutes dysfunction, after all? What family doesn't have problems? I'm certain my own daughters could give you an earful.

So, where to start? This is what my first-time clients ask all the time. They come into my office, which is on the third floor of a five-story Pepto-Bismol pink building on Royal Palm Way, their eyes wary, the fingers of one hand chipping at the wedding band on the other, as they perch on the ends of the upholstered gray-and-white chairs, their lips parting in anticipation, their mouths eager to give voice to their rage, their fears, their displeasure, and the first thing that tumbles out is always the same: Where do I start?

Usually, I ask them to describe the event that brought them to my office, the proverbial straw that broke the camel's back. They think for several seconds, then start slowly, building their case from the ground up, like a new house, piling detail upon detail, like blocks, one on top of the other, one indignity crowding against another, perceived slight over implied threat, the words spilling out so fast that they barely have time to fit them all into the space of an hour.

I've used a building analogy—Larry would be amused at this. Larry is my husband of twenty-four years, and he's a builder. A good portion of those spectacular new homes going up on golf courses across Palm Beach County are his. His profession is supposedly the reason we relocated from Pittsburgh to Florida some seven years ago, but I've always suspected that at least part of the reason Larry was so anxious to move down here was to get away from my mother and sister. He denies this, but since it was a large part of the reason *I* agreed so readily to the move, I have always found his denials suspect. It's pretty much a moot point anyway, since my mother followed us here less than a year later, and my sister several months after that.

My sister's name is Jo Lynn. Or at least, that's the name she goes

by. Her real name is Joanne Linda. But our father took to calling her Jo Lynn when she was just a child, and the name stuck. Actually, it suits her. She looks like a Jo Lynn, tall and blond and bosomy, with an infectious giggle that starts somewhere deep in her throat and ends up floating around her head like fairy dust. Even the deep, honey-coated Southern accent she's affected since moving to Florida seems more right, more genuine somehow, than the flat, cold tones of the North she spoke with for most of her thirty-seven years.

I said my father, but in fact he was only Jo Lynn's father, and not mine. My father died when I was eight years old. The way my mother tells it, he got up from the dinner table to get a glass of milk, remarked casually that he felt a hell of a headache coming on, and the next minute he was dead on the floor. An aneurysm, the doctor later pronounced. My mother remarried the following year, and Jo Lynn came along the year after that, just weeks after my tenth birthday.

My stepfather was a mean and manipulative man who relied more on his fists than his brains, assuming he had any. I'm sure it was from him that Jo Lynn acquired her lifelong habit of picking abusive men, although he was always very tender with her, his clear favorite. It was my mother who bore the brunt of his ill temper. Aside from a few well-placed cuffs to the back of the head, he largely ignored me. At any rate, my mother left him when Jo Lynn was thirteen and I'd already left home to marry Larry. My stepfather died the following year of pancreatic cancer. Jo Lynn was the only one of us who mourned.

And now I cry for my sister, as I have so often over the years. Technically, of course, she's only my half sister, and the ten-year age difference, coupled with her often erratic behavior, made it difficult for us to be close. But I will never forget the morning my mother first brought her home from the hospital, how she walked toward me cradling this small golden bundle in her arms and gently transferred her to mine, telling me I had a real doll to help care for now. I remember standing beside her crib for hours at a time while she slept, watching carefully for telltale signs of growth, as she moved inexorably from baby to toddler. She was such a beautiful child, so headstrong and confident, in the way small children have of knowing that they are absolutely right about ev-

erything, that it's still hard to reconcile that image with the lost soul she grew into, one of those people who wander aimlessly through life, always convinced that success and happiness are just around the corner. Except that she'd get distracted, forget what direction she was headed in, make a wrong turn, and end up on a dead-end street, no corners anywhere in sight.

I see traces of her in my older daughter, Sara, who also has to learn everything the hard way, and it scares me. Maybe that's why I'm on her back all the time, or so she says. Actually, Sara never *says* anything—she yells. She believes that the way to win an argument is to keep repeating the same thing over and over, each time louder than the time before. She's probably right, because eventually you either give in or run screaming from the room. I've done both more times than I care to admit. My clients would be properly horrified.

Sara is seventeen and stands just under six feet tall. Like Jo Lynn, she has big green eyes and huge breasts. I don't know where they came from. To be honest, I'm not all that sure where *she* came from. Sometimes, I look at her when she's in the middle of one of her tirades and wonder: Did the hospital make a mistake? Could this tall, wide-eyed, big-breasted creature screaming at me at the top of her lungs really be mine? There are days when I look at her and I think that she's the most beautiful thing on the face of this earth. Then there are other days when I swear she looks just like Patricia Krenwinkel. You remember her—she was one of Charles Manson's murderous gang, the sullen-faced teenaged killer with the long brown hair parted lazily down the middle, her eyes blank yet unforgiving, the same look I occasionally see on Sara's face. Sara wears clothes I swear I threw out twenty-five years ago, those shapeless, see-through, Indian caftans I have since come to despise, unlike Michelle, my fourteen-year-old, who will only wear clothes from Club Monaco and The Gap, and who carefully monitors each family altercation from the sidelines, commenting on the action later, like some skinny, adolescent Greek chorus. Or budding family therapist.

Is that why I have relatively few problems with my younger child? Do I want, as my elder daughter has suggested numerous times, that everyone be exactly like me? "I'm not you," she yells. "I'm my own

person!" And isn't that exactly what I've brought her up to be? But does her own person have to be so objectionable? Was I so rebellious, so rude, so downright miserable? I ask my mother, who smiles cryptically and assures me I was perfect.

Jo Lynn, she adds wearily, was another story.

"I wish on you a daughter just like you," I still hear my mother shouting at Jo Lynn in exasperation, something I've had to bite my tongue to keep from saying myself on more than one occasion. But whether out of spite or fear, my sister remained childless through three failed marriages, and I ended up with the daughter just like Jo Lynn. It doesn't seem fair. I was the one who played by the rules. If I was rebellious at all, I did so within all the prescribed parameters. I stayed in school, got my degree, didn't smoke, drink, or do drugs, and married the only man with whom I'd ever had sex. By contrast, Jo Lynn stayed in college only long enough to tune in, turn on, drop out, and was sexually active early and often. I became a family therapist; she became a family therapist's worst nightmare.

Why am I going into all this? Is this really the sort of thing the police will feel is relevant? I don't know. In truth, I don't know much of anything anymore. My whole life feels like one of those giant jigsaw puzzles, the kind that takes forever to put together, and then just when you're coming to the end, right at the point where you finally think you've got it, you discover that all the key pieces are missing.

With age comes wisdom, I distinctly remember hearing in my youth. I don't think so. With age comes wrinkles, I'm sure they meant. And bladder problems, and arthritis, and hot flashes, and memory loss. I'm not handling aging very well, which surprises me, because I always thought I'd be one of those women who grew old gracefully. But it's hard to be graceful when you're running to the bathroom every ten minutes or breaking into a sweat just after you've finished applying your makeup.

Everyone is younger than me. My dentist, my doctor, my daughters' teachers, my neighbors, the parents of my children's friends, my clients, even the police who came to question me—they're all younger than I am. It's funny because I always assume that I'm younger than everyone else,

and then I find out that not only am I older, I'm *years* older. And I'm the only one who's surprised.

Actually I surprise myself sometimes. I'll be all dressed up, feeling good, thinking I look great, and then I catch my reflection unexpectedly in a store window or a pane of glass, and I think: Who is that? Who is that middle-aged woman? It can't be me. I don't have those bags under my eyes; those aren't my legs; surely that's not my rear end. It's genuinely frightening when your self-image no longer corresponds to the image you see in the mirror. It's even scarier when you realize that other people barely see you at all, that you've become invisible.

Maybe that explains what happened with Robert.

How else can I explain it?

I'm doing it again, digressing, going off on one of my famous tangents. Larry says I do it all the time. I explain that I'm working my way up to the main point; he claims I'm trying to avoid it. He's probably right. At least, in this instance.

I'm about to have a hot flash. I know because I just got that horrible feeling of anxiety that always precedes it, as though someone has emptied a glass of ice water down my throat. It fills my chest, lies like a puddle around my heart. Ice followed by fire. I'm not sure which is worse.

At first I thought these feelings of anxiety were related to the chaos that was going on around me. I blamed my mother, my sister, Robert, the trial. Anything. But gradually I realized that these feelings of dread were immediately followed by tidal waves of heat that surged upward from the pit of my stomach toward my head, leaving me perspiring and breathless, as if I were in danger of imploding. I marvel at the strength of these interludes, at how powerless I am to stop them, at how little control I have over my own life.

My body has betrayed me; it follows an invisible timetable all its own. I wear reading glasses now; my skin is losing some of its elasticity, rippling like cheap fabric; there are thin lines around my neck, like the age lines of a tree. Things grow inside me, uninvited.

I was at the doctor's recently for a checkup. During the course of a

routine pelvic examination, Dr. Wong, who is tiny and delicate and looks all of eighteen, discovered several cervical polyps which she said had to be removed. "How did they get there?" I asked. She shrugged. "These things happen as we get older." She gave me the choice: she could schedule an operation in several weeks under a general anesthetic or she could snip them out right there and then in her office, no anesthetic at all. "What do you recommend?" I asked, not thrilled with either alternative. "How high is your pain tolerance?" she answered.

I opted to have the polyps out in her office. As it turned out, it was a relatively simple procedure, taking less than ten minutes, during which time the doctor explained clearly, and in more detail than I really needed, everything she was doing. "Now you might feel as if you have to go to the bathroom," I remember her saying seconds before my stomach began twisting into a series of tight little knots.

When she was finished, Dr. Wong held up a small glass jar for my inspection. Inside were two little round red balls, the size of large cranberries. "See," she said, almost proudly, "these are your polyps."

Twins, I thought giddily, then burst into tears.

I was supposed to call her office two weeks later to find out if there was a problem. I can't remember now whether I did or not. It was in the middle of all the craziness. It's quite possible I forgot.

Something is happening across the street. I can see it from the window. I'm sitting at my desk in the den, a small, book-lined room at the front of the house off the center foyer. Do the police want a description of the house? I'll include one, although surely they know it. They've been here enough times; they've taken enough photographs. But for the record, the house is a relatively large bungalow with three bedrooms and a den. The girls' bedrooms are to the right of the front door, the master bedroom to the left at the back. In between are the living and dining rooms, four bathrooms, and a large open space consisting of the kitchen, the breakfast nook, and the family room, whose back wall is a series of paneled glass windows and sliding glass doors overlooking the kidney-shaped backyard pool. The ceilings are high and dotted with overhead fans, like the one turning softly above my head right now, the floors large blocks of ceramic tile, interrupted by plush area rugs. Only the bedrooms

and den have wall-to-wall broadloom. The predominant color is beige, with accents in brown, black, and teal. Larry built the house; I decorated it. It was supposed to be our sanctuary.

I think I know what's going on across the street. It's happened before. Several large boys bullying a couple of smaller boys to come over, to knock on my door. The big boys are laughing, taunting the smaller ones, pushing them and calling them cowards, daring them to cross the street. Just ring the bell and ask her, I can hear them say, although no sound reaches my ears beyond their cruel laughter. Go ring her bell, then we'll leave you alone. The two younger boys—I think I recognize one of them as six-year-old Ian McMullen, who lives at the end of the street—straighten their shoulders and stare at the house. Another push and they're off the sidewalk and on the road, creeping up the front walk, their small fingers already stretching toward the buzzer.

And then suddenly they're gone, running madly down the street, as if being chased, although the older boys have turned and run off in the opposite direction. Maybe they saw me watching them; maybe someone is calling them; maybe good sense got the better of them. Who knows? Whatever it was that made them turn and flee, I'm grateful, although I'm already half out of my chair.

The first time it happened was just after the story hit the front pages. Most people were very respectful, but you always get a few who aren't satisfied with what they read, who want to know more, who feel they're entitled. The police did a good job of keeping most of them at bay, but occasionally young boys such as these made their way to my front door.

"What can I do for you?" I hear myself say, recalling their presence, feeling it still.

"Is this where it happened?" they ask, giggling nervously.

"Where what happened?"

"You know." Pause, anxious glances, trying to peer around my stubborn bulk. "Can we see the blood?"

It's around this time that I shut the door on their curious faces, although I admit the perverse temptation to usher them graciously inside, direct them toward the back of the house, like a tour guide, my

voice a melodic whisper, to point out the area on the family-room floor that was once covered in blood, and even now shows faint traces of blush, despite several professional cleanings. Probably I'll have to have those tiles replaced. It won't be easy. The company that manufactured them went bankrupt several years ago.

So, how did all this happen? When did my once steady and comfortable life begin careening out of control, like a car without brakes on a high mountain road, gaining speed and momentum until it crashes into the abyss and bursts into flames? At what precise moment did Humpty-Dumpty fall off the wall and shatter into thousands of tiny pieces, impossible to repair or replace?

Of course, no such moment exists. When one part of your life is coming apart at the seams, the rest of your life doesn't just sit back and patiently wait its turn to continue. It doesn't give you time to cope, or space to adjust and refocus. It just keeps piling one confusing event on top of the next, like a traffic cop rushing to make his quota of tickets.

Am I being overly dramatic? Maybe. Although I think I'm entitled. I, who have always been the steady one, the practical one, the one with more common sense than imagination, or so Jo Lynn once stated, am entitled to my few moments of melodrama.

Do I start at the very beginning, announce myself like a label stuck to a lapel: Hello, my name is Kate Sinclair? Do I say that I was born forty-seven years ago in Pittsburgh on an uncharacteristically warm day in April, that I'm five feet six and a half inches tall and one hundred and twenty-five pounds, that my hair is light brown and my eyes a shade darker, that I have small breasts and good legs and a slightly lopsided smile? That Larry affectionately calls me funny face, that Robert said I was beautiful?

It would be much easier to start at the end, to recite facts already known, give name to the dead, wipe away the blood once and for all, instead of trying to search for motivations, for explanations, for answers that might never be found.

But the police don't want that. They already know the basic facts. They've seen the end results. What they want are details, and I've agreed, as best I can, to provide them. I could start with Amy Lokash's

disappearance, or the first time her mother came to my office. I could begin with my mother's fears she was being followed, or with the day Sara's teacher called to voice her growing concerns about my daughter's behavior. I could talk about that first phone call from Robert, or Larry's sudden trip to South Carolina. But I guess if I have to choose one moment over all the others, it would have to be that Saturday morning last October when Jo Lynn and I were sitting at the kitchen table, relaxing and enjoying our third cup of coffee, and my sister put down the morning paper and calmly announced that she was going to marry a man who was on trial for the murder of thirteen women.

Yes, I think I'll start there.

Chapter

2

I remember it was sunny, one of those perfect Florida days when the sky is so blue it seems artificial, the temperature balancing on the comfortable side of eighty, with only a warm whisper of a breeze. I swallowed the balance of coffee in my cup, inhaling it as lovingly as a chain-smoker with her last cigarette, and stared out the back window at the large coconut palm that curved from behind the pool toward the terra-cotta tile roof of the house. It was the kind of picture you see on postcards that trill, "Having a wonderful time, wish you were here." The sky, the grass, even the bark of the trees, were so vivid they seemed to vibrate. Diamondlike sparkles of air reflected from their surfaces. "What a day," I said out loud.

"Hmm," Jo Lynn grunted from somewhere behind the morning paper.

"Look at it," I persisted, not sure why I was bothering. Was I looking for confirmation or conversation? Did I need either? "Look at how blue that sky is."

Jo Lynn's eyes flashed briefly over the top corner of the local news section of the *Palm Beach Post*. "Wouldn't you just love a sweater in that shade?" she asked, her voice a lazy Southern drawl.

Somehow this wasn't quite the response I'd been hoping for, although it was typical Jo Lynn, for whom nature was merely backdrop. I lapsed back into silence, debated whether to have another cup of coffee, decided against it. Three cups was more than enough, although I do love my morning coffee—my only real vice, I used to say.

I thought of Larry, out on the golf course since before 8 A.M. with prospective clients. Larry was relatively new to golf. He'd played a bit in college, was actually quite good at it, he confided, but gave it up for lack of time and money. Now that he had substantially more of both, and clients and business acquaintances were always inviting him out for a round, he'd taken it up again, although he wasn't finding it quite as relaxing as he remembered. The night before, he'd spent almost an hour practicing in front of the full-length bathroom mirror, trying to recapture the effortless swing of his youth. "Almost there," he kept repeating, as I grew tired of waiting for him to come to bed, and allowed myself to drift off to sleep, vague stirrings of frustration teasing at my groin.

He'd already left by the time I woke up. I got out of bed, threw on a short pink cotton robe, ambled into the kitchen, made a large pot of coffee, and sat down with the newspaper that Larry had been thoughtful enough to bring inside before heading out. The girls were still asleep. Michelle had been out with her girlfriends till after midnight. I didn't even hear Sara come home.

I was reading the movie reviews and enjoying my second cup of coffee when Jo Lynn showed up. She was in a lousy mood, she announced in lieu of hello, partly because she hadn't slept very well, but mostly because she'd been stood up the night before. Apparently her date, a former football player turned sporting goods salesman, who she said looked like a weathered Brad Pitt, had begged off at the last minute,

claiming a sore throat and achy limbs. So she'd gone to a bar and who should show up, looking healthy as a horse? Well, you know the rest, she told me, pouring herself a cup of coffee, settling in.

So there she was, in white shorts and revealing halter top, looking gorgeous as usual, despite her sleepless night, her shoulder-length blond curls gloriously askew—the freshly fucked look, she called it, although she hadn't been, she groused. That makes two of us, I almost confided, but didn't. I could never bring myself to discuss my sex life with Jo Lynn, partly because I didn't trust her to be discreet, mostly because there was nothing much to tell. I'd been in a monogamous relationship for almost a quarter of a century. To Jo Lynn, monogamy equaled monotony. I'd given up trying to change her mind. Lately, my words sounded hollow, even to me.

Jo Lynn, on the other hand, was always more than willing, eager even, to share the secrets of her love life with me. Details of her escapades flowed from her lips as briskly as water from a mountain stream. I tried to tell her that her love life was nobody's business but her own, but this was a concept she clearly didn't understand. I tried to remind her that discretion was the better part of valor; she looked at me as if I were crazy. I tried to warn her against disease; she scowled and looked away. I told her I really wasn't interested; she laughed loud and long. "Of course you're interested," she'd say, and of course she was right. "Just don't talk about it in front of the girls," I'd plead, to no avail. Jo Lynn loved an audience. She relished the effect she had on my daughters, who openly worshipped her, especially Sara. Sometimes they'd gang up on me, laugh at my so-called conservative ways, talk about dragging me onto one of those dreadful daytime talk shows they sometimes watched. "Girl, you need a makeover!" Jo Lynn would shout in the hyperextended voice of Rolonda or Ricki Lake, while Sara doubled over with laughter.

"He's cute," Jo Lynn was muttering now, her face buried so deep behind the morning paper that I wasn't sure I'd heard her say anything at all.

"Did you say something?"

"He sure is cute," she repeated, more clearly this time. "Just look

at that face." She spread the paper across the round glass top of the kitchen table. "I'm gonna marry that man," she said.

I stared down at the front page of the local news section. Three men stared back: the President of the United States, in Florida to confer with local politicians; a Catholic priest, lending his support to a projected gay and lesbian rights march; and Colin Friendly, the ironically named accused killer of thirteen women, sitting in a courtroom in West Palm Beach. I was afraid to ask which of the three she meant.

"I'm serious," she said, the long orange nail of her index finger tapping at the photograph of the accused murderer. "Just look at that face. He looks a little like Brad Pitt, don't you think?"

"He looks like Ted Bundy," I corrected, although, in truth, I couldn't make out what he looked like. I'd taken off my reading glasses and everything about the newspaper was a soft blur.

"Put on your glasses," she instructed, reading my mind, pushing the wire-rimmed half-glasses toward my face. The grainy black and white dots of the photograph immediately snapped into place, forming a clear, cohesive whole. "What do you see?"

"I see a cold-blooded killer," I pronounced, about to remove the glasses when her hand stopped me.

"Where does it say he killed anybody?"

"Jo Lynn, do you actually read the paper or do you just look at the pictures?"

"I read the article, smarty-pants," she said, and instantly we were both ten years old, "and it doesn't say one word about him being a murderer."

"Jo Lynn, he killed at least thirteen women . . ."

"He's *accused* of killing them, which doesn't mean he did it. I mean, correct me if I'm wrong, but isn't that why there's a trial?"

I opened my mouth to protest, thought better of it, said nothing.

"Whatever happened to 'innocent until proven guilty'?" she continued, as I'd known she would. Benign silence had never worked with Jo Lynn.

"You think he's innocent," I stated, a technique I often used with

clients. Instead of arguing, instead of trying to change their minds, instead of providing them with answers that might or might not be correct, I merely repeated their own words back at them, sometimes reframing those words in a more positive light, hopefully giving them time to discover the answers for themselves, sometimes just to let them know they'd been heard.

"I think there's a good chance he might be. I mean, just look at that face. He's beautiful."

Reluctantly, I studied the photograph. Colin Friendly sat between his lawyers, two faceless men conferring with each other behind his back, as the accused serial killer hunched forward, staring blankly toward the empty witness stand. What I saw was a man in his early thirties, his dark wavy hair combed neatly away from his finely chiseled features, a face that, under other circumstances, I might have regarded as handsome. I knew, from other pictures I'd seen, that he was over six feet tall and slim, almost wiry. His eyes were said to be blue, although never *just* blue, but always *piercing* blue or *intensely* blue, although today's photograph revealed nothing of the sort. But maybe it was hard for me to look at him objectively, even then.

"Don't you think he's gorgeous?"

I shook my head.

"You can't be serious. He looks just like Brad Pitt, only his hair is darker, and his nose is longer and thinner."

I stared at the thirty-seven-year-old woman sitting across from me. She'd gone from sounding like a ten-year-old to sounding like a lovestruck teen. Would she ever grow up? I wondered. Did any of us? Or did we just grow old?

"Okay, so maybe he doesn't look that much like Brad Pitt, but you've got to admit he's good-looking. Charismatic. Yeah, that's what he is—charismatic. At least, you have to admit that much."

"It's very hard for me to think of anyone who tortured and murdered thirteen women and girls as being either gorgeous or charismatic. I'm sorry, I just can't do it." I thought of Donna Lokash, a client of mine, whose daughter, Amy, had disappeared almost a year ago,

a possible victim of Colin Friendly's rage, although her body had yet to be found.

"You have to separate the two issues," Jo Lynn was saying, and I almost laughed. I was the one, after all, who was always talking about separating issues. "The fact that he's good-looking has nothing to do with whether or not he killed anybody."

"It doesn't?"

"No. One thing has nothing to do with the other."

I shrugged. "What do you see when you look at him?" I asked, genuinely curious. "Aside from Brad Pitt."

"I see a little boy who's been hurt." Jo Lynn's voice was solemn, genuine.

"You see a boy who's been hurt," I parroted, recalling Jo Lynn as a child, gently rocking a stray kitten back and forth across her bare tummy. It had given her ringworm. "Where? Where do you see that?"

The bright orange nail drew a small circle around Colin Friendly's mouth. "He has a sad smile."

I studied the photograph more closely, surprised to discover she was right. "Don't you think it's odd," I asked, "that, under the circumstances, he's smiling at all?"

"It's just boyish bravado," she said, as if she'd known Colin Friendly all her life. "I find it endearing."

I stood up, shuffled over to the kitchen counter, poured myself another cup of coffee. Clearly, I was going to need it. "Can we talk about something else?"

Jo Lynn swiveled around in her chair, held out her cup for me to fill. Her long tanned legs stretched toward me, the bright orange polish on her toenails peeking out from between the crossing leather bands of her white sandals. "You don't think I'm serious, do you?"

"Jo Lynn, let's not . . ."

"Let's not what? Talk about something just because it's important to me?"

I stared into my coffee cup, wishing I were back in bed. "This is important to you?" I asked.

Jo Lynn sat up straight, drew her legs back beneath her chair, pushed her lips into a Bardot-like pout that men usually found appealing, but which had always annoyed the hell out of me. "Yes, it is."

"So where do you want me to send the wedding present?" I asked, straining for levity.

Jo Lynn was having none of it. "Sure, make a joke. I'm just a big joke to you."

I took a long, slow sip of my coffee, the only thing I could think to do that wouldn't get me into more trouble. "Look, Jo Lynn, what is it you want me to say?"

"I want you to stop being so damned dismissive."

"I'm sorry, I didn't realize I was being dismissive."

"That's the problem. You never do."

My shortcomings weren't something I particularly wanted to get into at this hour of the morning. "Look, can't we just agree to disagree? It's a beautiful day. I really don't want to waste it arguing about some guy you've never even met."

"I'm going to change that."

"What?"

"I'm going to meet him."

"What?"

"I'm going to meet him," she repeated stubbornly. "I'm going to go down to that courthouse next week and meet him."

My patience was all but exhausted. This was worse than dealing with Sara. "You're going to go to the courthouse . . ."

"That's what I just said. I'm going to the courthouse. On Monday."

"And what do you think you're going to accomplish by going to the courthouse?" I asked, ignoring the little therapist's voice in the back of my head urging me to be quiet, to let Jo Lynn sputter on until she simply ran out of steam. "They're not going to let you talk to him."

"They might."

"They won't."

"Then I'll just sit in the courtroom and watch. I'll be there for him."

"You'll be there for him," I repeated numbly.

"As support. And stop repeating everything I say. It's very annoying."

I tried another approach. "I thought you were going job-hunting Monday."

"I've been job-hunting every day for the past two weeks. I've left résumés all over town."

"Have you followed any of them up with a phone call? You know you have to be persistent." I hated the sound of my own voice as much as the look on Jo Lynn's face told me she did. "God knows you can be persistent when you want to be."

"Maybe I don't want to be," she shot back. "Maybe I'm tired of working at a bunch of stupid low-paying jobs for a bunch of stupid low-lifes. Maybe I'm thinking of starting my own business."

"Doing what?"

"I haven't decided yet. Maybe opening an exercise studio, or a dog-sitting service, something like that."

I struggled to keep my face calm while digesting this latest bulletin. Jo Lynn had never attended an exercise class in her life; she lived in an apartment complex that didn't allow pets.

"You don't think I can do it."

"I think you can do anything you set your mind to," I told her honestly. At the moment, it was the thing about her that worried me the most.

"But you think it's a dumb idea."

"I didn't say that."

"You don't have to. I can see it all over your face."

I turned away, caught sight of myself in the dark glass of the wall oven. She was right. Even through the smoky glass, I could see how pale my skin had turned, how slack-jawed I'd become. Of course, it didn't help that my hair hung around my face like a limp, chin-length mop, or that the bags under my eyes had yet to shrink with the light of day. "You need money to start a business," I began, once again ignoring the tiny therapist pummeling her fists against the inside of my brain.

"I'll have money."

"You will? How? When?"

"When Mom dies," she said, and smiled, the same sad twisting of her lips as the killer in the morning paper.

For an instant, it felt as if my heart had stopped. I quickly lowered my coffee cup to the counter, took one shaking hand inside the other. "How could you say such a thing?"

And suddenly she was laughing, great whoops of glee that circled the air above my head like giant lassos, threatening to drop down and take hold of my throat, to jerk me mercilessly toward the ceiling, leave me kicking frantically at the air. "Lighten up, lady. Can't you tell when someone's kidding?"

"Kidding on the square," I said, then bit down hard on my lower lip. Our mother always said that.

"I never understood what that was supposed to mean," Jo Lynn said testily.

"It means you're kidding, but you're not really kidding. You're making a joke, but really you're serious."

"I know what it means," she said.

"Anyway," I insisted, "Mom's only seventy-five, and she's in great shape. I wouldn't count on her going anywhere for a while yet."

"I never count on her for anything," Jo Lynn said.

"Where is all this coming from?" I asked.

Now it was Jo Lynn's turn to stare at me with openmouthed disbelief. "It's always been like this. Where have you been all these years?"

"Well, how long is it going to go on? You're all grown up now. How long are you going to keep blaming her for things she may or may not have done over twenty years ago?"

"Don't minimize what she did."

"What *exactly* did she do?"

Jo Lynn shook her head, brushed several blond curls away from her cheek, pulled on the long gold loop earring that dangled from her right ear. "Nothing. She did nothing wrong. She was the perfect mother. Forget I said anything." She shook her head. The blond curls fell back across her flushed cheek. "It's just PMS talking."

That didn't mollify me. "Have you ever stopped to think that there is no such thing as PMS, and that this is the way you really are?"

Jo Lynn stared at me, green eyes narrowing, orange mouth pursing, as if she were giving serious thought to leaping across the table and wrestling me to the floor. Then suddenly her eyes widened, her lips parted, and she was laughing again, only this time the laughter was genuine and expansive, and I was able to join her.

"That was funny," she said, as I basked in her unexpected goodwill.

The phone rang. It was our mother. As if on cue. As if she'd been privy to our conversation. As if she knew our most secret thoughts.

"Tell her we were just talking about her," Jo Lynn whispered, loud enough to be heard.

"How are you, Mom?" I said instead, picturing her on the other end of the receiver, already showered and dressed, her short tightly curled gray hair framing her narrow face, dark brown eyes sparkling with expectation for the day ahead.

Her voice filled the room. "Magnificent," she trilled. That was what she always said. Magnificent. Jo Lynn mouthed the word along with her. "How are you, darling?"

"I'm good."

"And the girls?"

"They're fine."

"I'm good too," Jo Lynn called out.

"Oh, is Jo Lynn there?"

"She dropped by for a cup of coffee."

"Give her my love," our mother said.

"Give it back," Jo Lynn said flatly in return.

"Sweetheart," our mother continued, "I'm calling because I can't find that wonderful recipe I have for poach crumble, and I wondered if you had a copy of it."

"Poach crumble?" I repeated.

"Yes," she said. "Remember? I made it for you a few weeks ago. You said it was delicious."

"You mean the *peach* crumble?"

"Yes," she said. "Isn't that what I said?"

"You said . . . Never mind. It's not important. I'll look for it later and call you back. Is that okay?"

There was a moment's silence. "Well, don't wait too long." A hint of agitation crept into her voice.

"Is something wrong?" I mentally crossed my fingers. Please don't let there be anything wrong, I prayed. The day was already disintegrating around me, the sky steadily paling, leaking blue.

"No, nothing's wrong," she assured me quickly. "It's just Mr. Emerson next door. He's mad at me for something. I can't imagine what, but he's been quite unpleasant these last few days."

"Unpleasant? What do you mean?" I pictured old Mr. Emerson, charming, slightly stooped but still debonair, with a full head of thick white hair. He'd lived in the apartment next to my mother's for the two years she'd been a resident at the Palm Beach Lakes Retirement Home, a community for independent seniors. Mr. Emerson had always been an ideal neighbor, thoughtful, friendly, in possession of all his faculties. Of course, he was also closing in on ninety, so anything could happen.

"I thought I'd make him a peach crumble as a sort of peace offering," my mother continued. "But I can't find the recipe."

"I'll look for it and call you later," I told her. "In the meantime, don't worry about it. Whatever it is, he'll get over it in time."

"How much time does he have?" my mother quipped, and I laughed.

"Tell her I'm getting married," Jo Lynn said loudly as I was about to hang up the phone.

"What's that? She's getting married again?"

"You're gonna love him," Jo Lynn said, as I whispered hurried assurances to our mother that it was all a joke.

Jo Lynn became visibly indignant, the green eyes narrowing once again, the orange lips disappearing one inside the other. "Why did you tell her that? Why are you always trying to protect her?"

"Why are you always trying to hurt her?"

We stared at each other for what seemed an eternity, our unan-

swered questions suspended in the air between us like particles of dust in the sunlight. What's the matter with you? I wanted to shout. Can you really be serious about Colin Friendly? Aren't you tired of being abused by selfish losers? Who exactly are you punishing here? Are you really going to keep cutting off your nose to spite your face?

"What's going on here?" a voice asked sleepily from somewhere beside us. I turned around as Sara slouched into the kitchen, her feet bare, her Amazon's body slipping in and out of a navy silk teddy and boxer shorts. *My* navy silk teddy and boxer shorts, I realized, understanding now why I hadn't been able to find them in several weeks. Her eyes barely open and all but hidden by her long tangled hair, elegant arms extended in front of her, groping for the fridge like a blind woman, she opened the fridge door and extricated the carton of freshly squeezed orange juice, raising it to her lips.

"Please don't do that," I cautioned, trying not to scream.

"Chill," she said, one of those delightful teenage expressions I'd like to wipe from the face of this earth. "Get a life" is another.

"There are glasses in the cupboard," I advised.

Sara lowered the carton and opened the cupboard, careful to make sure that I caught the disdainful roll of her eyes as she reached for a glass. "So, what were you two making such a racket about before? You were laughing so loud you woke me up."

For a minute I couldn't imagine what she was talking about. It seemed so long ago.

"Your mother actually said something funny," Jo Lynn told her, reducing me instantly to the status of humorless crone. "About PMS. What was it again?"

"Well, I can't really take the credit for it," I qualified. "I heard it on a sitcom once."

"So, what was it?" Sara filled the tall glass with orange juice, downed it in one noisy gulp, then put both the carton and the empty glass on the counter.

"Uh-uh. In the fridge." I motioned. "In the dishwasher."

Another roll of the eyes as two sets of appliance doors clumsily opened and closed. "Never mind," she said, walking across the room,

glancing down at the newspaper spread out across the kitchen table. The President, the priest, and Colin Friendly stared back. "He's cute," Sara said, heading back toward her room.

"I'm gonna marry him," Jo Lynn called after her.

"Cool," Sara said, not breaking stride.

Chapter

3

Monday arrived. I had clients booked every hour from eight through six o'clock, with forty-five minutes off for lunch.

My office, in the heart of Palm Beach, only blocks from the ocean, consists of two small rooms and a smaller waiting area. The walls of each room are soft pink, the furniture predominantly gray. Stacks of recent magazines fill several large wicker baskets on either side of two padded benches that sit against the walls in the waiting room. I've made a point of keeping the magazines up to date ever since one of my clients walked tearfully into my office clutching a copy of *Newsweek*, asking if I knew that Steve McQueen had cancer. At this point, Steve McQueen had already been dead many years.

An eclectic group of pictures hang on the walls: a black-and-white photograph of a polar bear hugging a baby cub; a muted watercolor of a woman reading under the shade of a giant banyan tree; a bright reproduc-

tion of a well-known poster by Toulouse-Lautrec—Jane Avril, kicking up her leg to dance. Classical music plays in the background, not too loud, but hopefully loud enough to cover up the sometimes raised voices that emanate from behind the closed doors of my inner office.

Inside, three upholstered gray-and-white chairs sit grouped around a rectangular glass coffee table. More chairs can be brought in when required. There are some potted plants that look real but are actually replicas, since I have no talent with plants whatsoever, and I got tired of watching the real ones wither and die. Besides, on a symbolic level, dying plants seemed to reflect badly on my ability as a therapist.

On the coffee table sit a small tin of cookies, a large notepad, and a giant box of tissues. There is a video camera in one corner that I sometimes use to record sessions—always with the client's permission. A clock is on the wall behind my head, as well as several Impressionist prints: Monet's incandescent water lilies; a peaceful Pissarro village; an apple-cheeked Renoir girl standing on a swing.

There's another room at the back where I keep my desk, my phone, my files, a small fridge, some stacking chairs, and a treadmill, or "dreadmill," as I've come to refer to it. The treadmill has always struck me as a perfect symbol of the times: people walking as fast as they can, going nowhere. Even so, I try to spend at least twenty minutes a day on this awful contraption. It's supposed to relax my mind while toning my body. In fact, it only irritates me. But then, everything irritates me these days. I blame it on my hormones, which are in a state of constant flux, the magazines all tell me. These articles irritate me as well. It doesn't help that "women of a certain age," as I believe the French call us, are always being pictured in the accompanying illustrations as dried-up bare branches on a once-flowering tree.

Anyway, it was Monday, I'd been seeing clients all morning, and my stomach was growling its way through my last session before lunch. The couple sitting across from me had come for help in dealing with their teenage son, who was as sullen and difficult a fourteen-year-old as I'd ever encountered. After two sessions, he'd refused to come back, although his parents persisted, gamely trying to find some sort of compromise that everyone could live with. Of course, compromise only works if

all those involved are committed to it, and their son was committed only to wreaking havoc.

"He snuck out again after we'd gone to bed," Mrs. Mallory was saying, her husband sitting stiffly beside her. "We wouldn't even have known he was gone except that I woke up to go to the bathroom and I saw a light on. I went into his room, and you wouldn't believe it, he'd stuffed his bed with pillows to make it look like he was still in it, like they do in those prison movies you see on TV. He didn't get home until almost three in the morning."

"Where did he go?" I asked.

"He wouldn't say."

"What happened then?"

"We told him how worried we'd been . . ."

"*She* was worried," her husband corrected tersely.

"You weren't?" I asked.

Jerry Mallory shook his balding head. He was a neat man who always wore a dark blue suit and a gold-striped tie, in contrast to his wife, who usually looked as if she'd thrown on the first thing that tumbled out of the dryer. "The only thing I worry about is the police showing up on our doorstep."

"I don't know what to do anymore." Jill Mallory looked from me to her husband, who stared resolutely ahead. "He's making me a nervous wreck. I don't sleep; I yell at everyone. I yelled at little Jenny again this morning. Although I explained to her that even though I yell at her a lot lately, it doesn't mean I don't love her."

"You also gave yourself permission to keep yelling at her," I told her, as gently as I could. She looked at me as if she'd been shot through the heart with an arrow.

Jill, Jerry, Jenny, Jason, I recited in my mind, wondering whether the succession of J's had been deliberate. Jo Lynn, I found myself adding, picturing her in a crowded West Palm Beach courtroom, praying that common sense had kept her at home.

"Is there some way to force Jason back into counseling?" his mother asked. "Maybe a psychiatrist . . ."

I told her that wouldn't be a good idea. Teenagers are not great

candidates for therapy, for two main reasons: one, they have no insight into why they do things, and two, they have no curiosity about why they do things.

When the hour was over and the Mallorys had gone, I went into the other room, grabbed a tuna fish sandwich from the small fridge, and checked my voice mail. There were two hang-ups and seven messages: three from clients seeking appointments; one from the guidance counselor at Sara's school asking me to call at my convenience; two from my mother asking me to call as soon as possible; and one from Jo Lynn telling me she'd spent the morning in court, that Colin Friendly was even better-looking in person than in his photographs, that she was more convinced than ever of his innocence, and that I had to go with her to see for myself on Wednesday, a day I normally don't go into the office. I closed my eyes, took a deep breath, and called my mother.

There was a frantic edge to her voice I wasn't used to hearing. "Where have you been?" she asked. "I've been calling all morning. I kept getting that stupid machine."

"What's the matter, Mom? Has something happened?"

"It's that damn Mr. Emerson."

"What happened with Mr. Emerson?"

"He accused me of trying to poison him with that peach crumble I made for him. He claims he was up all night throwing up. I'm so upset. He's telling everyone in the building that I tried to poison him."

"Oh, Mom, I'm so sorry. You must be so disappointed. Here you went to all that effort." I imagined her bent over her kitchen counter, arranging slices of peaches in the pan in neat little rows. "Try not to worry about it. No one there is going to take him seriously."

"Do you think you could talk to Mrs. Winchell?" she asked, referring to the retirement home's administrator. "I'm just too upset, and I know if you phoned her and explained . . ."

"I really don't think that's necessary, Mom."

"Please." Again, that unfamiliar urgency clinging to her voice.

"Sure thing. What's her number?"

"Her number?"

"Never mind." Clearly my mother was in no frame of mind for such details. "I'll find it."

"You'll call right away?"

"As soon as I can."

"Thank you, darling. I'm sorry to be such a burden."

"You're never a burden. I'll speak to you later." I replaced the receiver, took a few quick bites of my sandwich, and flipped through my address book for Mrs. Winchell's phone number, deciding first to check in with my daughter's school. The guidance counselor came on the line just as an enormous piece of tuna glued itself to the roof of my mouth.

"Sara has been missing a lot of classes," he told me without preamble. "In the last two weeks, she's missed four math classes and two Spanish classes."

Oh God, I thought. Here we go again. Hadn't we been through this last year?

"I'll talk to her," I told the guidance counselor, feeling like a total failure, although I knew this was Sara's responsibility, not mine. Still, I felt responsible. Some family therapist, I thought, swallowing the rest of my sandwich, feeling it awkward and heavy as it lurched its way down my esophagus toward my stomach.

I called Mrs. Winchell, quickly explaining the reason for my call, and asking if she could pay Mr. Emerson a visit. Maybe he'd reached a point in his life, I suggested gently, when he needed to find a place that offered more supervised care. There was a moment's silence before Mrs. Winchell spoke. I found myself holding my breath, though I wasn't sure why.

"It's not quite as simple as that," she began, then stopped. I tried to picture her on the other end of the phone, but her silence was distracting. It took several seconds for a mental image of her to take shape. When it did, she emerged as a woman about a decade older than me, ebony-skinned and pretty despite a receding chin line, with short black hair and an engaging smile. "Actually, I've been meaning to call you."

"Is there a problem?" I coached reluctantly.

"We've had a few complaints," she began, "from some of the other tenants."

"Complaints? About Mr. Emerson?"

"About your mother," she said.

"About my mother?"

A long pause followed. Then: "There have been some problems over the last couple of months."

"What kind of problems?"

Another silence. Clearly, Mrs. Winchell was not someone who spoke before she was ready, a trait I've always admired in others but never quite mastered in myself. I checked my watch, then my appointment calendar. The name Donna Lokash was scribbled through the one o'clock slot.

"I'm sure you know your mother loves to bake . . ."

"Yes, of course. She's a wonderful cook."

Mrs. Winchell ignored the interruption. "And she's always been very sweet, making things for her friends and neighbors . . ."

Get to the point, I wanted to shout, but didn't, locating an errant cookie on my desk and stuffing it into my mouth instead.

"But I'm afraid that the last few times she's baked anything for anyone, they've gotten very sick."

My eyes creased toward the bridge of my nose. What was this woman trying to say? That my mother was deliberately poisoning her neighbors, as Mr. Emerson had accused? "I'm not sure I understand what you're getting at," I said.

There was another lengthy pause. I imagined the woman looking around her office, patting her tight dark curls, rubbing the tip of her nose. "It's probably just a case of old stomachs becoming increasingly delicate and not being able to tolerate such rich foods," she offered gently, "but I was wondering if you could suggest to your mother that she not bake anything for anyone for a while."

Already I could see the wounded look that would ambush my mother's features when I relayed Mrs. Winchell's request, and it broke my heart. "I'll talk to her," I said.

"There's something else," Mrs. Winchell continued.

I held my breath, said nothing.

"It's about the charges your mother has made with regard to one of our staff."

"I beg your pardon?"

"She's never said anything to you?"

I shook my head, then realized I would have to do more. "No, she's never said a thing."

"I think this might be too complicated for us to get into over the phone. It's probably better if we meet in person. Perhaps we could get together sometime soon, you, your mother, and I. Oh, and you have a sister, don't you?"

My mind instantly replayed Jo Lynn's message on my voice mail. *You have to see this man in person, Kate. He's even better-looking than his photographs, and I'm absolutely convinced he's innocent.* "Yes, I have a sister," I said.

"I think she should probably join us as well. We can talk things through, hopefully get to the bottom of everything."

My mother, Jo Lynn, and I, I thought, picturing Jo Lynn sitting in the courtroom, a one-woman cheering section, probably skipping lunch so she could get a seat closer to the accused for when court resumed in the afternoon. She'd be wearing all white, as usual, to highlight her honey-eyed complexion, and a short skirt to show off her legs. Not to mention the tightest of little tank tops. There was no way Colin Friendly was not going to notice Jo Lynn Baker. She'd make sure of that.

"The only day I have free is Wednesday," I told Mrs. Winchell, wondering how I was going to persuade Jo Lynn to come along.

"How's Wednesday at two o'clock?" Mrs. Winchell offered immediately.

"Fine."

"I look forward to seeing you then."

She hung up. I sat cradling the phone against my ear, wondering what was going on. My mother wasn't a troublemaker, and she'd never been one to complain, even when she had just cause. She'd suffered

years of abuse from my stepfather without saying a word, trying to protect my sister and me from things we already knew. Was that what she was doing now? Still trying to protect us?

I shook my head, inadvertently dislodging Sara from the recesses of my mind. Did a mother ever really stop trying to protect her child?

I returned the rest of my calls, then quickly exchanged my blue dress and flats for a gray sweat suit and sneakers, and stepped on the treadmill, gradually increasing its speed until I was walking a brisk four miles an hour, my arms keeping pace at my sides, my mind peacefully blank. It didn't take long, however, for my family to join me, their images attaching themselves to my arms and legs, like heavy weights, slowing my step, dragging me down.

Leave me alone, I admonished them silently, trying to shrug them off. This is my time alone, my time just for me, to unwind, to refresh, to tone and relax. I'll deal with your problems later.

But instead of fading away, their images grew bolder, more insistent. My mother appeared in front of me, like a genie escaped from a bottle, pushing her face just inches from my own, her arms clinging to me in a suffocating embrace; my daughter jumped on my back, knees circling my waist, hands clutching at my throat, riding me as if she were a small child, both women pressing so tightly against me I could barely breathe. Why was my daughter skipping classes? What was going on with my mother? And why were these things *my* problem? Why was I the one caught in the middle?

Don't expect any help from me, Jo Lynn warned, invisible hands tugging on my ankles, so that it felt as if I were trudging through deep snow. You're never there for me; why should I be there for you?

I'm always here for you, I said, kicking at her prone image, almost tripping over my own feet. Who stood by you through Andrew, through Daniel, through Peter, through all the men who repeatedly broke your bones and battered your spirit?

Yeah, but what have you done for me lately? she demanded, tightening her grip.

Don't bother with her, Sara admonished.

You'll deal with her later, my mother said.

Me first, said Sara.

No, me, my mother insisted.

Me.

Me.

Me. Me. Me. Me. Me.

I closed my eyes, anxiety tightening around my chest like a strait-jacket. "This is my time," I said out loud. "I'll deal with you later."

The anxiety suddenly lifted. I smiled, took a deep breath. You see, I reminded myself, sometimes all that's necessary is to voice these thoughts aloud. Almost immediately, however, the anxiety was replaced by a wave of heat so intense it felt as if someone were aiming a blowtorch at my brain. Perspiration soaked through my sweatshirt; my forehead grew damp; wisps of hair plastered themselves to the sides of my face. "Great. Just what I needed," I pronounced, adjusting the treadmill's speed, slowing it down too quickly, so that when it stopped, I almost fell off.

Steadying myself against my desk, I grabbed a soft drink from the fridge, and held it against my forehead until the room stopped spinning and the hot flush grew tepid, then disappeared. When I next glanced at my watch, it was almost fifteen minutes after one o'clock and I was still in my sweats. I quickly peeked into the waiting area, but Donna Lokash wasn't there. I was grateful, though worried. It was unlike Donna to be late.

My sweatshirt was halfway over my head when the phone rang. I yanked it off and answered the phone, standing there in nothing but my underwear. Donna's voice on the phone was garbled, crowded with tears. "I'm so sorry. I know I'm late. I was on my way out the door when the phone rang."

"Donna, what's wrong? Has something happened? Is it Amy?" Donna's daughter, Amy, had been missing for almost a year. I had a special interest in her disappearance, since Amy had attended the same school as Sara and had been in some of the same classes. I recalled the first time Donna Lokash came to my office, several months after Amy vanished. She remembered me from several parent-teacher meetings, she'd whispered, her thin frame hugging the doorway, eyes swollen al-

most shut from crying, further accentuating the grief-imposed gauntness of her face. She needed help, she said. She was having trouble coping.

"The police just called. They've found a body. There's a chance it could be Amy."

"Oh God."

"They want me to go to the medical examiner's office. They're sending a car for me. They asked if I could bring a friend. I don't know what to do."

I knew that Donna had drifted away from most of her friends since Amy's disappearance, and that her ex-husband lived in New York. He'd flown in when Amy first went missing, but had gone back after several weeks when Amy hadn't been found. He had a new wife and family to look after now. Donna had no one. "Would you like me to go with you?"

"Would you?" Her gratitude was so palpable I could almost hold it in my hands. "We'd have to go right now, which would mean canceling your other appointments. Of course, I'd pay you for your time and trouble. I wouldn't dream of asking you to do this without paying you for your time."

"Please don't worry about that. It's a slow day," I lied, drawing an invisible X through the rest of the day's appointments. "Tell me where to meet you."

"At the medical examiner's office on Gun Club Road. West of Congress. In front of the jail."

"I'm on my way." I hastily rescheduled the rest of my afternoon appointments, taped a note of apology to my office door for those I hadn't been able to reach, and left the office, heading for the county morgue.

Chapter

4

Twenty minutes later I pulled into the large entranceway of the Palm Beach County Criminal Justice Complex, an impressive array of sand-colored buildings that included the sheriff's office, various administrative offices, and the jail, a towering structure at the rear, nicknamed the Gun Club Hilton. Were it not for the rows of barbed wire that ran along the top of the prison gates, the complex might be mistaken for just another series of offices, like the South Florida Water Management District buildings directly across the street.

The medical examiner's office, a squat one-story structure at the front of the complex, had the look and feel of a building that didn't quite belong, like an old portable classroom that's been tacked on to a brand-new school, necessary but vaguely unwelcome. I found a parking spot nearby, switched off the car's engine, then sat staring out at the pond that stretched along the side of the road, my mind racing ahead to a sterile

room smelling vaguely of chemicals. I saw myself positioned slightly behind Donna, my eyes carefully averted, my hands on the sides of her arms, bracing her as the coroner pulled back a white sheet from a steel slab, exposing the gray face of a teenage girl, possibly her daughter. I heard her cry out, saw her sway backward, felt her collapse into my arms. The full, horrible weight of her grief fell on me, pressing against my nose and mouth like a pillow, robbing me of air, taking my breath away. I can't do this, I thought.

"If she can do it, you can do it," I admonished myself, scrambling out of the car and hurrying along the concrete walkway to the side entrance of the unimpressive building, pursued by another unwanted image, more terrible than the first: the coroner pulling down the sheet, the body of my own child staring lifelessly up at me. "Sara," I said, and gasped out loud.

A sharp quack sent the image scattering in all directions, like a bullet through a pane of glass, and I turned toward the sound. There, in a corner of the building, close to the door, a large Muscovy duck sat watch over a bunch of freshly hatched ducklings, their recently discarded eggshells lying broken and empty on the grass around them. I stared at the unexpected scene in amazement, afraid to approach too closely, lest I frighten the baby ducks and antagonize their mother. I watched them for several seconds, marveling at the fragility and resilience of life, and then I took a deep breath, and opened the door on death.

Donna Lokash was sitting in one of two steel-and-vinyl chairs along the off-white concrete-block wall of the small reception area, a uniformed police officer at her side. She was even thinner than the last time I'd seen her, and the lines under her clouded hazel eyes had deepened, forming large dark semicircles. Her brown hair was brushed back into a ponytail that spoke more of convenience than style, and the flesh around her fingernails had been picked raw, the nails themselves bitten to the quick. Donna jumped up, lunged toward me. "Did you see the baby ducks?" she asked, her voice giddy, incipient hysteria bracketing her words.

"I saw them."

"It's a good omen, don't you think?"

"I hope so," I told her. "Are you all right?"

She cast an unsteady glance around the room, dropped her voice to a whisper. "I feel a little sick to my stomach."

"Take deep breaths," I told her, then did the same.

The uniformed officer approached, extended his hand. He was of medium height with reddish-blond hair and a barrel chest. "Mrs. Sinclair, I'm Officer Gatlin. Thank you for coming."

I nodded. "What happens now?"

"I'll tell them you're here."

"And then what? Do I stay here or do I go inside with Mrs. Lokash?" I motioned toward the back room with my chin.

"Nobody's allowed back there," Officer Gatlin said.

"I don't understand."

"It's not like you see on television," Officer Gatlin explained gently. "We never allow anyone to actually see the body. A few of the more modern facilities in the country have special viewing rooms, complete with soft lighting, where you can view the body through a glass window. But this is an old building, and a small one. We don't have the space or the facilities."

"Then how . . . ?" I broke off, bit down on my lower lip.

"They'll bring out a photograph for you to look at."

"A photograph?"

"They won't let me see my baby," Donna said.

"We don't know yet that it's Amy," I told her.

"They won't let me even look at her picture," Donna continued, as if I hadn't spoken. She covered her mouth with her trembling hand, barely stifling a sharp cry.

"What do you mean?"

"We never let an immediate family member see the photograph," Officer Gatlin said. "It's too traumatic. That's why we ask them to bring a clergyman or a family friend, someone who knew the girl . . ."

"But I didn't know her," I said, the realization suddenly hitting me that I was the one expected to identify the body. "I mean, I only met her on a couple of occasions. I'm not sure I could . . ."

"I didn't know they wouldn't let me see her," Donna cried, rocking back and forth on the balls of her feet. "I don't know what to do. Oh

God, I don't know what to do. I don't know who else to call. I'm so sorry I dragged you into this, Kate. Please forgive me. I didn't know they wouldn't let me see her."

"I'll look at the picture," I said quickly, recalling the hours that Donna had spent in my office, poring over the family albums with me, pointing out Amy as a fair-haired infant, Amy as a pudgy little girl, Amy in a strapless prom dress, her light brown hair hanging in ringlets around her dimpled cheeks, Amy on her seventeenth birthday, brown eyes sparkling, just weeks before she disappeared. I grabbed Donna's hand, squeezed it tightly. "I should be able to recognize her."

Officer Gatlin nodded, walked toward the glass plate that separated the waiting room from the receptionist's office. *Push button for assistance*, a small sign read beside an imposing black button. He pushed the button, told the receptionist that I was ready to proceed.

"Why don't we sit down," I suggested to Donna, pulling out one of four chairs hovering around a round Formica table in the center of the room. She fell into it, and I lowered myself into the seat next to hers, concentrating on the details of the small room—a wine-colored mat that lay on the linoleum floor just inside the entrance, vertical blinds on the window, a water fountain in one corner of the room, two vending machines, one for soft drinks, the other for candies, against two of the walls, recessed fluorescent lights humming from the ceiling, illuminating a small, unimpressive landscape painting, a *No Smoking* sign printed in fifteen different languages, a small sign that read: *Sometimes it's the little things you do that make the big difference*—in an effort to ward off my mounting panic.

I'd never seen a dead body before, or even a picture of one, other than on the television news, and I didn't know how I was going to react to the sight of a teenage girl, a girl the same age as my older daughter, lying dead on a table, even if her death was presented via the distancing lens of a camera. And then another terrifying thought hit me. "Is there any trauma to the face?" I asked, struggling to keep my voice steady.

"We wouldn't show you the picture if there was," he said.

"How did the girl die?" Donna Lokash asked from her chair. She

was staring at the door to the back room, although her eyes were blank, and it was unlikely she saw anything at all.

"Multiple stab wounds," Officer Gatlin answered, his voice low, as if trying to minimize the impact of his words.

"Oh God," Donna moaned.

"When?" I asked.

"Probably several days ago. A group of kids found her body this morning in a park in Stuart."

"But Amy disappeared almost a year ago," I said. "What makes you think it's her?"

"She fits the general description," he said.

"What happens if I'm not able to make a definite identification?"

"We can check the dental records, if there are any," Officer Gatlin said. "Or we might ask Mrs. Lokash to bring in Amy's hairbrush, something with her fingerprints on it, lift the prints from that, compare the two."

The door at the back of the room suddenly opened. A tall, good-looking man with salt-and-pepper hair combed straight back off his face crossed into the waiting area, a photograph in his hand.

"Oh God, oh God," wailed Donna, rocking back and forth in her seat, arms clasped around her stomach.

"This is Fred Sheridan, one of the medical examiner's assistants," Officer Gatlin said, as I rose to my feet. "Are you ready, Mrs. Sinclair?"

"I'm not sure," I replied honestly.

"Take your time," Fred Sheridan said, his voice husky, full of gravel.

Several slow steps brought me to his side. I swallowed, closed my eyes, said a silent prayer. Please let me know one way or the other, I prayed, conjuring up a quick image of the last time I'd seen Amy, enlarging it, focusing in on each facet of her face, dissecting it piece by piece: the dimples on either side of her round mouth, the freckles dotting the sides of her upturned nose, bright eyes brown and wide apart. She was a pretty girl, of average height and weight, which meant she probably thought she was too short, too fat. I shook my head, opened my eyes. If

only they knew how beautiful they really are, I thought, thinking again of my daughter Sara, as I glanced down at the photograph in Fred Sheridan's outstretched hand.

"She was wearing a red barrette," Donna Lokash suddenly announced.

"What?" I turned away before the picture had a chance to register on my brain.

"When she went out that night, she was wearing a red barrette. It was just a silly plastic thing, a cupid sitting on a bunch of hearts, but she loved it. One of the kids she used to babysit for gave it to her, and she misplaced it, and was very upset, until I found it one morning when I was straightening up her room. It had fallen behind her dresser, and she was so excited when I showed it to her. She was wearing it in her hair, just above her right ear, the night she went out. She said it was her good-luck charm." Donna's voice broke off abruptly. She lapsed into silence, stared at the floor.

"Is this Amy?" Fred Sheridan asked gently, his words pulling me back toward the photograph.

The face I found myself staring at was young and round and surprisingly untroubled. No laugh lines interrupted the flat surface of her mouth; no worry lines tugged at the edges of her eyes. A blank slate, I found myself thinking. She hadn't even had a chance to live. Tears welled up in my eyes. I turned away.

"It isn't her," I whispered.

Donna emitted a strangled cry. Immediately, I returned to her side. She grabbed my hand, sobbed against it, her tears lying warm and wet on my skin.

"You're sure?" Officer Gatlin asked.

"Yes."

The girl in the photograph may have fit Amy's general description, but her nose pointed down instead of up and her lower lip was thinner, less prominent. There were no freckles on her ashen skin.

There was no red barrette.

"What happens now?" I asked.

"We keep trying to find out who she is," Officer Gatlin said, as Fred Sheridan retreated into the back room. "We keep our eyes out for Amy."

"My daughter didn't run away," Donna told him decisively.

"I'll give you a ride home, Mrs. Lokash," the officer said.

"I'll take her home," I told him.

Donna smiled gratefully. "I'm not sure I can stand up," she said.

"Take your time," I told her, as the coroner's assistant had earlier told me.

"What about you?" she asked as I helped her to her feet. "How are you doing?"

"Don't worry about me."

Officer Gatlin held the door open for us, and we stepped out into the sunlight. Into the land of the living, I thought. "Oh, look," Donna said, pointing to the spot where less than half an hour earlier the mother duck had been sitting with her newborn ducklings. All that remained now were a dozen empty and abandoned shells. Mother and children had vanished. "What happened to them?"

"The mother probably took them over to the pond," Officer Gatlin said. "There's another bunch getting ready to hatch around back, if you want to have a look."

"Can we?" Donna asked me, as if she were a small child.

"If you'd like."

We said goodbye to Officer Gatlin, and walked around to the back of the building. There, in a shaded corner, sat another large Muscovy duck, eggs fanned out around her.

"Look," Donna said, pointing. "There's a crack in that one. It must be getting ready to hatch."

"Pretty amazing."

"Can we watch for a few minutes? Would you mind?"

"We can watch." I sat down on the grass, tucking my legs underneath me, the skirt of my blue dress falling in folds around me. We sat this way for several minutes, as still as the eggs we were watching, neither of us speaking, each lost in her own private world. I thought of Sara and Michelle, how grateful I was for their well-being. I ached to hold

them in my arms, to tell them how much I loved them. Had they any idea? Did I tell them often enough? "How are you feeling?" I asked finally.

"I don't know," Donna said, her voice as lifeless as the girl in the photograph. "On the one hand, I'm so relieved, relieved beyond words, that it wasn't Amy." She sighed deeply. "But on the other hand, it would have been almost a relief if it had been, because at least that way I would have known once and for all what happened to her. There would have been some sense of closure. Not this waiting, all the time waiting," she said, her voice picking up urgency. "Waiting for the phone to ring, waiting for Amy to come walking through the door, waiting for her killer to come forward. I'm not sure how much more of this waiting I can stand."

"It must be so hard," I said, wishing I could say more, say something, *anything*, that might lessen her pain.

"The trial makes it harder," she said, and I knew immediately she was referring to the trial of Colin Friendly. "Every day I read about that animal in the newspaper, what he did to those women, and I wonder: Did he do the same thing to my little girl? And it's more than I can bear."

I moved to her side, cradled her in my arms.

"Do you know that he breaks their noses?" she said.

"What?"

"He breaks their noses. It's his trademark. Apparently, he doesn't always kill them the same way, but he always breaks their noses. I read that in the paper."

I recalled Colin Friendly's photograph in the *Palm Beach Post*. ("What do you see when you look at him?" I'd asked my sister. "I see a little boy who's been hurt," she'd said.)

"There are times when I want to burst into that courtroom and confront that monster myself," Donna was saying. "Demand that he tell me if he killed Amy. 'Tell me,' I want to scream. 'Just tell me so I know one way or the other, so I can get on with my life.' And then I think: No, I couldn't bear to hear him say he'd killed her, because if I know for sure that she's dead, what life do I have?"

I said nothing. Donna and I watched the mother duck as she stood

up and checked beneath her feathers, then repositioned herself slightly to the right.

"I keep thinking back to the night she disappeared," Donna said. "We had an argument before she went out. Did you know that? Did I tell you that?"

"No, I don't think you did."

"I didn't think so. I haven't told anybody. I'm too ashamed."

"Ashamed about what?"

"It was such a stupid argument. It was raining. I wanted her to take an umbrella; she said she didn't need one. I told her she was acting like a child; she said to stop treating her like one."

"Donna," I interrupted, "don't do this to yourself."

"But it was the last thing I said to her. Why did I have to make such an issue over a stupid umbrella?"

"Because you cared about her well-being. Because you loved her. And she knew that."

"Sometimes, when we'd argue, and it was always about little things, never about anything important, but everything always seemed so damned important at the time, I don't know, maybe because I was a single parent, and I always felt I had to make up for Roger's not being around, I don't know, I don't know what I thought anymore, but I remember . . . Oh God, do you want to hear something really awful? I remember that sometimes I thought it was just too much for me, that maybe she should go live with Roger, that it would be easier if she weren't around. Oh God, oh God, how could I think such a thing?"

"Every parent has thoughts like that from time to time," I tried to assure her, thinking of my mother and Jo Lynn, myself and Sara. "It doesn't make you a bad person. It doesn't make you a bad mother."

As if on cue, the egg we'd been watching cracked apart, and a scrawny creature, wet feathers plastered to its tiny, shaking skull, beak spread wide, eyes tightly shut, pushed itself into the open air, impatiently shucking off its protective shell, then collapsing onto its side with the effort, lying prone on the ground without moving.

"Is he dead?" Donna squealed.

"No, he's just too weak to move around yet."

Donna stared at the fallen duckling. "I have to know what happened to Amy," she said.

I said nothing. My mind was on Sara. Children drive you crazy, I was thinking, sometimes even make your life an absolute hell. But once they were part of your life, there was no life without them.

It was this thought more than anything else that persuaded me to accompany Jo Lynn to the courthouse on Wednesday.

Chapter
5

I arrived at the courthouse at just after eight o'clock Wednesday morning. Jo Lynn was already in line, near the front of the long queue that snaked its way through the lobby of the magnificent new peach-colored marble building in the downtown core of West Palm Beach. Jo Lynn had warned me to be at the courthouse at least two hours ahead of time in order to get a seat, but I'd refused to arrive before eight, and she'd agreed to hold a place for me. Cutting into the line, I got more than my share of dirty looks.

"Next week, you'll have to come early," Jo Lynn said, "or I won't save you a place."

I scoffed. "This is it for me."

Jo Lynn only smiled, lazily lacing a bright fuchsia scarf through her blond curls, then securing it with a saucy little bow at the side. The scarf matched her lipstick and sling-back, high-heeled shoes. In between, she

sported a clinging, low-cut white jersey dress with a thigh-high slit up the side. Standing next to her in my conservative, albeit fashionable, beige Calvin Klein suit, I felt like an old frump, the still-virginal maiden aunt who stands in judgment, showering her disapproval on everything the younger folks do. People walked by, smiled and nodded at Jo Lynn, scarcely aware of my presence.

It was the same whenever I went anywhere with Sara. Men craned their necks to get a better view of my daughter, visually pushing me out of the way. Why was I wasting my money on expensive designer fashion when it obviously didn't matter what I looked like? No one saw me anyway.

I pictured Sara, still flopped across her bed when I left the house, which meant she'd be late for school again today. Of course, her lateness yesterday had been my fault, she claimed. I was the one who started the fight, who had to butt my nose into her business. I reminded her that her business became mine when I got phone calls from the school. She told me to get a life. Despite the insights I'd received at the coroner's office, despite my best intentions and newfound resolve, the discussion went downhill from there. It ended with the front door slamming, Sara's final words reverberating down the otherwise quiet street: "Thanks for making me late for school, *Ms.* Therapist!"

A man approached, medium height, slightly scruffy in jeans and a lightweight navy sweater. He told Jo Lynn he was going across the street for a cup of coffee and asked if he could get her anything.

"Coffee would be great, Eric," she told him. "How about you, Kate?"

"Coffee," I agreed, smiling my appreciation. He didn't notice.

"Cream and two sugars, right?" he asked Jo Lynn.

"You got it."

"Just black for me," I said, but he was already on his way. "And who is Eric?" I asked her.

She shrugged. "Just a guy I met in line the other day. He's been coming since the beginning of the trial."

The trial was in its second week. According to news reports, it was expected to last until Christmas. I looked around, casually perusing the

faces of the others waiting behind me. Just a bunch of ordinary people, I
realized, awaiting their opportunity to glimpse into the heart of extraordinary evil. The young outnumbered the old; the women outnumbered the
men; the young women outnumbered everybody, undoubtedly drawn
here by the powerful twin magnets of revulsion and attraction. Did being
here make them feel safer, I wondered, more in control? Were they confronting their own worst fears, staring down their demons? Or were they
here, as was my sister, to ask for the demon's hand in marriage?

It was the first time I'd been inside the new courthouse, which had
been completed in May 1995. My eyes swept the foyer, trying to see it as
Larry might, with a builder's appreciation for detail, but all I saw was a
lot of glass and granite. Maybe I was too nervous. Maybe I already regretted my decision to be there.

Eric returned with our coffee. Mine, like Jo Lynn's, contained
cream and enough sugar to induce a diabetic coma. I smiled my thanks
and held the undrinkable thing between my palms until it grew cold. At
least Eric had remembered I was here.

About an hour later, a large contingent of men and women appeared, seemingly from out of nowhere, and swept past us through a set
of glass doors. "Press," Jo Lynn whispered knowingly as my eyes trailed
after them, my attention focusing on the profile of one man in particular,
thinking he looked vaguely familiar. He was about fifty, slim, maybe five
feet ten inches tall, with autumn-brown hair that matched his expensively tailored suit. My gaze accompanied him through the metal detectors and around the corner until he disappeared. "Too bad the judge
won't allow TV cameras into the courtroom," Jo Lynn was saying, sounding very knowledgeable about the whole proceedings. "Of course, if
there were cameras, I'd have to buy a whole new wardrobe. White
doesn't photograph very good on TV. Did you know that?"

"White doesn't photograph very *well*," I corrected, trying to decide
whether or not she was serious.

She looked stricken. "Well, who died and appointed you Mrs.
Grundy?" We didn't speak again until we'd passed through the metal
detectors ourselves and were in the crowded elevator on the way to the
courtroom on the top floor.

I didn't know what to expect, and I was astonished when I stepped out of the elevator and found myself staring out an expansive wall of windows at a truly spectacular view of the city, the Intracoastal Waterway, and the ocean beyond. A dreamscape, I remember thinking, as I proceeded down the long corridor, knowing I was walking into a nightmare.

The spectacular view continued inside the courtroom itself, where the entire east wall was made up of windows. The trial was taking place in Courtroom 11A, the so-called ceremonial courtroom, and the largest courtroom in the building. I'd never been inside a courtroom before and was amazed to discover how familiar it all felt. Years of watching fictional trials in the movies and on TV, plus the relatively new experience of Court TV, had rendered the arena more accessible, if not downright cozy. There was the judge's podium, flags to either side, the witness stand, the jury box, the spectator's gallery with room for about seventy-five people, everything exactly where I'd known it would be.

"Colin sits there." Jo Lynn indicated the long, dark oak table and three black leather chairs of the defense team with a nod of her head. "In the middle." She was already sitting on the edge of her seat, straining her body forward to get a better look, although there was nothing yet to see. We were in the third row of the middle section, just behind the prosecutor's table and the two rows reserved for the families of the victims. "We get a better view of Colin from this side," she explained.

I watched the courtroom fill, wishing that she would stop referring to the accused serial killer as if he were a close personal friend. "Wait till you see how handsome he is," Jo Lynn said. The shoulders of the woman sitting directly in front of us stiffened, her back arching, like a cat's. I turned toward the back of the room, stared absently at the cloudless blue sky, my face flush with embarrassment and shame.

It was several seconds before I realized that someone was staring back. It was the man I'd noticed outside, the man with the autumn-colored hair and expensively tailored suit. In profile, he'd appeared lean and angular, intense and inaccessible; full-face, he appeared kinder, softer, less formidable. Too many years of Florida sunshine had rendered his handsome face somewhat leathery, and there were crease lines around his full mouth and hazel eyes.

How could I know his eyes were hazel? I wondered, looking away, then immediately back again, staring at him outright, watching in awe as the years fell away from his features, like layers of paint being stripped from the side of a house. The grown man vanished; a boy of eighteen took his place. He was wearing a white track suit, a bright red number 12 stamped across his chest, the sweat of victory from his final race trickling down his cheeks and into his smiling mouth, as he accepted the congratulations of the adoring crowd around him. *Way to go, Bobby! Hey, guy, great race.* "Robert?" I whispered.

Jo Lynn's elbow pierced the side of my ribs. "That's the prosecutor, Mr. Eaves, coming through the door. I hate him. He's really out to get Colin."

Reluctantly, my focus shifted from the past back to the present, as the assistant state's attorney and his associates made their way up the left aisle of the courtroom to take their seats in front of us. They began opening and closing assorted briefcases, noisily setting up shop, ignoring our presence, as if we weren't there. Mr. Eaves was a serious-faced man with thinning hair and a gut that strained against the jacket of his dark blue suit. He undid the top button as he sat down. His associates, a man and woman who looked young enough to be his children, and enough alike to be siblings, wore similarly grave expressions. Their clothes were simple and nondescript. Rather like mine, I realized with a start, deciding I should have worn a scarf to brighten things up, wondering why I was even thinking such inane thoughts. Slowly, I let my gaze return to the back of the room.

The boy in the red-and-white track suit was gone. Back was the grown man in the expensive suit, now engaged in earnest conversation with the man beside him. I waited for him to turn back in my direction, but after a few minutes, he was still talking to the man next to him. No doubt I was mistaken, I told myself. Robert Crowe was a boy I'd dated back in high school, and hadn't seen since his family left Pittsburgh for parts unknown. I remember being so grateful they'd left the state—it made having been dumped slightly easier to bear. What would he be doing here now?

I shook my head, exhaled an angry breath of air, and stilled the foot

that was tapping nervously on the floor with an impatient hand, my heart pounding unaccountably fast. It had been over thirty years since I'd last laid eyes on Robert Crowe. Could he really still have this effect on me?

"Here he comes now," Jo Lynn announced anxiously, twisting around in her aisle seat, crossing one leg over the other, maximizing the effect of the slit in her skirt.

A concentrated hush fell across the courtroom as Colin Friendly entered the court from a door at the front of the room and was directed to his seat by an armed police officer. Immediately, his attorneys rose to greet him. The accused killer was dressed in a conservative blue suit with a peach-colored shirt and paisley tie, his dark wavy hair combed neatly off his face, looking exactly as he had in the photo in the weekend paper. I watched his eyes sweep effortlessly across the room, a hunter searching for his prey, I thought with a shudder as his eyes rested briefly on Jo Lynn.

"My God, did you see that?" she whispered, grabbing my hand, her long nails cutting into my flesh. "He looked right at me."

I struggled for air but found none. Without even trying, Colin Friendly had sucked up all the oxygen in the room.

"Did you see that?" Jo Lynn pressed. "He saw me. He knows I'm here for him."

The woman seated directly in front of us spun around angrily in her seat, then turned immediately away.

"What's her problem?" Jo Lynn asked indignantly.

"Good God, Jo Lynn," I stammered. "Would you just listen to yourself? Do you hear what you're saying?"

"What's *your* problem?"

The judge entered the room a few minutes later. Dutifully, we all rose, then retook our seats. Judge Kellner was suitably gray and judicious-looking.

Next came the jury, seven women, five men, two more women who served as alternates, all of them wearing badges that identified them as jurors. Of the fourteen, eight were white, four were black, two were somewhere in between. They were neatly dressed, although surprisingly casual. At least *I* was surprised. Of course, I was also the only one in the

courtroom, other than the lawyers and the defendant, who was wearing a suit. Except for Robert Crowe.

Again, my head spun toward the back of the room. This time, Robert Crowe was looking right at me. He smiled. "Kate?" he mouthed.

I felt my heart leap into my throat, my lungs filling with sudden dread, as thick as smoke. There is nothing to feel anxious about, I told myself. Just because you're in the same room with an accused murderer *and* an old high school sweetheart, this was not something to get unnecessarily worked up about.

In the next second, it was as if someone had taken a match to my insides. I felt my inner organs shriveling and disappearing inside invisible flames. Sweat broke out across my forehead and upper lip. I pulled at the collar of my beige blouse, debated taking off my jacket. "It's very hot in here," I whispered to Jo Lynn.

"No, it's not," she said.

The clerk called the court to order and the judge directed the prosecutor to call his first witness. The temperature in the room returned to normal. Jo Lynn squirmed excitedly in her seat as a studious-looking young woman named Angela Riegert was sworn in.

"Look at her," Jo Lynn muttered under her breath. "She's dumpy and homely and just wishes she could get a man like Colin."

As if he'd heard her, Colin Friendly slowly turned his head in my sister's direction. A slight smile played at the corners of his lips.

Jo Lynn crossed, then uncrossed her legs. "We're with you, Colin," she whispered.

His smile widened, then he turned his attention back to the witness stand.

"I'm gonna give him my phone number." Jo Lynn was already fishing inside her white straw purse for a piece of paper.

"Are you crazy?" I wanted to swat her across the back of her head, physically knock some sense into her.

Just like dear old Dad, I thought with disgust, marveling at the baseness of my instincts. I'd never hit anyone in my life, wasn't about to start now, however tempting it might be. I glared at the back of Colin Friendly's head. Obviously, he brought out the best in me.

Jo Lynn was already scribbling her name and number across a torn scrap of paper. "I'll give it to him during a break."

"If you do, I'll leave. I swear, I'll walk right out of here."

"Then I won't come with you to Mom's," she countered, bringing her fingers to her lips to quiet me.

She had me there. The only way I'd been able to persuade her to attend the afternoon's meeting was to agree to accompany her to court, although she insisted we change the time of the meeting to four o'clock so that she didn't have to "abandon Colin," as she put it, before court let out. She didn't know I'd already decided to tag along.

I still wasn't a hundred percent sure what exactly I was doing in that courtroom. Did I really think I might learn anything that might help Donna Lokash? Or was I trying to watch out for my sister, to protect her from Colin Friendly, to protect her from herself? Or was it simple curiosity? I don't know. I probably never will.

"State your name and address," the court clerk instructed the witness, a short, slightly overweight young woman, who looked nervous and uncomfortable, her small eyes refusing to look at the defense table.

"Angela Riegert," she said, barely audibly.

"You'll have to speak up," Judge Kellner said gently.

Angela Riegert cleared her throat, restated her name. It was only slightly louder the second time. The entire courtroom shifted forward, straining to hear. She gave her address as 1212 Olive Street in Lake Worth.

The prosecutor was on his feet, doing up the button of his dark blue jacket, the way you always see them doing on TV. "Miss Riegert, how old are you?" he began.

"Twenty," she replied, looking as if she weren't altogether sure.

"And how long had you known Wendy Sabatello?"

"We'd been best friends since the fourth grade."

"Who's Wendy Sabatello?" I asked.

"One of the victims," Jo Lynn said, the words sliding out of the side of her mouth.

I stared into my lap, not sure I wanted to hear more.

"And can you tell me what happened on the night of March 17, 1995?"

"We went to a party at someone's house. Her parents were away, and so there was this big party."

"What time did you get there?"

"About nine o'clock."

"And the party was in full swing?"

"It was starting to heat up. There were lots of people; the music was very loud."

"Did you know everyone?"

"No. There were a lot of people there I'd never seen before."

"Did you see the defendant?"

Reluctantly, Angela Riegert glanced toward the accused, then looked quickly away. "Not at first," she whispered.

"Sorry, could you repeat that?"

"I didn't see him till later."

"But you did see him?"

"Yes, he was in the backyard. I saw him when we went outside to get some air."

"Did you talk to him?"

"He talked to me."

"You wish," Jo Lynn scoffed.

"What did he say?"

"Not much. 'Nice party,' 'nice night,' that sort of thing."

"Was Wendy Sabatello with you at the time?"

"Yes. She thought he was cute."

"Objection, your honor," one of the defense lawyers protested, jumping to his feet. "Can the witness read minds?"

"She told me," Angela Riegert said clearly.

"Objection," the lawyer countered. "Hearsay."

"Overruled."

The witness looked confused, as if she weren't sure what exactly had transpired. She wasn't the only one.

"Did she say anything else about him?"

Angela Riegert nodded. "That he had incredible eyes."

"And what did you think?"

"I thought he was cute too, a little older than most of the other guys there."

"What happened then?"

The witness swallowed, bit down on her lower lip. "We went back inside."

"And did you speak to Colin Friendly again?"

"I didn't, no, but later on, Wendy said she was going back outside to talk to him."

"And?"

"It was the last time I saw her."

"She never came back in?"

"No. When I went to look for her later, to tell her I was ready to leave, she was gone."

"And the defendant?"

"He was gone too."

The prosecutor smiled. "Thank you, Miss Riegert." He nodded toward the defense. "Your witness."

The defense counsel was already on his feet, buttoning his jacket. He was an athletic-looking man, blond and thick-necked, the muscles of his arms clearly evident beneath the jacket of his gray silk suit. "Miss Riegert," he said, biting off each syllable, "was there any drinking at this party?"

Angela Riegert shrank back in her seat. "Yes."

"Drugs?"

"Drugs?" she repeated, clearly flustered.

"Marijuana? Cocaine?"

"I didn't see anyone doing cocaine."

"Were you drinking?" the attorney pressed.

"I had a few beers, yes."

"Were you drunk?"

"No."

"Did you have any marijuana?"

"Objection, your honor," Mr. Eaves protested. "The witness is not on trial."

"Goes to state of mind, Judge. It directly affects the witness's ability to identify my client."

"Objection overruled. Please answer the question, Miss Riegert."

She hesitated, looked close to tears. "I had a few tokes," she admitted.

"A few tokes off a marijuana cigarette and a few beers, is that what you're saying?" the defense attorney repeated.

"Yes."

"Were you stoned?"

"No."

"But you did go outside to get some air."

"It was hot inside, and very crowded."

"And outside?"

"It was better."

"Was it dark?"

"I guess."

"So," the defense lawyer stated, positioning himself directly in front of the jury, "it was dark, you'd been drinking and smoking marijuana . . ." He paused for effect. "And still you claim you can positively identify my client."

Angela Riegert pulled back her shoulders, stared directly at Colin Friendly. "Yes," she said. "I know it was him."

"Oh, Miss Riegert," the lawyer asked, almost as an afterthought, "do you wear glasses?"

"Sometimes."

"Were you wearing them that night?"

"No."

"Thank you. No further questions." The lawyer quickly returned to his seat.

"Well done," Jo Lynn said, and I was forced to agree. In less than a minute, Colin Friendly's attorney had neatly skewered Angela Riegert's testimony, introducing at least a modicum of reasonable doubt.

"You may step down," Judge Kellner instructed the witness. Angela Riegert took a deep breath, then stepped off the witness stand, Jo Lynn's eyes glaring at her as she walked past us out of the room.

"What a loser," Jo Lynn pronounced as the next witness was called.

"The state calls Marcia Layton."

I looked toward the center aisle at the same precise moment as Colin Friendly. For a fraction of a second, our eyes met. He winked boldly, then looked away.

Chapter

6

It was almost four-thirty by the time we reached our mother's apartment, located on Palm Beach Lakes Boulevard, several miles west of I-95.

"What's the big rush?" Jo Lynn asked, teetering on pencil-thin high heels behind me, as I ran across the parking lot toward the yellow structure that resembled nothing so much as a large lemon pound cake. "It's not like she's going anywhere."

"I told Mrs. Winchell we'd be here by four o'clock," I reminded her. "She wasn't happy. She has to be out of here by five."

"So, whose fault is it we're late?"

I said nothing. Jo Lynn was right. The fact that we were almost half an hour late was at least partly my fault. And Robert's.

He'd been waiting for me when we exited the courtroom at the end of the day. "I'm sorry I missed you at lunchtime," he apologized imme-

diately, while I tried not to notice how clear his hazel eyes were. "I had to rush off to a meeting."

"How are you? What are you doing here?" I asked, my voice an octave higher than usual. I was grateful that Jo Lynn wasn't beside me to witness my regression to adolescence, that she was still poised at the side of the courtroom doors, waiting for her chance to accost one of Colin Friendly's attorneys. She'd spent the better part of the lunch break composing a letter to the monster, having decided her phone number wasn't support enough. Colin Friendly needed to know why she was so convinced of his innocence, she told me. I told her she needed to have her head examined.

"What am I doing in Palm Beach or what am I doing in court?" The lines around Robert Crowe's eyes crinkled in a way that told me he was well aware of his effect on me, as he'd always been, and that he was amused, possibly even touched, by it. "I might ask you the same thing."

"I live here. In Palm Beach. Well, actually in Palm Beach Gardens. We moved here about seven years ago." Had he really asked for so much information? "And you?"

"My family moved to Tampa right after I graduated high school," he said easily. "I went off to Yale, then joined my folks in Florida after graduation, met a girl, got married, moved to Boca, got divorced, moved to Delray, got married again, moved to Palm Beach."

"So you're married," I said, and immediately wished the scales of justice would come crashing down on my head.

He smiled. "Four kids. And you?"

"Two girls."

"And a husband?"

"Oh yes, of course. Larry Sinclair. I met him at college. I don't think you know him," I babbled, wishing someone would stick a gag in my mouth. All my life, I've wanted to be a lady of mystery, one of those women who smile enigmatically and say little, probably because they have little to say, but everyone always assumes it's because they're so deep. At any rate, mystery has never been my strong suit. My mother always says you can see everything on my face.

Robert Crowe shook his head, revealing a number of gray hairs

around his temples. They made him look more distinguished, I thought. "Just the one husband?" he asked.

"Pretty boring," I said.

"Pretty amazing," he countered. "So, what brings you to court today?"

I glanced toward my sister, still waiting anxiously by the courtroom doors. "To tell you the truth, I'm not really sure. What about you? Are you a reporter?"

"Not exactly. I own a radio station, WKEY."

"Oh, of course." I hoped I didn't sound as impressed as I felt.

"Normally I wouldn't be here. We have reporters covering the trial, of course."

"Of course," I concurred.

"But I had a lunch meeting nearby, so I thought . . ." He broke off. "You're very beautiful," he said.

I laughed out loud. Probably to keep from fainting.

"Why are you laughing? Don't you believe me?"

I felt my cheeks grow crimson, my knees go weak, my body temperature rise. Oh sure, I thought, great time to turn into a red, quivering mass of sweat. That should impress the hell out of him. "It's just been a long time since anyone told me I was beautiful," I heard myself say.

"Larry doesn't tell you how beautiful you are?" He smiled, curling his lips around my husband's first name. He's playing with me, I thought.

There was a slight commotion at the door. Colin Friendly's attorneys were leaving the courtroom. "Mr. Archibald," I heard my sister call out, thrusting the letter she'd spent the lunch break composing at the lawyer in the gray silk suit, "I was wondering if you could make sure that Colin receives this. It's very important."

"Pathetic," Robert Crowe pronounced.

"What is?"

"Courtroom groupies. Every trial has them. The more gruesome the crime, the more ardent the bimbos." He shook his head. "It makes you wonder."

"About what?"

"About what kind of lives these poor deluded souls live. I mean,

look at that woman. She's not bad-looking; she probably wouldn't have any trouble getting a man, yet she chooses to go after a guy who gets his kicks from killing and mutilating women. I don't get it. Do you?"

I shook my head, although, in truth, I was barely aware of anything he'd said after "she's not bad-looking." Moments before he'd told me I was beautiful. Jo Lynn was merely "not bad-looking." Shallow thing that I was fast becoming, I couldn't get it out of my head.

"So, what does Larry's wife do when she's not attending sensational murder trials?" he asked.

The second mention of my husband's name snapped me out of my reveries. "I'm a therapist."

"That's right, I remember you were always interested in that sort of stuff." He managed to make it sound as if he'd actually been listening to anything I'd had to say thirty years ago. "So little Kate Latimer grew up to become the woman she always wanted to be."

Had I? I wondered. If so, then why was she such a stranger?

"Well, Kate Latimer, it's been very nice seeing you again after all these years." He leaned his face close to mine. Was he going to kiss me? Was I going to let him? Was I a total idiot?

"It's Kate Sinclair now," I reminded us both.

Cocking his head to one side, his eyes never leaving mine, he took my hand in his and brought it slowly to his mouth. His lips grazed the back of my hand. I don't even want to describe the effect this had on my body, which was already struggling to remain upright and in one piece. "Uh-oh," he said.

I froze. "What's the matter?"

"The bimbo is headed this way."

"Okay, we can go now," Jo Lynn announced, arriving at my side, eyes wandering between me and Robert Crowe.

"Jo Lynn," I said, "I'd like you to meet Robert Crowe. Robert, this is my sister, Jo Lynn Baker."

"Please shoot me now," Robert said simply, and I laughed. It felt good to be in control again.

"Am I missing something?" Jo Lynn asked. Her voice was light, but

her eyes flashed a familiar combination of anger and hurt. She didn't like to feel left out. She hated being laughed at.

"Your sister and I knew each other in high school," Robert said, as if this were explanation enough.

For some reason, this seemed to satisfy her. "Really? Well, then I guess you can thank me for this mini high school reunion. I'm the one who dragged her down here, and let me tell you, it wasn't easy." She leaned forward to shake his hand, her breasts all but spilling into the air between them.

"Yes, I seem to recall that it's pretty hard to get Kate to do anything she doesn't want to do." Robert's smile grew wicked. He'd spent six months in high school trying to seduce me, then dropped me like the proverbial hot potato when it became apparent I was a lost cause.

"We should get going," Jo Lynn stated, then leaned toward Robert, conspiratorially. "Our mom is terrorizing the tenants of the old folks home she lives in. We have a meeting."

"Interesting family," Robert Crowe said, as Jo Lynn led me away.

"So, did you sleep with him?" she asked on the way to the Palm Beach Lakes Retirement Home.

"No, of course not."

"But you wanted to," she persisted.

"I was seventeen; I didn't know what I wanted."

"You wanted to sleep with him, but you were such a goody-goody that you didn't, and you've always regretted it."

"For God's sake, Jo Lynn, I haven't thought about the man in years."

When I refused to discuss him further, Jo Lynn launched into a recap of the day's proceedings. Angela Riegert was a disaster as a witness, she pronounced; her testimony had been more helpful to the defense than to the prosecution. It didn't matter that she'd placed the defendant beside the victim shortly before the girl's disappearance; all the jury would remember was that Angela Riegert was a beer-guzzling, marijuana-smoking, half-blind half-wit.

Marcia Layton was similarly gutted, then tossed aside, as were the

rest of the day's witnesses, all of whom put Colin Friendly squarely in the vicinity of the murdered girls at the time they went missing. "Inconclusive," Jo Lynn pronounced stubbornly. "Eyewitnesses are notoriously unreliable."

There was no point in arguing. Jo Lynn had always believed exactly what she wanted to believe. She saw what she wanted to see. When she looked at Colin Friendly, she saw a lonely little boy with a sad smile, and she believed him to be innocent, as much a victim as each of the women he stood accused of murdering. Possibly more.

It had been the same way with Andrew and Daniel and Peter. Andrew, whom she married at eighteen, broke first one arm, then the other; Daniel, whom she married six years later, stole her money and cracked her ribs; Peter, whom she married just after her thirty-second birthday and divorced just prior to her thirty-third, threw her down a flight of stairs on their wedding night. Still, in the end, it was Andrew, Daniel, and Peter who did the walking. I tried to get her into therapy, but she would have none of it. "It's Mom's fault," she'd joke. ("Kidding on the square," our mother would say, shoulders slumping forward, accepting responsibility.)

"Would you slow down a bit," Jo Lynn whined as we reached the front door of the retirement home.

"Why'd you have to wear such high heels?" I asked, transferring my frustration from her to her fuchsia pumps.

"You don't like my shoes?"

The lobby was large and cheery, all white paint and green trees and chairs covered in bold floral prints. At least a dozen senior citizens sat in a row of white wicker rocking chairs, staring out the large front window, as if at a drive-in movie. Thinning hair, liver spots, stooped backs, and sunken faces, an old man fumbling with his fly, an old woman adjusting her teeth—I looked at them and saw the future. It scared me half to death.

Our mother was waiting for us outside Mrs. Winchell's office. "Where have you been? It's not like you to be late." She looked from me to Jo Lynn.

"Don't give me that look," Jo Lynn said immediately, her defenses, like fists, already raised.

"I was just thinking how nice it is to see you," our mother said.

Jo Lynn made a sound halfway between a laugh and a snort, and looked away.

"I'm sorry, Mom," I explained. "I met an old friend from high school."

"Who she wanted to sleep with, but didn't," Jo Lynn said.

"What?" said my mother.

"Jo Lynn . . ."

"It's true," Jo Lynn said, smiling at our mother. "Did she tell you I'm getting married?"

At our meeting Mrs. Winchell, whose tomato-red suit set off her velvety black skin but clashed with the rest of her predominantly canary-yellow office, made no effort to disguise repeated glances at her watch. She couldn't stay long, she'd stated before the meeting got underway; we were almost forty minutes late and, regrettably, she had a dinner engagement in Boca.

Got married. Moved to Boca. Got divorced. Moved to Delray.

"Perhaps you could tell your daughters your complaints regarding Mr. Ormsby," Mrs. Winchell began.

Our mother looked surprised, then confused. Clearly, she had no idea what Mrs. Winchell was talking about.

"Didn't you tell me that Mr. Ormsby was harassing you?" Mrs. Winchell prompted. "Fred Ormsby is part of our janitorial staff," she explained, checking her watch.

"He's a lovely man," our mother added.

"He hasn't been calling you at all hours of the night?"

"Why would he do that?"

It was Mrs. Winchell's turn to look confused. "Well, of course, he wouldn't. He didn't. I'm just repeating what you told me."

"No," my mother insisted. "Fred Ormsby is a lovely man. He would never do anything like that. You must have misunderstood."

"Then there's no problem?" my sister asked, jumping to her feet.

"Apparently not." Mrs. Winchell smiled, obviously relieved the meeting had reached such a surprisingly swift and satisfactory conclusion. If she had any other concerns, she wasn't about to get into them now.

"What did you make of that?" I asked my sister as we rode with our mother in the elevator up to the fourth floor.

Jo Lynn shrugged. "Mrs. Winchell obviously got her inmates confused."

"I don't trust that woman," our mother said.

Jo Lynn laughed. "You just don't like her because she's black."

"Jo Lynn!" I gasped.

"Mrs. Winchell is black?" our mother asked.

"How could she not know the woman is black?" I whispered as we exited the elevator and proceeded along the peach-colored corridor. "Do you think something's the matter with her eyes?"

"She just didn't notice."

"How can you not notice something like that?"

"Didn't anyone ever teach you it's not polite to whisper behind people's backs?" our mother asked pointedly, stopping in front of the door to her apartment, making no move to open it.

"What are you waiting for?" Jo Lynn said. "There's nobody home."

My mother reached into her pocket for her keys. She was elegantly dressed in a soft pink skirt and matching sweater set, highlighted by a single strand of pearls. "I was just thinking."

"About what?" I asked.

"About what I've done that would make Mrs. Winchell not like me." Her voice carried the threat of tears.

"She doesn't like you because you're Jewish," Jo Lynn said.

"I'm Jewish?" our mother asked.

"She's joking, Mom," I said quickly, glaring at Jo Lynn, feeling like Alice at the Mad Hatter's tea party.

"So was I," our mother said, smiling mischievously as we stepped into her small one-bedroom apartment. "Where's your sense of humor, Kate?"

I left it at the courthouse, I thought, my eyes taking in the room in a single glance. The living area contained a small love seat and matching

chair, with a glass coffee table crowded in between, and a standing lamp cramped into one corner. Pictures of me, my daughters, and Jo Lynn covered every available surface, including the windowsill that ran along the far wall, overlooking the parking lot below.

"It's like an oven in here. How high do you have the heat?" Jo Lynn moved to the thermometer. "It's eighty-three degrees. How can you stand it?"

"Older people feel the cold more," our mother said.

I took off my jacket, threw it across the back of the beige chair.

"What are you doing?" Jo Lynn said, scooping it up again, handing it back. "We're not staying."

"We can stay a few minutes."

"Of course you'll stay," our mother insisted. "We'll have some cake."

"Not a chance," Jo Lynn said. "You trying to poison us like you did old Mr. Emerson?"

Our mother was already on her way to the tiny galley kitchen, opening the fridge, removing a slightly lopsided angel food cake. "Oh, Jo Lynn," she said. "There you go again, kidding on the square."

"What's that?" I asked, coming up behind her, spying a large bottle of dishwashing detergent on the refrigerator's top shelf. "Mom, what's this doing in the fridge?"

Jo Lynn was immediately at our side. "God, Mom, is that what you've been cooking with?"

"Of course not," our mother scoffed, removing the detergent from the fridge, putting it by the side of the sink. "Don't you ever make mistakes?"

"Something's very wrong," I said as we were driving home. "She's losing it."

Jo Lynn waved dismissive fingers in the air. "She got confused."

I invited Jo Lynn over for dinner and was grateful when she said no. She wanted to relax and get a good night's sleep, she said, so she'd look fresh for tomorrow's day in court. It was important that Colin have attractive people around him to boost his morale. Besides, his attorneys might try to contact her, and she didn't want to miss their call.

"Whatever," I said, dropping her off at her low-rise apartment near Blue Heron Drive, watching till she was safely through the lobby's front door. My sister was pining for a serial killer and my mother kept dishwashing detergent in the refrigerator. Interesting family is right, I thought, recalling Robert's words, squirming in my seat as I turned the car back toward I-95.

Now, I am not anything like my sister. I am mature, levelheaded, not given to flights of fancy. If anything, I am too firmly grounded in reality. I have a clear understanding of my strengths and weaknesses; I've come to terms with my foibles and insecurities. I am decidedly unsentimental; I am definitely not a romantic. So, what did it mean that I was suddenly, inexplicably, overwhelmingly, desperate for a man I hadn't seen in over thirty years, a shallow jock who'd wooed me, then dumped me when I wouldn't put out? Why couldn't I get his sly smile out of my mind? "You're very beautiful," he'd said, the facile phrase repeating itself over and over in my head, attaching itself to Dwight Yoakam's country twang. Station WKEY, I realized, wondering when I'd changed the dial.

In fact, it doesn't require a great deal of psychoanalyzing to figure out my state of mind: I was getting older; my life with Larry had settled into a comfortable groove; I'd seen flashes of my own mortality in the face of my mother; my sister was driving me nuts. Robert Crowe was a harking back to my youth, my innocence, a reminder that my whole life lay before me. Plus, of course, he was a symbol of all that was desirable but unattainable, the one who got away.

Jo Lynn was right. I'd wanted to sleep with him very badly when I was seventeen. I'd been severely tempted on more than one occasion to throw caution to the wind, along with my morals and every article of clothing on me. I'm not sure what stopped me, other than the certainty that once I gave in, he would undoubtedly lose interest and move on. Well, he'd lost interest and moved on anyway. Then he'd moved away altogether and I never even had the chance to change my mind.

I'd lied earlier when I told Jo Lynn I hadn't thought about him in years. The truth was that I thought about him more often than I cared to admit, more often than I'd even realized. His features may have faded,

blurred, grown indistinct, but he was always there, lurking, a symbol of simpler times, of youthful ardor, of lost chances, of what might have been.

Dinner was already on the table when I arrived home. I was grateful to Larry, who was a better cook than I was, probably because he enjoyed cooking and I didn't. At any rate, he'd made some sort of chicken dish that Michelle didn't eat because she said it was too spicy and Sara didn't eat because she said she was getting fat. I wolfed down everything on my plate, and almost choked on a piece of chicken.

"Are you okay?" Larry asked.

"Do you need the Heimlich maneuver?" Michelle was already on her feet. She'd taken a St. John's Ambulance course the previous summer and was always asking if anyone needed the Heimlich maneuver.

"Sorry, sweetie, no," I told her.

Both Sara and Michelle left the table while Larry and I were still eating, Michelle to do homework, Sara to return to school. There was a rehearsal for an upcoming fashion show; she was in it and she couldn't be late. An interesting concept for Sara, I thought, who had no such qualms about being late for anything else.

Larry and I chatted briefly about our respective days, then lapsed into silence. I found myself studying him as he ate; he was a nice-looking man of average height and weight, growing bald with grace, his eyes a grayish blue, his complexion fair, his arms and legs on the thin side, any extra weight he'd acquired over the years having comfortably settled in around his stomach. He'd turned fifty the previous July with a minimum of fuss and even less angst. When I'd asked him how it felt to be fifty, he'd smiled and said simply, "It beats the alternative." How would Robert respond to a similar query? I wondered, trying to shake free of his memory as I cleared the table of food. But it was no use. Robert's presence pursued me into the kitchen as I cleaned up, crowded between Larry and me as we watched TV, followed me into the bedroom after I gave up waiting for Sara to come home.

Larry was already in bed. The fourteen decorative pillows that sit on top of the ivory bedspread during the day were now scattered rudely across the ivory carpeting. Larry hates the pillows. He says they're a pain

in the neck, and he's right, they are. But I love organizing them in the morning, arranging them in neat little rows, and truthfully, I don't really mind taking them off and stacking them at night. Probably, it gives me the illusion of control. Larry has no such illusions. He simply throws them into the air and lets them fall where they may.

I undressed and climbed into bed beside my husband, reaching for him in the dark. He sighed and stirred, turning onto his back, taking me into his arms, welcoming my touch. "Hi, funny face," he whispered as I kissed the side of his neck, my fingers drawing a slowly swirling line through the curly hairs of his chest, edging downward. A slight groan escaped his lips as I reached lower, cradled his penis in the palm of my hand.

I don't know why I always feel a little insulted when Larry isn't already fully aroused when I touch him, but I do. I know this is irrational, that it takes men longer to become aroused as they get older, that certain body parts no longer snap to attention at the merest whiff of sex, that gentle perseverance will pay off in the end. Still, it disappoints me, even angers me, if I'm being really truthful, that my mere presence beside him in bed is no longer enough. I know we've been married almost twenty-five years; I know my body isn't the same as the body he married; I know things have become somewhat routine; I know romance takes hard work. Haven't I already confessed I'm not a romantic?

So I pushed my hurt feelings aside and stroked him delicately, turning his penis over in my hand, kneading it, like a piece of Plasticene. I thought of swatting it, thought better of it. Definitely a mood killer. Instead, I took him gently in my mouth, feeling gratified when he grew quickly hard. Then I climbed on top of him and fitted him inside me, starting slowly, then picking up the pace, riding him with increasing urgency, as if there were someone chasing me, and perhaps someone was.

As Larry drifted off to sleep, I saw Robert watching me from one of two ivory chairs by the window, his Cheshire cat smile reflected brightly against the shadows. His image floated forward, whispered in my ear. Pleasant dreams, he said.

Chapter

7

As I struggle now to understand Sara's role in everything that happened, I ask myself if I could have done anything differently earlier on, something that might have warded off the chaos and tragedy that followed. Certainly the clues were all around me. The pieces of the puzzle that is my older child were all there. I had only to arrange them in their correct positions. Or would there always have been one or two pieces missing? And would finding them have done any good?

When Sara went out that night, supposedly to rehearse for an upcoming fashion show at school, I had no idea she was lying. Or maybe I did. Past experience had taught me to view everything Sara said as suspect. But, like a wife who has chosen to stay with her faithless husband, I had made a conscious decision to believe the things she told me until presented with conclusive evidence to the contrary. Sara being Sara, this usually didn't take long.

The first time I'd caught Sara in an outright lie was soon after she turned fifteen. We'd been out for dinner, it was raining, and Sara dropped her purse in the parking lot as we raced for the car. About ten empty packages of cigarettes tumbled out of the overstuffed leather bag and onto the wet pavement.

"They're not mine," she said, quickly scooping them up and stuffing them back inside her purse as I watched in awed silence.

"They're not yours," I repeated.

"They belong to a friend. She collects them."

Now most people would immediately dismiss this for the ridiculous fabrication it was and get in out of the rain. But when it's *your* kid with the ridiculous yarn, it's a different story. "Your friend collects *empty* cigarette packages?"

"Yes, and her mother would be really mad if she found out, so she asked me to keep them for her." Sara vaulted to her feet, the empty, and now soaking-wet, cigarette packages safely back inside her bag and out of sight. "I don't smoke," she insisted. "They're not mine."

I struggled to believe her. People collected all sorts of weird things, I told myself. Why not empty cigarette packages? If her friend's mother would be upset at this, well, then it was perfectly logical for her to ask Sara to keep them for her. This is what I actually tried to convince myself. And then common sense prevailed and the therapist took control. "You say you're not smoking, and I'd love to believe you," I began. "You know how dangerous smoking is, and *I* know I can't follow you around twenty-four hours a day. If you're going to smoke, you're going to smoke. I only hope that if you *are* smoking, you're smart enough to quit before you become addicted." And I left it at that. And, of course, she *was* smoking, and she *wasn't* smart enough to quit before she became addicted. Why was I surprised?

The ten empty cigarette packages were followed by the five full bottles of beer which I found in her closet while searching for the white blouse she'd asked me to iron. How dare I go snooping around her closet! she screamed later, as if I should have realized that her white blouse lay in a crumpled heap on the floor along with most of her other worldly

possessions. And, of course, the beer wasn't hers—she was merely keeping it for a friend.

There was the day she skipped school to go shopping in Fort Lauderdale, the weekend she snuck off to Miami to see the Grateful Dead. I'm sure I wasn't the only mother not to mourn the passing of Jerry Garcia, however much I might have enjoyed his music in my youth.

Sweaters disappeared from my drawers. Half our CDs went missing. Sara stole money from my purse and denied it outright to my face. The adoring creature who'd once looked at me with something approaching awe was replaced by a creature who glared at me with such utter contempt that it shook me to the bones. I told myself that this transformation was simply a rite of passage, that it was Sara's unconscious way of separating from me, of becoming her own person. But it still hurt. That's what the psychology texts don't prepare you for—how much it hurts.

Actually, it's the lies that hurt more than anything, because lies destroy trust, and it feels awful not to trust the people you love.

Not that the truth provided us with any great comfort. Sara blithely informed me, a few weeks after she turned sixteen, that she was no longer a virgin. Since she had no steady boyfriend, to say I was stunned was something of an understatement. I mumbled something about hoping it had been a pleasurable experience for her, then launched into a lecture about the dangers of unprotected sex in today's society, probably because I was afraid that if I stopped talking, she'd tell me something else I didn't want to hear. She assured me that she knew all about the threat of AIDS and the necessity for condoms, and insisted she wasn't a child. Then she asked me to drive her to the record store.

It was around this time that she also admitted to having experimented with drugs. Just a little grass and acid, she said with a shrug. Nothing to worry our old-fashioned little heads about. She reminded us that our generation had practically invented hallucinogens; I reminded her that they were still illegal, that she was playing with fire, and that we would send her packing should we ever find any drugs in the house. "That's what I get for being honest with you," she huffed in response.

She started getting phone calls at all hours of the night. Since we

only have one line, these phone calls woke up the whole house. I told Sara this had to stop; she said she couldn't be blamed for something over which she had no control. I told her it was her responsibility to tell people not to call after 11 P.M. She told me to mind my own business. The argument ended with Larry storming into her room and literally tearing her phone out of the wall. That pretty much took care of that.

The phone was how we found out that Sara hadn't gone to the school for any fashion show rehearsal. A friend, I suspect more than slightly inebriated, called at 2 A.M. to tell us that Sara had left her purse at the party, could we tell her not to worry? We said we'd be only too thrilled.

As it turned out, Sara had already realized she'd forgotten her purse and gone back for it, so she knew about the phone call and she was as ready for us as we were for her. Can you imagine? she lamented even before she was through the front door. She'd gone all the way to school only to discover the rehearsal had been canceled. A bunch of the kids, knowing how important this fashion show was—the proceeds were going to the United Way—and wanting to do the best possible job, decided to have a rehearsal of their own at somebody's house. There was no party. They'd selflessly worked their butts off all night, stopping only an hour ago when they were fully satisfied this was going to be the best fashion show ever. If we didn't believe her, she finished with a flourish, then that was our problem, not hers, and she felt sorry for us. By the time she was through, she'd worked herself into a self-righteous fury of almost biblical proportions. How could we not trust her? What kind of pitiful excuse for parents were we? And what were we doing talking to her friends anyway?

We grounded her for two weeks.

"Go to hell!" she shouted, storming into her room.

"Watch it," I warned.

"Watch this, *Ms.* Therapist!" Her door slammed shut.

"Make that three weeks," Larry yelled after her. The response was the sound of a shoe crashing against her still-vibrating door.

Seconds later, Michelle tiptoed out of her bedroom, fixed her father and me with her most baleful glance. "You know that grounding never works," she intoned, the seriousness of her message undermined some-

what by the teddy bear nightgown she was wearing. "Grounding only makes kids angry."

She's right, I thought. "Go back to sleep," I said.

Not that it's all been awful as far as Sara is concerned. Aside from the sheer creativity of some of her tirades, there is also a tremendous vulnerability, a genuine sweetness to Sara. Behind those enormous breasts beats the heart of a good kid. Sara is a child trapped inside a woman's body. She still isn't ready to come out.

I remember when she got her period for the first time. She was fifteen years old, which is late, and she'd long ago forgotten the mother-daughter discussion we'd had about such things. She took the pads I gave her, and skulked from the room, as if this appalling state of affairs was something I'd wished on her. The next morning, I asked if the pads had interfered with her sleep.

She looked horrified. "You mean you have to wear them at night?!"

I still laugh about that one, as I do when I recall her disgust some four days later. "How long does this go *on*?" she demanded indignantly. I didn't have the heart to tell her another thirty-five years.

One night, Sara was reluctantly helping me stack the dinner dishes inside the dishwasher. I'd lined all the glasses along one side. There was one left over, which I placed on the other side of the dishwasher. Sara immediately took a glass from my neat row and put it beside the single one. "I don't want it to be lonely," she explained.

It was all I could do to keep from crying. Instead, I hugged her and told her I loved her. Sara tolerated my embrace, mumbled something about loving me too, then left the room.

So, how does one reconcile the sweet innocent thing who worries about the feelings of dirty dishes with the foul-mouthed hellion who doesn't seem to understand that human beings have feelings too?

"The apple doesn't fall far from the tree," I tell my clients, seeking to reassure them—and no doubt myself—that eventually life returns to normal, that teenagers such as Sara do become human beings again. Provided they live long enough.

Is it true we get the children we need?

I wonder what my mother would say to that.

So, to answer my own question, I don't know whether or not I could have prevented much of what happened later had I acted differently in the beginning. Hindsight, as they say, is twenty-twenty. You do the best you can with what you've got. Sometimes it's good enough. Sometimes it isn't.

I steadfastly refused all Jo Lynn's entreaties to accompany her back to the courthouse, insisting that neither Colin Friendly nor her designs on him held any interest for me. In truth, I'd started following the case quite closely in the paper and on television. In the last week, the prosecutor had called a long string of witnesses to the stand, all of whom had been able, in one way or another, to connect the defendant to at least eight of the dead girls. An elderly man testified to having seen one of the victims giving Colin Friendly directions on the day she disappeared; a teary-eyed woman swore she'd seen him sitting on a bench in the park where her friend regularly walked her dog. The dog had been found by a group of children as he wandered aimlessly through nearby streets, dragging his leash behind him. His owner—or rather, what was left of her— had been discovered four months later by a group of campers near Lake Okeechobee. The medical examiner had since determined that she'd been raped, beaten, then stabbed some eighty-six times.

By Wednesday, the medical examiner had already been on the stand for two full days. In meticulous detail, he'd recounted each of the victims' injuries and how they'd been caused. He offered the forensic findings in dispassionate tones, unshaded by nuance, untouched by emotion. Victim number one, Marie Postelwaite, age twenty-five, and a nurse at JFK Memorial, had been raped, beaten, stabbed, and strangled with her own white panty hose, the knot twisted around her neck so tightly, she'd been almost decapitated; victim number two, Christine McDermott, age thirty-three, an elementary school teacher and mother of two, had been raped, sodomized, beaten, stabbed, and bitten repeatedly; victim number three, Tammy Fisher, age sixteen, grade eleven honor stu-

dent, was found raped, beaten, stabbed, her throat slashed from ear to ear; and on and on, through to victim number thirteen, Maureen Elfer, age twenty-seven and a newlywed, who'd been raped, sodomized, beaten, stabbed, and virtually gutted. Slight variations on the same grizzly theme.

The last thing I wanted to do, I'd told my sister when she called the night before, was to hear any of these gruesome details up close. It was enough to read about such awful things in the paper without having to listen to the muffled sobs of the victims' families as each fresh horror was recounted. Hadn't she had enough? I demanded.

"Are you kidding? This is only the beginning." The forensic evidence was highly suspect, probably tainted, she said knowingly. DNA was a notoriously inexact science. The medical examiner was in the prosecutor's pocket. Wait till the defense got a crack at him.

I thought of my visit to the squat building on Gun Club Road. I had told my sister about it, hoping it might scare some sense into her. It hadn't.

"Colin will be found innocent. You'll see," she insisted, still resolutely in his corner despite the fact that he hadn't responded to her note. At least somebody was thinking clearly, I thought, relieved.

"I wonder if they gave him my letter," she mused aloud in court that second Wednesday, as I squirmed around in my seat, my eyes drifting toward the back of the room, flitting casually across the representatives of the media.

Was that what I was doing here? Had I been hoping to see Robert again? Was that why I'd finally given in and agreed to spend another day in court?

Oh God, I thought with a shudder. I'm as bad as my sister.

"Do you think they'd do that?" Jo Lynn was asking.

"Do what?"

"Not give him my letter."

"I don't know," I said honestly, distracted by the powers of my own self-delusion.

"I think that would be illegal," she continued, "not giving someone

their mail. I mean, I wrote him a letter, which I entrusted to them, and I would think that they're under a legal obligation to make sure he gets it. Wouldn't you?"

"I have no idea." My voice vibrated impatience. I heard it. So did Jo Lynn.

"What's the matter with you? Disappointed because your boyfriend didn't show?"

My head snapped toward her, my eyes flashing anger, my cheeks flushing red. "Do you ever say anything that's not ridiculous?"

"Hit a nerve, did I?"

The door at the front of the courtroom opened and the prisoner was let in. He looked around, eyes taking in the entire courtroom at a glance. Beside me, Jo Lynn waved, a small fluttering of her fingers, followed by a tiny kiss she blew toward him. The corners of Colin Friendly's mouth creased into a smile as he reached out to grab the invisible kiss, his fingers tightening around it, as if around a young girl's throat. He was wearing the same blue suit he'd been wearing the first time I saw him, although his shirt was white and his tie navy, and I wondered if he received a fresh shirt and tie every day, and if so, who supplied them. I thought of asking Jo Lynn, decided against it. She'd probably use it as an excuse to comment on my own clothes, the fact that I was wearing a delicately floral dress I normally reserved for more formal social occasions, undoubtedly something she would attribute to the fact I'd hoped to run into Robert.

Jo Lynn was wearing a plunging white sweater and black leather miniskirt. Her hair was freshly washed and draped across her shoulders in layers of blond curls, like a heavy brocade. More than once I caught sight of people craning their necks in her direction. Jo Lynn appeared oblivious to it all, her total attention seemingly focused on the accused, but I knew she was aware of the scrutiny. And I could tell by the way she tossed her head and flicked her hair away from her face that she was enjoying it.

She was something of a celebrity here in Courtroom 11A. People talked to her. They asked her opinions of the previous day's proceedings. They asked whether or not she thought Colin would testify in his own

defense and whether or not she thought he should. I was amazed at how authoritative she sounded, at how much weight her answers were given. She'd always complained that I didn't take her seriously enough, and maybe she was right.

The medical examiner resumed his seat on the witness stand. He was a compact little man, standing no more than five feet four inches tall, with dark hair and an oblong face that looked as if it had been caught between the doors of a bus. His features were squished into the center of his face, his round wire-rimmed glasses propped awkwardly on the bridge of his nose. His name was Dr. Ronald Loring and he was about forty-five years old. Younger than me, I thought.

"We don't have too many more questions for you this morning, Dr. Loring," the prosecutor began, fastening the top button of his brown pinstriped jacket while approaching the witness.

Dr. Loring nodded.

"You've stated that the victims had all been raped and sometimes sodomized, is that so?"

"Yes, that's correct."

"Was there semen found in any of the victims?"

"There was semen found in the bodies that were sufficiently preserved." He listed the women's names.

"And did that semen match the sample of semen taken from Colin Friendly?"

"It did in many significant respects."

I glanced at Jo Lynn. She tossed her head, flicked her hair, pretended to be unaware I was looking at her.

There followed a lengthy discussion of the techniques used to analyze and identify sperm. It had something to do with bodily secretions and blood types and other variables I've forgotten. According to these variables, there was a seventy percent probability that Colin Friendly was the man who'd raped and sodomized these women.

"Seventy percent," Jo Lynn repeated, dismissively.

The same was true of the teeth marks that had been etched into the flesh of several of the victims. A mold had been taken of Colin Friendly's mouth. It closely—but not conclusively—matched the bite marks on the

bodies. Traces of saliva left inside the wounds pointed to—but didn't pinpoint—the accused. Despite this, there was no question in his mind, Dr. Ronald Loring pronounced, but that Colin Friendly had been responsible for the bites on the bodies of the dead girls.

What of the bodies that had decomposed beyond recognition, that were mere collections of bones by the time they were unearthed? the prosecutor asked. How could the doctor tell that these unfortunates had been murdered, let alone murdered by Colin Friendly?

Dr. Loring went into a lengthy discussion of the marvels of forensic medicine, how scientific techniques had become so sophisticated, they could often precisely pinpoint the exact time and cause of a person's death. He went into considerable detail regarding the methods his department employed. His voice was steady, his delivery dry. I could tell he was losing some of the jury, who looked bleary-eyed, one man's eyes threatening to close altogether.

"Mumbo jumbo," Jo Lynn muttered.

Aside from this, there were patterns to the violence that linked the accused to each of his victims, Dr. Loring continued, as the jury and the rest of the courtroom perked up. The women had all been severely beaten, their noses shattered. Multiple stab wounds circled the breasts of the victims, forming horizontal figure eights; the women's stomachs had been sliced open; they'd been stabbed directly, and repeatedly, through the heart.

The thirteen women Colin Friendly stood accused of killing had been murdered by the same man, the medical examiner concluded. That man was Colin Friendly.

"What a crock," Jo Lynn pronounced.

I couldn't help it. Like a hungry fish, I snapped at the bait. "How can you say that? Didn't you hear anything Dr. Loring said?"

"I heard him say 'seventy percent,' not 'one hundred,'" she snapped back. "I heard 'closely matched,' not 'perfectly matched.' Just wait till Mr. Archibald gets through with him."

Mercifully, the judge called a recess for lunch. I watched as Colin Friendly stood up, spoke briefly to his lawyers, then smiled over at Jo Lynn as he was led from the room.

"Hang in there, Colin," Jo Lynn said, underlining her faith in him with a nod of her head.

"I think I've heard enough," I told Jo Lynn. "Why don't we call it a day."

She looked indignant. "What's the matter? Your boyfriend doesn't show up, so you're gonna pick up your marbles and go home?"

"Don't be ridiculous."

"That's the second time today you've called me ridiculous. I'm not ridiculous. You're the one who's ridiculous, mooning over some guy who dumped you thirty years ago."

It took every ounce of self-control I had to keep from screaming. Instead, I took several very deep breaths, and grabbed my purse, signaling my intention to leave. Jo Lynn stood back to let me pass, and I stepped into the aisle.

"Excuse me, Miss Baker."

I turned to see the muscular, fair-haired attorney for the defense approach my sister. He leaned forward, whispered something in her ear, then walked away.

Immediately, we were surrounded by reporters, their cameras clicking wildly, like a gaggle of geese. I lowered my head, kept walking to the door. Jo Lynn followed after me, but slowly enough for the cameras to keep up.

"What did Jake Archibald say to you?" a reporter asked.

"It's confidential, I'm afraid," my sister replied, smiling sweetly, lips pursing, eyes slightly downcast. The eternal coquette.

"What exactly is your connection to Colin Friendly?"

"I'm just a friend who's convinced of his innocence."

"Even in light of this morning's evidence?"

"I think evidence can be planted and lab samples can be tainted. The Palm Beach County medical examiner's office is old and run-down," she said, subverting what I'd told her to support her case. "Their equipment is hardly state-of-the-art."

Serves me right, I thought, for confiding anything in her.

"Is Colin Friendly your boyfriend?"

"Really, that's much too personal."

"Tell us what Jake Archibald said to you."

Jo Lynn stopped, smiled at each of the reporters gathered around her, wet her dark red lips for the camera. "Really, guys," she said, as if these strangers were her best buddies, "you know I'd tell you if I could. Please, bear with me."

With that, she grabbed hold of my arm and pushed me out into the corridor.

"For God's sake," I whispered under my breath, "what were you doing in there?"

"Being polite. Like Mama taught us." She backed me into a corner, smiled teasingly. "Don't you want to know what Jake Archibald said to me?"

"No," I said.

"Liar," she said. "Go on, ask me."

I tried to keep silent, but my heart wasn't in it. In truth, I was desperate to know, and we both knew it. "What did he say?"

Jo Lynn's smile exploded across her face. "It's happening," she said as my body went numb. "Colin Friendly wants to see me."

Chapter
8

"Why don't you tell me what brought you here."

The dark-haired, middle-aged woman looked nervously toward her husband, whose eyes were all but glued to his brown Gucci loafers, then back at me. "I'm not sure I know where to begin." Again, she glanced anxiously at her husband.

"Don't look at me," he said without looking up. "I'm not the one who wanted to come here."

"You didn't want to come?" I repeated.

"This was her idea." A dismissive thumb jerked in the direction of his wife.

Lois and Arthur McKay sat across from me, their chairs angling toward opposite walls. They were a handsome couple—tall, immaculately groomed, almost regal in bearing. Probably they'd been breathtaking in their youth, the campus football hero and his beautiful

homecoming queen. They'd been married almost thirty years and had three grown children. This was their first visit.

"Why do you think your wife wanted to come here?"

He shrugged. "You'd have to ask her."

I nodded. "Lois?"

She hesitated, looked around, eyes dropping to the floor. "I guess I'm tired of being ignored."

"You're complaining because I play golf and bridge a few times a week?"

"You play golf every day and bridge three times a week."

"I'm retired. It's why we moved to Florida."

"I thought we moved here so we could spend more time together." Lois McKay took a deep breath, reached for a tissue, said nothing for several seconds. "It's not just the bridge," she said finally. "It's not just the golf."

"What is it?" I asked.

"About a year ago," Lois McKay began without further prompting, "I went for my routine yearly physical. The doctor discovered a lump in my right breast. She sent me for a mammogram. To make a long story short, the mammogram showed cancer. I had to have a mastectomy. Ask my husband what he was doing while I was in surgery."

"This isn't fair," her husband protested. "You said you didn't need me there, that there was nothing I could do at the hospital."

"Did you want him at the hospital?" I asked.

Lois McKay closed her eyes. "Of course I did."

"Did you or did you not tell me that I should go play golf?"

"Yes, that's what I told you."

"But you didn't mean it," I said gently.

"No."

"What stopped you from telling your husband that you wanted him with you?"

She shook her head. Several tears fell onto her lap, staining the skirt of her light green suit. "I shouldn't have to tell him."

"I'm supposed to read your mind?"

"I wanted him to *want* to be there," Lois McKay whispered.

"And you were hurt when he wasn't."

She nodded.

"I'm supposed to be a bloody mind reader," her husband reiterated.

"You're supposed to be there for me. You're supposed to care about whether I live or die. You're supposed to have the common decency to at least visit me in the hospital!"

"You didn't visit your wife while she was in the hospital?" I asked.

"She knows how I feel about hospitals. I hate the damn things. They make my skin crawl."

"Ask him the last time he touched me. Ask him the last time we made love." She continued without pause. "We haven't made love since before my operation. He hasn't come near me, not once."

"You were sick, for God's sake. First the surgery, then the radiation. You were exhausted. The last thing on your mind was sex."

"I'm not sick anymore. I'm not tired anymore. I'm just sick and tired of being ignored." She broke down into sobs. "It's like I don't even exist, like when they took off my breast, the rest of me disappeared as well."

For several seconds, the only movement in the room was the quiet shaking of her shoulders. I turned toward Arthur McKay. He sat absolutely rigid, the muscles in his face pulled tight against his scalp, like a death mask. "Were you scared when you found out your wife had cancer?" I asked.

He glared at me. "Why should I be scared?"

"Because cancer is a scary thing."

"I know all about cancer. My mother died of cancer when I was a little boy."

"Were you afraid your wife might die?" I asked.

His eyes flashed anger, his hands forming fists at his sides. He said nothing.

"Did you talk to your wife about how you were feeling?"

"She wasn't interested in how I was feeling."

"That's not true. I tried to talk to you many times."

"Look, what difference does any of this make?" he said. "It's all water under the bridge. There's nothing we can do to change it."

"What about now?"

"Now?"

"Are you scared now?"

Arthur McKay opened his mouth as if to speak, then closed it, said nothing.

"A mastectomy is a lot more complicated than most surgery. The loss of a breast has so many implications. For both partners. How did you feel about your wife's surgery? How *do* you feel?" I immediately corrected.

"I don't know," Arthur McKay said impatiently.

"I do," Lois McKay said, wiping at her tears with a fresh tissue. "He's repulsed by it. By me."

"Is that true?" I asked. "Are you repulsed by it?"

For one long, horrible second, Arthur McKay said nothing, then: "How am I supposed to feel?"

"How about grateful I'm alive?" Lois snapped.

"I *am* grateful you're alive."

"Grateful but repulsed."

Another interminable silence. Arthur McKay rose to his feet, began pacing back and forth in front of the window, like a caged tiger in a zoo. "This is just great. Now I'm an even bigger shit than I was before. It didn't seem possible, did it? You'd think you couldn't sink much lower than a guy who plays golf while his wife is on the operating table and then doesn't visit her in the hospital. But hey, we're just getting started. It seems this guy is actually repulsed by his wife's surgery. And he knows it's not going to change. He can't help the way he feels. And he's sick and tired of feeling guilty."

"Losing my breast didn't make me any less of a woman," Lois McKay said, tears streaming freely down her cheeks. "It just made you less of a man."

For several seconds, Arthur McKay stood absolutely still. Then he walked to the door, opened it, and stepped into the hall. The door closed behind him.

I jumped to my feet.

"Let him go," Lois said quietly, twisting the tissue in her lap.

"We can work through this," I told her, knowing only a few words were necessary to bring her husband back into the room.

She shook her head. "No. It's too late. Actually, it's a relief to finally get it all out in the open."

"He's terrified of losing you," I told her, knowing how strange those words probably sounded in light of the things her husband had said.

"Yes, interestingly enough, I think you might be right," she agreed, surprising me. "But I don't think it matters anymore."

"He may come around."

"I don't have that kind of time," Lois McKay said simply. "Besides, he's right—he can't help the way he feels."

"How do *you* feel?"

She took a deep breath, the words tumbling out of her mouth as she exhaled, like children tossed from a sled. I could almost see them hit the air. "Hurt. Angry. Afraid."

"Afraid of what?"

"The future." She shrugged. "Assuming I have one."

"You'll have one."

"A fifty-five-year-old woman with one breast?" She smiled, but it was a smile heavy with sadness, like a cloud threatening rain. Before she left, she scheduled a number of other appointments. Just for herself, she stressed. She'd be coming alone.

Moments after she'd left, I was out of my gray suit and into my sweats, marching determinedly on my treadmill. I wondered how I'd feel if faced with the loss of a breast. I wondered if Larry would react the same way as Arthur McKay.

I already knew the answer, at least as far as Larry was concerned. He wouldn't give a damn about the breast, any more than he would care whether I gained twenty pounds or lost all my hair. We'd met on a blind date in college. Some friends fixed us up. I was very reluctant—dating had never been my strong suit. At almost twenty-one, I was still a virgin, although less by choice, at this point, than by circumstance. I hadn't had a date in ages. My days were spent in classes, my nights at the library. I

went home only as a last resort. I'd go to bed hearing my stepfather's rants; I'd wake up to my mother's sobs. I think that's why I finally agreed to go out with Larry: anything to get out of the house.

We went out for dinner, a small Italian restaurant close to the university campus. He told me later that he fell in love with me that very first night. "Why?" I asked, anticipating a wealth of compliments regarding my eyes, my lips, my towering intellect. "Because you ate everything on your plate," he answered.

How could I not love him?

There were no games, no pretenses. His kind eyes were an accurate reflection of his generous spirit. I felt safe around him. I knew he'd be good to me, that he'd never intentionally do anything to hurt me. After all the abuse I'd witnessed at home, that was the most important thing to me. Larry was decent and honorable, and as moral a man as I would ever meet. I knew that he would love me no matter what.

I was on my treadmill when the phone rang. Normally, I'd let my voice mail answer it, and I'm not sure why I chose to jump off the treadmill and answer it myself. Probably I thought it was Jo Lynn, who'd taken to calling every day with a breakdown of the day's events. The prosecutor had spent most of the last week trying to convince the jury of the exactitude of DNA evidence, calling witness after witness to break down and explain the complicated and often tedious procedures involved in its testing. The defense had spent an equal amount of time trying to discredit the claims. Jo Lynn was getting antsy. She still hadn't met with Colin Friendly, was becoming convinced that there was a conspiracy afoot to keep them apart.

"Family Therapy Center," I said into the phone.

"May I speak with Kate Sinclair, please?"

"Speaking."

"Kate Sinclair," the voice said, "Robert Crowe."

Immediately my heart started to race and my breathing became labored, as if I were back on the treadmill.

"Hello? Kate, are you there?"

"Yes," I said quickly, ashamed and angry at my body's automatic response to the sound of his voice. Hadn't I just been waxing rhapsodic

about my husband's strong moral core? Where was my own? "How are you?"

"Great. I missed you in court this morning."

"You were there?"

"I was. You weren't."

"I can only go on Wednesdays."

"I'll keep that in mind. I saw your sister."

"She's hard to miss."

"That was an interesting mention she got in the paper the other day. 'Friendly's New Friend.' Catchy little phrase. What's the real story?"

"There isn't one." Was that why he was calling? To get the inside scoop?

"Well, you didn't miss anything today. The judge adjourned the trial until next week."

"He did? Why?"

"Apparently Colin has a touch of the flu. Poor baby wasn't feeling very well, so his lawyers asked for an adjournment. Who knows? Maybe he just needed a break."

"We could all use a break." I hoped Colin Friendly would develop pneumonia and die.

"That's exactly why I'm calling," Robert said, and I wondered for a moment whether I had missed part of the conversation. "I thought maybe I could take you out to lunch."

"Lunch?"

"How about next Wednesday? That's if you can tear yourself away from the courthouse."

"You want to have lunch?" I repeated, biting down on my tongue to keep from saying it again.

"I have an interesting proposition for you."

"What kind of proposition?"

"Something I think you'll like."

"Are you going to tell me what it is?"

"I will on Wednesday. Where should we meet?"

We agreed on Charley's Crab over on South Ocean Boulevard.

Twelve o'clock noon. I hung up the phone, wondering what the hell I was doing. "Oh God," I muttered, about to call Robert back, cancel our date, except it wasn't a date, I reminded myself, deciding I was being silly. It was just lunch. And an interesting proposition. What did that mean? "Guess I'll find out on Wednesday," I said, letting go of the phone.

Immediately it rang.

"You can't make it," I said into the receiver, convinced Robert had had second thoughts.

"Can't make what?" Larry asked.

"Larry?"

"Kate, is that you?"

I laughed, a strange combination of guilt and relief. "This one patient of mine, she can't seem to make up her mind whether she wants to come in or not." I stressed the word "she." Twice.

"She'll be there. How can anyone resist you?"

I tried to laugh, ended up coughing instead.

"You okay?" I could hear the concern in his voice. "You getting a cold?"

"I'm fine," I said, feeling awful. "What can I do for you?"

"Just checking to see if we're free a week this Friday night."

"I think so. Why? What's up?"

"A satisfied customer has invited us to dinner."

"Sounds good."

"Great. I'll tell him to count us in. Love you, funny face," he said, instead of goodbye.

"Love you too."

I hung up the phone. "Okay, you're going to call Robert Crowe back right this minute and cancel lunch. Enough of this foolishness. If he has anything interesting to propose, he can do it over the phone."

The door to my waiting room opened, then closed. I checked my watch, then my appointment calendar. Sally and Bill Peterson were early, and I was running late. Not a great combination. Hurriedly, I pulled off my sweatshirt, getting it tangled around my head. "Serves you right," I muttered, hearing the door to my inner office open, frantically tearing the

sweatshirt away from my face. Who on earth would just walk into someone's office unannounced and uninvited?

"Mother!" I gasped.

She backed against the wall, her face as gray as her uncombed hair,
her dark eyes wide with fear.

"Mother, what's happened? What's the matter?"

"Someone's following me."

"What?"

"Someone's following me," she repeated, glancing furtively around
the room.

"Who's following you? What are you talking about?"

"A man. He's been following me for blocks. He followed me into
the building."

In the next instant, I was in the outer hall, my head snapping
quickly to my left, then right. There was no one there. I walked down
the rose-carpeted corridor, past the elevator, approaching the stairway at
the far end of the hall with caution, then flung open the door. Again,
there was no one. I heard the sound of elevator doors opening, watched
as an attractive young woman got out, hurrying past me with a wary eye.
It was then that I realized I was wearing only sweatpants and a bra. "And
I'm the therapist," I announced.

"There's no man out there," I told my mother, reentering my office
and grabbing my sweatshirt, pulling it back over my head. I looked
around. My mother was nowhere to be seen. "Mother?" I walked into
the narrrow inner hallway. "Mother, where are you?" I pushed open the
door to my second office, expecting to see her standing by the window,
staring out at the magnificent palm trees along Royal Palm Way. But she
wasn't there. "Mother, where did you go?" Had she been there at all? Or
had my guilty conscience conjured her up to try to talk some sense into
me?

And then I heard the whimpering. Halting, muffled, as if trying
desperately not to be heard. It was a sound from my past I remembered
only too well, despite the passage of the years. It froze me to the spot.
"Mom?"

I found her sitting crouched behind the office door, her knees graz-

ing her chin, her face wet with tears, her eyes narrow slits, her mouth a large open wound. I rushed to her side, slid down beside her, surrounded her with my arms. She was shaking so badly, I didn't know what to do. "It's okay, Mom. It's okay. There's no one out there. You're safe now. It's okay. You're safe."

"He was there. He was following me."

"Who, Mom? Do you know who he was?"

She shook her head vigorously.

"Someone from your apartment building?"

"No. It was someone I'd never seen before."

"You're sure he was following you? Maybe he was just walking in the same direction."

"No," she insisted. "He was following me. Every time I turned around, he stopped, pretended to be looking in a store window. When I slowed down, he slowed down. When I walked faster, so did he."

I wondered whether I should call the police. Why would someone be following my mother? "Had you just been to the bank?" I asked, thinking an old woman was probably an easy target for robbers. Except that her bank was located close to her apartment building, which was on the other side of the bridge and miles away. It would have taken her all day to walk here. "How did you get here?" I asked.

She looked at me with blank eyes.

"Mom," I repeated, growing fearful, although I wasn't sure why. "How did you get here?"

The eyes darkened, flitted anxiously about the room.

"Mom, don't you remember how you got here?"

"Of course I remember how I got here," she said, her voice suddenly calm as she climbed to her feet and straightened the folds of her flower-print skirt. "I took a cab to Worth Avenue, did some window-shopping, then decided to walk over here to say hello. Along the way, some man started following me." She took a deep breath, patted her hair into recognizable shape. "Probably just wanted to snatch my purse. Silly me—I guess I overreacted. You'll have to forgive an old woman."

The door to my outer office opened, then closed. I looked warily in its direction, then back at my mother.

"It's just your next client," she assured me, running a calming hand across my cheek. "I'll go, let you get back to work."

I excused myself to Sally and Bill Peterson, and accompanied my mother downstairs, waiting until she was safely inside a taxi. "Mom," I ventured gently before closing the car door, "maybe you should see a doctor."

"Nonsense, dear. I'm perfectly fine." She smiled. "You're looking a little peaked, however. I think you work too hard." She kissed me on the cheek. "I'll talk to you later," she said, and seconds later, she was gone.

Chapter

9

Define sociopath."

The man on the witness stand—looking both distinguished and patriotic in a dark blue suit, white shirt, and red-striped tie—took a moment to consider his answer, although as an expert witness for the prosecution, he undoubtedly had his answer well prepared. "A sociopath is a person who is hostile to society," he began. "He feels little in the way of normal human emotions, except anger. This anger, combined with an almost total self-absorption and a complete lack of empathy for others, allows him to commit the most heinous crimes without any guilt or remorse."

"And a sexual sadist?"

Again a measured pause. "A sexual sadist derives sexual pleasure from inflicting pain."

"Do the two terms go hand in hand?" The prosecutor patted his brown paisley tie, looked toward the jury.

I followed his gaze, noted that the jury was paying strict attention. All it took was the mention of the word "sex," I thought, glancing over at Jo Lynn. She was wearing tight white jeans and a white tank top, the center of which was emblazoned with a bright pink heart.

"A sociopath is not necessarily a sexual sadist, but a sexual sadist is almost always a sociopath," came the reply from the witness stand.

"In your expert opinion, Dr. Pinsent, is Colin Friendly a sexual sadist?"

"He is."

"Is he a sociopath?"

"Most definitely."

Again, I looked at Jo Lynn, whose face was calm, even serene. Was she listening to this? Was she *hearing* it?

The prosecutor approached the defense table, stopping in front of the accused, staring at Colin Friendly as if he were seeing him for the first time. Colin Friendly smiled back pleasantly. He'd obviously recovered quite nicely from his bout with the flu. His eyes were clear; his color was good. Everything was back to normal. "But he doesn't look abnormal," Mr. Eaves observed, as if reading my mind. "In fact, Mr. Friendly seems as genial as his name would imply—handsome, polite, intelligent."

"Sociopaths are often quite intelligent," the witness explained. "And there's nothing that says they can't be good-looking. As for being polite, he's just giving you what he thinks you need to see."

The defense attorney was instantly on his feet. "Move to strike, your honor. The witness can't speak for Mr. Friendly."

"Sustained."

"Speaking in more general terms, Dr. Pinsent," the prosecutor continued, undeterred, "what do you mean when you say that sociopaths give people what they need to see?"

"Sociopaths are extremely manipulative. Their emotions run very shallow and they're intensely self-centered. But they can mimic the emotions they observe in others, and feed back the appropriate response, the

appropriate response being whatever would be considered normal under the circumstances. They play on people's assumptions of basic human decency. People attribute feelings to them that simply aren't there." He paused, looked directly at Colin Friendly. "Sociopaths are often highly articulate, very charming, and glib. They'll make you laugh, then stab you through the heart."

"Can you believe *anything* they say?"

"Oh yes. They're often quite truthful. As long as you keep in mind that their version of the truth is very self-serving."

"What produces a sociopath, Dr. Pinsent?"

Dr. Walter Pinsent rubbed his fingers across his chin and smiled. "I'm afraid that's a little like asking, 'Which came first, the chicken or the egg?' The eternal debate—are killers born or are they made?" He shook his head. "It's impossible to say conclusively one way or the other. There are many theories, of course, but they have a habit of changing with the times and the political climate. Sometimes we give more weight to the genetic theory, sometimes to the environment. We postulate about extra Y chromosomes and chemical imbalances. But lots of people have chemical imbalances; that doesn't make them murderers. And lots of people have an extra Y chromosome and they don't go around slicing up their fellow human beings."

"Does Colin Friendly have a chemical imbalance or an extra Y chromosome?"

"No, he does not."

"And what of the theory that environment is everything?"

Walter Pinsent cleared his throat, straightened his shoulders, tugged on his tie. "There's no question that our childhood is crucial in terms of our development. The seeds for everything we grow into as adults were planted when we were children. Almost all serial killers had truly appalling childhoods. They were neglected, molested, beaten, abused, abandoned, you name it."

"Is this true of Colin Friendly?"

"It is."

Jo Lynn leaned toward me. "Poor baby," she whispered, as I struggled to find a hint of irony in her words. There was none.

"Are there any characteristics that are common to all sociopaths?" the prosecutor asked.

"Research has shown that there is something we now refer to as the 'homicidal triad,' three elements that are present in virtually all children who grow up to become serial killers: cruelty to small animals; bed-wetting beyond the normally appropriate age; and fire-starting."

"And were these elements present in Colin Friendly's childhood?"

"They were."

"And is there any doubt in your mind, after meeting with the accused and studying his background and the many psychiatric reports made available to you, that Colin Friendly is a sexual sadist and sociopath, guilty of the crimes for which he stands accused?"

"No doubt at all," Dr. Pinsent replied.

"Thank you, Dr. Pinsent. Your witness, Mr. Archibald."

Mr. Eaves sat down, unbuttoned his jacket; Mr. Archibald rose to his feet, buttoned his.

"Dr. Pinsent, are you a psychiatrist?"

"No."

"A medical doctor?"

"No."

"A doctor of psychology perhaps?"

"No. My doctorate is in the field of education."

"I see." Jake Archibald shook his head, appeared confused, as if he couldn't quite comprehend what Dr. Pinsent was doing as an expert witness. This was purely for effect. The jury had already been told that Walter Pinsent was a special agent with the National Academy of the Federal Bureau of Investigation in Quantico, Virginia, and part of the Investigative Support Unit that specialized in profiling serial killers.

"How many times did you meet with the accused?"

"Twice."

"Twice." Jake Archibald shook his head, somehow managing to look subtly amazed. A neat trick, I thought. "And how long were these meetings?"

"Several hours each session."

"Several hours each session," the defense attorney repeated, this

time nodding his head up and down. "And this was enough time for you to come to the conclusion that Colin Friendly is a dangerous psychotic?"

"Sociopath," Dr. Pinsent corrected.

Jake Archibald chuckled derisively. So did Jo Lynn.

"You concluded after approximately four hours with my client that he was a dangerous sociopath and a sexual sadist?"

"I did."

"Tell me, Dr. Pinsent, would you have reached these same conclusions had you encountered Mr. Friendly in another context?"

"I'm not sure I understand the question."

"Let's say you encountered Mr. Friendly at a party, or ran into him on a holiday and spent a few hours talking to him. Would you have come away with the impression that he was a dangerous sociopath and sexual sadist?"

For the first time since he took the stand, Dr. Walter Pinsent looked less than sure of himself. "Probably not. As I've already stated, sociopaths are often very charming individuals."

"You consider Colin Friendly charming?"

"He seems very affable, yes."

"Is that a crime?"

The prosecutor raised his hand. "Objection."

"Sustained."

"Is it possible, Dr. Pinsent," the defense attorney pressed, "that you were influenced in your appraisal of Mr. Friendly by the fact that he was already under arrest, that your meetings with him took place in prison?"

"I was influenced by the things he told me."

"I see. Did Colin Friendly tell you he was guilty?"

"No."

"Did he, in fact, repeatedly protest his innocence?"

"He did. But that's typical of this type of personality."

"Interesting. So, what you're saying is that if he confesses his guilt, that means he's guilty, and if he says he's innocent, well then, that means he's guilty too. Damned if you don't, damned if you do. Reminds me a bit of the witch hunts in Salem."

The prosecutor jumped to his feet. "Your honor, move to strike. Is Mr. Archibald asking a question or making a speech?"

"Sustained."

"I'll rephrase that," Jake Archibald said, a noticeable bounce to his words. "Do you see serial killers under every bed, Dr. Pinsent?"

Mr. Eaves's ample backside barely had time to graze his seat before he was back on his feet again. "Objection."

"I withdraw the question," Jake Archibald said quickly. "I have no further questions of this witness."

"The witness may step down."

The judge called a ten-minute recess.

"Tell me you weren't fooled by that," I said hopefully to Jo Lynn, as people all around us stood up and stretched.

"Fooled by what?" She was squinting into her compact mirror, applying a fresh coat of lipstick to already very pink lips.

"By the defense attorney's attempt to throw a smoke screen over the evidence."

"What's that supposed to mean?" She raised the mirror, dabbed at her mascara.

"It means that Dr. Pinsent is about as expert a witness as anyone could find," I began.

She interrupted. "He's not a psychiatrist. Or even a medical doctor."

"He's a specialist with the Federal Bureau of Investigation."

"Since when did you become such a fan of the FBI?"

"I'm just saying that he knows what he's talking about."

"His is only one opinion."

"An expert opinion," I reminded her.

"You put too much faith in experts," she said. "Just because someone has a degree doesn't mean they know everything."

I took this as a direct dig at me. Jo Lynn was always trumpeting the value of practical experience over a university education.

Don't bite, I told myself, determined to be pleasant. "So, anything new?" I asked, looking for safer ground.

"Like what?"

I shrugged. "Have you had any calls about those résumés you sent out?"

She clicked her compact closed. "You know I haven't."

Strike one, I thought.

"Have you spoken to our mother?"

She dropped the compact into her purse. "Why would I do that?"

Strike two.

"Do you have a date for the weekend?"

She snapped her purse shut tight. "I have a date for Friday." She spun toward me, her mouth forming a provocative pout.

"That's great. Someone new?"

"Sort of."

"Anyone I know?"

"Someone you *think* you know."

"What does that mean?"

"It means that you think you know him, but you don't. It means you've got him all wrong. It means you don't know him at all. It means that you've been staring at the side of his face all morning."

Strike three.

The room darkened around me. Normal courtroom sounds gave way to a loud buzzing in my ears. I felt dizzy, faint. I gripped the bench on which I was sitting, digging my fingers into the hard wood. "Please tell me this is a joke."

Jo Lynn adjusted her tank top, repositioning the large pink heart so that it sat directly in the center of her large chest. "Why would I joke about something this important?"

Stay calm, I told myself. "When exactly did this come about?"

"Colin's lawyer called me last night. I would have phoned you, but it was late and I know you guys are sound asleep by ten o'clock."

"I don't understand," I stammered, "where is this 'date' taking place?"

"I'm not sure. Some holding room or something. They're gonna let me know."

"Jo Lynn, please," I said, unable to stop myself. "Don't you think

this has gone far enough? It's not too late to call the whole thing off. You don't have to go through with it."

"What are you talking about?" Her voice was indignant. "Why wouldn't I go through with it?"

"Because the man we're talking about is a cold-blooded killer."

"I don't agree."

"The evidence is overwhelming."

"I don't agree."

"You don't agree," I repeated.

"No, and I don't think the jury will either. Anyway," she said, waving at one of the reporters in the back row, "I don't want to talk about it anymore. Why do you always put a damper on everything?"

"I'm just trying to inject a little common sense into this mess."

Jo Lynn looked toward the front of the courtroom. "You always had more common sense than imagination," she said.

—

He was already seated when I arrived at Charley's Crab at twenty minutes after twelve. "Sorry I'm late," I said, collapsing into the chair the waiter held out for me, looking slowly around the large series of adjoining rooms, studying the framed photographs of prize fish that ran along one wall, admiring the large stuffed marlin that was mounted on another, gazing at the crowded bar, tracking the busy waiters as they maneuvered between booths and tables, zeroing in on the well-heeled patrons, with their large blond bouffants and fixed tight smiles. Anywhere but at the man sitting across from me.

"Considering that court doesn't get out till noon," he was saying, "you made very good time."

"I left early." I signaled for the waiter. An hour and a half early, I almost said, but didn't. I'd fled the courtroom after Jo Lynn's unpleasant revelation, and had been driving around ever since, trying to figure out what my sister was trying to prove by throwing herself at a sexually sadistic sociopath who would most likely die in the electric chair. If she

was trying to upset our mother, it wasn't working. Our mother had ignored all Jo Lynn's provocative pronouncements, carrying on as if there was nothing unusual or untoward about her younger daughter's recent behavior. On the other hand, if it was me Jo Lynn was trying to upset, I had to admit she was doing a damned good job.

The waiter appeared.

"Could I have a glass of white wine?" I asked.

The waiter looked confused. "You don't like the wine the gentleman ordered?"

For the first time, I looked at the man sitting across the table from me. Robert Crowe, looking suave, sophisticated, and generally drop-dead gorgeous, held up a bottle of California Chardonnay that had been cooling beside him.

"Thank you," I told the waiter, feeling like a total idiot. "This will be fine."

Robert said nothing, simply poured the wine into my glass, then clicked his glass against mine in a toast. "To the past," he said.

"The past," I agreed. It sounded safe enough.

"And the future."

I downed half the glass.

"Someone's either very thirsty or very uptight," he said.

"It wasn't an easy morning."

"You want to talk about it?"

"I want to talk about anything but."

"Talk about why you won't look at me."

I laughed, one of those awful, self-conscious barks that die upon contact with the air. "I'm looking at you."

"You're looking at my left ear," he said.

"And a very nice ear it is." I laughed, looked directly into his rich hazel eyes. Oh God, I thought, struggling to maintain eye contact, not to be the first to blink or turn away. Was there no end to my sophomoric musings?

I shouldn't have come. I should have followed my instincts and headed for home after leaving the courthouse. Instead I'd driven around

aimlessly for half an hour, then turned the car loose on I-95. I was almost at Pompano when I realized it was closing in on twelve o'clock, and I turned the car around, telling myself I was going home, but knowing the car was pointed toward the ocean and Charley's Crab.

Charley's Crab and Robert Crowe, I thought, and must have smiled because he picked right up on it.

"That's better," Robert said. "You have a beautiful smile."

"It's lopsided," I corrected.

"That's what makes it beautiful."

I blinked, looked away.

We ordered—grilled salmon for him, blackened swordfish for me. "And gazpacho," I said. Lots of garlic, I thought.

"So, tell me about the therapy business," he said.

I shrugged. "What can I say? Lots of people, lots of problems."

"What sort of problems?"

"Problems with parents, problems with children, marital problems, extramarital . . ." I broke off, took another long sip of my drink.

"And you solve these problems?"

"I do the best I can."

"How long have you been practicing?"

"Over twenty years," I said, feeling more secure now that we were on firm professional ground. "I started out as a social worker with the Pittsburgh Board of Education, then I left and opened up a family therapy clinic with a few other women. Eventually, we moved to Florida, and I set up shop on my own."

"Can't hold a job, huh?"

I thought of my sister, who'd flitted from one dead-end job to another all her life, from one dead-end relationship to another.

"Uh-oh," Robert said. "Storm clouds on the horizon. What are you thinking about?"

I really didn't want to talk about Jo Lynn. She'd taken up enough of my day as it was. "Just about how quickly time passes," I lied. It was easier. "What about you? How did you wind up owning a radio station?"

"I married it," he said simply.

I didn't know what to say, so I said nothing.

"Brandi's father owns a number of radio stations across the country." He smiled. "Beware of women whose first names are potable."

"I'll keep that in mind."

"Actually, her real name is Brenda. She was named after Brenda Marshall, who was an actress in the forties. Apparently, my father-in-law was a huge fan."

"She was married to William Holden," I said.

Robert Crowe regarded me with bemused admiration. "How did you know that?"

I shook my head. "The mind is a strange and wondrous thing. I can barely remember my telephone number, but I know Brenda Marshall was once married to William Holden."

"You're an interesting woman, Kate Latimer," he said.

I was about to correct him, decided not to bother. He knew what my name was. So did I. "So what does your wife do?"

"She shops, she lunches, she goes to exercise class."

"And looks after the kids," I added. "Four, I believe you said."

"Ages twelve through nineteen. Two boys, two girls."

"I'm sure she has her hands full."

"The oldest is away at college. The others are in school all day. We have two housekeepers. Trust me, Brandi's not overtaxed."

"Problems?" I asked, despite my best efforts not to.

"The usual, I guess."

"Is that why you asked me to lunch?"

He smiled, traced the rim of his glass with his fingers. "No. If it was therapy I wanted, I'd come to your office. I have something else in mind for you."

"Sounds interesting."

"I'm hoping you'll think so."

The waiter brought our lunch, refilled our glasses. For several minutes, we did nothing but eat and drink. "So," I began, fortified by my second glass of wine, "just what is it you have in mind for me?"

"Your own radio show," he said.

I dropped my fork. It bounced off my lap and onto the floor. A passing waiter immediately replaced it. "I don't understand."

"I haven't thought this through yet," Robert continued. "In fact, it wasn't until I saw you in court and you told me what you were doing that I thought about it at all."

"Thought about what exactly?"

"About you doing some sort of therapy show on the radio."

"You mean like on *Frasier*? A nightly phone-in show?"

"I'm not sure. Like I said, I haven't thought it through yet. That's one of the reasons I suggested lunch. I wanted your input."

"But I have no experience with radio."

"You know how to talk. You know how to give advice. And you have a great speaking voice."

"I don't have that kind of time. I have a job; I have a family."

"It doesn't have to be every night. It could be once or twice a week. And it doesn't have to be at night. It could be during the day. Wednesday." He smiled. "Your day off."

"But what would I do?"

"Be yourself. Answer questions. Help people with their problems."

"Why me?"

"Why not you? You're smart. You're beautiful. You're local. Look, I realize this is coming at you out of left field. Why don't you toss some ideas around in your head for a while. See what you come up with. Decide what kind of show might intrigue you, the kind of format you'd feel comfortable with. In the meantime, I'll mention the idea to a few of our producers, see if they can come up with anything. Think about it. That's all I'm asking."

"I'll think about it," I heard myself say.

"Good." He lifted his glass in another toast. "To interesting propositions," he said.

Chapter

10

Friday started out normally enough. Sara was still in bed when Larry, Michelle, and I left the house. I'd given up trying to wake her. Being on time for school was Sara's responsibility, not mine.

I knew to expect a phone call from the school informing me of Sara's lateness, so I wasn't surprised when I checked my messages during a five-minute break between sessions, and learned that the school had, indeed, called. I saw no point in calling back right away, reasoning that they weren't about to tell me something I didn't already know. Instead, I called home, trying to convince myself that the fact that no one answered the line was a sign that Sara was by now safely ensconced in her classroom. Or at least on her way. Or still sound asleep, a pesky voice whispered. I shushed it, as one shushes a small child, then ushered in my next clients. Outwardly, I was calm. Inside, I was screaming.

I wasn't the only one. Everyone who came into my office that day

was hollering about something. No one spoke softly. No one struggled to maintain composure. Everybody yelled—at one another, at themselves, at me. Perhaps it was a case of simple transference, my mood into their mouths; more likely it was the literally breathtaking humidity that had descended upon the Palm Beach area over the last twenty-four hours like a giant tarpaulin, threatening instantaneous combustion to anyone who ventured outside. Or maybe it was just one of those days.

By six o'clock that evening, I was exhausted. All I wanted to do was go home and crawl into bed, but I knew this was impossible. Larry had already committed us to a dinner party with "satisfied customers." I smiled. It was nice to know that someone, somewhere, was satisfied about something.

Before leaving my office, I again checked my voice mail for messages, and was dismayed to find that there were two more calls from Sara's school, one just after lunch, informing me that Sara had yet to show up at school, and another at the end of the school day to inform me that Sara had skipped a whole day of classes and was risking suspension. I checked my watch, knew it was too late to return the school's calls. Besides, what could I say? Maybe being suspended was just what Sara needed, some real consequences for her actions, but I wasn't convinced. Sara would shrug off the suspension as she did everything else. It was my life that would be placed on hold, not hers.

As I drove north along I-95, weaving restlessly through the Friday night traffic, worse now that the snowbirds had started their annual winter migration, I promised myself that I was going to remain calm when I confronted Sara. I would simply inform her that the school had called repeatedly about her truancy and that an explanation from her was neither wanted nor required. The school would deal with her on Monday. In the meantime, she was grounded. I knew that Sara would scream, swear, slam doors, the usual, trying to suck me into a fight. Whatever happened, I decided, exiting the highway at PGA Boulevard and heading west, I wasn't going to raise my voice. I was going to remain calm.

"What do you mean, she's not here?" I demanded loudly of my younger child not two seconds after I walked through the front door.

"Why are you yelling at me?" Michelle asked. She was standing in

the middle of the living room, to the right of the large glass-topped coffee table and between the two oversized tan-colored sofas, a cherry Popsicle at her mouth, coloring her lips blood red.

She looked like a beautiful porcelain doll, I thought, but didn't say. Instead I said, "Could you get off the carpet with that?" and proceeded into my bedroom. She followed me.

"Tough day?"

I smiled. Sara would have yelled at me; Michelle was worried about my day. "The worst." I looked toward the closed doors of the master bathroom, suddenly cognizant of the shower running. "When did Daddy get home?"

"A few minutes ago. He broke a hundred."

"A hundred what?"

"In golf. He broke a hundred. That's supposed to be good," she assured me, glancing at the carpeting beneath her feet and quickly stuffing the balance of the cherry Popsicle into her mouth. A thin line of red liquid dribbled down her chin, disappearing into her neck, as if she'd cut herself shaving.

I said, "It's nice someone had a good day."

"He said it was really hot, but that he thought it helped his concentration."

I undid the top buttons of my white blouse, flipped off my shoes, lay back against the army of decorative pillows. "Did he say anything about Sara?"

"Like what?"

Like where she's been all day, I wanted to shout, but didn't. Calm, I repeated silently. Calm was the answer. "Has she phoned?" I asked instead.

"What's the big deal about Sara?" A slight pout found its way to Michelle's mouth, further exaggerating the ruby outline of her lips. "Why are you always asking about Sara? Aren't you interested in *my* day?"

"Your day?"

"Yes, my day. I'm a person too, just like Sara, and I have days, just like everyone else."

I edged my back away from the pillows, my body on instant alert. I had been prepared for a scene with Sara, not Michelle. "Of course you do."

"Nobody ever asks about my day," she continued, as if she were a windup toy that someone had wound too tight and was now spinning out of control, unable to stop. "I asked Daddy how his day went, I asked you if you had a tough day, I always ask everybody, but does anybody ever ask about me?"

"Michelle . . ."

"No. You tell me to get off the carpet with my Popsicle . . ."

"Michelle . . ."

"You ask about Sara . . ."

"Honey, please . . ."

"Does anybody care that I got eighty-five percent in my math test? That I stood first in the class? No! Nobody cares!" She fled the room.

I was instantly on my feet. "Michelle, wait. Of course we care." Tripping over my shoes, a heel digging painfully into the sole of my right foot, I limped after her, watching the door to her bedroom slam shut. "Honey, please, let me in." I tapped lightly on her door, then more insistently. "Michelle, please let me in."

Slowly, the door to her room fell open. Michelle stood tearfully on the other side. I swayed toward her, my arms aching to encircle her skinny frame.

"Don't," she said softly, and I teetered momentarily on my toes before falling back on my heels, regaining my balance.

"You got eighty-five on your math test?" I repeated, my eyes welling with tears. "That's wonderful."

She didn't look at me. "It was the highest mark in the class."

"You should be very proud."

She backed into her room, plopped down in the middle of her queen-size bed, stared straight ahead. Unlike Sara's room, which was decorated in various shades of chaos, Michelle's predominantly pink-and-ivory room was as neat as the proverbial pin. Her bed was expertly made, pale pink-and-white-flowered pillows resting comfortably atop a matching quilted spread; the top of her wicker dresser was clear, save for a

pearl-encrusted jewelry box in the shape of a treasure chest; her clothes were hung in the closet and not strewn thoughtlessly on the floor. I winced. Even in the privacy of Michelle's own bedroom, Sara had a way of taking over, pushing her younger sister aside.

Gingerly, I approached the bed, sitting down only after I'd received the silent signal, a subtle nodding of Michelle's head that told me it was all right. "I'm sorry."

The nodding became more pronounced as one bright red lip disappeared inside the other, quivering. She turned away.

"Sometimes adults get so caught up in their own little worlds that they forget about the worlds of those around them," I began. "Especially when those around them are as capable and well adjusted as you are." I reached up, gently stroked the wavy brown hair that fell around her shoulders. She didn't pull away, for which I was very grateful. "We tend to concentrate all our energy on those who give us the hardest time, and that's not fair, because you deserve more. Lots more. And I'm sorry, honey. I'm really sorry. You're my sweet angel, and I love you so much. Please," I whispered, "can't I hug you?"

Silently, she fell against me. My nose immediately buried itself inside the folds of her soft brown hair, her smell as sweet to me as a newborn baby's. The heat from her slender body burned into my side, as fierce as a branding iron, welding us together. "I love you," I repeated, kissing the top of her head, once, twice, as many times as she would allow.

Michelle swiped a few errant tears away from her face, but she made no attempt to disengage. "I love you too."

We sat this way for some time, enjoying the intimacy, neither wishing to be the first to break away. For the first time all day, I was truly calm.

The peace was shattered with the sound of Larry's voice. "Kate?" he was calling. "Kate, where are you?"

"It's okay," Michelle said, squirming out of my arms, taking all tranquillity with her. Immediately, I felt my anger returning. What was Larry yelling about? Why did we have to go out tonight when all I

wanted to do was stay home? Where was Sara? What was she trying to pull this time?

"What's the problem?" I asked, greeting Larry at the doorway to Michelle's room. He was wearing a large beige towel around his waist and rubbing his wet hair with another.

"No problem." His deep voice filled the space between us, spilled over into Michelle's room. "Did Michelle tell you I broke a hundred?"

"She did."

"It was hot as hell out there, I tell you," he continued enthusiastically, following me back to our bedroom, an overgrown puppy at my heels. "But I don't know, all that humidity seemed to work for me. It made me really focus or something, I'm not sure. Whatever it was, it worked. I hit a ninety-eight. I would have gotten even lower if I hadn't blown up on the last two holes." He laughed. "I guess that's golf. It's a game of could-have's. How was your day?"

"Terrible. Do we have to go out tonight?"

He looked at his watch, still wet from the shower. "Sure do. In fact, we should be leaving in about ten minutes."

"Ten minutes? I have to take a shower, get dinner ready for Michelle."

"You don't have time for a shower, and Michelle can order a pizza."

"I'm not going anywhere without a shower," I said stubbornly, "and what about Sara?"

"You can take a long, leisurely bath when we get home from dinner, and what *about* Sara?"

"Do you know where she is?"

"Should I?"

"Somebody should," I said testily, knowing I was being unfair. "Apparently she didn't show up for school today."

Resignation replaced the elation on Larry's face. "Did you check the answering service to see if she called?" he asked.

I walked around the bed to the white phone that sat on the large, curved end table, quickly pressing the appropriate numbers to retrieve

my messages. There was only one message. It was from Jo Lynn. "Call me," was all it said.

Calling my sister was the last thing I wanted to do. Today was the day, after all, when Beauty was scheduled to meet the Beast, and I had no desire to hear the blow-by-blow. Already I knew more details than I cared to, that the meeting was to take place directly after court recessed for the weekend, that the place of assignation was to be the Palm Beach County Correctional Center on Gun Club Road, and that Romeo and Juliet would be separated by a wall of glass, speaking to each other through specially constructed phones. Just like in the movies, I thought, shaking my head at the irony of situating a penitentiary on a street named Gun Club Road. I closed my eyes, trying not to picture my sister and Colin Friendly, their hands pressed together against the glass of the partition that divided them.

"Well?" Larry was asking.

"No messages," I said. It was easier that way.

"Better start getting ready," he advised, already in his underwear and black knee-high socks.

"How can we go out without knowing where she is?"

"Easy." He slid his arms into a blue-and-white-striped shirt. "We just go. I am not about to let an inconsiderate child control my life. We'll deal with Sara when we get back."

He was right and I knew it, but I was in no mood for rational thought. "But we don't even know where she is."

"Even if we did," Larry said, "we don't have time to deal with her now. So, let's just get ready. This dinner is in Jupiter, and you know what the traffic's going to be like."

"Jupiter?!"

"Jupiter," he repeated, his lips curling into a smile. "Not Mars. It'll only take twenty minutes."

"Then I have time for a shower," I insisted, already on my way to the bathroom, pulling off my clothes as I walked, leaving them in a careless heap where they fell. Just like Sara, I thought, quickly locking the door behind me, and turning on the shower, welcoming the onslaught of hot water as it rained down, like tiny hailstones, on my head.

"Excuse me, can I use your phone?" The words were out of my mouth as soon as we walked through the door of our host's brand-new home in the gated golfing community of Windfall Village in Jupiter.

"Of course." The startled hostess, a plump brunette in toreador pants, pointed the way through her cavernous living room toward the kitchen. Deliberately ignoring Larry and the look I knew was taking root on his already unhappy face, I walked briskly across the marble-tiled floor, briefly nodding at the half dozen guests assembled around the grand piano and hurrying around the sweeping spiral staircase—one of two on either side of the house—to the marble-and-steel kitchen at the back. Two uniformed maids were preparing canapés and looked startled to see me. No more startled than Michelle was at the sound of my voice.

"Sara's not here," she told me, petulantly. I'd dragged her away from the umpteenth rerun of *Roseanne*. "Don't worry about her, Mom," she advised before hanging up. "You know she's fine. Don't let her ruin your evening."

It was already ruined, I almost confided, returning the phone to the waiting palm of one of the maids, who replaced it in its carriage, as if I couldn't be trusted to do it myself. And maybe I couldn't, I thought, catching sight of myself in the steel trim of the double oven, looking like a slightly deranged matron, my face distorted with aggravation, my hair still slightly damp from the shower, and not properly combed out. Who is that? I wondered.

Larry had stood over me like an impatient father while I applied my makeup, pointedly checking his watch as I fussed with the side zipper of my black cocktail dress. "It'll dry in the car," he'd protested when I reached for the hair dryer, taking it out of my hand and returning it to the drawer, ignoring my shrieks of protest. "You look fine," he insisted then, and again, repeatedly, in the car on the drive over, "fine" not being a word given to inspiring great confidence.

Not like "beautiful," I thought, thinking of Robert, knowing that he'd think nothing of being a little late for a dinner party, deciding that

he would have given me all the time I needed to get ready, probably even jumped in the shower with me, delaying us further. Or maybe we wouldn't have gone at all, I fantasized, reluctantly returning to Larry's side, allowing myself to be introduced to the general gathering, to be taken on the obligatory tour of the house that Larry built. "Beautiful," I said, then again: "Beautiful. Just beautiful."

We'd fought all the way to the party and we fought all the way home. "I can't believe how rude you were," he said as we raced along Donald Ross Road.

"I wasn't rude," I insisted.

"You don't call excusing yourself to use the phone every ten minutes rude?"

"I used the phone exactly three times."

"Four."

"All right, four. I used the phone four times. Guilty as charged." I thought immediately of Colin Friendly and Jo Lynn. According to Michelle, my sister had called a second time. I knew I'd have to call her in the morning, get the gory details of her jailhouse tryst whether I wanted to hear them or not.

"And what did it accomplish?" Larry persisted. "Nothing. Sara still isn't home, and you know what? She isn't going to be home when we get back, which is probably a good thing, since if she's there, I'm likely to kill her."

"I don't know how you can be so indifferent," I said, deliberately misinterpreting what Larry was saying. But I was angry, and it was easier to pick a fight with Larry—one I felt I stood a chance of winning—than to wait and have it out with Sara, where there was no chance at all.

He wouldn't rise to the bait. No matter how low I descended, and I descended pretty low, at one point accusing him of being more concerned about his clients than his daughter, he wouldn't bite. He wouldn't engage. The more he withdrew, the more I pushed. The tighter his hands gripped the steering wheel, the looser my tongue became. I yelled, I cried, I carried on. He said nothing.

What I wanted him to do, of course, was to stop the car and take me in his arms. Just pull over to the side of the road and hold me, tell me

that I was a wonderful mother, that I hadn't failed Sara, that everything was going to be all right, that I was beautiful. But of course he didn't do this. It's hard to tell someone she's beautiful when she's insulting your manhood, your profession, your fitness as a father.

When we got home, Larry went straight to our bedroom, not even bothering to check on Sara. He knew she wasn't home, as did I, though I insisted on checking anyway.

"She didn't phone," Michelle said from her bed. It was almost midnight and sleep was curled around her voice, like a kitten in a basket.

I approached Michelle's bedside, leaned over, and kissed her forehead, smoothing some hair away from her delicate face. She sighed and turned over. "Sleep well," I whispered, closing her door behind me as I left the room. If there were fireworks later, I didn't want Michelle to be disturbed.

Larry was already in bed, feigning sleep. My anger was spent; depression was settling in. "I'm sorry," I said, and I was, and he knew it, although that wasn't much consolation. What difference does it make that you don't mean the hurtful things you say? The fact remains that someone else hears them. And words hurt more than sticks and stones after all. They echo in the stillness of the mind long after other bruises have healed.

I lay down beside Larry on top of the covers, fully clothed for when I heard Sara come home. I wanted our confrontation to be on an even footing. Since Sara already had youth on her side, I didn't want to compound my disadvantage by being dressed in a nightgown.

Sara's curfew was two o'clock, although I'm not sure why I expected her to be on time. Does someone who skips a whole day of classes worry about being late for their curfew? Did Sara ever stop to weigh the consequences of any of her actions?

At this point, I wasn't really worried. I was angry, depressed, and disappointed, at her, by her, and in her, but not really worried. It wasn't the first time, after all, that she'd pulled this sort of stunt.

When the hour of her curfew came and went, I got out of bed and went back to her room, staring through the darkness toward her unmade queen-size bed. "Where are you?" I whispered, still fighting off worry,

trying desperately not to think of all the awful things that could have happened to her. I tried not seeing her lying bleeding in a ditch, the victim of a drunk driver who'd hit, then run; I tried not imagining her lying broken in an alley, the victim of a mugger's angry fists; I tried not hearing her screams as she was attacked by some sadistic rapist. I tried not seeing a photograph of her beautiful face, ashen and still, as she lay on a cold steel slab in the back room of the medical examiner's office. I tried, and I failed.

I stretched out across her sheets, the odor of stale cigarettes settling quickly on my skin. What was the matter with her? Didn't Sara know how many lunatics were out there just waiting for innocent young girls who thought they were invincible? Men like Colin Friendly, I thought with a shudder, obliterating his image by burying my face in the soft darkness of her pillow.

Surprisingly, I fell asleep. I dreamed of a girl I'd known in high school. She'd come down to Florida a year ago on holiday and I'd run into her at the Gardens mall. It was the first time I'd seen her since our graduation, but she still looked startlingly young. Full of energy and enthusiasm and proud stories about her family. Six weeks later, I heard she'd been killed in a traffic accident shortly after returning to Pittsburgh. Apparently she'd lost control of her car on an icy stretch of highway and hit a guardrail. The car had flipped over, killing her instantly. In my dream, she was waving at me across the frozen foods section at Publix. I'd lost my grocery list and she was laughing, telling me to stay calm, it would all work out.

When I woke up, Larry was sitting at the side of the bed, staring down at me. "I think we should call the police," he said.

Chapter

11

We decided to try Sara's friends first.

This wasn't as easy as it should have been. The people in Sara's life kept changing. Every year brought with it a fresh set of names. Old faces disappeared; new faces popped into view. No one seemed to stay around very long.

This was a pattern that had been established early in Sara's life. I remember her nursery school teacher taking me aside one afternoon during a get-acquainted tea and confiding that she'd never seen a child attack a classroom quite the way Sara did. Apparently, every afternoon Sara would climb off the little yellow bus that transported her from home to school and announce, "Today I'm going to play with so-and-so." Every day she chose a new playmate, and every day she was successful in winning that child over. The next day, she moved on to someone new. Sara never formed a lasting bond with anyone in particular, although

these temporary attachments were intense and heartfelt. But when each new day came, she moved forward, without ever looking back.

The move from Pittsburgh to Palm Beach hadn't affected her in any noticeable way. Sara, unlike Michelle, left no real friends behind. Several classmates wrote letters; Sara never answered them. She threw herself into her new life with typical enthusiasm and abandon, quickly making a new set of acquaintances, and sliding from one year into the next without the unnecessary encumbrances that lasting friendship often brings.

And so it was difficult to even think of whom Sara might be with. "Jennifer," I offered, mentioning a name I'd heard Sara mutter from time to time.

"Jennifer who?" Larry asked, a not unreasonable question.

I shook my head. I had no idea. Just as I had no idea what names went with Carrie, Brooke, or Matt. "I know Carrie's last name," I insisted, conjuring up the image of a young girl with waist-length blond hair and black jeans pulled tight across an ample backside. "She was here a few weeks ago. You remember her. Carrie . . . Carrie . . . Carrie Rogers or Rollins or something with an R." The fact that I couldn't recall the last name of even one of our daughter's so-called friends made me feel guiltier than ever. How can you call yourself a good mother, I could already hear the police declaim, when you don't even know who your daughter's friends are?

"Does she have an address book?" Larry asked finally, and we began searching through Sara's scattered belongings, as one might search through the rubble of a bombed-out building. We gathered up clothes from the floor, some dirty, some freshly laundered, picked up discarded tapes and closed open books. We found pencils and pennies and scrap pieces of paper, not to mention a half-eaten bran muffin under the bed.

"Look," I said, hearing a strange note of wistfulness creep into my voice as I held up four empty packages of cigarettes. "She's still collecting."

"Here it is." Larry pulled a tattered, black leather-bound book in the shape of a motorcycle jacket out from underneath several tubes of makeup. He opened the book, and we watched as flecks of baby powder drifted toward the carpet, like snow. "There's nothing under R," he said.

"Try C," I offered.

Sure enough, there was Carrie, scrawled across the page in dark green ink. No last name accompanied it. Maybe, I thought, Sara didn't know it either.

We returned to our bedroom and phoned Carrie. The voice that finally answered was heavy with sleep and smoke. It mumbled something unintelligible, more a prolonged sigh than an actual hello.

"Carrie?" I asked, my voice loud, demanding, the auditory equivalent of hands on her shoulders, shaking her awake. "Carrie, this is Sara's mother. Is Sara there?"

A long pause, then: "What?"

"Is Sara there?"

"Who?"

"Sara Sinclair," I shouted angrily. Clearly, this was a waste of time.

"Sara's not here."

"Do you know where she is?"

"What time is it?"

"Eight o'clock."

"In the morning?"

I dropped the receiver into its carriage. "Sara's not there."

We tried six other names before giving up. My hand was on the receiver, about to call the police, when the phone rang. "Sara?" I all but shrieked.

"Jo Lynn," came the unwelcome response.

My shoulders slumped forward; my head dropped to my chest. My sister was the last person on earth I wanted to deal with. "Jo Lynn, I'm sorry, I can't talk to you now. Sara didn't come home last night . . ."

"Of course she didn't come home," Jo Lynn said. "She's with me."

"What?" I barked. "Sara's with Jo Lynn," I told Larry quickly. He shook his head and collapsed on the bed.

"You'd know that if you bothered to return your messages."

"What?"

"I called you twice last night."

"You didn't say anything about Sara."

"I assumed you'd call me back."

I was about to protest, decided not to. The important thing was that we knew where Sara was and that she was safe. I was so grateful that I almost forgot that Sara had skipped a whole day of school. How long had she been with my sister? I wondered, seized by a different fear. "What's she doing with you?" The words emerged slowly, almost reluctantly, as if they had to be pushed from my throat.

"Promise you won't get angry," Jo Lynn began, as every muscle in my body began twisting into spasms.

"Please don't tell me she was with you all day."

"It was very educational for her. She's never been inside a courtroom before. Which is shameful, when you think about it. I mean, she's going to be eighteen on her next birthday."

Assuming she lives that long, I almost said, but didn't. It was Jo Lynn, after all, whom I wanted to kill. "You took her to court with you," I said, as Larry gazed up at the ceiling, his eyes frozen in disbelief, as if he'd been shot.

"Well, you wouldn't go with me."

So it was my fault, I thought, almost afraid to say another word. "Tell me you didn't take her with you to the jail."

"Of course I took her with me. What did you expect me to do—leave her alone in the middle of North Dixie Highway? That's not the greatest area, you know."

"You took her to meet Colin Friendly?"

"No, of course not. She waited in the waiting room. Wait till you hear about this visit, Kate. It was incredible."

"You took my daughter to the county jail," I repeated numbly.

"That is some amazing place," Jo Lynn babbled, oblivious to my hands reaching through the phone wires for her throat. "I was really nervous, but Sara was great. She was my navigator, directing me to the visitors' parking, and telling me to relax, that I looked beautiful, all that stuff that girlfriends are supposed to say."

"Sara isn't your girlfriend," I reminded her. "She's your niece, and she's half your age."

"What's age got to do with it?" Jo Lynn demanded testily. "Really,

Kate, you don't give your daughter enough credit. She says you treat her like a child, and she's right."

"I treat her like a child because she acts like one."

"You sound just like our mother."

"Someone has to sound like an adult."

"Anyway," Jo Lynn continued, "we had to walk across a bridge to get to the inmate visitation area. It was like a moat, you know, like around a castle. Actually, it's quite a pretty building," she said, one word running into the next, as if she were afraid I might hang up were she to take a breath.

I'd been considering doing just that, and I'm not sure why I didn't. I tried telling myself that I was waiting to speak to Sara, which necessitated wading through the rest of Jo Lynn's story, but I'm not sure that's the truth. Listening to Jo Lynn was akin to driving by the site of a bad accident. No matter how hard you tried not to look, you couldn't turn away.

"You go in the front entrance, and there are all these signs. *Stop! Read! The following personal items will not be allowed into the facility past the metal detector!* And then it lists fourteen things, fourteen! And you wouldn't believe what some of them are—cell phones, diaper bags, hats. Hats!" she shrieked with obvious disbelief. "And then you get to security, and there are these other signs, the usual ones about no smoking, stuff like that, but then this really funny one that says, *No Firearms, Ammunition, or Weapons of any kind beyond this point.* We had a good laugh about that one. I mean, who would be stupid enough to bring a weapon to a jailhouse?"

Probably someone stupid enough to bring their seventeen-year-old niece, I thought but didn't say.

"I told them my name and who I was there to see, and they looked at me like, I don't know, like with new respect or something, because I wasn't there to see some nobody who's robbed the local 7-Eleven. And I had to sign in and everything, and we sat down in this waiting area, which wasn't the greatest place in the world. Just a bunch of uncomfortable blue chairs, and the rest of the room was this icky shade of gray. But

there were vending machines, so I bought us some Cokes, but I only got to have a couple of sips before they called my name, and I had to leave my Coke behind because they won't allow any food or beverages into the visitors' rooms. Not even gum. Can you believe that?"

"So you left Sara in the waiting room by herself."

"There were other people there. It's not like I abandoned her. She was fine. She was enjoying herself."

"Can I speak to her?"

"She's still asleep."

"Then wake her up. And bring her home. Now."

"Why? So you can yell at her? She didn't do anything wrong."

"She skipped school," I reminded my sister. "She didn't come home last night."

"She was with me. And I tried to reach you. Several times. Trust me, she learned more yesterday out in the real world than she would have at school. She'll write an essay about it, get an A."

"You had no right . . ."

"Lighten up," Jo Lynn said. "It's over, and the kid had a great time. Don't ruin it for her."

"Just wake her up and bring her home," I instructed.

"Soon," Jo Lynn said stubbornly.

"Not soon. Now."

Jo Lynn's response was to hang up the phone. I turned toward Larry. He shook his head and walked from the room.

It was almost four o'clock when I heard Jo Lynn's car pull into the driveway. Larry had left the house at two for the driving range, afraid that if he waited one more minute for my sister to show up with our daughter, he would explode. I encouraged him to go. I was way past anger by this time.

Michelle was off with her girlfriends, and I was alone in the house. I moved from room to room, compartmentalizing my anger, tucking it away, like knickknacks into a drawer, rationalizing it out of reach. Sara

was safe, I told myself, and I knew where she was. No harm had befallen her. Missing one day of school wasn't the end of the world. She'd easily make it up. She'd spent the night with my sister, and my sister had called twice. It was my fault that I hadn't returned her calls. I couldn't be angry with my daughter for my sister's lack of judgment. And what was the point in being angry with Jo Lynn? Had it ever done me any good?

By four o'clock, I'd settled into an eerie calm. I would greet them at the door, thank my sister for bringing Sara home, get rid of her as quickly and as painlessly as possible, then wait till Larry got home to talk to Sara. We'd already agreed the best way to deal with her was without the fireworks she'd be expecting, and possibly even counting on. We would give her nothing to rage at. The less said, the better. Sara wasn't stupid; she knew what she'd done wrong. There would be consequences for her actions; it remained only for Larry and me to decide what those consequences might be.

Jo Lynn pushed past me as soon as I opened the front door.

"Where's Sara?" I asked, staring toward the old red Toyota leaking oil on my driveway.

"She's in the car."

I strained to see her through the glass of the car's dirty front window. "Where? I don't see anybody."

"She's hiding."

"Hiding? That's ridiculous. What does she think I'm going to do?" I was about to step outside.

"Don't go out there," she warned, her voice stopping me. "I promised her I'd talk to you first."

"I think we've talked enough," I said, calm giving way to anxiety.

Jo Lynn reached over and closed the front door. "I promised her," she repeated. "You don't want to make a liar out of me, do you?"

I'd like to make mincemeat out of you, I wanted to say, taking note of her white T-shirt and short shorts, her newly trimmed hair. I restrained myself, forced a smile onto my lips.

"You're angry," she said. Obviously my smile lacked a certain degree of sincerity, and besides, Jo Lynn had always been very good at stating the obvious.

"You got your hair cut," I said.

She fluffed at the sides of her blond curls. "This afternoon. You like it? It's only a few inches."

"It looks very nice."

"Look, I know I shouldn't have asked Sara to go with me without first clearing it with you," she said, catching me by surprise. Jo Lynn was not one who apologized easily. "But I was really nervous, and I didn't want to go alone, and I really needed someone to go with me, and I knew you wouldn't come."

"You're saying it's my fault?"

"No, of course it's not your fault. It's nobody's fault. There is no fault. I'm just saying that if you'd been a little more understanding, a little more sympathetic . . ."

"I would have gone with you, and you wouldn't have had to drag my daughter down with you," I said, completing her sentence. This was more the sort of apology from Jo Lynn that I was used to.

"Well, yes," she said. "I really needed you. And you weren't there for me."

I nodded, took a deep breath. I was no longer anxious. I was on fire. Beads of sweat broke out across my forehead and upper lip. Jo Lynn didn't notice.

"It was so incredible, Kate," she was saying. "It was the most amazing thing being there in that jail with Colin."

I opened my mouth to protest, then instantly thought better of it. The more I protested, the longer this scene would drag out. So I said nothing, wiped the perspiration from my lip, and waited for her to finish.

"I was wearing this new white dress I bought that I thought he would like, and I was right, he loved it. It's very classy, not too short, not too low-cut. Subtle, you know."

I nodded. My definition of subtle and Jo Lynn's definition of subtle were not to be found in the same dictionary.

"Anyway, I was a nervous wreck all afternoon. But Colin was really great, he kept looking over at me in the courtroom, giving me his little smile, like he was telling me not to worry, that it was all going to work

out fine. And, of course, Sara was so sweet. She was holding my hand, and telling me how cute he was, and how romantic the whole thing was, kind of like Robin Hood and Maid Marian, and making me feel better. And I was telling her not to believe all the awful things people were saying about him on the witness stand."

"So you went to the jail," I said, trying to hurry her along.

"We went to the jail, and I told you about the moat and the signs and everything."

"You told me."

"Well, the room where you visit with the prisoners is on the second floor. Longest walk of my life, I tell you." She giggled. "I was so nervous. It was this long room with a glass partition, and you sit on one side of the partition and the prisoner sits on the other and you talk into these phones. It's really silly. I mean, they've already made us leave everything behind, our cell phones, our diaper bags, our hats, for God's sake, so why do we have to be behind glass? They don't even let you touch. I mean, I think that's cruel and unusual punishment, don't you?"

I said nothing. *This* is cruel and unusual punishment, I thought.

"So, I'm waiting there behind the glass. There are a few other people in there too, talking to their husbands or whatever, but everybody stops and looks up when they bring Colin into the room. I mean, he's really a celebrity. He has this aura, you know." She paused. I assumed this was for effect, and I tried to look suitably impressed. "So, the guard directs him over to his chair, and all the while he's looking at me and smiling that sad little smile of his, and I'm thinking that he is so gorgeous, I'm about to wet my pants, and then he sits down and he picks up his receiver and I pick up mine, and we just start talking, like we've known each other all our lives. He has a little bit of a stutter that's just so endearing. He tells me how grateful he is for my support, how he loves coming to court every day because he knows he's going to see me, and how much he appreciates my faith in his innocence. He's so polite, Kate. He's a real gentleman. And he has a great sense of humor. I think you'd like him."

I cleared my throat to keep from screaming. I stared hard at the floor.

"He wanted to know all about me, the kinds of things I like, what I like to do. Oh, and he asked about you."

My head snapped up sharply, as if I were a puppet whose strings had been yanked. "What?"

"He remembers you from court," she said, her voice growing instantly defensive.

"And what did you tell him?"

"That you were my sister, that you were a therapist. He laughed about that, said he'd have to meet you one of these days."

I shuddered, felt my body grow cold.

"And he thought Sara was absolutely beautiful."

"Good God."

"He said that . . ."

"I'm not interested in anything else that monster had to say." I moved briskly to the front door and yelled toward the shadowy figure in the car. "Sara, get in here this minute."

"Don't get angry when you see what she's done," Jo Lynn began. "I think it looks spectacular."

"What looks spectacular? What are you talking about now?"

"It wasn't my idea."

If I hadn't already known that it was Sara in the front seat of the car, I probably wouldn't have recognized her. The creature who emerged from the red Toyota was familiar to me only by height and the size of her bosom. Her long brown tresses had been trimmed to shoulder length and bleached ash blond. The flowered-print Indian blouse and blue jeans had been replaced by a tight white T-shirt and red-and-white-checkered miniskirt.

"The clothes are mine," Jo Lynn offered unnecessarily. "That hippie stuff didn't exactly go with the new hair."

She looks like a hooker, I thought, too stunned to say anything out loud. Actually, I realized as Sara walked past me and straight into her bedroom, she looked just like Jo Lynn.

Chapter
12

We tried not to make too big a deal about Sara's hair, reasoning that anything negative we might say would only encourage her further, and anything positive would only be misinterpreted. I went so far as a meek "So, how does it feel to be blond?" Larry mumbled something about everybody needing a change now and then. It was left to Michelle, as usual, to state what was obvious: "My God, what did you do to your hair?" she screamed as soon as she saw her sister. "It looks awful!"

Actually, it didn't look awful. It just took some getting used to, and over the course of the next few weeks, we all sincerely tried. But Sara never makes things easy, and she was, by turns, remote, nasty, defensive, and hostile. Everything but contrite. Anything but sorry. We never got an apology for our night of anguish; we received no assurances she wouldn't put us through it again. For a while I tried pretending that she was a character in a play, dropped temporarily into our world to provide some

much-needed comic relief. But in the long run, it was hard to find her funny. Interestingly, she did write an essay for her English class about her day in court, as Jo Lynn had suggested. Naturally, she received an A. So much for consequences.

It was around this time that Larry started his gradual retreat from the rest of the family. At first, it was just Sara he avoided, reasoning that the less contact he had with her, the less chance of conflict, the less chance of heartache. So whenever possible, when Sara was at home, Larry wasn't. His workdays got longer, his golf games more frequent. The result of this, of course, was that Michelle and I saw that much less of him too, but in those weeks before Thanksgiving, this subtle shifting away from us went largely unnoticed. I was pretty busy myself. The holiday season, contrary to popular myth, is not a time of unrestrained joy and merriment. It does not bring out the best in people. In fact, just the opposite is true. My office calendar was booked solid through Christmas and into the new year.

And then there was the little matter of my mother and sister, both of whom I decided were, in their own unique ways, completely looney tunes. My sister continued her public vigil at the courthouse and her private visits to the jail. My mother expanded her list of complaints: if strange men weren't following her, they were banging on her door at all hours of the night, and whispering obscene messages over the phone; certain women on her floor were plotting to have her thrown out of the building; she was receiving smaller portions at mealtimes than any of the other residents; Mrs. Winchell was trying to starve her out.

She began calling me, both at the office and at home, at least fifteen times a day. Hers was the first call I received in the morning and the last one I took at night. One minute, she'd be hollering; two minutes later, she'd be as pleasant as could be. Often, she'd be crying.

I didn't blame my husband for not wanting any part of either my mother or my sister at this point. They weren't his family, after all. His family was quiet and sweet and had never given us any trouble. His mother, widowed a decade earlier, lived in South Carolina, two blocks from Larry's older brother, and next door to a lovely widower she'd been seeing for the last five years. We made occasional forays into each other's

territory, and such visits were always unfailingly pleasant. No, it was only my family that was ever, and increasingly, problematic. Had I been able to escape them, I would have. Hadn't I already tried?

So, I honestly didn't mind that in those weeks surrounding Thanksgiving, Larry was rarely at home. In a perverse way, I was probably even grateful. It was one less person to worry about.

Thanksgiving itself was strangely calm. The proverbial lull before the storm. We celebrated at our house, and everyone was on their best behavior. Larry was a genial host, expertly carving the turkey and making small talk with my mother, who was pleasant and talkative and minus her recent paranoia. Jo Lynn came conservatively dressed in a white silk shirt and black crepe pants, and refrained from mentioning either Colin Friendly or his trial, which was on a week's hiatus. Sara, whose dark brown roots were beginning to intrude rudely on her otherwise ashen mane, was helpful with the dishes and attentive to her grandmother. "Who is that sweet thing?" my mother whispered at one point during the evening, and I laughed, thinking she was making a joke, realizing only later that she really didn't know. At its conclusion, Michelle pronounced the evening a resounding success. "Almost like a normal family," she said, proffering her cheek for me to kiss good night.

As for Robert, we'd been communicating through our voice mail, never quite connecting. He'd call; I'd be tied up with clients. I'd return his call; he'd be in a meeting. He was thinking about me, he left word on my machine; I was thinking about his offer, I responded on his.

The Monday after Thanksgiving, there was a message waiting when I arrived at the office. "Enough of this nonsense," Robert's voice announced. "I'll see you at my office this Wednesday at noon. I'll take you around, introduce you to the gang, show you how we operate, then take you out for lunch. Have those ideas ready." He then left the station's address and directions on how to get there. There was no mention of my calling back to confirm. Since he already knew I didn't go into the office on Wednesdays, it was simply assumed I'd be available. That I might have made other plans was obviously not part of the equation.

As it happened, I'd already promised to take my mother shopping on Wednesday. We'll make a day of it, I'd offered after Thanksgiving

dinner, almost giddy with relief at how well the evening had gone. First we'd go Christmas shopping, then have lunch, I'd suggested. No way was I going to call her now and cancel just because I'd had a better offer. This wasn't high school, after all. Although it *was* business, I reminded myself, my hand already on the phone. "We can still go shopping in the morning," I told my mother.

"What a nice idea," she said, as if it was the first time she was hearing it.

I picked her up at ten o'clock Wednesday morning. She was already downstairs in the lobby, standing by herself just inside the front doors, casting furtive glances over each shoulder, anxiously clutching her purse. I waved. She looked startled, as if surprised to see me, then hurried outside. "Are you all right?" I asked, helping her into the front seat of my white Lexus, watching as her upper torso curved around her purse, as if protecting it from would-be thieves. "Mother?" I asked again, positioning myself behind the wheel. "Is something wrong? Are you okay?"

"I have something to show you," she whispered. Then: "Drive."

Slowly, reluctantly, I pulled out of the driveway onto Palm Beach Lakes Boulevard. "What is it?" I asked. "What do you want me to see?"

"I'll show you when we get there."

I was about to protest when I realized she was no longer listening, all her attention devoted to watching the road ahead. Quickly, my eyes absorbed her profile for any outward signs of disturbance, but her gray hair was freshly washed and neatly styled, her deep brown eyes were clear and focused, her small mouth was curled upward into a smile. Everything seemed normal. Only her posture, the way her body folded protectively over her purse, seemed out of place. Then I noticed her hands.

"What happened to your nails?" I asked, noting the dark purple smudges across her fingernails.

She glanced toward her long, slightly arthritic fingers, then displayed them proudly, as if surprised by what she saw. "Do you like them? The salesgirl at Saks assured me this polish is all the rage."

I reached over and rubbed the top of one thin nail. The so-called

polish came off on my fingers. "This isn't polish, Mom," I told her, wondering what the salesclerk had been trying to pull.

"It isn't?"

"It's lipstick." I rubbed at her other fingers. "You've put lipstick on your nails."

She shook her head. "No," she said adamantly. "You're quite mistaken. And now you've ruined it," she said, her eyes threatening tears.

"But, Mom," I began, then stopped, driving on in confused silence. Clearly, something was very wrong with my mother. Although she'd been just fine over the weekend, I quickly assured myself. Maybe the weekend had been too much for her. Older people didn't adjust as quickly to a break in their routine. Was seventy-five really all that old? What was happening to her?

We didn't speak again until I pulled the car into the Marshalls plaza on Military Trail. As soon as I turned the engine off, my mother spun around in her seat, her eyes flashing excitement, her fingers fluttering nervously in the air, like a child's. "Wait till you see this." She reached inside her purse, cradling something gingerly in the palm of her hand.

"What is it?" I could hear the nervousness in my voice.

My mother smiled proudly, then slowly opened her fist, revealing a small white egg. "Have you ever seen anything like it?" she marveled, as my breath constricted in my chest. She looked nervously around, as if afraid someone might be standing just outside the window, spying in on her. "They had some of these on the table at breakfast," she continued, "and I couldn't get over them. So, when no one was looking, I slipped one into my purse to show you. Just look at how perfectly it's shaped. Have you ever seen anything like it?"

"It's an egg, Mom," I said gently, staring at the small ovate object in disbelief. "Don't you know that?"

"An egg?"

"You eat them every day."

My mother stared at me for several long seconds. "Well, of course I do," she said, without changing her expression. She tucked the egg back inside her purse.

"Mom," I began, not sure what I was going to say, but terrified of the silence.

"Don't you look lovely," she exclaimed, as if seeing me for the first time. "Is that a new dress? Very fancy just to go shopping."

My hand automatically smoothed the folds of my newly purchased red-and-white-flowered print dress. "I have a luncheon meeting," I reminded her. "About doing a possible radio show. Remember, I told you about it."

"Of course I remember," she said. "Have you got Michelle's Christmas list?"

I suppose I should have realized at this point that there was something terribly wrong with my mother. Looking back, it seems incredible that I failed to recognize the obvious signs of Alzheimer's disease. Had she been the mother of one of my clients, no doubt I would have seen this much earlier, or at least considered the possibility, but this was *my* mother, and she was only seventy-five. And besides, usually she was fine. Usually she didn't go around stealing eggs from the breakfast table and applying lipstick to her fingernails. Usually she didn't accuse her neighbors of harassment or bake with dishwashing detergent. Usually she was fine, a little forgetful maybe, but then weren't we all? And it wasn't as if she didn't remember most things. Hadn't she been fine all weekend? Hadn't she just mentioned Michelle's famous Christmas list?

"I have it right here," I said, extricating the list from my black leather bag.

"She's such a funny girl," my mother said, and I laughed, although I wasn't sure why.

Normally, I received tremendous pleasure from Michelle's yearly list, which came complete with drawings of each requested item, their correct sizes, prices, and the stores where they could be purchased, along with an accompanying chart indicating preference. Items highlighted in yellow were deemed *nice*; those with an asterisk beside them were *nicer*, an arrow indicated *very nice*, and those marked with both an asterisk *and* an arrow were *the nicest*.

You always knew exactly where you stood with Michelle, I thought gratefully, clutching the list as if it were a lifeline.

Sara, it goes without saying, refused to make any list at all.

The morning progressed reasonably well. My mother snapped back into seeming normalcy; we managed to locate several of the items on Michelle's list with a minimum of difficulty; I was feeling more comfortable about my upcoming meeting with Robert. I even had a few ideas for what I'd now started to think of as "my radio show." So today's lunch was legitimate after all, I rationalized, leading my mother across the parking lot toward a small shop that specialized in golfing equipment.

Of course, I was as delusional about Robert as I was with regard to my mother.

"What's the best line of men's clubs you carry?" I asked the Greg Norman look-alike who offered his assistance. Guilt had nothing to do with my decision to buy my husband the best set of clubs currently on the market, I told myself, following the young man to the back of the store.

"Well, of course, that depends on your needs," he said as he walked. "But there's this new line of clubs called Titans that's just fabulous." He grabbed a long club with a large wooden head from its bag and began waxing rhapsodic about its particular virtues, his hand sliding up and down its smooth surface as lovingly as if it were a woman's body. "It's the perfect combination of titanium and graphite. For my money," he concluded, replacing the wood with an iron, assuming I knew the difference, "it's the best there is."

"How much is it?" I asked. It was, after all, *not* his money, but mine.

"Well, let's see," he began, scanning the store as if he didn't already have a price worked out in his head. His eyes suddenly widened, then froze, as if he'd been shot. "My God, watch out!" he yelled.

I heard the *whoosh* of the golf club before I actually saw it, felt the air beside me stir as it swept past me, the club missing my head by no more than six inches. Several young men suddenly appeared, seemingly

from out of nowhere, and all but wrestled my mother to the floor, tearing the golf club she was wielding, as if it were a baseball bat, from her hands.

"Kate!" she cried, a look of pure terror distorting her delicate features as strange hands seized her. "Help me! Help me!"

"It's all right," I yelled. "She's my mother." Looks of astonishment crossed the faces of the young men as they reluctantly released her. "It's all right," I repeated, as confused as everyone else. "She wasn't trying to hurt me."

"Hurt you?" My mother was whimpering now, her head bobbing up and down, as if attached to her body by wires, the bobbing accentuating the skin that hung in folds around her neck, like loose-fitting socks. "What are you talking about? I would never hurt you. I just wanted to try out that bat. Remember in high school, I was such a good hitter. The best on the team."

"It's okay, everything's fine," I assured the small crowd gathered around us. "She gets a little confused at times, that's all. Are you all right?" I asked her.

"You know I would never do anything to hurt you," my mother said as I led her from the store.

"I know," I told her. It wasn't until I was behind the wheel of my car that my knees stopped knocking together. And it wasn't until I'd dropped her safely back at her apartment that I could breathe.

———

"You look a little flushed," Robert was saying, his hand reaching over to touch my cheek. "Are you coming down with something?"

The touch of his hand on my cheek was almost more than I could bear. I closed my eyes, imagined us on a shimmering white beach, far away from mothers and daughters and husbands and wives. And sisters, I reminded myself, forcing my eyes open, firmly relocating us in his impressive suite of offices in the heart of Delray. "My mother thinks she's Babe Ruth," I said.

"Why do I think there's an interesting story there?" he asked, eyes twinkling.

"Because you're the media," I told him. "Everything's a story to you."

"Ah," he said, "but not always an interesting one. Why is it I find everything about you so interesting?"

"Because you haven't seen me in thirty years," I replied dryly. "Because you don't know me very well."

"Something I'd like to change."

For the second time that morning, I was finding it hard to breathe. I looked around his office, forced my eyes to absorb a host of inconsequential details: the walls were pale blue, the broadloom thick and silver, the top of his large desk a black marble slab, dominated by a large-screen computer. There were two blue-and-gray tub chairs in fashionable ultrasuede positioned in front of the desk, and several more in front of a full-size sofa that sat at the far end of the rectangular room. We were on the top floor of a twelve-story building; floor-to-ceiling windows faced east toward the ocean. It was the spectacular view that was responsible for my shortness of breath, I told myself, almost laughing out loud at this feeble attempt at self-denial.

A row of framed photographs graced the top of the oak credenza behind Robert's desk. I walked toward the pictures, casually perusing the happy family smiling back at me: a woman, dark-haired, petite, pretty enough without being beautiful, a slightly startled look about her eyes that indicated either surprise or plastic surgery; four children, two boys, two girls, their growth captured inside silver frames as they advanced from childhood through adolescence to young adulthood. "You have a lovely family," I said, although, without my reading glasses, the more minute details of their faces were lost on me.

"Thank you," he acknowledged. "And what about you? Any pictures of your girls?"

I fished around inside my purse, grateful for something to do with my hands. Immediately, I pictured my mother reaching inside her handbag and proudly proffering forth her wondrous new discovery. An egg.

Maybe she was right, I found myself thinking. There *was* something pretty wondrous about an egg.

"What are you thinking about?" I heard Robert ask, his eyes crinkling into a smile.

"Eggs," I told him, quickly resuming my search.

"Eggs," he repeated, shaking his head. "You're a woman of mystery, Kate Latimer."

I smiled. It was something I'd always wanted to be. "Kate Sinclair," I corrected softly, almost hopeful he wouldn't hear, finally locating a small red leather folder that contained pictures of Sara and Michelle, and extending it toward him. "These are at least a year old. Michelle hasn't changed that much, except she's even thinner now."

"She's lovely."

I studied the small photograph of my younger child: heart-shaped face and huge navy eyes; light shoulder-length brown hair and slightly sad little mouth. Of my two girls, Sara was the more striking, Michelle the more conventionally pretty.

"And this . . . ?"

"Is Sara," I said. "Her hair's different now. It's shorter, and blond."

"And you don't approve?"

I returned the red leather folder to my purse. Was I that transparent? "I like the cut," I qualified. "I'm not wild about the color."

"No pictures of your husband?" A mischievous twinkle danced in Robert's hazel eyes.

I moved to the window, stared out at the ocean, although I wasn't able to distinguish where the sky ended and the water began. What did it matter? It was all a miraculous shade of blue. "No," I said, wondering what I was really doing in Robert's office, feeling slightly guilty. "No pictures of Larry."

The intercom on his desk buzzed and his secretary informed him that a Mr. Jack Peterson was on the phone from New York. Robert excused himself to take the call, and I excused myself to go to the ladies' room.

I leaned against the large bathroom mirror. "What are you getting yourself into?" I asked my reflection, applying some fresh blush to my

cheeks, fluffing the sides of my hair. Do you need this in your life right now? Even if this whole thing is really about a job in radio, is that what you really want?

In truth, all I wanted was a semblance of normalcy back. I wanted a daughter with brown hair and a good report card, a sister with a steady job and no love life, a mother who wasn't acting like a visitor from another planet.

At least I'd been able to persuade her to see a doctor, I consoled myself, smoothing on a fresh coat of lipstick, recalling the magenta lipstick smudged across my mother's fingernails. At first, she refused to see a doctor, said she'd seen enough doctors, so I made it seem as if I was the one who required the appointment and wanted her along for moral support. "Of course, dear," she'd readily agreed. Unfortunately, the earliest appointment I could schedule was two months away.

Maybe by then the problem, whatever it was, would have sorted itself out, I told myself. Maybe in two months' time my daughter's hair would have returned to its brown roots, Colin Friendly would be on his way to the electric chair, and my mother would be herself again.

I had no way of knowing that things were only going to get worse.

Although maybe I suspected as much. Maybe that's why I decided not to let Robert introduce me to the station brass, not to join him for lunch, not to pursue some half-baked notion of radio stardom. Instead, I splashed some cold water on my face, in what was decidedly a symbolic cleansing gesture, returned my makeup to my handbag, and marched from the ladies' room.

Robert was waiting for me in front of the elevators. "Sorry about the interruption," he began, taking me by the elbow and leading me across the hall to the office of his station manager. "I can't wait to show you off," he said.

I allowed myself to be led through the labyrinth of offices that made up the twelfth floor, shaking hands with the various managers and office workers, touring the recording studios below, meeting the announcers and producers, those who worked on-air and behind the scenes. I have to admit I loved everything about it, the atmosphere, the people, the lingo, the buzz. Mostly, I loved the feel of Robert's arm on my elbow as he

guided me from one room to the next, from one unfamiliar situation to another, from new face to new face. It wasn't his touch so much as what that touch represented: the feeling of being gently led, of not having to do for myself, the knowledge that someone else was in charge, was making the decisions, was leading the way. That I was no longer responsible.

So I allowed myself to be seduced, as one always consents to a seduction, still insisting to myself as we left the station for the restaurant that Robert's interest in me was strictly professional and that my interest in him was strictly the same, a way of branching out, of spreading my professional wings.

Of course, that was before we had our lunch.

Self-delusion, rationalization, outright denial—they'll only take you so far.

Chapter
13

So, tell me, what are the secrets of a happy marriage?"

I stared across the table at Robert Crowe, searching for signs of irony in his bright hazel eyes. There weren't any. I tried to laugh, but the intensity of his gaze caused the laugh to stick in my throat. My hand fluttered to my face, returned to my lap, stretched across the table for another roll—my third.

He reached over, his palm covering the top of my hand. "You seem a little nervous."

Was he playing with me? "I guess I'm not sure how seriously to take you," I answered truthfully.

"And that makes you nervous?"

"I like to know where I stand."

"Take me very seriously," he said, removing his hand.

I was more confused than ever. I hadn't engaged in this kind of

elliptical banter in over twenty-five years. One of the things I'd always liked about my husband was that I'd known where I stood with him right from the very beginning of our relationship. There'd been no anxious nights by the telephone waiting for him to call. No emotional roller-coaster rides. So why wasn't it my husband I was flirting with across the table of a cozy little restaurant in Delray Beach?

"The secrets of a happy marriage," I repeated, trying not to think of how handsome Robert looked in his dark green suit. "There are no secrets. You know that."

"You've been married almost a quarter of a century," he reminded me.

"You've been married over twenty years yourself," I reminded him back.

"Who said I was happy?"

My mouth went suddenly dry. I looked around the dimly lit restaurant, decorated in shades of burgundy and pink, and wondered what was taking our food so long. We'd been sitting here, in a corner table at the back, for almost half an hour. We'd already tossed around a host of ideas for my so-called show: Was a daily hour-long format preferable to a weekly two-hour show? Would I interview various experts or go it alone? Should we concentrate on one topic at a time or should we open the phone lines and let the topics fall where they may? What about conducting real-life therapy sessions on the air? How about dramatizations? Was there a way to combine the two?

We'd reached no conclusions. Clearly, we had a long way to go in our discussions. It was obvious more such lunches would be necessary.

"You're not happy?" I asked, the question out of my mouth before I could stop it.

"I'm not *un*happy," he qualified. "My wife is a very nice woman; she's given me four beautiful children and a very successful career. I owe her a great deal. I know that."

"Do you love her?" I knew the question sounded naive, maybe even trite. But in the end, it was the only question that really mattered.

"Define love."

I shook my head. "Love means different things to different people. I couldn't presume to speak for you."

"Speak for me," he said. "Go ahead—presume."

I smiled, wishing I wasn't such a sucker for his easy charm. Get up now, I told myself. Get up out of your seat, and tell him you're not hungry, that this whole radio show idea is a bad one, that you're not fooled by his newfound interest in your therapeutic capabilities, and that you have no more intention of sleeping with him now than you did thirty years ago. Go ahead, tell him. Instead I stayed put, twisted restlessly in my seat, said, "I can only tell you what love means to me."

"Please do."

I swallowed. "I think that love is a combination of many factors—respect and tolerance and acceptance of the other person for who they are." My eyes shifted inexorably toward his. "And, of course, physical attraction."

"So, what happens when you have respect and tolerance and you accept the other person for who she is, but the physical attraction is no longer there?"

"You work hard to get it back," I said, somewhat stuffily, grateful beyond words when the waiter approached with our food.

"Be careful," the waiter warned, prophetically. "It's very hot."

I tore into my seafood pasta as if I hadn't seen food in weeks. It burned my tongue, seared the roof of my mouth. Still, as long as my mouth was full, I couldn't get into trouble, I reasoned, barely taking a breath between forkfuls. My tongue grew numb. The food lost all taste. I kept shoveling it in regardless, aware that Robert was smiling at me from across the table, that he was enjoying my discomfort.

"You're suggesting that I fake it?" he asked after a long pause.

"Why not? Women do it all the time."

"Are you speaking from personal experience?"

"I didn't say that."

"You didn't deny it."

"I'm not suggesting you fake anything," I said, my mouth on fire.

"That's good, because it's not always possible. From a strictly phys-

ical point of view," he added unnecessarily, as I struggled unsuccessfully not to imagine him naked. "The male body doesn't always cooperate with its best resolve."

"I don't think we should get into this," I said finally, swallowing, the pasta sitting like a lump of burning coal in the middle of my stomach.

"What are we getting into?" he asked.

"I'm not sure." I put down my fork, stared him straight in the eyes. "Why are you telling me these things?"

"I guess I was hoping you'd have some easy answers for me," he said, and laughed sadly. "The McDonald's School of Psychiatry. Quick and effortless. Over eight billion cured."

"McTherapy." I laughed. "Sounds like a good name for a radio show."

We lapsed into silence. I finished the balance of my pasta, felt it burn a trail through my esophagus, razing various internal organs on its way to my intestines, where it wrapped itself into a series of tight little knots.

"So, how do you do it?" he asked calmly, sipping on his wine.

"Do what?"

"Keep your relationship . . . what's the word they use? . . . vital?"

I sighed, more deeply than I'd intended. I understood that "vital" was a euphemism for "sexy."

"Do you love your husband?" he pressed.

"Yes," I answered quickly.

"You have the right combination of respect and tolerance and acceptance of one another?"

"Yes." One-word answers were about all I was capable of at the moment.

"And you still find each other physically attractive?"

"My husband is a very handsome man."

"And my wife's a very lovely woman. That's not what I asked."

"I still find my husband physically attractive, yes."

"And he, you?"

Did he? I wondered. "He says he does." Really? I asked myself. When was the last time he said that?

"You still make love?"

I reached for my water, took a long gulp, half hoped I would choke, have to be carried out of the restaurant. I glanced around the room, hoping for a diversion of some sort—a waiter dropping a tray, a couple breaking into a loud argument at a nearby table, someone's mother swinging a golf club at her head. "I really don't think that's any of your business."

"For sure it's none of my business," he agreed. "I'm asking anyway."

I tried not to smile, felt my lips wobbling all over my face. "We still make love," I answered.

"How often?"

"What?"

"You heard me."

"Yes, I did, and I have no intention of answering you."

"Not as often as you used to, I'll bet."

"Pretty safe bet after twenty-five years of marriage."

"And are you happy about that?"

"I'm not *un*happy about it," I replied, echoing his earlier phrase. Was that true?

He smiled.

Did he still have to look as handsome as he had so long ago? Couldn't he have grown fat or bald or dim-witted? Did he still have to move with an athlete's grace? Did his hips have to be so impossibly slim, his chest so impressively expansive? Did he have to look so damned . . . vital?

"My wife and I haven't made love in three years," he said.

"What?"

"You heard me."

"Yes, I did." Hadn't we already had this exchange? "I'm not sure what you want me to say."

"What would you say if I were your client?"

"I thought you once told me that if you wanted my professional advice, you'd make an appointment," I said, trying to shift the conversation to another level, one I could deal with safely in the professional confines of my office.

"Is that what you think I should do?" he asked.

"Is that what you need?" I asked in return.

"You're the therapist. You tell me."

"I think if you're unhappy with your situation, you should change it."

"I'm trying to," he said, provocatively.

I shifted uncomfortably in my chair, crossed one leg over the other. "You should talk to your wife about this. Tell her how you feel."

"You don't think I've done that?"

"I have no idea."

"My wife insists that part of her life is over. She's done her bit for posterity. She's gone forth and multiplied. Now all she wants is companionship and a good night's sleep."

"Maybe it's physical," I offered. "Some women going through menopause experience a decrease in their level of sexual desire."

"Has that happened to you?"

"We're not talking about me."

"I prefer talking about you."

"Have you tried courting your wife? Taking her out for dinner?" I persisted. Or lunch, I thought, but didn't say. "Sometimes all it takes is a few kind words. Try saying at least one nice thing to her every day. You'll see, it'll change your life."

"You used to drive me crazy," he said, sidestepping my advice, as if I hadn't spoken. "I'd come home from a date with you and head straight for the cold shower."

"You'd head straight for Sandra Lyons," I said, remembering how hurt I'd been when my girlfriend first informed me of his extracurricular activities, experiencing a slight twinge even now.

He looked surprised.

"Didn't think I knew about her, did you?"

"Everybody knew about Sandra," he said easily, recovering

nicely, taking a long sip of his wine. "She was the girl everybody knew."

"She killed herself shortly after you left town."

The wineglass almost slipped through his fingers. "What?"

I started to laugh, at first only a slight giggle, soon a great hearty guffaw. "I'm sorry," I said, then laughed even louder.

"You're laughing?!"

"I made it up. I'm sorry. I couldn't help myself."

"You made what up?"

"Sandra Lyons—she didn't kill herself." I tried to stop laughing, couldn't. "She's fine. At least she was fine the last time I saw her. I don't know—she could be dead by now." My laughter was verging on hysteria.

He looked horrified. "Why did you say she'd killed herself?"

"I'm not sure," I told him, still laughing, but that was only partly true. I'd been trying to shake him up. It wasn't fair that only one of us was a quivering mess.

He shook his head. "You're a strange woman, Kate Latimer."

"Sinclair," I corrected, the laughter suddenly freezing in my throat. Back to square one, I thought.

"Sinclair, right. Tell me, does your husband often see this side of you?"

"What side is that?"

"This twisted, rather sadistic side that, for some perverse reason, I'm finding extremely attractive."

I tried to laugh, couldn't. "I'm sure he sees it more often than he'd like."

Robert finished his wine, poured himself some more, studying me all the while. "Your husband's the only man you've ever been with, isn't he?" he said.

I felt suddenly exposed, as if he'd reached over and unbuttoned the front of my dress, laid bare all that was private and untouchable. Probably I should have slapped his face. I definitely should have gotten up and left. At the very least, I should have told him to shut the hell up, enough was enough. Instead I said, "What makes you say that?"

"I was always pretty good at reading people."

"My mother says my face is an open book."

"Your mother's right."

"Where is it written that my husband has been my only lover?"

Robert reached across the table, traced the line of my lips with his index finger. "Right here," he said, as a shiver raced through me, as strong as an electrical charge. "Aren't you ever curious," he asked, "what it would be like with somebody else?"

Oh God, I thought, I'm lost. If I didn't stop this and stop it now, I'd never find my way back. "No," I lied, pushing my chair back, just slightly out of his reach. His hand remained where it was, absently caressing the space between us. His touch lingered on my lips. I felt it as one supposedly feels the presence of a recently amputated limb. "I'm not curious."

"You've never been tempted?"

"I'm a married woman."

"Does that matter?"

"It matters to me."

"Has your husband ever been unfaithful?"

"No."

"You sound very sure."

"I *am* very sure," I said, and I was. There weren't many things I was sure of anymore, but I was sure of this: Larry would never cheat on me. It was something I'd never doubted in all our time together. "This is a very dangerous conversation," I finally acknowledged.

"What is?"

"This is. This—what we're doing."

"We're not doing anything."

"Yes, we are."

"What are we doing?"

"We're laying a foundation," I said, thinking of Larry.

"A foundation for what?"

"You know for what. Please don't be coy."

"Tell me."

"I'm not interested in an affair," I told him, pushing the words out of my mouth, hoping I sounded more convincing than I felt.

"An affair? That's what you think I want?"

"Isn't it?" Had I misinterpreted everything?

"I've never gotten over you, Kate," he was saying, his voice a soft blanket, inviting me inside. "I look at you, and I still feel the same sparks I did when I was a pimply-faced teenager."

"You never had a pimple in your life," I said.

"You're missing the point."

"I'm trying to."

"I want you, Kate," he said simply. "I've always wanted you. I think you want me too."

"I want a lot of things. It doesn't mean I'm going to get them. It doesn't mean those things are good for me."

"How do you know if you don't try?"

"And what would be the point of trying?"

"I don't know." He reached for my hands. I quickly put them in my lap. "I just know that something is missing from my life, and has been for a very long time. I thought I'd gotten used to it. I told myself that my life was full, that romance was for teenagers, all the stuff people tell themselves to get them through the night. But all that went out the window the day I saw you in the courthouse. There you were, every bit as beautiful as I remembered. And not only beautiful, but funny and smart and sexy as hell. It was like discovering my youth all over again, only better. I look at you and I feel that anything's possible. It's a feeling I'd forgotten. And I don't want to lose it. I don't want to lose *you*. I want you. Is that so wrong?"

"Oh God," I said, trying not to be overwhelmed. "That was quite a speech."

"I meant every word."

"I don't know what to say."

"You don't have to say anything right now. Just think about it."

"It'll be hard not to," I told him.

He smiled, then frowned, then smiled again, his hands retreating to

his sides. And suddenly he was on his feet, his arms extended, and I realized we were no longer alone, that someone else had joined us. "What are you doing here?" Robert was asking, sounding pleased by this unexpected interruption. I was amazed at how quickly he could shift gears. I was still locked in first, and slipping down that mountain road. "How did you know where to find me?"

The next voice was soft and unmistakably feminine. "I called the office; your secretary told me you'd probably still be here. I hope I'm not interrupting anything too important."

Of course I knew it was Robert's wife even before I turned around. "Actually, it's perfect timing. We were just finishing up," I told her, feeling dizzy and light-headed as Robert made the necessary introductions.

Brandi Crowe was an attractive woman approximately my own age. She was on the short side, maybe five feet three inches tall, and she wore a lot of makeup, especially around her eyes, which were small and gray and untroubled by lines. She had that vaguely surprised look I recognized from her photograph. I found myself checking her hairline for signs of recent surgery, but her hair—a shade too black, a touch too long—provided suitable camouflage. Her Chanel suit was the same shade of pink as the tablecloth.

"You're just in time for dessert," Robert said easily, pulling out a chair for his wife and signaling for the waiter.

"Well, I'll join you for some coffee, if you don't mind." His wife smiled in my direction. "I haven't had dessert in years. It's not fair, is it? I mean, look at Robert. He eats whatever he wants, and he never puts on a pound. I so much as look at a rich dessert . . ." Her voice trailed off. "Is that a new suit?" she asked her husband.

He shook his head, but the slight blush that appeared unexpectedly on his cheek told me otherwise. So, he'd bought a new suit for our lunch, I thought, twisting the buttons of my newly purchased red-and-white-floral dress.

"Do you work at the station?" Brandi Crowe asked as the waiter cleared away the dishes from our main course and passed around the dessert menus.

"Kate's a therapist," Robert explained. "I've been trying to talk her into doing a little something for us."

Brandi Crowe looked confused. "Really? In what capacity?"

We ordered coffee and several slices of Key lime pie, and Robert explained the general concept of what he had in mind. "McTherapy," he announced finally, and I smiled in spite of myself.

"Sounds great," she enthused. "I'd certainly listen."

"Well, the idea's still in its infancy," Robert said.

"It's by no means a sure thing," I said.

Robert smiled and looked away.

A slight chuckle escaped Brandi Crowe's carefully outlined lips. Her upper lip was very full, I noticed, wondering whether she'd had collagen injections, then wondering what she was chuckling about. "When my husband decides he wants something, absolutely nothing gets in his way." She chuckled again, an increasingly irritating sound. "This is a done deal." She reached over, patted her husband's hand. I felt a jolt through mine.

My gaze dropped to the pink linen tablecloth, and stayed there until the aroma of freshly brewed coffee forced my head back up. The waiter slid a slice of Key lime pie under my nose. The pie was tall and yellow and topped by a great lather of whipped cream.

"You're skinny," Brandi Crowe was saying. "You can eat that. If I were to eat it, it would go straight to my hips. I have to work like the devil to keep the pounds off."

"You look great," I told her, and meant it. Despite what the media tries to tell us, not everyone has to be six feet tall and a hundred and twenty pounds. Immediately, I pictured Sara, wondered whether she was in school, what she was doing. Couldn't be any worse than what her mother was doing, I realized.

"That looks delicious," Brandi said, eyeing her husband's piece of pie. "Let me just steal a forkful."

"What about your diet?"

"You're right. I'll hate myself in the morning." She sat back in her chair, watched me shoveling the Key lime pie into my mouth with the same abandon with which I'd earlier attacked my seafood pasta. In sec-

onds, the whole thing was gone. Brandi Crowe looked vaguely stunned. "So, how did this whole idea come about?" she asked. The look on her face told me she was beginning to doubt my credentials.

"Actually, I knew Kate from high school," Robert said. I couldn't help but admire his cool. He was sipping his coffee and eating his Key lime pie just like normal people do.

"Really? You mean in Pittsburgh?"

I listened to Robert's account of our accidental reunion at the courthouse, watching his wife's reactions, searching for any signs of intimacy between them, for telltale clues as to whether or not they were sleeping together, subtle glances, furtive touches. But aside from that first pat on the hand, the jolt of which I still felt in my palm, there was nothing to give them away. They might be sleeping together; they might not.

What difference did it make? I asked myself angrily, swallowing my coffee in one prolonged rush and jumping to my feet. "I'm sorry, but I really have to get going. I'm supposed to meet my husband," I lied, glancing at my watch for added authenticity.

"Maybe the four of us could get together one night for dinner," Robert's wife suggested.

I must have mumbled something positive, because she said she'd call and we'd set something up. Then I went out and bought my husband the most expensive set of golf clubs I could find.

Chapter
14

For the next few weeks, Colin Friendly was everywhere: on television, on the front pages of the newspapers, on the covers of both local and national magazines. The trial was winding down and there was much speculation as to whether Colin Friendly would take the stand in his own defense. The rumors were contradictory and many. According to the *Fort Lauderdale Sun-Sentinel*, he would most assuredly take the stand; according to the *Miami Herald*, his lawyers would never allow it. The *Palm Beach Post* came down solidly in the middle: Colin Friendly would take the stand, and it would be against his lawyers' advice.

About one thing, almost everyone was certain—Colin Friendly would be found guilty. The only real question was how many minutes it would take the jury to arrive at its guilty verdict. Of course, my sister remained unshakable in her belief not only that Colin Friendly would be found not guilty but that he *was* not guilty.

"Did you see the profile in the *Post* this morning?" she asked me, her voice on the phone low and threatening tears. The trial had adjourned for lunch, and she'd caught me in between clients. "They had so many things wrong. Really, half their information was incorrect. And it makes me so mad because they think they can just get away with it, and of course, they can, because what's Colin gonna do—sue them?"

I said nothing, knowing no response was required.

"They said he's six feet two inches tall. Since when? The fact is he barely tops six feet. They say he weighs a hundred eighty pounds. Well, maybe he weighed that before he was arrested. He's lost at least fifteen pounds in that awful jail because the food's so bad. But the newspapers like to paint a picture of this big, threatening guy, so they add an inch here, a few pounds there, and pretty soon he's Hulk Hogan. Well, you saw him, he's not threatening-looking at all."

"I don't think his height and weight are really major issues," I ventured.

"They're deliberately misleading. And, what's more important," she countered, "they're indicative of the kind of shoddy reporting that passes for journalism in this country these days. They said his mother's name was Ruth. It wasn't. It was Ruta. At first, I thought maybe it was a typo, but they kept repeating it, so, obviously, it was just carelessness. They said he came from poverty, but his great-grandparents were really rich. They lost it all in the Depression, of course, but still, they could have mentioned it. I mean, if they can't get the simplest of facts right, then how can you believe anything they print? How can you take anything they say seriously?"

"I thought the reporters were your friends."

"Oh, please, you tell them one thing, they print something completely different. They're always getting their quotes wrong or taking things out of context. They have their own agenda."

"And what is that?"

"To see Colin Friendly in the electric chair. But it isn't going to happen. You'll see. He'll be acquitted. And when he is, I'll be right there waiting for him."

"I have to go now," I told her, not wanting to hear the familiar litany again.

"The only thing they got right," she continued, as if I hadn't spoken, "is that he had a terrible childhood. You couldn't help but cry when you read it. Wasn't it sad? Didn't you cry?"

"I didn't read it," I lied. A mistake. Jo Lynn now felt compelled to provide me with all the details I'd supposedly missed.

"Well, his mother was crazy. I mean really crazy. She got kicked out of the house when she was fifteen, got pregnant at sixteen, and was already a drunk and a doper by the time Colin was born. She'd shoot up right in front of him, have men back to her room, and have sex with them while Colin was watching. She didn't even know for sure who Colin's father was.

"When he was really little, she used to lock him in the closet whenever she went out. Sometimes she'd disappear for days at a time, and Colin wouldn't have anything to eat. And if he had to go to the bathroom, well, he'd just have to go in his pants. Isn't that pathetic? No wonder he was a bed-wetter until he was eleven. Of course, she'd punish him whenever he wet the bed, do awful things like rub his nose in it, like a dog. And she kept moving all the time, so Colin never got a chance to make any friends, and he was really shy. He started to stutter, and his mother would make fun of him and beat him. She was really awful."

"No wonder he hates women," I said.

"Oh, but he doesn't hate women," Jo Lynn exclaimed. "Which is really an amazing thing, when you think about it. He loves women."

"He loves women," I repeated, my voice as dull as a matte finish on a photograph.

"He had this great neighbor, Mrs. Rita Ketchum, and she was really nice to him. She taught him that most women weren't like his mother."

"I thought you said they moved around all the time."

"This was later, when he was a teenager, living on his own in Brooksville."

"I don't remember the article mentioning her."

"You said you didn't read it."

"I glanced at it," I qualified.

"You read every word. Why won't you admit it?"

"How does he explain the kittens he tortured as a child?"

"Colin never tortured anything. Some other kids had been at those kittens. Colin just put them out of their misery."

"And the fires he started?"

"Kid stuff. Nobody ever got hurt."

She had all the answers. There was no point trying to argue. For whatever her reasons, my sister had decided that Colin Friendly was nothing more than a sadly misunderstood young man, and no amount of logic or evidence to the contrary was going to convince her otherwise.

"Is he going to testify?" I asked.

"He wants to, but his lawyers don't think it's a good idea. Not because they think he's guilty," she added quickly. "It's because when Colin gets nervous, he stutters, and his lawyers don't want to put him through the ordeal of a cross-examination."

"Probably a good idea."

"I think the stutter's kind of sweet. And I think it would show the jury how vulnerable he is, that he's a human being, not this awful monster they keep hearing about."

"So you've advised him to testify?"

"I said I'd support him no matter what his decision. But I think it's really important to him that he makes people understand."

"Understand what?"

"That he didn't kill those women." Jo Lynn's voice was filled with exasperation. "That he could never do the awful things they say he did."

"When do they think the trial will be over?" I didn't think I could take too many more conversations like this one.

"Two weeks tops. The prosecution should wrap things up tomorrow, and then it'll be the defense's turn. If all goes according to plan, Colin will be out by Christmas."

"And if he isn't?"

"He will be."

"And then what?"

"Then we can get on with our lives."

"Sounds good to me."

"Will you come with me to court on Wednesday?"

"Not a chance."

"Please. It would mean a lot to me."

"Why?" I asked. "You know I don't share your high opinion of the man."

"I want you to hear what Colin has to say firsthand. I honestly think if you just listen to him, I mean *really* listen to him, like you do with your clients, then you'll change your mind about him."

"I doubt that."

"It's really important to me, Kate."

"Why is it important?"

There was a second's silence. "Because I love him."

"Oh, please . . ."

"I do, Kate. I really love him."

"You don't even know him, for God's sake."

"That's not true. I've been sitting in that courtroom for almost two months. I know everything about him."

"You know nothing."

"I've been visiting him every week."

"You talk to him through a glass partition."

"That's right, I do. And he talks to me. And we really understand each other. He says I know him better than anybody."

"That's because he's killed everybody else!" I shouted in total frustration.

There was another, longer pause. "That was beneath you," Jo Lynn pronounced. "I would have thought that with your professional training, you'd have a little more compassion."

"Look, Jo Lynn," I said, trying another approach, "you're the only one that matters to me in this equation. I don't want to see you get hurt again."

Her voice softened. I could almost see the relief in her face through the phone lines. "But I'm not going to get hurt. He loves me, Kate. He says I'm the best thing that ever happened to him."

"I'm sure you are," I told her honestly.

"You know what he told me when I went to see him on Friday?"
I shook my head, said nothing.
"He said I looked as sweet as the first strawberry in spring."
I smiled despite myself.
"You're smiling. I can tell you're smiling. Isn't that just the most darling thing you ever heard? I mean, when was the last time that Larry ever said anything that romantic to you?"

It's been a while, I thought, but didn't say. I felt a sudden twinge as my thoughts shifted from Larry to Robert.

"So, you can stop worrying about me. I'm gonna be fine. If Colin and I can get through this, then we can survive anything. I want you to be happy for us, Kate. And I need you to be there for me. Can you do this for me just this one last time? I'll even go visit Mom with you this weekend. How's that for a deal?"

I closed my eyes, lowered my forehead into the palm of my hand. "Okay, you got me," I said softly.

"Thank you, Kate," she said. "You won't regret it."

"I'll see you Wednesday," I told her, knowing she was wrong.

Some interesting facts about the Palm Beach County Courthouse: With almost 700,000 square feet of floor space, it is the largest such structure in the state of Florida and one of the largest in the nation; it was designed by Michael A. Shiff and Associates and Hansen Lind Meyer, Engineers, and built by the George Hyman Construction Company; the exterior portico arch is 52 feet high and the interior waterfall is 30 feet tall; the vaulted roofs atop the building were designed to echo the twin towers of the Breakers Resort Hotel directly to the east in Palm Beach proper.

I gleaned this knowledge from a brochure I'd taken from the information desk in the lobby, while waiting to get into court on Wednesday morning. I also learned that the courthouse was designed with 44 courtrooms and the potential to expand to 60 when two empty floors are built

out, and that a central recording studio handles audio from all the courtrooms piped to the studio and put on long-playing tapes. To review a portion of testimony in a courtroom, the judge merely phones the studio and asks for a playback. Amazing, I thought, smiling at the gray-haired old man standing behind the information desk. He was wearing a bright red vest emblazoned with the words "Clerk of the Court, Volunteer." He winked. I felt ancient.

Some other interesting data: There are now 3,780 attorneys practicing in Palm Beach County; the county's courts handled 311,072 cases filed the previous year, two-thirds of them traffic-related; more than 3 miles of shelves are needed to house the 3.6 million court files; there are 55 miles of telephone cable and 40 miles of computer cable; there are 56 holding cells for prisoners standing trial.

According to the brochure, the prisoners enter the building via jail buses that park in their own garage. They reach the courtrooms through a maze of holding cells, electronic lockdowns, special elevators and corridors. The deputies guarding the prisoners are outfitted with special infrared sensors that sound an alarm and automatically seal off an area if a deputy is knocked down. The state-of-the-art security system includes 274 video cameras, more than 200 infrared detectors, 200 intercoms, and more than 300 card-key doors.

At eight o'clock that morning, we were permitted entry into the main corridor. We stepped through the tall, heavy glass doors and through the metal detector, heading toward the bank of elevators to our right. The crowd was bigger than usual, although I recognized numerous faces from my previous visits. Eric was still supplying my sister with her morning cup of coffee. According to Jo Lynn, he hadn't missed a day. There were several others, and she pointed out each one, who showed up faithfully every morning. I wondered what these people would do once the trial was over. Did they have jobs or families to return to? Or would they simply find a new courtroom to visit, a new prisoner to focus their attentions on? In a way, the trial was a kind of drug, I understood, glancing across the wide corridor at the large auditorium-like room where potential jurors waited to hear if their names would be called. Would

these judicial groupies experience a kind of withdrawal when it was all over? Would I? I wondered, realizing how much of my own life this trial had absorbed.

A well-stacked law library was located beside the jury office and across from the cafeteria. The cafeteria was open between eight and five, and always smelled of Javex. Two large escalators ran up and down on opposite sides of the corridor. There were more guards and another metal detector at the Quadrille Street entrance. I'm not sure when I became aware of such details. Perhaps they passed through me by osmosis as I waited for the elevator to take us to the eleventh floor. But such unnecessary facts were now a part of my life, and I was likely to retain them, in much the same way I would always know that Brenda Marshall had once been William Holden's wife.

"Do you ever worry about things?" Jo Lynn asked as we stepped out of the elevator and began the long march to the courtroom at the far end of the hall.

"What kind of things?" I asked.

"Silly things, things you shouldn't be worried about."

"Like what?"

"I don't know." Jo Lynn stared out the long windows as we walked down the hallway, the heels of her brown sandals clicking against the gray and black squares of the marble floor. She was wearing a white sweater and a long brown linen skirt, with buttons up the front, although the buttons were undone to her thighs. Tanned bare legs flashed briefly, then disappeared, with each step.

"Tell me," I said, genuinely curious. It was unlike Jo Lynn to be overly introspective.

"You'll think I'm crazy."

"I already think you're crazy."

She made a face. "You're 'kidding on the square,' " she said, her voice an exact duplicate of our mother's.

"What do you worry about?" I asked.

We passed through the large double doors and into the small, dark anteroom that preceded Courtroom 11A. "Like here," she said, stopping unexpectedly. "It's so dark. I sometimes worry about what it would be

like if it were always this dark. Sometimes, I close my eyes and pretend that I'm blind, like we used to do when we were kids, and I think: What would happen if when I opened my eyes, I still couldn't see? I mean, don't you think that would be awful? Not to be able to see anything, to be a prisoner of the darkness?"

"It would be awful not to see," I agreed, not sure where this was coming from. We stepped into the courtroom, were greeted immediately by a wall of sunlight. Jo Lynn walked directly to our seats, unmindful of the spectacular view. "What else do you worry about?" I asked, taking my seat beside her.

"I worry about getting cancer," she said.

"That's a pretty normal fear," I told her.

"Ovarian cancer, like Gilda Radner," she said.

"There's no history of ovarian cancer in our family," I assured her.

"Cancer's just so sneaky, don't you think? I mean, here's Gilda Radner, she's a famous TV star with a movie star husband, she has everything, and then one day maybe she gets a pain in her lower back or something, and she goes to the doctor and discovers that she has ovarian cancer, and a few months later, she's dead. Or that friend of yours from Pittsburgh, the one who was killed in that awful car accident? Here she was, driving along, probably listening to the radio, maybe even singing along, and one minute she's fine, and the next minute she's dead. And I hate that. I really hate that."

"It's a reminder of our own mortality."

"What?"

"We all worry about things like that occasionally," I said instead.

"You don't," she stated.

"Of course I do."

Her eyes searched mine for signs I might be mocking her. "You never seem like you worry about anything."

"I have the same worries as everybody else. Don't you think I'm human?"

She fidgeted uncomfortably in her seat. "It's just that you always seem to have everything under control. You know everything . . ."

"I don't know everything."

"Yes, you do. Or at least, that's the impression you give. Kate Sinclair, the woman who has everything, knows everything."

I listened to her voice for signs of bitterness, but there were none. She was just stating the facts as she believed them.

"But it's not true."

"Of course it is. Kate, face it. You're hopelessly put-together. You have the perfect life—a husband who adores you, two terrific kids, a great career, a gorgeous house, a designer wardrobe."

I stared guiltily down at my navy Donna Karan pantsuit.

"You have it all," she said. "No wonder it's so hard for Sara."

"Sara? What are you talking about?"

"You're a tough act to follow, Kate," she explained. "It's hard enough being your sister."

I was having trouble keeping up with the sudden shifts in the conversation. Hadn't we started out talking about Jo Lynn? How did we end up talking about me? And what did Sara have to do with anything? "What do you mean, it's hard for Sara? What is?"

"Being your daughter, knowing how high your expectations are, knowing that she'll never measure up."

"Did Sara tell you this?"

"Not in so many words, but we've talked about you a lot. I understand the sort of things she's going through."

I felt a stab of anxiety, like an ice pick to the heart. "The only expectations I have for Sara are that she go to school and be reasonably pleasant to live with."

"That's not true. You want her to be just like you."

"No, I don't."

"That's what she thinks."

"But it's not true. I just want her . . ."

"To be happy?" Jo Lynn said, our mother's voice resurfacing. "No—you want *you* to be happy *with* her. Michelle makes you happy because she's just like you. She has the same style as you. She wants the same things. But Sara's different, and you have to let her live her own life."

"Why are we talking about Sara?" I demanded testily.

Jo Lynn shrugged, looked away.

The courtroom was filling up. It was becoming uncomfortably warm. I undid the buttons of my jacket, fanned my face with the brochure I'd taken from the information desk in the lobby.

"So, what do you worry about?" Jo Lynn asked, as if daring me to prove I was human.

"I worry about the kids," I told her. "And about our mother."

"She'll outlive us all," Jo Lynn said dismissively. "Besides, that's too ordinary. Tell me something crazy that you worry about, something that doesn't make any sense."

"I worry about words losing their meaning," I heard myself say, surprised to be voicing these thoughts out loud. "That I'll be reading a book or the newspaper or something, and it'll be like reading a foreign language, the words won't make any sense."

"That's pretty crazy," Jo Lynn agreed, seemingly satisfied.

"And I worry about losing pieces of myself," I continued, even as I felt her interest waning, her attention drifting away. "That as I keep giving pieces of myself to everyone else, there won't be anything left over at the end of the day for me, that there won't be anything left *of* me." That I'll look in the mirror one morning, I continued silently, and there won't be anyone looking back.

"Oh God, there he is," Jo Lynn said, rising in her seat, waving toward the front of the courtroom.

Like a vampire, I thought, snapping out of my reverie, directing my attention to the real-life vampire coming through the door beside the judge's podium, a handsome man in a conservative blue suit, not unlike my own, a man whose greatest pleasure was sucking the life's blood from defenseless women and girls. And this man was smiling at my sister.

The clerk quickly called the court to order and we all rose as the judge assumed his seat at the podium. "Is the defense ready to proceed?" Judge Kellner asked.

Jake Archibald was on his feet, doing up the top button of his tan jacket. "We're ready, your honor."

"Call your first witness."

There was a collective intake of breath from the gallery of spectators as we waited to see who that witness would be.

The lawyer paused, took a deep breath of his own. "The defense calls Colin Friendly to the stand."

Chapter
15

S tate your name, please."

The accused killer leaned toward the slender black microphone in front of the witness stand and spoke softly into it, his eyes sweeping across the room before settling on the jury box. "Colin Friendly."

"And do you normally reside at 1500 Tenth Street in Lantana, Florida?"

"Yes, sir. I had an apartment there before I was arrested." His voice was pleasant, his accent subtle and melodious. He spoke slowly, carefully enunciating each word.

"What's your occupation, Mr. Friendly?"

"I worked for a waterproofing company."

"In what capacity?"

"I was a foreman."

"And what sort of hours did you work?"

"Whatever hours the job required. Usually from eight till four. Sometimes later."

"Five days a week?"

"Sometimes seven," Colin Friendly stated. "It all depended on how busy we were."

"How old are you, Mr. Friendly?"

"Thirty-two."

"And what is your level of education?"

"I have two years of college."

"What college is that?"

"Florida State University."

"Have you ever been married?"

"Not yet." He smiled directly at Jo Lynn.

Jo Lynn squeezed my hand. My stomach turned over.

"Mr. Friendly," his lawyer began, "you're well aware of the charges against you?"

"I am."

"Is there any truth to those charges?"

"None."

"Did you rape and murder Marie Postelwaite?"

"No, sir."

"Did you rape and murder Christine McDermott?"

"No, sir."

"Did you rape and murder Tammy Fisher?"

"No, sir."

"Did you rape and murder Cathy Doran?"

"No, sir."

"Did you rape and murder Janet McMillan?"

"No, sir."

I found myself counting off each successive name on my fingers, my body growing increasingly numb.

"Did you rape and murder Susan Arnold?"

"No, sir."

"Did you rape and murder Marilyn Greenwood?"

"No, sir."

"Did you rape and murder Marni Smith?"

"No, sir."

"Did you rape and murder Judy Renquist?"

"No, sir."

Jo Lynn leaned toward me, whispered in my ear. "Look at his eyes. You just know he's telling the truth."

I looked at his eyes, saw only evil.

"Did you rape and murder Tracey Secord?" Jake Archibald continued.

"No, sir."

"Did you rape and murder Barbara Weston?"

"No, sir."

I stared at the jury. All eyes were riveted on the accused, all ears hanging on the defense's heartbreaking litany. Could there possibly be one among them who agreed with my sister? And if there was one, could there be more? Was there any chance that Colin Friendly might be acquitted, that he could walk from this courtroom a free man?

"Did you rape and murder Wendy Sabatello?" the defense attorney asked, almost at the end.

"No, sir."

"Did you rape and murder Maureen Elfer?" he concluded, the last of the thirteen unfortunate women.

"No, sir," came the automatic response.

Did you rape and murder Amy Lokash? I added silently. Did you smash her nose, stab her repeatedly, and leave her to die in some hostile swamp? Will we ever learn the truth about what happened to her?

"I could never hurt anybody," Colin Friendly said, as if speaking directly to me.

"Thank you, Mr. Friendly," his lawyer said. "No further questions." Jake Archibald returned to his seat, unbuttoned his jacket, nodded toward Howard Eaves, who rose to his feet, buttoning his.

"You could never hurt anybody," Howard Eaves repeated, speaking before he was fully out of his chair.

"No, sir."

"What about your mother?"

"My m-mother?" Colin Friendly stuttered briefly.

"Oh, see what that miserable man's done," Jo Lynn whispered. "He's upset him. It's okay, baby," she coached. "It'll be all right."

"Didn't you break your mother's nose, send her to the hospital?"

"Objection, your honor," the defense counsel stated, rising reluctantly to his feet. "Irrelevant and prejudicial."

Howard Eaves smiled, patted his thinning hair. "Colin Friendly opened the door to this line of questioning when he stated under direct examination that he would never hurt anybody. The state can prove otherwise. Goes to credibility, your honor."

"I'll allow it," Judge Kellner pronounced.

"Did you break your mother's nose and send her to the hospital?"

Colin Friendly lowered his head. "That was a l-long time ago, sir. I didn't mean to hurt her."

"Didn't you beat her so badly that she had to be hospitalized for almost a week?"

My sister squirmed indignantly in her seat. "The witch. She deserved it after the things she did to Colin."

Colin Friendly looked embarrassed, even ashamed. "I don't know how long she was in the hospital. I felt so terrible about what happened, I left t-town."

"Where is your mother now, Mr. Friendly?"

"I don't know, sir."

"Isn't it true that she went missing about six years ago?"

"Not to my knowledge, no."

"Well, let me ask you this: When was the last time you saw your mother?"

Colin Friendly shook his head, spoke with measured slowness. "It's been a long time."

"Six years?"

"Maybe."

"Did you have anything to do with her disappearance?"

Again, Jake Archibald was on his feet. "Objection, your honor. We have no proof that anything untoward has happened to Mr. Friendly's mother, nor is he on trial for anything concerning her."

"Sustained."

"Well done," my sister said, as Jake Archibald resumed his seat.

Howard Eaves was undaunted. He faced the jury while directing his questions at the accused. "Tell me, Mr. Friendly, did you know any of the murdered women?"

"No, sir."

"You'd never met any of them?"

"Not to my knowledge. I was p-pretty busy working," he continued, then swallowed, as if trying to swallow his stutter. "You don't meet a lot of women in the waterproofing business." He flashed one of his patented little half-smiles toward the jury. Several responded with little half-smiles of their own.

"What about the testimony of the witnesses who placed you near some of the victims at around the time of their disappearances?"

"They're m-mistaken, sir."

"You never attended a party at 426 Lakeview Drive in Boynton Beach?"

"No, sir."

"You never spoke to a young woman named Angela Riegert?"

"No, sir."

"And yet she positively identified you."

"She m-must be confusing me with s-somebody else."

"You never left the party with Wendy Sabatello?"

"I wasn't at the party, sir," Colin Friendly replied clearly. "Why would I be there? I'm a l-lot older than those kids."

"And what about Marcia Layton, who testified having seen you in Flagler Park on several occasions?"

"It's p-possible she saw me," he admitted. "Sometimes when I'd be working, I'd go to a nearby p-park to have my lunch."

"Did you meet Marni Smith in the park?"

"No, sir."

"Did you ask directions from Janet McMillan?"

"No, sir. I've l-lived in Florida all my life. I pretty much know where everything is."

"So, you're saying that, to the best of your knowledge, you've never had any contact with any of the murdered women?"

"None, sir."

"And all the witnesses who have positively identified you are mistaken," Howard Eaves stated rather than asked.

"Yes, sir."

"Seems strange, doesn't it? That so many people would have identified you incorrectly."

"A l-lot of people look the way I do," Colin Friendly volunteered.

"You think so?"

"There's nothing very special about me."

"Unfortunately, that's all too true," the prosecutor said.

Jake Archibald immediately objected, and Howard Eaves retracted his comment.

"How do you explain the seventy percent probability that it was your semen found in many of the victims' bodies?"

Colin Friendly shook his head, his lips a cruel snarl. "Seventy percent's barely a passing grade."

"Are you disputing the conclusions of the medical examiner?"

"If he says it's my semen, then he's wrong."

"And the bite marks on several of the victims? How do you explain how closely they match the mold taken of your mouth?"

"Close only counts in horseshoes," Colin Friendly said without a trace of stammer. The snarl twisted into a smirk. He winked boldly at my sister, then settled back in his chair, as if he'd somehow gained the upper hand.

"How do you explain the close matchup with your saliva?"

"It's not my job to explain it, Mr. Eaves."

"But if you had to make a guess . . ."

"I'd say that someone obviously made a mistake."

"I suggest that someone is you, Mr. Friendly."

"I suggest that someone is you, Mr. Eaves," came the immediate retort.

A slight gasp rippled through the courtroom.

"You think you're smarter than I am, don't you, Mr. Friendly?"

"I can't say I've given the matter much thought, Mr. Eaves."

"In fact, you think you're smarter than most people, isn't that correct?"

"Most people aren't very smart," Colin agreed, clearly starting to enjoy himself.

"And it's fun tricking them, isn't it?"

"You tell me, Mr. Eaves. Seems like you're the one interested in tricking people."

"It's a great feeling having the power of life and death over people, isn't it, Mr. Friendly?"

"You're the one here with that kind of power, sir, not me."

"No. That power rests with the members of the jury."

"Then I can only hope they'll be more interested in the truth than you are," Colin stated coolly.

"And the truth is?"

"That I'm not guilty, sir."

Jo Lynn leaned toward me. "He's very polite, don't you think?"

The prosecutor thrust a large color photograph of one of the dead girls into Colin Friendly's face. "You didn't do this?"

Jake Archibald was immediately on his feet. "Objection, your honor. This is unnecessary. The witness has already answered the question."

"Overruled."

"Your honor," Jake Archibald said, "may we approach?"

The two adversaries approached the bench.

"Damn that Mr. Eaves," Jo Lynn whispered. "He'll stop at nothing to get a conviction." She crossed, uncrossed, then recrossed her legs, her skirt flipping back and forth, exposing first one thigh, then the other, then the first again. "But I don't think the jury's buying it. See that woman, the one in the middle in the second row, I think she's on our side."

I looked toward the middle juror in the second row. She was younger than the other members of the jury, maybe thirty years old, with pale skin and badly styled blond hair that did nothing to enhance her generally nondescript features. I realized that I'd never noticed her before, and wondered if not being noticed was something she'd grown used to. Would she be the type to be charmed by the likes of Colin Friendly? Was this trial her chance to step into the spotlight, to grab for her fifteen minutes of fame, to force a nation's attention her way by being the lone hold-out for an acquittal? Would her obstinacy force a retrial?

I shuddered, not having considered the possibility of a hung jury until now. Anxiety tugged at my heart. Why couldn't the forensic evidence have been more conclusive? "Close only counts in horseshoes," I heard Colin repeat. All it took was one not-guilty vote, I realized. And then what? Another trial? More months of anguish for the victims' families and friends? More months of headlines and depressing news reports? More months of my sister haunting courtooms and visiting jails? I sighed deeply. I didn't think I could go through it again.

"Something the matter?" Jo Lynn asked, eyes scanning the room.

"It's hot in here."

"No, it's not. You're just warm because your boyfriend's here."

"What?" I spun around. Robert smiled at me from his seat at the back. Oh God, I thought, perspiration breaking out across my forehead. When had he come in?

"Relax, Kate. Nobody's going to spill your little secret."

"I don't have any secrets," I hissed between clenched teeth.

Jo Lynn smiled. "Tell it to the judge," she said.

"The objection is overruled," the judge was saying, sending the lawyers back to their battle stations. "The witness may answer the question."

"This isn't your handiwork?" Howard Eaves repeated immediately, handing the photo to the defendant.

"No, sir."

"What about this?" The prosecutor pushed a series of pictures into Colin's hands. "You didn't leave those bite marks on Christine McDermott's buttocks? You didn't slit little Tammy Fisher's throat?"

"No, sir. I c-certainly did not."

"And yet, I notice that you have no trouble looking at the photographs."

"Objection, your honor," Jake Archibald protested.

"Sustained."

"I c-could never do anything like that." Colin Friendly looked directly at my sister. "You have to believe me, Jo Lynn."

"I believe you, Colin." Heads snapped toward us as my sister rose to her feet.

"Sit down, young lady," the judge ordered, banging on his gavel, as excited whispers spun circles around us.

"It doesn't matter what anybody else thinks," Colin continued, "as long as I know you believe in me."

The entire courtroom now pivoted in our direction. I found myself holding my breath. Oh God, I thought, please let this be all a bad dream.

"I love you, Jo Lynn," Colin Friendly was saying over the mounting din. "I want to marry you."

"Order in the court," Judge Kellner bellowed.

"I love you too," my sister cried. "There's nothing I want more than to be your wife."

The courtroom erupted, people laughing, hooting with surprise, reporters scrambling for the door, everyone on their feet at once.

"Sit down," the judge ordered my sister, "or I'll hold you in contempt."

"Please, no," I muttered, feeling sick to my stomach.

In the next instant, I was pushing past my sister into the aisle and out of the courtroom.

"We'll take a half-hour recess," I heard the judge shout as I reached the darkness of the small anteroom.

"Kate, hurry," a voice beckoned. "This way." An arm pulled me into the corridor, guided me into the sanctuary of the empty courtroom next door.

"Oh God," I cried, my body heaving, my breath coming in short, angry bursts. "Were you there? Did you see what happened?"

"I was there," Robert said.

"Did you see what they did? Did you hear what they said?"

His arms reached for me. "Kate, try to calm down."

"She told that monster she'd marry him. Right out in open court, my sister stood up and told the world she loves a crazy man, that she wants to marry him."

"Kate, it's all right, it'll be all right."

I was sobbing now. "Why is she doing this, Robert? What is she trying to prove? Does she want the publicity, is that it? Does she want to be a star on *Hard Copy*? Does she want to make the front page of the *National Enquirer*? What is the matter with her?"

His arms were around me. "I don't know what her problem is, but you can't let it get to you."

"You don't think that she'll really marry that monster, do you? I mean, you don't think that the jury will actually find him not guilty, that there's any chance they'll let him go."

"I don't think there's a chance in hell of that happening."

"I want him to die," I cried. "I want him to die and get out of our lives."

"Ssh," Robert said gently as I buried my face against his chest. "Don't worry. It'll all be over soon."

He held me tight against him, one hand stroking the back of my hair, as if I were a small child who'd scraped her knee and needed comforting. My own arms reached around him, clung to him as if I were drowning, as if he were the only thing keeping me afloat. His lips grazed the sides of my cheeks, kissing away my tears, assuring me without words that everything would be all right, that he was there to ensure that nothing bad could ever happen to me again.

And then he was kissing me, really kissing me, full on the lips, and I was kissing him back, with a passion that astounded me. Suddenly, I was a sophomore in high school and he was a senior, and our lives were just beginning and everything was right with the world.

Except that we were no longer in high school, our lives were half over, and my world was quickly disintegrating into dust. "This is the last thing I need," I told Robert, breaking free of his embrace, trying to make sense of what was happening.

But even as I regained my composure and walked from the room, past the throng of reporters who crowded the corridors clamoring for my sister's attention, and toward the bank of waiting elevators, I knew it was too late, that there was a very good chance my world would never make sense again.

Chapter

16

I tried burying myself in my work. It wasn't easy. Everywhere I looked, there were my sister and her "fiance," as she had taken to referring to him on television and in print. Their pictures tormented me from the front pages of every newspaper and tabloid in town; Jo Lynn gave interviews to *Hard Copy* and appeared twice on *Inside Edition*, although on both broadcasts she mercifully refrained from mentioning she had a sister. Since our last names were different—she went by her second husband's name because she liked the sound of it with Jo Lynn—no one made the connection between us. Because we never traveled in the same circles, her newfound notoriety was not a problem to me either socially or professionally. Still, I was embarrassed—I like to think more for her sake than for mine, but truthfully, I'm not sure—and deeply concerned about both my sister's mental state and her well-being.

Sara, of course, pronounced the situation "cool"; Larry, as usual, ignored the whole business; Michelle asked simply, "What's *wrong* with her?" As for my mother, she seemed oblivious to the commotion raging around her younger child. She never commented on the many stories in the newspapers or the ubiquitous interviews on TV. When I asked if she'd seen Jo Lynn's picture on the front page of the *Palm Beach Post*, she said only that I should save her a copy, then never mentioned it again. Only Mrs. Winchell called to voice her concerns, her main worry being that all the publicity might adversely impact on the Palm Beach Lakes Retirement Home should it become known that Jo Lynn's mother was a resident, and perhaps we might consider moving her someplace else. She needn't have worried. Jo Lynn showed no inclination to share the spotlight.

Robert phoned on an almost daily basis, but I was afraid to return his calls. Surely my life was chaotic enough without the addition of an extramarital affair, although his messages made no mention of what had happened between us. He asked only if I'd come up with any ideas, professionally speaking, and said nothing about the decidedly unprofessional kiss we had shared. Actually, I did have an idea I thought was pretty good, but I was growing increasingly fearful of both him and the media, and was no longer sure I wanted any part of either. Besides, if I were to have my own show, then surely, at some point, some ambitious reporter would discover the connection between my sister and me. Indeed, Jo Lynn would probably be my first caller.

"My sister's always criticizing me," I could hear her shout across the airwaves. "She doesn't approve of my choice of clothes or my choice of men. She doesn't think I'm capable of making an adult decision without her input. Just because she's a professional, she thinks she knows everything. She's always telling me what to do and I'm sick of it. What do you advise?"

"I'm sorry, what did you say?" It was almost six o'clock one evening, and Ellie and Richard Lifeson, a young couple in their late twenties, were staring at me expectantly across the coffee table in my office, obviously awaiting some inspired words of wisdom to tumble from my

lips. I realized that I had no idea what we'd been discussing, and silently cursed Jo Lynn, blaming her for my inability to concentrate. Immediately, I was back in the courtroom, watching as the accused serial killer proclaimed his love for my sister for all to hear. What had Colin Friendly hoped to prove with his little stunt? What had he been trying to gain? Sympathy? Support? What? "What?" I asked again, as Ellie and Richard Lifeson exchanged worried glances. "I'm sorry, could you repeat what you just said?"

"She's always telling me what to do, and I'm sick of it," Richard Lifeson repeated.

"I don't tell him what to do," his wife protested.

They were a nice-looking couple, fresh-faced and well scrubbed. They'd been married three years; it was the first marriage for both; they had no children; they were contemplating divorce. I checked my notes to reacquaint myself with the particulars of their situation, then my watch to determine how much of the session I'd already missed.

"Are you kidding?" Richard Lifeson asked. "Tell her what happened right before we got here."

"Why don't *you* tell me," I suggested, concentrating on his wide forehead, his square jaw, in a concerted effort to keep Colin Friendly out of my office, out of my thoughts.

"I wanted to buy some potato chips," he began, "and she tells me to get that new low-fat kind. I don't like the low-fat kind, they have no taste, and why should she care, she doesn't eat them anyway. But, of course, what kind do I end up having to buy? Guess."

"I never said you had to buy them. I just made a suggestion."

"Her Majesty never suggests anything. She issues proclamations."

"There he goes again, putting me down. He's always putting me down. I can't say one thing to him without his putting me down."

"Like what?" Richard Lifeson asked. "When do I put you down?"

"Try last night when we went to my niece's ballet recital," Ellie Lifeson answered before I could step in. "After it was over, he asked me which dance I liked best and I told him I liked the one with the swans, and he said, 'That just shows how little you know about ballet.' And we

end up in this huge fight, so, of course, we go to bed angry, and we don't make love. Again," she added pointedly.

"You going to order me to make love to you now?" Richard Lifeson demanded.

"Okay, wait, wait," I said calmly. "There are a lot of issues here. Let's try to take them one at a time. First, with regard to the potato chips: Ellie, you think you're being helpful; Richard, you think she's being dictatorial. This is a gender issue. Women think they're making suggestions. Men hear them as orders."

"I'm not allowed to make suggestions?"

"I know it won't be easy, Ellie, but try to curb your desire to help out. And, Richard, you have to learn to stand your ground. If you don't want low-fat potato chips, you have to say so."

"And get into a huge argument?"

"You get into a huge argument anyway," I told him. "Maybe not about the potato chips, but all that repressed anger is going to come out somewhere."

"She's the one who's always angry."

"Because you're always putting me down."

"Try to avoid words like 'always' and 'never.' They're counter-productive and inflammatory. And, Ellie, remember that nobody can put you down unless you allow it. Let me show you how the conversation after the ballet recital could have gone. Ellie, I'll be you; you be Richard. 'So, Richard,' " I began, addressing my comments to Ellie, " 'which dance did you like best?' "

Ellie automatically deepened her voice, speaking as if she were Richard. " 'I liked the modern one at the end. What about you?' "

" 'I liked the one with the swans,' " I told her.

" 'That just shows how little you know about ballet,' " Ellie huffed.

" 'You didn't like it?' "

" 'I thought it was terrible.' "

" 'That's very interesting,' " I said. " 'I liked it. I guess we have different tastes.' "

Ellie and Richard stared at me in silence.

"You see?" I said. "Nobody gets put down; nobody fights."

"It's that simple?" Richard asked.

"Nothing's simple," I told him. "It's a whole new way of relating, a brand-new vocabulary. It'll take time to learn, even more time to put into practice. But eventually, it gets a little easier."

They looked skeptical.

"I promise," I said.

At home, Larry and I were at each other's throats.

"Sara's teacher called today," I announced one evening as Larry sat, feet comfortably up on the ottoman, watching a hockey game on TV. The girls were in their rooms, supposedly doing homework.

"What did she have to say?"

"Who said her teacher is a woman?"

"Sorry, I just assumed."

"Are all teachers necessarily female?"

"Of course not. What did this teacher have to say?"

"She said that Sara has been . . ."

"*She?*" Larry asked. "So, her teacher *is* a woman?"

"This one is, yes."

"The one who called."

"Yes. What's the big deal?"

"You're the one who made it a big deal," he said.

"Are you interested in what she had to say or not?"

"Yes, I said I was."

"I don't remember you saying any such thing."

"Maybe if you paid attention."

"You're saying you don't get enough attention?"

"Just tell me what Sara's teacher had to say," he said.

"She said that Sara has been acting very strangely."

"She just noticed?" He smiled.

I refused the chance to smile back. "Stranger than usual," I said.

"How so?"

"Nothing she could put her finger on."

"That's helpful."

"Are you going to treat this whole conversation as a joke?"

"I'm certainly not going to get all worked up about it."

"You never do."

"What's that supposed to mean?"

"It means that I'm starting to feel like a single parent around here."

"Excuse me? You want to clarify that statement?"

"It means you're never here."

"I'm *never* here?"

"You're always on the golf course."

"I'm *always* on the golf course?"

"When you're not at work," I qualified.

"Oh, so I work. Well, thanks for noticing."

"It really doesn't bother you that our daughter is failing?"

"She's failing?"

"She failed her last two English tests."

"Have you talked to her about it?"

"Why should I be the one who talks to her about it?"

"All right. Do you want me to talk to her about it?"

"And just what would you say?"

He was on his feet. "I don't know. I guess I'll find out when I get there."

"I don't think you should put her on the defensive."

"I wasn't planning to put her on the defensive."

"Just tell her that her teacher called and that she's very concerned about Sara's recent behavior."

"If you're going to tell me what to say, why don't you talk to her yourself?"

"Because I always talk to her, and I'm tired of being the one who takes care of everybody's problems. I do it all day at work, and when I come home, I'd like somebody else to shoulder a little bit of the responsibility. Is that too much to ask?"

"Apparently, since you won't let me do it."

"I'm just trying to help you. Is your ego so frail that you can't take a few simple suggestions?"

"Is your ego so inflated that you can't imagine I might not need them?"

"You're really a bastard sometimes, you know that?"

He flipped off the television, walked out of the family room.

"Where are you going?"

"To bed."

"I thought we were having a discussion."

"The discussion is over."

"Why? Because you say it is?"

"That's right."

I followed him into our bedroom. "That's very mature."

"I thought one of us should be."

"Meaning?"

He reached the bed, started throwing pillows into the air. "I don't want to fight with you, Kate. I don't have the strength. I'm tired. You've been on my back all week."

"I've been on your back?"

"Yes."

"How could I be on your back when you're never here?"

"I don't know, but you manage." He tossed the remaining pillows on the floor. One landed close to my feet.

"Watch that!" I yelped, as if I'd been injured.

He looked startled. "Watch what?"

"You almost hit me with that."

"What are you talking about? It's nowhere near you." He pulled down the covers of the bed, started undressing.

"Don't you dare go to sleep," I told him.

"Kate, it's been a long day. You're obviously all worked up about something, and I don't think it has anything to do with either Sara or me."

"Oh, really? And when did you earn your psychology degree?"

"Let's stop before we say things we'll regret."

"I don't want to stop. I want to know what you think I'm so worked up about."

"I don't know. Maybe your sister, maybe your mother, maybe something happened at work that I don't know about."

"Or maybe it's you," I shot back.

"Maybe it is," he agreed. "Maybe you're right, and I'm the problem. I accept it. You've made your point. You win. I'm a rotten human being."

"I never said you were a rotten human being."

"I'm sure you were getting to it."

"Don't put words in my mouth."

"I'd like to put a gag in your mouth."

"What?" I gasped. "Are you threatening me?"

Anger flushed his cheeks bright red. "I'm suggesting that we both shut up and try to get some sleep."

"You're telling me to shut up?"

"I'm telling you to get some sleep."

"I don't want to get some sleep."

"Then shut the fuck up!" he shouted, and climbed into bed.

And then he didn't say another word. No matter what I said or did, how much I tried to provoke him, how hard I tried to pull him back into the fray, he wouldn't bite. Instead, he withdrew, burying himself inside his covers as if inside a cocoon. The harder I tried to drag him out, the farther he retreated.

I accused him of being a poor husband, a bad father, an indifferent son.

He sighed and turned over.

I accused him of caring more for his golf game than his family.

He put a pillow over his ears.

I said he was selfish, childish, and mean.

He brought the comforter up over his head.

I told him he was being passive-aggressive.

He feigned sleep.

I told him to go to hell.

He pretended to snore.

I stormed from the room.

We didn't speak for three days.

It didn't help that I knew Larry was right. He wasn't the problem. Maybe I would have liked it had he spent more time at home on the weekends, but, truthfully, I didn't begrudge him his golf games. Maybe I was even a little jealous. At least Larry had somewhere to go, a place to escape the insanity that seemed everywhere around us. I had nowhere. Work didn't help—it only compounded my confusion. I was so busy being in control at the office that I was losing it at home. Larry was my scapegoat, and for a while, he seemed to understand this, but there's only so much understanding a person can have.

What I really wanted was for Larry to take me in his arms, as Robert had done that morning in the courthouse, and to tell me that everything was going to be okay: Sara would get out of high school and into the college of her choice; my mother would slough off her alien skin and become the woman I'd known and loved all my life; my sister would get off the front pages and back to her senses; Colin Friendly would die and we'd get on with our lives. Was that too much to ask?

But even when Larry did just that, it wasn't enough.

"It's okay," he said one evening as I cried softly against his shoulder. The trial had concluded that afternoon, and despite predictions of a speedy verdict, the jury had been out for over five hours. Reporters were now speculating that if a verdict wasn't returned within the hour, the jury would be dismissed for the weekend.

"What could possibly be taking them so long?" I asked.

"I think they're just going over all the evidence, and that by this time on Monday, it'll all be over," Larry said, telling me what he knew I needed to hear. "Colin Friendly will be on death row; your sister will be back to normal. Well, normal is a relative concept when it comes to your sister," he said, and I laughed gratefully. And then we were kissing, softly at first, and then with greater urgency.

It had been several weeks, I realized, since we'd made love. In fact, the last time a man had kissed me this way, it hadn't been Larry at all, but Robert. "Oh God," I said guiltily.

Of course, Larry misinterpreted my guilt for passion, and suggested

we go into the bedroom. It was Friday night and the girls were both out for the evening.

"Do you think this is a good idea?" I asked between kisses, as he led me into our room, stopping beside our bed.

"Best idea I've had in weeks," he said, sending the fourteen decorative pillows to the floor with one wide sweep of his arm.

"What if the kids come home?"

"They won't."

"What if they do?"

"I'll close the door," he said, leaving my side to close the door. In the next instant, his lips were back on mine, and his hands were at my breasts, undoing my blouse. "I've missed you," he said, slipping the blouse off my shoulders and onto the carpet.

"I've missed you too," I told him, as his fingers gently teased my nipples through the lace of my bra. "That tickles," I said, feeling mildly irritated, though I wasn't sure why.

His fingers fidgeted with the hooks of my bra.

"I'll do it," I said.

"No, let me," he urged softly. "I'm just a little out of practice, that's all." He struggled for several more seconds before I ran out of patience and reached behind me to unsnap the recalcitrant hooks.

"I wanted to do that," he said.

"Don't whine," I started to say, but he covered my mouth with his kisses, and pushed me down on the bed, his lips moving to my bare breasts, fastening themselves on my nipples.

In the past, this was always something I enjoyed. Now it annoyed me. As Larry sucked on first one breast, then the other, I found myself growing increasingly angry. "That tickles," I said again, squirming away from his insistent mouth.

He moved on, undoing the zipper of my gray trousers and sliding them easily off my hips.

"Careful with those," I admonished as he tossed them aside, his fingers tracing the outline of my lace panties, his lips returning to my nipples. I felt nothing, no sexual stirring of any kind. Just growing irritability. I tried fantasizing: I was a slave girl being auctioned off to the

highest bidder. There were perhaps a dozen men pawing me, lifting my skirt to inspect the merchandise, exposing me to their hungry eyes . . .

It didn't work. I tried another. I was a college student whose professor had given her a failing grade. What could I do? I begged him. I'd already told my parents I was getting straight A's. I could come to him after class, he told me, wearing nothing but a garter belt and stockings . . .

I shook my head, pushed Larry's head away from my breasts. Nothing was working.

Larry pulled my panties down, buried his head between my thighs. I waited anxiously to feel some release, felt nothing but frustration.

"That hurts," I told him after several minutes.

"Just relax," he said. "You're so uptight."

"I'm uptight because you're hurting me."

"How am I hurting you?"

"You're applying too much pressure."

He shifted his weight, adjusted his position. "How's this? Better?"

"You're not in the right place," I said, my voice testy.

"Show me."

"I don't want to show you."

He raised himself on his elbows. "What's wrong, honey?"

"You're not in the right place," I repeated stubbornly, knowing I was being unfair, knowing the right place was anywhere away from me. "Let's just forget it. It's not going to work."

"Let me try again," he said.

"No," I said loudly, drawing my legs together, staring toward the window. I didn't have to see his face to feel the hurt on it.

The phone rang.

"Don't answer it," Larry pleaded softly.

I reached over, grateful for the interruption, and lifted the receiver to my ear. "Hello," I said as Larry turned away.

"Kate, oh God, Kate." It was Jo Lynn. She was sobbing.

"What is it? What's happened?"

"The jury came back. They just announced their verdict."

I held my breath. Was she sobbing from disappointment or relief?

"I can't believe it, Kate. They found him guilty. Guilty!"

I closed my eyes. Thank God, I uttered silently.

"Are you all right?" I asked my sister as Larry edged his body off the bed.

"I can't believe it," she repeated. "How could they do that when he didn't do it? It's so unfair."

"Do you want to come over?" I asked as Larry walked from the room.

I could feel her shaking her head. "No. I don't know what to do."

"I think you should go home, get a good night's sleep . . ."

"They found him guilty," she cried, not listening to me. "He's my whole life. Oh God, Kate, what am I going to do now?"

Chapter
17

Two days before Christmas, my mother disappeared.

I was in the middle of an argument with Sara when the phone rang. "Could you get that?" I asked. We were in the family room, and I was on my knees, stacking the last of the Christmas presents around the tall, ornament-laden spruce tree.

Sara remained where she was, in the middle of the room, impossibly long legs planted firmly apart on the tile floor, stubborn hands poised on improbably slim hips. She was wearing elasticized black leggings, a cherry-red, too short, too tight tank top, and ankle-length black boots with three-inch heels that exaggerated her already considerable height. Her hair, like parchment paper, had yellowed from continual exposure to the sun, except for the dark roots that framed her oval face like a wide headband. To say she was a formidable-looking opponent would be something of an understatement. In fact, she was terrifying. "The an-

swering machine will pick it up," she said, not budging. "Why won't you give me any money?"

"Because I don't feel like paying for my own Christmas presents again this year," I told her truthfully, as the phone fell mercifully silent. "I think you're old enough now to be buying gifts for people with your own money."

"What money?"

"Money you're supposed to have saved. Christmas isn't exactly a surprise. You've had lots of time to prepare. Michelle's been saving her money for months." I knew it was a mistake the minute the words were out of my mouth.

"Sure, compare me with Michelle, why don't you?" Sara threw her arms into the air, in a gesture that was simultaneously threatening and full of defeat.

"I didn't mean to compare you with Michelle."

"You're always comparing us. Little Miss Perfect, she can't do anything wrong. Little Miss Bitch," she sneered.

"Sara! Stop it right now. Leave your sister out of this."

"You're the one who brought her in."

"Yes, and I'm sorry."

"So nobody will get any presents from me this year because I don't have any money," she repeated.

I shrugged. "That's too bad."

"Yeah, you sound really broken up about it."

The phone rang again.

"You're determined to embarrass me, aren't you?" Sara continued, trying a new approach. "Just because I'm not organized like Michelle, because I'm different than you guys, you're trying to punish me."

God help me, I thought, clambering to my feet, heading for the phone on the counter that separated the kitchen from the family room. "Hello."

"Mrs. Sinclair?"

"Yes."

"Thank God. I tried you a few minutes ago and got your machine."

"Mrs. Winchell?" I asked, connecting a face to the harried voice on

the other end of the line. "What's wrong? Has something happened to my mother?"

There was an ominous silence. "Then she's not with you?"

"If I were Michelle, I bet you'd give me the money," Sara raged, pacing back and forth in front of the counter.

"What do you mean?" I asked Mrs. Winchell.

"I mean, if I were Michelle, there wouldn't be any problem," Sara said.

"We can't find your mother," Mrs. Winchell said.

"What do you mean, you can't find my mother?" I demanded. "Would you stop that!" I shouted at my daughter, whose pacing came to an abrupt halt.

"I beg your pardon?" Mrs. Winchell asked sheepishly.

"Don't yell at me," Sara snapped.

"Please tell me what happened," I urged Mrs. Winchell.

Mrs. Winchell cleared her throat, paused, cleared it again. "Your mother didn't come down for breakfast this morning, and when we went to check on her, we discovered she wasn't in her apartment, and her bed hadn't been slept in. I was hoping that she was with you, what with Christmas and everything, and that you'd just forgotten to inform us."

"She isn't here." My eyes shot aimlessly around the room, as if my mother might be hiding behind the large silk palm tree in the corner.

"Is there any chance she's with your sister?"

"None," I said, then promised to check with her anyway. "Have you searched the building?"

"Who's missing?" Sara asked. "Is Grandma missing?"

"We're searching it now."

"I'll be there as soon as I can."

"I'm sure we'll find her," Mrs. Winchell said, although the quiver in her voice told me otherwise. "If she's wandered off somewhere, she can't have gotten very far."

If she's been walking all night, she could be halfway to Georgia by now, I thought as I punched in my sister's number, picturing my mother walking along the center line of the freeway, falling off a bridge into the Intracoastal Waterway, or wading fully clothed into the ocean.

"Jo Lynn, is Mom with you?" I asked as soon as I heard my sister's voice.

"Is this a joke?" she asked in return.

"She's missing. I'll pick you up in five minutes," I said, hanging up before she could object, grabbing my purse, and running for the door.

"I'm coming with you," Sara said, right behind me.

I didn't object. Truthfully, I was grateful for the company.

"Have you found her?" I demanded as my sister, my daughter, and I stormed into Mrs. Winchell's office. We must have been quite a sight— my yellow-haired Amazonian daughter with her black roots, three-inch heels, and forty-inch bosom, my similarly endowed sister, her hair wild and uncombed, with her white mini-dress barely grazing the top of her thighs, and me with no makeup, blue jeans, and crazed visage, all of us towering above poor, petite Mrs. Winchell, who took several instinctive steps back when she saw us.

"Not yet," she said, her dark face pinched with worry, "but I'm sure we will."

"How can you be sure," Jo Lynn said, "when you have no idea where she is?"

"Have you notified the police?" I asked.

"Of course. They're keeping their eyes open for her. So far, they haven't found . . ."

". . . any bodies," Jo Lynn said.

"Anyone matching her description," Mrs. Winchell corrected.

"Half of Florida matches her description," my sister told her.

"And in the meantime," I interrupted, "what's being done?"

"We've searched all the common rooms, and the kitchen, and the garage. So far, nothing. We have staff checking all the floors."

"I don't understand, how could this have happened?" I knew the question was pointless, but asked it anyway.

"It's hard to keep track of everyone twenty-four hours a day. This isn't a hospital. It's strictly a facility for assisted living," Mrs. Winchell

reminded me, as I marveled over the phrase "assisted living." "The residents are free to come and go as they please. We check on them every morning, of course. If someone doesn't come down for breakfast and they haven't previously informed us, then well . . ." Her voice drifted off. "I'm sure she'll turn up."

"Bad pennies always do," Jo Lynn said, only half under her breath.

I almost smiled. Despite the circumstances, it was nice to know that my sister seemed to have snapped out of her self-imposed mourning and was back to her usual caustic self. Our mother always managed to bring out the best in her, I thought, wondering where on earth she could be.

It was almost two hours before they found her.

A janitor discovered her hiding behind the central air-conditioning unit in the main utility room. She'd somehow managed to squeeze between the unit and the wall, a not inconsiderable feat, considering the tiny amount of space, and it took three workers almost half an hour to extricate her. When they finally brought her to Mrs. Winchell's office, she was bruised and whimpering, and the front of her mint-green dress was dirty and torn.

"My turn to hide now?" Jo Lynn asked when she saw her.

I rushed to my mother's side, took her in my arms, hugged her gently to me. "Are you all right?"

"Hello, dear," she said. "What are you doing here?"

"What happened, Grandma?" Sara asked, laying a gentle hand on her grandmother's back. "Why were you hiding behind the air conditioner?"

"Someone was after me," my mother confided with a wink. "But I tricked them."

"Were you there all night?" I asked.

"I don't know," she answered, rubbing her arms. "Maybe. I'm a little stiff."

"You must be hungry," Mrs. Winchell said. "I'll arrange to have some breakfast sent to your room, and of course we'll get you all cleaned up and have a doctor look at you."

"Who was after you?" Sara asked.

"I don't know." My mother's unsteady hands reached over to

stroke Sara's hair. "You're a pretty thing, aren't you?" she said. "Are you new here?"

I watched Sara's features crumple even as her eyes grew wide. "Don't you recognize me, Grandma?" she asked, her voice as small as a child's. "It's me, Sara, your granddaughter."

"Sara?"

"I've changed my hair color," Sara explained.

"So you have," my mother said, and smiled. "I think I'd like to lie down now." Watery eyes swept across the room. "Would you mind? I seem to be very tired."

"Of course not," I told her. "You rest for a while. We'll see you later."

〜

"It was the hair color," Sara said as we crossed the parking lot to my car. "That's why she didn't recognize me. It's my hair."

"Time to get those roots done, kid," my sister said.

"My mother won't give me any money."

I unlocked the car door. We climbed inside, Sara beside me, Jo Lynn in the back. Jo Lynn's hand instantly flopped over the front seat, waved five twenty-dollar bills beside Sara's head. "Here. My treat. Christmas comes a day early."

"Wow. This is so cool."

"You're in a good mood," I said, deciding not to be angry with Jo Lynn's impromptu generosity.

"Our mother is safe," she said sarcastically, flopping back in her seat. "All is right with the world."

"Who do you think was after her?" Sara asked.

"Her conscience," Jo Lynn said.

"Her conscience?" Sara repeated.

"What's that supposed to mean?" I asked.

"It means I'm hungry," Jo Lynn said. "It means we stop for lunch. My treat."

"I don't have time," I began.

"Everybody has time to eat," Jo Lynn pronounced. "What kind of example are you setting for your daughter? You want her to turn into one of those scrawny anorexics?"

I didn't think there was much chance of that, but I agreed to stop for lunch.

"We'll go to the mall," Jo Lynn said as I turned onto I-95. "That way, we can eat, Sara can get her hair done, and we can do some last-minute Christmas shopping."

"Not me," Sara said. "Mom won't give me any money to buy presents."

"Mean Mommy," Jo Lynn said, and laughed. "Don't worry, kid, I have lots of money. You can buy whatever you want."

"And where is all this money coming from?" I asked. "Did you get a job?"

Jo Lynn made a sound halfway between a laugh and a snort. "You don't want to know," she said.

I decided she was probably right, so I said nothing further.

Sara, however, had no such qualms. "Where'd you get the money?" she asked.

Jo Lynn required no further prompting. She lurched forward, leaned her elbows on the back of the front seat, rested her head on her hands. "I promised the *Enquirer* an exclusive. They paid me half the money in advance."

"An exclusive what?" Sara asked as I tried to block my ears to the inevitable.

I could feel Jo Lynn's smile burning a hole in the back of my neck. "An exclusive on my wedding," she said.

"What is it going to take to convince you that the man you're so intent on marrying is a homicidal maniac?" I asked Jo Lynn as soon as Sara took off to get her hair done. We were sitting in the crowded food court on the second level of the Gardens Mall, Jo Lynn taking her time with a piece of apple pie, me on my fourth cup of coffee.

"Nothing you could say would ever convince me, so you might as well stop wasting your breath."

"Don't you understand that the man would just as soon kill you as look at you?"

"Don't *you* understand that I really don't appreciate these kinds of comments?"

"And *I* don't appreciate you undermining my authority."

"What authority do you have where Colin is concerned?"

"I'm not talking about Colin. I'm talking about Sara."

"Whoa! Hold on a minute." Jo Lynn made a sweeping gesture with her hands, elegant magenta nails fluttering before my face. "When did we make the switch?"

"I told Sara I wasn't giving her any money this Christmas . . ."

"How can you not give the kid money to buy Christmas presents?" Jo Lynn interrupted.

"That's not the point."

"The point is it's my money," Jo Lynn said, "and if I want to give money to my niece so she won't be embarrassed on Christmas morning, then that's what I'll do. Don't be such a grinch. She'll probably buy you something fabulous."

"I don't need anything fabulous."

"You need something, that's for sure."

"Some sane relatives might be nice."

Jo Lynn swallowed another piece of pie. "So, what do you think is the matter with the old girl anyway?"

"I don't know."

"What's your educated guess?"

She underlined the word "educated," making it sound vaguely obscene. I closed my eyes, took a deep breath, and released it slowly. When I opened them, I noticed several teenage boys looking our way, snickering behind closed fingers.

"You don't think it could be Alzheimer's, do you?" Jo Lynn asked.

It was a possibility I'd deliberately refused to consider, and one that, even now, I admitted to my vocabulary with only the greatest of reluctance.

"She has all the symptoms," Jo Lynn continued. "She's disoriented; she's paranoid; she's forgetful."

"That doesn't necessarily mean . . ."

"You said yourself she was losing it when we found the dishwashing detergent in her fridge."

"Still . . ."

"She didn't recognize Sara."

"It was her hair."

"It wasn't her hair."

"I know," I said, admitting defeat.

"So, you think it's Alzheimer's?"

"I think there's a good chance."

"Damn!" Jo Lynn snapped, pushing what was left of her apple pie halfway across the table with an angry flip of her fingers. "Damn it to hell. That makes me so mad."

I was surprised by the ferocity of Jo Lynn's reaction. I'd expected her to treat this latest development regarding our mother with her usual degree of casual disinterest.

"There's no point in getting angry about it," I told her. "If it's Alzheimer's, then, unfortunately, there's not much we can do. We just have to make sure she's as comfortable as possible."

"Why would I want to do that?"

Now I was really confused. "You don't want her to be comfortable?"

"I want her to get exactly what she deserves."

"Meaning?"

"Why couldn't she get cancer like everybody else?"

"Jo Lynn!"

"A little suffering is good for the soul. Isn't that what they say?"

"You want her to suffer?"

"Why shouldn't she? What makes her so damn special that she should get off scot-free?"

"She's your mother."

"So, what does that mean? That I'm just supposed to forgive and forget? That the past gets wiped clean? She won't remember it, so I might as well pretend it never happened? Is that what you're telling me?"

"What is it you want her to remember? I don't understand."

"Of course you don't." Jo Lynn shook her head, dislodging several angry tears. "You never have."

"I'd like to try," I said honestly.

Jo Lynn jumped to her feet. "What's the point? You said it yourself. We can't change anything."

"That's not true. Some things can be changed."

"The past?"

"No, not the past."

Jo Lynn nodded her head vigorously up and down, her mouth a bitter pout. "So she just gets away with it."

"Gets away with what? What are you talking about?"

"Excuse me, miss," a voice said from somewhere beside us, and we turned to see a brown-haired boy of about fifteen, wearing cutoff jeans at least four sizes too large and a baseball cap worn back to front and pulled low across his forehead. "Are you Jo Lynn Baker?"

"Yes." Jo Lynn swiped at her tears with the back of her hand, forced a smile onto her lips.

The teenager looked back at his buddies. "It's her," he yelled excitedly. "I told you." He grabbed a napkin off our table and thrust it toward her. "Could you autograph this for me? I don't have a pen."

Jo Lynn fished inside her purse for a pen, then quickly scribbled her signature on the crumpled serviette. "Have a good Christmas," she called after him, her smile now wide and genuine. "Wasn't that sweet?"

"Gets away with what?" I pressed.

But Jo Lynn was already weaving her way between the tables of the extended food court toward the escalator. "Forget it," she called back. "Everybody else has."

⚯

It was almost midnight by the time I got to bed, and it took several hours for me to fall asleep, the events of the day ringing in my brain, like a malfunctioning alarm. I'd finally lapsed into merciful unconsciousness when I felt something sweep across my face, soft and

gentle, like a chiffon scarf. My hand extended lazily to brush it aside, my eyes still firmly closed. Seconds later, it happened again, only this time it was more a tapping against my skin, like water dripping from a leaky faucet. My fingers brushed the air in front of my face, finding nothing. I turned over, refusing to wake up. Something tickled the back of my neck. I swatted it, felt the sting of my fingers as they connected with my skin, jolting me awake. Reluctantly, I opened my eyes, sat up in bed, stared impatiently through the darkness, saw nothing. "Great," I muttered, glancing over at Larry, wrapped peacefully inside the covers. He hadn't touched me since our last disaster. I knew he was waiting for me to make the first move, to be the one to take him in my arms, to coax him into passion, but I couldn't seem to work up the necessary enthusiasm. I lay back against the pillow, exhaled a deep breath of troubled air, reclosed my eyes.

Almost immediately, something danced lightly across my closed lids. A spider? I wondered, shaking my head in an effort to dislodge it. Possibly a mosquito, I thought, as once again I forced my eyes open.

He was leaning over me, smiling through the darkness, the knife dancing in his fingers as it played with the air around my face. I opened my mouth to scream but he shook his head no, and the scream died in my throat. "I thought we should get better acquainted," Colin Friendly said. "Seeing as we're going to be family."

"How did you get out of jail?" I heard myself ask, amazed at my ability to speak.

His smile stretched eerily across his face, his pale skin almost translucent. "You really think that a bunch of video cameras and infrared sensors are gonna be enough to keep me away from you?"

"I don't understand. What do you want with me?"

He brought the knife to the tip of my chin. "Brought you a little Christmas present." He grabbed my hand, brought it to the front of his pants.

"No!" I screamed, pulling my hand away as he climbed onto the bed. I looked helplessly toward Larry. What was the matter with him? Why didn't he wake up?

"He can't help you," Colin Friendly stated, blue eyes slicing through the darkness, as deadly as the knife in his hand.

"What do you mean?"

"Take a look," Colin Friendly instructed, his free arm reaching across the bed to tear the blanket away from my sleeping husband. I saw Larry's open eyes, his parted lips, the deep red line that slashed across the center of his throat.

"No!" I screamed as Colin Friendly pushed himself on top of me. "No!"

I bolted up in bed, my screams bouncing off the walls.

Miraculously, Larry didn't wake up. "It was a dream," I marveled, my hands on my heart, as if to contain its wild beating. "It felt so real."

Larry stirred, groaned, refused to wake up.

"I'm going to check on the girls," I said to the darkness, climbing out of bed.

The house was dark and quiet. I walked toward the girls' bedrooms, knowing I was being silly, but needing to see them sleeping soundly in their beds. You can't protect them forever, I told myself, peeking in on Michelle, kissing her warm forehead, her hand reaching up in sleep to brush my kiss aside. Just as I had done moments ago in my nightmare, I realized with a shudder, pushing open the door to Sara's room, approaching her bed, leaning forward to touch her cheek.

It took me a moment to realize that Sara's bed was empty. "Sara?" I called, checking her bathroom. "Sara?" I flipped on the overhead light. Her bed hadn't been slept in.

I was racing back through the living room toward my bedroom, about to rouse Larry, when I saw a tiny light coming from the back patio, and thought I heard voices. I stopped, stood absolutely still, listened as the soft voices floated to my ears. "Sara?" I hurried toward the sliding glass door at the back of the family room, pushed it open, stepped outside.

Sara, still wearing the clothes she'd had on earlier in the day, was sitting in one of two chaise longues, a lit cigarette dangling from her fingers. She stared at me defiantly, almost daring me to object.

"What are you doing out here?" I asked instead.

"What does it look like?"

"I don't understand. It's late. You know you're not supposed to smoke anywhere on the property."

"Oh, give the kid a break," my sister said, leaning forward on the other chaise longue.

"Jo Lynn! What's going on?"

"You haven't heard the news?"

I shook my head, too dazed to speak.

"A juror at Colin's trial announced she's been having an affair with one of the prosecutors. The whole case has been thrown out of court. Colin's a free man."

"What?!"

"You heard me. He'll be out by morning. I came by to celebrate." She lifted a champagne glass into the air. "You don't mind," she said. "I helped myself."

I stumbled back inside the house. "No, this can't be. It can't be." I ran into the bedroom. "Larry, wake up. Something terrible's happened." I reached his side, prodded his shoulder beneath the blanket. "Larry, please wake up. Colin Friendly is a free man. He'll be out of jail by morning."

Larry's body shifted beneath the covers. He breathed deeply, pushed the blanket aside, sat up in bed. "Well, don't you look as sweet as the first strawberry in spring," Colin Friendly said, his hand reaching for my throat.

I screamed. Or at least I thought I did. Probably the scream was silent, because Larry didn't wake up. He lay there, his sleep undisturbed, as I sat crying beside him, my breathing labored and painful, perspiration soaking my skin, my mind trying frantically to distinguish between the nightmares of my sleep and those of my daily existence.

"Larry, are you awake?" I whispered, needing the comfort of his arms.

But he either didn't hear me or pretended not to. I lay back against the damp pillow, as cold and alone as if I were lying in my grave, and waited for morning.

Chapter

18

"Tell me again who these people are and why we're having dinner with them," Larry said as we pulled the car into the large parking lot in front of Prezzo's, a trendy Italian restaurant located in a long strip plaza at the corner of PGA Boulevard and Prosperity Farms.

The parking lot was crowded and there were no spaces close to the restaurant. We drove slowly, looking down each successive aisle, our eyes peeled for an empty spot. A light rain was falling. "Robert and Brandi Crowe," I reminded him. "I knew him in Pittsburgh."

"Right." Larry nodded, but his voice was flat, disinterested. "And you ran into him at the courthouse."

"Right," I agreed. "There's one." I pointed toward a car that was just pulling out of a space at the side of the enormous Barnes & Noble bookstore that occupied one corner of the lot.

"And the reason for this dinner?"

"Does there have to be a reason?"

Larry pulled the car into the space just vacated and turned off the engine. The rain was falling harder now. We hadn't brought an umbrella. "I guess I should have let you off in front of the restaurant," he said.

"Too late now."

"I can go back." He restarted the engine.

"Don't be silly," I said. "A little rain won't kill me."

"If you're sure," he said.

"I'm sure."

Which was pretty much the extent of most of our conversations in the past weeks. Excessive, forced politeness over the minutest of inconsequential things. A careful treading of the waters. Saying just enough to be understood, not risking the one word that might lend itself to misinterpretation.

"We should probably wait a few minutes," he advised.

"Sure." I stared out the front window at the rain. It wouldn't last long, I decided. The rain in Florida was often ferocious and brief. Like a doomed love affair, I thought, picturing Robert, wondering if he and his wife were similarly trapped, if they sat staring wordlessly out the front window of their car, waiting for a lull in the weather so that they could escape the confines of their car, of their life together.

There's nothing lonelier than an unhappy marriage, I thought, then wondered when I had started to consider my marriage an unhappy one. I glanced at my husband, hoping to catch the flicker of a smile in his face, some sign of reassurance, a ray of hope regarding our future, but his head was pressed back against his headrest and his eyes were closed.

We'd endured rough patches before, I reminded myself: the months following Sara's birth, when she was colicky and kept us up all night (and we were too tired and confused to make love); the months preceding our move to Palm Beach, when we were trying to convince our families and ourselves of the rightness of our decision (and we were too tired and confused to make love); the weeks that followed first my mother's move down here and then my sister's, when we wore ourselves out trying to accommodate them (and were too tired and confused to make love).

Was there a pattern here? And were we not making love because we

were tired and confused, or had we grown tired and confused because we'd stopped making love? Did everything ultimately come down to sex? No matter how old we were?

Nothing ever really changes, I thought. We are who we were. Our pasts are always with us, our personalities chronic, like a lingering illness. No need to look over our shoulders. The past is right in front of our eyes, setting up roadblocks, blocking the way to a happy future.

My mind raced back through more than thirty years. Another parked car in the rain. A deserted strip of country road instead of a crowded parking lot. Robert and I in the front seat of his father's black Buick, his lips on mine, his tongue halfway down my throat, his hands reaching for my breasts. "Let me," he whispered, and again, more urgently, "Let me."

And I might have. I was so close. Why not? I screamed silently at my conscience. Robert was the boy all the girls wanted, and he wanted me. I'd heard the rumors about Sandra Lyons, the girl he sometimes went to see after he drove me home. Was I driving him into her arms? Was I prepared to lose him? All my friends were doing it. What would be so wrong?

I let his hand sneak higher, held my breath. It felt so good. I was so close. "Let me," he said again.

And then that awful knocking on the window. A flashlight shining on our faces, two strangers peering in. We scrambled to fix our clothing, regain our composure. We'd heard all the apocryphal stories of young couples ambushed in lovers' lanes. By thieves, by killers, by monsters with deadly hooks in place of arms. Was that to be our fate?

"You all right?" a uniformed police officer asked me as Robert rolled down the car window.

I nodded, too frightened to speak.

"Would you like a ride home with us, miss?"

I shook my head.

"This isn't a good spot to be," the second policeman said to Robert.

"No, sir," Robert agreed.

"I'd get this girl home right now if I were you."

"Right away," Robert said, starting the car engine.

"Drive carefully," the officer said, slapping the top of the car with the flat of his hand, sending us on our way.

"What do you think?" Larry was asking now, his voice snapping me back into the present, as if I were wrapped inside an elastic band.

"What?"

"I said, it doesn't look like it's going to stop."

I stared at the rain beating down on the front window, aware of my heart pounding wildly in my chest. He was right. The rain was coming down as strongly as before. I checked my watch. It was ten minutes after eight.

"Do you think we should make a run for it?"

"Let's give it another few seconds," I said. What were we doing here anyway? *This isn't a good spot to be.* How had I allowed myself to be talked into having dinner with my prospective lover and his wife? Had I had any choice? "Pick a day, any day," Brandi had chirped over the phone the previous week. What could I say? And when had I started thinking of Robert as my prospective lover?

Probably around the same time I decided my marriage was unhappy, I told myself, understanding how one such decision necessarily impacts on the next. The last time I'd thought of going too far with Robert, the police had intervened. This time, I doubted there would be any cavalry riding to my rescue.

Larry restarted the car. "I'm going to drop you off."

"We'll lose our spot."

"Maybe we'll find something closer."

We did. Right in front of the restaurant.

"Tell me again these people's names," Larry said as we pushed open Prezzo's heavy glass doors, shaking the rain from our heads.

"Robert and Brandi Crowe." My eyes darted skittishly around the noisy, crowded room.

"And you knew her from high school."

"I knew *him*," I shouted over the noise, spotting Robert in a corner booth on the other side of the room. He was on his feet, waving. "There they are."

We began snaking our way through the crowd in front of the bar,

which was normally the focal point of the large, well-lit room, but which tonight was all but hidden by the crush of well-toned, well-tanned bodies milling ten deep around it, vying for one another's attention. There were a trio of blondes in coordinating tight red dresses, a brunette in an emerald-green sweater, a redhead in a black plunging neckline and white thigh-high boots. The men wore expensive gold jewelry under open-necked silk shirts in a variety of hues, and black trousers, as if they were students at the same exclusive private school. "Do you have a license to carry that smile?" I heard one man ask as I passed by, but I didn't bother to turn around. I knew he wasn't talking to me.

Robert was waiting for us with his hand extended. Behind him was a large red poster of white noodles wrapped lovingly around a fork. "You must be Larry. It's a pleasure to meet you. Kate speaks very highly of you," he said, shouting in order to be heard.

Larry smiled, shook Robert's hand, shouted back, "I understand you knew each other from high school."

"That we did." Larry and I slid into one side of the booth, upholstered in subtle green and beige stripes, opposite Robert and his wife. "Larry, this is my wife, Brandi."

"Nice to meet you," Larry said.

"A pleasure," Brandi agreed, then looked over at me. "That's quite the deluge out there."

For a moment I thought she was referring to the crowd, then I realized she meant the weather, and self-consciously swept my hair free of any possible remaining raindrops. "We've been waiting in the car, hoping it would let up."

"I think this is an all-nighter," Brandi said.

We were actually talking about the weather, I thought, avoiding Robert's eyes by concentrating on his wife. Yellow Valentino had replaced pink Chanel, although her eyes were still heavy with blue shadow, obviously a personal trademark. Her black hair was brushed away from her face and secured with a beaded black headband. She was trying to look ten years younger than she was, and as a result, looked ten years older. It was sad, I thought, hoping I wasn't making the same mistake.

"You're looking very lovely," Robert said, as if reading my mind,

and I buried my face in the menu, thanking him without looking up. I'd already taken in every detail of his appearance when I first spotted him across the room: the brown slacks, the tan shirt, the hair falling carelessly across his forehead, the wondrous smile. *Tell me, do you have a license to carry that smile?*

I realized, in that instant, that I had no idea how my husband was dressed, and glanced guiltily beside me. Larry was wearing an old dark green floral shirt that had always been one of my favorites, but which now seemed rather dull, even a trifle shabby. His thinning hair seemed sparser than usual, and his forehead was red and peeling slightly from too much golf and too little sunscreen. Still, he was a handsome man. I wished that he would look over at me and smile, give me some indication that he was still on my side, that he wouldn't let me do anything foolish.

Was my foolishness his responsibility?

I should have told him how nice he looked before we left the house. *Say something nice to your spouse every day*, I always advise clients. *It'll change your life.* But I was too busy thinking of other ways to change my life.

"You look very glamorous in black," Robert continued.

"Thank you," I muttered as the waiter approached to take our drink order.

"That's quite the scene, isn't it?" Brandi Crowe pointed with her chin toward the bar. "You should have seen what it was like before you got here. There was this young guy with a little girl. She was about three years old, and I heard him tell these two women that he was her uncle, and of course they were oohing and aahing, and making a huge fuss over her."

"The better to show off their qualifications for motherhood," Robert quipped.

"And next thing you know, he's got both women's phone numbers, and they're taking care of his niece while he supposedly uses the men's room, but is actually off trysting with bachelorette number three. It was amazing."

"It was quite a display," Robert agreed.

"The kid's probably not even his niece." Brandi laughed. "He probably borrows her from a neighbor to meet girls."

"Sounds like something I might have done," Robert said.

"I doubt that would have been necessary," I heard myself say, then bit down hard on my tongue.

Brandi reached over and patted her husband's hand, the gesture unleashing the same kind of havoc in my body as the first time I'd seen it several weeks earlier. "Yes, I understand my husband was quite the lady-killer back in his high school days. You have to tell us all about him."

"I'm afraid I didn't know your husband that well," I lied, doubting that Robert would have said much about our past relationship to his wife.

"Well, you obviously made quite an impression if he remembered you thirty years later."

"I'm the one who remembered him," I told her.

"Amazing, running into each other in court like that," Brandi said.

"So, what do you think of our boy getting the chair?" Robert asked, deftly switching the subject.

"I couldn't be more thrilled," I said, truthfully.

"How's your sister taking it?"

"As you might expect."

"Your sister?" Brandi asked.

"Jo Lynn Baker," I said, assuming this was explanation enough.

It was. "Oh my God," she whispered, then glared accusingly at her husband. "You didn't tell me that."

The waiter returned with our drinks and a list of the night's specials, the conversation drifting back to the weather, the sports pages, and the joys of life in southern Florida. I cocked my head, feigned interest in the small talk, probably even contributed to it, but my mind was elsewhere, back in Jo Lynn's messy one-bedroom apartment, where I'd spent most of the morning listening to her rail hysterically against a justice system that could so heartlessly condemn a man to die for crimes he didn't commit.

"How could they do it?" she sobbed repeatedly, yesterday's mascara streaking her swollen, unwashed face. She'd been crying since the

previous afternoon's sentencing hearing, when the judge had dispatched Colin Friendly off to the Florida State Prison in Starke to await execution without so much as a by-your-leave. "Of course, his lawyers are planning an appeal."

I held her while she cried, said little. I wasn't there to gloat. Colin Friendly had been found guilty and sentenced to die, and my sister, probably the only person in the world who hadn't been prepared for this eventuality, was in torment. Why she'd put herself in this position, how she could love such a man, why she did any of the crazy things she did, all this was now irrelevant. Out of sight, out of mind, as the saying goes, and my sister's attention span was limited at the best of times. She would weep for him, maybe even make the trip up to Starke to visit him once or twice, but eventually, Jo Lynn would grow tired of the long drive, the longer wait, the lack of a normal life. Eventually, she'd accept the inevitable, proceed with her life, forget about the man on death row.

Colin Friendly, I assured myself, tuning back in to the conversation around the restaurant table, was now safely out of our lives.

"I find the names of the streets so fascinating," Robert was saying. "Military Trail, Worth Avenue, Gun Club Road."

"Prosperity Farms," I chimed in.

"Exactly," Robert said.

"I don't think there's anything particularly fascinating about any of those names," Brandi Crowe said. "Military Trail was probably just that a long time ago; the same is likely true of Gun Club Road. Worth Avenue was undoubtedly named after somebody important, and has nothing to do with all the expensive stores on it, and this part of Palm Beach was all farmland at one point, and the largest one was probably called . . ."

"Prosperity Farms," Robert concluded with a shake of his head. "You're right. Nothing very interesting there, I guess."

Brandi Crowe slipped her arm around her husband's shoulder and laughed as my fists formed tight little balls in my lap. "In case you hadn't realized it, my husband is the last of the romantics." She laughed again, withdrew her arm. My hands relaxed. "So, what do you think of your wife becoming a big radio star?" she asked Larry.

"A big radio star?" Larry repeated.

"You mean she hasn't told you?"

"I guess not." Larry turned to me, waited for an explanation.

"Well, nothing has been decided yet," I stammered.

"I thought you had it all worked out," Brandi said to her husband.

"I've made your wife an offer," Robert said to Larry. "I think she's waiting to see it in writing before she makes any announcements."

"What kind of offer?"

"To host her own phone-in show," Brandi Crowe explained.

"My wife is a therapist," Larry said.

"Exactly," Robert told him. "She'd be giving advice."

"Like on *Frasier?*" my husband asked.

"We haven't decided on a format," Robert said.

"Well, actually, I do have an idea I think is pretty good." A wide smile stretched across my face for the first time that evening.

"What's your idea?" Robert's smile was almost as big as mine.

"A weekly two-hour spot which would combine love songs with advice to the lovelorn." I spoke rapidly, nervous excitement creating a slight wobble in my voice. Until then, I hadn't realized how excited I was about the idea, how eager I was to throw myself into something new. "Every week, we pick a different topic, choose some appropriate songs, and intersperse the songs with the live phone-ins asking for my advice. The music can be used to illustrate a point, or underline it, or the song can be the advice itself, like *Stand by Your Man* or *Take This Job and Shove It*, depending on what the show's about. The list of topics is endless— drinking, loneliness, marriage, cheating . . ." I broke off, coughed into the palm of my hand. "What do you think?"

Larry shrugged. "It's different."

Brandi smiled. "It's interesting."

"It's great," Robert said.

"When would you have time to do this?" Larry's voice was a glass of cold water, dampening our enthusiasm.

"Well, naturally, we'd have to work around Kate's schedule," Robert began.

"You've never done anything like this before," Larry said.

"That's the whole point," I told him. "It would be a challenge."

"You don't think you have enough challenges in your life at the moment?"

I fell silent. What was the matter with him? Had he always been such a wet blanket?

"Ideas like this take months to develop," Robert said. "We're in the very beginning stages. And we haven't even started contract negotiations."

"Should I be hiring an agent?" I joked. Kidding on the square, as my mother would say.

"Uh-oh," Brandi said, and laughed, once again snaking her arm across her husband's shoulders. "Something tells me you're going to have your hands full with this one."

~~

"Don't fuck this guy," Larry said, his voice measured and calm, his anger restrained and simple.

"What? What are you talking about?"

"You tell me," Larry said as we climbed into the car. The downpour had ceased, but a light drizzle persisted.

"I don't know what you're talking about."

"Are you sleeping with him?"

"What?"

"You heard me."

"You can't be serious."

"Do I sound as if I'm joking?"

"You think I'm sleeping with Robert Crowe?"

"Are you?"

"No, of course not. Where is this coming from?"

"You tell me."

"There's nothing to tell."

"This is just some guy you knew from high school," Larry said.

"Yes."

"Who you just happened to run into one day at the courthouse."

"Yes."

"And he just happens to own a radio station."

"His wife's father . . ."

"And he offers you your very own show. Just like that. Out of the blue," he continued, not interested in my clarification.

"More or less," I conceded.

"How much more?"

"What?"

"Why would he offer you your own show? You have no experience. He hasn't seen you in thirty years. What's he really after, Kate?"

"This is very insulting," I said, and actually managed to be offended.

"I'm not an idiot," Larry said.

"Then stop acting like one." My voice was shaking, although whether it was shaking more with indignation or guilt, I'm not altogether sure. Was I really so transparent? And did just thinking about having an affair make me guilty as charged? Maybe I should be on my way to the state prison in Starke along with Colin Friendly.

Larry started the car and we drove home without speaking. I flipped on the radio, tried to make my mind a blank, to lose myself in the music. "Here's an old favorite," I suddenly heard my voice crackle across the airwaves. "*Your Cheatin' Heart* by Hank Williams. Callers, the phone lines are now open. Have your questions ready."

Chapter
19

It was around this time that I started having recurring dreams. There were two of them, different in content, though equally disturbing. In the first one, I'm lying facedown on my bedroom floor, my hands tied with a rope behind me, my sister sitting on the small of my back, bouncing up and down, riding me as if I were a pony, as a faceless stranger ransacks my drawers, throwing a seemingly endless supply of bras and panties into the air, letting them fall where they may.

In the second dream, I'm walking alone along a sunny strip of sidewalk, my steps propelled by a feeling of buoyancy, of being almost lighter than air. In the next instant, I am absolutely convinced that with a little effort, I can actually take flight, and so I start flapping my arms wildly up and down, angling my body to forty-five degrees, my chin thrust forward and leading the way, my neck and shoulders following, as if skiing off a high jump. And suddenly my legs actually leave the

ground, and I am suspended in the air, maybe a foot or two off the sidewalk, and I flap my arms even more furiously, trying to sustain the momentum, to increase my speed, to gain greater height, to fly through the air. I'm so close. "Let me," I cry, even as I feel my feet returning to the ground, my flight aborted, my energy spent.

It's not hard to figure out what these dreams mean: the perceived loss of control, the outside forces keeping me down, my desire to break free, to escape the underpinnings of my life, the oblique references to Larry and Robert, the not so oblique reference to my sister. Even my dreams are transparent, it would seem.

The dreams became a constant, alternating with one another on a nightly basis, occasionally doubling up, like an old-fashioned double bill at the movies. They interrupted my sleep, woke me at three in the morning, like a colicky infant, and hung on till it was time to get up. Occasionally, I awoke from one of these dreams dripping with perspiration, the skin between my breasts glistening with sweat, the sheets around me damp and cold. I forgot what it was like to sleep through the night.

Interestingly enough, it was during this time that Larry and I started making love again. I woke up one night, sweaty and breathless from my attempts to take flight, and he was sitting up in bed beside me. My thrashing had awakened him, he said matter-of-factly, and I apologized, which he said wasn't necessary. I smiled gratefully, and told him I loved him. And he took me in his arms and told me he loved me too, that he was sorry for his part in our recent estrangement, and I apologized for mine. And we made love. And it was nice and familiar and comforting, and I hoped that would put an end to the dreams, but it didn't.

The subconscious, it would appear, is not so easy to fool as our waking selves, and the truth was that I didn't want lovemaking that was nice and familiar and comforting. I wanted lovemaking that was furious and unfamiliar and exciting. The kind of lovemaking that transports you, makes you think that anything is possible, the kind of lovemaking that can save your life. Or destroy it.

I wanted Robert.

Don't fuck this guy, I heard Larry say, even as I fucked him daily in

my mind. Robert was everywhere around me, his voice in my ear, telling me what to say, his eyes behind mine, showing me where to look, what to see, his hands at my breasts, dictating the beat of my heart. I made love to my husband, but it was Robert who slept inside me at night, who guided my hands when I showered in the morning, and if I tried scrubbing myself free of him, which I did only rarely, he clung to me stubbornly, coating my body, like a soapy residue, refusing to give way.

As for Robert himself, he was mercifully out of town, first at a media convention in Las Vegas, then reluctantly, on some sort of cruise, organized on behalf of one of his wife's pet charities. He'd be gone just over three weeks, he told me over the phone before he left. He'd call as soon as he got back. By which time, I assured myself repeatedly in the interim, I would have returned to my senses.

I kept hoping the same would hold true for Jo Lynn, who, during the month of January, made weekly treks to Starke, driving up on Friday and staying at a motel not far from the penitentiary, then spending the allotted six hours with her "fiancé" on Saturday, before making the five-hour drive back home. She had few kind words to say about how the state prison operated. What could possibly be the harm, she demanded indignantly, in allowing the inmates visitors on both Saturday and Sunday, and not forcing them to choose either one day or the other? And talk about cruel and unusual punishment, did we know that the state of Florida didn't allow conjugal visits? Not that this would stop her from going ahead with her wedding plans, she insisted.

Probably it was that blind, stubborn insistence that propelled me into action, although I had no idea what I was doing, or what I thought I could accomplish. One afternoon, I simply picked up the phone, punched in 411, and waited for the recorded voice to come on the line.

"Southern Bell," the cheery voice obliged. "For what city?"

"Brooksville," I heard myself say.

"For what name?"

"Ketchum," I answered, spelling the name of Colin Friendly's neighbor, the one who'd tried to help him, who'd supposedly taught him that all women weren't like his mother. "Rita Ketchum." Why did I want to speak to her? What good did I think talking to her would do?

Seconds later, a human voice replaced the recorded message. "I show no listing for a Rita Ketchum," the woman said, her voice decidedly less cheerful than the recording she replaced. "Do you have an address?"

"No, but how big is Brooksville? There can't be very many Ketchums."

"I have a listing for a Thomas Ketchum on Clifford Road."

"Fine," I told her.

The recorded voice returned, relayed the phone number, offered to dial it directly for a nominal charge. I accepted, not trusting my fingers to do the job.

The phone rang once, twice. Assuming I had the right number, what was I planning on saying to Rita Ketchum? *Hello, I understand you taught Colin Friendly all he knows about love?*

The phone was answered on its fourth ring. "Hello," a young woman said, a baby crying in the background.

"Is this Rita Ketchum?" I asked.

The voice grew suddenly wary. "Who is this?"

"My name is Kate Sinclair. I'm calling from Palm Beach. I need to speak to Rita Ketchum." Except for the baby crying in the background, there was silence. "Hello? Are you still there?"

"My mother-in-law isn't here. May I ask why you want to speak to her?"

"There are some questions I'd like to ask her," I said, growing uneasy.

"Are you with the police?"

"The police? No."

"What kind of questions do you want to ask her?"

"I'd rather discuss this directly with Mrs. Ketchum."

"I'm afraid that won't be possible."

"Why is that?"

"Because nobody's seen or heard from her in almost twelve years." In the background, the baby began screaming.

"She disappeared?"

"Twelve years ago this May. Look, I really have to go. If you want to call back this evening, you can speak to my husband."

"Thank you," I said, too stunned to say anything else. "That won't be necessary."

"So what are you saying?" Jo Lynn demanded over the phone only minutes later. "That just because some woman ran away from home, Colin had something to do with it?"

"For God's sake, Jo Lynn, what is it going to take to get through to you?" I said angrily. "The woman didn't just run away from home. She disappeared. Of course Colin had something to do with it."

"Colin would never hurt Mrs. Ketchum. He loved her."

"The man is incapable of love. He makes no distinctions between feelings, between people. If he could kill the one woman who tried to help him, what makes you think you'll be any different?"

Her answer was to hang up the phone. I lowered my head into the palms of my hands and cried.

On February 5, I took my mother to our scheduled doctor's appointment. Dr. Caffery's office, located on Brazilian Avenue in Palm Beach proper, is a small series of examination rooms off a larger waiting room, the whole area decorated in gradations of pink. Like the womb, I thought, ushering my mother inside and pushing her toward the receptionist's desk.

"Hi, I'm Kate Sinclair," I announced. "This is my mother, Helen Latimer."

"Hello, dear," my mother said to the receptionist, who was about twenty-five, with short black hair cut on the diagonal and half a dozen assorted gold loops and studs running up each earlobe. Her nameplate identified her as Becky Sokoloff.

"We have an appointment," I said.

"Have you been here before?" Becky asked.

"No, this is our first visit."

"You'll have to fill out these forms." Becky pushed several sheets of paper across her blond-wood desk. "Why don't you have a seat for a few minutes. The doctor is a little behind schedule."

I took the forms and directed my mother to the row of bright pink chairs that ran along the pale pink wall. Several women were already waiting, and one glanced up from her magazine with a weary smile, her eyes indicating that the doctor was more than a *little* behind schedule. "Would you like a magazine, Mother?" I didn't wait for her reply, just grabbed a handful of magazines from the long, rectangular coffee table that sat in the middle of the room, and plopped them into her lap.

My mother promptly folded her hands on top of them, like a human paperweight, making no move to open them. I studied her for several seconds, deciding that she looked well. Her skin color was good, her dark eyes bright, her gray hair combed and curled. She seemed in good spirits. No one was plotting against her, nobody was following her, everything was "magnificent," she'd trilled on the drive over from her apartment, then lapsed into silence, other than to ask how the girls were getting along, a question she repeated at least five times.

"Mom, don't you want to read a magazine?" I reached under her hands and extricated the latest edition of *Elle*, opening it to a page of naked breasts in quite an astonishing assortment of shapes and sizes.

"Oh my," my mother and I both said, almost as one. Immediately, I flipped to another page. More breasts. Some barely covered, some simply bare. And still more: here a breast, there a breast, everywhere a breast-breast, I sang silently, flipping quickly through the entire magazine. A seemingly inexhaustible supply.

What every well-dressed woman is wearing, I thought, turning my attention to the forms the receptionist had handed me, starting to fill in the blanks. Name, address, phone number, place and date of birth. "Mom, what year you were born?" I asked without thinking, then bit down on my tongue. She had trouble remembering what she had for breakfast. How was she going to remember what year she was born?

"May 18," she said easily, "1921."

I felt strangely elated by the fact my mother knew the date of her birth. Maybe she wasn't in such bad shape after all, I rationalized, even though I knew that Alzheimer sufferers often had no trouble recalling even the minutest details of their distant pasts. It was their short-term memory that deserted them. I tried another question, deciding that short-

term memory was vastly overrated. "Are you allergic to any medications?"

"No, but I'm allergic to surgical tape."

"Surgical tape?"

She leaned against me, as if about to confide something highly confidential. "We didn't find that out until after my cesarean with Jo Lynn." She laughed. "The doctors put regular surgical tape across my stomach to hold the stitches from the operation in place, and of course, nobody thought a thing about it until a few days later, when I started to itch something terrible, and they took off the bandages, and discovered that my stomach was covered in these horrible, angry red welts. Oh, it was terrible. I thought I'd die, I was so itchy. And there wasn't much the doctors could do for me, except to lather my skin in cortisone cream. It was months before those welts went down. I looked terribly ugly, what with this big scar and those angry red welts covering my stomach. Your father hated it."

It was the most I'd heard my mother say in months, and I couldn't help but smile, despite the mention of my stepfather. "Do you think much about him?" I heard myself ask.

"I think about him all the time," she answered, surprising me, although I'm not sure why. She'd been married to the man for fourteen years, had a child with him, been regularly beaten to a bloody pulp by him—why wouldn't he still be part of her thoughts? Hadn't I held on to my memories of Robert all these years?

"He was such a handsome man," she continued, without prompting. "Tall and dashing and very funny. You inherited your sense of humor from him, Kate."

It was then that I realized she was talking about *my* father, and not Jo Lynn's. "Tell me about him," I said, partly to find out how much she recalled, but mostly because I was suddenly hungry to hear news of him, as if I were a small child waiting for word of her handsome and brave father, off fighting a distant war.

"We met at the end of World War II," she said, repeating a story I'd heard many times before. "My father gave him a job in his textile factory,

and Martin eventually worked his way up to foreman. He was so smart and ambitious, he would have become foreman even if he hadn't married the boss's daughter." Her eyes suddenly clouded over. "But then my father lost the business, and my parents had to sell their house, and my mother never forgave him. Do you remember your grandmother?" she asked.

An image of a heavyset old woman with strawlike hair and thick ankles flashed before my eyes. "Vaguely," I said. I was only five years old when she died.

"She was a very strong woman, your grandmother. There was no gray in her world, only black and white. Something was right, or it wasn't. If you made your bed, you had to lie in it."

"That couldn't have been very easy for you," I heard the therapist in me reply.

"We learned. If you made a mistake, you had to accept the consequences. You couldn't just pack up your things and run away."

"Is that why you stayed with my stepfather even after he started beating you?" I knew the question was too simplistic, but I asked it anyway.

"Your father never beat me," she said.

"My stepfather," I repeated.

"Your father was a wonderful man. He was a foreman at my father's textile plant until my father lost the business, then he took a job with General Motors during the day and went to law school at night. He'd always wanted to be a lawyer. Isn't that interesting? We've never had a lawyer in the family. But he died before he could graduate." She smiled sadly at the receptionist.

"It shouldn't be too much longer," Becky Sokoloff automatically replied.

"We were finishing our dinner," my mother continued, as I watched the scene play out in my mind. "You were in your room, getting ready for bed. Your father and I were still at the dining-room table, taking our time over dessert. It was so rare, you see, that we got to spend a whole evening together, and so we were lingering over our dessert, just talking and

laughing. And your father got up to get a glass of milk, and suddenly he said that he felt a hell of a headache coming on. Those were his exact words, 'I feel a hell of a headache coming on.' I remember because it was very unusual for him to swear, even a simple word like 'hell.' And I was about to suggest that he take a few aspirin, even though he didn't like pills, but I never got the chance. He stood up, took two steps, then collapsed onto the floor."

I said nothing, watching as her eyes flickered with the passage of time, as if she were watching an old newsreel.

"Do you know what I did?" she asked, not waiting for an answer. "I laughed!"

"Laughed?"

"I thought it was some sort of joke. Even after I called for an ambulance, even on the ride to the hospital, I kept expecting him to open his eyes. But he didn't. The doctor told me later that he was dead before he hit the floor."

I reached over and hugged her, felt the outline of her skeleton beneath the soft cotton of her blue dress. When had she become so frail? I wondered, as her body bent to my embrace. And how long before these memories, now so strong, ultimately faded, then disappeared?

So the past gets wiped clean? Jo Lynn had demanded in the mall the day before Christmas. *She won't remember it, so I might as well pretend it never happened?*

Pretend what never happened?

She just gets away with it.

Gets away with what? I wondered, as I'd been wondering ever since that afternoon.

"Mom," I began.

"Yes, dear."

"Can I ask you something?"

"You can ask me anything, dear."

I paused, not sure how to pose the question, deciding finally that the most direct approach was probably the best. "What exactly happened between you and Jo Lynn?"

"Something's happened to Jo Lynn?" Her eyes flashed immediate concern.

"No, she's fine."

"Oh, I'm so glad."

"I mean, what happened between the two of you a long time ago?"

"I don't understand." My mother's eyes grew restive, flitting fearfully around the room.

"You two have never really gotten along," I began again, trying a different approach.

"She was always such a headstrong little girl. You could never tell Jo Lynn anything."

"Tell me about her."

"Don't get me started," my mother said, and laughed, the fear in her eyes vanishing as quickly as it had appeared.

"She was a cesarean delivery," I coaxed, waiting.

"That's right," my mother marveled. "I had a terrible time after she was born because I had an allergic reaction to the surgical tape."

"And she was headstrong and you could never tell her anything . . ."

"She had a mind of her own, that's for certain. I couldn't get her to wear a dress for love or money. I'd put her in all these pretty, frilly little things, the kind you always loved, and she'd rip them off, wouldn't have anything to do with them. No, she only wanted to wear pants. She was such a handful. Not like you. You were such a good baby. You loved your little dresses, but not our Joanne Linda. No, she had to wear the pants in the family." She laughed. "That's what your father used to say anyway."

"My stepfather," I qualified.

"Jo Lynn could do no wrong as far as he was concerned. He let her get away with murder. Whatever she wanted, he made sure she got. Spoiled her terribly. Always took her side whenever there was an argument." She shook her head. "She never got over my leaving him. I know she blames me for his death."

"He died of pancreatic cancer. How can she blame you for that?"

"She blames me for everything."

I looked toward the receptionist, then over at the two women waiting in the chairs across from us. "What else does she blame you for?" I asked.

My mother smiled and said nothing, her eyes drifting back to the bare bosoms on the pages of *Elle*. "Oh my," she said.

⌒

"That's what she told you?" Jo Lynn asked over the phone later that afternoon.

"She says you blame her for his death."

"She would say that."

"Do you?"

"He died of cancer."

"That's beside the point."

"There is no point. Not to this conversation, anyway. What did the doctor say?"

"Not much. She's going to run a bunch of tests. Apparently, Alzheimer's is one of those diseases that they identify more by a process of elimination than anything else."

"What kind of tests?"

"EKG, CAT scan, MRI, mammogram."

"Mammogram? Where'd that come from?"

"Dr. Caffery feels we might as well do a complete physical. She wants me to have one too," I added.

"You? Why? Aren't you feeling all right?"

"She thinks I might be starting menopause," I admitted.

"What?"

"It's no big deal," I lied.

"So, are you coming up to Starke with me this weekend?" The question was deceptively casual in its delivery, as if we'd been discussing this for some time and were simply tying up a few loose ends.

"You must be kidding," I answered.

"I thought you might find it interesting."

"Not a chance." There was an awkward silence. "You could do me a favor, though," I said, surprising myself.

She waited, said nothing. I could almost feel her body tense.

"You could ask your boyfriend what he did with Rita Ketchum."

There was another pause, this one redolent with silent fury. "You know what?" Jo Lynn asked, her voice edgy and cold, like chipped glass. "If you have anything you want to ask my *fiancé*, I suggest you ask him yourself."

Chapter
20

Which may, or may not, explain what I was doing sitting beside my sister as she raced her old red Toyota up the Florida Turnpike toward the state prison outside Starke the following Friday night.

"Don't you think you should slow down a bit?" I fidgeted in my seat, eyes darting through the darkness for state troopers along the side of the highway. "I thought the police had this area pretty well covered."

"They never stop me," Jo Lynn said confidently, as if surrounded by an aura of invincibility. "Besides, I'm not going that fast."

"You're doing almost eighty."

"You call that fast?"

"I think you should slow down."

"I think you should relax. I'm the driver, remember?" She lifted both hands off the wheel, cracked her knuckles, stretched.

"Get your hands on the wheel," I said.

"Will you please calm down. You'll make me so nervous, I'll have an accident."

"Look, you've been driving for almost three hours," I said, watching the speedometer stubbornly climb, trying a different approach. "Why don't you let me take over for a while."

She shrugged. "Sure. Next time we stop for gas, it's all yours."

I stared out the front window at the battery of signs that regularly interrupted the flat stretch of road along the ink-blue sky, most of them announcing the imminent arrival of Disney World, located just outside the city of Kissimmee, twenty miles southwest of Orlando.

"You want to go there?" Jo Lynn asked.

"Where?"

"Disney World. We could go on Sunday."

I shook my head in amazement. The state penitentiary one day, Disney World the next.

"Or we could do Universal Studios. I've always wanted to go there, and it's around here somewhere."

"I think I'll pass."

"What about Busch Gardens? It's supposed to be terrific."

"We were there about five years ago," I reminded her. "Remember? You went with the kids on that water ride and everybody got drenched."

Jo Lynn squealed with delight. " 'The Congo River Rapids' ride! I remember. That's the place with all the animals. It was great. Let's go there." Her head snapped toward me, her eyes appealing longingly to mine.

"Would you please keep your eyes on the road."

"Party pooper." Her eyes returned to the highway stretching monotonously before us. "How about one of those alligator farms? You know, the ones you hear about where some poor kid always falls off the bridge and gets eaten?"

"You're not serious."

"Of course I'm serious. I love that sort of stuff."

"I can't," I told her, watching the enthusiasm drain from her face, like liquid from a straw. "I promised Larry I'd be home tomorrow night."

Actually I hadn't promised him any such thing. In fact, Larry had encouraged me to wait until Sunday to make the long drive home. But I knew my tolerance level for my sister would take me only so far.

"You're such a wet blanket," Jo Lynn said, her mouth a pronounced pout.

"I'm here, aren't I?"

She scoffed. "Colin doesn't know anything about what happened to Rita Ketchum. You'll see."

What about Amy Lokash? I thought, but didn't say. What about the scores of other women who crossed his path and disappeared? "Where is this place anyway?"

"It's either in Raiford or Starke, depending on who you talk to," Jo Lynn explained. "Between Gainesville and Jacksonville, in Bradford County. Another couple of hours and we should be at the motel."

"I don't think I've ever been to Bradford County," I said.

"Well, it's one of the state's smallest counties," Jo Lynn pronounced with the authority of a tour director. "Its early settlers were farmers from South Carolina and Georgia. The main businesses are truck crops, tobacco, timber, and livestock. The largest private employers include manufacturers of work clothing, wood products, and mineral sand. Population around 23,000, about 4,000 of whom live in Starke, which is also the county seat. Raiford's even smaller."

"My God, where'd you learn that?"

"Are you impressed?"

"Yes," I said honestly.

"Would you still be impressed if I told you I made it all up?"

"You made it up?"

"No," she said grudgingly. "But I kind of wish I had. Actually, the manager of the motel we're staying at supplied me with the details."

"What else do you know?"

"About this area?"

I nodded, though it was my sister who fascinated me far more than the data she was reciting.

"Well, Starke is twenty-four miles away from the nearest airport, which is in Gainesville, and there are three colleges and universities

within fifty miles of the county, as well as three community colleges and two vocational schools."

"Not to mention the state penitentiary," I added.

"Actually, there are five prisons between Starke and Raiford," she said, her voice adopting a world-weary tone. "There's the North Florida Reception Center, for newly arriving prisoners from the north, the Central Florida Reception Center, the South Florida Reception Center, as well as the Union Correctional Institution, which is just across the river from Florida State Prison. Colin will probably be transferred there when there's a vacancy."

"I thought he was on death row."

Even in profile, I could feel the glare in Jo Lynn's eyes. "They have death rows in both places," she said slowly, between newly clenched teeth. "The executions, however, take place in Florida State Prison. If Colin were to be executed, and he won't be, then he'd have to be transferred back again."

"What's happening with his appeal?" The Florida Supreme Court, which automatically reviews all death sentence convictions, had already upheld Colin's sentence.

"His lawyers are appealing to the U.S. Supreme Court."

"And if they refuse to hear the case?"

"Then there's a hearing before the governor and his cabinet. If the hearing is denied and the death warrant is signed by the governor, then we petition the Florida Supreme Court a second time with briefs stating that new evidence is available."

"Even if there isn't?"

"If that petition is rejected," Jo Lynn continued, ignoring my question, and continuing on as if she were a recorded message, "then Colin's lawyers go to the trial court and insist that the defendant didn't get a fair trial the first time and that he should get a new one. If that fails, we go back to the Florida Supreme Court for a third time with a request to stay the execution."

"And if that fails?"

"You needn't sound so hopeful." Jo Lynn straightened her shoulders, tightened her grip on the steering wheel. "If that fails, we go to the

federal district court, where we say that the defendant deserves a stay of execution or that the sentence is unfair. If this court refuses to do anything, then we go to the U.S. Eleventh Court of Appeals in Atlanta, requesting that the execution be stopped. And if that doesn't work," she said softly, "there's a final appeal to the U.S. Supreme Court. If that fails, Colin gets the chair. Would you like to hear about that?" she asked, continuing before I had a chance to object.

"Florida began using the electric chair in 1924. Prior to that, hanging was the execution of choice. Between 1924 and 1964, when executions were temporarily halted because of court battles challenging their constitutionality, Florida electrocuted 196 people. The oldest was fifty-nine; the youngest three were sixteen. Two-thirds of the total were black. Electrocutions resumed in September of 1977, and today there are more than 340 residents living on death row.

"The executioner, a private citizen whose identity is never disclosed, is hired from a host of applicants for the job. He wears a mask when he throws the switch, and makes the princely sum of 150 dollars per execution.

"As for the death chamber itself, it's pretty basic. A twelve-by-fifteen-foot room whose only furniture is this massive oak chair bolted down to a rubber mat. The source of power for this chair is a diesel generator capable of producing 3,000 volts and 20 amps, although I'm not sure I understand the distinction. At any rate, it's irrelevant because a transformer behind the chair turns those 3,000 volts and 20 amps into 40,000 watts, which is enough to shoot the body temperature of the person in the chair up to 150 degrees."

"My God."

"Once in the chair, the prisoner faces a glass partition behind which is a small room with twenty-two seats, twelve of which are for official witnesses picked by the warden, and the rest of which are for reporters. Just before the execution, the prisoner is taken to a so-called prep room, where his head and right leg are shaved for electrical attachments, just like you see in the movies. What you don't see is that his head is also soaked with salty water to assure good contact. Of course, when he's in the chair, his head is covered with a rubber hood. There are also rumors

that a tight rubber band has been fitted around the inmate's penis and a pack of cotton wadding stuffed up his ass. Oh, and did I mention that behind Old Sparky, as the chair is affectionately known, are two telephones, one for the institution and the other for the governor in case he changes his mind at the last minute?"

"Unbelievable," I said, trying to rid my mind of the graphic images that were filling it.

"Less than four minutes after the prisoner enters the death chamber, he's toast. The body is then slipped into a dark coat, ready for burial. The state of Florida is nothing if not efficient."

"I don't believe it," I said.

"I'm not making any of this up," she said.

"That's not what I mean."

"What *do* you mean?"

"I mean you're amazing," I told her.

"What's *that* supposed to mean?"

"It means I think you're amazing. I can't believe you know all this stuff."

She shrugged. "I've been doing a little reading, that's all. I can read, you know."

"But you actually *remember* everything. That's the amazing part."

"What's so amazing? I have a photographic memory. No big deal. Besides, I have kind of a vested interest in all this."

"Have you ever thought about going back to school, becoming a lawyer?" The idea was forming as I spoke.

"Are you nuts?"

"No, I'm serious," I said, warming to the idea. "I think you'd make a terrific lawyer. You have a great mind. You have all these facts and figures at your fingertips. God knows, you know how to argue. I bet you wouldn't have any trouble at all swaying a jury to your point of view."

"I flunked out of college, remember?"

"Only because you never tried. You could go back, get your degree."

"Degrees aren't everything," she said defensively.

"No, of course they're not," I agreed quickly. "But you'd be a

natural. I mean, you should have heard yourself. You're really good at this stuff. I bet you'd do great. You could go back to school, get your law degree, then defend Colin yourself. If anyone can keep him out of the electric chair, it's you." My sister, the lawyer, I thought. My brother-in-law, the serial killer.

A slow smile crept onto Jo Lynn's face. "I probably would make a good lawyer."

"You'd be great."

She took a deep breath, held the smile for several seconds, then allowed it to tumble from her lips, like a baby's drool. "No," she said quietly. "It's too late."

"No, it's not," I insisted, even as I knew it was. "We could make some inquiries when we get back home, find out what you'd have to do, how much it would cost. Larry and I could loan you the money. You'd pay us back as soon as you started raking in the dough." *Raking in the dough?* I asked myself, knowing I'd traveled beyond the realm of reason into the territory of giddy.

"I bet Mom would give me the money," Jo Lynn stated, and I held my breath. She'd made me promise not to discuss our mother during the trip, and I'd reluctantly agreed. Now she was the one bringing her up. Was she opening the door, beckoning me to step through?

"I bet she'd be happy to."

"She owes me," Jo Lynn said. "Oh, good, there's a service station." She quickly transferred lanes and pulled off at the next exit.

The brightly lit service station contained both a gas station and a Burger King. "I'll take care of the gas if you go get us something to eat," Jo Lynn said as we opened the car doors and climbed out.

I arched my back, stretched my legs. "Oh, that feels so good."

"You stupid idiot," a girl's voice screamed, and for an instant, I thought it was Jo Lynn screaming at me. But when I looked across the top of the car at Jo Lynn, I saw that her attention was directed at the young couple standing by the car in the next aisle, a blue Firebird as bruised as the young girl's arms.

The girl couldn't have been more than sixteen, her boyfriend only marginally older. Both were pale-skinned, fair-haired, and painfully thin,

although the boy's arms were muscular and veined, as if he'd been pumping iron. His cheeks were flushed with anger; his fists clenched at his sides. "Who are you calling an idiot?" he raged.

"Who do you think?" the girl challenged, emboldened perhaps by those of us watching nearby.

"I don't need this kind of crap from you," the boy said, opening the car door. "Now, get in the goddamn car. We're outta here."

"No."

"You want me to just leave you here? Is that what you want? 'Cause I'll do it. I'll drive off and leave you in the middle of goddamn nowhere."

I was debating with myself whether or not there was anything I could say or do that might defuse the situation when my sister came up behind me and whispered in my ear. "Stay out of it," she said.

"Maybe we should call the police," I said.

"Maybe we should mind our own business," she countered, directing my attention to the Burger King. "I'll have a cheeseburger, large fries, and a jumbo Coke."

I went to the bathroom, splashed water on my face, stared at my tired reflection in the mirror, noting the deep bags tugging at my eyes. "Turning into an old crone," I whispered.

There was a line at the Burger King counter and it took almost ten minutes for my order to be placed and delivered. "What kept you?" Jo Lynn asked as I handed her the cheeseburger, fries, and soft drink. She slid into the passenger seat while I walked around the car to the driver's side. If I saw the thin wisps of dishwasher blond hair in the back seat, my subconscious refused to acknowledge it until I was behind the wheel of the car and halfway out of the lot. "Where's your food?" Jo Lynn asked, unwrapping hers.

"I didn't get anything."

"Want some?"

I shook my head. "I'm not very hungry."

"I wasn't talking to you," she said, and I screamed as a thin hand reached across the front seat from the back.

I spun around, saw the young girl with the bruised arms staring back at me, pale green eyes wide and frightened.

"For God's sake, watch where you're going," Jo Lynn admonished with a sly smile. "You want to get us killed?"

I clutched the wheel as tightly as I could, more to keep from strangling my sister than for safety's sake. Hadn't she told me, just moments ago, to mind my own business? What was she doing inviting a stranger into our car? Didn't she know how dangerous it was to pick up hitchhikers?

"This is Patsy," my sister said by way of introduction. "Patsy, this is my sister, Kate."

"Hi, Kate," the girl said, taking a large bite out of my sister's burger and a long sip of her Coke, before handing them back. "Thanks for the ride."

"Where exactly are we taking you?" I managed to ask, wincing as my sister fastened her lips around the same straw the young stranger had just relinquished.

"Wherever," Patsy said, her voice a low growl. "It doesn't much matter."

"Patsy's boyfriend took off without her," Jo Lynn explained.

"Stupid idiot," Patsy said.

"Where do you live?" I asked.

She shrugged. "I'm not sure," she said. "Nowhere now, I guess."

This answer was somewhat less than satisfactory. "Where are you from?"

"Fort Worth."

"Fort Worth? Fort Worth, Texas?"

"Way to go, Katie," my sister said. "Give that girl a silver star."

"How'd you get all the way over here?" I asked, trying to push my voice back into its normal register.

"Drove," came the disinterested reply. Patsy reached forward, grabbed a handful of fries from the container that my sister was stretching over her shoulder.

I watched through the rearview mirror as Patsy flopped back against her seat, stuffing the fries into her mouth, then rubbing her bruised arms, closing her eyes, heavily outlined in black pencil. "With your boy-

friend?" I asked, despite the look on my sister's face that told me to be quiet.

"Yeah, the stupid idiot."

"What about your parents?"

"Kate, this is none of our business," Jo Lynn interjected.

"Do your parents know where you are?" I persisted.

"They don't care where I am."

"You're sure of that?"

Patsy laughed, but the sound was hollow, and echoed pain. "I haven't seen my dad since I was a little kid, and my mother has a new boyfriend and a new baby. She probably doesn't even realize I'm gone."

"How long ago did you leave?"

"Two weeks."

I thought immediately of Amy Lokash, pictured her mother, Donna, cowering tearfully at my office door on the day of her first visit. "Have you called her? Does she know you're all right?" Even without looking at Patsy, I could see the confused mixture of defiance, loneliness, and stubborn pride playing havoc with her delicate features.

"I haven't called her."

Don't you think you should? I wanted to scream, but didn't, knowing it would only put the girl on the defensive. "Do you want to?" I asked instead.

Patsy said nothing for several seconds. "I don't know." She leaned her forehead against the glass of the rear side window.

"What's stopping you from just picking up the phone and calling home, telling your mother that you're safe?" I asked.

"What's the point?" Patsy countered sullenly. "She'll only yell at me, tell me she was right about Tyler all along."

"That's what's stopping you?"

"I don't want to hear it again."

"*Was* she right about Tyler?"

"Yes," came the barely audible mumble from the back seat.

"So, are you going to let Tyler call the shots here or what?" I asked, after a slight pause.

"Tyler's the stupid idiot, right?" Jo Lynn asked, and I smiled gratefully for her subtle support.

"Maybe I'll call her," Patsy said, reaching for a few more fries. "I'll think about it."

"Just a phone call to let her know you're okay," I continued, thinking again of Donna Lokash, how easily this could be her child, praying that a similar insanity had overtaken Amy, that she was even now hitchhiking across the country, unmindful of the pain she was causing, the anguish she'd left behind. But alive.

I fought back the sudden threat of tears as I realized how alien our children were becoming to us. E.T., phone home, I thought.

We said nothing for the next few minutes, Jo Lynn slurping up the balance of her Coke to the rhythm of Garth Brooks and Shania Twain, occasionally passing her drink to the back seat, along with what was left of her cheeseburger and fries. The odor of fast food permeated the car, sinking into the seats like water into soil, lingering long after the food was gone, reminding me that I hadn't eaten since lunch. Probably I should have eaten something when I had the chance. It would be close to midnight before we got to the motel in Starke.

"Hey," Patsy suddenly shouted, her hand extending over the top of the front seat, her finger pointing excitedly toward the side of the road. "The next exit is for Disney World."

"We're not going to Disney World," I told her.

"Where *are* you going?" That there might be other options had obviously never occurred to her.

"We're on our way to Starke," I said.

"Starke? Where's that?"

"Bradford County, between Gainesville and Jacksonville," my sister clarified.

"I don't want to go to Starke," Patsy said, sounding in that instant very much like Sara. "I want to go to Disney World. That's where Tyler and I were headed when we got into that stupid fight."

"Why don't you come with us instead," I suggested. "Then you can call your mother from the motel."

"I want to go to Disney World," Patsy insisted. "It's the whole

reason I came to Florida in the first place. Just pull the car over and let me off. I can hitchhike the rest of the way."

"Don't you know how dangerous it is to hitchhike?" I began, then stopped. Was there really any point in arguing with her, trying to make her see reason, to change her mind? I signaled, pulled the car over to the side of the road, and stopped.

"I don't think this is such a good idea," Jo Lynn said suddenly. "I mean, there are lots of looney tunes out there, just waiting to pick up young girls." If Jo Lynn was aware of the irony inherent in her advice, she gave no sign.

"I'll be fine," Patsy insisted, with all the arrogance of youth. "Thanks for the ride and the food and everything." She opened the door, climbed out. "I'll call my mother after I ride 'The Pirates of the Caribbean.' "

"You do that," I said, watching Patsy in the rearview mirror as she proffered her thumb into the air. I drove off before I could see anyone stop to pick her up.

"How could you let her do that?" my sister demanded angrily, assuming the mantle of motherly worry I normally wore. "How could you just let her get out of the car like that?"

"Are you suggesting that we should have held her against her will? I believe that constitutes kidnapping."

"She's a minor, for God's sake. How could you just let her go like that? Aren't you worried what might happen to her?"

I thought of Amy Lokash, of Sara, Michelle, my mother, even Jo Lynn. All the women in my life passed quickly before my eyes, like the last images of someone who is drowning. "Can't save everyone," I said.

Chapter
21

We left the motel for the prison at precisely eight-thirty the following morning. Visiting hours were from nine till three, and Jo Lynn was determined to be there for every minute of those six hours. Although the prison was only eleven miles west of Starke on State Road 16, she'd already warned me that it would take about twenty minutes to pass through all the gates and various security checks, which made leaving the motel by eight-thirty an absolute necessity.

When Jo Lynn awakened me at seven-thirty that morning, she was already showered and dressed in the white miniskirt and tank top that had become something of her trademark, her makeup meticulously applied, her hair gloriously askew. I stumbled around the garishly appointed room, with its heavy red curtains and deep purple bedspreads, amazed I'd slept so soundly. For the first time in months, I'd actually

slept through the night—no dreams, no pesky trips to the bathroom. Was it because I was so exhausted, both mentally and physically, from the long drive up from Palm Beach? Or was it because I was almost afraid of opening my eyes to face this new day? I stepped into the shower, allowing the surprisingly satisfying torrent of hot water to envelop me.

"Hurry," Jo Lynn prompted later, as I zipped up the fly of my navy slacks and reached into my overnight bag for my orange blouse. "Is that what you're wearing?" she asked, then laughed.

"Something wrong with this?"

"No, it's perfect." She laughed again, watching as I did up the buttons, then quickly ran a brush through my hair. I thought of applying a bit of blush, a stroke of lipstick, then decided against it. Jo Lynn was in a hurry, and besides, there was nobody I wanted to impress. "We'll stop for an Egg McMuffin on the way," she said, picking up the cooler stuffed with the various cheeses and chicken salad sandwiches she'd made herself—Colin's favorite—and pushing me out the motel room door toward the car.

Probably because we'd driven at night, I'd failed to notice how drastically the scenery had changed once we'd transferred off the turnpike onto Highway 301. I saw now that here, in the heart of rural north-central Florida, truck farms and scraggly pines had replaced the orange groves and majestic palm trees of the southeast coast. "I didn't realize the area was so poor," I said, perhaps disingenuously, as we made our way along the state road toward the prison, Jo Lynn behind the wheel.

"Looks a bit like the backwaters of Georgia," Jo Lynn agreed, and I wondered when she'd last seen the backwaters of Georgia.

"It's so hot," I marveled, trying to find a radio station that was broadcasting something other than the latest farm reports, the air hanging fetid and bloated around me, like a drowned man draped across my shoulders. I heard a huge roar and turned my head, half expecting to see an enormous tidal wave gathering force behind me; instead I saw a massive tractor-trailer riding up our tail, then drawing precipitously close to the side of our car.

Jo Lynn looked up and waved to the driver and his male passenger,

both of whom were practically hanging out their window to get a better look at my sister's bare legs. "I like to give 'em a flash of thigh," she confided as they sped past.

"You think that's such a good idea?" I asked, not expecting, nor particularly wanting, any reply. The road opened onto a broad plain. Cattle grazed along the roadside, some standing up, others lying down.

"It might rain," Jo Lynn pronounced.

I stared through the window at the cloudless blue sky, as waves of heat bounced, like pebbles, from the road across the hood of the car. "Rain?"

"If the cows are all standing up, it means it's going to be sunny. If they're all lying down, it's going to rain. If some are up and some are down, then the weather's going to be changeable."

"Something else you picked up from the motel manager?" I asked.

"No," she said. "From Daddy."

I tried not to look surprised by the sudden intrusion of my stepfather into the conversation.

"He used to take me for drives in the country sometimes, and we'd see all these cows grazing, just like these guys are doing, and he'd say that if all the cows were standing up, it was going to be sunny, and if they were all lying down, well, you know the rest. These cows are owned by the prison, by the way."

"Are those prisoners?" I asked, suddenly cognizant of small gangs of men working along the side of the road, supervised by uniformed guards wearing sunglasses and carrying shotguns.

"This ain't Oz," Jo Lynn said, chuckling at my discomfort.

And suddenly the prison stretched before us, actually two prisons, one to either side of the stream, ambitiously named New River, that divided Union and Bradford counties. The Union Correctional Institution was situated to the right, Florida State Prison to the left, each identified by huge signs in front of double rows of chain-link fences topped with razor ribbon, and differentiated by color: Union Correctional was a series of concrete block buildings painted an indifferent beige; Florida State Prison was a sickly pastel lime green.

Jo Lynn pulled the car into the designated parking area, turned the

engine off, and dropped the keys into her straw purse. "We have arrived," she said solemnly, throwing open her door. "Everybody into the pool."

I followed Jo Lynn toward the main gate, our pace brisk in order to keep the horde of insistent insects at bay, mindful of the guard watching us, rifle in hand, from the watchtower high above our heads. As we approached, the gate opened, and we stepped through. Immediately, it closed behind us, and I instantly felt sick to my stomach. Another gate sputtered noisily open, beckoning us further inside. We're entering hell, I thought, hearing the second gate clang shut behind us as I followed my sister down the concrete walkway to the double doors of the prison itself.

I don't remember pushing open the doors, or even stepping across the wide threshold. All I remember is standing in a small waiting area, staring at a large man in a tiny glass-enclosed booth, who sat in front of a crowded control panel, smiling at Jo Lynn as she strode purposefully toward him. "Hi, Tom," she said easily.

"Hi, Jo Lynn, how're you all doing today?"

"Just fine, Tom," Jo Lynn answered. "Want you to meet my sister, Kate."

"Hello there, Kate," Tom said.

"Hello there, Tom," I said in return, marveling that people actually talked this way, that *I* was talking this way.

"You know the routine," Tom said to Jo Lynn.

"Sure do," Jo Lynn said, offering him both her purse and the cooler.

Tom spent the next ten minutes going through each and every item in our bags. He inspected the contents of the cooler, actually unwrapping the cheeses and breaking them into smaller chunks and opening the halves of the chicken salad sandwiches to peer inside, before moving on to our purses, studying our driver's licenses as if committing each detail to memory, checking us both carefully against our photographs, even though he'd obviously recognized my sister from her past visits. "He does this every week," Jo Lynn whispered over the constant clanging of prison doors.

"Nice seeing you again," Tom said to my sister, motioning us

toward a third barred gate and a metal detector. "A pleasure to meet you, Kate."

We had to rid ourselves of our shoes, our belts, our keys, our sunglasses, and any pens and loose change we might be carrying, and once through the metal detector, a guard accompanied us through yet another loudly clanging gate and down a long yellowy-beige corridor with a shiny linoleum floor. "The prisoners wax and polish this floor every day," Jo Lynn confided.

There were some steps and still another gate controlled by a guard in a glass-enclosed booth, and suddenly we were in the heart of the prison, a four-way intersection called Grand Central. To our right were floor-to-ceiling bars, beyond which were the cellblocks of the prisoners. "That's where they keep the electric chair." Jo Lynn pointed through the bars toward a closed door at the very end of the long, wide hall.

Several prisoners walked past us on their way to work at the prison laundry, wearing blue prison-issue dungarees and blue work shirts. "We go this way," Jo Lynn motioned, and we followed another guard into the so-called visiting park off the main corridor.

A variety of cooking smells assaulted my nose, one blending into the next, rendering them indistinguishable. "We're in the same wing as the kitchen and the mess hall," Jo Lynn said. "In fact, this visiting park *was* the old mess hall. You'll see, it looks just like a high school cafeteria."

She was right. The room was large, nondescript, filled with maybe thirty or forty stainless-steel tables and chairs. The only thing that distinguished it from a school cafeteria was the fact that these tables and chairs were bolted to the floor. "See that watercooler over there?" Jo Lynn pointed toward the large glass watercooler in one corner of the room.

I nodded.

"Keep your eye on it," she advised.

"Why? Does it do something?"

"Wait till the prisoners get here. You'll see." She checked her watch, pointed to her left. "They'll be bringing them in anytime now. I gotta use the facilities," she announced abruptly, placing the cooler on

one of the tables and marching quickly to the rest room just outside the door.

I looked around, pretending to casually peruse my surroundings, but actually concentrating my attention on the other men and women waiting for the arrival of their friends and loved ones. There were about a dozen of us, the women outnumbering the men by a ratio of three to one, the blacks outnumbering the whites by perhaps the same ratio. All the younger women wore dresses, as opposed to slacks, although none were quite as provocatively attired as my sister. One older black woman, wearing black from head to toe, so that it was hard to distinguish where her skin left off and her clothing began, was crying softly against her husband's shoulder; another woman, whose lips were pierced by a series of small gold loops and whose arms were covered by a series of ink-blue tattoos, paced anxiously back and forth behind a nearby table.

"You okay?" I asked my sister when she returned, looking slightly flushed.

"Oh sure."

"You rushed out of here so fast, I was afraid something might be wrong."

She waved away my concern with a sharp flick of her wrist. "I just had to get something."

"Get something?"

She slid into one of the chairs and leaned both elbows on the stainless-steel top of the table, nodding toward the seat across from her for me to sit down. "I brought Colin a little present," she said out of the side of her mouth, eyes on the guard at the doorway.

"A present?"

"Ssh! Lower your voice."

"What kind of present?" Images of guns stuffed inside bras and knives secreted inside lush layer cakes danced before my eyes, although I knew this was absurd. We'd passed through two metal detectors, and there was nothing other than cheese and chicken salad sandwiches inside Jo Lynn's cooler. Nor had I noticed any gifts when Tom went through her purse. "What kind of present?" I asked again.

She slipped her hand inside her straw bag and pulled something out, which she was careful to conceal from the guard. When she was confident no one was looking, she opened the palm of her hand, showing me a smooth oblong container filled with about six hand-rolled cigarettes.

"Marijuana?!"

"Ssh!" She immediately returned the container to her bag. "Do you have to yell everything?"

"Are you crazy?" I demanded. "Bringing that stuff in here."

"Will you lower your voice and stop acting like some silly schoolgirl. Everybody does it."

I looked anxiously around me, at the black woman crying on her husband's shoulder, the girl with the lip rings and tattoos pacing nervously behind the next table. "But how did you sneak it past the guards? Tom went through our bags with a magnifying glass."

"I stuffed it up my snatch," she said, and giggled. "Close your mouth. Flies will get in."

"Your vagina?"

"Vagina," she echoed, her mouth twisting with disdain. "God, Kate, who but you uses words like vagina anymore?"

"I don't believe this."

"You'd be amazed to find out what goes on in places like these."

"But how does Colin get them back to his cell?"

"Trust me, you don't want to know."

"I think I'm going to be sick."

"You can't be sick now. Here they come. Remember to keep your eyes on the watercooler."

I looked quickly from the door to the watercooler and back again to the door as several guards—tall, burly, vaguely menacing—escorted a coterie of about ten men into the room. All were dressed in the same blue prison garb, with one notable exception—Colin Friendly. Like me, he was wearing blue pants and an orange top.

Now I understood why Jo Lynn had laughed at my choice of clothes. Orange T-shirts were what distinguished the prisoners on death row from the other inmates.

My fingers went self-consciously to the neck of my orange blouse,

as I watched my sister leap from her seat to embrace the convicted serial killer, his hands sliding down to cup her rear end, his palms catching the hem of her short skirt, momentarily exposing the rounded bare flesh of her buttocks. I realized, in that instant, that when Jo Lynn had rid her body of its hidden contraband, she'd also removed her panties. "Oh God," I moaned as they broke from their embrace and walked toward me.

Colin Friendly seemed taller than I remembered him from court, and while somewhat thinner, he was definitely more muscular. Probably he'd been working out, I thought as I rose unsteadily to my feet, my hands resolutely at my sides, trying to decide how I would react were he to offer his hand in greeting.

He didn't.

"Colin," Jo Lynn said, hanging on to his arm, "I'd like you to meet my sister, Kate. Kate, this is Colin, the love of my life."

"Nice to meet you, Kate," he said easily. "Your sister talks about you all the time."

Or words to that effect. Truthfully, I'm not exactly sure what was said that morning, or during most of our time together in that so-called visiting park. The hours pass through my brain with the swiftness and cruelty of an ambush. I remember our conversation in fits and starts, a few choice words here, a chilling phrase there, most topics blending one into the other, one hour disappearing inside the next.

"You don't look much like sisters," Colin was saying as we took our seats, Colin beside Jo Lynn, their hands in each other's laps, despite the rules against touching. Prisoners were permitted opening and closing embraces, nothing in between, but the three guards who were present often looked the other way, and a wide variety of indiscretions were taking place, all of which I tried hard not to notice.

"Different fathers," I told him.

"So Jo Lynn tells me."

"Isn't he the most gorgeous thing you've ever seen?" Jo Lynn said, and giggled, like an adolescent. She leaned toward him, her bosom grazing the side of his arm, and wiped a dark curl away from his high forehead.

He laughed with her. "You're the most gorgeous thing I've ever seen, that's for sure," he told her without a trace of self-consciousness, as if I weren't privy to their conversation, as if they were the only two people in the room. "You have no idea how jealous everybody is of me back on the row. They know I have the most beautiful, sexy woman in the world waiting for me every Saturday."

"I'm wearing your favorite underwear," she told him, and I drew a huge intake of breath as I saw his hand sneak beneath her short skirt, and the laughter spread to his cold blue eyes.

"I hope you're taking real good care of your baby sister," he said without looking at me, "until I get out of here."

I said nothing, tried to look elsewhere, saw similar gropings at other tables.

"You gotta make sure she's eating right and getting plenty of exercise and sleep."

"You shouldn't be worrying about me," Jo Lynn said. "You've got enough to worry about in here with all these perverts."

He laughed. "Yeah, we got 'em all in here. Sodomites, pederasts, necrophiliacs, faggots. We even have guys that drink their own urine and eat their own shit. One guy likes to smear the stuff all over his body. Disgusting son of a bitch if there ever was one. I stay away from him, I tell you."

"Colin is in R Wing now," Jo Lynn said, glancing briefly in my direction, "but when he first got here, they put him in Q Wing, which is where they house all the nut cases. Colin's lawyers got him out of there pretty damn quick."

"It was a scary place," Colin agreed, shaking his head, his hand disappearing farther under my sister's skirt. "Here they pretty much leave me alone."

"Colin lets them think he's guilty," my sister explained.

"Smart move," I mumbled.

"One of the perks of being on death row is that we get our own cells."

"You're a lucky man," I said.

Colin's head slowly turned from my sister to me, his eyes piercing

through mine like a pin through a butterfly. "Your sister told me you had kind of a sarcastic sense of humor. I see what she means."

I said nothing, surprised and dismayed that my sister had discussed me in any kind of detail at all.

"You don't approve of me, do you?" he asked some time later, and it took me a moment to realize he was serious.

"Does that surprise you?" I asked in return.

"Disappoints me," he answered.

"You're a convicted murderer," I reminded him.

"He's innocent," Jo Lynn said.

"I'm innocent," he repeated, eyes twinkling.

I nodded, fell silent.

"I brought you a present," Jo Lynn said as we were eating our sandwiches, her voice a singsong. She indicated her purse with a nod of her head.

"Brought you something too," Colin told her, reaching into the pocket of his blue pants.

Jo Lynn squealed with delight as he produced a handful of letters. "Oh good, fan mail," she trilled, laughing as she opened the first letter. " 'Dear Colin,' " she read aloud, " 'you are the handsomest man I have ever seen. Your eyes are like sapphires, your face the visage of a Greek god.' Visage? That's one of your words, Kate." She laughed. "Don't you just love this stuff?" She tore into the next one. " 'Dear Colin, do not despair. As long as you accept Jesus and take Him to your heart, God will forgive you your sins and evil deeds.' Stupid woman," Jo Lynn proclaimed. "Colin didn't commit any evil deeds." She opened another letter, read silently for several seconds. "Oh, this is the best one yet. Listen to this, Kate. I bet you can identify with this one. 'Dear Colin, I am fifty years old with brown hair and hazel eyes, and friends tell me I still have a pretty good figure.' " She glanced knowingly in my direction. " 'I know I'm a married woman with a husband who loves me, but the truth is, the only man I want is you. I think about you night and day. I long to suckle you to my breast, to cradle you in my arms, to give you all the love your mother denied you.' What do you think, Kate?"

"I think the woman wants a baby, not a man," I answered, embarrassment staining my cheeks, like the blush I hadn't bothered to apply.

Jo Lynn handed the letters back to Colin. "Thanks for showing them to me, sweet buns."

"You know I don't keep any secrets from you," Colin said.

"Just don't go writing any of these crazies back," Jo Lynn cautioned.

"You don't have to worry about a thing from me, babe," he told her. "You know that."

"I know I love you."

"Not half as much as I love you."

"Now!" Jo Lynn suddenly hissed across the table, motioning with her chin toward the watercooler in the far corner of the room. I watched as one of the inmates snuck in behind it with his wife, another inmate and his wife positioned in front of it, perhaps blocking, perhaps guarding, perhaps simply waiting their turn. Seconds later, the cooler began shaking, the water inside it sloshing from side to side, like waves in a turbulent sea.

"What happens if they get caught?" I asked.

"You worry too much about consequences," Jo Lynn said. "Besides, it's the state's fault for not allowing conjugal visits."

"A guy's gotta do what a guy's gotta do," Colin Friendly said, squeezing my sister's thigh.

"You haven't . . ." I started, then stopped, deciding I didn't want to know.

"Gone for a drink of water?" Jo Lynn teased. "No, we haven't. Not yet, anyway."

"We're saving ourselves for our wedding night," Colin said, and they laughed.

I jumped to my feet, although I'm not sure what I was planning to do. One of the guards looked over, his eyes an inquisitive squint. I smiled, pretended to stretch, then sat back down. "Have you set the date?"

"Not yet. There's still a lot of things that have to be arranged. Blood tests, shit like that. But it'll be soon," Jo Lynn assured me.

"A simple thing like getting married, and they make it so difficult."
Colin shook his head in dismay. "Have you asked your sister yet?"

"Asked me what?"

"To be my matron of honor," Jo Lynn said hopefully.

I swallowed hard, looked away, tried not to burst into tears. She
couldn't be serious, I thought, knowing she was. "I don't think that
would be a very good idea."

"Why don't you give yourself some time to think about it," Colin
advised, eyes boring into mine. "We'd sure appreciate your support."

"I'd sure appreciate knowing what happened to Amy Lokash," I
said, shocking not only my sister and her so-called fiancé but myself as
well. I'd been planning to ask about Rita Ketchum, not Amy. Obviously,
my subconscious had other plans.

"Amy L-lokash?" Colin stuttered for the first time all day.

Jo Lynn rolled her eyes in disgust. "What are you trying to pull,
Kate? Who the hell is Amy Lokash?"

"She's a seventeen-year-old girl who disappeared about a year ago. I
thought you might know something about it."

"This is ridiculous," my sister raged. "Colin, you don't have to
answer any of her stupid questions." In the next instant, Jo Lynn was out
of her seat and on her way to the rest room, adjusting her skirt across her
bottom as she walked.

"Isn't she the juiciest thing you ever saw?" Colin marveled, eyes
trailing after Jo Lynn until she disappeared.

"Why don't you just leave my sister alone."

"Say 'please,' " he said, casually, almost as if he hadn't spoken.

"What?" Maybe I hadn't heard him correctly.

He swiveled toward me. "You heard me. Say 'please.' " A sneer
tugged at the corner of his lips. "Make that 'pretty please.' "

I said nothing.

"You want me to leave your sister alone, you gotta do something for
me. Say 'pretty please.' Go on, say it."

"Fuck you," I said instead.

He laughed, ran his tongue across his upper lip. "Maybe in time."

My body went instantly cold as I recalled my earlier nightmares. My

heart beat wildly, its errant pulse reaching inside my brain, as noisy and relentless as a massive tractor-trailer, so loud against the inside of my ear that I could barely hear the sound of my own voice. "This is all a sick game to you, isn't it?"

"I don't play games. I play for keeps."

"Did you kill Amy Lokash?" I asked, struggling to regain control.

Colin Friendly leaned closer, rested his elbows on the table. "Cute kid, dimples, wore a little red plastic barrette in her hair?"

I grabbed the side of the table for support, felt it cold against the palms of my hands. "Oh God." I thought of Donna Lokash, wondered if I'd have the courage to confide in her the certainty of her daughter's fate. "She was just a baby, for God's sake. How could you hurt her?"

"Well, you know what they say," Colin said lazily. "Old enough to bleed, old enough to butcher." He paused, allowing several seconds for this latest obscenity to sink in. "You familiar with John Prince Park?" he asked.

I shook my head, too numb to do anything else.

"Real pretty park. Just east of Congress between Lake Worth and Lantana roads. You should go there sometime. There's barbecues and picnic benches, and a bicycle path, even a playground. Real pretty sight. Right on Lake Osborne. You know Lake Osborne?"

"No."

"Too bad. It's a pretty big lake, one of those long and winding numbers. A couple of little bridges. Real scenic. Lots of people fishing from the shore. Or you can rent boats. You should do that sometime, Kate. Rent a boat, take a little ride out to about the middle of the lake, where it's deepest."

"What are you saying?"

"Your daughters would really like it," he said, smiling widely. "You've got a daughter Amy's age, don't you? Real attractive girl, if I remember correctly."

I held my breath.

"And a younger one too. Michelle, right? Maybe one day, you, me, Sara, and Michelle, we could all get together, have some fun. I've never had a mother-daughter act before."

"Bastard," I muttered.

"So they say."

"I hope you rot in hell."

He smiled. "Does that mean you won't be coming to the wedding?"

I'm not sure what I said next, if, in fact, I said anything at all. I wanted to lash out, to slap that stupid smirk off his face, to pummel him lifeless. Instead I fled the room, as helpless as any of his victims, crying as I raced toward the parking lot, bugs swarming around my face, seagulls screeching overhead, a slight rain starting to fall. By the time Jo Lynn appeared, at just after three o'clock, I was soaking wet, my orange blouse clinging to my arms, like Saran Wrap, my hair plastered against my head, like seaweed.

"The cows were right," my sister said, unlocking the car door. Neither one of us said another word for the duration of the long ride home.

Chapter

22

Four days later, I stood on the shore of Lake Osborne, watching the police drag the area from small, flat-bottomed boats. A dive team, complete with scuba gear, had been in the water for the better part of the morning.

"What are they looking for?" a woman asked, coming up beside me.

"I'm not sure," I said, truthfully. Amy Lokash had been missing, and presumably in her watery grave, for almost a year. What could the police hope to find?

Unless Colin Friendly had weighted down her body, or encased it in cement, Amy's body would have floated to the surface within days of its disposal. No such body had been found, the police were quick to assure me when I reported my conversation with the convicted serial killer.

"He's just playing with you," one police officer told me. But they agreed to search the area anyway.

Generally speaking, spectators aren't allowed close to such a scene, but John Prince Park is a large public area, and easily accessible from a variety of spots. It's impossible to close off the area entirely. In any event, it wouldn't have been necessary. It was the middle of the week in the middle of February. There were only a smattering of people in the park: a young mother pushing her toddler on a nearby swing, oblivious to everything but each other; two men strolling arm in arm, who took off as soon as they saw the police; a man drinking from a paper bag, too far gone to care if anyone saw him or not; several joggers, pausing briefly in their run to ask what was going on, then be on their way.

I wasn't sure why I'd come. Maybe I was hoping for some concrete evidence that I could present to my sister before it was too late. Maybe I was looking for some closure for Donna Lokash. Or maybe I was just putting off getting on with my own life, which today meant picking up my mother for our scheduled mammograms.

By noon, the divers had returned to the surface shaking their heads, and it was becoming obvious that the police were about to call it quits, not having turned up anything but an old tire and several stray pairs of men's shoes. Colin Friendly might have killed Amy Lokash, but he hadn't thrown her body into Lake Osborne. The police were right—he'd been playing with me.

An hour later, I was standing naked from the waist up, watching as expert, but indifferent, fingers placed first my right breast, then my left, between two cold surfaces, and squished them flat as a pancake. Smile for the camera, I thought, as I listened to the buzz of the large X-ray machine.

"Okay, we're done," the technician said, releasing my breast as I restarted my breathing. "Have a seat in the waiting room. Please don't get dressed until I make sure the X-rays are all right."

I slipped my arms back through the blue hospital gown that hung around my waist, and shuffled into the hallway, over to the waiting area, where my mother sat among four other women, all dressed in similar

smocks, waiting for either their turn to be photographed or their permission to get dressed.

"How're you doing, Mom?" I asked, sliding into the seat beside her, leaning my head back against the cool blue wall, breathing deeply.

She smiled pleasantly, eyes unfocused, staring toward the Matisse print on the wall across from us. "Magnificent."

I released a deep breath of air. "You've had mammograms before, haven't you?" I stated more than asked.

"Of course," she said.

"Be sure to let the technician know if she hurts you."

"Of course, dear."

"They don't really hurt."

"Of course not."

Such was the extent of most of my mother's discourse these days. Still, it was more than my sister had said to me since our return from Raiford. I'd tried to tell her what had transpired while she was out of the room, carefully repeating the things Colin had said, then had to sit and listen while she rushed to his defense, as I'd known she would—I'd provoked him, deliberately misunderstood him, put words into his mouth. I told her she was crazy; she told me I was jealous. We hadn't spoken since.

The technician appeared, clipboard in hand. She was tall and thin, with long, stringy red hair pulled into a ponytail, and she looked no older than Sara. I realized I hadn't really noticed her before, despite the intimate nature of our encounter. To me, she was just a pair of hands, as no doubt, to her, I was just a pair of breasts. We took from each other only what we needed, no more, no less. So easy, I thought, to separate the part from the whole.

"Mrs. Latimer?" The technician looked around the room, which was small and windowless, though not unpleasant. My mother said nothing, continued staring dreamily into space.

"Mrs. Latimer," the technician repeated.

"Mom," I said, nudging her arm. "She's calling you."

"Of course." My mother rose quickly to her feet, didn't move.

"Follow me, please," the technician told her, then looked at me. "You can get dressed now, Mrs. Sinclair."

"The tests were negative?" I asked hopefully.

"Your doctor will discuss the results with you," she said, as I'd known she would. "But the X-rays are fine. I don't have to redo them."

Thank God, I thought, watching as my mother followed the technician to the door.

"I'll wait here, Mom," I said.

"Of course, dear," she answered.

I changed back into my street clothes, a white cotton sweater over gray pants, fixed my hair, reapplied my lipstick, returned to my seat in the waiting area, and closed my eyes. Immediately, I pictured Colin Friendly's mocking smile, and opened my eyes again, grabbing the latest issue of *Cosmopolitan* from a nearby end table, and concentrating all my attention on the latest Cosmo girl. She was wearing a royal blue negligee against a royal blue background; her hair was long and dark, her eyes brown and sultry, her cleavage deep and bountiful.

I remembered when Sara was about ten years old, and I found her standing in front of the bathroom mirror studying her naked chest. "When I grow up," she asked seriously, "am I going to have big breasts or nice little ones like yours?"

I told her the odds favored the little ones, not the last time I've seriously misjudged my older daughter, whose breasts have been known to enter a room a full five seconds before she does. I used to joke that had I had big breasts, I could have ruled the world. Kidding on the square, my mother would say, and she'd be right.

When my mother reentered the waiting area, she immediately began removing her hospital gown, exposing herself to the startled women in the room. The women looked away, pretended to be coughing, reading, elsewhere.

"Mom, wait," I said, rushing to her side, tugging the gown back up across her shoulders. "Didn't the technician tell you to wait until she was sure the X-rays came out?"

My mother smiled. "Yes, I believe she did."

"Then why don't we sit down for a few minutes." I led her to the row of upholstered navy chairs. "How'd it go?"

"I didn't much care for it," she stated, and I laughed.

"Did it hurt?"

"I didn't much care for it," she repeated, and I laughed again, because she seemed to be expecting it.

"I didn't much care for it," she said a third time, and we lapsed into silence until the technician appeared and told my mother her X-rays were fine and that she could get dressed.

"You can get dressed now, Mom," I repeated when she failed to respond.

She immediately began pulling the gown from her shoulders.

"Not here, Mom. In the changing room."

"Of course, dear."

I led her toward the small changing room, my heart heavy, as if I'd swallowed something undigestible and it was sitting there in my chest, refusing to go down. I knew what was happening. By this point, I'd done quite a bit of reading about Alzheimer's disease, and my reading had told me roughly what to expect. The long and the short of it was that my mother was becoming my child. She was regressing, gradually losing pieces of herself, shedding her identity as a snake sheds its skin. Soon there would be nothing left of the woman she once was. She would forget everything—how to read, how to write, how to speak. Her children would become strangers to her, as she would become a stranger to herself. One day, her brain would simply forget to tell her heart to breathe, and she would die. It would remain for the rest of us to try to salvage the pieces of her she'd discarded, to fit them back together, to make her whole again, at least in our memories.

At the time, it felt as if my mother's deterioration had occurred very suddenly, but, looking back, the signs had been there for years. She'd often seemed vague, occasionally confused, her conversations cheery but essentially empty. She forgot things, mispronounced words, occasionally forgot them altogether.

Didn't we all? I'd told myself, not paying particularly close atten-tion. And if talking to her was sometimes like talking to the woman on

the weather channel, well, so what? Weather, food, constipation—these were probably hot topics in assisted living communities. She'd had enough turmoil in her life, I rationalized. If she wanted to speculate endlessly about the weather, she was entitled.

And, of course, there were times that she was rational, witty, and seemingly normal, when flashes of her old self would appear to remind us that she hadn't disappeared completely, that part of her was still hanging on, fighting to get through. A piece of her here, a piece of her there. She tossed them toward me, like bread crumbs to a hungry bird. Maybe, like Hansel and Gretel, she was trying to leave a path, a way to trace her steps back home, back to the self she had lost.

"Are you ready?" I asked after several minutes, knocking on the door to the changing room.

There was no answer, so I knocked again, gently pushing the door open. My mother was standing in the middle of the tiny cubicle, totally nude, arms protectively covering her sagging breasts, her ribs clearly delineated, her flesh mottled, heavily veined, her skin the color and consistency of skim milk. "I'm cold," she said, looking at me as if it were my fault.

"Oh God, Mom, here, let me help you." I stepped into the tiny changing area, closing the door behind me, tried to gather up her clothes from the floor.

"What are you doing?" Her voice was edgy, on the verge of panic.

"I'm trying to find your underwear."

"What are you doing to me?" she demanded again.

"Ssh, Mom," I cautioned. "It's all right. I'm just trying to help."

"Where are my clothes?" she shouted, spinning around in the cramped space, knocking me against the wall.

"They're right here, Mom. Try to calm down. Here are your panties." I held out a pair of voluminous pink underpants. She stared at them as if they were a foreign object. "You just step into them," I said, directing first one foot, then the other, inside the legs of the panties, then pulling them up over her hips.

Fitting her inside her brassiere took another five minutes, as did getting her into her ivory-colored dress. When we finally emerged from

the cramped cubicle, I was soaking wet and breathing hard. "Are you all right, dear?" my mother asked as we exited the building. "You look a little peaked."

I laughed. What else could I do?

"You look a little peaked," she repeated, then waited for me to laugh again, and so I obliged, although the joy was gone, another piece lost.

"Jo Lynn called me last night," my mother said as I was driving her back to her apartment.

I tried not to sound too surprised. Time had become a relative concept to my mother. Last night could mean anything—last night, last week, even last year. "She did?"

"Said she was getting married next week."

"She said that?" This time there was no disguising my surprise. Or my dismay.

"I thought she was already married."

"She's divorced."

"Yes, of course, she's divorced. How could I have forgotten?"

"Jo Lynn's been married three times," I reminded her. "It's hard to keep track."

"Yes, of course."

"She told you she was getting married next week?"

"I think that's what she said. Daniel Baker, she said. A nice boy."

My shoulders slumped. I tightened my grip on the steering wheel. "Dan Baker was her second husband, Mom."

"Is she marrying him again?"

"Are you sure she told you she was getting married next week?" I pressed.

"Well, now, maybe I'm not. I thought that's what she said, but now I don't know. Whatever happened to Daniel?"

"They got divorced."

"Divorced? Why? He was such a nice boy."

"He beat her up, Mom."

"He beat her?"

"Yes, Mom."

Tears filled my mother's eyes. "We let him beat her?"

"We didn't have much choice. We urged her to leave him. She wouldn't."

"I don't remember," my mother said, pounding her fists against her lap in obvious frustration. "Why don't I remember?"

"It's over, Mom. It happened a long time ago. They got divorced. She's all right now."

My mother stared anxiously out the car window, her fingers twisting the fabric of her dress. "What's happening to me?" she asked, her voice high, birdlike. "What's happening to me?"

I swallowed, not sure what to say. Dr. Caffery had discussed the various possibilities with her, including Alzheimer's disease, a conversation my mother had seemingly forgotten. Was there really any point in going over it again?

"We're not sure, Mom," I told her. "That's why you're going for all these tests. It could be something physical, some blockage somewhere, maybe a tumor of some kind that they can remove, or maybe you're just starting to forget things. It happens when people get older. It doesn't necessarily mean it's Alzheimer's," I qualified, more for my benefit than for hers. "I know how frustrating it must be for you, but we'll get to the bottom of all this soon, and hopefully there will be something we can do about it. You know medical science. It moves so quickly, they could find a cure before they even know what you have."

My mother smiled and I patted her hand reassuringly. She closed her eyes, drifted off to sleep, and I drove the rest of the way with only my thoughts for company. My mother would be all right, I told myself. This was just a temporary problem, not a permanent condition, and certainly not irreversible. Before long, one of these X-rays would turn up something, and it would be small and entirely treatable, and my mother would be her old self again, all the pieces neatly back in place.

I pulled into the parking lot of the Palm Beach Lakes Retirement Home, turned off the ignition, gently nudged my mother awake. She opened her eyes, smiled lovingly. "Jo Lynn called last night," she said. "She's getting married next week."

"Relax," Larry was saying, as I paced back and forth behind the kitchen counter.

"Please don't tell me to relax."

"I'm sure Mrs. Winchell will reconsider."

"I'm sure she won't."

"Kate, stop pacing. Let's sit down, talk this out."

"What's there to talk about?" I plopped down on the family-room sofa, jumping immediately back up again, resuming my pacing, this time in front of the TV. "You didn't see her. You didn't hear her. She was very adamant. She said that she has a responsibility to the other residents, that the whole building could have burned to the ground."

"She's exaggerating."

"She doesn't think so. She says that if old Mr. Emerson hadn't smelled something burning in my mother's apartment, then they wouldn't have discovered the pot she left on the burner, and the whole building would have gone up in flames."

"Everyone forgets to turn a burner off now and then," Larry argued, the same words I'd used earlier in the afternoon with Mrs. Winchell.

"Palm Beach Lakes Retirement Home is an assisted living community," I said, repeating Mrs. Winchell's words verbatim. "It is not a nursing home. It is not equipped to deal with Alzheimer sufferers."

"Grandma has Alzheimer's?" Sara asked, bringing a stack of old papers into the kitchen, dropping them into the garbage can under the sink.

"We don't know that yet," Larry told her.

"What are you doing?" I asked.

"Cleaning my room," Sara said.

"You're cleaning your room?"

"It's a mess. There was nowhere to study."

"You're studying?"

"We have a big test in a few weeks."

"You're studying for a test?"

"I thought I'd give it a try," Sara said, and smiled. "Will Grandma be all right?"

"I hope so," I told her. "Meanwhile, I have to find her a new place to live."

To my shock, Sara walked to my side and drew me into a warm, comforting embrace. "It'll be all right, Mom," she reassured me, as I had reassured my mother earlier. I hugged her tightly to me, relishing the feel of her skin against mine, burying my face into the elegant bend of her neck. How long had it been since she'd allowed me to hold her this way? I wondered, realizing how much I'd missed it.

"I love you," I whispered.

"I love you too," she said.

For a few minutes, it seemed that everything would be all right.

Chapter

23

Wednesday morning found me lingering over my second cup of coffee and looking forward to a day of total self-indulgence: a much-needed, long-anticipated massage at ten, a facial at eleven-thirty, followed by a hairdresser's appointment, a manicure and a pedicure. I thought of my mother, putting lipstick on her nails, then pushed her out of my mind. Wednesday was *my* day, my oasis in the desert, my day to unwind and regroup. It seemed I hadn't had such a day in an eternity.

The phone rang.

I debated answering it, almost didn't, gave in after the third ring. "Hello." I crossed my fingers, praying it wasn't the masseuse calling to cancel our appointment.

"Just wanted to tell you how nice it was seeing you the other day," the male voice said.

"Who is this?" The muscles across my back contracted painfully. I already knew who it was.

"How was L-lake Osborne?" Colin Friendly asked.

I said nothing, my eyes shooting instinctively to the windows, to the sliding glass door.

"And how are my lovely nieces-to-be?"

I slammed down the receiver, my hands shaking. "Damn you!" I screamed. "Damn you to hell, Colin Friendly! You leave my daughters out of your sick fantasies." I began pacing, turning around in a series of increasingly small circles, until I felt my head spin and my knees grow weak. "Don't let him get to you," I said aloud, collapsing into a waiting chair, hating his newfound power over me. "There's no way I'm going to let you torment me," I said, reaching for the phone, about to call the prison officials in Starke, when the phone rang again.

I stared at it without moving. Slowly, I plucked it from its carriage, brought it gingerly to my ear, bracing myself for the familiar stutter, said nothing.

"Hello?" a woman asked. "Hello, is someone there?"

"Hello?" I asked in return. "Mrs. Winchell?"

"Mrs. Sinclair, is that you?"

For an instant, I considered telling her that I was the cleaning lady, that Mrs. Sinclair wasn't home, and wouldn't be back till the end of the day. "What can I do for you?" I asked instead.

"I was just wondering if you'd been able to find other accommodations for your mother," she began without further preamble.

I informed her politely that I'd made inquiries into several upscale nursing homes in the area, but that there were no current vacancies. In a sympathetic, yet firm voice, Mrs. Winchell told me that I'd have to look farther afield, and recommended several nursing homes I hadn't tried, one in Boca, another in Delray. Boca, I told her immediately, was out of the question. It was too far away. I might consider having a look at the one in Delray.

"Please do," she said. She didn't need to add "as soon as possible." The tone of her voice said it all.

I poured myself another cup of coffee, took my time drinking it,

refusing to think about either Mrs. Winchell or Colin Friendly, then made my bed, arranging, then rearranging, the fourteen decorative pillows that graced it, trying out new groupings, ultimately returning the pillows to their original configuration. It was only then, when there was no more coffee to drink, no more pillows to disturb, and nothing left to straighten, that I phoned the nursing home in Delray, and, much to my chagrin, was able to get an immediate appointment.

There goes my day, I thought, reluctantly canceling my various appointments. Why did it always have to be me? I groused. Why couldn't Jo Lynn assume at least some of the responsibility as far as our mother was concerned? Did she have anything better to do with her time? If she could spend between ten and twelve hours every weekend driving up to north-central Florida and back, surely she could spend thirty minutes driving to a nursing home in Delray. And she could damn well tell her psychotic boyfriend to leave me and my daughters alone. On a sudden impulse, I picked up the phone and called my sister, although I hadn't spoken to her since our ill-fated excursion to the state pen.

"Your fiancé called me this morning," I said, instead of hello.

"Yes, I know."

"You know?"

"He told me he was planning to apologize for any misunderstanding there might have been . . ."

"Misunderstanding?" I repeated incredulously.

"I told him it would be a waste of time."

"If he ever calls me again, I'll complain to the warden. They'll cancel his phone privileges altogether," I warned, discovering how easy it was to threaten the already vulnerable.

"Thanks for your call," Jo Lynn said icily.

"I'm not finished."

She waited. I could see her eyes rolling toward the ceiling with disgust.

"Mrs. Winchell says Mom can't live at Palm Beach Lakes anymore."

"So?"

"So we have to find her somewhere else to live."

Silence.

"I've made an appointment with this nursing facility in Delray. It's called the Atrium."

"Fine."

"It's for eleven o'clock this morning. I thought you should be there."

"Not a chance."

"I just thought you might like to have a look at where Mom might have to go," I persisted.

"She can go to hell as far as I'm concerned."

"Jo Lynn!"

"So can you." She hung up.

"Jo Lynn . . ." Once again, I slammed the receiver down, only to watch it bounce off its carriage and tumble toward the floor, where it jerked to a sudden stop mere inches from the carpet, hanging by its white cord, like some misguided bungee jumper. "What the hell is the matter with you?" I scooped up the receiver, dropped it into its carriage, plopped down on the side of my bed, and stared out the window at the curving coconut palm. "Why couldn't I have a normal sister?" I shouted.

I was still screaming as I drove down to Delray. Screaming and speeding, for which I was duly pulled over by a waiting police officer and ticketed. "Any idea how fast you were going?" he asked. Not fast enough, I thought.

Mrs. Sullivan was a moon-faced, pleasant-voiced woman of around sixty. She had brown hair, brown eyes, and legs the size of toothpicks under an otherwise sturdy frame. She graciously showed me around the grounds, which were well manicured and attractively landscaped, then the building itself, a relatively new structure that was low and white and Mediterranean in feel. It didn't look like a nursing home, I tried to convince myself, refusing to allow the vaguely medicinal scent permeating the halls to penetrate my nostrils, ignoring the low wails I heard emanating from behind the closed doors of several of the spacious rooms, pretending not to notice the empty eyes and slack jaws of the residents lined up in wheelchairs against the walls. "Hello there, Mr. Perpich," Mrs. Sullivan said gaily, receiving no response from the white-haired,

toothless old man whose body was twisted and gnarled, like the trunk of a long-dead tree.

How could I abandon my mother to a place like this? I asked myself as I raced to my car. "Don't be silly," I said out loud, fumbling with my keys. "There's nothing wrong with this place. It's a perfectly acceptable place, nicer than the ones you looked at in Palm Beach." What was I always telling clients in similar positions? You have to think about yourselves. Your mother will be happier there. She'll have people to look after her. You won't have to worry about her falling down the stairs or getting enough to eat. You can get on with your life.

Sure. Easy for you to say.

How could I get on with my life when the woman who gave me that life was losing her own? How could I abandon her to clean but sterile hallways, leave her sitting in a wheelchair for hours at a time, staring into space, into a past she could no longer connect with, into a future that held no hope. She could last for years this way, I reminded myself, her life effectively over, death a slow tease away. I couldn't put my life on hold indefinitely. Yet she was my mother and I loved her, no matter how many pieces of her former self were missing. I wasn't ready to let go.

Still, it was clear she could no longer stay where she was. If I wasn't prepared to put her in a nursing home, that left only one other alternative. "I was wondering how you'd feel about my mother moving in with us for a while," I rehearsed into the rearview mirror, seeing my husband's eyes widen in alarm. "It would only be temporary. A few weeks, maybe a few months. No longer than that, I promise."

"But you're gone all day. Who's going to look after her while you're at work?"

"We could hire someone to come in. Please, would you do it for me?"

I knew he would. No matter what his reservations, I knew that ultimately Larry would do whatever he thought would make me happy.

So, what was I going to do? I asked myself repeatedly as I drove aimlessly through the streets of Delray. The office building that housed radio station WKEY suddenly appeared before me like a mirage in the desert. Had I been heading here all along?

"This is a pleasant surprise," Robert said as I stepped inside his office. I heard him close the door behind me.

I turned around and into his arms, his face a handsome blur as his lips fastened on mine, my body collapsing into his with an eagerness I hadn't anticipated. "I can't believe I'm doing this," I heard myself say, but the words never made it past my mouth as I swayed, ever closer, against him.

He pulled back, just slightly, pulling me with him, like a magnet. "Why didn't you tell me you were coming?"

"I didn't know myself."

"I have a lunch appointment in a few minutes."

"I can't stay."

He kissed the side of my mouth, the tip of my nose. "I would have kept my schedule free."

"Next time."

"When?"

"What?"

"Next time—when will it be?"

He kissed my forehead, my cheek, the side of my neck. "When?" he repeated.

"I don't know. My life is such a mess right now."

"Messes become you. You look sexy as hell."

"I look sexy or I look like hell?"

"You're driving me crazy, you know that."

And then he was kissing me again, this time full on the lips, our mouths open, his tongue circling mine, and suddenly I was seventeen years old, and he was pressing my body against the hard bricks of the high school we attended, his knee pushing my legs apart as his hand tried to sneak underneath my blouse. "No, I can't," I said, pulling back, hitting my head against the window of his twelfth-floor office, snapping rudely back into the present tense. "You have a lunch appointment," I said quickly, trying to catch my breath, tucking my blouse back inside my skirt. "And I really should get going."

"We have a few minutes," he said, pinning me against the glass. "Tell me what you want," he whispered.

"I don't know what I want."

"I think you do."

"Then you tell me."

He kissed me, one of those soft, lingering kisses that leave you limp. "No, you tell me. Tell me what you like."

"I like it when you kiss me," I managed to say.

His tongue grazed the outline of my lips. "What else do you like?" His tongue grew more insistent, pushed its way between my teeth. "Tell me what else you like."

"I don't know."

"Tell me what you want me to do."

"I don't know."

"Tell me when we can be together."

"I don't know."

"How about next week? I'll arrange to take next Wednesday off. We'll go somewhere special, spend the day making love."

"I can't next Wednesday."

"Yes, you can."

"I can't. I have a doctor's appointment."

"Cancel it."

"I can't. It was the only way I could get my mother to go." His lips muffled the last of my words.

"When, then?"

"I don't know."

He pulled abruptly away. For an instant I felt as I had during my mammogram, as if part of my flesh were being ripped from my body. Robert straightened his tie, smiling sadly. "We're not kids anymore, Kate," he said. "There's only so long I can play this game."

"I'm not playing," I told him, my body aching for his return.

"What are you doing?"

"Everything's just moving a little fast for me."

"It's been thirty years," he reminded me, and I smiled. "Look," he said, walking to his black marble desk, leaning against it, "I don't want to pressure you into doing anything you don't want to do . . ."

"I don't know what I want," I interrupted.

"I think you do." The intercom on his desk buzzed. Robert reached over, pressed the necessary button. "Yes?"

His secretary's voice filled the room, ricocheted off the floor-to-ceiling windows. "Melanie Rogers is here."

"Send her in," he said easily, eyes glued to mine. "The next move is up to you, Kate." The door to his office opened and in walked a beautiful woman with dark red hair and a wide, full mouth. "Melanie," he said, kissing the side of her cheek, as he had mine only moments ago.

I raised my hand to my face, stroked the place where his lips had lingered, felt it burn.

"I'm sorry I'm late." Her voice was soft, hypnotic.

"Don't be sorry. It worked out perfectly. Let me introduce you to an old friend. Melanie Rogers, this is Kate Sinclair. We go back a very long way."

I don't remember Melanie's reply. I only remember thinking she had the greenest eyes I'd ever seen, and wondering what she was doing having lunch with Robert.

I muttered something like "I won't keep you," then headed to the door.

"I look forward to hearing from you again soon," Robert said as I stepped into the reception area. Seconds later, the door to his office closed behind me.

‗‗

My mother moved in with us that Friday night.

She'd had another run-in with poor Mr. Emerson, this time attacking him with his own cane, whacking him against the side of his head and actually knocking him to the floor. Both Mr. Emerson's family and Mrs. Winchell were now demanding that my mother be removed from the Palm Beach Lakes Retirement Home. Mr. Emerson's family actually threatened to press charges if this wasn't done immediately.

There was no question as to where to move her. We had no choice. She had to stay with us. "She can have my room for the weekend," Sara offered, having made plans to spend the time studying for her history test

with a friend from school. Without my prompting, she'd even supplied me with the name, address, and phone number of that friend, and granted me permission to check with the girl's mother to make sure it was all right.

"How long do you think this will last?" Larry marveled.

"I'll take whatever I can get," I said.

My mother appeared disoriented by the move. She kept asking when it was time to go home. I told her she'd be spending some time with us. She said, "That's fine, dear," then five minutes later asked if it was time to go home.

"She's going to drive you nuts," Larry whispered, carrying his new set of clubs to the front door.

"Who's that?" my mother asked, her head swiveling after him.

"That's Larry, Mom. My husband."

"Where's he going?"

"Not going anywhere, Mom," he answered. "I'm just getting everything ready for tomorrow."

"Good idea," she said, although the blank expression in her eyes indicated she had no idea what the idea was, let alone whether it was good or bad. "Is it time to go home yet?"

I tucked her into Sara's bed at around ten o'clock that night, and she fell asleep almost instantly. "Sleep tight," I told her, as I used to tell Sara.

"Think she'll sleep through the night?" Larry asked as I crawled into bed beside him.

"I hope so."

"Did you call Mrs. Sperling?"

"I said I was just checking to make sure that Sara wasn't an imposition, and she said that Sara is a joy to have around."

"Are you sure you called the right number?"

I laughed, settled into the crook of his arm, drifted off to sleep. At three-thirty, I awoke to find my mother wandering the house. I returned her to Sara's bed, went back to my own. This was repeated every hour until, at six-thirty, I decided I might as well get dressed. Larry left for his

golf game at seven. My mother asked who that nice man was and where he was going.

When Michelle woke up, she offered to take my mother for a walk, and they left the house hand in hand. I finished making my bed and moved into Sara's room, picking up the covers my mother had kicked to the floor and straightening the tousled sheets. Sara had done a great job tidying up. "You can actually see the floor," I marveled, picking up my mother's housecoat and heading for the small walk-in closet.

I almost didn't see the books. They were hidden behind some clothes in the far corner, and I was half out of the closet before I realized they were there. I'm not sure what made me look closer. Maybe it was just the novelty of finding books in a closet, or maybe it was my suspicious nature as far as Sara was concerned. At any rate, I picked up the books, opening them to confirm what I already knew: they were a history text and a world atlas. Didn't Sara need these for her test?

I walked to the kitchen and quickly called the Sperlings. The line was busy. I hung up and tried again. Still busy, as it was five minutes later when I tried a third time. "You're being silly," I told myself. "Her friend has the same books; what do they need with two sets of texts?" But even as I found reasons to reassure myself, my fingers continued punching in the Sperlings' phone number. "Damnit," I said, giving up when I heard the front door open and close.

"Something wrong?" Michelle asked from the foyer.

"I have to go out for a few minutes," I told her, returning to Sara's room and gathering up the history books. If she didn't need them, fine. That would be just fine, I told myself, asking Michelle to look after my mother, assuring my mother I'd be back before she knew I was gone. "You're being silly," I repeated as I drove to the Sperlings'. "This is not the same thing as finding those empty packages of cigarettes. This is not like finding those bottles of beer. This isn't the same thing at all. Sara has no reason to lie to you. She's turned over a new leaf." And if she hadn't? "You spoke to Mrs. Sperling. She was expecting Sara. Sara's a joy to have around. Remember?"

The Sperlings lived in the gated community of Admiral's Cove off

PGA Boulevard. I pulled my car up to the front gate, gave my name to the serious-faced security guard in the access booth. He peered at his clipboard. "I'm afraid your name's not on the list."

"Mrs. Sperling's not expecting me. But my daughter is visiting for the weekend, and she forgot her books." I indicated the books on the seat beside me.

"Just a minute, please." The guard retreated to his station and used the phone. "I'm afraid the line is busy. If you'd like to pull your car over to the side there, I can try again in a few minutes."

I pulled my car into the designated spot and waited, wondering who was on the phone for so long and would they ever get off. A minute stretched to five, then ten. "Just go home," I told myself. "Sara obviously doesn't need the books. What are you trying to prove?" She's going to think you're checking up on her, I continued silently, and that's going to make her very angry. Is that what you want? Especially now when everything has been going so well? I looked toward the guard, watching his lips move as he talked on the phone.

As I was about to signal the guard my intention to leave, he hung up the phone and stepped out of the booth.

"Mrs. Sperling says your daughter isn't here," he announced, approaching my car.

"I don't understand," Mrs. Sperling said to me over the phone in the guardhouse a few seconds later. "Soon after Sara arrived, she got a phone call. She said it was from you, and that something was wrong with her grandmother, and you needed her back home. She said she'd meet you at the front gate."

I listened in silence, too numb to speak.

"I'm so sorry. I don't know what to say," Mrs. Sperling continued. "You don't think anything's happened to her, do you?"

"I'm sure she's fine," I said, my voice expressionless, as if someone had sat on it, flattened the life right out of it.

"Do you have any idea where she is?"

"I know exactly where she is," I said, returning the phone to the guard's waiting hand and climbing back into my car, staring at my lifeless eyes in the rearview mirror. "She's at a wedding."

Chapter 24

The scene unfolds as if in a nightmare—in fits and starts, images fading in and out, no conjunctives to connect one event with the next, to provide context. I see my sister, dressed in a short, yet surprisingly traditional white wedding dress, a shoulder-length veil covering, but not hiding, her radiant smile. I see Colin Friendly, dressed in blue dungarees and death row orange T-shirt, laughing as my sister walks to his side, his eyes looking past her to the beautiful young girl who follows behind. The girl is wearing layers of black and white, much like her hair, whose dark roots are encroaching ever further into her blond curls. Her forest-green eyes are huge and curious; her mouth quivers uncertainly into a smile.

Close-ups of body parts: eyes, mouths, breasts, hands, fists, teeth.

Men in standard blue prison garb stand to either side of the spectacled prison chaplain, who cradles the Bible between steady palms.

More close-ups—stainless-steel tables and chairs, their legs bolted

to the linoleum floor. Human legs mingle—white high heels, black Doc Martens, brown loafers, scuffed prison sneakers.

I watch helplessly as the chaplain opens his mouth to speak.

Do you take this woman?

Can't somebody stop this?

Do you take this man?

Run. Now—while you still can.

If anyone knows just cause why this man and this woman . . .

Is everybody crazy? Why am I the only one to object?

Let him speak now or forever hold his peace.

I'm screaming. Why can't anybody hear me?

He hears me. Colin hears me.

Fists clench beside blue prison dungarees. Piercing blue eyes narrow with hatred.

Long manicured fingers, nails painted bubble-gum pink stretch into the air. Fists unclench, slip a thin gold band on the third finger of the outstretched hand. The hand proudly displays the ring for all to see.

Sound effects: oohing and aahing, laughter. Someone breaks into song. *She'll Be Coming 'Round the Mountain.*

And now by the power vested in me by the state of Florida . . .

Don't do it. There's still time to get away.

I now pronounce that you are husband and wife.

A clock clicks noiselessly on the wall behind them. It has no face.

Colin, you may kiss your bride.

Lips connect, bodies sway together.

More laughter, cheering, congratulations all around.

Whoopee! Colin exclaims as Jo Lynn laughs, draws Sara happily into her arms.

I guess that makes us family, Colin says to Sara, beckoning her forward.

I guess so, Sara says, rough arms surrounding her as I press my hands against my temples, trying to squeeze such images from my brain.

Of course, I don't know exactly what happened that afternoon, because I wasn't there, and I've never asked for the specifics. I know only that a wedding took place, that my sister married the man of her dreams

and my nightmares, that my daughter acted as maid of honor, that several inmates served as witnesses, that one broke into song, that it was all perfectly legal, that my sister was once again legally wed.

The tabloids made much of the wedding. A picture of Jo Lynn in her wedding dress graced the front page of the *Enquirer*. Another inside photo showed her proudly displaying her wedding band, a ring she'd purchased, and paid for herself. "As soon as Colin gets out," she was quoted as saying, "he's going to buy me a diamond eternity band. This marriage," she went on to say, "is forever."

Till death do us part.

Mercifully, the tabloids hadn't been allowed inside the prison, and so there were no pictures of Sara, although it was reported that Jo Lynn's niece served as her maid of honor, an indication, the paper surmised, of her family's support.

"It was everything I've always wanted in a wedding," my sister babbled. "Low-key and beautiful. There was just so much love in that room."

The paper then gave a brief description of Jo Lynn's three previous marriages, and even carried an interview with Andrew MacInnes, husband number one, who opined that Jo Lynn had always been a little wild and reckless, and a handful for any man. He didn't bother mentioning that his way of dealing with her wild and reckless nature was to beat her senseless.

My sister's courtship with Colin Friendly was rehashed and reprinted: her steadfast loyalty, her continuing support, her unwavering belief in his innocence. If you didn't know the man had been convicted of torturing and killing thirteen women and girls and was suspected in the disappearance of scores of others, you'd swear they were writing about a modern-day Romeo and Juliet, a pair of star-crossed lovers whose misguided enemies were intent on keeping them apart.

Not that Colin's history was ignored. Gruesome and lurid details of his killing spree filled page after page. Under a profile of Jo Lynn, Colin's penchant for breaking the noses of his victims was duly noted, something the psychologists who'd testified at his trial had traced back to his boyhood, when his mother had held his nose in his own waste. These same

psychologists now speculated on Colin's motives for marrying my sister, and hers for marrying him. Stability, image, friendship, they postulated on Colin's behalf. Publicity, loneliness, a martyr complex, they proffered with regard to Jo Lynn. They gave conflicting opinions as to whether or not they thought the marriage would last. "It stands as good a chance as any," one proclaimed.

The Saturday afternoon I found out that Sara wasn't at the Sperlings', I called the prison, hoping to prevent the marriage from taking place. But the wedding was already over. My sister had left the premises. Colin was back in his cell.

I sat up all night waiting for Sara to come home, even though I knew she wouldn't be back till the following day. She was at the Sperlings', after all, studying hard for a test. She wasn't due back till Sunday evening.

"Come to bed," Larry urged on several occasions. "You were up all night last night. You need your sleep."

"I can't sleep."

"You could try."

"She might come home."

"She won't."

"She might."

"What are you going to say to her when she does?"

"I don't know."

That much, at least, was the truth. I didn't have a clue what I was going to say to my older daughter. Was there any point in reminding her, yet again, that lies destroy trust, and that, despite the fact I would always love her, with every lie I liked her less? Would she care that she was making it harder and harder for us to believe anything she said, that she was wiping out whatever goodwill she'd managed to acquire?

Was there any point in asking her why she did these things, why she would deliberately go against our explicit instructions that she have nothing further to do with my sister and Colin Friendly? Had she learned nothing from the last episode except to make her lies more elaborate?

I shuddered with the knowledge that she'd been setting me up for

weeks: cleaning her room, helping around the house, doing her homework, actually being pleasant to be around. I remembered the feel of her
body in my arms when she'd comforted me about my mother, the overwhelming tenderness I'd felt toward her. I'd feasted for days on that
feeling. I have my little girl back, I told myself.

But it was all a ruse. A way to soften me up, get me to drop my
defenses, leave my suspicions at the door. Of course, you can stay the
weekend with your friend. I know how hard you've been working for this
test. I know how much you want to do well. Take care of yourself, darling. Don't study too hard.

I heard the rustle of pajamas, turned to see Michelle walking toward
me, eyes half closed in sleep. "Is everything all right?" she asked.

"Fine, sweetie," I told her. "I just can't sleep."

"Are you worried about Grandma?"

"A little."

"I just looked in on her. She's sound asleep."

"Thank you, doll."

"Her blanket was on the floor, so I picked it up."

"You're a good thing."

She sat down on the sofa beside me, burrowed deep into my side.
"I think I've decided what I want to be when I grow up," she said, as if
this were the most logical thing to be discussing at almost three o'clock in
the morning.

"Really? What's that?"

"A writer," she said.

"A writer? Really? What kind of writer?"

"A novelist, I think. Maybe a playwright."

"That's a great idea," I told her. "I think you'd make a wonderful
writer."

"You do? Why?"

"Because you're sensitive, and observant, and beautiful."

She groaned. "You don't have to be beautiful to be a writer."

"You have a beautiful soul," I told her.

"Of course, I'd finish my education first," she reassured me.

"I think that's a smart move."

"I was thinking of Brown, or even Yale. Do you think I'm smart enough to get into an Ivy League college?"

"I think they'd be lucky to have you."

I brushed some soft hairs away from her face, planted a gentle kiss on her forehead, stared toward the front door. How could I have two children so completely unalike? How could two children raised in the same household by the same two parents, in essentially the same way, be so totally different?

It had been that way right from the beginning, I realized, thinking back. Sara had been a difficult baby, demanding of my total attention. Michelle had been the easiest baby in the world, happy just to be included. Sara demanded to be fed every few hours; Michelle waited patiently until I was ready. Sara refused all efforts at toilet training, peeing in her pants until she was almost seven years old; Michelle trained herself at thirteen months. So, what else was new? Had anything really changed?

"You're thinking about Sara, aren't you?" Michelle said.

I closed my eyes, shook my head. Even in the dark, I was transparent. "Sorry, sweetie."

"Don't worry about her, Mom. She's all right."

I patted her hand. "I guess so."

"She's not at Robin's house, is she?"

"No."

"I didn't think so."

"Why? Did she say anything to you about where she was going?"

Michelle's head shook from side to side. "No, she just asked if she could borrow my black-and-white top—you know, the one with the matching sweater."

"How could she borrow your top? It would be way too small."

"She likes them that way."

"What did you tell her?"

"I told her no. I said, why would she need to borrow my top just to go study?"

"What did she say?"

"She said I was a stupid bitch."

"What?"

"It's all right. I'm used to it."

"Used to what?"

"She always calls me a stupid bitch. Sometimes worse."

I was horrified. "Why haven't you told me this before?"

"Because I have to learn to deal with these things myself. Isn't that what you would have told me? That deep down, my sister loves me very much, and that I'm a smart girl, I'd figure out how to deal with her?"

I smiled sadly. That was exactly what I would have told her. But that was before my daughter had run off to serve as maid of honor for my sister's marriage to a serial killer. Now I wasn't sure what I knew about anything. "I'm so sorry, sweetie. You don't deserve that. She has no right to call you names."

"She had no right to take my top and matching sweater, but she did anyway."

"She took your top after you said no?"

"I looked everywhere. They're gone. So are three of my tapes."

"Your tapes?"

"Nine Inch Nails, Alanis Morissette, Mariah Carey."

"Oh God."

"She'll bring them back. Of course, the tapes'll be ruined, and my clothes will be all stretched out and reek of cigarettes."

"I'll get you new ones," I told her.

"I don't want new ones. I just want her to stop taking my things."

"I'll talk to her."

"That won't do any good."

"Maybe it will."

"Has it ever?"

"I don't know what else to do," I admitted after a pause.

"Can I have a lock put on my closet?"

I stared through the darkness at my younger child, amazed at how innately practical she was. "Yes, we can do that."

"Good."

"How'd you get to be so smart?"

Michelle smiled. "Can I tell you something terrible?" she asked.

I held my breath. "How terrible?"

"Pretty terrible."

"About Sara?"

"About me."

I felt a strange combination of fear and relief. What could Michelle possibly tell me about herself that could be so terrible? And if there was something truly terrible about her that I didn't know, did I really want to hear it? Now? "What is it?" I asked.

For a second, she was silent, as if debating with herself whether or not to proceed.

"You don't have to tell me," I said hopefully.

"Sometimes I hate her," she confided.

"What?"

"Sara," Michelle clarified. "Sometimes I hate her."

That's it? I thought, with great relief. That's what's so terrible? "You hate your sister?"

"Sometimes. Does that make me an awful person?"

"It makes you pretty normal."

"Is it normal to hate your sister?"

"It's normal to be angry at somone who steals from you and calls you names," I said.

"It's more than that. Sometimes, I really, really hate her."

"Sometimes I hate her too," I said.

Michelle's arms reached around my waist, hugged me tightly. Two wounded comrades-in-arms, I remember thinking, kissing the top of her head.

"Can I tell you something else?" she asked, her voice shaking with the threat of tears.

"You can tell me anything," I told her.

"You remember when I was in grade five?" she asked.

I nodded. "Yes."

"And Mr. Fisher gave me the butterfly's cocoon to take care of over the Christmas break?"

"I remember."

Michelle had brought home a glass jar that contained a butterfly's cocoon that was attached to the side of a small stick. Every day, she watched over that jar, checking the cocoon for signs of growth, fretting over it the way a mother worries about her newborn baby. "I don't think it's right," she announced one day. "I think the cocoon's supposed to be higher."

"I think you should leave it alone," Sara advised.

"I think it should be higher." Michelle reached inside the jar, adjusted the cocoon with her fingers. "That's better."

When Michelle proudly returned the jar to the teacher, he told her that something had dislodged the cocoon and that the butterfly inside had died. "These things happen," he told her. "Don't blame yourself."

"It was my fault," Michelle said now, crying softly. "I moved the cocoon and so the butterfly died. Sara was right."

"Oh, my sweet baby."

"She said to leave it alone. I didn't listen."

"You've been worrying about this all these years?"

"I never told Mr. Fisher I moved it."

I rocked her back and forth, as I had when she was small, more for my benefit than for hers, even then. "It would be wonderful if we could go back and change things, correct all our mistakes, make everything right."

Michelle sniffed loudly. "But we can't."

"No, we can't. If we did, we'd be so busy rewriting the past, we'd have no time left for the present."

"What things would *you* rewrite?" she asked.

"Oh my. That's much too big a question for this hour of the night," I told her. "Besides, you only torture yourself when you start asking questions like that. We all make mistakes. The trick is to do the best you can."

"I think you've done really well," Michelle offered graciously.

"Thank you, sweetie. Have I ever told you that when I grow up I want to be exactly like you?"

She laughed through her tears, gave another loud sniff, hugged me tighter.

We heard footsteps, turned as one toward the sound, watched as my mother emerged from the shadows, clad in a white flannel nightgown, the dim light of the quarter-moon dancing across her face. "Hello, dear," she said, coming over and sitting on my other side. "Is it time to get up?"

"It's three o'clock in the morning, Grandma," Michelle told her.

"Of course it is," my mother said.

"We should all be in bed."

"Where's your father?" my mother asked, looking around.

"He's asleep," Michelle answered.

"Where's your father?" my mother repeated, and I realized it was me she was addressing.

"He's dead," I reminded her gently.

"Yes," she said, her gray head nodding up and down. "I remember that. We were having dinner one night, finishing our dessert, and he stood up to get a glass of milk, and said he felt a hell of a headache coming on. Those were his exact words—a hell of a headache. I remember because he almost never used profanity."

"Hell isn't a profanity," Michelle said.

"It isn't?"

"No. Not now."

"Well, it was. It was then," my mother told her with a certainty that surprised me.

Three generations of women lapsed into silence. Past, present, and future, together in the darkness before dawn. I remember thinking that I'd never felt so helpless.

God grant me the serenity to accept the things I cannot change, I found myself praying, the strength to change the things I can, and the wisdom to know the difference.

Chapter
25

Needless to say, I didn't sleep at all that night. When Larry woke up at eight o'clock the next morning, he found me still sitting on the living-room sofa, my eyes open and glazed over, staring blankly toward the front door. I was alone. I had a vague recollection of Michelle guiding my mother back to bed at some point during the night, then coming back to kiss my forehead before retreating to her room. I remembered little else. My mind was mercifully blank. One hour had drifted seemlessly into the next. The sky had gone from black to gray to blue without any input from me. I was alive to face another day.

"Have you been up all night, funny face?" Larry asked, sitting down beside me, the pillows of the sofa shifting to accommodate him, his terry-cloth bathrobe grazing my bare arms.

I turned away, trying to escape the sound of his voice, the weight of his concern falling heavy into my lap, like an unwanted child.

"Sara's fine, you know," he continued. "You can bet that *she* didn't lose any sleep."

"I know that."

"Why don't you get back into bed for a few hours. You might surprise yourself and fall asleep."

"I don't like surprises," I told him stubbornly, deliberately missing the point.

"You know what I mean," he said.

I nodded, but didn't move.

"How can you even think of confronting Sara when you haven't slept in two days?"

"I'll be fine."

"Have you reached any conclusions about how to deal with her?"

"Other than shooting her, you mean?" I asked, and he smiled.

"Shooting's good," he said. My turn to smile. "I have some thoughts on the matter," he continued. "If you're interested," he added, waiting.

"Can we talk about them later?"

"Can you promise not to do anything until I get home?"

"Where are you going?"

"Golf game, remember? I'm teeing off at nine twenty-one."

"Nine twenty-*one*?"

"Tee-off times are scheduled every seven minutes."

I shook my head in seeming wonder, although the truth was that I really didn't care. Still, it was easier—and far less dangerous—to talk about golf than about our older daughter.

"I don't have to go," he volunteered.

"Why wouldn't you go?"

"If you'd rather I stayed home . . ."

"No. What's the point in that?"

"If you wanted company. If you didn't want to be alone."

"I'm not alone."

"If you wanted *my* company," Larry qualified.

I turned to him, tried to smile. "I'll be fine. You go. Break a hundred."

He rose to his feet, swayed unsteadily, his body a reflection of his state of mind. "I should be back by two. Maybe we could go to a movie."

"Maybe," I said.

He excused himself to get dressed. I went into the kitchen and made a large pot of coffee. An hour later, I was on my fourth cup, and Larry was on his way to the golf course. I checked on my mother and Michelle, relieved to find them both still sleeping soundly. Maybe Larry was right, I decided, climbing into my bed, crawling between the sheets, and pulling the covers up around my chin. Maybe a few hours' sleep would be enough to restore my perspective, if not my faith.

But the four cups of coffee had done their work, and there was no way I was going to fall asleep. After about half an hour, during which time I twisted my tired body into every conceivable position, and counted enough sheep to stock herds on both sides of the Atlantic, I finally gave up and headed for the shower, from which I emerged, some twenty minutes later, wetter but none the wiser.

Larry returned home at just after two o'clock—his score a disappointing 104—to find me sitting in basically the same position in which he'd left me. "I know you moved, because you're wearing different clothes," he noted with a sad smile. "Did you check the paper?"

"The paper?"

"To see what movies are playing."

"I can't go to a movie."

"Why not?"

"What am I supposed to do with Michelle and my mother?"

"They'll come with."

"And Sara?"

"She's not invited. Come on," he cajoled. "We'll take in a movie, then grab some fajitas at Chili's. You know how much Michelle loves Chili's."

"What if Sara gets home while we're out?"

"Then she'll wait for us for a change."

"I don't think that's a good idea."

"What's not a good idea?" Michelle asked, coming into the room,

plopping down into the opposite sofa, long skinny arms dangling between long skinny legs.

"I thought we'd go to a movie around four o'clock, then have something to eat."

"Chili's?" Michelle's voice literally chirped with anticipation.

"One fajita combo coming up," Larry said. "Why don't you check the paper and talk to Grandma and decide what movie you want to see."

Michelle was instantly on her feet. "Grandma," she called in the direction of Sara's room. "We're going to the movies."

"I can't go," I told Larry.

"Of course you can," he insisted.

"All right, then, I don't *want* to go."

"You *want* to sit here and stew until Sara comes home?"

"I need some time to think."

"You've been thinking for the past twenty-four hours. Has it done any good?"

"That's not the point."

"What *is* the point?"

"The point is that going to a movie is not high on my list of priorities right now."

"Maybe you should reexamine your priorities."

"What?"

"You heard me."

"Our daughter deceives us, defies us, and disappears for the weekend, and you want me to go to the movies instead of being here when she gets home. Those are your priorities?"

"There'll be plenty of time to confront Sara later. Right now you're wound so tight . . ."

"I'm not wound so tight. Please don't tell me I'm wound so tight. You have no idea what I'm feeling."

"Tell me." He sat down beside me. Immediately, I jumped to my feet.

"I'm frustrated," I said, the words flying from my mouth, like spit. "I'm frustrated and angry and hurt." I began pacing back and forth between the two living-room sofas, anxiety gnawing at my chest, like a rat

on a rope. "I trusted her, damnit! I believed her. I fell for all the lies. She got me—again! What? Am I stupid? All she has to do is smile at me and I'm ready to buy her the store?"

"You're her mother," Larry said simply.

"I'm an idiot," I raged. "And she's nothing but a goddamn liar."

"And you think this is the right frame of mind for you to be dealing with her?" Larry asked logically.

"You'd rather not deal with her at all, is that it?"

"I didn't say that."

"What are you saying?"

"I'm saying that you need a breather. You've been sitting here stewing in your own juices all day. You need to get out of this house for a few hours, get your mind on something else. You're not going to accomplish anything with Sara when you're this angry."

"And then what?" I demanded. "After the movie and the fajitas. What happens then?"

"We come home. Hopefully Sara will be here. We'll listen to what she has to say . . ."

"More lies."

"Then we'll decide—calmly—what we're going to do."

"Such as?"

There was a minute's silence. The anxiety curled around my heart like a snake, beginning its slow squeeze.

"I think Sara has to understand the seriousness of what she's done," Larry began, "the fact that this kind of behavior can no longer be tolerated."

I shook my head. Hadn't we been through all this before? Sara understood exactly what she was doing. It was Larry and I who had yet to come to terms with our level of tolerance.

"I think we should cancel all her privileges for the remainder of the school year," Larry continued. "That includes her allowance and any extracurricular activities. When she's not at school, she's at home, it's as simple as that."

"You really think she's going to go along with that?"

"If she doesn't, she'll have to find somewhere else to live."

The simple statement took my breath away. "What?"

Larry got to his feet, walked to my side, put his hands on my arms, forced my eyes to his. "What other choice is there, ultimately?" he asked.

"You're suggesting we kick our daughter out of the house?"

"I'm suggesting we give her the choice—either she chooses to live by the rules of this household or she chooses to live elsewhere. It's as simple as that."

"Stop saying that," I shouted, pushing his arms away, resuming my angry pacing. "Nothing is simple where Sara is concerned."

"Then, at the very least, we have to make it less complicated where *we're* concerned." He looked toward the ceiling, then back at me. "Who calls the shots here, Kate? Who sets the limits? You're the therapist. You know this is exactly how you'd advise a client."

"This is our seventeen-year-old daughter we're talking about. You're saying we should just throw her out on the street?" I pictured Sara huddled around an open fire on some deserted corner. The flames from the fire reached out for me, searing the lining of my lungs.

"That's not what I'm saying."

"You know what she'll do if we kick her out, don't you? She'll just move in with Jo Lynn. That's what she'll do. God, it's so hot in here." I pulled roughly at the collar of my beige cotton sweater.

"Did you say that Jo Lynn is coming to live with us?" my mother asked, walking sprightly into the room, Michelle at her side.

"Oh God," I muttered.

"We picked a movie," Michelle announced. "It starts at three-fifty."

"I don't think I can take too much more of this." My voice emerged as a thin wail, scratching the air like nails on a blackboard.

"Mom, what's wrong?"

"Something the matter, dear?" my mother asked.

"There's nothing the matter," I snapped, the heat sweeping through my insides with the unrestrained fury of a brush fire. "It's just so fucking hot in here!" In the next instant, I ripped my sweater up over my

head, threw it angrily to the floor, then stomped on it, before kicking it halfway across the room. I looked up to find my husband, my mother, and my daughter staring at me as if I were nuts.

"It *is* a little warm in here," my mother said.

"Mother!" Michelle's eyes had grown so large they threatened to overtake her face. "You said the F-word."

"You know what," Larry said, clearly flustered by my outburst. "I think we need to clear out of here and give your mother some space."

"Oh, that's just great," I said. "Rats deserting the sinking ship."

Larry raised his hands into the air, then dropped them lifelessly to his sides. "I thought that's what you wanted," he said.

"There are rats?" my mother asked. Wary eyes skirted the tile floor.

"Of course, that's what you do best, isn't it?" I said, looking directly at my husband.

"What are you talking about?" Larry asked.

"When the going gets tough, the tough go golfing. Or to the movies. Isn't that what they say?"

Larry turned toward my mother and Michelle. "Michelle, honey, we still have some time before we have to leave. Why don't you take your grandmother out for a little walk."

Michelle's eyes moved from me to her father and back again, as if she were courtside at a tennis match. "Come on, Grandma," she said finally, leading my mother toward the front door.

"Are we going to the movies?" my mother asked as the door closed behind them.

"You have something you want to say to me?" Larry said after they were gone.

I retrieved my sweater from the floor, used it to wipe the sweat from between my breasts. "Are you sure you have time? I mean, you don't want to be late for the movie."

"You have something to say, say it."

"It's just so easy for you, isn't it?"

"What is?"

"To pick up and leave."

"It's just a movie, Kate. Not everything has to be such a big deal."

"No, I recognize that our daughter isn't as big a deal as breaking a hundred . . ."

"Okay, let's stop this right now," Larry warned.

"I thought you said if I had something to say, I should say it."

"I changed my mind."

"Too late."

"It will be if you don't stop this right now."

"What—you're threatening me? If I don't conform to the rules of the household, you're going to throw me out too?"

"Kate, this is crazy. Listen to yourself."

"No, you listen. For the last few months, my life has been steadily falling apart. And where have you been? On the golf course."

"That's not fair."

"Maybe not, but it's true. I've been dealing with my mother, my sister, the kids, these goddamn hot flashes," I continued, "and meanwhile you've been making yourself scarcer and scarcer. Oh, you say all the right things, you make all the right sounds, but you're never actually here when I need you."

"I'm here now," he offered softly.

"Only long enough to shower and change your clothes, then it's off to the movies, off to Chili's."

"What do you want from me, Kate?" he asked. "What do you want me to do? Tell me, because I honestly don't know anymore. I feel like, no matter what I say or do, it's gonna be wrong. It's like I'm always walking around on eggshells. I'm afraid to open my mouth, in case I say the wrong thing; I'm afraid to touch you, in case I touch you in the wrong spot, and you fly off the handle. You say I'm never here. Maybe you're right. Maybe my way of dealing with all that's been going on is to just get away from it. Is there really that much to be gained by confronting everything head-on?"

"I don't know," I admitted, pressing my sweater against me, feeling the sudden chill from the air-conditioning system creeping along my bare arms. "I don't know anything anymore."

"You know that I'm not suggesting that we throw Sara out on her ear," Larry continued softly.

"I know that."

"I guess I'm just looking for a little peace. God knows, it's been a long time since she's given us any joy."

"She's not here to give us joy," I reminded him.

"Not part of her job description, I guess," Larry agreed sadly. "Come to the movie with us, Kate. Please. It'll be good for us."

"I can't," I heard myself say as tears dropped down my cheeks. "I just can't. But you go. Really. It's all right. You go."

I left him standing in the middle of the room and went into the washroom, splashed water on my face, then pulled my sweater back over my head. I stared at my reflection in the mirror over the sink, studying the lines beneath my eyes, like the tiny but persistent river lines on a map, I thought, standing there until I heard the front door open and close. When I returned to the living room moments later, Larry was gone, and I was alone. I sat back down on the sofa and waited for Sara to come home.

⌒

She walked through the door at exactly three minutes after six o'clock, her battered brown leather knapsack draped carelessly across one shoulder. She was wearing the same tight jeans and bosom-hugging striped jersey she'd been wearing when she left two days earlier, and her hair hung loosely around her face in several shades of careless blond. "Oh, hi," she said, stopping when she saw me, a hint of blush flashing across her pale cheeks. "You scared me. I almost didn't see you sitting there. Why don't you turn on some lights?"

"I've been waiting for you," I said, my voice surprisingly, eerily, calm.

She glanced slowly from side to side. "Is everything okay? Grandma . . . ?"

"She's fine."

"Good." She took several steps toward her room.

"Did you bring Michelle's sweaters back?"

"What?"

"And her tapes?"

"I don't have any of Michelle's tapes, and why would I take her sweaters? They don't fit me." Sara managed just the right degree of indignation. For a split second, I thought maybe Michelle might be mistaken.

"Then you wouldn't mind showing me the contents of your knapsack," I pressed.

"Of course I'd mind. I said I don't have any of Michelle's things, and I don't. What—you don't believe me?"

"Apparently not."

She shook her head, as if my suspicions were beyond belief, as if I myself were beneath contempt. "Well, that's your problem."

Oh, she's good, I thought, rising to my feet. She's very good. "No, I'm afraid it's *your* problem."

"There's nothing in my knapsack but a lot of books," Sara protested.

"History books?" I asked.

"I have a big test tomorrow. Remember?"

"Oh, I remember."

"And I still have a few things I want to go over, so if you'll excuse me . . ."

"Don't you think you've studied enough? I mean, you've been at it all weekend." My voice was soft, conciliatory.

"I just want to go over everything one more time." Sara punctuated her lie with a modest laugh for extra authenticity, took several more steps toward her bedroom.

"When are you going to stop lying to me, Sara?"

The simple question stopped her cold. Her back arched, stiffened, like a cat's when threatened. "I don't have Michelle's stupid sweater or her dumb tapes," she enunciated carefully, as if each word were an effort, her back still to me.

"And you were at the Sperlings' house all weekend, studying for a test."

"You know that. You spoke to Mrs. Sperling."

"Yes, I did. Several times, in fact."

Slowly, Sara spun around to face me. When she stopped, I could see her eyes still moving, trying to process this latest bit of information, readying a fresh line of defense. "When did you speak to her?"

"Yesterday afternoon."

"You were checking up on me?"

I laughed. Her indignation was truly inspirational.

"Don't laugh at me," she warned.

"Don't lie to me," I said in return.

"I didn't lie to you. I did go to the Sperlings'."

"Yes, but you didn't stay there very long, did you?"

A pause, but only a slight one. "I couldn't. Something came up."

"Yes, I know," I sympathized. "Your grandmother. You were needed back home."

Sara rolled her eyes, glanced from side to side, as if searching for the proper alibi. "Something came up," she repeated. "It was important."

"I bet it was. Why don't you tell me about it."

Sara shifted her weight from one foot to the other. "I can't," she said.

"Why not?"

"I can't betray a confidence."

Again, I almost laughed, this time managing to keep it in check. "You can betray my trust but you can't betray a confidence?"

"I didn't mean to betray your trust."

"You just didn't care."

"Of course I care."

"Where did you go?" I asked.

Sara lowered her gaze to the floor, then slowly lifted her face back to mine. Even in the fading light, I could see the tears glistening in her eyes. She's in pain, I thought, aching to take her in my arms. Despite everything, it was all I could do to keep my feet still, my hands at my

sides. "A friend of mine is in trouble," she began, and my hands instantly lost their desire to comfort, clenching into tight, angry fists. More lies, I thought, fury spreading like a cancer through my brain, all but blocking out her words. "She's been seeing this guy her parents don't like, and they want her to break up with him, and she wants to, but she's afraid she might be pregnant." A pause. A gulp. The threat of more tears. "She really needed someone to talk to. What could I do, Mom? It was pathetic. She was almost suicidal. She turned to me because she knows you're a therapist, and I guess she thought that maybe some of your wisdom might have rubbed off on me, that I'd be able to help her."

I gasped at the sheer wonder of how her mind worked, the speed with which it concocted these convoluted stories, her effortless ability to suck me into each elaborate scenario, flatter me into becoming at least partly responsible. After all, if I weren't a therapist, none of this would have happened. If it hadn't been for my profession, my expertise, my *wisdom*, Sara wouldn't have been dragged into this mess, she wouldn't have had to skip out on the Sperlings, she wouldn't have had to lie. "And were you able to help her?" I asked, continuing the charade.

"I think so." She smiled, relaxed her guard. "Anyway, I'm really sorry I had to lie. But I did manage to get some studying done anyway. I think I'm going to do really well on this test."

"You studied?" I asked. "Without any books?"

"What do you mean, without books? I had my books with me." She patted her knapsack in confirmation.

"Your books are in your closet," I said, tired of the charade.

"What?"

"Your books—they're in your closet. You want me to get them?"

"No, I don't want you to get them." Sara's voice swept across the house like a broom. "Who said you could go into my room?"

"Your grandmother has been using that room," I began, but she didn't let me finish.

"What were you doing snooping around in my closet?"

"I wasn't snooping."

"God, Mom, how can you expect me to respect you when you don't show me any respect?"

"I show you plenty of respect."

"How? By sneaking into my room? By rifling through my things?"

"I did not sneak into your room. I did not rifle through your things."

"What were you doing in my closet?"

"This is not about me," I reminded her, trying to regain control.

"The minute I leave this house, you're in my room, snooping around, calling the Sperlings, checking up on me. You call that trust? You call that being honest? You're such a hypocrite."

"Watch it," I warned.

"What do you want from me?" she demanded, as Larry had demanded earlier. "I've told you the truth. I didn't want to. It meant betraying a confidence, but I told you anyway."

"You told me nothing."

"I was with my girlfriend."

"The same girlfriend who collects empty cigarette packages?"

"What? What are you talking about?" Concern softened the angry lines around her eyes and mouth. "Mom, are you all right?"

"I know where you were, Sara," I said, my voice filled with so much rage, humiliation, and disappointment, it wobbled. "I know you weren't with any pregnant suicidal girlfriend. I know you were with my sister. I know you went to her goddamn wedding."

The room fell suddenly silent. If I expected more tears, apologies, pleas for forgiveness, I had the wrong child. Sara stared at me with undisguised contempt. "If you knew all along where I was," she said, her voice low, firm, resolutely unapologetic, "then why this stupid charade? Who's really the liar here, Ms. Therapist?"

"Don't you dare talk to me that way."

"Then stop all these stupid games."

Frustration froze my tongue. It lay fat, heavy in my mouth. I should have listened to Larry, gone with him to the movies, dealt with Sara after we got home, Larry at my side. I was too tired to deal with her alone, and Sara was much too wily an opponent. Everything Larry said had been right.

"I'm going to my room," Sara said.

"You're sleeping in the den," I told her, surprising both of us.

"What?"

"Grandma has your room. I don't think it would be wise to move her. She's confused enough." This was probably true, although I hadn't given the matter any previous thought.

"Fine," Sara said. She swayed toward the den.

"And while you're there," I continued, unable to stop myself despite my best intentions, despite my years of professional training and *wisdom*, "you might give some thought as to whether you really want to be a part of this family anymore."

"What?" The look on Sara's face told me she thought I'd lost my mind. "What on earth are you jabbering about now?"

"As of this moment, all privileges are suspended."

"What?"

"You heard me. No more privileges."

"You give a dog privileges," Sara shot back. "People have rights."

We have rights too, I heard Larry say.

"No more allowance," I continued, fueled by her protest. "No more going out on weekends. For the rest of the school year, you're either at school or at home," I said, repeating Larry's words.

"Go to hell," Sara said succinctly.

"No," I said. "You're the one who'll be looking for new accommodations. You either play by the rules of this household or you find somewhere else to live. It's as simple as that."

Sara looked me straight in the eye. "Fuck you," she said.

In the next instant, I watched myself literally fly across the room at Sara, my feet off the floor, my arms outstretched. I landed almost on top of her, my fists falling like hammers across the back of her head, her neck, her shoulders, any part of her they could find. Sara screamed, tried to escape, her hands reaching up to protect herself from my blows. We were both screaming and crying, as my fists continued to pummel her flesh.

"Stop it, Mom!" she was screaming. "Stop!"

I pulled back in absolute horror, stared into Sara's startled, tear-stained face. "Sara, I'm so sorry," I began.

"Fucking bitch," she said.

Without thinking, I hauled back and slapped her hard across the face, so hard the palm of my hand stung, and the sound echoed throughout the house. I watched a torrent of angry wet tears wash the years from Sara's face. The teenager became the adolescent, then the child, then the infant at my breast. My baby, I thought, as she pulled herself up to her full Amazonian height and slapped me right back.

I stared at my older daughter in astonishment, my cheek, my insides, on fire. "If you ever hit me again," I told her slowly, my voice surprisingly calm, "then you're out of here."

"You hit me first," she protested.

"If *I* ever hit you again," I continued without missing a beat, "then you're out of here."

"What? That's not fair."

"Maybe not, but it's *my* house."

"You're crazy," Sara started screaming. "You know that? You're crazy."

It was around this time that Larry brought my mother and Michelle home.

"She's crazy," Sara was yelling, as Michelle cradled my mother in the front foyer. "I'm going to call the police. I'm going to call Children's Aid."

"What happened?" Michelle asked, temporarily abandoning my mother to come to my aid, eyes shooting daggers at her sister.

"Oh, here she is," Sara intoned. "Little Miss Perfect."

Somehow, Larry managed to settle us all in our rooms, as a referee manages to restore order in the ring, returning the combatants to their respective corners. He calmed my mother, reassured Michelle, tended to Sara's invisible bruises, made sure everyone was breathing normally. Eventually, the house fell silent, grew dark.

"Are you all right?" Larry asked later, climbing into bed beside me.

I lay on my side, staring at the fuzzy glow from the moon through the bedroom curtains. "No," I said.

It was as simple as that.

Chapter
26

Don't feel guilty," Larry advised me often over the course of the next few days.

But, of course, I did feel guilty. How could I not? I'd hit my child, not once, but repeatedly. I'd used my fists on her back and shoulders, my open palm on her face. That beautiful face, I thought. How could I have slapped it?

"You were provoked. She had it coming," Larry said.

And that was true. I was provoked; she did have it coming.

That still didn't make it right.

"You taught her that she can push people only so far," Larry said.

"The only thing I taught her is that I can't control my temper."

"Stop being so hard on yourself, Kate."

"I'm the adult in this equation."

"She's seventeen," he reminded me. "She's six feet tall."

"I'm her mother."

"You don't call your mother a fucking bitch."

"I hit her."

"She hit you back."

Strangely enough, of all the things that were said and done that night, the fact that Sara had hit me bothered me the least. Maybe because I've always believed that if you hit someone, you have to be prepared to be hit back.

It was something my mother never did.

A torrent of deliberately repressed memories rushed back at me. I heard the front door of my childhood open, saw my stepfather walk through. *Hello, darling,* my mother greeted him. *You're late.*

Are you complaining?

Of course not. I was just worried. Dinner was ready an hour ago.

Dinner is whenever I get home.

It's on the table.

It's cold.

I'll warm it up.

You know I hate warmed-over food. I don't work hard and pay good money for meat to have it warmed over.

Don't get all worked up. I'll make you something else.

You think I have all night to wait until you make something else?

It won't take long.

You don't think I deserve a decent meal when I get home?

Of course you do. That's why I try to make everything nice for you.

Then why isn't everything nice?

It is. It's just that you were late.

You're saying it's my fault?

Of course not. These things happen. I understand.

You understand shit.

I'm sorry, Mike. I didn't mean . . .

You're always sorry. You never mean. You never think, *that's your problem. Why do you do these things?*

Please, Mike, calm down. You'll scare the children.

Fuck the children.

Please watch your language.

My language? Oh, that's right, isn't it? Your first husband, fuck his sainted memory, he never swore, did he? Well, what are you going to do, wash my mouth out with soap? Is that what you're going to do?

Please, Mike.

You know what? That's a damn good idea. That's exactly what I'm going to do. I'm going to wash your mouth out with soap. Then next time you think of getting smart with your husband, you'll think twice.

No, don't, please don't!

What's the matter? Don't you like the taste? I bet it tastes better than that shit you were going to serve me tonight, you stupid bitch.

I closed my eyes, tried not to see the bruises along the side of my mother's mouth the next morning, the red marks on the side of her neck and arms, the angry scratch along her chin.

What did you do to my mother? I demanded on another such occasion.

Ssh, Kate, my mother warned, *it's nothing.*

What are you talking about? I never touched your mother. What lies have you been telling the kid, Helen?

I didn't tell her anything. It's okay, Kate. I tripped on the carpet. I fell against the side of the door.

Clumsy idiot, my stepfather said.

She's not a clumsy idiot, I told him. *You are.*

Even now I can feel the sharp cuff of his hand as it snapped across the back of my head. I'll never do that, I vowed in that instant. I'll never hit a child of mine.

"I'm no better than he was," I told Larry.

"Stop beating yourself up about this," he said.

An interesting choice of words, I thought. "I'm a therapist, for God's sake."

"You're a therapist," he repeated. "Not a saint. Kate, has anything even remotely like this ever happened before? No. It happened once. You were provoked and you lost control."

He's not always this way, I could hear my mother tearfully intone. *There are times when he's gentle and thoughtful and funny. It's only sometimes when he's under a lot of stress. Or I provoke him and he just loses control.*

"It doesn't wash," I told Larry, as I had told her.

Was violence contagious? Was it passed down from one generation to the next, like some dreaded inherited disease? Was there no escape?

I canceled my appointments for the next two days, barely got out of bed. Sara refused to acknowledge my presence. She went to school, came home, stayed in the den until dinner, ate in silence, then returned to the den when dinner was through. I was the invisible woman, a role that was somewhat familiar to me, although this time was different, because this time my invisibility was something that had been deliberately imposed.

"Can I talk to you?" I asked from the doorway several nights later.

"No," Sara said. She opened a book, pretended to read.

"I think it's important that we talk about what happened."

"You beat me up, that's what happened."

"I didn't beat you," I began, then stopped. "I'm so sorry."

"I don't want to talk about it."

"Leave her alone," Larry said gently, coming up behind me and guiding me away from Sara's door. "You have nothing to apologize for."

"She'll start talking to you again as soon as she wants something," Michelle said.

"Is it time to go home?" my mother asked.

"I'm trying to find somewhere nice for you, Mom," I told her, realizing I'd have to make some decisions soon regarding her future. It was increasingly obvious that she couldn't stay here. "But first, we have a doctor's appointment tomorrow, remember?"

Of course she didn't remember. She wouldn't remember two minutes from now or two minutes after that. She had no idea why I was waking her up so early the next morning, or where we were headed as I drove south along Dixie Highway looking for Dr. Wong's office.

"How are you feeling?" I asked her.

"Magnificent," she said. "Where are we going?"

"To the gynecologist. It's just a routine examination."

"That's nice, dear."

It wasn't so nice, as it turned out. It was in Dr. Wong's office that she discovered my twin polyps and promptly removed them. "I'm sure there's nothing to worry about, but I'll send these off to the lab, just in

case," she said, as I struggled to bring my legs together. "Why don't you call my office in two weeks. We should have the results back by then."

I nodded, opened the door to the waiting room to see my mother rifling through the morning newspaper, a photograph of Jo Lynn proudly displaying her self-bought wedding band occupying a prominent spot on the front page. I felt sick, clutched my stomach.

"I'll give you some pills for the cramping," Dr. Wong said. "And no sex for a week," she advised on my way out.

No problem, I thought, thinking of Robert as my mother and I walked slowly toward the parking lot. I fought the urge to curl into a fetal ball in the middle of the warm gray pavement. Good thing Robert and I hadn't made those plans for this afternoon, I thought, and almost laughed.

"How are you feeling, Mom?" I asked, securing her seat belt around her.

"Magnificent. How about you, dear?"

"I've felt better," I confided.

She smiled. "That's good, dear."

I got home, settled my mother in front of the TV in the family room, and crawled into bed. Within minutes, I was asleep, dreams of Sara circling my head, like a plane awaiting permission to land. Mercifully, I don't remember the particulars. I only remember that at some point we got into a horrible fight and began exchanging blows, Sara's right fist catching me square in the groin. I awoke with a start, the pain in my stomach excruciating. I ran toward the bathroom, watched as blood leaked into the toilet bowl from between my legs. "Charming," I said, swallowing another pill, then heading back to bed.

The phone rang. It was Larry. "How'd it go?" he asked, and I told him. "Why didn't you call me? I would have picked you up."

"It wasn't necessary."

"You don't have to deal with everything by yourself, Kate."

"No sex for a week," I said.

He sighed. What else is new? the sigh said.

"I'll try to be home early," he offered.

"No need."

"Don't shut me out, Kate."

"I'm not." I was.

I replaced the receiver, lay back against the pillow, fantasized about sex with Robert. In my fantasy, we were in one of the recently renovated rooms at the Breakers hotel, a large sun-filled room overlooking the ocean, the waves lapping through the floor-to-ceiling windows toward our king-size bed, as we kissed and caressed one another with the utmost tenderness. That's as far as the fantasy went, maybe because of the cramps I was experiencing, or maybe because Sara kept pushing her way into the hotel room, eventually crowding Robert out of our bed, banishing him to one of the older rooms at the front of the hotel, her voice blocking out the soothing sound of the ocean.

I replayed the scene with Sara, reliving every detail of what had happened, the shouts, the sarcasm, the slaps, then played it through again, this time with a different script. In this newly edited version, I kept my cool, refused to take the bait, held my temper firmly in check. Whenever Sara tried to suck me in or drag me down, I stepped aside. I simply explained that we knew the truth about where she'd been, and detailed the consequences of her lies. Ultimately Sara saw the error of her ways and accepted responsibility for her acts. We ended the encounter with a tearful embrace.

How's that for a fantasy?

At three o'clock, the doorbell rang. I pushed myself out of bed, and answered it, thinking it must be Larry and wondering why he didn't use his key. But it wasn't Larry. It was Jo Lynn. Please let this be another dream, I prayed, taking note of her conservative blue pantsuit and tied-back hair.

"I'm in disguise," she said, reading my face. "The reporters are driving me crazy."

"Fancy that," I said, then wished I hadn't. I had nothing to say to my sister. What was she doing here?

"You look awful," she said, stepping inside before I could stop her. "You sick or something?"

"I had some unexpected surgery this morning," I answered. What was the matter with me? Could I never keep my mouth shut?

"Surgery? What kind of surgery?"

"Just minor."

"Yick," she said, not interested in the specifics.

"What are you doing here, Jo Lynn?"

"Uh-oh, you're mad. I can hear it in your voice."

"You're so perceptive."

"You're so sarcastic. Come on, Kate. Surely you're not surprised. I've been telling you my wedding plans for months."

"How could you do it?" I demanded.

"I love Colin. I think he's innocent."

"I'm not talking about your idiot husband," I shouted. "I'm talking about my daughter."

There was silence. "Colin's not an idiot," Jo Lynn said.

I groaned.

"So, you like my new name? Jo Lynn Friendly. Has kind of a nice ring to it, don't you think?"

I said nothing.

"What—you're not going to talk to me?"

"I'd rather not."

"Oh, don't be such a tight-ass, Kate. I needed a maid of honor, you said no, so I asked Sara, and she graciously agreed. It was a joyous occasion, for God's sake. A wedding."

"A wedding that took place behind bars."

"Don't be so melodramatic."

"You expressly went against my wishes."

"You're making a mountain out of a molehill."

I took a deep breath. The last thing I needed now was a fight with my sister. "What are you doing here, Jo Lynn?" I asked again.

"I'm looking for our mother."

I glanced toward the family room. Our mother was sitting in exactly the same position in which I'd left her hours earlier. She hadn't moved, even at the sound of Jo Lynn's voice. "Mom?" I asked, walking quickly toward her.

On the television, an impossibly good-looking young couple were

arguing about their father's impending remarriage on one of the daytime soaps. Our mother seemed to be watching, her hands folded neatly in her lap, her feet placed firmly on the floor. Her eyes were open and her jaw slack, a small spittle of drool trickling toward her chin.

"Is she dead?" Jo Lynn asked, leaning over me as I leaned over our mother.

"Mom?" I asked, holding my breath, touching her shoulder.

Her eyes flickered briefly, then closed. The breath in my lungs escaped with a relieved whoosh. I gently wiped the drool from her face, then backed into Jo Lynn's arms. I quickly extricated myself, stepped aside. "She's asleep."

"She sleeps with her eyes open?"

"She drifts in and out."

"Creepy."

I reached for the remote-control unit, about to turn off the TV.

"Don't do that," Jo Lynn squealed. "That's Reese and Antonia. Their father is about to remarry his second wife, who they've always hated because she's a former stripper who once tried to kill them by setting their house on fire. But she's okay now. She went back to school, became a psychiatrist. You got any coffee?"

I flipped off the TV. "No."

"Then make some." Jo Lynn plopped herself down on one of the wicker chairs in the breakfast nook. "You know you're dying for a cup."

She was right. I walked to the kitchen and did as I was told.

"It's amazing what goes on on some of these soaps," Jo Lynn said without a trace of irony. She nodded toward our mother. "So, what's the old girl's prognosis?"

"So far, the doctors haven't found anything physically wrong with her," I said, too weary to do anything but let this visit run its course. "How'd you know she was here?"

"I tried her apartment and was told the number was no longer in service. So I checked with Mrs. Winchell."

"Why the sudden interest in our mother?"

"I can't be interested?"

I shrugged, watched the coffee as it dripped into the glass pot.

"So, aren't you going to ask me what it was like behind the water-cooler?" Jo Lynn squirmed in her seat.

"No," I said.

"Come on, you're dying to know."

"No, you're dying to tell me. There's a difference."

"It was fabulous," she said. "Well, maybe not fabulous in the technical sense. I mean, it was pretty cramped behind there and we were pretty rushed, but that made it all the more exciting, in a way. You just know that under the proper circumstances, Colin is a dynamite lover."

What was taking the coffee so long? I wondered, my eyes widening, willing the coffeemaker to pick up speed.

"You think we should wake the old girl up?" Jo Lynn asked.

"What for?"

"I want to talk to her."

"What for?" I repeated.

"Do I need your permission to talk to my own mother?"

"Of course not. It's just that anything anybody says to her goes in one ear and out the other."

"Maybe," Jo Lynn said.

"Not maybe. That's the way it is. I'm the one who's with her all the time. I'm the one who talks to her."

"Maybe you're not saying anything very interesting."

I sighed, shook my head. She was probably right. "Can I ask what it is you want to talk to her about?"

Jo Lynn pursed her lips, twisted her mouth from side to side, as if weighing the pros and cons of taking me into her confidence. "I guess I can tell you since it was your idea in the first place."

"My idea?"

"About going to law school."

"What?"

"I've thought a lot about what you said, and I've decided it might not be such a crazy idea after all."

"You're serious?"

"I *do* listen to what you say, you know," she told me. "Occasionally."

"And you've decided you want to go back to school," I repeated numbly. Surely, this conversation wasn't really taking place. Surely, I was back in bed, the covers up around my ears, my insides cramping to protest the surprise pruning of internal weeds. On Saturday, my sister had married a serial killer; today, she was applying for law school. Fantasies had given way to hallucinations. I was as nutty as the rest of my family.

"I think you were right," Jo Lynn was saying. "It's the only way I can really help Colin, get him out of that terrible place."

"It won't be easy," I warned her.

"I know it won't be easy. First, I have to finish my degree."

"First you have to apply."

"I know that," she said impatiently. "But I'm determined, and you know what I'm like when I'm determined."

"It means at least five years of school."

"Do I have anything better to do?"

"No, I guess not."

"What's your problem?" she asked. "You're the one who suggested it, who made it sound like such a great idea."

"It *is* a great idea."

"I thought you'd be thrilled."

"I am. It's just that . . ."

"You're still mad at me because of Sara."

"You don't give people a lot of time to catch their breath."

"Part of my charm." Jo Lynn looked toward our mother. "So, think she'll spring for it?"

I reached into the cupboard, grabbed two mugs, filled them with freshly brewed, steaming-hot coffee. "Spring for what?"

"The tuition."

I handed Jo Lynn her mug, sipped gingerly from my own, the steam searing my eyelashes shut.

"What's the matter? You don't think she'll give me the money?"

I opened my eyes. "I'm not sure she has the money to give."

Jo Lynn jumped to her feet, hot coffee from her mug spilling over the back of her hand. She didn't seem to notice. "What are you talking about? Of course she has money."

"Most of what she had is gone," I tried to explain. "Her medical expenses will probably eat up the rest."

"Goddamn her anyway. She couldn't just die?"

"Jo Lynn!"

She was pacing now, turning in small circles between the table and the kitchen counter. "Oh, spare me your righteous indignation. You can't tell me you haven't thought the same thing."

I was about to protest, but didn't. The truth was that there had been times over the last number of weeks when I thought death might have been kinder, for all of us.

"What about you and Larry?"

"What?"

"You said you'd loan me the money, that I could pay you back when I was *raking in the dough*. Didn't you mean it?"

I hesitated.

She pounced. "You didn't mean it, did you? It was just one of those things you say to make you feel good about yourself, but you have no intention of actually doing."

"That's not true."

"Will you loan me the money or won't you?"

"Hold on a second," I said, trying to slow things down. "Aren't we moving a little fast here? What's the urgency?"

"Why wait? I want to get the ball rolling."

"This is very implusive," I told her. "Are you sure you've thought it all through?"

"I don't see what the big deal is. It was your suggestion that I go to law school. I'm taking you up on it. I thought you'd be thrilled. I'm finally going to do something with my life. I'm finally going to amount to something. Or is that the problem? Are you so used to being the omnipotent older sister that you don't really want me to succeed?"

I downed the contents of my mug, felt my throat sting. When had

this conversation become about me? "Look," I began. "You've caught me off guard, and this probably isn't the best time to be asking for favors in any case. Leave it with me for a few days. I'll discuss it with Larry when I think the time is right."

"Who are you kidding? The time will never be right." In the next second, Jo Lynn was on her way to the front door. "I don't understand," she said, waving her hands in frustration. "I mean, what is it you want from me?"

I stood there helplessly as the door slammed in my face.

Chapter
27

I'm thinking of going to South Carolina next week," Larry said, as we lay side by side on our backs in bed, hands folded across our stomachs, not touching, staring at the ceiling fan whirring gently overhead.

"To see your mother?"

"That, and to play golf. My brother called, invited me up for a few days. Invited us, actually."

"I can't go," I said quickly.

"I told him I didn't think you'd be able to make it."

"It's a bad time," I said. "There's just too much going on."

"That's what I told him."

I heard the disappointment in his voice, ignored it. "But you can go. You haven't seen your family in a while. I'm sure your mother would be thrilled."

"I think I will go," he said, after a pause.

"I think it would be good," I said. "Have you given any thought to Jo Lynn's request?"

"Nope."

"Are you going to?"

"Nope."

"You don't think you're being just a tad shortsighted?"

"Nope."

I took a deep breath, released it slowly, louder than was necessary.

"Look, Kate. After the stunt she pulled, I'm not prepared to give your sister the time of day, let alone the kind of money she's talking about."

"It's not a gift. It's a loan."

"Sure. Like she's actually going to go through with five years of college. Like I'm actually going to see the money again."

"I know we'd be taking a big chance," I agreed, "and, at first, I thought it was ridiculous too, but then I thought about it some more, and I thought that maybe it's not so ridiculous, that maybe this time she might actually pull it off, and I *am* the one who suggested it, who gave her the idea in the first place, who gave it the big buildup, convinced her she could do it."

"That doesn't make you responsible, Kate," Larry said. "You are not your sister's keeper."

"I just think it might be her last chance."

"If she really wants to go to law school, let her get a job and pay for it herself. There are lots of people out there putting themselves through college."

"I know, but . . ."

"Look, Kate, I know she's your sister, and that you'd like to help her out, and I won't stop you. I mean, if you have the money and you want to give it to her, there's nothing I can do, but don't ask me to contribute. I can't, and I won't."

"Fine," I said. But it wasn't.

"You know what amazes me?"

Larry's question was rhetorical. It didn't require an answer.

"What amazes me is how easily you let yourself get sucked in. She

does it to you every time. One minute, you're so mad at her, you never want to see her again; the next minute, you're ready to give her the moon."

"She's my sister."

"She's a flake. She always has been. The difference is that now she's a *dangerous* flake."

"Dangerous?"

"Yes, dangerous. Women who flirt with serial killers are misguided; women who marry them are crazy; women who involve their teenage nieces in their craziness are dangerous."

"I just thought if there was anything I could do to help her . . ."

"There isn't. You can't." He sat up, leaned on one elbow toward me. "Kate, you know as well as I do that you can never pull people like Jo Lynn up. They can only drag you down."

He leaned over to kiss me. I turned my head away, flipped over onto my side, faced the window.

"Well, in another week, I'll be out of your hair," he said sadly, flopping back down. "You'll have a few days on your own to decide what you want to do."

He didn't say about what. He didn't have to. We both understood what he meant.

The next day, I picked up the phone and called Robert, told him of Larry's plans. We agreed to meet the following Saturday. At the Breakers, we concurred. A room with an ocean view.

~

The letter arrived within minutes of Larry leaving for the airport. I stared at it for several seconds without opening it, puzzled by the unfamiliar handwriting, the lack of a return address. I carried it into the kitchen, cutting my finger on the envelope as I carelessly ripped it open, watched as a tiny drop of blood stained the page.

Well, I guess it's official now, dear Katie, the letter began. *We're family.* My eyes shot to the bottom of the plain white piece of paper, my

hands shaking, my heart pounding. *Love, Colin* was scribbled with obscene clarity across the bottom of the page.

"No!" I cried, eyes returning in growing horror to the main paragraph.

Well, I guess it's official now. We're family, I read again, forcing myself to continue. *Kissing cousins, you might say. I got to admit I like the sound of that. Anyway, I just wanted you to know how sorry I was that you couldn't make the wedding, but wanted to let you know that Sara did you real proud. That older girl of yours is really something. Why, she's as sweet as the first strawberry in spring.*

My eyes filled with angry tears. I wiped them away, continued reading.

I know I'm not one of your favorite people, Katie girl, but you're sure one of mine. One day, I hope to prove that to you. In the meantime, just know I'm thinking about you. Love, Colin

"No, no, no, no!" I shouted with increasing ferocity, ripping the letter into as many pieces as my shaking fingers could manage, watching the tiny scraps of paper fall to the tile floor, like flakes of confetti, realizing only too late what I'd done, immediately down on my hands and knees, trying to gather the pieces together, giving up moments later in disgust. "Great," I moaned. "Just great. That was really smart." I took a deep breath. Talk about destroying the evidence. How could I call the police now? Instead, I called my sister.

"You gave him our address?" I declaimed as soon as I heard her voice.

"He said he wanted to try one more time to make amends," Jo Lynn explained.

I told her what the letter said.

"I think that's so sweet," she said. "What's the matter with you, Kate? He's trying so hard. Can't you give him a chance?"

I hung up the phone, more resigned than surprised. She called right back.

"Have you decided whether or not you're going to lend me the money for law school?" she asked, as I shook my head in disbelief.

"I haven't talked to Larry yet," I lied.

"Why not?"

Were we actually having this conversation? "He had to go out of town for a few days. He'll be back Monday. I'll talk to him then."

"Monday's too late."

"Too late? What are you talking about?"

This time, she was the one to hang up.

"Figures," I said out loud, although nothing did. I checked my watch, realizing that if I didn't leave for work now, I'd be late for Mrs. Black, a new client I'd scheduled for one o'clock. I'd canceled my morning appointments so that I could drive Larry to the airport, but he'd said there was no need, he'd already arranged for a limo. I headed for the front door, the set of golf clubs I'd bought him for Christmas leaning against the wall of the foyer, like a silent rebuke. He'd taken his old set with him to Carolina. "I'll have better luck with these," he'd said, without kissing me goodbye.

Could I blame him? I'd been dreadful to him for months, closing myself off, freezing him out.

"You should have gone with him," I told myself, unlocking my office door, trying to block out unwanted images of Colin Friendly by imagining how Mrs. Black might look, what her problem would be. So many problems, I thought. So few solutions.

Moments later, I heard the door to my outer office open and close. I rose to my feet, went out to meet Mrs. Black.

She was standing in the middle of the waiting room, and it took a moment for my brain to register who she was, despite the fact that I recognized her immediately. You know how it is when you meet someone in one set of circumstances, and don't expect to see them in another. Such was the case with the woman who stood before me now, smiling at me from behind layers of blue eye shadow, her too black hair falling into a stiff flip at her shoulders. She was wearing a peach-colored suit with matching peach-colored stockings and pumps. The effect was somewhat startling, like an overripe piece of fruit. "Hello, Kate," she said.

"Brandi," I acknowledged, watching the encounter from some-

where inside my head, struggling to keep my voice its normal timbre. What on earth was she doing here? "How are you?"

"Not so great."

"Oh—I'm sorry to hear that." Actually, I was sorry to hear anything. Brandi Crowe was the last person I wanted to see. Wasn't I planning to sleep with her husband the day after tomorrow?

She smiled, clasped her hands together nervously, then dropped them to her sides. What did she want? Had Robert told her of our plans? Had a reservation clerk from the Breakers phoned her, tipped her off?

"Is there a reason you're here?" I asked reluctantly.

"I need to talk to you."

"To me?"

"Professionally," she said.

"I'm so sorry," I said quickly. "I'm completely booked this afternoon." Had I ever felt so grateful to be so busy?

"I have an appointment."

"You do?" I scanned my memory for mention of her name. Surely, I wasn't so out of it that I wouldn't have noticed the name of my prospective lover's wife in my appointment calendar.

"Mrs. Black," she said, and smiled apologetically. "Not very original, I'm afraid."

Of course. My new client. "Good enough to fool me," I heard myself say.

"I was afraid you wouldn't see me if I gave you my real name. And I didn't want Robert to know I was coming."

I held my breath.

"I apologize for the charade."

"No need." The words slid out as I was forced to exhale. I ushered her inside my inner office, trying to collect the thoughts that were madly scrambling around inside my brain, realizing that she must have called my office weeks ago for this appointment, long before I'd arranged my upcoming Saturday tryst with her husband. There was no way she could know anything about our plans for the weekend. I almost laughed with relief. "Have a seat."

She arranged herself neatly in one of the chairs across from my own, crossed, then uncrossed her peach-tinted legs. "I feel a little self-conscious."

"Are you sure I'm the person you should be seeing?"

"Yes," she said quickly. "You strike me as a good listener. And Robert speaks very highly of you."

Silently, I debated the ethics of counseling my lover's wife. Of course, he wasn't my lover yet, nor had I decided to take his wife on as a client. Brandi's visit would hopefully prove to be only a one-time thing. "It's just that you might feel more comfortable talking to someone you don't know," I ventured, understanding it was I who would feel more comfortable.

"No, really, I'm sure I'll be quite comfortable talking to you."

"Good." I forced a reassuring smile onto my lips, picked up my notebook, readied my pen. "What can I do for you?" It appeared I had no choice but to listen to what she had to say. I could always recommend another therapist later, I rationalized.

Brandi Crowe looked around the room. "I don't know where to start."

"Why don't you begin with whatever it was that brought you here."

She laughed, though her eyes were already filling with tears. There was a long pause, during which she swallowed several times. "God, I'm so embarrassed. It's such a cliché."

"Somebody once said that a cliché is something that's been true too many times. There's no need to be embarrassed."

"Thank you," she said, and smiled, swallowed again. "I don't know who I am anymore." She shrugged helplessly, tears falling toward the collar of her peach jacket.

I grabbed a tissue and handed it to her. She took it gratefully, dabbed at her eyes, careful not to disturb her makeup. "Why don't you start by telling me a little bit about who you *were*," I said.

"You mean my childhood?"

"I know your father owns a string of radio stations," I prompted.

She nodded her head up and down in confirmation. "Fourteen."

"And your mother?"

"She died when I was twenty-one. She committed suicide."

"My God, how awful."

"We weren't very close, but yes, I guess it was pretty awful."

"Do you have any brothers or sisters?"

"Two sisters. Both older. One lives in Maui, the other in New Zealand."

"They couldn't get much farther away."

She laughed. "I guess that's right."

"So, you don't see them very often."

"Almost never."

"How do you feel about that?"

"All right, I guess. We don't have a lot in common."

"How did your mother kill herself?" I asked, genuinely curious. Brandi Crowe was a much more interesting woman than I'd originally imagined.

"She hanged herself in my father's office." Her voice was distant, dispassionate, as if she were talking about a stranger, and not her mother. "I think she was trying to get his attention." She shook her head. "It didn't work. He decided not to go into the office that day. One of the cleaning staff found her."

"Their marriage was obviously not a happy one," I commented.

"My father was happy enough. He had his radio stations, his family, his women."

"His women?" The pen in my hand began to wobble. I laid it down across my notepad.

"My father is one of those larger-than-life characters you see in the movies. Big, brash, demanding. He's not easily satisfied. Oh, he's slowed down a bit now. He's older, can't run around quite as much anymore. Not that he doesn't try."

"And your mother knew he was unfaithful?"

"We all knew. He didn't go out of his way to keep his affairs a secret."

"How did that make you feel?"

Brandi Crowe tilted her head, stared toward the window. "Diminished," she said finally.

An interesting choice of words, I thought. "In what way?"

"I don't know if I can explain it. I guess I took his cheating personally, as if he wasn't just cheating on my mother, but on me too. It made me feel as if I wasn't very important."

"Have you ever talked to him about this?"

She laughed bitterly. "My father's a very busy man. Besides, he's not interested in anything I have to say. He never has been."

"Did he remarry?"

"Several times. Right now, he likes to say he's between ex-wives."

"Sounds like a very selfish man."

"Oh, he is. That's part of his charm." She shook her head, dislodged several fresh tears. "It's funny."

"What is?"

"I swore I'd never get involved with anyone remotely like him, and look what I did."

"What did you do?" I asked, despite my intense desire not to.

"I married Robert," she said simply.

"You think Robert is like your father?"

"He's exactly like my father."

My turn to swallow, tilt my head, look toward the window. "In what way?"

"He's handsome, smart, charming, selfish, self-absorbed, arrogant. Arrogance is a very sexy quality in a man, don't you find?"

"There's a difference between arrogance and confidence," I said, flinching at the reference to sex.

"Robert is both confident and arrogant, wouldn't you agree?"

"I don't know him well enough," I hedged.

"But you knew him in high school," Brandi said quickly. "What was he like then?"

"Handsome, smart, charming, selfish, self-absorbed," I said, parroting her words. "Arrogant," I added truthfully.

She smiled. "And very sexy, right?"

"And very sexy," I admitted, sensing it was pointless to lie.

"I saw him coming a mile away," Brandi continued. "I told myself, whatever you do, stay clear of this one. He's dangerous. But of course,

that was part of his appeal. I knew his reputation. Hell, I knew his history with women the minute I laid eyes on him. It was my father all over again. But even though I knew rationally that I'd never change him, something deep inside me must have thought I could. Something inside me obviously was trying to prove that I was not my mother, that I could give the story a happy ending." She laughed. "You see, I've read all the self-help books. I have a pretty clear understanding of my own motivations."

"You're saying that you think Robert is cheating on you?"

"I *know* he's cheating on me."

"How do you know?" I bit down hard on my tongue.

"He's been cheating on me for almost twenty years," she said.

My pen rolled off my lap and onto the floor. I reached down awkwardly to pick it up.

"It started within a year of our wedding. His receptionist, I think it was. It went on for about six months, then it ended."

"He told you about her?"

"Oh no. I said he was arrogant, not stupid."

"How did you find out?"

"I'm not stupid either," she said simply.

"Did you confront him?"

She shook her head. "When you confront something, you have to deal with it. I wasn't ready to do that."

"And now?"

"I love my husband, Kate. I don't want to lose him."

"How do you think I can help you?" I asked finally.

"Tell me what to do," she said.

"I can't do that."

"I knew that's what you were going to say." She tried to laugh, but the sound that emerged was brittle, shattering upon contact with the air. "It's just that I'm running out of ideas. God knows, I've tried everything, turned myself inside out to please him." She pulled at the stiff flip in her hair. "I wear my hair this way because Robert likes long hair. He hates gray, so I have touch-ups every three weeks. I own every anti-wrinkle cream on the market, and I go to exercise class three times a week. But,

you know, there's only so much you can do. I'm forty-six years old; I've had four children. My muscle tone is never going to be what it was." She reached up with her right hand, pulled her hair away from her ear. "Four years ago, I had a face-lift. I don't know if you can see the scars."

"No," I said, reluctant to look until it became obvious that she wasn't going to release her hair until I did. "It's a very good job," I muttered.

"It hurt like hell, let me tell you. I felt as if I'd been hit by a truck. My face and neck were covered with bruises for months. They don't tell you that beforehand. They tell you to expect a little discomfort, a little swelling. You might have bruises for a week or two. Hah! I was a mess for months. Although, that was nothing compared to the tummy tuck I had last spring."

"You had a tummy tuck?"

"You name it, I've had it. The face-lift, the tummy tuck, the liposuction, the boob job."

"You had your breasts enlarged?"

"After four children, my breasts weren't quite what they were, and Robert, well, you've seen him, he looks as good as he did thirty years ago. He has that slim, athletic body that never seems to put on a pound, and I looked, well, I looked like a middle-aged woman who'd had four children. I couldn't blame him for looking elsewhere."

"Was it easier to blame yourself?"

"I guess it was. That way, I felt more in control, as if there was something I could do that would make Robert look at me the way he used to. But you know what I've realized?" she asked, then waited.

"What's that?"

"That my husband doesn't want what he's used to. That's precisely the point. It's not a question of my looking younger, or even better. Some of the women Robert's been involved with over the years were older than me. A few weren't even very attractive. What makes them so appealing to him is that they're new, they're something he's never had. They don't have to be young, as long as that's how they make him feel."

I lowered my eyes, counted to ten. "What about your sex life?"

My wife and I haven't made love in three years, I heard Robert say.

"It's fine."

"Fine? What does that mean?"

"It means it's good. It's always been good."

I pulled at the top button of my blouse. "So, you still make love."

"Oh yes, that's never been our problem. You look surprised."

"No." I struggled to make my face a blank. "No," I said again, realizing this was true. "I'm not surprised."

"The frustrating thing is that I honestly thought we'd turned a corner. The kids are getting older. They're more independent. We've been getting along better than we have in a long time. His last affair was almost a year and a half ago. And now this."

"This?"

"It's starting again. He's having an affair. Or he's about to."

"How do you know?"

"All the signs are there. Trust me, I know."

"Do you know with whom?" I held my breath.

"It doesn't matter with whom," she said dismissively.

"What *does* matter?" I asked.

"What matters is that I don't think I can go through it all again. The lies, the deceit, the casual disregard of my feelings. I don't know that I can just sit back and pretend it isn't happening, and that scares me because I've been Mrs. Robert Crowe for so long, I'm not sure I exist on my own anymore. I've done everything I can to make my husband happy. I've turned myself inside out to please him. I've pumped stuff into my body and sucked stuff out so many times that there are days when I look in the mirror and I barely recognize myself. It's like there's nothing left of me anymore." She stood up, walked slowly to the window, stared at the street below. "What does it say about me, that I've tolerated his infidelities for all these years?" She didn't wait for an answer. "You want to know what's really scary?"

"What's that?"

"I'm just like my mother."

Her answer caught me off guard. "What makes you say that?"

"My mother committed suicide," she said, her eyes focused and dry. "In my own way, so have I. It's just taken me a little longer to die."

Chapter
28

B astard!" I was screaming, punching the steering wheel as I drove home along I-95. "Lying bastard. *My wife and I haven't made love in three years!* And you believed him." I slapped at the rearview mirror, watched my image tilt, then disappear. "Idiot!"

How could I be so stupid? Was I still as hopelessly naive as I'd been thirty years ago, at least where Robert was concerned? Except that thirty years ago I'd known I wasn't the only one. I'd known all about his visits to Sandra Lyons. And I'd pretended I didn't. Just as his wife had been doing all these years. Pretending that things didn't exist, losing ourselves in the process.

At least she doesn't know it's you, I thought, straightening the rearview mirror, watching my eyes jump into view, widen with alarm. "Or does she?" Perhaps her visit to my office had been calculated well in

advance, then executed with the subtle precision one might expect from someone with so much experience in these matters.

"I'm not stupid," I heard Brandi say, sad gray eyes reflecting through mine in the rearview mirror.

Objects in the rearview mirror are closer than they may appear, I knew, feeling Brandi's breath mingling with my own, reexperiencing the touch of her hand in mine as we shook hands goodbye. "I don't think that I need to come back," she'd said as she was leaving my office.

"Beware of women whose names are potable," Robert said. Of course, he'd said a lot of things. Were any of them true?

My wife and I haven't made love in three years.

Well, maybe they hadn't. Maybe it was Brandi, and not Robert, who was the liar in this equation. Maybe Robert had been a good and faithful husband all these years, despite a cold and unloving wife.

"Do you really believe that?" I asked myself out loud.

I glanced at the woman in the car next to mine, also talking to herself. Probably on a speaker phone, I decided, realizing she was likely thinking the same thing about me. All these crazy women driving along America's highways talking to themselves. I laughed. So did she.

Was Brandi laughing as well? Had she left my office chuckling with the knowledge that she'd accomplished her mission, shaken up the competition, stopped her husband's would-be mistress dead in her tracks? Was it possible that *everything* she'd said had been a lie, that she'd concocted the whole story from top to bottom, her father's philandering, her husband's affairs, even her mother's suicide?

I changed lanes without signaling, eliciting a loud horn and a raised middle finger from the driver behind me. I didn't have to make any decisions right now, I told myself. I had till Saturday to decide what to do about Robert. "Your wife came to see me," I rehearsed, afraid to say more.

For the duration of the drive, I concentrated on making my mind a blank. Every time a thought came in, I pushed it out. Every time an image appeared, I wiped it away. By the time I arrived home some fifteen minutes later, I was exhausted from all the pushing and wiping, and

I felt a bad headache lying in wait behind my eyes. All I wanted to do was climb into a hot Jacuzzi, then crawl into bed.

The beat-up red car was parked in the middle of my driveway, leaving me no room on either side to get in. "Great. Just what I need." I backed up, found a spot on the street. "What are you doing here, Jo Lynn?" I asked the growing darkness.

The front door opened as I approached the house. Michelle stepped outside, a veritable poster girl for The Gap, in light khaki pants and cropped moss-green sweater. She closed the door behind her, met me halfway down the front walk. "I thought I better warn you," she said.

"What's going on?"

"Jo Lynn's here."

"I can see that. Where's Grandma?"

"She's asleep."

"What's Jo Lynn doing?"

"She's cooking dinner."

"She's cooking dinner?"

Michelle shrugged. She's *your* sister, the shrug said.

"When did she get here?"

"About an hour ago."

I checked my watch. It was almost seven o'clock. "Is Sara home?"

"She's helping Jo Lynn."

"She's helping?"

"I'll taste your food first," Michelle said.

I laughed, though the laugh was bittersweet. "I don't think that will be necessary." I leaned over, kissed her on the cheek. "But thanks for the offer."

"I think that whatever happens," Michelle advised as we approached the front door, "the important thing is for you to stay calm."

"Nothing's going to happen," I said. Was I seeking to reassure my daughter or myself?

"Well, you know what Jo Lynn is like. For sure she'll say something to upset you. Just don't let yourself get sucked in."

I stared at my younger daughter in absolute wonderment. Where

had this wise little creature come from? At the same time, I felt ineffably sad. My fourteen-year-old child was trying to protect me. Protecting me wasn't her job. It was *my* job to protect *her*. "I'll be fine, doll," I said.

Michelle smiled. "Chin up," she said as I pushed open the door.

"Jo Lynn?" I stepped into the foyer. Honey, I'm home, I thought, but didn't say.

"I'm making stir-fry," she called from the kitchen. Her voice resonated warmth, intimacy. What are families for? it said.

"Smells good." I forced my shoulders back, my feet forward. Michelle was right behind me.

Jo Lynn stood in front of the stovetop, stirring a large pan filled with vegetables and small pieces of chicken. She was wearing white jeans and a loose-fitting black V-necked sweater. Sara was standing beside her in blue jeans and a skimpy denim shirt, tending to a steaming pot of white rice. As soon as Sara saw me, she dropped the cover on the pot, spun on her heels, and left the room. "You didn't set the table for dinner," Jo Lynn called after her.

"I'll do it later."

"Now, please," Jo Lynn said.

Amazingly, Sara turned around and came back. Jo Lynn gave me an easy smile. See how simple that was, the smile said, as Sara quickly set the table for five.

"Larry's out of town, right?" Jo Lynn asked.

"Till Monday." Was that why she was here—to check up on my story?

"Anything else you want me to do?" Sara asked her aunt, as if I weren't there, as if I didn't exist.

"Not at the moment."

"Then I can go?"

"Sure. I'll call you when dinner's ready. And thanks."

Sara nodded, refusing to look my way as she walked from the room.

"Why'd you kick Sara out of her room?" Jo Lynn asked immediately. "You could have given our mother the den."

The muscles in my stomach tensed. I looked over at Michelle, who

was leaning against the family-room sofa, carefully monitoring the scene. "Smile," she mouthed silently, pushing her lips up with her fingers, as if to underline the word.

"It won't be for much longer," I said.

"A girl's room is pretty sacred ground," Jo Lynn continued, speaking to me as if I'd never been a teenage girl. "You have to learn to respect a kid's privacy, you know, if you want the kid to have any respect for you."

"Is that so?"

Michelle cleared her throat, the forced smile tightening on her lips, her eyes bulging with the effort.

"I just remember how I hated for anyone to go into my room, that's all," Jo Lynn said, then: "Wait until you taste this stir-fry. It's the best. I've become quite the cook, you know."

"Great."

"It's practice more than anything else. I mean, anybody who can read, can cook. At least that's what Mom used to say."

"Since when did you listen to anything Mom had to say?"

"I've been trying out all these recipes lately," she continued, as if I hadn't spoken, "for when Colin gets out."

"Great," I said again. It seemed like the only thing I could say that wouldn't get me into trouble. I was wrong.

"Why do you keep saying 'great'? You know you don't mean it. You know that the last thing you want is for Colin to get out of jail."

"It's great that you're enjoying cooking so much," I said.

"I didn't say I was enjoying it."

Again, I glanced over at Michelle. She lifted her chin with the back of her hand. I followed her silent instructions and pushed my chin up.

"Something wrong with your neck?" Jo Lynn asked.

"It's a bit stiff," I said quickly.

"That's because you don't know how to relax. You've never learned to roll with the punches. Stop trying to be so perfect all the time."

"I'm not trying to be perfect."

"You know what your problem is?" Jo Lynn laid down the fork she was using to stir the vegetables. "You bring your work home with you."

"That's probably true," I agreed.

"You're so used to telling people how to run their lives, and I'm not saying there's anything wrong with that, don't get me wrong, it's part of your job, but it's easy to forget that not everybody back home is interested in your opinion."

I pulled a large platter out of the cupboard and handed it to my sister. What I really wanted to do was break it over her head. "What are you doing here, Jo Lynn?"

"Cooking you dinner."

"Why?"

"I guess it's my way of saying 'I'm sorry.' "

I almost laughed. My sister had a unique way of apologizing. "That's the only reason you're here?"

She shrugged, as if what was about to follow was incidental, unimportant. "I need to talk to Mom."

"About what?"

"Dinner's ready," Jo Lynn called out, transferring the stir-fry and the rice from the stove to the platter, depositing the steaming platter on the table in the breakfast nook. "Come and get it."

"I just don't think you should say anything to upset her," I said before anyone came back.

"This is really none of your business." Jo Lynn punctuated her rebuke with a sweet smile.

Sara was the first one at the table. She filled her plate and was already eating before anyone else had a chance to sit down.

"Don't you think you should wait till everybody gets here?" I asked.

"Go ahead—eat," Jo Lynn said, pouring water into everyone's glass. "Since when do we stand on ceremony here? You too, Kate—help yourself."

"I'll wait for the others."

"Suit yourself. But it tastes better hot." Jo Lynn began heaping the stir-fry chicken and vegetables onto her plate.

"What's this?" my mother asked, Michelle guiding her into the room. "A party?"

She was wearing a pale pink shirtdress, her gray curls slightly flattened from sleep. She looks just like my mother, I thought.

"Yes, Mom," Jo Lynn answered. "It's your party, you can cry if you want to."

"Cry?" my mother asked, oblivious to the reference to the old Lesley Gore hit.

"Eat," my sister said.

"Something smells wonderful."

"It tastes even better," Sara offered, as Michelle helped my mother into a chair.

"Yes, Kate is a wonderful cook," my mother said.

Jo Lynn scooped up an enormous helping of chicken and vegetables and dumped them onto our mother's plate. "*I* made the dinner," she said.

"Did you, dear? Good for you."

Jo Lynn lifted her water glass into the air. "I'd like to propose a toast." She waited, a smile forming, then freezing on her lips, while we raised our glasses. "To new beginnings." We clicked glasses.

"Is this a party?" my mother asked.

"Yes, Grandma," Michelle answered.

My mother took a few tentative bites of her food. "You don't have to be afraid of it," Jo Lynn said. "It's not going to bite back."

"It's delicious," our mother pronounced. "Kate is a wonderful cook."

"Jo Lynn made the dinner, Grandma," Sara said.

"Of course, dear."

The rest of the meal passed in merciful silence. When it was over, my mother complimented me on the delicious dinner. "It was a lovely party."

"Party's not over yet," Jo Lynn said as Sara and Michelle cleared the table and stacked the dishes in the dishwasher. "We have a little business to discuss."

"Business, dear?"

"Jo Lynn, please . . ."

"Kate, butt out. This doesn't concern you."

"Would you like to watch some TV, Grandma?" Michelle asked from the kitchen.

Jo Lynn's eyes flashed daggers toward my younger child. "Call off the dogs, Kate."

"You know she's not going to understand anything you say," I said.

"So, what else is new?"

"And even if she does understand, she won't remember it."

"She doesn't have to remember it. And you don't have to stay."

"I'm not going anywhere."

"Suit yourself. But stay out of it." Jo Lynn twisted our mother's chair around so that it faced hers. "Mom, listen to me. This is no big deal. I just need some money."

"Money?"

"Yeah, you know, that evil green stuff you've been hoarding away for years."

"Jo Lynn, please . . ."

"Shut up, Kate."

"She doesn't have any money."

Our mother glanced warily toward me. "That was a lovely dinner, Kate."

"*I* made the dinner," Jo Lynn said, her hands on the sides of our mother's chair, her face mere inches from our mother's. "Thank me, not Kate."

"Kate is a wonderful cook."

Angry tears filled Jo Lynn's eyes. "Kate is wonderful at everything she does. We all know that. But Kate is not part of this discussion. Now, do you remember what I just said?"

"Of course, dear."

"Good. Because this is very important to me. I've decided to go back to college, to become a lawyer. What do you think about that?"

"I think that's wonderful, dear."

"And in order to do that, I'd need money. Money that I don't have. So I'm asking you to lend me some."

Our mother smiled.

"It's not a lot of money. A few thousand dollars is all I need right now."

"Right now?" My voice was sharp, like the crack of a whip.

"I asked you to stay out of it, Kate," Jo Lynn warned.

"But why do you need a few thousand dollars right now? You haven't been accepted anywhere yet. You haven't even applied."

"You have to send in a check with your application."

"Not for a few thousand dollars, you don't."

"Times have changed since you went to school, Kate," she reminded me.

"Not that much, they haven't. Why do you need two thousand dollars?"

"Correct me if I'm wrong," Jo Lynn said, "but isn't this conversation between Mom and me? Didn't you already renege on your promise to loan me the money?"

"What's really going on here, Jo Lynn?" I demanded.

"That was a lovely dinner, Kate," our mother said, eyes flitting nervously between her two daughters. "I think I'd like to go to my room now."

"Sure, Mom," I said quickly. "Michelle, why don't you help Grandma . . . ?"

"Michelle, stay right where you are," Jo Lynn said. "Grandma isn't going anywhere until this is settled."

"For God's sake, what's the point?" I asked, "You can see you're just upsetting her."

"*You're* the one who's upsetting her. I was doing fine."

"She doesn't understand what's going on."

"She understands plenty. Don't you, Mom?"

"Of course, dear." Our mother shifted uneasily in her chair.

"You heard her."

"That's her answer for everything," I tried to explain.

"What's the matter, Kate?" Jo Lynn snapped. "Afraid there won't be as much left for you to inherit?"

"Inherit? What are you talking about? There's not going to be any money to inherit."

"All I need is two thousand dollars, Mom. Surely you can spare that much. It's not like I've asked you for anything before."

"That was a delicious dinner," our mother said, her voice thin, her hands flitting nervously about her lap.

"You're scaring her," I said.

"Is Kate right?" Jo Lynn asked. "Am I scaring you?"

"I think I'd like to go to my room now."

"You can go anywhere you like as soon as we get this settled."

"For God's sake, Jo Lynn, enough is enough. I think it's time you went home."

"Is the party over?" our mother asked.

"Yes, Mom, the party's over."

"The party's still going strong," Jo Lynn stated, her voice harsh, strangely desperate. "Look, I don't think that any of you realize how important this is to me. It could be my last chance. You wouldn't want to deprive me of that, would you? I mean, think how proud you'd be, Mom. You could tell all your friends about your daughter the lawyer."

"Of course, dear."

"If you tell me where you've hidden your checkbook, I can get it for you."

"My checkbook," our mother repeated, looking at me.

"Don't look at her. Look at me. Just tell me where it is, and I'll get it for you. I'll fill it all out. All you have to do is sign it."

"Of course, dear."

"Where is it? Is it in your purse?" Jo Lynn was on her feet, hurrying toward Sara's bedroom.

"What's all this about?" Sara asked warily, the first words she'd said to me since our altercation.

"I'm not sure," I answered truthfully.

Jo Lynn returned with our mother's purse. "I can't find your checkbook. Where do you keep it?"

"I have her checkbook," I said, preparing myself for the fireworks that were sure to follow.

"What do you mean, you have it? What are you doing with it?"

"There's no money, Jo Lynn. And there's no point in arguing about it."

"Goddamnit, who put you in charge?"

"Why don't we all calm down," Michelle ventured.

"Shut up, Michelle. This is none of your business."

"Don't tell her to shut up," Sara said, taking the words out of my mouth.

Jo Lynn threw her hands into the air. "Oh, great. Gang up on me, why don't you?"

"I'll make you a deal," I offered. "Bring me the application. I'll write out a check for the application fee, and we'll take it one step at a time."

"That's not good enough."

"What do you mean, it's not good enough?"

"Stop treating me like a child."

"How is that treating you like a child?"

"You want to see the application; you want to write the check. You always have to be in control."

"Do you want the money or don't you?"

She ignored me, fell to her knees in front of our mother. "Please, Mom, this is really embarrassing for me. Can't you just lend me the money. Don't make me beg."

Tears filled our mother's eyes. "That was a lovely party."

"Don't do this, Mom," Jo Lynn said. "Please don't do this."

"She can't help it," I said.

"She *can* help it." Jo Lynn pushed herself off her knees, began pacing back and forth in front of our mother's chair, a caged tiger in a small cell, claws extended, ready to leap, go for the jugular. "You're not going to do this, Mom. This time you're not going to get away with it."

"Get away with what?" I demanded. "What has she ever done to you?"

"Nothing!" Jo Lynn shouted. "She does absolutely nothing! Isn't that right, Mom? Isn't that right? You do nothing!"

"I do nothing," our mother repeated, a faint glimmer of understanding creeping into her eyes.

"You just sit there, and do nothing. Just like you've always done."

"I do nothing," our mother agreed.

"When your husband comes home and screams at you, you do nothing. When he hits you and washes your mouth out with soap, you do nothing."

"Nothing."

"When he terrorizes your children, you do nothing."

"I do nothing."

"Jo Lynn, what's the point of bringing this up now?" My voice was a painful whisper. It literally hurt to speak.

"The point is that she did nothing! All those years, she did nothing."

"And she paid for it. God knows, she paid for it."

"No—*I* paid for it! *I'm* the one who paid for it." Tears began falling the length of Jo Lynn's cheeks.

"What are you talking about? You were his favorite. He never touched you." The second the words were out of my mouth, I knew they were wrong. "Oh no," I said. "Please, no."

"Welcome to the real world, Ms. Therapist," my sister said.

"I did nothing," our mother said, rising slowly to her feet.

"That's right, Mom. You did nothing." Jo Lynn looked toward the back window, as if the past were projected on the glass, like a movie on a screen. "All those nights he came into my room to 'kiss me good night,' all those times he left your bed to come into mine, all those rides in the country on Sunday afternoon. 'You see those cows over there?' he'd say, while his hand was pushing its way between my legs. 'When all the cows are standing up, it means it's going to be sunny, and when all the cows are lying down, that means it's going to rain.'"

"Oh God," I said, feeling weak, gutted. "I had no idea."

"No, but *she* did." Jo Lynn glared at our mother, whose eyes were

fixed on the back window, watching the same old movie as my sister. "And she did nothing."

"I didn't know," our mother whispered. "I didn't know."

"Don't tell me you didn't know," my sister shouted. "You knew. You knew. You just pretended it wasn't happening. What did you think, that if you ignored it, it would go away? Is that what you thought?"

"I didn't know."

"How could you let him get away with it? How could you let him do the things he did to me? You're my mother. You were supposed to take care of me. You were supposed to protect me."

"He was always so kind to you," our mother said, crying now. "So loving."

"Oh, he was loving, all right."

"I was so envious. I used to think, if only he would be so kind, so gentle, with me."

"You knew," Jo Lynn insisted. "Don't try to tell me you didn't know."

"It wasn't until you were almost thirteen years old that I began to suspect there was something more."

"What was your first clue, Mom? The nightmares I kept having, my poor grades, the blood on my sheets?"

For a moment, the silence was absolute. Sara reached over to Michelle, drew her into her arms.

"It was the way he looked at you," our mother said finally. "You were bending over to pick something up, and I caught the look in his eyes, and suddenly I knew. I left him the next day."

"It was too late by then." Jo Lynn wiped her nose with the back of her hand. "It was too late."

Our mother sank back down into her chair, burying her head in her hands.

"But you went to see him," I reminded my sister. "After he got sick, you went to the hospital. You cried when he died."

"He was my father," Jo Lynn said simply.

No one said another word.

Chapter

29

That night I dreamed I was running through a large open field. The sky was mauve, threatening rain, the grass dry and yellow. In the distance, Jo Lynn was singing: *You can't catch me. You can't catch me.* I raced toward the sound, tripping over a large black-and-white cow that was lying on the ground. As I scrambled to my feet, I saw Sara sitting on the back of another cow. She was crying. I ran toward her, my path suddenly blocked by two rows of thick barbed wire that sprang up between us.

Colin Friendly stood in a high tower, the long rifle in his hands pointed at my daughter's head. "Don't worry," he told me. "I'll take care of her."

"All the cows are lying down," a voice said from somewhere behind me.

I spun around. My stepfather was leaning against the side of a mas-

sive banyan tree. In one hand, he held a bottle of beer; in the other, he held Michelle.

"That means it's going to rain," Michelle said, as my stepfather's hand tightened across her chest.

I bolted up in bed, my heart pounding, my body soaked in sweat. In the next instant, I was on my knees in the bathroom, throwing up into the toilet. "Son of a bitch," I whispered between heaves. "Goddamn son of a bitch."

How could I not have known? How could I not have suspected? My sister had been dropping hints for years. The pieces were all there. All I'd had to do was find them, gather them together, arrange them into a cohesive whole. Had I been blind or just stupid? And what of my mother? Had she known all along, as Jo Lynn had accused, or had she left as soon as her suspicions were aroused? Did it matter anymore? The damage had been done.

I thought of calling Larry and decided against it. It was almost two in the morning. I'd wake up the whole house, scare his mother half to death. And why? So that I could share this latest bulletin about my increasingly demented family? What did I expect him to do? What could any of us do now?

It had taken over an hour to get everyone settled after Jo Lynn raced from the house in a torrent of tears, her body doubled over in pain, rubbery legs threatening to collapse under her. "Please stay," I begged as she hurled herself into her car. "You can sleep in my bed. Please, Jo Lynn, you shouldn't be driving. You shouldn't be alone."

Her answer was to lock the car doors and bolt backward out of the driveway, narrowly missing my car parked on the darkened street. I tried phoning her ten minutes later, got her answering machine. "Hi, this is Jo Lynn," her voice purred seductively. "Tell me everything."

"Please call me as soon as you get home," I told her, calling back ten minutes later, leaving another such message, calling every ten minutes until I finally gave up at just after midnight. Clearly, she didn't want to talk to me. What more, after all, was there to say?

"Do you think she's all right?" Michelle asked.

"I don't know," I said.

"Do you think Grandma knew?"

"I don't know."

"Why didn't Jo Lynn ever say anything to anyone?"

"I don't know."

Did I know anything?

"Why couldn't you just give her the money?" Sara demanded. "It's not like you can't afford it."

"That's not the point," I said.

"The point is that she asked you for help and you wouldn't give it to her."

"I've tried to help her."

"Yeah, some therapist *you* are."

I didn't argue. She was right.

Somehow I managed to guide my mother into Sara's room, get her out of her clothes and into her nightgown. I tucked her into bed, leaned forward to kiss her soft, tear-stained cheek. "Are you okay, Mom?" I asked, but she made no reply, simply lay there, her eyes open, tears continuing to fall. When I looked in on her again half an hour later, she hadn't moved.

The next morning, I drove to Jo Lynn's apartment.

"Can you let me into her apartment?" I asked the superintendent, a tall man with a long, angular face and dark, sunken eyes. "She was pretty upset last night. I just want to make sure she's okay."

"How do I know you're her sister?" he asked, viewing me skeptically.

"Who else would I be?"

"Reporter," he replied lazily, not bothering to pronounce the *t*. "You guys been hounding her pretty good since the wedding."

"I'm not a reporter."

"You don't look like her sister."

"Look, I'm just afraid she might have done something to hurt herself." I broke off, too tired to argue, then turned, about to walk away.

"Wait," he called after me. "Guess I can let you in."

"What changed your mind?" I asked as he unlocked the door to my sister's second-floor apartment.

"If you were a reporter," he said, standing aside to let me enter, "there's no way you would have given up so easily."

"Jo Lynn," I called from the doorway, then held my breath. "Jo Lynn, are you here?" I pushed one foot in front of the other, afraid to linger, to look too closely, in case I saw something my mind was unprepared to accept. "Jo Lynn," I repeated, inching forward, the superintendent fast on my heels, like an overly friendly puppy.

In typical Jo Lynn fashion, her apartment was both organized and chaotic. Organized chaos, I thought, my eyes flitting across the well-worn blue-green carpeting, the fading floral-print sofa and matching armchair, the coffee table whose glass top was completely hidden by stacks of old newspapers and the latest tabloids. More discarded newspapers lay scattered across the top of a black Formica bar. A stained white sweater was draped over one of two barstools, while a pair of cerise sandals, one with a broken strap, lay on the floor, one on top of the other.

"Doesn't look like she's here." The superintendent peered over my shoulder as I peeked into the kitchen. More newspapers stretched across the top of the kitchen table, a pair of large scissors beside them, along with an open scrapbook and an empty container of glue. I glanced at the scrapbook, saw Colin Friendly winking at me from the open page, and turned away quickly, noting the row of old cereal boxes that stood in a line on the countertop, along with an empty milk carton. A young girl's picture stared at me from the side of the milk carton. MISSING, it read above her gap-toothed smile. I ran from the room, my eyes filling with tears.

"You all right?" the super asked.

I shook my head, images of Jo Lynn suddenly dropping before my eyes, like a succession of grisly snapshots from the morgue. There she was in the bathtub, her wrists slashed and dripping blood onto the white tile floor; or over there, hanging from the shower stall, an oversized, gaily colored beach towel for a noose; or there, lying on her bed, skin ashen, mouth open, hands folded primly across her ample bosom, dead from an overdose of sleeping pills.

"Would you do me a favor?" I asked. "Would you please check the other rooms for me?"

He hesitated, swayed, ultimately left my side.

"You better come in here," he said several seconds later.

My knees buckled, almost gave way. "Oh God," I said, grabbing the side of the bar, knocking over several sections of newspaper, watching them fall to the floor by my feet. Colin Friendly stared up at me, eyes directed up my skirt. "Oh God," I said again, kicking at his head, watching his face split in two, as the paper ripped apart. "Is she . . . ?"

"She's not here," the superintendent answered. "Doesn't look like she slept here last night."

The laugh that escaped my mouth was one of relief. It quickly turned into a sob that caught in my throat and died as I approached my sister's bedroom, staring toward her queen-size bed, which was neatly made and covered with a childlike blue gingham comforter. A stuffed apricot-colored teddy bear sat on top of a ruffled gingham pillow.

"Looks like a little girl's room," the super said, stealing my thoughts, as I caught my reflection in the mirror atop Jo Lynn's dresser, across from her bed. Pictures of Colin Friendly lined the sides of the mirror, poking out at all angles from the metal frame, forcing themselves into my world, my reality. Wherever I looked, he was there. Laughing at me.

"Her clothes are gone," the super said.

"What?"

He motioned toward the closet. "She say anything to you about taking a vacation?"

I shook my head, my hands slapping against her empty hangers, running across deserted shelves, pulling open abandoned dresser drawers. But aside from a few old blouses and scarves, there was nothing.

"Doesn't look like she's coming back," the super said, once again usurping the thoughts swirling around my brain, like fallen leaves in the wind.

Where could she have gone? Why had she taken all her clothes?

"Her rent's due next Wednesday," the super said.

"I'm sure she'll be back by then," I muttered, anxious now to be on my way. "She goes away every weekend," I reminded us both, trying to fit the pieces of this latest puzzle together, to determine what Jo Lynn

was up to. Had she decided to find an apartment closer to the penitentiary? Was she moving in this weekend? Was that why her clothes were gone? Was that why she needed money? First and last months' rent, a security deposit, I listed silently, as the super followed me out of Jo Lynn's apartment and locked the door after us. These things add up, I told myself. It was expensive to start a whole new life. "If you see my sister, would you tell her I was here, and that I need to talk to her? It's urgent."

"Doesn't look like she's coming back," the super repeated ominously as I headed to my car.

"Where are you, damnit?" I shouted into the empty interior of my car.

"She went to visit Colin," Larry assured me when I phoned him in South Carolina. "Stop worrying about her, Kate. She's in Raiford, surrounded by armed guards and police officers. She couldn't be in a safer place."

"You think so?"

"I know so."

"Thanks," I told him. "I'm glad I called."

"So am I."

"How's the family?"

"Terrific."

"And the golf?"

"Great."

"Great," I repeated. "Terrific."

"Everybody sends their love."

Send it back, I heard Jo Lynn say. "Say hi to everyone," I said instead.

"I will," he said, then: "I miss you. I love you very much. You know that."

"I know that," I told him. "I love you too."

On Saturday, I went to the Breakers to meet Robert.

I told myself I was going because I needed to know the truth, that unless I confronted Robert, I would never know for sure if the things Brandi had told me were true, and then I would spend the rest of my life wondering and regretting. I'd been wondering for too long as it was, and my whole life was rapidly degenerating into one huge regret.

"Have you heard from Jo Lynn?" Sara asked, coming into my bathroom as I was applying a coat of newly purchased deep coral lipstick.

I jumped, dropped the lipstick to the countertop, watched it leave a large orange circle on the almond-colored marble. Death row orange, I thought, quickly wiping the stain off the counter with a damp cloth, then tossing the lipstick into my purse, trying to appear casual, matter-of-fact. "No, she hasn't called."

"What are you going to do?"

"What *can* I do?"

Sara shrugged, leaned against the wall. She was wearing cutoff jeans and one of those loose-fitting Indian blouses she used to favor.

"Look, I have to go out for a few hours," I said, determined not to think about my sister for the balance of the afternoon. When she was ready, she would resurface. She always did.

"You look nice."

"Thank you." I tried not to sound too surprised by the compliment, wondering if Sara could somehow see through my beige Armani pantsuit and ivory silk shirt to the delicate pink French lace bra and panties beneath.

"Where are you going?" Sara asked.

"I'm looking at some places for Grandma," I lied, hating myself.

"I thought you were doing that tomorrow."

"Tomorrow too," I said, thinking that we hadn't had such a long conversation in months, wondering why it was taking place now.

"Do you think you'll find something?"

"I hope so," I told her, my heels clicking on the marble floor as I exited the bathroom.

"Where'd you get those shoes?"

God, she didn't miss a thing. "I bought them a few weeks ago. What do you think?"

"They're kind of high," she said. "I've never seen you wear such high heels."

"I thought I'd try them. For a change."

"When will you be back?" she asked.

"Soon. A few hours. Maybe less," I said. Maybe more, I added silently. "Why?"

"Just wondered." Again, she shrugged, didn't move.

"Is everything all right?" I asked reluctantly, guiltily. Normally, I would have jumped at the opportunity to reopen the lines of communication between us, especially since it was Sara making the overtures. But why did it have to be *now*? "Is there something you want to talk about?"

"Like what?"

"I don't know. You seem kind of at loose ends."

"What does that mean?" Her body tensed, ready to take offense at any possible slight.

"It doesn't mean anything." I didn't have the time, or the patience, to deal with this now. "I really have to get going."

"Maybe we could go to a movie later," Sara said, following me to the front door.

"You want to go to the movies? With me?"

"Well, I don't have any money, and you won't let me go out with my friends," she said logically.

"Right," I said, understanding the situation somewhat better now. "We'll see when I get back."

"Don't be long," she said as I climbed into my car.

They must have some kind of built-in radar, I thought as I backed out of the driveway, some subtle warning device that signals when their world is about to shift. Don't we all? I wondered, realizing how often I'd ignored mine.

Twenty minutes later, the twin towers of the Breakers Golf and Beach Club shot into view. Immediately I thought of the new Palm Beach County Courthouse, whose vaulted roofs had been designed as an architectural echo. God, why was I thinking of that now? This was hardly the time to be thinking about my sister or her lousy taste in men.

An uncomfortable thought squeezed its way into my brain, like an earthworm through wet soil. My sister and I weren't so different after all, it said. We were both pining for undesirable men. My sister was ruining her life for one. Was I about to do the same thing for another?

I found a parking space at the front of the hotel between a black Rolls-Royce and a chocolate-brown Mercedes and walked briskly along the U-shaped driveway, past the large fountain of sculpted water nymphs, to the entrance of the grand old hotel, a magnificent structure that fairly shouted old money. I hurried past the valets and bellhops with their crisp white shirts and navy epaulets, noting the many luggage carts, golf clubs, and potted palms lined up along the portico as I followed the red carpet through the tall Ionic columns and glass doors into the long expanse of lobby, its vaulted fresco ceiling dotted at regular intervals by huge crystal chandeliers, the marble floor all but covered by richly textured area rugs. There were tapestries on the walls, enormous floral arrangements on tall marble stands, comfortable groupings of sofas and chairs, even small tables set up for chess and checkers. I walked toward the long counter of the registration desk, my feet cramping inside my high heels.

I was early, I knew without having to check my watch. Robert wouldn't be here yet. Even so, I glanced furtively around, careful not to make direct eye contact with any of the hotel's many other visitors. I could spend the next half hour browsing through the exclusive boutiques that were located just off the lobby, or I could stroll around the grounds, visit the bar at the back, off the main dining room. Larry and I had come here for dinner once, not long after we'd moved to Palm Beach. Over the years, we'd occasionally talked of checking ourselves in for a weekend. We never had. Now, here I was, about to check in with another man.

I lowered myself into a nearby antique chair, my body immediately obliterated by a hulking hydrangea plant whose bright pink flowers all but leapt into my lap. I heard laughter, turned sharply, the pointed end of a narrow green leaf catching the side of my eye. A young couple was standing not more than six feet away from me, wrapped in each other's

arms, their lips pressed tightly together, their bodies swaying to imaginary breezes, as bemused onlookers tiptoed gingerly around them, careful not to disturb their passion. Next to the registration desk, a young boy of about six was standing beside his mother, pointing at the couple and laughing. His mother admonished him not to point, then looked away, although seconds later I noticed she looked back, sad eyes lingering.

That's what I want, I thought, knowing she was thinking the same thing. To be young and desperately in love, to need someone's arms around me so badly it hurt, to literally ache for the feel of his lips on mine, to be that desired, that carried away, that oblivious to the rest of the world. To be seventeen again.

This was my fantasy: Robert and I in each other's arms, his eyes gazing lovingly into mine, his lips delicately kissing the sides of my mouth, the bend in my neck, my fluttering eyelashes, my cheeks, the tip of my nose, his hands cupping my face, his fingers twisting through my hair as his tongue twisted gently around mine, our kisses growing deeper, yet softer, always softer.

The reality would be different. It always was. Oh, there might be deep tender kisses, but they would be mere preamble to the main event, and they could only linger so long, time being of the essence. Sara was waiting for me at home; Robert, no doubt, had plans with his wife. We couldn't be gone too long without arousing suspicions. And so, soft lingering kisses would give way to increasingly insistent caresses. Clothes would be unbuttoned, shed, and discarded. Limbs would entwine, flesh merge. A different flesh than I was used to, a different way of being touched. And it would be wonderful. I knew it would be wonderful. And when it was over, we would lie in each other's arms, mindful of the moments ticking away, trying to avoid the growing reality of the wet spot beneath us.

That was the difference between fantasy and reality. A fantasy contained no consequences, no mess. When it was over, you felt great, not guilt. Fantasies didn't leave wet spots.

That's what I wanted. I wanted the fantasy.

I didn't need any more reality. I had too much as it was.

I pictured Robert and me sitting on opposite sides of the bed, not speaking, no longer touching, struggling to get back into our clothes. I knew I'd feel awful. I felt awful enough now.

"What am I doing here?" I whispered, catching a long leaf in my mouth, feeling it slither across my tongue. And then I saw him.

He walked through the front door with a comfortable stride, long arms swinging casually at his sides. He was wearing navy pants and a white polo shirt, muscles impressively on display. His hair fell roguishly across his forehead. His lips curled into a natural smile. Could he look more beautiful? I wondered, as every muscle in my body cramped. Was it possible to want someone so much and like him so little?

I gasped, quickly covering my mouth to prevent the sound from escaping, as the truth of my latent observation hit me square in the gut, like a boxer's fist. And the truth was that I really didn't like Robert very much, that I never had, and that was the reason I hadn't slept with him thirty years ago. It was why I couldn't sleep with him now.

Robert strode confidently across the lobby, eyes straight ahead, looking neither right nor left. He didn't see me. I wasn't surprised. The truth was that I was invisible to Robert, that I'd always been invisible. How could you see someone, after all, when the only thing you saw when you gazed into their eyes was the glory of your own reflection?

That was the truth. That was the reality.

I watched Robert speak easily to the clerk behind the registration counter, then glance carelessly around the large lobby. Get up, I told myself. Get up and announce your presence, tell him you've had a change of heart. Instead, I burrowed in deeper behind the potted plant, knowing I was being silly, that even if I wasn't going to go upstairs with him, at least I owed him the courtesy of an explanation.

Except that something kept me rooted to that antique seat as surely as if I'd been potted myself. For despite my recent epiphany and new-found resolve, I knew that if I left that chair, if I confronted Robert, then I was lost, it was game over, I was as good as naked and lying smack in the middle of the wet spot. And so I remained in my chair, hidden by the

giant hydrangea, watching as my would-be lover signed the register and took possession of the room key, smiling securely as he headed for the elevators.

And then I raced for the front entrance of the hotel as if someone were after me, as if my life depended on it.

Perhaps it did.

Chapter

30

I phoned Jo Lynn as soon as I got home. Her machine was still picking up, so I called the motel in Starke where she usually stayed. The manager informed me that she hadn't seen Jo Lynn in several weeks, then hung up before I could ask her the names of other motels in the area. "Great," I muttered, debating whether or not to call the police, maybe the penitentiary, deciding against both alternatives. What would I say after all? What could they do?

"I take it she didn't call?" I asked my daughters.

They shook their heads.

I thought of Robert, wondered if he was still waiting for me at the hotel, if he'd ordered champagne, if he was growing restless, bored, worried, angry. "Did anybody else phone?" I asked.

"Like who?" Sara said.

"Nobody in particular." I noticed she'd washed her hair, changed

into a pair of surprisingly presentable beige pants and matching sweater. "Still want to go to the movies?"

"I guess so." Sara's voice strained for indifference, almost succeeded.

"How about you, Michelle? Feel like a movie?"

"Can't," she said. "I'm going over to Brooke's, remember?"

"That's right. I forgot." I looked around. "Where's Grandma? Is she sleeping?"

"She's in her room," Sara said. "She's been acting kind of funny."

"What do you mean, funny?"

"Hi, darling," my mother said, as if she'd been standing in the wings, waiting for her turn to resume center stage. She shuffled into the kitchen, purse in hand. "Did I hear you say we're going to the movies?"

Sara selected a popular movie, and the theater, at barely four o'clock in the afternoon on a beautiful sunny day, was almost full. We managed to find three seats together near the front. "Is this okay for you, Mom?" I asked.

She said nothing. She hadn't spoken a word since we left the house.

"Was she this quiet while I was gone?"

Sara nodded. "Except for every so often, when she suddenly screams."

"She screams?"

"Every so often."

"Why didn't you tell me this before?"

"I *did* tell you."

"You said she was acting funny. You didn't say anything about screaming."

"Sshh!" someone said, as the houselights dimmed.

She screamed the first time during one of the previews. It was a piercing wail, like a siren, and it scared me half to death, not to mention the people around us, all of whom literally jumped out of their seats.

"Mom, what's the matter?!"

"Is everything all right?" the woman directly in front of us asked.

"Mom, are you all right?"

Wide eyes stared at the screen. She gave no reply.

"She's fine," I assured those around us.

She screamed again about ten minutes into the feature presentation, once again scaring those people in our immediate vicinity half out of their wits, and causing a general outbreak of nervous giggles in the surrounding rows, not to mention a pronounced smattering of "sshh's." Two people at the end of our row got up and moved.

"I'm sorry," I whispered into the general darkness. "I'm very sorry. Mom, what's the matter? Does something hurt you? Do you want to leave?"

"Sshh!" someone hissed loudly.

My mother said nothing, settled back in her seat, her demeanor outwardly calm, her demons seemingly exorcised. I tried to relax, to pay attention to what was happening on the screen, but it was a bit like waiting for the other shoe to drop. I sat stiffly, my body on full alert, poised to whisk my mother out of the theater at the next outburst. It never came. Instead, she drifted off to sleep, awoke as the final credits were rolling.

"How are you?" I asked her as the lights went up.

"Magnificent," she said.

At least she'd kept my mind off Robert, I realized, as we walked up the aisle. I wondered how long he'd stayed at the hotel, and whether he'd tried calling my house to see if I was there, if everything was all right. Had he checked the hospitals, called the police, contacted station WKEY for the latest in accident reports?

As soon as we reached the pay phone in the lobby, I checked my answering machine for messages. There weren't any.

We went to a tiny Italian eatery in the same plaza as the movie theater. The restaurant was brightly lit and decorated in the colors of the Italian flag—red, white, and green. We ordered a large pizza with everything on it, and a Gorgonzola salad to share. "So, did you find a place for Grandma?" Sara asked as we waited for our food to arrive.

"What?" I was staring out the front window into the parking lot, wondering where Robert was now, and what he was doing. I wasn't really surprised he hadn't called. Nor, I realized with no small measure of relief, was I especially disappointed.

"I asked if you found a place for Grandma to live."

"No," I said, staring across the table at the stranger who used to be my mother. The harsh light in the small room accentuated the blankness in her eyes, and gave the rest of her features an eerie glow. She looked almost otherworldly, an alien creature dropped into our midst. I recalled the promo line from an old horror movie: *First they come for your body, then they come back for your mind.* Except that, in this case anyway, reality seemed to work in reverse. It was my mother's mind that had been taken, while her body remained reasonably intact. No, I thought, staring at the woman who'd given me life almost a half century ago, staring *through* her, this woman was not my mother. The porcelain-skinned creature with the empty, cavernous eyes bore no relation to my mother at all.

We ate in silence, listening to a man at the next table loudly critique the movie we'd just seen. An interesting concept but a mediocre script, he pronounced, probably the result of too many writers and too much studio meddling. The actors were adequate, but no more; the direction lacked focus. There were too many weird camera angles, no real vision. Decidedly, a minor effort. Rating: C+.

Sara made a face, took another bite of her pizza, dripped tomato sauce and cheese down her chin. "What did you think of the movie, Grandma?" she asked.

"I didn't know," my mother replied, eyes growing fearful.

"You don't know if you liked the movie?"

"I didn't know," my mother repeated, her hands leaving her pizza to scratch at the air.

I reached across the table, clasped my mother's hands in mine, brought them back down. "It's okay, Mom. It's okay now."

"What's happening?" Sara asked.

"I tried to protect you," my mother said. "I always tried to protect you." She rose halfway out of her seat.

"I know that, Mom."

"It's a mother's job to protect her child."

"It's okay, Mom. It's okay."

"I would never let anyone hurt my babies."

"I know that, Mom. Sit down. Please, sit down." My hands guided her back into her chair.

"I had to have a cesarean section, you know," she said. "I had an allergic reaction to the surgical tape. My skin is very sensitive."

"I know."

Her hands began frantically pawing at her stomach. "I'm horribly itchy. I'm not supposed to scratch."

"I'm scared," Sara said.

"It's all right, honey. Grandma's just a little confused."

"Don't be scared, Jo Lynn," my mother whispered, her hand leaving her stomach to caress Sara's cheek. "Mommy's here. I'll protect you."

After dinner, we guided my mother back to the car and strapped her into the rear seat. As soon as I started the engine, the radio came on, the sound of country music immediately filling the air. "How can you listen to this garbage?" Sara said, flipping through the various channels, eliciting a beat here, a chord there, each gone before anything had a chance to register on my brain. What difference did it make? I thought, catching a stray fragment of spoken word.

He apparently escaped . . .

Sara punched in another channel. The sound of heavy metal assaulted my ears. She quickly switched to another station. *You can take my heart, my achy breaky heart . . .*

She switched again.

"Wait a minute, what was that?"

"Mom, please don't make me listen to Billy Ray Cyrus."

"Not that. Before. The news."

"I don't want to listen to the news."

"Sara . . ."

"Okay, okay."

It took several seconds before we relocated the news, and by that

time, the announcer had moved on to the weather. *Another beautiful sunny day for South Florida.*

"Find another channel."

"What are you looking for?" Sara asked.

"I thought I heard something."

"What?"

"Just find the news."

We found it, then listened in stunned silence as the story unfolded. *A dramatic escape took place earlier today at the Florida State Prison in Raiford. Colin Friendly, the convicted killer of thirteen women and the suspected killer of many more, escaped while being transferred to the neighboring Union Correctional Institution.*

"Oh God."

Officials are remaining tight-lipped about what exactly happened, but it appears that the notorious death row inmate was aided in his daring daytime escape by his wife, the former Jo Lynn Baker of Palm Beach.

"Oh God, no. Please, no."

"Jo Lynn helped him escape?" Sara asked incredulously.

Apparently, Colin Friendly was able to overpower one of his guards with a knife that had been smuggled into the prison. Police have issued an all-points bulletin for the getaway car, a 1987 red Toyota, license plate number YZT642, that belongs to the killer's wife. If anyone sees this vehicle, you are urged to call the police immediately. Under no circumstances should you approach the vehicle directly. Colin Friendly is armed and considered extremely dangerous.

"I don't understand," Sara said. "Why would Jo Lynn do such a thing?"

"Because she's a moron," I shouted, slamming the steering wheel with my fists, accidentally connecting with the horn, feeling its sharp blast like a stab to my heart.

Once again: Colin Friendly has escaped from the Florida State Prison and is believed to be in the company of his wife, the former Jo Lynn Baker, who married Friendly in a recent jailhouse ceremony. They fled in the bride's 1987 red Toyota, license plate YZT642, and were last seen heading northwest. Police have set up roadblocks throughout the state, and are advising that should you see the couple, you call them immediately. They are considered armed and very danger-

ous. Under no circumstances approach them directly. And now, in other news . . .

"What's going to happen now?" Sara asked.

"I don't know."

"Do you think that's why she wanted the money so badly, so that she could help him escape?"

"It looks that way."

"Where do you think they're going?"

"I don't know. Northwest, the announcer said. Alabama, maybe. Georgia. I don't know."

"Do you think she'll try to get in touch with us?"

"I don't know." God, I was getting sick of saying that.

"You don't think there's any chance they'll come back here, do you?" Sara asked.

"No," I said, because I knew that's what she wanted to hear.

From the back seat, my mother started screaming.

⌐⌐

As soon as we walked in the front door, I called Brooke's house and asked to speak to Michelle. I was going to tell her to take a cab home, or better yet, to spend the night with Brooke.

"She's not here," Brooke's brother told me, his voice nasal and bored, barely audible above the television blaring in the background.

"What do you mean, she's not there?"

"They went out a while ago."

"Do you know where they went?"

"I heard them say something about a party."

"Whose party? Where?"

"I don't know."

"Can I speak to your mother?" It was more demand than question. Stay calm, I tried to tell myself. There was nothing to worry about. Colin Friendly was headed northwest, not southeast. He wasn't crazy enough to come back to Palm Beach. There was nothing for me to worry about.

"There's nobody home but me," the boy said. I pictured him

sprawled out lazily on the family-room sofa, a bowl of potato chips at his side.

I hung up the phone, not sure what to do next.

"Don't worry, Mom," Sara said. "You know Michelle. She'll be home by curfew."

I checked my watch. It was barely eight o'clock. Michelle's curfew was almost four hours away. Could I last that long? I checked my answering machine for messages. No one had called.

"What are you so worried about?" Sara asked, eyes growing fearful.

"I'd just feel better if I knew where she was."

My mother began crying, swaying unsteadily from side to side. "I think I'd like to go home now," she said.

"It's okay, Mom. Everything's okay."

I asked Sara to get my mother ready for bed, and stay with her until she fell asleep. Then I marched into the family room and quietly placed a call to the police.

"My name is Kate Sinclair," I began, my voice a whisper so as not to alarm my older daughter.

"I'm sorry," said the officer who answered the phone. "You'll have to speak up."

I repeated my name, more loudly this time, then spelled it. "My sister is Jo Lynn Baker," I told him. "Jo Lynn *Friendly*," I immediately corrected, picturing the officer snap to attention on the other end of the line.

"Your sister is Jo Lynn Friendly?" There was a slight chuckle in his voice that told me he didn't quite believe me.

"Yes, and I'm concerned that Colin Friendly might be headed this way."

"And which way is that?" Again, the annoying chuckle wrapped around each word.

I gave him my address. "I'm not making this up," I told him.

"What makes you think Colin Friendly might be heading back to Palm Beach?"

I told them about Colin's phone call, his letter.

"Did you report these things to the police?" he asked.

"No. I guess I should have."

"You have the letter?"

"I tore it up," I said sheepishly.

"Can you hold on a minute?" He put me on hold before I could object.

I grabbed the remote-control unit, flipped on the TV. Immediately, Colin Friendly's murderous face filled the screen, alternating with video footage of my sister at the courthouse. "Where are you?" I hissed at the screen. "Where the hell are you?"

The officer came back on the line. "We're sending someone over to talk to you," he said.

At 1 A.M., I was still sitting in front of the television, listening to tales of Colin's horrible exploits and staring at his killer smile. The police had come and gone. And Michelle still wasn't home.

By one-thirty, I was pacing the floor of the living room, and debating whether or not to call Larry in South Carolina. By two o'clock I was in tears, and wondering whether to check back with the police. They'd promised to patrol the neighborhood, despite the fact they were convinced Colin Friendly was heading in the opposite direction. So far, I hadn't seen one police car drive by.

By two-thirty, when I finally heard Michelle's key twisting in the front lock, I was such a mess that I didn't know whether to hug her or yell at her. So I did both.

I ran toward her, arms extended, tears streaming the length of my face. "Where the hell have you been?" I was hugging her so tightly she couldn't answer. "Do you know how late you are?"

Immediately, she began to whimper. "I'm sorry, Mom. We were at a party, and I had to wait until someone could give me a lift home."

"You could have taken a taxi. Or called me. I would have picked you up."

"It was so late. I thought you'd be asleep. I didn't want to wake you."

"Do you have any idea how frantic I've been?"

"I'm sorry, Mom. I'm so sorry."

"It's two-thirty in the morning."

"It'll never happen again."

"You're damn right it'll never happen again."

"What are you going to do?"

"I don't know." A familiar whiff reached my nostrils. "Have you been smoking?"

"No," she said immediately, backing out of my reach.

"You reek of cigarettes."

"Lots of kids at the party were smoking."

"But not you."

"Not me. Honestly."

I closed my eyes, rubbed my forehead. Was I crazy? Only minutes ago I'd been frantic that something might have happened to her; now I was upset that she might have been smoking. I was too old for this, I thought, double-locking the front door. Menopause and teenage girls— they definitely didn't mix. "Go to bed," I said. "We'll deal with this in the morning."

"I'm really sorry, Mom."

"I know."

"I love you."

"I love you too. More than anything in the world." Once again, I hugged her tightly against my breast. "Now get some sleep."

I watched her walk away, wiping tears from sleepy eyes. Sooner or later, I thought, heading into the kitchen for a glass of ice water, they're gonna get you.

I stared out the back window at the kaleidoscope of stars sprinkled across the black sky, finding the brightest one, making a wish. "I wish everything would go back to normal," I said, walking back toward the living room, past the spot by the breakfast nook that, less than eight hours later, would be covered in blood.

Chapter

31

I undressed, washed my face, brushed my teeth, and crawled into bed, exhaustion coating me like a layer of heavy dust. It filled my nose and mouth, crawled inside my pores, sank beneath the layers of my skin, inhabited my insides, like a tapeworm, growing fat even as its host withers and dies.

Surprisingly, I slept very well.

There were no dreams, no disturbances, no waking up in the middle of the night, agonizing over bad choices or bad memories. I thought of nothing and no one—not Larry or Robert or Colin Friendly, not Sara or Michelle or Jo Lynn, not my mother or my father or my stepfather. No one. As soon as my head hit the pillow, my mind went totally, mercifully blank.

When I opened my eyes, it was eight o'clock the next morning, and the sun was pushing through my bedroom curtains, like a large fist. "Just

another day in Paradise," I said, swinging my legs out of bed and heading for the bathroom, fending off the intrusion of serious thought as I showered, dressed, and fiddled with my hair until it gave up and went totally limp. Only reluctantly did I leave the confines of my bedroom, stepping trepidly over the threshold into the main living space, hands crossed protectively over my chest, as if guarding my heart.

I stared at the front door. On the other side, the morning newspaper lay waiting, my sister no doubt featured prominently on the front page. I staggered, closed my eyes, turned away from the door. "Not before I've had my coffee," I said, extending my arms, as if I could physically keep reality a comfortable distance away.

I'm not sure what I was thinking as I prepared the morning coffee. Probably I was trying very hard not to think, which only made things worse. Had my sister really had anything to do with Colin Friendly's escape? How far was she prepared to go to help him? What would happen to her once Colin Friendly was apprehended, as no doubt, sooner or later, he would be? Would the police file criminal charges against her? Would she go to jail? Or would they judge her to be unstable, force her to seek psychiatric help? Was there even the slightest possibility that something good might come of this fiasco?

I glanced toward the TV in the family room. Maybe my sister and Colin Friendly had already been apprehended. How long could they hide, after all? They weren't the most inconspicuous of couples, and would have attracted attention even if their faces hadn't been plastered across the front pages of newspapers for months. Jo Lynn's weathered red Toyota was hardly the ideal choice of a getaway car. Surely, by now, someone had spotted them. "So turn on the TV and find out," I said, but didn't move. Whatever the news was, it wouldn't be good.

Instead I reached for a coffee mug, selecting one with a pink flamingo etched into its side, china tail feathers serving as a handle, and *Beautiful Palm Beach* scribbled in black along its side. I filled the oversized mug with steaming coffee and carried it into the family room, where I lowered myself gently into the sofa and sat staring out the large expanse of floor-to-ceiling windows at the backyard. Another one of those

magic days, I thought, where the blue of the sky is so intense, it almost hurts the eyes. "Wouldn't you just love a sweater in that shade?" I heard Jo Lynn ask, and felt the mug in my hands about to slide through my fingers.

I gripped the flamingo's tail tighter, almost snapped it off. "Relax," I told myself. "The day has yet to begin."

"Who are you talking to?" a voice behind me asked, and I jumped, the coffee flying out of the mug and into the air, as if it were lava erupting from a volcano. It burned my hands and slashed across the front of my yellow T-shirt like a knife, the resultant brown stain bearing an uncomfortable resemblance to dried blood. "Are you all right?" Sara asked, rushing forward, taking the mug from my hands, depositing it on the coffee table. "I'm sorry. I didn't mean to scare you."

"I'm okay," I told her. "I just need a wet cloth."

"I'll get it." Sara was instantly in the kitchen, at the sink, back at my side, swatting at the front of my T-shirt with the wet dishrag. "I'm really sorry," she said, tears forming in the corners of already swollen eyes.

"It's okay, Sara. Really, I'm fine."

"You're sure?"

"I'm sure."

"I'm really sorry."

I studied her face, still beautiful despite the swollen eyes and lack of sleep. I knew she was apologizing for more than the coffee.

"I know," I said. "I'm sorry too."

"I don't know what comes over me sometimes. I just get so angry."

I said nothing.

"I love you," she said.

"I love you too."

"Do you?" she asked plaintively.

"Always."

Sara bit down on her bottom lip. It quivered beneath her teeth, broke free of her grasp. "How can you love me when I'm such an awful person?"

"You're not an awful person, Sara."

"Michelle never acts the way I do."

"Michelle's different than you are."

"She's so together. She knows who she is. She knows what she wants."

"What do you want?"

"I don't know. I don't know anything. I'm so stupid."

"You're anything but stupid."

"Then why do I do these things?"

"I don't know," I told her honestly. "Maybe it would help to talk to a therapist."

"You *are* a therapist."

"I'm also your mother. The two don't seem to mix."

Sara tried to smile, though her lips refused to hang on to it, and it slid off the side of her face. "Is there any news about Jo Lynn?"

I shook my head. "I don't know. I've been afraid to find out."

Sara quickly scooped up the remote-control unit from the coffee table and turned on the TV, flipping through a number of Sunday morning sermons before finding the news. I listened absently as a boyishly handsome announcer filled me in on the latest in global politics, then began a detailed report on the environment. With the flick of a button, he was gone, replaced by another boyishly handsome announcer. A major late-winter storm was about to hit sections of the Northeast, threatening to dump a possible three feet of snow on the area, he intoned, as images of high winds and swirling snow filled the screen.

And suddenly the snow disappeared into the Florida sunshine, and I found myself staring at a dilapidated old red Toyota, parked in front of a seedy-looking motel and surrounded by a virtual horde of state troopers. "My God," I said, holding my breath, inching forward, my hands digging into the back of the sofa.

"Police report that they have located the vehicle they believe was used to aid in the escape of Colin Friendly from the Union Correctional Institution in Florida yesterday afternoon," the announcement began. "A 1987 red Toyota, believed to belong to Jo Lynn Baker, recent bride of the convicted serial killer, was found parked in a wooded area near the fam-

ily-owned and -operated Wayfarer's Motel just outside of Jacksonville, Florida, early this morning."

"Jacksonville?" Sara asked, echoing my thoughts. "They only got as far as Jacksonville?"

"Police are refusing to speculate whether the fugitive couple are still in the Jacksonville area," the announcer continued, as pictures of Colin Friendly and my sister filled the screen. "They wish to remind the public that both Colin Friendly and his wife should be considered armed and extremely dangerous. If you see them, or have any information as to their whereabouts, contact the police immediately. Under no circumstances should they be approached."

"How could she do this?" I muttered, sinking onto the arm of the sofa.

"Do you think they'll get away?"

"No."

"What's going to happen to her?" Sara asked.

"I don't know."

"This just in," the announcer continued, unable to disguise the excitement in his voice. He's probably been waiting his whole life to say, "This just in," I thought, as once again my breath constricted in my chest. "Police have confirmed that the body of a man matching Colin Friendly's description has been found in the wooded area behind the Wayfarer's Motel near Jacksonville."

"My God."

"What about Jo Lynn?" Sara asked.

"I repeat: police say they have recovered the body of a man believed to be Colin Friendly in a wooded area behind the Wayfarer's Motel on the outskirts of Jacksonville, close to where the red Toyota belonging to his wife, the former Jo Lynn Baker, was spotted earlier this morning. Police are refusing further comment at this time, but promise to have a statement later in the day. Stay tuned for further developments as they occur. In other news . . ."

"He's dead?" Sara asked. "Colin Friendly is dead?"

"I can't believe it."

"Do you think Jo Lynn killed him?"

"Jo Lynn couldn't kill a bee if it were getting ready to sting her."

"Then where is she? What's happened to her?"

"I don't know." I stood up, sat back down again. "I don't know what to do."

"What to do about what?" Michelle asked, coming into the room, neatly dressed in denim shorts and a lime-green shirt. "What's happening?"

"Colin Friendly's dead and nobody knows what's happened to Jo Lynn," Sara told her.

"What?!"

"Maybe there's something in the morning paper," Sara said. "Where is it?"

"It's still outside."

"I'll get it," Sara volunteered, heading for the front door.

The phone rang. Michelle ran into the kitchen and answered it. It was Larry.

"You've heard?" he asked as Michelle handed me the phone.

"Just now—on the news."

"Any word about Jo Lynn?"

"Nothing."

"Okay, listen, hang tight. I'm on my way to the airport. I'm on standby for an earlier flight. I'll be home as soon as I can. Don't try to talk me out of it."

"Hurry," was all I said.

"Colin Friendly's dead?" Michelle repeated.

"Apparently."

"Good." The front door opened and closed. "What's it say in the paper?" Michelle called out.

There was no answer.

"Didn't they deliver the paper?" I asked, rounding the corner into the breakfast nook.

What I saw next is carved deeply into my brain, like ancient hieroglyphics on the inside of a cave: my older daughter, in white sloppy shirt and boxer shorts, the newspaper dangling from her limp hand, uncombed

multihued hair falling into wide, swollen eyes, tears falling into her open mouth, head thrust back, a long jagged-edged knife held across her throat.

"Oh, they delivered the paper, all right," Colin Friendly said, smiling face pressing against Sara's tear-stained cheek, one arm snaked around her waist, holding her firmly in place, the other around her neck, his hand pressing the knife to her jugular. "But you know how newspapers are. They never get anything right."

For a moment, everything stopped—the humming of the refrigerator, the birds singing in the backyard, the blood running through my veins, my very breath. In the artificial silence, I registered Colin Friendly's startling blue eyes, his wavy hair and twisted smile, the oddly conservative blue shirt and black linen pants that hung loosely on his wiry frame, the powerful hands that escaped from under cuffs a shade too long, the long slender fingers that were curled around the black handle of a long serrated knife, the jagged edge of which was pressed against my daughter's tender flesh.

"Who's here?" Michelle asked from the kitchen, coming into the breakfast nook, freezing momentarily when she saw the nightmarish tableau, then abruptly bolting for the sliding glass door at the back of the family room.

"Stop!" Colin Friendly called out. "Or I'll slit her throat right here and now. Don't think I won't."

Michelle came to an immediate halt.

"That's a good girl," Colin said. "Now, come on back here. Join your mama. Thatta girl."

Michelle walked slowly back to my side, pushing one foot in front of the other with great difficulty, as if she were walking through mud. I grabbed her to me, held on tight, too numb to speak, the sight of my older daughter with a knife at her throat rendering me as helpless as if I'd been bound and gagged. Where were the police? Was it possible that the patrol car had spotted Colin Friendly hiding in the bushes and was, even now, radioing for backup?

"We thought you were dead," Michelle said to Colin Friendly.

He laughed. "Yeah, well, I was kind of hopin' you'd think that."

A small squeal escaped Sara's mouth. Fresh tears fell the length of her cheeks.

"Please let her go," I said, finding my voice, weak and cowering in a corner of my throat, pushing it out.

"Let her go?" he asked incredulously. "Hell no. She's one of the reasons I came back here."

"I'm sorry, Mommy," Sara cried, although her lips never moved.

Colin Friendly tightened his grip around her waist. "Isn't that cute? The way all little girls cry for their mommy when they're in trouble? Wendy Sabatello cried for her mommy, and Tammy Fisher, she did too. Oh, and that little girl you were so interested in, Amy Lokash, she cried for her mommy. It always gives me kind of a little thrill, you know."

"You're a monster," I whispered.

"Yeah, well, you always knew that, didn't you, Mommy?" he said. "Lucky for me your sister never believed you."

"Where is Jo Lynn?"

"Back in Jacksonville. She didn't feel up to making the trip back here."

"Is she all right?"

He smiled. "You think I'd hurt the one woman who stood by me, who believed in me, who helped me escape?"

"You killed Mrs. Ketchum," I said, remembering the neighbor who'd tried to help him.

The smile grew into a laugh. "Yeah, I did, didn't I?"

Sara squirmed in the killer's arms. He pressed the knife harder against her throat, drawing a small bead of blood.

"Oh God," I moaned.

"Yeah, he's a big favorite too," Colin said. "I hear his name a lot. God and Mommy—they run kind of neck and neck."

"Why are you here?" Michelle demanded. "What do you want from us?"

"Feisty little thing, isn't she?" Colin winked at me, grinned widely. "It's going to be fun doing you, sweetheart. Bet I'll be your first," he continued, as I fought the urge to throw up. "And your last." He

laughed, clearly enjoying his power over us. He hasn't stuttered once, I realized. "That's why I'm here, darlin'," he went on. "That's what I want from you. From all of you, even Mommy here." His voice was like a lasso, encircling us, tying us together, pulling us toward him. "I've been thinking of little else since I went to prison. You all been my nourishment, what's been keeping me going. Plus, of course, I missed my goody box."

"Your goody box," I repeated, wondering if the police were anywhere in the vicinity, trying to stall for time.

"Yeah, the box where I keep all my little souvenirs: Tammy Fisher's ankle bracelet, Marie Postelwaite's panties, Amy Lokash's plastic red barrette. Lots of interesting stuff. I got it buried in the backyard of my old apartment building in Lantana. Shouldn't be too hard to find, especially with the police convinced I'm heading north."

"How did you get here?"

"Well, I couldn't very well drive your sister's fire-engine red piece of shit, now could I? So I borrowed some guy's car. He didn't mind. What does a dead guy need with a car anyway?" He smiled widely. "That's the guy they found in the woods. The one they think is me. Probably because I didn't leave him much of a face. He was nice enough to swap clothes with me before he died."

A soft whine filled the air as Sara slumped in Colin's arms.

"Don't faint on me, girl," he said. "Not yet." He drew the knife up toward the underside of her chin, as if he were a barber giving a shave. A faint sound, somewhere between a gasp and a sigh, escaped Sara's lips. "You hear that?" Colin asked. "That cute little sound? It must run in the family. Your sister made that same little sound," he told me. "Right before I smashed her nose in."

"Oh God."

"There's that name again."

"You killed my sister?" Tears filled my eyes, temporarily blinding me. I tried wiping them away, but the room remained blurred, one object bleeding into the next, like ink on a wet piece of paper. I saw Colin Friendly, his wavy dark hair disappearing into Sara's dark roots, the whiteness of his skin merging with the whiteness of her shirt, the knife

dancing unsteadily at her throat, so that it seemed as if there were many knives, many throats. The room lost focus, perspective, balance. It threatened to overturn, crumble, disappear.

"Now, I didn't say I killed her," he said evenly. "I just said I broke her nose."

"What have you done to her?"

"It's funny how some people react when they know they're going to die," he said, ignoring my question. "Some people get all panicky, and they yell and cry and carry on. Then there are others who try to reason with you. You kind of play along with them for a while, make them think like they might be getting through to you, and they relax a little bit, get all hopeful, and then there's that wonderful moment when they realize you're going to kill them anyway, and you watch the hope sink in their eyes, kind of like a ship going down in the ocean. That's usually when they start pleading." He laughed, a kind of manic cackle that hacked at the air, like a machete. "I think I like that part the best of all." He swayed, eyes dreamy, as if savoring the memory. "They give you all these reasons not to kill them—they want to live, they're young and they got their whole lives ahead of them, they got their children or their widowed mothers to look after. Shit like that. Janet McMillan, she was cryin' about her two little kids, and your friend Amy Lokash, she worried about her mother. Hey, you still want to know where to find her?" he asked suddenly, continuing before I had a chance to speak. "Remember when I sent you off on that wild-goose chase to Lake Osborne?"

I nodded.

"Well, it really wasn't such a wild-goose chase after all. Amy's there, all right. Just not in the water. I buried her beside that little building they have there for the kids' summer camp. You must have seen it."

"I saw it," I acknowledged, picturing the squat wooden cabin surrounded by trees.

"Couple of months from now, kids'll be dancing on her grave."

Once again, my eyes filled with tears—for Amy, her mother, my daughters, myself. Jo Lynn. "Did you kill my sister?" I asked.

"If I did, she deserved it. She couldn't do nothing right. She didn't

bring me one dime of the money she said was lyin' around here, money I know you'll be kind enough to provide me with before I go."

"Did you kill my sister?" I repeated.

"Yeah, I did," he said easily. "And you know, she didn't beg or plead or try to talk me out of it or anything. She just gave that cute little sound and looked at me with those big green eyes like she'd kind of known what was going to happen all along. She wasn't nearly as much fun to kill as you all are gonna be." Without loosening his grip on my daughter, he managed to reach into the pocket of his pants and pull out the wedding band my sister had purchased for herself and worn with such proud defiance. "For my goody box," he said.

I tried to contain my growing panic, to figure out what I could do to protect my daughters from this monster. It was obvious the police weren't going to help us. But there were three of us, I told myself, and only one of him. And even though he held a knife to my daughter's jugular, we were only steps away from the kitchen and knives of our own. Perhaps there was some way to distract him, overtake him, surprise him before he had time to react, before he could plunge the knife into Sara's throat.

And then I saw her. She first appeared in the corner of my eye, like a speck of dust, and then grew, like a shadow, assuming shape and form and three dimensions, her gray curls flat and uncombed, her nightgown falling loosely from her shoulders, her slippered feet making no sound as she crept along the tile floor behind Colin Friendly, her brown eyes clear and focused.

"Grandma!" Michelle gasped before she could stop herself.

"What?" Colin Friendly asked, spinning around.

And then everything exploded.

I didn't actually see the golf club in my mother's hands until it came slicing through the air at Colin Friendly's skull. It connected with bone-shattering fury, pushing one cheekbone into the other, almost tearing the hair from his scalp, blood spilling copiously from his right ear. I lunged toward Sara, pulled her screaming from Colin Friendly's grasp as he staggered sideways, the knife dropping from his hand as the club

swooped down again, this time with even greater ferocity, slicing across his jaw, shattering his teeth, so that they flew from his mouth, like niblets of corn, blood gushing down his chin as if from a fountain. The club came down yet again, this time with hammerlike precision across the center of his face, bringing him to his knees in a pool of his own blood, his nose shattered. He looked over to where I stood huddling with my girls, and tried to laugh, although instead of sound, there was only blood. And then he fell forward at our feet.

I ran to my mother, as the club dropped from her hands, kissed her, hugged her tightly to my chest. "I'll protect you," she whispered, as Michelle and Sara joined in our embrace, their bodies surrounding us, clinging to our sides like plastic wrap. "I'll protect you."

By the time the police arrived, her eyes had clouded over. She greeted the officers with a polite smile, and dozed against my shoulder as I tried to tell them what happened.

Chapter

32

The media had a field day. For the next several weeks, we were literally besieged by hordes of reporters from around the world. TV cameras took root on our front lawn, grew like ivy around the house, scaling the windows, burrowing into every nook and cranny of the cream-colored exterior. Everywhere we went, microphones were pushed toward our mouths, strobe lights exploded in our faces, people whispered behind our backs. We issued terse "no comments" to the hundreds of questions posed. It was easier than trying to explain we didn't have any answers.

Even now, four months later, I have no answers. I'm still struggling to understand what happened.

The only thing I know for certain is that my sister is dead.

At first, I tried to deny it. I told myself that Colin Friendly was lying, that once again he'd been playing with me, enjoying my torment, and that, in reality, Jo Lynn was alive and well, that she'd sneaked away

from his bed in the middle of the night, was even now hiding out in the wooded area behind the Wayfarer's Motel near Jacksonville. Even if Colin Friendly was telling the truth, I rationalized further, Jo Lynn was a strong woman, and somehow she'd managed to survive his brutal attack. She might have to spend a few weeks in a hospital, recovering from her wounds, but she'd get better. Even after the police reported finding a woman's body in Room 16 of the now-infamous lodging, I told myself that it wasn't Jo Lynn. The police had been wrong about the body of the man they'd initially identified as Colin Friendly. They were wrong now, or so I tried to convince myself. Until such denials became impossible.

I went to the medical examiner's office, but they wouldn't let me see her body, wouldn't even show me a photograph. There was significant trauma to the face, the police officer explained, even though I was no longer listening, having heard it all before. Did they remember me? I wondered absently, recalling my visit with Donna Lokash, at the time never dreaming, as I glanced reluctantly at the photograph of the teenage girl lying dead on a steel slab in the back room, that one day my sister would be lying on that same slab. Or was I lying to myself about that as well? Had I somehow known all along?

What else had I known all along? I ask myself now. Had I known, somewhere deep down in my gut, the things that happened between my stepfather and Jo Lynn all those years ago? Certainly the clues were there, all the missing pieces of the puzzle that was my sister. Looking back on it now, it seems inconceivable that I could have missed them. Jo Lynn was always dropping hints. All I had to do was bend down and pick them up. Was it possible I'd deliberately ignored them?

Some therapist you are, Sara shouted at me, and maybe she was right. As a therapist, I should have known. Had Jo Lynn been a client, and not my sister, I would have at least suspected the truth, but, like the shoemaker's children who go without shoes, this was simply too close to home.

Ultimately, they identified my sister from her fingerprints, and her body was cremated. Ashes to ashes. Dust to dust. For a while, it felt as if she'd never existed, that there'd never been this exotic creature named Jo Lynn. And maybe this is as close to the truth as I'm likely ever to get.

Because from the time my stepfather first laid his perverted hands on her, the real Jo Lynn, the Joanne Linda she was born, ceased to be. In her place grew a disturbed young woman with a penchant for high drama and low self-esteem, a woman who'd learned from childhood that to be abused meant to be loved.

The fact was that Jo Lynn had never known safety from a man. Not from her father, not from husbands one through three, all of whom had only underlined the concepts she learned in childhood: that it was acceptable to hurt the ones you love, that dangerous men are often the most attractive, that hard fists are more persuasive than soft words. Colin Friendly was merely an extension of the men who'd preceded him. It could be argued that my sister's marriage to Colin Friendly was as logical a move as any she'd ever made.

Is this sufficient to explain why she would willingly throw herself at a man who would, quite literally, just as soon kill her as look at her? Was she, as the tabloids have proclaimed, that desperate for attention? For publicity? For love?

I don't think so. I think this is too simple an explanation for her behavior, and that somehow it misses the point.

I think that, strange as it may seem, Colin Friendly was someone my sister thought she could control. He was in prison, after all, sentenced to die in the electric chair. Even if he managed to escape death, he would spend the rest of his life behind bars. In a subtle, but very real way, this fact rendered the vicious serial killer one of the safest men my sister had ever known.

Or perhaps she thought she could save him, that if she loved him hard enough, believed in him strongly enough, supported him ardently enough, she would be his salvation, and that by saving him, she could somehow save herself as well.

Could anything have saved her? Could I?

I don't think so, but then, that's always been part of my problem. I think too much. What about how I feel? Isn't that what I'm always asking my clients—how do you *feel*?

Well, how *do* I feel?

I feel like pulling all the dishes from the cupboards and hurling

them against the tile floor, watching them smash into a million pieces. I feel like standing in the middle of the road and screaming at the top of my lungs, daring cars to hit me. I feel like running as fast as I can, as far as I can, until my legs give out and my body cries for mercy, and then screaming some more. I feel helpless. I feel angry. I feel frustrated. I feel sad. So sad. Sadness fills my lungs, like water. I feel as if I'm drowning. I'm scared. Jo Lynn has abandoned me. She was wild and reckless and just a little bit crazy. And as long as she was those things, I didn't have to be. I could play it safe, be the good girl, the common sense to her imagination. And now she's gone, and I feel as if a wild animal has torn a huge chunk of flesh out of my side.

Part of me is missing.

I never told my sister that I loved her. And she never told me.

How could two sisters have so much insight into each other, and so little into themselves?

I don't have the answer. The lady with all the answers doesn't have any. What will my clients think?

Actually, I don't have any clients. I've decided to take some time off, maybe a year, maybe more. Reconsidering my options, I believe is the phrase most commonly used. I've been working since I graduated from university, and I need a break, although, to be perfectly truthful, this sabbatical is as much a result of outside forces as inner convictions. Within days of the story breaking in the papers, most of my clients called to cancel their scheduled appointments. I don't blame them. It's hard to entrust your life to a therapist who can't control her own.

Of course, my projected radio show came to naught. Robert called to say that the powers that be at the station had decided that, in light of all the recent publicity, now was probably not the best time for me to be launching such a high-profile career. He talked about the need for credibility in broadcasting, without actually saying that mine had been seriously undermined. He never said a word about what happened—what *hadn't* happened—at the Breakers. He wished me all the best; I wished him the same.

Yesterday, I was flipping through the channels on my car radio, and I caught the end of Faith Hill's bloodless rendition of *Piece of My Heart*,

immediately followed by a husky, and strangely familiar, voice: "We're talking about heartache today on WKEY-FM's Country Counselor. The call lines are now open. If there's anything you want to tell me about the last time you lost a piece of your heart, or you need some advice on finding it again, or you just want to hear a song about it, then call me right now. I'm Melanie Rogers, and I'm here to help."

I recalled the honey-voiced redhead with the emerald-green eyes I'd met in Robert's office. "Let me introduce you to an old friend," Robert had said by way of introduction. "Melanie Rogers, this is Kate Sinclair. We go back a very long way." All the way back to high school and Sandra Lyons, I thought, understanding that some things never change.

It seems almost inconceivable to me now that I could have seriously considered jeopardizing my marriage to Larry for someone like Robert. The truth is that I love my husband, that I always have. I can't imagine life without him. Lately, Larry and I have been talking about leaving Florida, going back to Pittsburgh. We've never made any real friends here, and Larry says he misses the change in seasons. His golf game is the pits, he claims, and besides, he can no longer look at a golf club without thinking of my mother and Colin Friendly.

It's still amazing to me that Colin Friendly survived the attack, although I really shouldn't be surprised. People like Colin Friendly always survive. It's the innocent who perish. I read in the paper the other day that the Florida Supreme Court turned down his latest request for a stay of execution. If I remember correctly the things Jo Lynn told me, that would leave the federal district court, the U.S. Eleventh Court of Appeals in Atlanta, and the U.S. Supreme Court. It's a long process. It could drag on for years.

My mother is in a nursing home now, and something of a celebrity, although she doesn't seem to understand what all the fuss is about. She hasn't spoken since that morning she took a club to Colin Friendly's head, and I'm pretty sure she has no memory of the incident. I'm not even sure she knows who I am anymore, although she always looks pleased to see me when I visit.

Sara and Michelle often accompany me on these visits. Sara's hair is

back to basic brown, her wardrobe an eccentric combination of hooker and hippie. Michelle has discovered black. They've been staying pretty close to my side these days, which is normal considering what we've been through. I confess to loving this renewed closeness. I savor every minute, partly because I know it won't last much longer. Several times lately, I've caught the whiff of cigarettes on Michelle's breath, and heard the hint of impatience in Sara's voice. I know they're getting ready to resume their lives. I'm bracing myself, trying to prepare for this eventuality, knowing that whatever course they choose, it is out of my control. I can't protect them forever. I can only tell them how much I love them.

Therapy has helped. Sometimes we all go together; sometimes we go individually. After years of listening to everyone else's problems, I've rediscovered the joys of talking about my own. But it's a long road back to normalcy, and I know it'll take time. I'm only grateful we have that time. For people like Donna Lokash, that time is gone forever.

The police found Amy Lokash's remains buried beside the day camp center in John Prince Park, exactly where Colin Friendly said they'd be, and they located his so-called goody box, filled with items belonging to each of his victims, all neatly labeled with the victim's name and date of death. Nineteen in all, including a hair curler belonging to his mother and a silver cross that once hung around Rita Ketchum's neck.

And so the police can now indisputably link Colin Friendly to the disappearances of six more women. Six more cases closed.

Incidentally, I just heard on the news that Millie Potton was found limping along the shoreline of Riviera Beach in her underwear, sunburnt and confused, but otherwise seemingly healthy. I'm glad. I was worried about her.

I think that's everything. I'll probably edit out some of the more personal revelations before I hand this over to the police. I'm not sure that any of this is what they were expecting. But I've tried to provide substance, context, explanations. I've searched my memory and bared my soul. I'm sure there are still some pieces missing. But I've done my best. Hopefully, it will be of some use.

At any rate, it's time to pick up the pieces. And go on.

1-2003

Please remember that this is a library book,
and that it belongs only temporarily to each
person who uses it. Be considerate. Do
not write in this, or any, library book.